A SHORT HISTORY OF
WESTERN LEGAL THEORY

A
SHORT HISTORY
OF
WESTERN LEGAL
THEORY

by
J. M. KELLY

CLARENDON PRESS · OXFORD

Oxford University Press, Walton Street, Oxford OX2 6DP

Oxford New York Toronto
Delhi Bombay Calcutta Madras Karachi
Kuala Lumpur Singapore Hong Kong Tokyo
Nairobi Dar es Salaam Cape Town
Melbourne Auckland Madrid

and associated companies in
Berlin Ibadan

Oxford is a trade mark of Oxford University Press

Published in the United States
by Oxford University Press Inc., New York

First published 1992
Reprinted 1993 (twice)

British Library Cataloguing in Publication Data
Data available

Library of Congress Cataloging in Publication Data
Kelly, J. M. (John Maurice)
A short history of Western legal theory / J.M. Kelly.
Includes index.
1. Jurisprudence—History.   2. Law—Philosophy—History.
3. Political science—History.   I. Title.
K215.E53K45   1992   340'.1—dc20   91–36905
ISBN 0–19–876244–5
ISBN 0–19–876243–7 (pbk.)

Printed and bound in Great Britain by
Biddles Ltd, Guildford and King's Lynn

Foreword

' "Man is born free, yet everywhere he is in chains":
words like these [of Rousseau] gave what might be
called the plain chant of natural rights, as Locke had
intoned them, a polyphonic charm.'

The tone of the passage itself is unmistakable: only John Kelly could have written a sentence at once so graceful and so resonant, so replete with learning and so refined in its choice of words. He conducted a lifelong love affair with the English language (among others); he may sometimes have felt with Auden that:

> *Time that is intolerant*
> *Of the brave and innocent.*
> *And indifferent in a week*
> *To a beautiful physique,*
> *Worships language and forgives*
> *Everyone by whom it lives.*

But only sometimes, because he also knew the inadequacy of language itself as a vehicle of feeling and we can glimpse as well in the sentence his passion for music, above all when it was at its most complex and many layered, as in the masterpieces of his beloved J. S. Bach.

All this may seem far away from the ineluctable and mighty issues at the heart of Western jurisprudence with which he wrestled in this, his last book. Yet as he brings before us with his own incomparable gifts of exposition the intellectual struggles of these great men, of Plato and Montesquieu, of Aquinas and Voltaire, of Locke and Bentham, we are repeatedly made conscious by him of how much of all of this is a battle with words.

He had indeed edged away with distaste from the verbal contortions typical of some contemporary Anglo–American jurisprudence and only a severe sense of duty can have compelled him, in the last chapter of this book, to follow some of the writers concerned on to what he describes with characteristic acerbity as 'a sort of course in mental and moral athletics, sweating around the cinder track of mid-twentieth century linguistic analysis and late twentieth century political issues'.

But his purpose was to give students an accessible guide, hitherto unavailable in English, to the history of legal theory in the West and he was too generous and open-minded a person not to recognize the many adventurous and exhilarating perspectives which modern scholars have given us on basic legal problems. His primary concern, however, was to make us see jurisprudence in its historical setting and, in so doing, he has vividly illustrated the recurrent preoccupation of the thinkers who dominate his text with certain themes. Whether it be the natural law of Aquinas, the *grundnorms* of Kelsen or whatever, we can see in his pages the constant search of writers on law for a coherent framework which explains its part in human life and activity. So too we can observe the haunting of the Western mind by still unanswered questions. What is the justification of punishment for crime? Should the law concern itself with private morality? Can we ensure that law is not simply, as the Marxists once said, a structure to support capitalist and bourgeois values?

In illuminating these themes, he has drawn not merely on his knowledge of jurisprudence over the centuries, but on his wide familiarity with the literature of the classical world and of later eras. He has with astonishing skill painted the historical background which is essential to his main themes and, although he writes deprecatingly in the introduction of his own lack of qualifications as a historian, I think the reader of these pages is likely to be far more impressed by the wide range of his reading and the dexterity with which he has related the development of jurisprudence to the convulsions which have marked millennia of history.

Understandably there was not room for everything. As I read his account of the dispute between the Pope and William of Ockham as to how the Franciscan Order reconciled its ownership of property with its vows of poverty, I wondered if he had got round to reading Umberto Eco's enchanting medieval detective story, *The Name of the Rose*, in which that controversy figures prominently. And there may be other areas—parallels between what was happening in legal theory and in other realms of thought and activity—which he would have found time to expand. But now that torrent of intellectual activity, of scintillating wit and monumental erudition is stilled forever. It is some comfort to know that generations of students will have Kelly on their shelves, keeping fit company with other great writers who have made all of us who work in the law aware of its part in the history of our civilization.

John Kelly came to University College, Dublin, in 1949 on an open scholarship in ancient classics: a year later I followed him by the same route. But our paths diverged for a while as students, since he continued with the classics, while I moved over to history. It was the dramatic society, I think, which brought us together again: John had an austere disapproval of our activities as time-wasting, but too many of his college friends were involved for him to cut himself off completely with Thucydides and Tacitus. He had, in fact, secured himself the position of prompter in 1949 for a tour to Oxford and Cambridge. As a result he knew *The Playboy of the Western World* by heart and allusions to it were liberally strewn through his conversation over the ensuing decades. Then, as he began to study for the bar, I saw more of him. In those days, the Law Faculty of UCD was a strictly part-time school, the most prominent member of which, Professor Patrick McGilligan, a spare figure with a pure Derry accent uncorrupted by fifty years living in Dublin, had considerable influence on John. His attention was engaged by the Irish Constitution, on which McGilligan lectured, but which was then almost ignored by most practising lawyers. And McGilligan was also one of the first of many people who were to be the subject of John's incomparable gifts as a mimic—always a sign with him, the least malicious of men, of his affection and respect for the target.

The travelling studentship which he was awarded in 1953 brought him back into the classical fold, but with the legal dimension still present. In Heidelberg, he encountered the richness of the German tradition of Roman law studies which was to be another enduring interest. But it was also a time of intellectual and emotional maturing: he had grown up in the stiflingly isolated Ireland of the 1940s and the novel which he subsequently wrote based on this period is a touching and funny account of a young Irishman finding his way in life with the sympathetic assistance of more than one German girl.

His work in Heidelberg resulted in the first of his studies of Roman law which were to bring him an international reputation in that field. The period which followed in Oxford was to reawaken his interest in the Irish Constitution now fostered by Robert Heuston, who supervised a thesis subsequently published under the title *Fundamental Rights in the Irish Law and Constitution*. In

Oxford, he forged many enduring friendships, but a conflict was also emerging which was to dominate his life between the world of learning which he loved so much and the attractions of the plane of action. He returned to Dublin to practice for a time at the bar and found in the Law Library (and on the bench) a rich gallery of figures to add to his ever increasing repertoire of imitations. But the seduction of the academic life was still potent and he returned to Oxford in the 1960s as a fellow. It was again a crucial period in his life: he married Delphine and his happy and rewarding life as a husband and father began.

Later in the 1960s he returned to UCD to lead the revitalized and full-time law faculty, built up largely through the dedication of its then Dean, William Finlay. There is not space to detail John's contributions to the establishment of Irish legal studies on a radically new footing: one project which must be mentioned, however, is the launching of the new *Irish Jurist*, on which he lavished so much time and thought.

But the world of affairs still beckoned. His career as a politician began, first as a senator, then as a Dail deputy and successively as Chief Whip, Attorney General and Minister for Industry and Commerce. He brought to Irish political life a gift for oratory, coruscating wit and sharpness of debate which was almost without equal since the foundation of the state. More importantly, he fought against some of the least endearing features of Irish life: hypocrisy, double standards and self-righteousness. Political allies and opponents alike acknowledged his honesty and integrity and his decision to leave political life was widely lamented.

What public life gained by John's dedication, the academic world lost: yet even when he was most fully preoccupied by politics, he continued to produce work of outstanding quality. In particular, *The Irish Constitution* was the most comprehensive work yet published on its subject and reflected at many points the practical knowledge he had gained from his years in active politics.

His novel about Germany had been published under the banal title of *Matters of Honour*, the publisher's preference over John's more allusive choice, *Heidelberg Man*. There was another, which I read in typescript more than thirty years ago, and which portrayed with entrancing accuracy the life of the young Dublin middle class in those days. I am not sure why it was never published and I hope some day to see it in print.

At least we have in his writings much by which we can remember him. But nothing can bring back those darting, mischievous glances behind the glasses, the talk bubbling with fun and an endless relish for the absurdity and oddness of life itself. He was one of those rare people who seemed to brighten a room when he came in and, when he was taken from his family and friends with such cruel abruptness just a year ago, the many who loved him could only console themselves with the knowledge that life would have been so much poorer if they had not known him. And even someone as self-critical as he must have been content with what he had achieved: he was entitled to be at rest.

> *The bright day is done,*
> *And we are for the dark*

18 December 1991   RONAN KEANE

Preface

This book is an attempt to offer students of law and politics a guide of manageable size to the history of the leading themes in the legal theory of Western civilization.

The idea of writing it came from my own teaching experience at Dublin. Under the rubric Jurisprudence, or Legal Theory, lecturers are notably freer to choose their own material and method than when dealing with the practical parts of the law. The lack of a fixed conventional content in the subject can be seen in the very different plans adopted by those who have written textbooks in the field, as a quick glance at Dias, Friedmann, Lloyd, Paton, Salmond, and Wortley will demonstrate. My own preference is to try to take my class through the history of the main themes of legal theory, starting with the Greeks and going up to the present day. But the approach of most of my colleagues in the common-law world is different. They prefer to concentrate on contemporary legal theory, on the doctrines of legal philosophers still alive, or not long dead.

This conception of jurisprudence, at any rate as a subject in a law-school syllabus, comes through for instance in an examination paper which I recently saw set for the Final Honour School (i.e. final examination for the primary law degree) at Oxford. There were sixteen questions, of which candidates were required to answer three. The questions, as one would expect, were mostly of formidable sophistication, and I could only feel glad that I did not myself have to satisfy those Oxford examiners. Anyone to whom they awarded a first-class mark must certainly have had a first-class brain and received first-class tuition. On the other hand, it would have been possible for the candidate, no matter which three questions were selected, to write first-class answers even if suffering from the delusion that the world began around the year 1930.

I think this is a pity. I am not a historian, and today I am sorry that I did not try to make myself one by private reading in my student years. I would not even attempt to explain the reasons why a sense of the past, of the remote roots and the patterns of growth of our world and the ideas which govern it, is important for a student if he is to be an educated adult and citizen of his country. But I believe it strongly; particularly in the case of law students, whose discipline becomes every day more specialized and more engrossed by modern statute-based mechanisms, operated by a technique which needs be learnt only once. The jurisprudence they are taught ought, therefore, to give a humane foundation to what will be their life's profession; instead of which, it seems to me, they are nowadays mostly given a sort of course in mental and moral athletics, sweating around the cinder-track of mid-twentieth-century linguistic analysis and late twentieth-century political issues. If one needed a graphic representation of this historical parochialism, and if one were permitted to seek it in a different dimension of existence, I would propose the well-known and brilliant Steinberg illustration for a 1976 *New Yorker* cover: it is the world seen from the *New Yorker* offices: in the foreground Ninth Avenue, complete with cars and pedestrians, litter bins, traffic lights, delivery vans, the entrance booth to a parking lot; a block further west, a corner of Tenth Avenue is visible, with a gas station; then the Hudson River, with the funnel of a moored ship; at the far side New Jersey; then a bleak plain, relieved by a few vague cactus-shaped mountains, representing the rest of the United States, with Washington, DC, Texas, and Chicago perfunctorily pencilled in; then a stretch of water, smaller than the Hudson River, for the Pacific Ocean; and finally three low, disconsolate humps labelled 'Russia', 'China', and 'Japan'.

Of course there are already excellent textbooks which do not neglect the historical dimension of legal theory: I have relied heavily on Friedmann's *Legal Theory* and Lloyd's *Introduction to Jurisprudence* in advising students on reading, as well as on H. F. Jolowicz's excellent *Lectures on Jurisprudence*, which it would be a well-deserved tribute to their author's memory to expand and update. But what I would have wished for, and in the end have tried to produce myself—though a trained philosopher or historian would have been far better qualified to attempt it—is something which would have performed at however humble a level for legal theory what Bertrand Russell's *History of Western Philosophy* does for that subject: namely, a simple, chronologically sequential, account of the legal theories produced by, and in their turn influencing, the main epochs of Western history.

When I started work, no modern book of the kind seemed to

exist in English, apart from the translation of C. J. Friedrich's too condensed *Geschichte der Rechtsphilosophie*. There were, indeed, some in German, Italian, Spanish, and Dutch; but for various reasons none of them would have met the case even if translated. Guido Fassò's *Storia della filosofia del diritto* is the best of them; but it is a three-volume work, therefore too grand in scale for a student; it is in places too Italocentric for readers of other nations; above all, it is twenty years old, and so has caught only a few drops from the cataract of Anglo-American jurisprudence of recent years. After I was well launched, I discovered the Swedish scholar Stig Strömholm's *Short History of Legal Thinking in the West* (1985). This has been something of a lifeline for my students; but there is virtually no quotation from the actual writings of significant figures; there are no footnote references to sources or further reading; often he seems to be signalling to people of his own level of sophistication, rather than to students with only dim notions of what distinguishes the seventeenth century from the twelfth. Above all, Strömholm draws his history to a close in 1900. There is, indeed, a lot to be said for not attempting the history of one's own age; Bertrand Russell, for one, evidently thought so, as his own book's second edition (1961) does not so much as mention Wittgenstein, who died ten years earlier; the last two philosophers he discusses, William James and John Dewey, were born in 1842 and 1859 respectively. All the same, even at the risk of inflating what a later age may dismiss as trivial or ephemeral, or neglecting something whose true status I have missed, I think I should at least have a shot at telling students what is actually going on in the name of jurisprudence.

This brings me to the first of a few personal explanations. This book is divided into ten chapters dealing with ten slices of the time separating Homer's world from that of Gorbachov. The last of those ten chapters, which is a good deal longer than most of the others, tries to cover the years since the middle of the twentieth century. But it is not intended to be, and cannot be, a complete, still less a critical, survey of Western jurisprudence in the last few decades. Such surveys exist in several excellent contemporary works, and I do not attempt to compete with them on what would be a necessarily miniature scale. So several of the figures familiar today on legal theory's Ninth Avenue will not be found between these covers, or will be so small as to be, perhaps, unrecognizable.

Secondly, I have certainly not succeeded in mentioning all the important subjects of legal theory in my ten successive periods. The more I worked on this modest book, the more I came to feel the boundlessness of the theme; and that an entire liberal education (and an excellent undergraduate honours course), extending beyond law into general history, philosophy, politics, economics, anthropology, even aesthetics, could be built around the history of legal theory. A work adequate to anchor such a course could easily be projected on a scale sufficient to absorb several lifetimes and fill many volumes. But in a book of barely 500 pages, something has to give. I have tried in each chapter—on the Russell model—to offer, after a short sketch of the general and intellectual history of the age, an idea of what was felt and written about the main problems of law. Therefore (although some themes emerge only late, while others drop out of sight earlier) I try to follow through, in separate sections in each chapter, matters such as the basis of the state, the source of the ruler's authority and of legal obligation, the relation of custom and legislation, the idea of natural law and of natural rights, the rule of law, the concept of equity, the essence of justice, the problems arising from the value of equality, the nature of law itself, the status of property, the proper object and scope of criminal law, the theory of a law to govern nations, and one or two more. My array of themes, while I hope not arbitrary or eccentric, is of course selective; and I might, I suppose, have added to this list matters such as legal personality, the theory of contract, the theory of succession, the theory of evidence . . . But where to stop?

Thirdly a word about the material I have used. In the early chapters there is virtually nothing consciously composed as 'legal theory', because such writing scarcely existed before the end of the Middle Ages. Therefore, in order to present the legal 'thought' of early Europe, one has to reconstruct it by trawling the actual practice of law or state, or the work of men whose main purpose was to theorize not about law, but about society, or ethics, or theology, or politics. Indeed, except perhaps for the pages on the twentieth century, a lot of the material has as much claim to be ranked under the history of political as of legal thought. But a clean separation of those areas is not possible. If one looks at the Carlyles' massive *Medieval Political Theory in the West,* or Sabine and Thorson's *History of Political Theory,* one will see that law, especially what we could classify as constitutional law, is the backbone of their respective stories, and could not be excised without the collapse of the whole. Ideas of fundamental law and rights, of the social contract, of the rule of law, of the limits of state power, are central to the interest of the political scientist, but no less so to that of the jurist.

Lastly, while I have tried to offer a picture of legal theory in Western history generally, I am conscious of how heavily English-language jurisprudence predominates as the twentieth century progresses. I suspect this has something to do with the very generous staffing of British and American law schools compared with those of France, Germany, or Italy. But it may have to do also with deeper causes in the philosophical or political traditions of the common law and civil law worlds respectively. On this level there appears to be—amazingly in an era of progressive European integration—a barrier greater than mere language differences could explain between Anglo-American jurisprudence and that of the European continent. For instance: in the same year, 1985, there appeared both the fifth edition of Lloyd's *Introduction to Jurisprudence* and the fourth edition of Helmut Coing's *Grundzüge der Rechtsphilosophie* ('Outlines of Legal Philosophy'). In his chapter on contemporary theory, Coing says 'particular attention should be drawn to the significant contribution made above all by Niklas Luhmann towards establishing a theory of law' (this is his legal sociology, which he then describes). But Lloyd, although his Index of Authors contains about 800 names, has no mention whatever of Professor Luhmann. Conversely, Lloyd naturally gives huge prominence to H. L. A. Hart and a good deal also to Ronald Dworkin; but in Coing's work Hart gets four lines, Dworkin not one. To the Continental eye, it is the writers of the common law world who are out of the main stream: an Italian reviewer of *The Legal Mind: Essays for Tony Honoré* (1986) wrote that, on entering the world inhabited by the contributors of papers in the field of jurisprudence in this collection, the Continental lawyer felt himself as an Alice in Wonderland, and wondered if much was to be gained by Anglo-Saxon legal science through persisting in its 'traditional splendid isolation from Continental legal experience'.

J.M.K.

The book, apart from some footnote references, was virtually complete before John Kelly's sudden death. We had talked and corresponded about it. The following extract from his last letter to me helps to put his aims in perspective.

I am sorry if my preface gives the impression that I am critical of Anglo-American jurisprudence of recent years. On the contrary, I think it is an astonishing flowering, and I only wish my own wits would stretch to fully understanding it all and perhaps being able to take up this issue or that. My problem is that the growth is so luxuriant that in the modern jurisprudence course it seems to blot out everything else; and my book is an unpretentious effort to adjust the student's perspective. Perhaps there is too much sailing under the flag 'jurisprudence' and it might more rationally be divided into two teaching subjects: (*a*) history of legal theory; (*b*) modern philosophy of law. At any rate I think law students should not graduate without knowing a little about how we arrived where we are. *Vixere fortes ante Hart et Dworkin multi.*

He was especially keen that I should read the book and advise him on it. I have accordingly made a few corrections and added some references, but the views expressed are wholly his.

TONY HONORÉ

The publishers would like to thank Tony Honoré for having so willingly taken on the task of reading and checking the typescript before sending it to press. They would also like to thank Mr Ernest Metzger of Brasenose College, Oxford for successfully tracking down some several dozen references which were missing from the author's last draft.

Thanks are also due to Faber & Faber for their permission to quote from *In Time of War, Commentary from Journey to a War* (1939), by W. H. Auden.

Contents

I

The Greeks

GREECE AS A STARTING-POINT

The reason why Greece has a special place in the history of civilization is not merely that most departments of literature and the visual arts were there raised to levels which later ages agreed to regard as classical, that is, as permanent standards of excellence. It is also because the Greeks were the first people—at any rate, the first of whom Europe retains any consciousness—among whom reflective thought and argument became a habit of educated men; a training for some, and a profession or vocation for others, not confined to observation of the physical world and universe—in which the Egyptians and Babylonians had long preceded them—but extending to man himself, his nature, and his place in the order of things, the character of human society, and the best way of governing it.

Other ancient peoples had contained priests and prophets whose teaching or whose poetic insights included perceptions of human nature and moral precepts; a lot of the Old Testament of the Jews, for example, could be put into that category. Similarly, other ancient peoples, since they had laws, must have had some capacity to reason about the function of a law and how best to make it achieve a particular purpose; this can be presumed of the civilizations of Mesopotamia, from whose ruins the great code of the Babylonian King Hammurabi (about 1800 BC) and the laws of Eshnuna (about 200 years older still) have been excavated. This epoch antedates the high period of Greek civilization by roughly 1,500 years. Nevertheless it was among the Greeks that the objective discussion of man's relation to law and justice became an activity of the educated mind and was recorded in a literature which has been part, ever since, of a more or less continuous European tradition. It is therefore with the Greeks that the history of reflective jurisprudence in the West, or European legal theory, must begin.

SOME COMPARATIVE CHRONOLOGY

If we focus on the period in ancient Greece which is best illumined by historians, orators, and philosophers, say from the death of Pericles to the deaths of Alexander the Great and Aristotle (in rough, round-number dates, 420–320 BC), and look at the rest of Europe from the Greeks' point of view, we will see first of all that the Romans, the other great people of European antiquity, scarcely featured on their horizon. In the time of Pericles Rome was still no more than a largish town near the mouth of the modest river Tiber, its people one of the nations of the Italian peninsula speaking a dialect of the Italic family (in Rome's case, that of the district called Latium, i.e. Latin); though Rome even then had experienced the influence of Greece, partly mediated by the powerful and mysterious Etruscan civilization to its north, partly perhaps directly through the proximity of the many Greek cities to its south (Greek colonization of the coasts of southern Italy and Sicily had begun as far back as the eighth century BC and is attested still today by the Greek-derived names of such towns as Naples, Palermo, Taranto, Agrigento, and Syracuse). But Rome's power at that time extended no further than its immediate hinterland, an area far smaller than even the smallest Irish county today contains; the wars with the Carthaginians which started Rome on the path of imperial expansion, and the conquest of overseas provinces, still lay 100 years or more in the future. Indeed it is unlikely that many of the Greeks of 420 BC, other than those living in southern Italy, would even have heard of Rome. The earliest event in Roman history of which Greeks seem to have taken any notice was the sack of the city in 387 BC by raiding Gaulish Celts; the Romans themselves made no major stir in mainland Greece until 100 years later, when the Greek King Pyrrhus of Epirus, adventuring into southern Italy, was defeated by them.

As for the further reaches of Europe to the west and north, they were for the Greeks of our period a more or less unknown wilderness, inhabited by what they called barbarians (*barbaroi*, the word supposed to mimic foreigners' clumsy speech). They knew in a general way about the Scythians who lived in the area of today's southern Russia; and about the Celts, a race without stable political frontiers or institutions, but whose settlements (as we know from modern archaeology) stretched at that time across central Europe from the Black Sea to Ireland. But ancient Greek geography was on the western and northern sides confined to the Mediterranean seaboard; their world more or less ended in the ocean beyond the straits of Gibraltar. The historian Herodotus, writing just before the beginning of our period, mentions the Danube, the Pyrenees, and the continental Celts, but neither Ireland nor Britain. Eratosthenes, who was librarian at Alexandria a hundred years after our period, mentions Ireland (Iernē) and Britain, presumably relying on information from merchants at the end of a trade chain, but says nothing about these islands. At the time of the Peloponnesian war (431–404 BC) between Athens and Sparta, which is a fully historical period for Greece, and even (though in a much more imperfect way) for Rome, Ireland is shrouded in historical darkness; archaeology and philology suggest that at that epoch the migrations of Celtic peoples to these islands had begun, but the subsequently dominant Gaelic wave of migrants to Ireland did not arrive until about 250 years later. Thus the brilliant noonday sun of classical Athenian civilization coincides chronologically with the modest, rustic dawn of the Roman republic, and with the fabulous small hours of the Irish night, the dark silence broken only by legendary echoes of the Fir Bolg and the Tuatha Dé Danann.

THE POLITICAL STRUCTURE OF ANCIENT GREECE

During the whole period with which we are concerned the Greeks did not live in a single Greek state. In the seventh, sixth, fifth, and fourth centuries BC the people who spoke one or other dialect of the Greek language, and who recognized in their linguistic and cultural affinities a common Hellenic nationality, were distributed over the mainland of Greece, the islands of the Aegean, the coast and coastal islands of Asia Minor to the east, and the coasts of Sicily and southern Italy to the west; there were a few Greek settlements also on the Mediterranean shores of France and Spain, in Libya and Egypt, and in the Black Sea. These Greeks lived in hundreds of 'cities' (*poleis*), one of which—Athens—was of considerable size even by modern standards, but which varied greatly, down to something hardly bigger than a large village of the modern world together with a small immediate hinterland. These cities were essentially independent political entities; transient relationships and regional ascendancies might subject one city to another, a subjection expressed perhaps in the obligation to supply a tribute of money or ships, or in a forced military alliance, or in the dominance in the subject city of the faction favouring the stronger one; but these conditions, even when multiple subjections to a single ascendant city made it possible to speak of an Athenian 'empire', never implied the extinction of the independent personae of the other cities, which remained in theory autonomous, i.e. able to make their own laws and decide their own policies.

Accordingly, when we speak of Greek literature or (still more) of Greek law, we mean something quite different from the idea in the phrase Roman literature or Roman law. Greek literature and poetry exhibit a strong dialectal variety, whereas the Romans made their own Italic dialect, Latin, the standard for the Italian peninsula and for much of the Mediterranean world which they ruled. Similarly, while Roman law means the law which was elaborated within a more or less unitary master-state, 'Greek law' is a much looser expression, meaning the various codes or rules originating in a large number of independent political units inhabited by people of Hellenic language and culture. Certain features of broad family resemblance between the legal institutions of different cities can be seen, but in the classical era a unified Greek legal system never existed because no unified Greek state existed.

In any treatment of Greek civilization, including Greek law, there is a tendency for Athens to bulk very large, and often to seem synonymous with Greece itself. This is because, of the hundreds of Greek city-states, Athens was by far the greatest, in population, in power and influence, in wealth, in art and literature, until her defeat in the long Peloponnesian war with Sparta inaugurated a rapid decline. Even this decline is, in the area important for our subject, not obvious; for it is to the century which follows the Peloponnesian war that the great names of Athenian rhetoric belong, the orators Demosthenes, Lysias, Isocrates, Isaeus, as well as two of the great figures of Athenian philosophy, Plato and Aristotle; Plato's teacher, Socrates, was put to death soon after the end of the war. The infancy of Greek philosophy had been mostly led in the cities of Ionia (as the Greeks called the western coastal fringe of Asia Minor, modern Turkey); but its maturity, expressed in those names, is essentially Athenian; as, too, is the fifth-century maturity of Greek tragedy

(Aeschylus, Sophocles, Euripides), comedy (Aristophanes), historiography (Thucydides), and sculpture (Pheidias). Because of Athens having been thus brilliantly illumined for us by the literature of the fifth and fourth centuries, we know more about the life and politics of the city, including its legal life, than we do about the corresponding elements of any other Greek city (quite apart from the fact that the militaristic culture of Athens's rival, Sparta, was so philistine that there was no Spartan literature anyway). It is, however, altogether wrong to assume that a constitutional or legal rule evidenced at Athens was mirrored in a similar rule everywhere else. Despite the features of broad family resemblance mentioned above, Greek cities differed as widely in their political systems— which ranged with numerous gradations from kingships through tyrannies (most of them, in our period, in Sicily) and oligarchies to democracies, in many places with frequent revolutions from one system to another—as they did in dialect; their legal systems, though we are very imperfectly informed about most of them, probably reflected this variety in regimes.

THE SOURCES FOR GREEK LAW AND LEGAL THEORY

The materials for the history of Greek law are not to be found in Greek legal texts; the Greeks, so fertile in so many areas of the intellect, never produced a practical legal science; the Roman jurists were to be the first to give this to the world. Indeed such a thing as a Greek legal treatise does not exist, nor is there any hint that such a thing was ever written, even at Athens, or that any school of legal instruction ever operated there. What laws the people of Greece lived by must be gathered elsewhere; the best source is the physical remains of law-codes or statutes engraved on stone or bronze, of which archaeology has uncovered a scattering all over the Greek world, most no more than problematical fragments, only one—the code of Gortyn in Crete of about 450 BC—both large and well-preserved. Other evidence must be gathered wherever it can be found, chiefly in various departments of literature: a good deal, for example, is known of the law of Athens from the speeches of the fourth-century orators, while the works of historians, philosophers, and even dramatists also provide useful material. Much of the knowledge of the law of later, Hellenistic Egypt has been provided by the numerous papyri (documents made from the papyrus reed) which have been excavated there. As for the very earliest period at all accessible to us, however, the poems of Homer and Hesiod contain our only clues about legal life.

The position in regard to legal theory, as distinct from actual law, is similar. There was no such thing as a recognized and distinct branch of philosophy of specifically legal orientation; such questions as the origin and basis of the state, the source of obligation in law, or the relation of law to some higher or more fundamental standard, were not discussed in monographs on those themes alone, or by theorists specializing in them. Greek ideas on such matters are indeed recorded in great quantity, and are the first shoots of an intellectual growth which later ages cultivated in a more specific and organized way; but they must be gathered from a variety of literary sources, many of them quite unconscious contributions to the history of jurisprudence, a science for which the Greeks did not even have a name (just as there was no Greek word for 'law' as an abstract concept). Thus not only philosophical works—although these are certainly the most important—but also the work of poets, dramatists, and historians must be drawn on to provide the first chapter in that history.

ARCHAIC GREEK IDEAS ON LAW AND JUSTICE

The earliest coherent body of evidence we have about Greek life and thought is furnished by the Homeric epics, the *Iliad* (about the siege of Troy) and the *Odyssey* (about the wanderings of the Greek Odysseus trying to get home after the Trojan war); these poems seem to have been put into the form in which we know them about 800–700 BC, but this form represents the concretization of a long tradition of orally transmitted epic poetry, and it is agreed that the poems reflect a much earlier epoch of Greek society, very roughly 1300–1100 BC, the era to which the 'siege of Troy' (which from the evidence of archaeology may have been a historical event) can be assigned.

This archaic society already rests on 'cities', each with a political organization consisting of king, council of elders, and people. It is a society living according to an understood pattern, in which the supernatural plays an important part, and in which various moral virtues or faults are celebrated or deplored; but in which the idea of law, in a sense which the word conveys immediately to the modern mind—or conveyed to the Romans, or even to the Greeks of a later age—is fluid and elusive. We seem to be seeing, in Homer, the formative stage in the idea of law; indeed, if we appraise Homeric society from the standpoint of our own conception of law as something known, certain, and objective, we are seeing Europe in a pre-legal condition.

There is no 'legislature'. The king does not 'make' laws, in the sense of rules which the people must obey. There is no apparent consciousness of custom as something normative. Instead, there is *themis*: a word whose force is difficult to grasp, but which is applied to an area at the centre of which is perhaps the idea of a god-inspired decision or directive or finding. This finding is not arbitrary, but reflects a shared sense of what is proper. It is the word used to convey rulings of the gods as well as of kings; and 'as the gods came to be regarded as good in the sense of just and virtuous, so did *themis* take on the meaning of what was not so much expedient as morally incumbent upon gods and men alike. Thus *themis* began to imply some wider principle of which it was at once the expression and application', wrote J. W. Jones; 'from the first there is in *themis* always the assumption of a society of thinking beings, whether of gods or men, and of some sort of collective social conscience'.[1]

Side by side with *themis*, we find in the Homeric poems the notion of *dikē*, a word which in the Homeric era had not acquired its later clear senses (abstract justice or a lawsuit or a judgment) but nevertheless had a somewhat sharper edge, a 'severer countenance'[2] than *themis*. '*Themis* is a law of the heavens, *dikē* the earthily law which imitates it', wrote R. Köstler; 'the former rests on divine institution (*themis* from *tithēmi* = I place, set), the latter on direction from the law thus instituted (*dikē* from *deiknumi* = I point out, indicate), and is therefore derivative law which comes into effect through the sentence of the judge.'[3] This formulation of the shadowy relationship between the ideas is perhaps too compact, but, of the two concepts, *themis* is the more venerable, the more associated with supernatural beings or their inspiration of human

[1] J. W. Jones, *The Law and Legal Theory of the Greeks* (Oxford, 1956), 29–30.
[2] R. Hirzel, *Themis, Dike und Verwandtes* (Leipzig, 1907), 57.
[3] R. Köstler, 'Die homerische Rechts- und Staatsordnung', in E. Berneker (ed.), *Zur griechischen Rechtsgeschichte* 180.

rulers, *dikē* the word which later had a set of fully secular and practical senses and derivatives. To quote Köstler again, 'with the growth of an earthly legal system, the gods' legal system recedes, and, even in the Homeric epics, the concept *themis* is increasingly supplanted by that of *dikē*'.[4]

These hazy conceptual embryos, *themis* and *dikē*, are the symbols of a world not yet conscious of law (though familiar with the judicial decision of disputes, as the famous scene on the shield of Achilles attests).[5] Even the notion of custom—although the shared moral or emotional responses which *themis* and *dikē* presuppose might suggest that something like custom was understood—does not show through in the Homeric poems as having in principle what we would call the force of law. The word *nomos*, which in a later age signified custom (and, later still, a statute-law) does not occur at all in Homer. Of anything that can be called a theory of law, or reflection on the nature of society or the state or government, there is no trace in these epics, which otherwise transmit a very full idea of how Hellenic society lived and thought in the late second millennium BC.

In the age following Homer, in the eighth–sixth centuries BC, though the works of Hesiod and the lyric poets reflect a conception of justice—Hesiod (eighth century) complains of the evil of 'crooked judgments'[6]—there is still no sign that the concept of law has emerged. The commonest later word for law, *nomos*, does indeed appear in these poets; but as well as 'custom' it has a variety of other meanings, of which the central and unifying feature (going back to the root of the verb *nemō* = I apportion, distribute) is the idea of measuring out or allotting, in contexts from a musical measure to a pasturage of land, and including something like the idea of an arrangement being accepted as a proper apportionment. Modern authors have tried to build impressionistically the bridge between this elusive family of ideas and something which we can more easily understand as customary *law*; thus de Romilly: '*Nomos* effectively reconciles and combines the abstract ideal of order, and that simply of custom observed in practice';[7] and Jones: 'Until the age of the Athenian democracy, *nomos* preserved much of its old

---

[4] R. Köstler, 'Die homerische Rechts- und Staatsordnung', in E. Berneker (ed.), *Zur griechischen Rechtsgeschichte* 180.   [5] Homer, *Iliad* 18. 497 ff.

[6] *skoliai dikai*: Hesiod, *Works and Days* 224–6.

[7] *La Loi dans la pensée grecque* 23.

sense of any living group's way of life. But in group life there is always a tendency to identify what is habitually done with what ought to be done; to confuse "is" with "ought".'[8]

THE AGE OF THE LAWGIVERS

The earliest European appearance of something which obviously corresponds with our 'law' in the positive, statutory sense is with the famous lawgivers Dracōn (late seventh) and Solōn (early sixth century BC). This is the era in which, all over the Hellenic world, and undoubtedly related to the recent development of the art of writing, the first efforts were made to inscribe in permanent and public form rules which formerly had the vaguer status of custom, the interpretation or even the statement of which was vulnerable to distortion through the self-interest of the aristocracies which ruled in most Greek cities and whose members were the repositories of whatever justice there was.

These earliest recorded positive laws are called at first not *nomoi* (*nomos* apparently still meant, in its sense nearest to this subject, merely custom) but *thesmoi*, which, like *themis*, is a formation from *tithēmi*. The dramatist Euripides, writing in the late fifth century, presents the emergence of written laws as a progressive achievement, tending to equalize the ground of rich and poor; laws, once publicly written up on stone or bronze, were equally knowable and accessible to all, and so no longer subject to the arbitrary statement or interpretation of a closed and privileged caste.[9]

STATUS (AND ORIGINAL QUASI-SANCTITY) OF STATUTE-LAW

The earliest phase of Greek legislation was associated with individual lawgivers such as Dracōn and Solōn at Athens, (the perhaps mythical) Lycurgus at Sparta, Charondas at Catana, Zaleucus at Locri. But the later legislative process, at any rate in cities which were democracies, rested on a majority vote of the people. Democratic legislation seems also to have led to a

---

[8] Jones, *Legal Theory* (see n. 1), 34.   [9] *Suppliants* 429 ff.

broadening of the meaning of *nomos* so as to include law, in what
now became the only recognized sense, i.e. statute, as well as mere
custom. Once the wave of codes had passed over the Greek world,
statute came to be thought of not just as a more effective vesture for
law, but as its only source; there is no trace of custom being looked
on as an independent or even complementary source of law. Indeed
the prejudice in favour of statute reached the point that, where an
ancient rule was actually practised although not contained in a
contemporaneously existing written law, it was attributed to a
former lawgiver, even if he was a mythical one.[10]

The Athenian democracy of the fifth century evidently saw in its
nomoi, its laws, a characteristic feature which proudly distinguished
them, as other Greeks were for the same reason distinguished, from
their non-Greek ('barbarian') neighbours; the latter, of whom the
Persians defeated at Salamis and Marathon bulked the largest in the
Greek eye, were ruled by tyrants guided only by their own
arbitrary discretion, while the Greeks—to use the words put by the
historian Herodotus into the mouth of Dēmaratos the fugitive king
of Sparta conversing with Xerxes the king of the Persians—
'although free, are not free in everything: they have a master,
namely the law, which they fear even more than your subjects fear
you'.[11] To see in this claim the earliest recorded expression of what
we call the 'rule of law' is perhaps too simple, but it does convey a
definite sense of an objectified law, concrete now where formerly it
was a vague amalgam of debatable custom and unpredictable
inspired 'findings'. The literary tradition of the fifth and fourth
centuries, de Romilly wrote, 'implies a heightened sense of a
common law which the citizens had been able to give themselves,
and from which they expected both order and liberty. Even then,
liberty was defined for them as obedience to the laws'.[12]

This sense of a proud distinction in the possession of written laws
may have something to do with the strong difference in attitude
towards statute law between the Greeks and the medieval and
modern (and to some extent even the Roman) world. Whereas no
particular sanctity attaches, in the modern eye, to the original text of
an enactment, in the sense that no inhibition is felt about amending

---

[10] H. J. Wolff, 'Gewohnheitsrecht und Gesetzesrecht', in E. Wolf (ed.),
Griechische Rechtsgeschichte, 112.

[11] *Histories* 7. 104. See also Euripides, *Medea* 536–8, *Orestes* 487.

[12] Romilly, *La Loi* (see n. 7), 23.

it, perhaps frequently, in response to changed conditions, the Greeks were at first averse to altering their laws. A general predisposition in favour of the stability and permanence of a law once made is attested both by passages in literature (Aeschylus, Thucydides, Aristotle)[13] and by evidence about rules actually governing the process of proposing a new law (which necessarily must repeal or modify the old one). The most extreme example is reported by Demosthenes about the Locrians, a Dorian people living in the toe of Italy, who were reputed to have been the first of all the Greeks to adopt a written code; anyone who proposed an alteration in their laws had to make his proposal with a rope around his neck, which, if his proposal was rejected, was drawn tight.[14] The Athenians, who were of the other (Ionian) branch of the Greek family, had no such spectacularly drastic law; but the process of legislation in Athens was hedged around with formidable barriers. Someone proposing a new law had first to bring a sort of prosecution (*graphē*) against the old law which it was to replace, and risked being himself prosecuted for what might be called unconstitutional behaviour, in the *graphē paranomōn*, if he neglected some requisite formality or if his proposal could be represented as offending against some fundamental value.

In the following age this austerity was relaxed, at any rate in the era of Athens's incipient decline; new laws multiplied, the legislative process was degraded to an engine of political warfare, and even the recording of new laws became chaotic, so that it was often uncertain whether a supposed law existed or not, or whether a directly contradictory law might coexist with it. A further source of confusion was the unclear relationship of *psēphismata* (resolutions, decrees) to *nomoi*, statutes more strictly so called; the most that can be said is that *nomoi* were envisaged as permanent general dispositions, while *psēphismata* were *ad hoc* or supplementary or effectuating measures; though Aristotle uses the word in the sense of something which modifies a general law to meet the equity of a particular case,[15] and *psēphismata* are occasionally themselves included in the category of *nomoi*. It is however clear from the expressions of the orators that this picture of uncertainty, and of the transfusion of the legislative process by political expediencies of

[13] See Friedemann Quass, 'Nomos und Psephisma', *Zetemata*, 55 (1971), 20–1.
[14] Demosthenes, *Against Timocrates* 139.
[15] *Nicomachean Ethics* 5. 10. 6.

the moment, was regarded as a shameful decline from the standards of an earlier age which had looked on the ancestral laws as immutable.

THE EMERGENCE OF LEGAL THEORY: ORIGIN OF THE STATE AND OF LAW

When the Greek philosophers first began to reflect on the human condition rather than on the physical universe, they found themselves and their neighbours already living in cities, many of them so old that their foundation was entangled in myth. How was this organization to be accounted for? The answer might be interesting not only in the same sense as some other pattern in nature might call for explanation, but also because it might suggest prescriptions for the conduct men ought to adopt in their mutual association.

Since urban existence in Greece appeared immemorial, it could not be accounted for purely as a matter of history, and admitted only hypotheses. Plato (427–347 BC) in his relatively early work *Protagoras* addressed the problem briefly, explaining that while primitive man had the capacity to feed himself, he was unable as an individual to defend himself against wild animals; at this stage he was still without 'civic skill' (*politikē technē*), the faculty of living in community with others; men learned however the necessity of combining in order to defeat the threats of the wild, and saved themselves by founding cities. This did not work too well at first because of men's ill behaviour to one another; but ultimately Zeus bestowed on them the mutual respect and sense of justice which made civic existence feasible.[16] In his last work, the *Laws*, much the same idea is presented at greater length. Here Plato visualized men's primordial political acts as having vanished in the Deluge (a Greek as well as a Jewish idea), after which a fresh start had to be made. Food was plentiful, and there was no need to compete for it; and because of men's desolate condition, they were friendly to one another. They had no need of formal laws, but lived by custom and patriarchal rules, their groupings coagulating progressively into larger communities and finally into something like national polities.[17]

---

[16] *Protagoras* 322 BC.   [17] Ibid. 677 ff.

Plato's (ultimately more influential) disciple Aristotle (384–321 BC) also presented the origin of civic existence as an organic development, resting for him on the progressive and natural accumulation of units, starting with the family, and thence evolving into the city or state (*polis*) through the union of neighbouring villages.[18]

Of permanent importance in Aristotle's conception is his emphasis on the *natural* character of this familial and social coagulation. Deploying his idea that the nature of everything is to reach always towards its own perfection in the achievement of its purpose, he presented the city-state as the perfected framework for leading the good life, and man's instinct to combine in such an organization as something natural to him for this reason. In a passage culminating in a very famous phrase he characterizes man as a creature tending by his nature to a civic existence:

The partnership finally composed of several villages is the city-state; it has at last attained the limit of virtually complete self-sufficiency, and thus, while it comes into existence for the sake of life, it exists for the good life. Hence every city-state exists by nature, inasmuch as the first partnerships so exist; for the city-state is the end of the other partnerships, and nature is an end, since that which each thing is when its growth is completed we speak of as being the nature of each thing, for instance of a man, a horse, a household. Again, the object for which a thing exists, its end, is its chief good; and self-sufficiency is an end, and a chief good. From these things therefore it is clear that the city-state is a natural growth, and that man is by nature a being inclined to a civic existence (*politikon zōon*).

But this characteristic of man as a being impelled by his natural instinct to live in an ordered community with his fellows does not make him a mere analogue, in his order, of other kinds of gregarious animal; for (unlike bees and so on) 'man alone has perception of good and bad and right and wrong and the other moral qualities, and it is partnership in these things that makes a household and a city-state'.[19]

This presentation of human nature as one tending to organized association of the kind which the Greek city-state embodied—to civic existence, in what seems the best rendering of the phrase *politikon zōon* which when translated as 'political animal' is so often misunderstood—did not exhaust the Greek contribution to the theory of the individual's role *vis-à-vis* the rest of society and the

---

[18] *Politics* 1. 1 ff.   [19] Ibid. 1. 1. 8–9, 11.

state. It was in the consideration of this problem, in the form of the question as to whence the citizen's obligation to obey the law arose, that Greek philosophy foreshadowed the most pervasive and most fruitful of European political and legal theories, that of the 'social contract', the idea that submission to government and law, the fundamental civic duty, rests on a supposed original agreement to which the individual citizen remains by implication a party.

This notion, so far as we can trace its beginning, surfaced in the demoralized climate of Athens at the end of the Peloponnesian war, afflicted by disease and defeat, and in a famous and tragic setting. Athens at that epoch contained a school or movement of minds called then and since by the name sophists, the word *sophistes* deriving from the adjective *sophos* (wise), but intended to convey a disparaging modulation of the idea of wisdom implying something like superficial cleverness allied with moral rootlessness. A position maintained by the sophists (and suggested perhaps by the ambiguity of the word *nomos*) was that, since human customs are widely and visibly different from place to place,[20] laws (even in the sense of deliberate statutory regulation of human behaviour) might perhaps be regarded as equally relative and contingent. In other words, does a law (*nomos* in the later sense of statute) have any more compelling moral content than an observed custom (*nomos* in the former sense), which might easily have been otherwise, and in fact *is* otherwise among people living on the other side of a sea or mountain range? Why should disobedience to law be wicked, when no one could rationally stigmatize in this way the non-observance by one tribe of a custom recognized by another? Sophists tended to answer that all law is merely conventional, contingent, accidental, variable; this observation, evidently valid for mere custom, had however the effect of fixing law itself with the character of relativity and indifference, and thus of floating it off from the moral moorings which provide the sense of duty to obey it.

To this *nomos*, which was no more than conventional, the sophists contrasted nature (*physis*), which was immutable. This was not what a later age meant by the 'law of nature' discoverable by reason, but rather the natural physical universe and the instinctual nature of its human inhabitants, which were unvarying everywhere. This formula, which in one aspect was just a piece of observation,

---

[20] See, for a famous instance, Herodotus 3. 38 (respective customs of Greeks and Indians for the disposal of their dead).

developed a moral dimension as soon as the sophist Antiphon[21] presented human nature as being to dominate those weaker than oneself, and to follow one's own interest, the consequence of which being that law was a violence done to nature inasmuch as it inhibited the unchecked pursuit of self-interest (since law itself was a purely conventional system which might have been shaped otherwise in some other place). He saw people as having an interest in obeying the law only if they were being observed by others (if unobserved, and so able to disobey with impunity, there was no reason not to do so). This, as we would say, anti-social teaching caused an indignant reaction; the comedian Aristophanes satirized the demoralization and lack of respect for the laws (generally then blamed on the sophists) by showing a son beating his father and justifying himself by the example of animals which attack their parents.[22] But the overall effect of sophistic doctrine, at its strongest in the era of Athenian defeat at the close of the fifth century, was to take the moral stuffing out of the not yet fully developed idea of law, and so to deprive any part of a legal system of any permanent, rationally defensible authority.

The first philosopher to challenge the sophistic position was Socrates (469–399 BC), who ended his life having been condemned to death for reasons which are still obscure—ostensibly for 'corrupting the youth', but probably at least partly because of the spirit of critical detachment towards received ideas and ancestral beliefs which the whole tribe of philosophers—Socrates as well as the sophists—displayed. In prison under sentence, and waiting to be given the fatal draught of poison, Socrates could, apparently, have easily escaped; his friends were anxious to arrange this, and the authorities (it is suggested) might have been glad enough to turn a blind eye to the frustration of a sentence which some of them now regretted. Plato's dialogue *Crito* shows Socrates's friend of that name trying to persuade him to grasp the chance of life; Socrates firmly refuses, determined to remain obedient to the laws of his city, though he was himself the innocent victim of their unjust operation. He imagines the laws as personified, and as arguing with him the basis of his duty to obey them, a duty resting indeed on 'convention', but in a far deeper and morally weightier sense than that intended by the sophists; convention in the sense, in fact, of

[21] *On Truth*, fr. 44A (Diehls).   [22] Romilly, *La Loi* (see n. 7), 108 ff.

implied but none the less binding contract. Socrates had had the benefit of those laws all his life; if he had not wished for their protection, he could have left Athens and gone to live elsewhere; and so by his conduct he has tacitly agreed to respect them. 'We regard someone who remains here' (he imagines the laws addressing him),

> having seen what sort of justice and government we operate, as having in effect agreed to be bound by our measures; and the disobedient citizen as being unjust in three ways: he injures us as his parents, as his educators, and also by breaking his agreement to obey us (while failing to persuade us that we are in the wrong).[23]

And this disobedience, if Socrates were to take the chance of escape, would amount (say the laws) to 'doing what in you lies to destroy the laws and with it the whole state'.[24] This quixotic determination to uphold the laws even at the unjust sacrifice of his own life gives peculiar force to the element of agreement, of contract, as the rock on which both state and laws are founded.

In fact the sophists' view of human nature had itself also produced a contractual formula for the state's origin. In his *Republic* Plato has Socrates debating the nature of justice with Glaucon, who, stating the position that human nature tends to commit injustice where it can get away with it while avoiding its infliction by others, says:

> So, when men do wrong and are wronged by one another and taste of both, those who lack the power to avoid the one and to take the other determine that it is for their profit to make a compact with one another neither to commit nor to suffer injustice; and this is the beginning of legislation and covenants between men, and of their calling lawful and just what the law commands, and of the fact that this is the genesis and nature of justice, a compromise between the best, which is to do wrong with impunity, and the worst, which is to be wronged and to be impotent to get one's revenge.[25]

Both the more and the less high-minded view of the state and its laws being rooted in mutual agreement continued to resound in the following century. It is possible to assign to the materialist side of the line the argument used by Demosthenes in his speech *Against Meidias* which concludes[26] with an appeal to the court's members to reflect that the personal security of each of them depends on the

---

[23] *Crito* 12–14.   [24] Ibid. 11.
[25] Plato, *Republic* 358e–359a.   [26] *Against Meidias* 223 ff.

solidarity of all in upholding the law (in breach of which Demosthenes had himself been assaulted)—a plain invocation of self-interest as recommending obedience to law. Aristotle, on the other hand, who rejected the theory that the state grew from the exigencies of man's purely animalic nature, saw human beings as essentially different from other animals in having a natural tendency to associate in a civil structure, a formula which, though not explicitly contractual and indeed brought into the field against the sophist position, must still imply, in the simultaneous expression of people's civil natures, some understood pattern of concerted forbearance and co-operation.

LAW AS A COMMAND

The question 'what is law?' which bulks so large in modern legal theory seems scarcely to have occurred to Greek thinkers. In the classical era of Athenian philosophy the expression 'the laws' conveyed a meaning, and evoked a response, clear enough for purposes of their discourse, without analysis of the kind which would identify a precept as falling either inside or outside the category of *nomos*. Yet Greek literature is not absolutely without mention of the matter; it surfaces, though inconclusively, in a form foreshadowing that which in the early nineteenth century Austin (following Bentham) would give it. Aristotle focuses on the character of law as being a 'kind of order' (in the sense of orderly regulation: *taxis tis*); good law must mean good order.[27] But law has compulsive force (*anankastikē dynamis*),[28] he says, being the rational product of mind and consideration.

Here note of compulsion, of the law's imperative quality, is perhaps only glimpsed in a text which is difficult anyway. But some years earlier Xenophon reports a supposed conversation between Pericles and the young Alcibiades in which two of the central problems of jurisprudence are touched on. One is the relation of law to the expression of a political superior's command (the other being whether the existence of a political superior's command is enough to confer the character of law on what he decrees). In reply to Alcibiades's question of what law is, Pericles says first that 'all

[27] *Politics* 7. 4. 5.   [28] *Nicomachean Ethics* 10. 9. 12.

those measures are laws, which the body of the people in assembly has approved and had inscribed, laying down the conduct to be observed or to be avoided'. Alcibiades points out the inadequacy, or inaccuracy, of this definition. The authority of the people, stipulated by Pericles, cannot be essential to the meaning of 'law', he says, because in an oligarchy, too, 'all the decrees of the dominant group in council also carry the name of law', and this goes even for a tyranny, since a tyrant's statute also is called *nomos*. Accordingly, what seems to be a law would, on Pericles's definition (says Alcibiades), be a mere exercise of force and therefore in effect a piece of lawlessness (*anomia*). Pericles concedes that what has been constrained by force, and does not rest on persuasion, is indeed violence rather than law, whether it is formally inscribed or not.[29] But note that this whole conversation, whether envisaging the decrees of a democracy, an oligarchy, or a tyranny, presents a law as essentially a command or prohibition issued by political authority. Similarly the orator Lycurgus, a younger contemporary of Xenophon, says that laws are too brief to give instruction, they merely declare 'what must be done' (*ha dei poiein*: the phrase which Xenophon also uses).[30] There is no evident consciousness here of 'law' encompassing rules of other kinds. The only sign in recorded Greek thought that—to use phrases coined in modern times by H. L. A. Hart—a distinction was appreciated between 'primary' rules of obligation (commands and prohibitions) and 'secondary' ones such as 'power-conferring' rules (these being also law), is to be found in Aristotle's classification of the types of 'corrective justice', as will be seen below.

ELEMENTS WHICH CONDITION LAW IN PRACTICE

The Greeks were conscious of the variations between the laws of different peoples, and some of them used this fact to deny any moral duty to obey a particular law of one's own city. Aristotle, however, at the close of his *Ethics*[31] and by way of introduction to his *Politics*, visualizes collections of different cities' laws as being serviceable to public men 'capable of studying them critically, and of judging what measures are valuable or the reverse; and what kinds of laws are

---

[29] *Memorabilia* 1. 2. 40–6.   [30] Lycurgus, *Against Leocrates* 102.
[31] *Nicomachean Ethics* 10. 9. 21.

suited to what kinds of people'. The latter clause is meant to render an over-terse Greek phrase (*poia poiois harmottei*), and, if it is correct, it does suggest that Aristotle recognized the necessity for laws to be adapted to the different characters and circumstances of the people they were to govern.

The perception of law as the expression of the interest of the dominant class, associated in the modern world with the Marxist critique of bourgeois society, appears in ancient Greece both in the frequently reiterated principle that legislation should be for the benefit of the whole people (of which more below), and in the observations in Plato suggesting that the dominant element in a state tends to make laws benefiting itself. In his *Republic* the uncouth sophist Thrasymachus is presented advancing the thesis that 'each form of government enacts the laws with a view to its own advantage', thus consecrating the legislation 'that which is for their—the rulers'—advantage, and the man who deviates from this law they chastise as a law-breaker and a wrongdoer'.[32] Socrates contests his conclusion that justice is in fact the interest of the stronger, while not contradicting his observation as to what happens in practice. In his late work, the *Laws*, the same view is presented as being a generally held opinion.[33]

THE RELATION OF LAW TO A HIGHER STANDARD

A central problem of jurisprudence is whether a law, in order to be recognized as such, need conform only to formal criteria, or whether its validity depends also on its not infringing some permanent, higher, 'natural' standard. In other words, even assuming in general terms that the state and its laws are entitled to obedience, does this mean that any measure whatever, as long as it bears the formal marks of enactment, is entitled to this obedience, however repugnant it may be to the subject's moral values? Or is there a transcendent standard which is paramount?

This question, on which Christian theory has had no doubts since the early Middle Ages, and which lies at the root of all modern discussion of 'fundamental rights', was not posed by ancient Greek

[32] Plato, *Republic* 338d, e.   [33] Plato, *Laws* 715a.

philosophy, but does appear in Greek literature. It is raised in mid-
fifth century Athenian tragedy, in the *Antigone* of Sophocles, where
it is presented in the form of a celebrated dilemma, handled by the
poet so easily as to make us suspect that it was a commonplace even
in his time. A civil war had divided two brothers, one of whom died
in attacking Thebes, the other in its defence. The king forbids the
burial of the former, wishing to leave his body to be devoured by
beasts; but thus also, according to Greek religious ideas, preventing
his soul from finding the repose which only burial—even a token
interment under a handful of earth—can ensure. Antigone, the dead
brothers' sister, is impelled by piety to disobey; she puts earth on
the body lying exposed on the plain, and is arrested. The king asks
her whether she knew of his order, and, if so, why she disobeyed it.
She replies:

> . . . These laws were not ordained of Zeus,
> And she who sits enthroned with gods below,
> Justice, enacted not these human laws.
> Nor did I deem that thou, a mortal man,
> Couldst by a breath annul and override
> The immutable unwritten laws of heaven.
> They were not born today nor yesterday;
> They die not; and none knoweth whence they sprang.[34]

Eternal laws of supernatural origin are mentioned by Sophocles also
in another passage,[35] though not in a context of similar dramatic
confrontation. But otherwise the *Antigone* passage, although much
cited in later classical literature,[36] is isolated. It contains a thought
which never surfaces among the philosophers writing on the theme
of law, nor among the orators pleading before courts of law. In
general, Greek thought knew nothing of the idea that there exists a
range of values, which, if human laws should conflict with them,
render those laws invalid.

Nevertheless the Greeks reveal, in two ways, a belief in the idea
of something transcending positive laws, something which is
'naturally' right and proper, something classifiable as 'natural' law
or justice. Firstly, Aristotle actually enunciated[37] the theoretical
distinction between that which is naturally just (*to physikon
dikaion*) and that which is just only in consequence of having been
prescribed by positive law (*to nomikon dikaion*):

---

[34] *Antigone* 453–7.   [35] *Oedipus Rex* 865 ff.
[36] Aristotle, *Rhetoric* 1. 18. 2.   [37] *Nicomachean Ethics* 5. 7. 1.

Of political justice [*to politikon dikaion* = something like 'the rules governing citizens'] one sort is natural, the other conventional; and the natural sort has the same force everywhere and does not depend upon one's opinion being for or against it, whereas the conventional sort of rule, while initially it does not matter whether it is fixed one way or the other, once it *is* fixed, ceases to be a matter of indifference; such for instance as [various arbitrarily fixed amounts of ransoms, sacrifices, etc.].

But the example of a natural rule which he gives is an unfortunate one for our purposes; it describes not a natural law in the moral order, but a 'law' of the physical universe—something that we would call a law only in a metaphorical sense—namely, the fact that fire burns in the same way in Greece as in Persia. He does not venture on examples of 'natural' rules in the area of human behaviour; and, while he says later in the same passage that 'there is such a thing as natural justice', he calls it 'variable' in the same way that purely conventional rules are variable, and again gives an example from physical rather than moral nature: the fact that, though most people are born right-handed, they can make themselves ambidextrous.

Secondly, a series of Greek literary passages suggests that a certain range of relationships was felt to involve 'natural' rights and duties (though without asserting the invalidity of conflicting positive laws). The family relationship was seen as carrying with it the natural duty of children to give honourable burial to parents[38] and to support them in old age, just as the parents had been under a natural duty to sustain their children in infancy.[39] Again, while Aristotle admitted that all men were born free by nature, and had difficulty in justifying the institution of slavery (universal in the ancient world), enslavement was regarded as the natural consequence of capture in war.[40] The rights of intestate succession were attributed to the natural circumstances of blood relationship;[41] the right of self-defence was equally located in nature,[42] and, as will be seen, punishment for wrongdoing which exactly matched the mode of the offence (symmetrical retribution) was considered to be what nature suggested.[43]

---

[38] See Jones, *Legal Theory* (see n. 1), 59 ff.   [39] Ibid.
[40] *Politics* 1. 4–5.   [41] Jones, *Legal Theory* (see n. 1), 62.
[42] Ibid.
[43] See below at the end of the section on 'The Theory of Punishment'.

THE PURPOSE AND SCOPE OF LAW

As has been seen, philosophers could recognize the element of self-serving class interest in the actual governance of states. But the references we possess to the subject show that legislation intended to benefit only a section of the people, or the ruling interest, was disapproved of. The theme is not as often heard as it was to be in the early Middle Ages, when churchmen had to admonish the half-barbaric German masters of Europe that their temporal rule was entrusted to them by God for their subjects' sake, not for their own arbitrary pleasure. Plato both in his *Republic* and in his *Laws* emphasizes the conferring of *general* benefit as the proper role of law. In the earlier work he shows us Socrates, locked in conflict with the ill-conditioned Thrasymachus, drawing an analogy between the office of a ruler and the professions of a physician and a pilot, seen strictly as such. Just as the latter, in their professional character, consider the advantage of patients and sailors in their charge rather than their own, so 'neither does anyone in any office of rule, in so far as he is a ruler, consider and enjoin his own advantage but that of the one whom he rules and for whom he exercises his craft, and he keeps his eyes fixed on that, and on what is advantageous and suitable to that, in all that he says and does'.[44] In the *Laws* he condemns regimes in which power is jealously monopolized by the victorious interest; these, he says,

we, of course, deny to be *politeiai* [here meaning something like 'constitutional systems'], just as we deny that laws are true laws unless they are enacted in the interest of the common weal of the whole state. But where the laws are enacted in the interest of a section, we call them *stasiōteiai* [a word he has coined from *stasis* = faction, as we might say 'factionalities'] rather than *politeiai*; and the 'justice' they ascribe to such laws is, we say, an empty name.[45]

In these passages, taken in isolation, Plato may be thinking of laws with the sort of functional range familiar to a Greek city. If the code of Gortyn in Crete were typical (it is mentioned only because it is the most complete set of Greek city-laws to survive) they would deal with various departments of crime, property, succession, contract, and so on, and would have some kind of analogues,

---

[44] Plato, *Republic* 342d, e.   [45] Plato, *Laws* 715b.

however remote, in the legal systems of modern states. But Plato's idea of what law, in a more or less coercive sense, could be got to do did not end with such pedestrian functions. He assigned to law not merely the regulation of conditions inherent or at least common in human society, but also the deliberate training (in the gardener's quite as much as in the teacher's sense) of that society towards an ideal state of perfection. Thus he visualized law in an extra dimension which, although various regimes have tried to make it a reality, the West has on the whole rejected.

The conception of a state in which law has this dimension was made articulate by Plato; but it existed in practice already in his time in the most individual of all Greek states, Sparta, and Sparta is thought to have been his inspiration. This city, a byword then as now for rigorous austerity, enforced its manners by education and training on the young, and maintained them among them as adults. These manners had no basis in what we might recognize as a religious morality, but were geared to the production and constant renewal of a militarist and irresistible state. Other Greeks, glimpsing, as they thought, something of the pristine simplicity and manliness of their race in a milieu which must have resembled that of a philistine boarding-school, felt a sneaking admiration for Sparta, expressed in Plato's case by his proposing something like the Spartan model for his ideal polity and its rulers.

These rulers ('guardians') are central to the whole system.[46] The first generation of rulers is to be selected by the legislator, who will also divide the remaining population into the second class (soldiers) and the third (common people); thereafter an official myth will be propagated, according to which these three categories correspond to a divinely preordained classification. The further breeding in the ruler class is to be governed by rigorous eugenic regulation, by which weaklings will be either avoided or eliminated. Between the rulers—who may, incidentally, be of either sex—a communism not only of property but of sexual partners and of children is to be observed. Anything like the nuclear family, the concept around which so much of Christian and even of non-Christian law and ethics revolves, will not be in the picture. The education of young people is to be subject to the most minute regulation, with certain modes of music excluded from the curriculum as tending to

[46] *Republic* 374 ff., 395 ff.

encourage softness or frivolity; the body is to be trained to endure hardship, the spirit to show courage; the formation of the intellect is to be aimed at producing rulers who will be philosophers (the 'philosopher kings', in a phrase commonly used to sum up this idea of Plato's). The formidable austerity and the (to us, repellent) conformity which Plato sought for—and in some measure found in his Spartan model—was, however, not visualized as harnessed to the sort of imperialist or racialist ideology with which we might expect to find it associated in the twentieth century. It was simply a regime which he rather naïvely thought would produce a noble state in which justice could best be achieved. Thus it was a regime complying certainly at first sight with the doctrine that laws should be for the general benefit; but (at any rate, as we would think) conflicting with it at a deeper level because established at too great a cost in human freedom and dignity.

This conception of law stretched to encompass so ambitious a function as engineering a new kind of state is not echoed by other classical Greek philosophers; though Aristotle in his *Ethics* also seems to attribute to law a function formative as well as regulatory, namely that of training in virtue.

It is difficult [he says] to obtain a right education in virtue from youth up without being brought up under right laws; for to live temperately and hardily is not pleasant to most men, especially when young; hence the nurture and exercises of the young should be regulated by law . . . We shall need laws to regulate the discipline of adults as well, and in fact the whole life of the people generally; for the many are more amenable to compulsion and punishment than to reason and to moral ideals. Hence some persons hold that, while it is proper for the lawgiver to encourage and exhort men to virtue on moral grounds, in the expectation that those who have had a virtuous moral upbringing will respond, yet he is bound to impose chastisement and penalties on the disobedient and ill-conditioned, and to banish the incorrigible out of the state altogether.[47]

The Rule of Law

The ideal of the state whose authorities act in accordance with pre-existing, known laws, not arbitrarily or without regard to those

---

[47] *Nicomachean Ethics* 10. 9. 8–9.

laws, is not made explicit in this abstract form in classical Greece. Nevertheless the substance of the ideal is often expressed by philosophers and historians. The *general* sovereignty of law rather than arbitrary rule was (according to Herodotus, cited above reproducing a dialogue between a Spartan and a Persian) felt as a proud distinction of free Greek cities. Its *specific* sovereignty over rulers themselves comes through in passages which show them in fact acting subject to it, or which prescribe such subjection as essential to good government.

Thus Plato in his *Laws* makes the main speaker, an Athenian, call magistrates the 'servants' of the laws, thinking this a vital condition for the ideal system: 'For wherever in a state the law is subservient and impotent, over that state I see ruin impending; but wherever the law is lord over the magistrates, and the magistrates are servants to the law, there I descry salvation and all the blessings that the gods bestow on states.' His interlocutor, a Cretan, agrees with him.[48] Aristotle in his *Ethics* says 'we do not permit a man to rule, but the law' (as a man tends to rule for his own benefit and thus becomes a tyrant).[49] In his *Politics* he says the laws, if rightly enacted, ought to be sovereign, with discretion left to rulers only in matters of detail which general laws cannot cover exhaustively (though he appears also to say that the laws are not to be sovereign if they 'go off the rails', i.e., perhaps, if they turn out to be completely unsuitable).[50] Obedience to law is a high point of praise of rulers: Aristotle in his work on the constitution of Athens commends the sixth-century autocrat Pisistratus for having ruled in accordance with the laws (of Solōn, according to Plutarch)[51] and taken no advantage for himself; and reports that the principal Athenian magistrates, the archons, take an oath on entering office to govern according to the laws;[52] any private citizen may prosecute an official for failure to observe them.[53] Plutarch (writing admittedly four centuries later, and in the Roman world) strikes the same note in his praise of ancient Greek rulers; as well as Pisistratus, he mentions in the same sense the Theban Pelopidas and the Corinthian Timoleon for having governed in accordance with law. It is true that Plutarch's attitude towards

---

[48] *Laws* 715d.

[49] *Nicomachean Ethics* 5. 6. 5. The Greek word *tyrannos* means an absolute ruler, but not necessarily with the suggestion of oppressiveness or cruelty which the English derivative carries.

[50] *Politics* 3. 6. 13, 3. 10. 5. See also 3. 9. 3–5, 3. 10. 10.   [51] *Solon* 31.

[52] *Athenian Constitution* 16. 8, 55. 5.   [53] Ibid. 57. 3.

statesmen who bend the law to favour their friends is ambivalent—in his life of Themistocles he appears to disapprove it, but to countenance it in his life of Aristides.[54] This is perhaps a special context. In general, the Greek mind, as far as is accessible to us through those writings, believed the ruler of a city ought to be governed by its laws.

ARISTOTLE'S ANALYSIS OF JUSTICE

The nearest thing to conscious legal theory in classical Greek literature is to be found in the fifth book of the *Nicomachean*[55] *Ethics* of Aristotle, devoted to an analysis of justice and equity. Justice, Aristotle thought, 'can only exist between those whose mutual relations are regulated by law, and law exists among those between whom there is a possibility of injustice, for the administration of the law means the discrimination of what is just and what is unjust'.[56] But justice, he wrote in a classification which became celebrated, is of two kinds: 'distributive' and 'corrective'. By distributive justice he meant 'that which is exercised in the distribution of honour, wealth, and the other divisible assets of the community, which may be allotted among its members in equal or unequal shares.[57] Allowing for the far greater range of material regulation characteristic of the modern state, we might say this definition corresponds evidently with 'legislative justice', the kind we expect to see displayed in statutes or other governmental measures which distribute benefits or impose burdens in patterns and proportions which we can accept as fair or rational having regard to the subject-matter; the kind—to use a phrase which has entered Irish constitutional jurisprudence from the United States— which is free of 'invidious discrimination'. Aristotle's meaning emerges from some general propositions, for example, that equals are to be treated equally, unequals unequally;[58] that justice is proportion, injustice is disproportion.[59] He presents this in a sort of formula: a just distribution involves, in the simplest case, a pair of persons and a pair of 'shares', and so involves at least four terms in a

---

[54] Plutarch, *Pelopidas* 26, 31, *Timoleon* 10, *Themistocles* 5, *Aristides* 2.
[55] So called because dedicated (it appears) to Aristotle's son Nicomachus.
[56] *Nicomachean Ethics* 5. 6. 4.   [57] Ibid. 5. 2. 12.
[58] Ibid. 5. 3. 6.   [59] Ibid. 5. 3. 14.

'geometrical proportion', i.e. 'one in which the sum of the first and third terms will bear the same ratio to the sum of the second and fourth as one term of either pair bears to the other term'.[60] He does not, however, descend to discussing a hypothetical concrete situation to be regulated by law, which will of course not respond to measurement against an abstract formula, but only to a legislator's instinct of fairness.

'Corrective' justice, on the other hand, is not legislative justice, but rather what we might call judicial justice, the justice of the courts. Corrective justice is putting right something that has gone wrong, restoring an equilibrium where the just balance has been disturbed. Here the formula is simpler, an arithmetical rather than a geometrical proportion, since the respective qualities of the persons involved are immaterial:

For it makes no difference whether a good man has defrauded a bad man or a bad man a good one, nor whether it is a good or a bad man that has committed adultery; the law looks only at the nature of the damage, treating the parties as equal, and merely asking whether one has done and the other suffered injustice, whether one inflicted and the other has sustained damage. Hence the unjust being here the unequal, the judge endeavours to equalise it: inasmuch as when one man has received and the other has inflicted a blow, or one has killed and the other been killed, the line representing the suffering and the doing of the deed is divided into unequal parts, but the judge endeavours to make them equal by the penalty or loss he imposes, taking away the gain ['gain' being used to include the condition of having inflicted, and so far got away with having inflicted, an injury].[61]

This corrective justice, moreover, comes in two forms: where it intervenes in situations which are 'voluntary', and where it does so in situations which are 'involuntary'. These words, by themselves too compressed to convey much meaning, he explains like this:

Examples of voluntary transactions are selling, buying, lending at interest, pledging, lending without interest, depositing, letting for hire; these transactions being termed voluntary because they are voluntarily entered upon. Of involuntary transactions some are furtive, for instance, theft, adultery, poisoning, procuring, enticement of slaves, assassination, false witness; others are violent, for instance, assault, imprisonment, murder, robbery with violence, maiming, abusive language, contumelious treatment.[62]

[60] Ibid. 5. 3. 10–13.   [61] Ibid. 5. 4. 3.   [62] Ibid. 5. 2. 13.

The distinction between 'voluntary' and 'involuntary' transactions corresponds superficially with the distinction which we would recognize between contract, on the one hand, and tortious or criminal wrongs, on the other. It is, however, interesting in particular because it corresponds also, roughly if not completely with that insisted on by H. L. A. Hart between 'power-conferring' rules, which do not fit the conception of law as a system purely of commands backed by sanctions and issued by a political superior, and 'primary rules of obligation', which do; despite the passages both in Aristotle and in other writers, mentioned above, which show the Greek mind, like Austin, visualizing law in terms of an imperative.

Law and Equity

In the fifth book of the *Ethics*, in which Aristotle discusses justice, he also deals with 'equity' (*epieikeia*) as something distinct from it. The conception of equity, he says, is not generically different from that of justice; what is equitable is in fact itself just, but not according to law; rather it is a correction of legal justice, because a law speaks in general terms, and, because of the natural irregularity and variety of the material it tries to regulate, it cannot provide a perfectly just treatment for every possible case:

When, therefore, the law lays down a general rule, and thereafter a case arises falling somewhat outside the general model, it is then right, where the lawgiver's words have turned out to be too simple to meet the case without doing wrong, to rectify the deficiency by deciding as the lawgiver would himself decide if he were present on the occasion, and would have enacted if he were aware of the case in question.[63]

Effect is given to equity in this sense, he says, not by changing the general law but by a popular vote (*psēphisma*) which bends, *ad hoc*, its application,[64] also, apparently, by an arbitrator agreed on by the parties to a dispute, because in another work, the *Rhetoric*, he says that what is fair and equitable, though just, is a sort of justice which 'runs alongside' legal justice, which is why people prefer an arbitrator, who looks to equity, rather than a judge who must stick

---

[63] *Nicomachean Ethics* 5. 10. 5.   [64] Ibid. 5. 10. 6.

to the strict law; indeed this is why (he says) such a thing as an arbitrator was invented.[65]

On the other hand, there is no analysis of *epieikeia* in terms which relate it to a 'natural' sense of justice, or to any moral hierarchy in which the prompting of conscience, the spirit of a law, is preferred over its letter. It is clear also that those expressions of Aristotle do not amount to evidence of an actual recognition, in the legal practice of Athens or anywhere else, of a dual system of law and equity such as is familiar in English and, in a somewhat different form, in Roman legal history. On the contrary, it can be demonstrated from some actual cases known from the orators that, even where the facts disclosed some element such as bad faith, which in the English or Roman systems might have given ground for an equitable defence or equitable relief of some kind, the Athenian courts were tied to the letter of the law and had no jurisdiction to deploy principles of equity in opposition to it.[66]

EQUALITY BEFORE THE LAW

This value—sometimes represented by the word *isonomia*—cannot be sought in the non-existent formal jurisprudence of classical Greece, but that the Greek or at any rate the Athenian mind gave it conscious weight is clear. To this mind the kind of levelling, anti-aristocratic egalitarianism expressed in the modern tag 'one man is as good as another' was certainly foreign. Aristotle quotes verses of the venerated Solōn, for example, in which this archetypal Greek lawgiver disclaims all willingness to allow the base to have equal shares in the country with the noble;[67] and in the celebrated funeral oration delivered by Pericles and reported by Thucydides the statesman mentions it as a proud feature of the Athenian system that personal merit will lead to honour and preferment. But in the same passage[68] Pericles says that, despite a hierarchy of rank based on merit, 'as regards the law, all men are on an equal footing so far as concerns their private disputes'. Dracōn—according to Demosthenes—forbade the enactment of laws aimed at particular individuals; Demosthenes says the theory behind this was that, 'as everyone shared in the rest

---

[65] Ibid. 1. 13. 19.
[66] See Aristotle, *Rhetoric* 1. 15. 5–6, which appears to suggest this.
[67] *Athenian Constitution* 12. 3.   [68] Thucydides 2. 37.

of the state, so all should share equally in its laws'.[69] Another verse
of Solōn quoted by Aristotle shows him, in spite of his resolve not
to place evil citizens on the same plane as good, boasting of having
enacted laws equally for both kinds, 'shaping an even justice for
each'.[70] Plato in his *Menexenus* says (perhaps echoing the passage
from Pericles's speech cited by Thucydides) that 'our equality of
birth by nature impels us to seek equality under the law, and to give
way to one another in nothing except reputation for goodness and
understanding'.[71]

Due Course of Law, Elementary Standards of Justice

There is no technical Greek expression corresponding to our notion
of 'due course of law'. On the other hand, we know that to put
someone to death without his having been judged or condemned
(*akriton kteinein*) was considered an outrage; passages in Herodotus[72]
and Demosthenes[73] mention such summary executions in the same
breath as the violation of women as typical manifestations of a
tyrant's rule. The point here is not simply that no formal
pronouncement of sentence has preceded an execution, but that no
trial, and hence no finding of guilt according to understood modes,
has taken place: this is the force of *akritos* (= unjudged, from
krinein, to judge).

As for those understood modes, or judicial criteria, again there is
no formal doctrine about the weight of evidence, or about what we
today call natural justice. But the substance of the most notable
feature of natural justice—the obligation to hear both sides of a
case, and to give an accused person a chance to exculpate himself—
was recognized in a general way. The Athenian judicial oath
(attributed by Demosthenes to Solōn) contained a promise to listen
equally to prosecutor and defendant,[74] and Aristophanes the comic
playwright seems to reproduce a general feeling that both sides of
every case should be heard (though in a passage where the sentiment
is countered by the view that this is unnecessary if the matter is

---

[69] Demosthenes 23. 86, 24. 59.   [70] *Athenian Constitution* 12. 4.
[71] *Menexenus* 239a.   [72] *Historiae* 3. 80. 5.
[73] Demosthenes 23. 27, 76, 81.
[74] Demosthenes, *Against Timocrates* 149–51.

already manifest and 'cries aloud').[75] It is true that there are passages also in Aristophanes and Euripides which present the principle of hearing both sides in the light of a precept of wisdom rather than of justice.[76] Nevertheless, when all the disapproving references to condemnation without trial or hearing are assembled it is clear that there existed—at any rate among the Athenians—a strong, even if not professionally organized feeling in favour of regular, impartial judicial procedures.

Again, the instinct against trying someone a second time on a charge on which he has already been tried, or in general opening up an issue which has already been judicially disposed of, is evidenced in Athens, this time actually in a law. In one speech Demosthenes, without purporting to cite any statute, says in general that the laws declare that suit may be brought once only against the same person for the same acts.[77] In another speech he cites a statutory text to the same effect, the context of which appears to show that the principle applied quite generally, in matters which we would call either civil or criminal, so as to rule out a second proceeding on an issue already judicially decided.[78] Whether the principle was recognized with the same emphasis everywhere else in the Greek world is not certain.

THE THEORY OF PUNISHMENT

The administering of punishment in the most primitive age was probably instinctive and unreflecting, the product of a victim's feelings and those of his kin, or, in cases grave enough to draw the whole society into the process, the product of a sense of outrage or danger. It is an important step when calm reflection is applied to the infliction of punishment, and objective reasons of policy are found to justify it. This stage in Western thought is recorded first in Plato, for whom punishment had two aspects: the corrective, tending to force the wrongdoer to mend his ways; and the deterrent, tending to discourage others from imitating him.[79] Of these two values, the one which most often appears thereafter is the deterrent; this is a commonplace with the Attic orators of the succeeding age. Thus

[75] *Wasps* 919 ff.
[76] See J. M. Kelly, 'Audi Alteram Partem', in *Natural Law Forum*, 9 (1964), 104–5.
[77] Demosthenes 38. 16.
[78] Ibid. 24. 54.   [79] Plato, *Gorgias* 525a.

Demosthenes in his speech against Androtion tells the judges that the sight of the guilty man paying the penalty for his many crimes will be a salutary lesson for everyone else to behave with more moderation.[80] This almost educational element in punishment is stressed also by Lycurgus: young people, he says, are much influenced by seeing the guilty punished and the good rewarded; the sight of the punishment causes them to avoid it through fear.[81] And Aeschines in his accusation of Ctesiphon says that when a wicked pimp of his sort pays the penalty, 'other people have received instruction'.[82]

Long afterwards, the Roman writer Aulus Gellius in the early second century AD purported to reproduce Greek doctrine on this subject, or at any rate he uses Greek words to denote what he says are three aims of punishment.[83] Apart from correction and deterrence, he mentions a third, *timoria*, which he says means the vindication of the victim's honour, which would be impugned if the culprit went unpunished. (This seems to be a confusion arising from association with the word *timē*, honour; *timoria* just means punishment, and it is doubtful if the Greeks meant it to include what Gellius describes. Significantly, he points out that Plato did not mention this element among his justifications of punishment.)

The Greek mind addressed also the relation of punishment to the wrongdoer's state of intent. The notion which seems elementary in the modern world, that guilt and liability to punishment depend on the state of mind which accompanied the injurious act—expressed in the criminal law of the common law world by the maxim 'actus non facit reum nisi mens sit rea'—was by no means axiomatic in the ancient world. Indeed, the irrelevance of intent, in the archaic Greek perception, comes through in legend: for example in the story of Oedipus, who killed his own father unwittingly (in fulfilment of a prophecy which had led the father to abandon him as an infant), pollution and guilt were felt to attach to him despite the involuntary quality of the patricide. However, the code attributed to Dracōn in late seventh-century Athens recognized degrees of homicide related to the state of mind of the person causing the death:[84] an achievement transcending the purely legal frame, and reflecting with

[80] Demosthenes, *Against Androtion* 614.
[81] Lycurgus, *Against Leocrates* 149.
[82] Aeschines, *Against Ctesiphon* 246.
[83] Aulus Gellius, *Noctes Atticae* 7. 14.   [84] *IG* i². 115.

particular clarity the level which civilization had for the first time reached. These degrees distinguished premeditated murder, unintentional killing in an athletic contest or something like killing under provocation, and killing in self-defence. The words of the statutes, as reproduced by Demosthenes,[85] may not be original in all points, and the total scheme does not convey to the modern eye a clear and well-organized picture, but there is no doubt that Dracōn's laws, though a byword for severity, do exhibit a consciousness of the factor of intent, of greater or lesser guilt related to the subjective condition of the doer's mind and to the effect upon it of surrounding circumstances.

In later centuries the materiality of intent to liability to punishment is universally recognized. Thucydides reports the Athenian demagogue Cleon, in a speech urging the massacre of allies who had revolted from Athens, saying that 'they knowingly plotted against us, and did not just injure us involuntarily: because that which is unintentional is forgivable'.[86] This position is given formal theoretical status by the philosophers. Plato in his late work, the *Laws* (although expressing the view, which need not be explored in the present context, that no one ever really *wishes* to commit a wrong) still acknowledges, as something too well-established to be overridden, that 'voluntary and involuntary wrongs are recognized as distinct by every legislator who has ever existed in any society, and regarded as distinct by all law'.[87] Dealing with the specific case of homicide, he proposes more subtly differentiated categories: involuntary killing, for example through an accident of sport, in which the agent is to be free of pollution on performing ritual purifications; a killing 'without intention', but apparently in some degree culpable, perhaps something like a common-law manslaughter; and a killing 'in passion', in which he would distinguish an act committed under a sudden impulse of rage, and one which is premeditated. The demarcation between these categories is not as clear as a statute might make it; but the general principle is stated that the act which resembles the greater evil should receive a greater, that resembling a lesser evil a lesser punishment.[88] The relevance of intent to the measure of punishment is kept up in later provisions which he advances for killings of

---

[85] Demosthenes 20. 158, 23. 22, 28, 54, 60.
[86] *Histories* 3. 40.   [87] *Laws* 861a, b.
[88] Ibid. 865–7. See also Aristotle, *Athenian Constitution* 57. 3.

persons in special degrees of closeness to the killer (friends, family, etc.).[89] Aristotle in his *Nicomachean Ethics* considers it necessary to define that which is voluntary and that which is not, an exercise, as he says, useful also for a lawgiver who has to distribute rewards and punishments.[90] Lawgivers 'chastise and punish all who do evil, unless duress or innocent ignorance has been the cause of their acts'.[91] His contemporary, the orator Demosthenes, confirms the position of the philosophers, and even gives it an express basis in nature:

Among other people I find this sort of distinction universally observed. If a man has gone wrong wilfully, he is visited with resentment and punishment. If he has erred unintentionally, pardon takes the place of punishment . . . This distinction will be found not only embodied in our statutes, but laid down by nature herself in her unwritten laws and in the moral sense of men.[92]

On the other hand, if the condition of not appreciating what one is doing is itself caused by the doer's own behaviour, as where drunkenness or culpable ignorance of the law underlies the injurious act, then that condition, according to Aristotle, ought to be no excuse.[93] Aristotle also records a law of Mytilene in the sixth century punishing drunken assault more severely than sober; the lawgiver, taking note of the fact that men are more insolent when drunk, had regard rather to the public benefit (by this harshly deterrent measure) than to the excusing factor which intoxication might represent.[94]

The proportioning of punishments to the seriousness of offences— quite apart from the role of intent in estimating their seriousness—is a principle which the Athenian philosophers do not treat specifically. On the other hand, it seems an easy corollary of general rules enunciated by Plato and Aristotle about proportion and measure. For the former, as has been seen, to treat unequal things equally, i.e. as though they were in fact equal, produces inequality, unless there is due measure.[95] Aristotle's treatment of justice requires things equal to be treated equally, things unequal unequally; shortly afterwards he says justice is proportion, injustice what is contrary to

---

[89] *Laws* 877.
[91] Ibid. 3. 5. 7.
[93] *Nicomachean Ethics* 3. 5. 8.
[95] *Laws* 757.

[90] *Nicomachean Ethics* 3. 1. 1.
[92] Demosthenes, *De corona* 274–5.
[94] *Politics* 2. 9. 9.

proportion.[96] The matter is expressly mentioned by Plutarch in his life of Solōn; the great lawgiver repealed measures of his forerunner Dracōn which did not, in their severity, distinguish between trivial and major offences, and designed his own legislation so as to reflect that distinction in the scale of punishments.[97]

It is worth, finally, mentioning in this connection an idea which runs through ancient law (and folklore) and turns up also in Greek thought: that of making the punishment fit the crime, not in the sense merely of proportion just noticed, but in the sense of retaliation on the offender in the same mode as that in which he offended. Plutarch, admittedly a late source, and admittedly writing about a half-legendary figure, the founding king of Athens, says that Theseus administered a justice which was modelled on the wrongdoer's injustice.[98] A firmer indication that the idea had a place in Greek criminal theory is provided by Plato in his *Laws*: to suffer the same evil as one has inflicted he calls 'justice according to nature' (*kata physin dikē*), the mode of punishment which nature itself suggests.[99]

THEORY OF PROPERTY

The Athenian philosophers were aware of the moral and political dimensions of ownership of material resources, and in their works on the ideal state proposed ways of looking at property and (in Plato's case) of legally regulating it. It may first be emphasized that they did not suggest that a right of private property was an attribute of man by nature; this position, as will be seen, was first maintained in the early years of the Christianized Roman Empire, and even then had to compete with a strong strain of communist[100] doctrine within the Church; it did not finally become the orthodoxy of Christian Europe until the High Middle Ages.

Plato in his *Laws* visualizes an ideal community (with an actual ideal number of households, namely 5,040), whose lawgiver was to display the same spirit as that which proposed a totalitarian scheme of education in the *Republic*. He was to ordain a community of wives and children, and also, in some measure, of property; for all

---

[96] *Nicomachean Ethics* 5. 3. 6 and 14.
[97] *Solon* 17.
[98] *Theseus* 11.
[99] *Laws* 870d, e, 872d, e.
[100] In the sense of common ownership of all property.

the land available to this new-founded city was to be brought into a pool, and then parcelled out in lots, as far as possible equal, between the citizens. These allotments, however, were not to be regarded with the jealously proprietorial attitude of a freeholder; the division was to take place 'with some such thought as this, that he to whom a lot falls is yet bound to count his portion the common property of the whole society'.[101] Plato recognizes that a complete equality of property between the new citizens will be impossible, as the settlers will each arrive with different quantities of wealth. He does not propose an expropriation and redistribution of the goods arriving in the city in this way, nor a prohibition on acquiring future goods through gift, or business enterprise, or treasure trove. But there must be a limit on the development of inequalities between property classes:

In a society which is to be immune from the most fatal of disorders which might more properly be called distraction than faction, there must be no place for penury in any section of the population, nor yet for opulence, as both breed either consequence. Accordingly the legislator must now specify the limit in either direction. So let the limit on the side of penury be the value of an allotment; this must remain constant . . . The legislator will take this as a measure, and permit the acquisition of twice, thrice, and as much as four times its value.

Any surplus over and above four times the basic minimum share is to be surrendered (by compulsion of law) and 'consigned to the State and its gods'.[102]

Within those limits, however, Plato was willing to see private property respected: 'I would have no man touch my property, if I can help it, or disturb it in the slightest way without some kind of consent on my part; if I am a man of sense, I must treat the property of others in the same way.'[103] Indeed he himself admits, in a different passage, that the instinct of ordinary people is against interference with the free play of private ownership: at the foundation of the Dorian[104] cities, he says, when the first lawgivers were trying to effect changes in land-tenure, and the general cancellation of debts (the Greeks called the latter *seisachtheia*, 'shaking off of burdens') in order to 'establish a certain equality of

---

[101] *Laws* 739–40.   [102] Ibid. 744–5.   [103] Ibid. 913a.
[104] The cities of Crete, the Peloponnese, and southern Italy inhabited by people of the Dorian branch of the Greek race, were thought to have pioneered legislation. The legendary Minos of Crete was the archetype of lawgivers.

possession', they encountered bitter resistance.[105] In Athens, the principal magistrate elected for the year similarly used to swear, according to Aristotle, that he would protect men's possessions.[106]

Aristotle's own treatment of property is far more pragmatic and cautious. He has no time for doctrinaire communism, for simple reasons of common sense: 'Property should be in a certain sense common, but, as a general rule, private; for, when everyone has a distinct interest, men will not complain of one another, and they will make more progress, because everyone will be attending to his own business.' A levelling communism, on the other hand, extinguished enterprise, makes likely an inefficient administration of the community's wealth, and diminishes both the motive and the capacity for private liberality.[107] All the same, no justification for the institution of private property at any higher level is offered by him; property of some kind is 'necessary for existence',[108] but not necessarily—except for the practical reasons just mentioned—in the form of individuals' exclusive ownership of whatever quantity of material goods they can amass.

Two forms of property rights caused Aristotle to pause; one was property in slaves, who were a universal feature of the ancient world, and one around which its economy was organized. Slaves were indeed living property:

> but is there anyone thus intended by nature to be a slave, and for whom such a condition is expedient and right, or rather is not all slavery a violation of nature?
> There is no difficulty in answering this question, on grounds both of reason and of fact. For that some should rule and others be ruled is a thing, not only necessary, but expedient; from the hour of their birth, some are marked out for slavery, some for rule.[109]

This is what he calls 'natural' slavery, not a very happy rationalization, but perhaps the only possible one in practice, of what he saw around him. Another sort of slavery, as generally recognized in the ancient world as the concept of slavery itself, is merely conventional: that resulting from capture in war; and here he admits that there are powerful arguments, which others have advanced as based on nature, for condemning the pretension of anyone to reduce another to slave condition by the mere exercise of force.[110]

---

[105] *Laws* 684d, e.
[106] *Athenian Constitution* 46. 2.
[107] *Politics* 2. 3, 5.
[108] Ibid. 1. 4.
[109] Ibid. 1. 4–5.
[110] Ibid. 1. 6.

The other area in which private property seemed to Aristotle to call for qualification was that of commerce. He explains in his *Nicomachean Ethics* the function of money[111] is to act as a measure, to make things commensurable—because their value is expressed in terms of different quantities of the same medium of exchange—and so to equalize them.[112] But, just as Christian philosophers were later to do, he appears to regard as respectable the employment of money only to facilitate exchanges between primary producers. The role of a middleman, a retail trader, is for him somehow censurable. But worst of all is usury, the lending of money at interest. This is because the use of money, not as a medium of exchange, but merely to beget more money (the Greek word for loan-interest is *tokos*, the primary meaning of which is 'offspring') is unnatural.[113]

---

[111] At Aristotle's date, money had in Greece no very ancient history. The earliest coins date from about 600 BC; metal ingots go back to an earlier date.

[112] *Nicomachean Ethics* 5. 5. 14.   [113] Ibid. 1. 3. 2–3.

2

The Romans

ROME AND ITALY

At the beginning of the previous chapter an attempt was made to place the classical period of Greek civilization in chronological context with Rome and with northern Europe; and at that epoch, as has been said, Rome was still in the earliest stage of its history. The Italian peninsula contained not merely the Roman people, who occupied only the area of the 'seven hills' near the mouth of the Tiber and its immediate hinterland, but also other political communities of similar or closely related blood and speech (i.e. other members of the Italic branch of the Indo-European family) as well as other powerful and strongly individual civilizations. The seaboard of southern Italy and most of Sicily was dotted with cities founded, from the eighth century onward, by Greek colonists; this area was essentially an integral part of the Greek world. Central Italy, mainly the region of the modern Tuscany which takes its name from them, was inhabited by the mysterious Etruscans, of non-European, perhaps Phoenician origin, whose culture had been strongly influenced by that of Greece (it was via the Etruscan adaptation of the Greek alphabet that the Romans acquired theirs), Etruscan power stretched at one time to Rome, and the Etruscans seem to have installed there the royal dynasty whose last representative, Tarquinius Superbus, was expelled in 509 BC. In the north of Italy lived the Celts, more closely related linguistically to the Italic peoples than any other, whose restless aggressiveness—their commonly received image in the ancient world[1]—carried them, too, to Rome, which they sacked in 390.

[1] See T. G. E. Powell, *The Celts* (London, 1958), 73–4. The great German scholar of classical antiquity, Theodore Mommsen, wrote of the Celts that 'they shook all empires, and founded none': *History of Rome*, trans. W. Dickson (London, 1908), i, bk. 2, ch. 4.

In the course of the fourth and third centuries the power of Rome grew from this modest beginning until it had become the dominant force in Italy. The pattern of this development was the gradual building of a network of relationships, mostly of alliance, with neighbouring peoples; the planting of colonies and settlements; and the progressive extension of Roman citizenship. This development was occasionally marked by wars, as this or that people revolted from an alliance which was in fact one of dependence, but on the whole the progress of Rome to supremacy in Italy was not a naked military conquest. A generous policy in regard to the grant of citizenship, and a prudent restriction of authority's exercise to what was necessary for military security—there was no attempt to impose a uniform system of local government, judicature, or religion—helped to produce a genuinely harmonious Italy, Roman in its standard language, sentiment, and allegiance.

In the mid-third century Rome became embroiled with Carthage, an ancient and powerful Phoenician city in north Africa, near the modern Tunis. The scene of the first hostilities was Sicily, where Carthage's commercial interests had involved her; and when the wars with Carthage (the 'Punic' wars) had ended, over 150 years later, with the destruction of that city, Rome had become the dominant power not just in Italy but in the Mediterranean. Sicily had become a Roman province; and provinces had been created also in northern Africa, Spain, and southern Gaul. In later times the Romans pushed into northern Gaul and the Low Countries, into the Balkan peninsula, across the Bosphorus into Asia Minor, ultimately as far as the Black Sea and the Euphrates. With the bringing of Egypt under Roman domination, after the civil wars which followed the murder of Julius Caesar and ended in the deaths of Antony and Cleopatra in 30 BC, the whole of the civilization ringing the Mediterranean, and much territory far beyond, was a Roman empire. Even then, Roman expansion was not complete; the first century AD saw the addition of Britain and of Dacia (the area of the modern Romania). The only part of main continental Europe where the Romans never made substantial and durable inroads was the land of the Germanic peoples, north of the Danube and east of the Rhine; those peoples, in later ages, were to overthrow the Roman order and empire, and lay the foundations of the principal nation-states of modern Europe.

THE ROMAN STATE

The early Roman state, after the expulsion of the kings, was a republic: not an egalitarian democracy such as the modern world knows, but strongly marked by the dominance of an aristocracy. It was, however, a republic at least in the sense that public office was elective, and that the legislature consisted of all adult male citizens; there were, until near its end, annual changes of magistrates, if always within the governing class. The general pattern by which this republic's constitution evolved is fairly well known to us; though it was never incorporated in a written charter or law ('constitutions' in this sense are a modern invention), and even the conception of a constitution, as we understand it (or of what the Greeks called a *politeia*) was perhaps not a distinct notion to the Romans, even if the phrase *ius publicum*, 'public law', did adequate duty for it in most contexts.

We know most about the republic in its final phase, the age of Caesar and Cicero in the last century BC. Here we see it as a polity in which the supreme position of prestige and authority is occupied by the Senate, a body composed originally of the heads of the chief families (*senatus*, from *senis* = an old man, literally therefore means 'council of elders'); its natural shrinkage in numbers made up by recruitment from the upper class, and annually supplemented by the inclusion of each person elected to a higher magistracy: not, strictly, a legislature, yet enjoying a virtual legislative authority.[2] The power of enacting *leges*, laws properly so called, lay with the people, marshalled in different modes of assembly for different purposes; but this power was used very infrequently.[3] Moreover, a Roman assembly had a very different character from a modern parliament; it could not initiate, debate, or amend a proposed law, but could merely accept or reject a bill proposed by a magistrate (who would previously have sought the Senate's approval for it). The executive

---

[2] Gaius, *Inst.* 1. 4: 'A resolution of the Senate (*senatusconsultum*) is what the Senate commands and lays down; it has the force of statute (*lex*), even though this has been questioned'. The position of the senate is justified by Cicero, *De republ.* 2. 9, 10.

[3] In the entire period of the republic—say from 509 to 28 BC—we know only about 30 *leges* by name (the content of far fewer, the text of fewer still). There must have been *leges* of which no record survived, but these would hardly augment this total significantly. See W. Kunkel, *Introduction to Roman Legal and Constitutional History* (Oxford, 1973), tr. J. M. Kelly (2nd edn.), 131.

power lay with elected magistrates, ranging in political weight from the annually elected pair of consuls (or, in point of dignity, from the quinquennially elected censor) through the praetors, whose special responsibility was the supervision of the administration of justice, to quaestors, who were treasury officers, and lesser magistrates such as aediles, who discharged a sort of police function in public streets and markets. The section of the population originally distinguished from the patrician aristocracy, namely the *plebs*, had officers of its own called tribunes, who might exert considerable political weight. The overseas provinces were administered by governors who were former consuls or praetors, sent after their year of office at home to command for a further year abroad; they were said to govern 'in the quality of' consul or praetor respectively (*pro consule*, *pro praetore*), and were hence called proconsul or propraetor.

Justice was administered in a scheme of judicature contrasting strongly with modern patterns. First, there were on the civil side several different jurisdictions which did not exactly compete or overlap, but whose coexistence cannot be explained on theory, only by reference to their origins and to the typical settings in which they are found operating. Secondly, judges were not, either on the criminal or on the civil side, permanent and salaried office-holders, but members of the propertied class acting in an honorary capacity. They were selected from case to case, *ad hoc*; and, in private litigation, could be assigned only with the agreement of both parties on who was to be their judge, so that the single judge who tried an action on a contract, for example, resembled rather a modern arbitrator than a judge. The praetor's role here—although, as will be seen, of cardinal importance in the development of Roman law— was reformative, regulatory, and supervisory rather than judicial.

Political rivalries, arising in the context of disputed social reforms, became violent in the second century BC, and there set in a period of about ninety years of continual disturbance and civil war, in which abnormally prolonged military commands, repeated tenures of the consulship by the same person, and quasi-dictatorships signalled the debility and approaching collapse of the old constitution; this had evolved in a medium-sized city-state, and despite improvised adaptations it could not contain violent rivalries played out on a world stage. The era of the struggles and successive autocracies of Marius and Sulla, of Pompey and Caesar, of Antony and Octavian, has been called that of the Roman revolution; the republic, as we conventionally understand it, ended, and the age of the emperors (the Roman empire, in the sense of a form of government rather than of an extent of territorial dominion) succeeded. But it was a very special and, at first, a very subtle kind of revolution; and, as the ghost and image of the Roman empire exercised a powerful influence on the political and legal thought of Europe in later ages, it is worth considering the genesis and the nature of this polity.

The two most significant revolutions of modern ages, those of France at the end of the eighteenth century and of Russia at the beginning of the twentieth, were characterized by the total destruction of the old regime, its system, and its symbolisms. The same is true of the American revolution of 1776–87 and that in Ireland in 1916–22; these, while less totalitarian in spirit and method, still held up deliberately the indicia of a conscious break with the past and a repudiation of the old sovereignties. The Roman revolution, on the other hand, was consummated in a spirit of painful anxiety to suggest that nothing essential had changed. This was due to the character and policy of the state's new master, Julius Caesar's great-nephew Caius Octavius, later called Caius Julius Caesar Octavianus, or Octavian, and, after his attainment of unchallenged political supremacy, given by the Senate in 27 BC the title implying divine appointment and that by which he is known to history, Augustus.

Augustus, reckoned by us the first of the Roman emperors (though in his own time referred to by what was a much less formal word, *princeps*, 'the chief'), appears to have had a genuine reverence for ancestral Roman laws and manners, and this alone might have led him to preserve everything in the old constitution which was not inconsistent with his own permanent ascendancy. But, if so, it was a course which political calculation would in any case have suggested; the soothing appearance of restoration could effectively conceal the disturbing reality of revolution.

On the surface, indeed, nothing had changed. The Senate still met; indeed, it now entered an era of peculiar prestige. The magistrates were still annually elected. The people's assembly, which had long been in abeyance as a legislature, was actually brought into renewed operation, perhaps as a piece of romantic antiquarianism on Augustus's part, in order to enact some laws in the area of family manners and morals, and to inhibit the racial dilution of the citizen body by excessive emancipations of slaves.

The old system of judicature still functioned as before, its procedures actually rationalized. But a silent, hardly visible transformation, even transubstantiation, had in fact taken place; because every part of the constitution now contained a new, tacit term, namely acquiescence in the will of an individual. Augustus himself left an account of his public life, still preserved in two official inscriptions which he had set up at Ancyra (the modern Ankara in Turkey) and Antioch in Syria; he neatly and frankly described his position with the words 'Post id tempus auctoritate omnibus praestiti, potestatis autem nihilo amplius habui quam ceteri, qui mihi quoque in magistratu conlegae fuerunt': 'after that time [i.e. *his restoration of the state*] I excelled all others in personal authority, but enjoyed no more official power than did the other persons who were my colleagues in this or that magistracy.' The crucial fact expressed by these words is that there has been a shift in the state's centre of gravity, from constitutionally based, regular magistral office to the undefined power of an individual resting on his own personal authority: in other words, not to put too fine a point upon it, from republic to monarchy.

This idiosyncratic revolution, viewed politically, was a virtually total success. Pockets of old republican sentiment survived, but the least suspicion that they contained the germ of active opposition led to ruthless repression. On the other hand, a population weary of three generations of civil strife was willing to accept the new order; the Roman circles which cultivated literature, in particular, supported the Augustan revolution, and figures such as Virgil and Horace placed their poetic genius at its service. To the last, the Roman emperors never claimed the title of king, apparently because of its association in the folk-memory with the Tarquin dynasty expelled in 509 BC. But, for practical purposes, this distaste for kingship yielded to appreciation of the order which monarchy could ensure; though there was perhaps also a certain conditioning for it in the sight of the Hellenistic kingdoms of the near East which were still flourishing long after the breaking up of the Macedonian empire of Alexander.

Viewed as an experiment in government, the new Roman order was of permanent significance for Europe. Augustus and his successors avoided demolishing the old republican structure, but they effectively created a new one alongside it, dependent on and drawing its force from the emperor's personal authority, the *auctoritas principis*. With the new institution of entirely new prefectships, not by legislation but by the personal appointment of the emperor the foundations of a modern-looking administration were laid; and, as the emperors gradually developed (or rather usurped, as this had to be done out of thin air and without legal basis in the republic's constitution) a jurisdiction in the administration of justice both civil and criminal, something like a hierarchy of courts, with a system of appeals, emerged for the first time. The only area in which it could be said the new order conspicuously failed, at least according to a standard that the modern world would think vital, was the matter of succession; in peaceful times this generally followed the deceased emperor's wishes, to which he had given expression in life by adopting as his personal heir the man to whom he intended the empire to pass; but it was a system inherently vulnerable to dispute, and the military origins of the revolution, never entirely shaken off, tempted many commanders to induce their men, usually by a promise of money rewards, to raise them up as pretenders by acclaiming them *imperator*.[4] Successions disputed in this way were the reason for the non-stop civil wars of the third century AD, and contributed, along with other factors, to the ultimate decay of the western empire and its destruction by the peoples of the north.

ROME'S ENCOUNTER WITH GREEK CULTURE

At the time when Rome was advancing towards dominance in Italy, Greece was on a course of dependence and decline. This was associated with the rise of the Macedonians, a wild northern people regarded as barely within the Hellenic family at all; and with the conquests of Philip and Alexander, who reduced the free cities of Greece in the later fourth and third centuries to a subjection from which they never recovered. With political decline went also a darkening of Greek civilization.

---

[4] This word, originally used for acclaiming a victorious general, became a sort of personal name of Augustus, and looked on as 'inherited' from his adoptive father Julius Caesar. This unprecedented evolution lent the word a political colour: it came to carry a sense indistinguishable from the bearer of the supreme authority in the state. Its military origin made it sound easily in the mouths of the armies which now, when they agreed to support the pretensions of their general, in shouting 'imperator' meant 'emperor' in the modern sense. See F. De Martino, *Storia della costituzione romana*, 5 vols. (Naples, 1972–5), iv. 212 ff.

This was, however, the era in which the vigorous Roman state, once almost beneath the notice of an Athenian, began fully to appreciate the world of the Greek intellect. The Romans had indeed long been aware of the civilization of Greece, since they were in close and constant contact with it through their neighbours in the Greek cities which fringed the coasts of southern Italy and Sicily; and an ancient tradition asserted that, as early as 450 BC, the commission which was to draw up the written code of laws afterwards known as the Twelve Tables travelled from Rome to Athens to study the laws of Solōn and actually incorporated some of those in their work. In the second century BC the Romans were drawn militarily into Greece: their first victorious appearance there wore the guise of liberation, as the philhellenic general Flaminius proclaimed Greek freedom (albeit under Roman protection); but fifty years later, after a series of provocations, another Roman general, Mummius, destroyed Corinth and reduced Greece to the condition of a Roman province.

While these events were unfolding on the military and political plane, something like a reverse conquest was taking place in the sphere of the intellect. Educated Romans could see that their own native forms of literature and art were primitive compared with what they could see in the Greek world. Greek models in epic, in lyric poetry, in historiography, in tragedy and comedy, in philosophy and rhetoric, in the visual arts and architecture, were admired and studied; they found a following notably in the so-called 'Scipionic circle', an influential aristocratic group called after its central figure Scipio Aemilianus Africanus (185–129 BC). Imitation of those models soon transformed every department of Roman intellectual life; the genius of the individual Roman poet or sculptor was his own, but the frame within which he worked, the standards he set himself, were supplied by Greece. It is this reception of Greek culture into the Roman world that makes it possible to speak of the classical world as a 'Graeco-Roman' continuum; and it was the paradoxical conquest of Rome by the Greek spirit, at the very time that Greece was falling politically under Roman dominion, that in later years inspired Horace's epigram 'Graecia capta ferum victorem cepit' ('captive Greece took captive her wild conqueror').[5]

***

[5] *Epist.* 2. 1. 156. The sentence continues: 'et artis intulit agresti Latio' 'and brought the arts to rustic Latium').

One particular event which took place in the course of this conquest stood out in the Roman memory as peculiarly important, as it is frequently mentioned by later writers, especially Cicero. This was the visit of an embassy sent by the Athenians in 155 BC to petition the Roman senate for the reduction of a fine laid upon them in an arbitration for an offence against another Greek people. The embassy consisted of three leading Athenian philosophers, heads respectively of three philosophical schools. In addition to carrying through successfully their embassy with the senate, they held public lectures in which their skill in organizing and presenting their themes made an immense impression on their Roman audiences. They themselves, in turn, were impressed by the receptiveness which the Athenian style of classifying material and presenting argument found among their hearers; and their account of Rome after they returned home seems to have led to the migration of other Athenian philosophers to this new setting. One of these in particular, Panaetius, a follower of the Stoic philosophy, became the companion of Scipio himself.

A Stoic philosophy became the principal influence on the Roman educated class, and on the Roman lawyers (so far as they responded to extraneous influences at all, which is much in debate), and hence contributed to what legal theory the Roman world can show, a little needs to be said about it here. The founder of the Stoic school was Zeno, from Citium in Cyprus, who lived from about 333 to about 264 BC and thus represents the generation after that of Aristotle. The name of the school of philosophy which he inaugurated is taken simply from the open public building in Athens where he assembled with his disciples, the *Stoa Poikilē*, the 'painted porch'. His teaching contained elements derived from different sources; its central message was that everything in nature is to be explained by reason; and every act must be justified by reason. The wise man, therefore, must live in accordance with the reason which is identical with nature; his conduct in accordance with that principle will enable him to rise superior to the application of any force or temptation. It is this element of sovereignty, of serenity, available to everyone who practises such wisdom, that provides the link with the modern usage of the word 'stoic', meaning calm steadfastness in adversity. It is thought that this element also made the philosophy particularly attractive to the Greece of those latter days, the old world of its city-state civilization submerged by the Macedonian conquest, the old bearings lost: here was a training in individual character that would reward its practitioner with a vital inner independence. On the other hand, although the decline of Greece went chronologically with the rise of Rome, the Stoic philosophy found a most congenial soil in the Roman temperament too; the streak of austerity, of simplicity, of indifference to good or ill fortune, which the Romans liked to admire in themselves or their ancestors, represented a rather similar disciplining of self. Other doctrines also, as will be seen, were of Stoic origin, and sometimes find their way into Roman legal texts or Roman legal philosophy. At any rate, the Stoic view of the world virtually conquered the mind of the late Roman republic and of the early empire; almost all the Roman jurists, whose profession began fully to emerge at about the epoch of the Scipionic circle, followed Stoic teaching, as did those Romans who themselves wrote on philosophic themes: Cicero at the end of the republic, Seneca in the first century AD, the emperor Marcus Aurelius in the second.

THE GREEK IMPACT ON ROMAN LAW

Apart from becoming familiarized with philosophic themes which had obvious legal relevance, the Romans derived from the intellectual method of their Greek instructors important lessons in the organization of legal material. But before anything more is said about this, something must be said about the impact of Greek models on concrete Roman rules of practical law.

This impact was nil, or virtually nil. It was the one area in which the Greeks had nothing to teach their intellectual captives. As was seen in the former chapter, the Greek cities had laws, and traditions of lawgiving. But nowhere was there a legal science or any very sophisticated legal technique. A mid-fifth-century Greek law-code, such as that of Gortyn in Crete,[6] might be as elaborate and as extensive in scale as the Twelve Tables enacted by the Roman legislative commission at about the same date; but the subsequent life of a Greek system was led without any jurists' profession to guide, organize, expound, and develop it. Moreover, at any rate in Athens if we can judge from the speeches which have survived from the fourth-century orators of whom Demosthenes was the most

[6] These laws, inscribed in columns of writing on a wall of dressed stone blocks, represent the only Greek code to survive more or less in its entirety.

famous, litigation was conducted less in the spirit of a contest about the objective applicability of a legal norm than as a rhetorical match in which no holds were barred. Even in Athens we do not know the name of a single person who worked as a legal adviser (rather than as a court orator), or who taught law to students, nor the name of a single book on a legal subject. We are not aware that such persons or such books even existed, and we might not unreasonably conclude, since this is an era well illumined by history in most respects, that they did not.

In Rome, on the other hand, apparently already some time before the first encounter with the Greek mind (at any rate in the intense form in which Scipio's circle studied it), there were the beginnings of a legal profession of a kind that never existed in Greece and remained, indeed, unique in the world until the rise of the common lawyers in the high Middle Ages. This profession, pursued in some measure through a sense of public duty and the responsibilities of their class by men of rank engaged in the running of public affairs, was entirely secular, even though its remoter origins may lie partly in the functions of the Roman priesthoods in an era when cult ritual, magic, and the activation of legal forms were different aspects of the same complex of ideas, namely, those connected in the involvement of the gods in bringing about results in human affairs. By the later republic all traces of this primitive association had disappeared. The lay jurists, who from about the mid-second-century BC became known to us individually by name, pursued the entirely secular and practical tasks of expounding rules of law, drawing up formulas for legal transactions, and advising magistrates, litigants, and judges. They also taught their science to the generation of students who would follow them, and they began to publish: commentaries, monographs, collections of their opinions, introductory textbooks for students. For a period of nearly 400 years, from the last century of the republic until the turmoil of the third century AD, the science of these jurists represents—together with the Roman genius for imperial government—the most characteristic flower of Roman civilization, and the one least indebted to foreign models, evidently growing spontaneously from some part of the Roman national spirit without parallel elsewhere in the ancient world.

These jurists pursued a science which was the opposite of theoretical. The formulation of great first principles and grand generalities was quite foreign to them. They were strictly practical, concentrating on the concrete individual cases in regard to which they had been consulted as to the law (hence their name *iuris consulti*, 'persons consulted about the law'), and giving their view tersely, without rhetorical or philosophical flourish, mostly also without any full statement of reasons (though often citing in support the congruent opinions of other or earlier jurists). Anyone seeking the underlying principles of their work in a particular area of law must do so by careful collation from the vast sediments of their case-material and commentaries, perpetuated in a later age in the *Digest* of the Byzantine emperor Justinian.

These jurists, then, practised a science unknown to the Greeks, who therefore could not impress them. Direct Greek contributions to Roman law, accordingly, are nearly non-existent; apart from the tradition, not verifiable or even likely apart from one or two minor matters, of conscious borrowing from Athens when the Twelve Tables were compiled, it would be possible to point in, say, AD 200, at the end of the age of the jurists, only to a couple of marginal matters of commercial law for which a Greek model must be admitted. And yet it would be wrong to say that the Greek intellect, as distinct from rules of Greek law, made no contribution to the Roman legal achievement; because the Roman jurists in fact owed extremely important elements of their *method* to the adoption of tools which they encountered in Greek philosophy and grammar, and perhaps to some extent also in Greek rhetoric.

The most important of these, one with which the study of Plato and Aristotle would have acquainted them, was the so-called dialectical method: this means the organization of material in an orderly system by a process of division and sub-division into genera and species, arrived at by establishing differences (*diairēsis*) on the one hand, and analogies or affinities (*synagōgē, synthesis*) on the other. On this process, which the Stoic school also practised, the Greeks had already built, through analysis of their own tongue in accordance with it, the science of grammar. 'This discernment of kinds', wrote Schulz,

was to lead on to the discovery of principles governing the kinds and explaining individual cases . . . [The study especially of grammar] provided [the jurists] with models showing how to reduce to a system an extensive and unwieldy material . . . Not only does dialectic subsume individual phenomena under their genera; it is also an instrument of discovery, suggesting, when applied to jurisprudence, problems which have not actually occurred in practice.[7]

The republican jurists who learnt this method from their study of Greek works began also to essay definitions (though later, classical jurists fought shy of definition)[8] and the most famous of them, Quintus Mucius Scaevola, at whose feet the young Cicero sat, actually wrote a short collection of them which he published in a book with a partly Greek title: *Liber singularis horōn.*[9]

In addition to the dialectic process, it may be that Roman ideas on the interpretation of statutes or other legal instruments and transactions were influenced by lessons and themes from Greek philosophy and rhetoric. Some aspects of interpretation belong more naturally under the head of Roman 'equity', but at the purely mechanical level we may note that the Roman jurists very often had recourse to the etymology, the real or supposed[10] derivation of a word, in order to explain its legal force. It is true that they might have spontaneously hit upon this technique; but in fact it was a commonplace among the Greek philosophers, the Stoics in particular, who taught that all words have a natural meaning which their etymology will elucidate. In an age when the newly fashionable Stoic philosophy had made so many conquests, especially among the pioneer jurists, the Greek practice probably either inspired or at least reinforced the Roman one.

Another interpretative rule ultimately given canonical force by inclusion in Justinian's *Digest* requires that words should be understood in the sense in which they are generally employed, and not in some sense which may have been special to the person using them in a particular case.[11] This too may have a partly Greek origin, though at least one jurist is reported as having favoured the reverse conclusion, and in fact, whatever its practical advantages, it does not assort easily with the Greek insistence on the primacy of the spirit over the letter. The Roman lawyers do not seem to have treated interpretation of words as a clear department of law in its own right;

[7] F. Schulz, *History of Roman Legal Science* (Oxford, 1946), 62–3, 68.

[8] 'Omnis definitio in iure civili periculosa', wrote the 2nd-cent. AD jurist Iavolenus (D. 50. 17. 202); 'rarum est enim, ut non subverti posset' ('all legal definitions are dangerous for a definition can rarely escape being discredited').

[9] *Horōn*, genitive plural of *horos*, 'definition'.

[10] Some of the jurists' etymologies were absurd, as for instance Gaius's explanation of *mutuum* (a loan) in *Inst.* 3. 90.

[11] Celsus, D. 33. 10. 7. 2.

it has been observed that neither the *Institutes* of Gaius nor the *Epitome* of Ulpian, all that survives of textbooks for beginner law students from the classical periods, deal with this subject at all.[12]

GREEK PHILOSOPHY AND ROMAN EQUITY

Roman equity, in the sense here intended, covers more than just that department of Roman law which has always excited interest because of its similarity to the jurisdiction developed by the English chancellors. It is meant here to convey also in a more general way the impact on Roman theory and practice of Greek ideas about the superiority of the spirit to the letter, and the importance of the will or intention rather than mere words; and about the *epieikeia* which the Romans rendered as *aequitas*, meaning that which is fair or conscionable, and a value co-ordinate with *ius*, the strict law. Indeed it is easier to trace the Greek influence in the honouring of these general standards than in the operations of the praetor—the Roman analogue of the English chancellor—because the beginnings of the praetor's jurisdiction antedate the reception of Greek philosophy in Rome, and other forces might very probably have set it on a course of equitable creativity even if that reception had not taken place when it did. No doubt the more general principles, too, might have been independently evolved; but the presence ready-made of a philosophical armoury of fashionable provenance makes it likely that they are in fact deploying themes learned from the Greeks.

The contrast between words and intention (between *verba* and *voluntas*) was a Stoic commonplace, and is often drawn by the Roman jurists in giving primacy to the latter. The late classical jurist Papinian declared it 'settled doctrine that in the agreements of contracting parties regard should be had rather to the intention than to the words'.[13] Three statements on the intention to be imputed to a statute are made by Celsus, who flourished about AD 120: 'to know the laws does not mean just grasping the words, but their force and scope';[14] 'laws are to be interpreted generously, to the end that their purpose be upheld';[15] and 'if the wording of a law is ambiguous, it should be understood in the manner which is not

---

[12] J. Himmelschein, 'Studien zu der antiken *Hermeneutica Iuris*', *Symbolae Friburgenses in honorem O. Lenel* (Leipzig, 1935), 396.
[13] D. 50. 16. 219.   [14] D. 1. 3. 17.   [15] D. 1. 3. 18.

objectionable, especially since the law's intent could be gathered from this'.[16] The Stoic emphasis on the primacy of intention probably played a part in shaping rules of concrete law; for instance, that intention determined whether a particular case of physical control of a thing was to rank as *possessio* (in the technical sense which entitled the *possessor* to a legal remedy to protect his possession) or as mere *detentio*, bare physical control. Very likely, too, the Aristotelian and Stoic teaching on will and intention underlay the introduction, in the last century of the republic, of the actions and defences based on *dolus* and *metus* (fraud and duress) in order to frustrate the effectuation of transactions brought about by those prime types of vitiation of the will.

The role of *epieikeia*, Romanized as *aequitas*, is more subtle. The conception of 'equity' as a standard coexisting with law, and having the function of adjusting or supplementing it, was known from Aristotle; but just as the Greek *epieikeia* had no status in the actual practice of the Athenian courts, so *aequitas* conveyed no separate standard recognized by the Roman system as qualifying the law. Certainly the word 'aequum', as used by the jurists, does not mean anything like 'equitable' in the English sense implying a contrast with strict common law and qualifying it. Indeed, 'aequum est' can sometimes mean no more than 'the correct course is' (to do this or that).[17]

Yet the Aristotelian distinction between strict law and equity was a commonplace. It served as a stock theme for training purposes in the Roman schools of rhetoric; Cicero, in a treatise on rhetoric, says that cases offering scope for upholding either standard were put up by teachers, making their pupils practise by arguing at one moment for the letter of the law, at another for *aequitas*, something which here means a less rigid standard ('alias scriptum, alias aequitatem defendere docentur').[18] He reports an episode from a time before his own birth, in which two prominent jurists are drawn into a dispute (by a client who had consulted them both in succession, and got opposite opinions); Galba tries to show Crassus he is wrong, citing many instances and parallels, and putting up arguments based on equity as against the strict law ('multa pro aequitate contra ius').[19] The essence of equity, though not raised to the status of a legal doctrine, might be respected in a Roman court, in which the

[16] D. 1. 3. 19.
[17] e.g. D. 3. 5. 2.
[18] *De oratore* 1. 57. 244.
[19] Ibid. 1. 56. 239–40.

advocates would naturally deploy the weapons with which their education in Greek philosophy and rhetoric had furnished them. Thus Cicero also reports a case in which one party, who had resold to the person from whom he had originally bought it a piece of land which was subject to an easement, was being sued for failure to disclose the existence of this encumbrance. Strictly speaking, the law required such disclosure; but as it had existed at the time when it had been sold by the man who was now repurchasing it, who therefore knew about it perfectly well, was there not a case for treating the rule requiring declaration as inapplicable in these circumstances? Cicero says one orator pressed for the law to be upheld, the other argued for equity ('ius Crassus urguebat, aequitatem Antonius').[20] We do not know how this case went in the end; but we do know that in a celebrated will-suit, the so-called *causa Curiana* of 92 BC, the same Crassus argued successfully for an interpretation of a will which respected the testator's obvious intention rather than following the literal wording of the testament.[21] Cicero also reports that the maxim 'summum ius summa iniuria'—'the strictest application of the law is the greatest injustice' more or less renders the sense—was a trite proverbial expression.[22] Something virtually identical turns up in the comic dramatist Terence in the early second century BC, and since Terence drew his material largely from the Greek playwright Menander, it is quite likely that we are seeing a Romanized version of a Greek perception.

A theory of equity, then, formed part of the Romans' intellectual armoury, even though in a form which was not admitted among the explicit norms of Roman law. There was, however, a formal route by which what would today be called equitable values were *in fact* introduced into the law, namely, the jurisdiction of the praetor, already mentioned; though this jurisdiction did not exist for this purpose only. It was an absolutely central element in Roman administration of justice, the importance of which cannot be exaggerated. The question of the extent to which the work of the praetor was influenced by ideas consciously picked up from philosophy is impossible to answer; but inasmuch as the praetor, being simply a politician with perhaps small knowledge of law, had to rely on the guidance of jurists, it is highly likely that ideas first

---

[20] *De officiis* 3. 16. 67.   [21] *De oratore* 1. 39. 180.
[22] *De officiis* 1. 10. 33.

articulated by philosophers percolated into his creative activity at their inspiration.

Without being himself a judge, the praetor was the gate of access to judicial hearing and decision; it was before him that the issues between the parties were clarified, whereupon he reduced them to a simple, one-sentence formula, expressed as a command to the judge: depending on which of the alternative positions of the parties he found justified, he was either to make the appropriate decree against the defendant, or absolve him—i.e. dismiss the plaintiff's action. Thus far, it would be possible to imagine a modern jurisdiction, in which every litigious issue had to be processed by a special official before trial, as not essentially different from this part of the praetor's operations. For the most important of his functions, however, there is no modern analogue. This is because in the modern democracy there is a clear distinction between lawmaking and law-administering functions; the peculiarity of the Roman praetor, however, was that out of his supervisory role in the administration of justice there grew what for all practical purposes was a legislative power. This happened in gradual stages by a process of usurpation which was simply acquiesced in.

The key to this development lies in the fact that the praetor was the absolute, uncontrolled master of civil legal process. All actions were initiated before him, and the hearing of an issue by a judge was authorized by him; if he chose to deny a plaintiff the action he sought, there was no one to whom an appeal could be brought, and the plaintiff remained shut out from relief. Alternatively he might effectively guarantee the plaintiff's ultimate failure by letting him go ahead, but building into the written programme for the hearing (the conditional command to the judge, called the *formula*) a special defence, related to some plea which the defendant had raised, and directing the judge to dismiss the action if he found the facts did sustain that plea. From accumulated single instances, as may be imagined, firm practice emerged; thus by the last century of the republic a regular special defence, based on the plea that the plaintiff's behaviour had been or was now unconscionable, called the *exceptio doli*, had emerged, and sufficed to frustrate a plaintiff who might have the strict letter of the law on his side; a similar defence based on duress (*metus*) was established around the same time. Again, where someone who had purchased property and had actually got possession of it, but without the conveyancing formality requisite for property of that type, was sued for possession by someone claiming on the vendor's civil-law ownership (which still subsisted because of the ineffective conveyance), the praetor created, so to speak out of the air, a special defence called the *exceptio rei venditae et traditae*, which cut the Gordian knot of civil law by simply directing the judge, if he found that the property had been the subject of a contract of sale and had been physically handed over to the buyer, to dismiss the action founded on the seller's title notwithstanding that, at civil law, this title was perfect.

These are instances of the simplest kind of praetorian intervention, the evolution of special defences; but the praetor also created new actions for plaintiffs whose cases fell outside the four corners of the existing civil law. Thus, to recur to the hypothesis of the defective conveyance just mentioned, if the purchaser is not just being sued on the vendor's title, but has actually been put out of possession before the lapse of time would have made him civil-law owner anyway,[23] he can seek a completely new action invented by the praetor, which used the device of a fiction (the so-called *actio Publiciana*, after the praetor Publicius who made the innovation): the dispossessed purchaser could sue the dispossessor, and the *formula* directed the judge to *assume*, for the purpose of the case, that the time necessary for civil-law ownership to arise in the purchaser anyway by lapse of time *had in fact elapsed*. Naturally the availability of these procedural devices to someone with a formally defective conveyance undermined the whole system of conveyancing formalities by making them irrelevant in practice; and so, in the result, the praetor effectively repealed the old law on the subject. Another striking praetorian creation, one used by the Romans themselves as a textbook example, was the action available to either party where *X* had, as a volunteer (or busybody), undertaken some transaction on *Y*'s behalf without request from *Y* or even his knowledge; as, on this hypothesis, there is no contractual link between the parties, the action of mandate is not available to either party if some grievance arises in consequence of *X*'s well-meant officiousness; but this gap was filled by some praetor (we do not know exactly when) who simply announced, in the edict or programme of action which every magistrate might issue at the

---

[23] By 'usucapio'.

beginning of his year of office,[24] that in such a case he would grant an action on foot of it. These examples could be extended by very many more; all showing what is, in effect, a straightforward enactment of substantive law via the creation of procedural remedies.

The praetor's function in importing equitable values into the administration of justice, and by that route into substantive law, was summarized in the second century AD—long after the creative period of the praetorship had ended—by the jurist Papinian in terms which seem to contain an echo of Aristotle's explanation of *epieikeia*. 'Praetorian law', he wrote, 'is what the praetors introduced in order to assist, or to supplement, or to correct the civil law' ('adiuvandi vel supplendi vel corrigendi iuris civilis gratia').[25]

ROMAN THEORY OF NATURAL LAW

What might be called the vocabulary of the natural-law doctrines of the medieval Catholic church (and of later secularized natural-law theory) was formed in the pre-Christian Roman world. Both the philosophers and the lawyers of that world contributed to it. However, the Roman philosophers—a term which in this context includes scarcely anyone except the many-sided Cicero—used the concept of nature in a way very different from what the Roman jurists meant by it; and the jurists' usage, in its turn, was not uniform. All these different employments of 'nature' represented at the same time so many expressions of legal theory, and they must be disentangled from one another.

It is in Cicero, writing in high-minded academic detachment, that we encounter a conception of natural law which not only strongly resembles the Christian teaching but, very likely, actually contributed something to the formation of that teaching. In his treatise *De legibus* ('On the Laws'), certainly influenced both by Aristotelian and by Stoic doctrine, he presents nature as the source of precepts to the human individual, a source accessible to every such individual

---

[24] In the case of the praetorian office, although in theory each succeeding praetor could issue an entirely fresh programme, in fact a stock edict was gradually built up, carried on from one praetor to the next. By the 1st cent. BC this (in effect) standing edict was regarded as stable enough to compose commentaries on.

[25] D. 1. 1. 7. 1.

through his or her reason; and this provision for human conduct has its origin in God. According to the definition of law which he attributes to 'the most learned men',

law is the highest reason, implanted in nature, which commands what ought to be done and forbids the opposite. This reason, when firmly fixed and fully developed in the human mind, is Law. They believe that Law is understanding; whose natural function it is to command right conduct and forbid wrongdoing . . . The origin of Justice is to be found in Law, for Law is a natural force; it is the mind and reason of the intelligent man, the standard by which Justice and Injustice are measured . . . In determining what Justice is, we may begin with that Supreme Law which had its origin ages before any written law existed or any state had been established.[26]

In another passage he argues that even if there had been no written law against rape in the reign of the last Tarquin (king of Rome), Tarquin still violated the 'eternal law' by his outrage on Lucretia:

For reason did exist, derived from the nature of the universe, urging men to right conduct and diverting them from wrongdoing, and this reason did not first become Law when it was written down, but when it first came into existence; and it came into existence simultaneously with the divine mind. Wherefore the true and primal Law, designed for command and prohibition, is the right reason of the high God.[27]

In the most celebrated of all such passages—and there are many such, not just in the *De legibus* but scattered throughout his other works[28]—he wrote:

True law is right reason in agreement with nature, diffused among all men; constant and unchanging, it should call men to their duties by its precepts, and deter them from wrongdoing by its prohibitions; and it never commands or forbids upright men in vain, while its rules and restraints are lost upon the wicked. To curtail this law is unholy, to amend it illicit, to repeal it impossible; nor can we be dispensed from it by the order either of senate or of popular assembly; nor need we look for anyone to clarify or interpret it; nor will it be one law at Rome and a different one at Athens, nor otherwise tomorrow than it is today; but one and the same Law, eternal and unchangeable, will bind all peoples and all ages; and God, its designer, expounder and enacter, will be as it were the sole and universal ruler and governor of all things; and whoever disobeys it, because by this act he will have turned his back on himself and on man's very nature, will pay the

---

[26] *De legibus* 1. 6. 18–19.   [27] Ibid. 2. 4. 10.
[28] *De republ.* 3. 22. 33.

heaviest penalty, even if he avoids the other punishments which are adjudged fit for his conduct.

We owe our knowledge of this passage to the Christian writer Lactantius (c. 250–317), who calls Cicero's description of God's law 'almost divine'.[29]

Cicero the court advocate and politician dealt in the ordinary law of murder, outrage, partnership, etc. without more than a very rare reference to a higher law; but Cicero the philosopher assigned to the positive laws of humans an altogether subordinate place by comparison with the law of nature. The mere fact that a measure has been enacted by a commonly accepted method does not of itself entitle it to respect as being just, or perhaps even to the title of 'law' at all if it defies higher principles:

The most foolish notion of all is the belief that everything is just which is found in the customs or laws of nations. Would that be true, even if those laws had been enacted by tyrants? . . . [or if a law proposed] that a dictator might put to death with impunity any citizen he wished, even without a trial. For Justice is one; it binds all human society, and is based on one Law, which is right reason applied to command and prohibition . . .[30]

If the principles of justice were founded on the decrees of peoples, the edicts of princes, or the decisions of judges, then justice would sanction robbery and adultery and forgery of wills, in case these acts were approved by the votes or decrees of the populace.[31]

It is agreed that laws were invented for the safety of citizens, the preservation of states, and the tranquillity and happiness of human life, and that those who first put statutes of this kind in force convinced their people that it was their intention to write down and put into effect such rules as, once accepted and adopted, would make possible for them an honourable and happy life; and when such rules were drawn up and put in force, it is clear that men called them 'laws'. From this point of view it can be readily understood that those who formulated wicked and unjust statutes for nations, thereby breaking their promises and agreements, put into effect anything but 'laws'.[32]

These strong expressions stop short of actually imputing invalidity, as distinct from injustice, to laws infringing the higher law. Nevertheless their rhetorical feeling is considerable, and it is easy to see how they provided for the later, Christian world a framework to

[29] *Inst. div.* 6. 8. 6–9.
[31] Ibid. 1. 16. 43–4.
[30] *De legibus* 1. 15. 42.
[32] Ibid. 2. 5. 11.

which a more absolutist role for natural law could readily be fitted.[33]

On the positive side, Cicero presents several legally material principles as derived from the law of nature (much as the Greeks had referred to nature, as has been seen, some of their own standards and practices). The right of self-defence is the most obvious instance;[34] others are the prohibition against cheating or harming others,[35] and the precept that one must positively defend others from harm.[36]

If we move now to the Roman jurists we see that, although they very frequently speak of natural law and natural reason (*ius naturale*, *naturalis ratio*) as well as using the word 'natural', in certain cases, to qualify concepts like possession and obligation, they mean by this usage, in almost every case, something quite different from Cicero's concept of a primordial higher law. When they speak of natural law or natural reason underlying some rule or institution they are talking not of the law or reason of God, but of the nature of things on the ground, things as they are, things for which common sense, the facts of life, the essence of business relations, and so on, 'naturally' suggest the appropriate legal treatment. 'For "natural" was to them', wrote Ernst Levy, 'not only what followed from physical qualities of men or things, but also what, within the framework of that system, seemed to square with the normal and reasonable order of human interests and, for this reason, not in need of any further evidence.'[37] It might not be too crass a comparison to say that the relation between Cicero's eternal, divinely inspired natural law and the practical natural law of the jurists somewhat resembles the relation which was to emerge, at the dawn of modern times, between the divinely appointed natural law of Aquinas and the medieval Catholic church, and the secular, rationalist natural law on which Grotius was to build a law of

---

[33] 'It is primarily Cicero's account of natural law which represented the Stoic position for Christians like Lactantius and Ambrose and so influenced the Middle Ages . . . [Ambrose and Augustine] took natural law from Cicero, baptised it, and handed it on for preservation to the Church': G. Watson, 'The Natural Law and Stoicism', in A. Long (ed.), *Problems in Stoicism* (London, 1971), 228, 235–6.

[34] *Pro Milone* 4. 10.

[35] *De officiis* 3. 17. 68, 3. 5. 26, 3. 6. 27.   [36] Ibid. 1. 7. 23.

[37] 'Natural Law in Roman Thought', *Studia et Documenta Historiae et Iuris*, 15 (1949), 7.

nations, and which dominated the legal theory of the seventeenth and eighteenth centuries.

This practical 'natural' law of the jurists suggested to them, as self-evident, rules for the care of the property and persons of children and lunatics; the admission of all blood relations to the possibility of intestate succession (originally this was confined to persons related only through a common male ancestor); the right of self-defence; the voidness of contractual promises to perform that which was in physical nature impossible. A slightly different category centred not so much on the physical nature of things and human instincts, as on generally shared, instinctive perceptions of what was a fair and simple rule to use in this or that legal setting; as Levy puts it, 'nature is here the order inherent in conditions of life as the Romans saw it'.[38] In this category belonged principles such as that a man's position may be improved without his knowledge or consent, but not made worse; that the party who bears the cost or burden of a relationship should also have the benefits of it, and vice versa; and that the first taker of something previously owned by nobody became its owner. (Where X made a product out of Y's raw materials there was disagreement among the jurists as to whether or not X became owner of this newly emerged thing; each side to the debate thought it was supported by natural reason.)

This entirely practical, common-sense employment of the concept of nature by the jurists linked up in their minds with an element in the Roman legal system which arose in one important area of legal practice, namely commerce (in the broadest sense) with foreigners on Roman territory, or between such foreigners themselves. This element was called the *ius gentium*, 'the law of (all) nations', as distinct from the *ius civile*, 'the citizen-law', i.e. that pertaining only to Romans. The *Institutes* of Gaius, an elementary student's textbook of the second century AD, opens with the following exposition of this duality:

All peoples who are governed by laws and customs make use partly of law which is peculiar to themselves, partly of law which is common to all men. What each nation has established as law for itself is the law peculiar to itself, and is called its civil law (*ius civile*), that is, the law peculiar to that state (*civitas*); but what natural reason has established among the law of the nations (*ius gentium*), that is, the law which all nations use. Thus the

---

[38] Ibid. 9.

Roman people uses partly its own special law, partly law which is common to all men.

This passage, taken in isolation, would suggest that the Romans had taken a scientific interest in the legal systems of other peoples, and by comparative study had established that certain rules were the same everywhere. In fact this is not the case. The Romans, like other ancient peoples, took very little interest in the institutions of their neighbours; Tacitus's account of the institutions of the Germans is an unfortunately isolated exception; it did not occur to Caesar, for instance, or any of his officers to leave what would have been priceless to us, an account of the legal and political institutions of Celtic Gaul or Britain. What Gaius meant by *ius gentium* was, in fact, a body of native Roman rules which were (exceptionally, because in principle Roman law was applicable only to Roman citizens) applied in disputes either between foreigners on Roman territory, or between a Roman and a foreigner. This extension of Roman rules to persons who were not Roman citizens took place, probably, during the third and second centuries BC, when Roman domination of Italy was complete, but before Roman citizenship was extended to the entire Italian population. In other words, in an era when it was necessary for Romans to do business with large numbers of non-Roman neighbours in the same peninsula, not to speak of non-Romans with whom commerce brought them into contact elsewhere in the Mediterranean world.

This necessity was met not by reflecting on what natural reason suggested in order to compose an international commercial code, but simply by applying, outside their original sphere, such ordinary Roman rules as seemed suitable, in other words, those that were simple, of minimum technicality, and in approximate conformity with the common sense and practice of the neighbouring peoples. Thus the quite formless transference of ownership in all kinds of movable property (except slaves and gregarious farm animals), by merely handing the thing over (*traditio*), was reckoned an item of *ius gentium*, although it was the Romans' own native way of doing this; so was the equally formless loan of money (*mutuum*);[39] so was the Roman mode of creating a binding unilateral obligation by the mere exchange of an exactly corresponding verbal question and

---

[39] *Mutuum* included also loans of commodities (e.g. seed-corn) for repayment in due course in the same kind and quantity.

answer (*stipulatio*); and so were the (commercially highly important) contracts of sale, hire, mandate, and partnership, which could be created by simple, formless agreement, howsoever expressed (much like an English simple contract, except that the Romans had no doctrine of consideration); these latter contracts, called 'consensual' from the fact that consensus was their only prerequisite, may however have first entered Roman law from the sphere of foreigners' litigation, which was supervised by a special praetor, the 'foreign' praetor (*peregrinus*).

This entirely practical development not only received the sort of bogus aura of comparative science which Gaius gives it; it was given also an equally adventitious philosophic tone by the jurists, who were inclined to identify the dualism *ius civile/ius gentium* with the contrast—familiar to them through their conventional education in Greek rhetoric and philosophy—between positive law (*to nomikon dikaion*) and natural law (*to physikon dikaion*). By this route a kind of circle was closed, at least in part; the pedestrian, practical working-out of a body of Roman rules suitable for application to foreigners, inflated *post factum* with theory, rose into the rarified atmosphere in which Cicero's philosophy of the law of nature hovered above the earth. The only exception from the identification of *ius gentium* with *ius naturale*, or its subsumption in it, was slavery. Although it had to be admitted that by nature men were born free, the universal practice of the ancient world (not merely the Roman) was contrary to this doctrine; and indeed the Romans' use of the word 'natural', as opposed to 'civil', in describing the quasi-possession or quasi-rights of a contractual type which might be imputed to a slave, gave, as Ernst Levy pointed out, the game away; when natural and civil law came, as here, into collision, the Roman lawyers were in no doubt that the latter prevailed, and the former went to the wall.[40]

THE ROMAN CONCEPTION OF THE STATE

The Greeks, as has been seen, had no word for the abstract concept which we call 'the state'; the word which did duty for it was simply *polis*, 'the city', the only setting in which political organization was

[40] 'Natural Law' (see n. 37), 17–18.

familiar to them. The Roman word *civitas* seems to come nearer the abstraction, as does the phrase more commonly used in this context, *res publica*, in which *publica* is simply an adjective formed from *populus*, the people; indeed Cicero underlines this association by putting into the mouth of the main speaker in a philosophical dialogue the words 'est igitur res publica res populi'. There was however also an official phrase, used from at least the middle republic, to serve as the state's constitutional name: *senatus populusque Romanus* (abbreviated in inscriptions and on coins, etc., to *SPQR*), which expressed the dual residence of power in the senate and in the people.

The Roman lawyers, true to their strictly practical disposition, did not trouble themselves with speculation as to the historic or moral basis of this state or the society of which it was an aspect. But Roman philosophy—unoriginal here as elsewhere—kept alive Greek theory on this subject. The earliest representative writer here seems to be Lucretius (99–55 BC). He was a follower of the Athenian philosopher Epicurus (a much younger contemporary of Aristotle); and in his single known work, a long poem called *De rerum natura*, he expounds the Epicurean system, centred mainly on the finiteness of human existence and the mortality of the soul, with its corollary suggestion that the self-contained, calm enjoyment of pleasure was the proper end of life. Unlike Epicurus himself, however, he included in this monumental work a theory of the emergence of society and settled laws not very different from the suggestions of Plato in his *Protagoras* and *Laws*. Initially, wrote Lucretius, man lived in no community, but simply supported himself from the fruits and berries in which the earth abounded; then an instinct for friendship brought people together; these human bonds he calls by a word with contractual overtones, as it usually means 'treaty' (*foedera*). With the discovery of gold, turbulent greed and ambition brought mankind into chaos; so that, although formerly they had been able to live (in the pre-community condition) without either law or custom, now

some of them, by precept, brought about the creation of a ruler and the establishment of laws, and made people willing to use them. For the human race, weary of spending life in violence, was grown weak through its hatreds; and this made it the more willing spontaneously to submit to the strictness of law and rule . . . The man who, by his acts, violates the common bonds of peace [*communia foedera pacis*] does not find it easy to live a quiet and orderly life.

From this beginning—the weariness of disorder and universal hostility—human progress, including submission to laws, was learnt by experience, little by little.[41]

Cicero, a slightly older contemporary of Lucretius, was familiar with his work, and when, probably in the last year of Lucretius's life, Cicero wrote his treatise on the state (*De republica*), he included in it several passages which transmit a conception of the origin of political society with a quite strong contractual slant which Lucretius had conveyed in much vaguer terms. The state is presented, first, in more general terms not unlike those of Lucretius: it is the ultimate fruit of man's instinct to associate with his fellows, broadening out from the primary associations of marriage and parenthood. That instinct is the 'origin of the city, and, as it were, the seed-bed of the state' ('principium urbis et quasi seminarium rei publicae');[42] once one had explained this natural social instinct of man, the 'source of laws and of law itself' ('fons legum et iuris') could be discovered.[43] In the *De republica*, however, he goes further:

Not every assemblage of men howsoever brought together makes up the *populus*, but an assemblage of a great number allied together in binding agreement [*iuris consensu sociatus*] and in a sharing of interests [*utilitatis communione*]. And the first cause of their coming together is not so much their individual weakness as the natural social instinct of men; for the human race is not one of solitary wanderers.[44]

Note here not merely an echo of the Aristotelian notion of human beings as creatures tending naturally to civic society (the *politikon zōon*), but the certainly deliberate legal references. When to this passage another phrase from the *De republica* is added—'a single bond of law, and an agreement and partnership in coming together, which is what makes a people' ('unum vinculum iuris [ac] consensus ac societas coetus, quod est populus')[45]—Cicero can probably be seen as alluding to the Roman 'consensual' contract of partnership (*societas*), of which the sharing of the partners' goods (*communio*)

---

[41] *De rerum natura* 5. 1141 ff.; passages summarized but not quoted are 5. 958 ff., 1011 ff., 1448ff.

[42] *De officiis* 1. 17. 54.

[43] *De legibus* 1. 5. 16.

[44] *De republ.* 1. 25. 39.

[45] Ibid. 3. 31. 43.

was an aspect. That in restating, in Roman terms, the social-contract
theory of the state's origin which had already appeared among the
Greeks, Cicero was conscious of his forerunners is perhaps proved
by his express dissent from the idea—first put forward by the
sophists—that the weakness of individuals had been their motive in
entering the primordial social bargain.

In this contract-based state there is (unlike the polity imagined
long afterwards by Hobbes as under an absolute ruler whose
dominion all have acquiesced in) no room for tyranny. Cicero
represents tyranny, indeed, as the negation of the state itself: 'where
all are oppressed by the cruelty of a single man . . . would anyone
call it a state (*res publica*)? . . . It must be said that, where a tyrant
rules, the state is not so much defective as non-existent.'[46] A similar
thought is expressed later by Seneca, when he visualizes an original
golden age subverted by vice and sinking under tyranny: it was
then, and as tyranny's antithesis, that the need for laws arose.[47] But
Seneca lived into an era in which, as J. W. Gough pointed out,
'while contractarian thought and phraseology were evidently still in
being, the whole political atmosphere was one of absolutism and
submission';[48] he was forced, under Nero, to commit suicide.

THE IDEAL NATURE OF LAW

As has been seen, Cicero the philosopher wrote of law in an
idealized way as inseparable from the reason implanted by nature in
human kind; the jurists, on the other hand, found an employment
for the concept of the 'natural' only on the practical, working level
of that which was simple and obvious, having regard to the actual
conditions of life and society. But occasionally the jurists, too, in
their rare attempts to define or describe what they practised, briefly
touched the idea plane. A famous instance is the opening passage of
Justinian's *Digest*, which records the second-century AD jurist
Ulpian as citing an earlier jurist, Celsus, as having 'neatly'
(*eleganter*) defined law (*ius*) as the 'ars boni et aequi', a phrase
whose sense is hard to reproduce in English, but which means
literally 'the art of the good and right'.[49] A few sentences further on,

[46] *De republ.* 3. 31. 43.   [47] *Epistulae morales* 90, §§ 3, 5, 36, 38, 40.
[48] *The Social Contract* (Oxford, 1957), 21.   [49] D. 1. 1. 1.

Ulpian is again quoted, on justice: this consists in 'the steady and constant will to give each one what is his by law' ('constans et perpetua voluntas ius suum cuique tribuere'); and the fundamental precepts of that law are, 'to live honourably, not to injure others, and to render to everyone what is his' ('honeste vivere, alterum non laedere, suum cuique tribuere').[50] The Greek inspiration of these maxims seems unmistakable.[51]

THE SOURCE OF LEGAL OBLIGATION

The forms in which Roman law subsisted varied somewhat from one era to another; but broadly speaking, they included the statutory type, functionally comparable with modern statute; the edictal form, i.e. the lawmaking reforms and innovations and adaptations associated with the praetorship (described above, and bearing some comparison to the English chancellors' construction of equity); the uniquely Roman form of *responsa prudentium*, or the opinions of recognized jurists; and, in a very modest position,[52] custom. In the republic the 'statutory' types of law consisted of *leges* properly so called, i.e. measures enacted by the popular assembly; *leges* slightly less properly (though commonly) so called, because more strictly *plebis scita*, measures adopted by the *concilium plebis*, to which the force of law attached; and *senatus consulta*, resolutions of the senate, in form mere directives to magistrates, but in practice looked on as having the force of law. In the empire these statutory forms were joined by the *constitutiones principum*, i.e. the emperors' measures, which came in different formats, but all accepted as law, and in fact soon supplanting all the other lawmaking modes.

The Roman theory on the source of validity of law (all from the time of the empire, by which time the *princeps* was the only legislative organ that mattered) is curiously two-faced. On the one hand, much in the way that Cicero had thought the state itself required to be sustained by popular consent, we find the jurist Julian, writing in the time of Hadrian, emphasizing the democratic

---

[50] D. 1. 1. 10, pr., 1. 1. 10. 1.   [51] Cicero, *De legibus* 1. 5. 18.
[52] It is not mentioned by Gaius at all in his enumeration of sources of law, only by Justinian's *Institutes* (1. 2. 9).

nexus between law and its subjects in a passage where he attributes legal efficacy to custom as well as to statute:

Immemorial custom is, rightly, observed as though it were statute law; this is the law which we call established by usage. For, since the only reason that even statutes bind us is that they are accepted in the people's opinion, it is only right that rules which the people has accepted without any writing at all, should bind everyone; for what does it matter, whether the people has made its will known by a vote, or by the fact of what actually happens?[53]

A couple of generations later a very different note was struck by the famous Ulpian (about 215 AD), perhaps reflecting the accelerating trend from 'principate' to 'dominate'. In a phrase which would have been unthinkable to Cicero, but which served thereafter until the French revolution as the most venerable axiom in absolutism, he wrote 'quod principi placuit, legis habet vigorem' (the emperor's will has the force of statute); this was incorporated in Justinian's *Digest*.[54] On the other hand, this same *Digest* passage also quotes Ulpian's essentially democratic rationalization even of this principle of absolutism; he followed the phrase just quoted with the words 'utpote cum lege regia, quae de imperio eius lata est, populus ei et in eum omne suum imperium et potestatem conferat': 'seeing that, by the "royal statute" concerning the emperor's authority, the people surrender to him and confer upon him all their own authority and constitutional power'. This 'royal statute', supposed to have been enacted by the old Roman popular assembly for the benefit of the first *princeps*, Augustus, is known to be a later fiction designed to legitimize retrospectively the actuality of the emperor's power; but it still ranks as evidence of the need officially felt to explain power in terms of the people's will, and so of an inarticulate theory of this kind, surviving so to speak (since Justinian's compilers perpetuated it) in the catacombs of the late Roman mind.

THE CONCEPTION OF STATUTE-LAW

Early Roman statute-law, of which the instance towering over all others was the fifth-century BC Twelve Tables, perhaps enjoyed the same presumption of semi-permanency that early Athenian laws did; at any rate it was seldom changed, let alone regularly tinkered

---

[53] D. 1. 3. 32.   [54] D. 1. 4. 1, pr.

with. But what was it thought to *be*? *Lex*, though a narrower term than *ius*, we find defined in terms which modern analytical jurisprudence would probably think inadequate. It appears predominantly as a command. Cicero calls the conception *lex* 'right reason in commanding and prohibiting'.[55] The third-century jurist Modestinus is cited in the *Digest* as saying: 'The effect of a statute is to command, to prohibit, to permit, or to punish.'[56] Less clear, and also unsatisfactory, is the definition given by Papinian, the leading jurist of the preceding generation: 'A statute is a general ordinance [the fruit of] lawyers' counsel; the repression of offences committed deliberately or ignorantly; [or] a general commitment of the public faith of the state'.[57] Nevertheless those essays at definition, the first two over-terse, the other awkward, no doubt covered well enough the tenor of most if not all of the *leges* with which jurists dealt in practice.

It is worth noting briefly and finally in this connection that, though Ulpian for example, sees lawyers as priests dedicated to making people good, neither Cicero nor any other Roman writer followed Plato in visualizing how as serving to shape the state or citizens according to any detailed plan. In this omission one may perhaps again see the strictly practical, unpretentious, sober bent of the Roman legal mind.

THE RULE OF LAW

The ideal of the state governed according to known rules which bind rulers and ruled alike appears among Roman writers in far feebler form than among Greek. Yet until the final establishment of the imperial autocracy the theme is occasionally heard. The best and earliest instance is found in Cicero's speech *Pro Cluentio*—his defence of a client charged with poisoning—where, in contesting the accuser's indignant demand that a formal differentiation made by the law between senators and those of lesser rank should be ignored, Cicero says that, even if this differentiation were wrong,

it is a far greater shame, in a state which rests upon law [*in ea civitate, quae legibus contineatur*], that there should be a departure from law [*discedi ab legibus*]. For law is the bond which secures these our privileges in the

[55] *De legibus* 1. 12. 33.   [56] D. 1. 3. 7.   [57] D. 1. 3. 1.

commonwealth, the foundation of our liberty, the fountain-head of justice . . .
The state without law would be like the human body without mind . . . The
magistrates who administer the law, the judges who interpret it—all of us,
in short—obey the law in order that we may be free.

And he goes on to a series of rhetorical questions designed to
emphasize the dependence of the entire apparatus of the courts on
law. 'Look round at all the departments of the state', he adds, 'and
you will find everything happening according to the rule and
prescribed measure of law (*omnia legum imperio et praescripto
fieri*)'.[58] In the following century Seneca, the great Roman representative of Stoicism, in his treatise on clemency admonishes the
emperor (Nero) to behave as if he were answerable to his own
laws;[59] a theme which, perhaps in part reinforced by the memory of
Seneca's words, will frequently be heard after the fall of the Western
empire and Europe's passage under the rule of half-barbarian kings.

As the imperial position hardened into formal absolutism, a
doctrine arose which had never been heard in the republic, namely
that the emperor was above the law (or, as Ulpian put it in a terse
and famous maxim soon after AD 200, 'freed from the laws':
'*princeps legibus solutus est*'.[60] Ulpian's contemporary, the historian
Dio Cassius, explains what is meant by this

prerogative which was given to none of the ancient Romans outright and
unreservedly, and the possession of which alone would enable them to
exercise [all their formal functions] and others. For they have been released
from the laws, as the very words in Latin[61] declare; that is, they are free
from all compulsion of the laws and are bound by none of the written
ordinances.[62]

This Roman authority was later appealed to in justification of
absolute regal power up to the time of Louis XIV and beyond. The
competing principle of the rule of law, however, as will be seen, was
ultimately to prevail in the Western world.

EQUALITY BEFORE THE LAW

While Cicero could eloquently state the principle of law's sovereignty,
he lived in a system which recognized within the law a large range of

---

[58] *Pro Cluentio* 53. 146–7.   [59] *De clementia* 1. 4.   [60] D. 1. 3. 31.
[61] Dio Cassius wrote in Greek.   [62] *Roman History* 53. 18. 1.

formal differentiations according to rank; and neither he nor any of the jurists expressed the idea of equality before the law in the sense of the impermissibility of such formal discriminations. On the contrary, Cicero thought that the recognition in law of degrees of rank was necessary to a well-ordered polity. In his treatise on the state, pointing out the strengths and weaknesses respectively of monarchies, oligarchies, and democracies, he says of the latter that 'when the people control everything, then, however much justice and moderation they may act with, still even equality itself is inequitable when it has no regard to degrees of rank (*cum habet nullos gradus dignitatis*)'.[63] In the Athenian democracy after the fall of the Areopagus, he thought, the reason why the state declined in splendour was that the people did not respect difference in rank.

In practical legal life something like what Cicero meant was observed in several quite open ways. There is good reason to think, for instance, that the full-dress criminal trials by the standing courts called *quaestiones*, such as the famous trial in which Cicero prosecuted Verres, ex-governor of Sicily, for extortion, were not laid on for the lower orders of the population; the delinquencies of humbler citizens received, probably, short shrift from minor magistrates who were expected to keep order among the lower classes without fuss.[64] In the field of civil law there were contexts in which differences of rank were expressly recognized as justifying varying treatment of parties; for example, the delict *iniuria*, which embraced a range of acts the common feature of which was insult or outrage, became aggravated (with consequent inflation of damages) into *iniuria atrox* if the injured party were someone of conspicuous rank such as a magistrate.[65] Leave to bring the *actio de dolo*—imputing fraud to the defendant and resulting in a mark of infamy if the action succeeded—was not given to everyone: not to children or freedmen as against their parents or patrons (this can be seen as a gesture to decency) but also not to 'a person of low rank as against someone of high station, for example to a plebeian as against a highly respected man of consular rank, or to a wastrel and rake, or some other kind of low character, as against a man of irreproachable

---

[63] *De republ.* 1. 27. 43.
[64] See Kunkel, *Untersuchungen zur Entwicklung des römischen Kriminalverfahrens in vorsullanischer Zeit* (Munich, 1962), 9, 21 ff.
[65] Or a parent or patron, to whom special respect was owed: D. 47. 10. 7. 7–8.

life'.[66] Apart from these open, formal discriminations, the social inequalities of Roman life affected the operation of Roman justice; much evidence shows the socially disadvantaged party as not enjoying access to the same kind of justice as his adversary.[67]

All the same, in a curious way the ideal of equality somehow coexisted with the reality just described. Cicero, who defended a legal system which should discriminate according to rank, also gives in his sketch of an ideal code of law a philosopher's appreciation of the principle of equality. He proposes to reproduce in this code a provision which the Twelve Tables (he says) actually contained: *privilegia ne inroganto*, which means '[The magistrates] shall not propose laws directed against individuals'. The context as well as other evidence makes it clear that what is here in mind is something in the criminal sphere, a *legislative* condemnation of an individual person, like the English acts of attainder in the era which the revolution of 1688–9 concluded. Cicero however (who had himself once been the object of a personal decree of banishment) justifies the prohibition of *privilegia* on reasons broad enough to transcend the criminal area: 'Our ancestors provided an admirable rule for the future: they forbade the passing of laws aimed at individuals, which is what a *privilegium* is. For what is more unjust than such a law? since the sense of the very idea of law is that it is decreed and prescribed for all.'[68] In his speech *Pro Milone* he appears to combine this idea with his views on distinctions based on rank: 'let there be', he says, 'a difference between the higher and lower grades of society; but let a criminal homicide be governed by the same laws and the same penalties'.[69] And in one of his works on rhetoric he defines *aequitas* as that which in like circumstances demands a like legal treatment (*paria iura*).[70] Marcus Aurelius, too, the philosopher-emperor, mentions something probably best rendered 'equality before the law' under its Greek name (*isonomia*, mentioned in the former chapter) when he lists, at the beginning of his *Meditations*, the various good examples he has had the opportunity to imbibe from others: to Severus, his relation by marriage, he attributes 'the conception of a state with one law for all, based upon individual equality and freedom of speech'.[71]

---

[66] D. 4. 3. 11. 1.
[67] See J. M. Kelly, *Roman Litigation* (Oxford, 1966), chs. 2, 4, 5.
[68] *De legibus* 3. 19. 44.   [69] *Pro Milone* 7. 17.
[70] *Topica* 4. 23.   [71] *Meditations* 1. 14.

The Theory of Punishment

Roman opinion on the subject of the objects of punishment was evidently formed by Greek mentors. In his tract on mercy addressed to Nero, Seneca enumerated three bases for it. Injuries done to others, he says, should be punished by the emperor for the same reasons as they are punished by law: the reformation of the delinquent, the giving of a warning example to others, or so that, by the removal of the criminals (*sublatis malis*), everyone else may live in greater safety.[72]

A century later the Roman writer of miscellanies Aulus Gellius discusses the reasons for punishment assigned by Plato in his *Gorgias* (mentioned in Chapter 1), namely correction and deterrence, and wonders why another one, namely the vindication of injured honour, was not expressed in his list.[73] To this he gives the Greek name *timōria*, associating it with the Greek word for honour or estimation, *timē*; but *timōria* is the ordinary, general Greek word for punishment, and its Greek usage does not seem to reflect any conscious association with Gellius's idea. Perhaps, however, the plausible-looking etymology gave form to what genuinely was a Roman trait, namely the sensitiveness about injured dignity which, as has been seen, could aggravate an *iniuria* into *iniuria atrox*.

When we come to the question of the relation of the infliction of punishment to a wrongdoer's state of mind, it is possible to present some information based on our scraps of knowledge about the earliest Roman legislation. The grammarian Festus, in explaining the meaning of the word *paricidas*, purports to cite a law attributed to the second of Rome's supposed seven kings, Numa Pompilius, who (if he existed at all) would have been legislating in the early seventh century BC, earlier even than Dracōn at Athens, which alone makes the attribution unlikely. Festus' quotation,[74] though linguistically archaic, is not archaic enough for so remote a date; but it could conceivably be a linguistically modernized version of an ancient law antedating the Twelve Tables. At any rate he says this law qualified as a *paricidas* or murderer only someone who

---

[72] Seneca, *De clementia* 1. 22. 1. As penal imprisonment in the modern style was not a part of the Roman criminal system, *sublatis* must mean 'put out of the way' in a sombre sense.

[73] *Noctes Atticae* 7. 14: above, Ch. 1 at n. 83.   [74] L. 247.

'knowingly and with evil intent has caused the death of a free man' ('qui hominem liberum dolo sciens morti duit'). A likely supposition is that *dolo sciens*, the mental element, is an attempt to reproduce the similar element of deliberateness given special treatment for the first time in the law of Athens by Dracōn. Whether or not this is so, it does point, like Dracōn's rule, to a decisive advance in legal civilization.

The Twelve Tables are also credited with recognizing the distinction between voluntarily and involuntarily causing harm. The penalty of burning to death, inflicted (according to Gaius)[75] for arson, was exacted, under the Twelve Tables, only where the arsonist had acted *sciens prudensque* ('knowingly and with foresight of the consequences'); but, says Gaius, if the burning was an accident, he had merely to make good the loss or, if he could not afford this, got a mild beating. Also, in a context which is not clear because the cited fragment is too small, the Twelve Tables according to Cicero[76] contained a clause about the throwing of a weapon: if it 'fled his hand rather than that he threw it' ('si telum manu fugit magis quam iecit'), a ram was 'substituted'—almost literally, a 'scapegoat' to take the place of the person who has been merely the physical agent of death or injury and would (had the deed been deliberate) have had to face the vengeance of his victim's family.

These early traces of a native breakthrough in legal sophistication— they must be called that, because the necessity of mentioning the distinction in statute law suggests that in the preceding age it was not recognized—served Cicero the philosopher as well as Cicero the orator: in his treatise *De inventione* he produces the generalization that 'intention is what must be looked at in all things', nothing being more unworthy than the punishment of someone who has not been at fault.[77] Cicero's actual phrase in this text ('in omnibus rebus voluntatem spectari oportere') seems to be echoed in a rescript of Emperor Hadrian: 'in maleficiis voluntas spectatur non eventus' ('with crimes, regard is had not to the event but to the intent');[78] it is likely that both Cicero and the emperor were presenting a home-produced principle in a vesture borrowed from Stoic philosophy, in which the primacy of the intent was a commonplace. Generally, in classical Roman law the state of mind of someone causing injury

[75] D. 47. 9. 9.   [76] *Topica* 17. 64; also *Pro Tullio* 21. 51.
[77] *De inventione* 2. 101.   [78] D. 48. 8. 14.

was central also in civil-law contexts; the jurists' writings abound with distinctions related to this element, referred to by a range of words such as *dolus, fraus, culpa, animus, mens, voluntas, consilium, sponte.*

Due Course of Law

It is not easy to produce anything like a clear Roman statement of the value which we call 'due course of law'; perhaps as good a statement of it as can be found comes from a surprising source, the *Golden Ass*, or *Metamorphoses*, by Apuleius of the second century AD. This is a kind of novel; and at one point in the tale we see magistrates preventing a lynching, saying that a proper judgment must be given in the proper legal manner ('civiliter sententia promeretur'), after a trial had been held duly and in accordance with inherited tradition ('rite et more maiorum'), with consideration of the pleas raised on both sides ('utrimquesecus allegationibus examinatis'). On no account should the 'condemnation of someone unheard, after the example of wild barbarians or unrestrained tyrants', be allowed to intrude into a time of peace such a dreadful precedent.[79]

The reference here to condemnation without a hearing touches, of course, the central value in 'due course of law'; and the Roman texts which show this act as something deeply disapproved of are numerous, though they mostly come from lay rather than legal writers, suggesting that for the jurists the principle of hearing both sides of a case was too obvious to need stating. They do not need to be individually cited; one or two will serve as representative.[80] Tacitus reports an effort on the part of the senate to have a man who had been a notorious informer under Nero condemned unheard; other senators retorted that 'time should be allowed, the charges published; and that even the most odious and guilty defendant should, as was customary, be heard' (*more audiendum*).[81] The

---

[79] *Metamorphoses* 10. 6.
[80] For other instances see J. M. Kelly, 'Audi Alteram Partem', *Natural Law Forum*, 9 (1964), 105 ff.
[81] *Histories* 2. 20.

roughly contemporary Seneca stated the principle in terms once cited by a modern Irish judge:

> Quicunque aliquid statuerit, parte inaudita altera,
> Aequum licet statuerit, haud aequus fuerit:

(Whoever shall have given judgment, leaving one of the parties unheard, will not have acted justly, even if his judgment in fact does justice.)[82]

THEORY OF PROPERTY

At the moment when Roman law first yields historically reliable data, i.e. the era of the Twelve Tables or a little earlier, say the late sixth century BC, the institution of private property is already clearly established (though within a social system which recognized a capacity to own property only in the *paterfamilias*, the family patriarch). It is, however, agreed that at an earlier stage some form of tribal or collective ownership of land existed; and we are told that during the kingship only very small plots of land were allotted to individuals for transmission by inheritance.[83] Only very sparse traces of anything like a theory of private property, whether of its origin or of its justification, appear in Roman literature. The picture drawn by Lucretius of the origin of society and laws, already adverted to, suggests a primeval condition in which all wants could be satisfied from the bounty of the earth, a condition then disrupted by the effects of greed after the discovery of gold; the order subsequently imposed by men on themselves to avert chaos implies the protection of the individual in the enjoyment of what is 'his'. Similarly Cicero, in the only explicit ideology of property that Roman literature seems to contain, compares the world's goods to the seating in a theatre: 'just as, though the theatre is something publicly owned,[84] yet one can properly say that the seat that each person has taken is "his", so in the state or in the world, though

---

[82] *Medea* 199–200. The Irish judge was Mr Justice Gavan Duffy, in *Maunsell* v. *Minister for Education*, 1940 IR 213; 73 ILTR 36.

[83] Varro, *De re rustica* l. 10; Cicero *De republ.* 2. 14. 26: De Martino, *Storia della costituzione romana* (see n. 4), i. 24 ff.

[84] 'Theatrum cum commune sit': theatres were reckoned in the category of *res publicae*; they belonged to the city, not to individuals.

these too are common property, still no argument of right can be opposed to the idea that each man's goods should be his own.'[85]

RUDIMENTS OF INTERNATIONAL-LAW THEORY

The Romans in the republican period had a special priesthood, the *fetiales*, charged with functions affecting the public faith and credit with other peoples; they administered a system containing rules about the declaration of war, the making of peace treaties, and so forth. This *ius fetiale* appears to have rested on understandings common to all the peoples of Italy (even the non-Italic Etruscans).[86] But apart from this we find in Cicero the concept of a law governing the relations of peoples generally, at least in the rudimentary contexts of war and the transactions incident to war:

There is even such a thing as a law of war [*ius bellicum*]; and the terms of an oath must often be observed with an enemy . . . Regulus[87] would have had no right to violate by perjury the terms and agreements made with a foreign enemy: the Romans were dealing with an open and recognized enemy, and it is to this category that the whole *ius fetiale* applies, as well as many generally observed rules [*multa iura communia*].[88]

One of those generally observed rules appears to surface in the middle of this passage, where Cicero distinguishes between an oath taken to an enemy nation, and a promise of ransom made to pirates; because 'a pirate does not fall within the concept of a lawful enemy, but is the common enemy of all the world; and with a pirate there is no common basis for either faith or oaths'.[89] Rather than regard Cicero as describing what actually was a sort of international common law which might have been expounded in the same way at Carthage as at Rome, it is better to understand him here as presenting pure Roman doctrine. The sacredness of an oath to an enemy—which the Romans on several occasions upheld against

---

[85] 'Sic in urbe mundove communi non ad versatur ius quo minus suum quidque cuiusque sit': translated freely.

[86] P. Catalano, 'Cicerone *de off.* 3. 108 e il così detto diritto internazionale antico', *STAR* (1964).

[87] This famous Roman, captured by the Carthaginians, had been allowed to return to Rome to discuss the release of captured Carthaginians, on his oath to return to Carthage if these were not freed. He actually advised the senate against their liberation, and returned to Carthage and his death.

[88] *De officiis* 3. 107–8.   [89] Ibid.

their own interest—reflected their own fundamental value of *fides*, the imperative quality of which, on the conduct of state or citizens, was not dependent on reciprocity. Implicit, however, is the theoretical proposition that this doctrine ought to be respected as self-evident by others.

3
The Early Middle Ages
(to 1100)

The expression 'Middle Ages' is a loose one. In special contexts, for example, when we use a phrase like 'medieval chivalry' or 'the great medieval cathedrals', we may be pointing at a period of three or four hundred years. But in a larger sense the Middle Ages are the whole interval between the end of the Roman empire in the west and the rise of modern Europe, signalled most notably by the Renaissance, the great geographical discoveries, and the Reformation, about a thousand years later. If we try to describe the life of legal theory during this vast extent of time, it will be convenient to divide those thousand years into three periods. These do not necessarily correspond with self-contained 'periods' with distinct political or cultural characteristics that a historian might think significant; historians indeed tend to reject the 'periodization' of what for them is a seamless continuum. All the same, the breaking up of the past into manageable fragments seems, in a work like this, the only reasonably simple way to present our material.

The first 'period', then, of the Middle Ages must be that which arises from the events of the late Roman empire and, spanning what used to be called the 'Dark Ages', runs up to the age of the first Crusade, the formal schism between the Christian churches of East and West, the great contest between the Popes and the German Emperors, the Norman conquests of England and later of Ireland: in round figures, therefore, up to about 1100.

THE LATE ROMAN EMPIRE AND AFTER

1. The Division of the Empire

Three events of late Roman history—all three contained within the fourth and fifth centuries AD—may fairly be called of cardinal importance in the sense implied by the derivation of the word 'cardinal' from the Latin word for a hinge: they were the hinges upon which a gigantic door of history turned, closing the era of the Graeco-Roman pagan world centred on the basin of the Mediterranean, opening that of the Western Christian world whose centre of gravity lay more and more to the north of the Alps. Those three events were, firstly, the formal division of the Roman empire into a western and an eastern half; secondly, the roughly contemporaneous adoption of Christianity as the official religion of the empire; and thirdly, the destruction and conquest of the western empire by the Germans.

The division of the empire into eastern and western spheres was originally intended as a governmental reform to restore order from the chaos which had characterized the whole course of the third century. In the second there had been a whole series of strong and enlightened emperors, among whom the name of the philosopher-emperor Marcus Aurelius has remained the most famous in later ages. But the chronic weaknesses of the system survived these benign rulers: above all, no proper system for securing a peaceful and orderly succession, together with an increasing reliance on mercenary armies; with the result that the death of an emperor encouraged the ambitions of pretenders who struggled for the imperial purple with the support of armies bought by the promise of booty. In the third century the empire was laid waste by the civil wars unleased by the non-stop vacancies in the imperial throne (usually caused by murder). Economic desolation, especially in the West, and administrative dislocation, led first the emperor Diocletian (284–305), once he had restored peace after those generations of turmoil, to devise a system based on two co-ordinate emperors or *Augusti*, one for the east and one for the west, each having a junior colleague, or *Caesar*, designated as his successor. This system based on four rulers did not in fact even survive its inventor; but the idea of splitting the military and governmental responsibilities of the gigantic empire on geographical lines did survive, and became a reality under Diocletian's successor Constantine (306–37). Constantine gave this reality the most conspicuous of possible symbols by establishing a new capital for the eastern empire—a new Rome—on a strategic site at the mouth of the Bosphorus; there already was a small city here, an ancient Greek colonists' foundation called Byzantium, but Constantine, in refounding and enlarging it, named it after himself. As Constantinople it intrigued and dazzled the Middle Ages (though the peculiar culture of which it was the centre, and the state and society of which it was the capital, are usually described as Byzantine, evoking the more ancient name of the site).

It was not part of the plan of either Diocletian or Constantine that this reorganization of the empire in twin spheres should lead to their separation; both rulers considered themselves emperor throughout the whole extent of the Roman territory, from the borders of Scotland to the Euphrates. But in fact there were powerful factors at work, of an economic and cultural character, which pulled the two halves of the empire apart, and institutionalized their separation to the point that rivalry and conflict, rather than co-operation, was the normal state of their relations for the short period that the western empire still survived after the division. Firstly, the eastern empire's economy had suffered much less, in the years of turmoil since 200 or thereabouts, than had that of the West; the latter had sunk back into conditions so primitive that even its coinage, even the standardized metal medium of exchange which originally superseded barter of goods for goods, was itself increasingly replaced by a reborn barter economy; the apparent reason for this being the stresses generated by the invasive pressure of German peoples on its frontiers and the crushing financial burden of repelling them. Secondly, while administrative disintegration in the West had favoured the rise of powerful local interests able to defy central authority, in the East the empire had proved better able to keep its grandees—and the Church—in a condition of obedience. Thirdly, perhaps more important than either of the other factors, the cultural world amid which the eastern empire subsisted was essentially a Greek world; at its core were the Greek-speaking territories once part of the empire of Alexander; the soil of the western empire was that on which the Latin culture was dominant. After the separation of East from West the Greek character of the empire based on Constantinople came through virtually undisguised; it might, once the West had fallen, remain the one and only 'Roman' empire, but the language of its administration was Greek, and its ruler in later ages was often called the Greek emperor. With the disappearance of every last reminiscence of the Roman republic, too, and of its pristine standards of simplicity—the corresponding memories of free Greece had disappeared long before—the tone of the empire centred on the ancient Byzantium became more and more oriental as its contacts and undistracted views towards the east led to an absolute monarchy characterized by forms and rituals of abject submission, and to a worship of the ruler's person, of a kind which in the classical age of Rome or of Greece would have excited only disgust. Yet this east-Roman, Byzantine empire survived the collapse of its western twin half by a thousand years, though in a condition of continual contraction and advancing debility, until the capture of Constantinople by the Turks in 1453, barely a generation before the discovery of America.

The culture of this Eastern Roman empire, though it has always appeared stifling and even sinister to the modern Western European mind, is of enormous importance for the history of European civilization (and of European jurisprudence). Its distinctness from that of the West provided the cultural underlay for the schism of Greek or 'Orthodox' from Latin or 'Catholic' Christendom; and for the mutual sense of strangeness of Eastern and Western Europe indicated by the separate Latin and Cyrillic alphabets (the latter devised, on the basis of the Greek alphabet, by the missionaries through whom the Eastern Church Christianized most of the Slav peoples). The Eastern empire preserved in its Byzantine form the Greek language and with it the physical remains of classical Greek literature and science; in that era of fragile manuscript transmission, almost all knowledge of this vast culture had disappeared in the West when the Western empire lapsed into semi-barbarism with the German conquest; but at the epoch of the Renaissance it was chiefly from the libraries of the Byzantine empire that Greek learning, and scholars able to interpret it, once again reached the West. And, of central importance in the history of law, it was in the Eastern empire, under the emperor Justinian (527–65), that the mass of the inherited writings of the classical Roman jurists (which came to an end in the turbulence of the third century) was edited and compiled into the *Digest* which bears his name. This work, although promulgated in Italy during Justinian's brief reconquest of parts of the Western empire from German power, was apparently as good as unknown throughout the West during the Dark Ages, but it was rediscovered in the late eleventh century (at the end of the period covered by this chapter) and ultimately became the basis of the whole civil law of continental Europe and, later, of the many distant lands to which it was exported by colonialism or by cultural penetration.

2. The Christianization of the Empire

The tiny Christian communities formed while Christ's apostles were still alive—like those to whom St Paul addressed his epistles—were scarcely noticed by the official Roman world until the end of the first century, and even then were not clearly distinguished from Jewish communities. Both Christians and Jews worshipped only one God; whereas the pagan Graeco-Roman world was characterized by polytheism, a view of the supernatural which left room for an infinite variety of deities. For this reason alone, they stood out as foreign bodies in the empire. In addition to this, Christians held that all gods except their own were false; and it was this doctrinal totalitarianism which led them, necessarily, to refuse worship to the pagan deities. In other words, while the Graeco-Roman pagans did without an organized theology, and were easily tolerant towards new or strange cults, the Christians took their God, and the exclusive truth of his revelation, seriously. This, in the eyes of official Rome, was anti-social, disruptive, and a threat to civic and military discipline; and explains the official hostility to Christians which frequently became exasperated to the point of cruel persecution.

Those persecutions, however, were intermittent enough to allow early Christianity to spread rapidly; to develop a hierarchical Church organization which was a major factor in Christianity's strength; to attract converts not only among the urban poor (to whom Christ's message was especially compelling) but also among the educated upper classes, who (as will be seen) quickly proved able to meet paganism on intellectually level, and better than level, terms. By the late third century the numbers of the Christians were very large, in some parts of the empire, notably Italy, though still a minority of the population. Appreciable proportions of Roman armies now consisted of Christians; and (an event traditionally supposed to have been crucial) the emperor Constantine believed he had won the battle of the Milvian Bridge against a claimant to the empire (AD 312) by the help of the Christians' God. There then followed, first, a general toleration of Christians, next the establishment of Christianity as the official religion of the empire; though Constantine himself received baptism only on his deathbed.

3. The Fall of the Western Empire

The Romans had never succeeded in bringing within the empire much of the territory to the east of the Rhine and to the north of the Danube, in other words, of the territory of modern Germany. A certain presence of a defensive kind was indeed established in a narrow belt on the German side of those rivers; but beyond that belt, and stretching north to Scandinavia and east to what is now Poland, the country was inhabited by a variety of peoples of Germanic speech and culture, among whom the more ancient Celtic inhabitants of central Europe had been absorbed. These Germans were not savage forest-dwellers (as they are sometimes represented); they had settled villages, settled agriculture on land cleared of trees, a wide range of simple industrial techniques; archaeology has brought to light great quantities of their relatively sophisticated artefacts. But in comparison with the inhabitants of the Mediterranean-centred Graeco-Roman world their civilization was primitive, and they ranked by the standards of that world as barbarian. Writing was virtually unknown among them, so that they were without literature. They had no architecture, apparently, beyond the humblest techniques for the construction of small, non-durable huts. Their artefacts were far inferior in sophistication to those of the Roman world, from which they imported luxury goods, probably in exchange for slaves and simple primary products. They had no cities and no coinage. But they were physically hardy and had all the military virtues.

These peoples—themselves under pressure from wilder races to their east—had been pressing on the Roman frontiers since Caesar's conquest of Gaul. Their contacts with the Romans were not uniformly hostile ones: apart from the trading just mentioned, the Romans began to recruit them as army auxiliaries. This recruitment did not take place man-by-man; far more likely, they were recruited by the troop and tribe. In this way they learnt Roman military technique and warlike technology; but were able also to look over the frontier into the incomparably richer and more comfortable Roman world, which they beheld not in apprehension—they had inflicted notable defeats on Roman incursions into the German interior—but with the ambition of predators. In the third century a major series of German attacks on the empire's perimeter was beaten off only with difficulty. Thereafter the Romans thought to protect the northern frontiers by the dangerous expedient of installing whole German tribes as defensive colonies within the frontiers. The Western empire was by now in a state of chronic economic and administrative paralysis; and these tribes began to prey on the empire they were meant to guard. Their encroachments mounted in tempo, became unstoppable; the empire in its debility accepted the trend, and its highest military commands were now commonly held by men of barbarian origin. With the sacking of Rome itself by Alaric the Goth in 410, and the deposition of the last emperor of the West, Romulus Augustulus, in 476, the fall of the Western empire was complete. On its ruins arose a patchwork of German kingdoms, ancestors of the main nation-states of modern Western Europe.

THE KINGDOMS OF EARLY MEDIEVAL EUROPE

The most significant and enduring of the kingdoms, in this entirely new European dispensation, was that of the Franks. These people, whose name means 'free men', came from the area of modern central western Germany; but their establishment across the Rhine, on the Romano-Celtic territory of Gaul, gave their name to the modern France and the French, and that of their first king to the later French monarchy: there was no unbroken line of descent, but the name Louis was simply a modern form of the name of the Frankish chief Chlodovech, or Clovis (466–511), and its use evoked the high antiquity of the French kingship. The Franks at first shared the territory of the modern France with other Germanic peoples: the Burgundians, whose kingdom was in central eastern France, and the Visigoths (= 'western Goths'), whose realm, centred in Spain, stretched also far beyond the Pyrenees into southern France. The Frankish kingdom however soon grew into a huge domain which, in the reign of their greatest king, Charlemagne (768–814), included virtually all of the modern France, Belgium, Holland, western Germany, Switzerland, Austria, and the greater part of Italy. In a unique stroke which was intended both to aggrandize the Frankish dynasty and to revive, by fusion in it, the ancient Roman empire, Charlemagne had himself crowned emperor by the pope in Rome on Christmas Day, 800; this empire, however, fell to pieces soon after his death; and by the treaty of Verdun (843) it was divided between his descendants, in such a way as to separate France from Germany for ever. The Frankish kings thereafter rarely enjoyed more than nominal sovereignty over powerful provincial dukedoms; one of these was that of Normandy, the home of the Normans or 'Northmen'—more Germanic invaders—who in the course of the ninth century sailed into the rivers of western France and established themselves there, at the same epoch as other Northmen (mostly called Danes) were gaining a destructive foothold in Ireland and England.

Spain had been in the hands of the Visigoths since before the final collapse of the Western Roman empire. But soon after 700 Spain was invaded by the Arab lords of north Africa—this was the era of early militant Islamic expansion—and the Visigothic monarchy overthrown. Almost the whole peninsula became an Arab kingdom, with its capital at Cordoba; it was the home of an advanced culture, whose representatives were responsible not only for transmitting to Western Europe specifically Arabic sciences and arts, but also for mediating the earliest smatterings of Greek philosophy to reach the West since the barbarian tide had submerged it. The remnants of the Visigothic power, driven back within a few counties under the Pyrenees, however, before the end of the eighth century, commenced the recovery of Spain; this 'Reconquista' had by 1100 brought half of the peninsula back under Christian rule.

The first barbarian conqueror of Italy was Odoacer, chief of a tribe called the Sciri; it was he who deposed the last emperor in 476. Soon, however, his kingdom was taken from him by the eastern Goths, or Ostrogoths, who arrived in Italy from the direction of the modern Hungary and northern Yugoslavia, and whose king, Theoderic, established his capital at Ravenna. The Ostrogothic kingdom did not last long; in the mid-sixth century the Eastern Roman emperor, Justinian, undertook a partial (and transient) reconquest of a large part of the West, overthrowing the Ostrogoths in Italy, and retaking the north African coast (which had fallen to yet another German nation, the Vandals), and a small part of southern Spain. This Byzantine reconquest of Italy was then nullified by the incursion and establishment of a still fiercer German tribe, the Lombards, whose original home had been on the Elbe; they set up a kingdom in 568 with its capital at Pavia near Milan, comprehending all the peninsula except for a few Byzantine enclaves (the last of them, Bari, falling only in 1071 to the Normans who had established themselves in Sicily and southern Italy). Meanwhile the Lombard kingdom of northern and central Italy was, in its turn, brought in 774 under Frankish sovereignty, and formed part of Charlemagne's empire; and it was at this period, too, that the pope was assigned a belt of territory as his temporal possession (the 'patrimonium Petri'). Most of Italy remained in Frankish hands until the mid-tenth century, and then passed for 300 years to the German emperors who had succeeded to the crown of Charlemagne. To be the object of foreign ambitions, and the scene on which foreign rivalries were played out, remained the destiny of Italy until the national resurgence of the nineteenth century brought independence and unification.

The German homelands which had never been brought within the Roman empire contained at the time of the Western empire's fall a number of nations of which the most important were the 'eastern' Franks, who lived in what now corresponds with the western part of reunited Germany. To their north, roughly on the ground occupied today by the Netherlands and north-west Germany, lived Friesians, Angles, and Saxons. The empire of Charlemagne had included all these peoples; but after the division effected in 843 the eastern Franks, separated now politically from their cousins who had crossed the Rhine, formed the kingdom from which ultimately the German empire, or, more formally, once Charlemagne's imperial title had passed to it in the early tenth century, the 'Holy Roman Empire of the German Nation' emerged. But the German emperor, although accorded a pre-eminent rank, coexisted with a number of powerful monarchs of less exalted formal title. He was an important force in his own right throughout the Middle Ages, when pope and emperor were the two dominant figures on the European scene; but after the Reformation had destroyed the religious unity of Europe, and especially of Germany, the imperial position declined sharply in significance, vesting at last in the Austrian Hapsburgs until, after a life of a thousand years, it was abolished in 1806 by Napoleon.

In Britain the Roman occupation had ended soon after 400, as the last legions were withdrawn to assist the defence of the continental empire; shortly afterwards the eastern half of England was in the hands of Angles and Saxons from northern Germany. The British Celts, less Romanized than those of Gaul, continued an independent existence in Wales and Scotland; in England they were culturally submerged by the invaders. Among the kingdoms into which Anglo-Saxon England was divided, that of Wessex in the south ultimately predominated, evolving into the kingdom of England, King Alfred (849–901) its most famous representative. In the ninth century England was invaded by Vikings and Danes; from 1013 until 1042 it was ruled by Danish kings. The Anglo-Saxon monarchy was restored, but soon afterwards the country was again conquered, this time by Normans descended from the Northmen long settled in the French province which bears their name, Normandy. The English nation and monarchy of subsequent ages essentially proceed from the fusion, under Norman kings after the conquest of 1066, of the Norman invaders with their other Germanic predecessors, Anglo-Saxons and Danes, in whose world the ancient Celtic element had been silently absorbed.

Ireland had been untouched by the Romans; and, as the last waves of a tide barely cover the remotest part of the beach, so the flood of the German migrations submerged her to a lesser depth than countries nearer its source. The Anglo-Saxons never settled there; Danish settlement was confined to harbours at river-mouths; only with the Normans were deeper inroads made. The Christianization of the country, associated with the mission of the Romanized Briton St Patrick ascribed to the year 432, gave Ireland the use of writing and with it the beginnings of its history and literature. The strongly individual Irish church furnished a large Irish missionary presence in Europe, especially in the Frankish kingdom, from the seventh to the ninth centuries, important in halting the relapse into paganism occurring in many places, and in consolidating civilization and learning: in this form the country became woven into the larger tapestry of early medieval Europe.

CHRISTIANITY AND THE LATE ROMAN WORLD

By comparison with the classical centuries of Graeco-Roman civilization, or with that of the Europe formed by the Renaissance, the centuries which immediately followed the collapse of the Western Roman empire were a period of intellectual stagnation. This night was lit, sparsely, only by the Christian Church, whose bishoprics and especially—once the great movement begun by St Benedict (c.480–542) got under way—whose monasteries were the centres of whatever education the Western world could still provide. Literacy of any kind was virtually confined to clerics, if only because a priest must at least be able to read the Gospels and expound them; even the most enlightened king was commonly unable to write his own name (Charlemagne, the best example, despite sincere patronage of learning, never himself learnt to write). It is, therefore, the Fathers of the Church who provide in their writings virtually the only vestiges of political and legal theory in the early medieval world, all secular literature on this and most other subjects having ceased.

Even these Church Fathers, however, by so much as handling such themes, had moved some distance from the ground of the original Church and the message of its founder. Christ's message had nothing to do with the world's laws, nor could it be brought under the concept of 'censorial jurisprudence'. On the contrary, a considerable part of it consisted in the rejection of legalism, the arid attachment to the letter of the law of the Old Testament which characterized the Pharisees. Christ explicitly suggested the ultimate irrelevance of the things that were Caesar's; and declared the whole of the law contained not in a code but in the precept of love. The justice of which he repeatedly spoke was not the justice which a human judge tries to establish between litigants, but a total virtue not reducible to lawyerly norms.

Nevertheless the idea of normativity, of regulation, of subordination, soon percolated into the Christian Church, if only because that Church itself was an organization, and, as such, could not escape having rules. But the points at which Christians found themselves at odds with the pagan world required them to address the intellectual axioms of that world—about the nature of the state, the source of the right to govern, the law of nature, the institutions of property which the implications of Christian teaching made questionable—and, in doing so, Christianity evolved a legal and political theory of its own. It was not monolithic and uniform, and not in all respects original, as some of its content was ancient philosophy relaunched in Christian dress, but it provided those ancient ideas with the force of religious faith and ensured in this way their survival throughout the centuries in which religious faith was the central factor in Western life.

THE CONCEPTION OF THE STATE IN THE
POST-ROMAN WORLD

The Romans, as has been seen, had an only rudimentary conception of the state: the words *res publica* came nearest to expressing the idea, though this could occur in contexts where it was better rendered by a more general phrase like 'society' or 'the public interest'. The state seen as an entity distinct from its most important components (the senate and people), and with an abstract value which not only the Roman but also every other political society must possess, is almost completely absent from their thought, Cicero alone having attempted to express the state's essence and purpose. Only in the Christianized later empire—and therefore in a setting belonging more to the coming medieval world—did there emerge anything like a theory of the state as a familiar branch of philosophy.

The earliest Christian attitudes to the state appear in the New Testament. As has been said, Christ's message was on a quite different level, calling to a life which transcended state and laws, but this did not imply provoking rebellion or disaffection. Although the point of the text is to stress the limits of Caesar's authority, and the higher importance of the sphere beyond the sway of earthly rule, Christ did command the 'rendering unto Caesar of the things that are Caesar's';[1] and, by saying to Pilate 'Thou wouldst not have any power over me at all, if it had not been given thee from above', he appeared again to countenance the legitimacy of temporal government.[2] St Paul admonished the Christians of Rome in the most explicit terms to be submissive to temporal authority:

authority comes from God only, and all authorities that hold sway are of his ordinance . . . The magistrate is God's minister, working for thy good . . . It is not for nothing that he bears the sword; he is God's minister still, to inflict punishment on the wrong-doer. Thou must needs, then, be submissive, not only for fear of punishment, but in conscience.[3]

In the second century the Church Fathers Irenaeus and Theophilus of Antioch recognized the positive role of the state.[4]

---

[1] Mark 12: 13–17.   [2] John 19: 11.   [3] Rom. 13: 1–7.
[4] Irenaeus, *Adversus omnes haereses* 5. 24; Theophilus, *Ad Autolycum* 1. 11.

Other tones were, however, heard from Christian writers from the earliest times, representing the state in a far more negative way. The Apocalypse of St John showed the Roman state, at any rate, as diabolical;[5] Tertullian (*c.*150–225) gave form to political protest against religious repression by the Roman state. This attitude might be natural in the era of persecutions; but, while many of the Church Fathers judged individual rulers rather than the institution of earthly rule as such, a negative view of the state survived even after the empire itself had become officially Christian. Many writers presented the state more or less as a necessary evil, countenanced indeed by God himself, but with its roots in human sin. Lactantius, writing about 300, regarded the power of a ruler as the consequence of man's having fallen away from God; Theodoretus (*c.*393–460) wrote that laws were necessitated by man's sin, and that, for the protection of the innocent and the punishment of those who would oppress their neighbours, legislators and judges were unavoidable. The greatest of the Fathers, St Augustine of Hippo (354–430), visualized the City of God, the *civitas Dei*, against which was set the *civitas terrena* of infernal origin, which had to be penetrated by the other in order to lose its godless character and become tolerable (though even then only as an unhappy necessity); a state devoid of the justice flowing from the eternal law was nothing but a system of organized banditry.[6] And yet, the state's protective function, he wrote, however unholy the conditions which had required its exercise, represented a duty laid upon it by God.[7] This combination of the recognition of the divine origin of political authority with a pessimistic rationalization of what made it necessary remained standard throughout the early Christian world and into the Early Middle Ages; though it was increasingly overlaid by absolutist doctrine which, by elevating the role of the ruler and prescribing unconditional submission to him, gave emphasis rather to the state's legitimacy than to its origins.

THE SOURCE OF TITLE TO GOVERNMENT

As was seen in Chapter 2, the advancing autocracy of the Roman emperors had, as early as about 200, been bolstered by juristic

[5] Revelations 16: 10, 17: 1, 3–7.   [6] *De civitate Dei* 15. 5, 4. 4.
[7] Ibid. 19. 15.

doctrine; the will of the *princeps*, Ulpian had written, makes law. This compendious statement of the absolutist position overshadowed the justification which Ulpian appended, namely the supposed irrevocable conferral of this authority on the emperor by the people; and the atmosphere of the late empire, in which the last democratic forms had been shed by monarchs now more aptly called 'lords and masters' than merely 'chiefs', was not one in which anyone sought to remobilize the original and fundamental authority of the people which Ulpian's formula still appeared to salute. The German invasions, however, brought on to the old Roman lands nations with quite other traditions, and kings of those nations who, at any rate at first, raised no such pretensions about their position as the Roman emperors had entertained. A long perspective on political and legal theory in the early medieval world seems therefore to reveal a competition between two opposed conceptions of the source of authority and law within the state.

These competing conceptions have been labelled the 'descending' and the 'ascending' theories of government. The 'descending' theory means the view according to which power is originally centred in the ruler, who is beholden to no human being for it (though in its Christian guise the theory imputes to God its original bestowal on the ruler), and whose subjects have no role in moderating or imposing conditions on its exercise, but must simply submit. On the 'ascending' theory, power derives ultimately from the people, from whom it is delegated upwards to rest in the ruler's hand: this ruler not being absolute, but, in conformity with the source of his authority, bound to respect the people's laws which are antecedent to him. By the neat if oversimple affiliation of each of these theories to one of the two main cultural elements in Europe at the outset of the Middle Ages, the descending theory is characteristic of the Roman, the ascending theory of the Germanic tradition.

That Germanic tradition is not easy to document, as it was, after all, the tradition of illiterate barbarians to whom anything like conscious political theory can hardly be imputed. Allowance must be made not only for the scarcity of historical materials, but also for the favourable light in which German institutions appeared to the romantic eye of later Europe, or even to the more austere of the first Roman observers. Thus Gibbon, in giving an account of the political and social manners of the Germans who burst upon the world stage in the fourth and fifth centuries, speaks with admiration of their fierce independence, their attachment to the hard conditions of a life in which the high points were days of battle and personal valour the greatest virtue, and the far from subservient attitude to their kings, who were restrained by the powerful force of tribal opinion within the four corners of the ancestral laws. But the colours for this picture Gibbon had to borrow—for want of another source—from the description which the Roman historian Tacitus had given of the Germans just before AD 100, one which has been generally thought in some degree influenced by that writer's wish to present a dramatic contrast between the proud and vigorous simplicity of those invincible barbarians, and the corrupt and debilitated society which he believed he saw around him in the Roman world.

These German peoples, according to Tacitus,[8] took their kings on the basis of their high birth ('ex nobilitate'), but the power of those kings was not unlimited or arbitrary ('nec regibus infinita aut libera potestas'); and some decisions rested with the people, who listened in their assembly to their kings, respecting the weight and authority which attached to their counsels, but not their power simply to give orders ('audiuntur auctoritate suadendi magis quam iubendi potestate'); their chief's proposal, if unpopular, was shouted down ('si displicuit sententia, fremitu aspernantur'). This picture of monarchy limited by important democratic checks, even if coloured by Tacitus' own sentiments, has never been suspected in regard to its general accuracy. The Germans who dominate the history of Western Europe after the fall of the western empire were seen at first to reflect, despite the lapse of four centuries since Tacitus had written his *Germania*, something of the same political feeling—the 'ascending' view of government—that he described.

The Germans, however, were not quite as austere or incorruptible as Tacitus had imagined. Modern archaeology, far from confirming their supposed contempt for gold and silver, has shown the houses and tombs of their chieftains containing impressive quantities of precious metals and luxuries, in which there was a busy trade northwards from the Roman world. The comforts and riches of that world, perhaps even its milder climate, enticed them to break in upon it; and in various ways they soon adapted themselves—in ways material to legal and political theory as in others—to the

[8] *Germania* 7.

civilization on which they had intruded. Most of them had been, more or less, converted to Christianity (often in the form of the Arian heresy) while still relatively quiescent on the empire's frontiers; though after their conquest of it large areas lapsed again into paganism. (These areas were reclaimed, in the period 600–800 or so, by the efforts of missionaries, among whom the Irish— themselves still uninvaded—were the most prominent.) With this conversion there came also an absorption of the more articulate and sophisticated Roman and Christian culture, most obvious in the fact that throughout the Western continent, in France, in Italy, in the Iberian peninsula, Germanic speech nowhere became the finally dominant tongue: the provincial dialects of Latin prevailed and were adopted by the conquering race, and the foundations of the modern Romance languages were laid down in the lands lying under the rule of the Germanic Franks, Burgundians, Visigoths, and Lombards.[9]

With this cultural and religious absorption there went an absorption of the political ideas which the late Roman world, and the Church, had received ultimately from the Roman imperial jurists, chief among them the idea that power descended from the ruler (in Christian terms, after it had been entrusted to him by God) in a hierarchical transmission, to be exercised over his subjects: in a manner, however (again in Christian teaching), showing mindfulness of the divine origin of the royal power. This 'theocratic', Christian version of the descending theory of government is given repeated expression by the early medieval writers, of whom Sedulius 'Scotus' (the Irishman) who lived at the court of the bishop of Liège about 850,[10] may serve as a typical example. In his work *On Christian Rulers* he exhorts

the pious ruler fervently to strive to obey the will and holy commands of the Supreme Master of all things by whose divine will and ordination he does not doubt himself to have risen to the summit of authority . . . An upright ruler acknowledges that he has been called by God . . . For what are the rulers of the Christian people unless ministers of the Almighty?[11]

[9] The only part of conquered Western Europe in which Germanic speech took permanent root was Britain under the Anglo-Saxons, perhaps because Britain had been less thoroughly Romanized than the continental provinces.

[10] For an account of him, and some of his poetry, see Helen Waddell, *Medieval Latin Lyrics* (Harmondsworth, 1952).

[11] *De rectoribus christianis*, ed. S. Hellman, in *Quellen und Untersuchungen zur lateinischen Philologie des Mittelalters* (Munich, 1906), i. 19 ff.

There thus was laid down in the Early Middle Ages, and universally accepted, the notion, firstly, of human sovereignty and hence of the legitimacy of human legislation and government, and secondly, of the derivation of this sovereignty from God. It depended in no sense on the will or consent or delegation of subjects, who merely had the duty to obey, but no rights to assert as against their sovereign. 'As a result of the overpowering influence of Christianity', wrote Walter Ullmann,[12] 'the Germanic peoples adopted the theory inherent in Christian doctrine—which was almost wholly of a Latin-Roman complexion—and the ascending theme was, so to speak, driven underground, not to emerge again as a theoretical proposition until the late thirteenth century'. Once it had done so however, it was to remain the pulse of constitutional reform up to and throughout the era of revolution in England, America, and France; and its remote origins, supposed to lie in the forests once inhabited by 'our German ancestors', supplied a pleasing romantic touch to the rhetoric of Anglo-Saxon writers on both sides of the Atlantic.

THE IDEAL STANDARD FOR LEGISLATION AND GOVERNMENT

The theocratic, 'descending' conception of government of the Early Middle Ages did not mean a general intellectual surrender to arbitrary rule; several strands of doctrine, traceable already in that era, tend towards the limitation of the ruler's power at least in theory. One of these amounted to the principle that, while the king was not answerable to his subjects, he was answerable so to speak *for* them, and ought to exercise his rule in their interest. Very early in the post-Roman era the centrality of the interest of the governed, as the prime standard for government, was stated by St Isidore of Seville (*c.*560–636) in an elaborate recipe for right law which became canonical:

Now a law will be honourable, just, capable of being obeyed, in accordance with nature and in accord also with ancestral practice, adapted both to its time and to its place; necessary, useful and clear (so as to contain nothing to

---

[12] *A History of Political Thought: The Middle Ages* (Harmondsworth, 1965), 13.

trip people up through misunderstanding) not framed for the advantage of any individual, but for the common benefit of the citizens.[13]

This formula, in which the climax lies in the element of subserving the common good, was much cited by later writers; as also was St Isidore's definition of a king, confining entitlement to that name to the ruler who is just:

Kings get their name from ruling (*reges a regendo vocati*) . . . and he who does not correct (*qui non corrigit*, 'who does not bring things into the right way') does not rule. Thus the name of king is held through doing right, and is forfeited by doing wrong. Whence the ancients had a proverb: You shall be king if you do right, and not otherwise.[14]

Sedulius the Irishman, among others, echoes this etymology.[15] The Visigothic kingdom in Spain and southern France, of which St Isidore was one of the greatest ornaments, produced a significant volume of legislation; the code of Ervig (681) is one in which the king has almost entirely escaped from his historically populist origins (i.e. the primitive Germans' conception of kingship as constitutionally limited) and the theory of kingship which emerges from the laws is unashamedly theocratic. But this was considered to involve no justification of arbitrariness in his rule; on the contrary, God had set up his government as a remedy for the consequences of man's sinful fall, and its purpose was thus the amelioration of the wretched condition to which rejection of the divine law had brought the human race. In other words, as King Reccared (586–601) had said, Almighty God had granted him his kingship for the benefit of his peoples ('pro utilitatibus populorum'), or, as King Ervig said, to save his country and relieve its inhabitants ('ad salvationem terrae et sublevationem plebium'). The theme of the common welfare—including of course spiritual salvation—as the prime purpose of government and kings recurs constantly in the Visigothic laws.

CONTRACTUAL THEORY OF THE RIGHT TO GOVERN

Closely allied with the axiom that the benefit of the subjects is the purpose of the institution of the ruler, though not emerging in

---

[13] *Etymologiae* 5. 21.   [14] Ibid. 9. 3.
[15] *De rectoribus christianis* 2.

explicit form until the end of the period covered in this chapter, is
the idea that the relationship between ruler and ruled is to be
conceived as in essence one of contract. As has been seen, a few
passages in the literature of classical Greece and Rome had already,
in very general terms, presented political society in terms of an
agreement or pact between citizens. In the earlier Middle Ages,
however, there surfaces for the first time a rather different—and
much more explosive—doctrine: namely, that although the kingly
office itself is of divine origin, the basis on which a particular
monarch occupied his throne was one of mutual compact with
his people.

This image was in part suggested by the oaths which medieval
kings commonly swore at coronation, to do justice and to respect
the laws, and the oaths of allegiance which were sworn to them by
their greater subjects on the same occasion. It was easy to represent
these forms as expressing the mutuality, the reciprocal consideration,
which was the essence of the normal contract. But there was a
further factor in the landscape of the Middle Ages from roughly the
ninth century onwards which must have predisposed to a contractual
interpretation of the king–subject relationship, and that was
feudalism. This phenomenon, which is impossible to reduce to a
single formula because it appeared in very many different models,
grew out of the conditions of society after the collapse of
Charlemagne's empire. It was a variegated pattern of social and
economic ties, serving to give people the sort of order, and the sort
of structure of mutual support, which the rudimentary Western
European kingships—struggling with the assaults of Northmen and
Magyars—were not strong enough to provide. Central and common
to all the forms taken by feudalism was a bilaterality of obligation:
the vassal owed allegiance to his lord, but his lord in turn owed
protection and support to his vassal, and if the lord failed in his duty
to provide this, the vassal was thought entitled to renounce his
allegiance. It cannot be said that medieval theory consciously
extended this idea by analogy so as to take in also the king–subject
relationship; but it seems likely that the universal familiarity of
feudal patterns of reciprocal obligation made easy its construction
on contractual terms, particularly in the light, too, of the universal
teaching as to the good ruler's duties towards his people.

In the eleventh century there broke out the long conflict between
the popes and the German emperors over the question whether the

temporal ruler had the right to appoint bishops (the so-called Investiture Conflict); it called forth huge quantities of polemical pamphlets on both sides, and for the first time since the collapse of the Western Roman empire there were laymen to be found among the controversialists who deployed political theory in support of their own side. The paroxysm of the struggle came in 1076, when Pope Gregory VII deposed the German emperor Henry IV. Among the partisans of the papal claims was the German monk Manegold of Lautenbach who, while acknowledging the divine origin of kingship and the reverence due to kings, defended the right of Henry's opponents to resist him because of his evil conduct, and construed the papal deposition as no more than a formal authentication of what had happened anyway once his subjects had justifiably renounced their allegiance. For, he wrote,

since nobody can make himself king or emperor, the people raise up some man above themselves for one purpose only, that he should rule and govern them on principles of just government, rendering to each his due, cherishing the good and removing the evil-doers, weighing out justice to all. But, indeed, if he breaks the agreement by which he is elected (*si pactum, quo eligitur, infringit*) and rushes to disrupt and confound the things which he was appointed to keep in order, the reasonable conclusion is that he releases the people from their duty of obedience, seeing that he was the first to abandon the bargain (*cum fidem prior ipse deseruerit*) which bound one party to the other in faithfulness.[16]

Earlier medieval theory had been against admitting any right in subjects to rebel against their king, no matter how tyrannical he was. Gregory the Great, who was pope from 590 to 604, wrote that even to criticize, let alone to resist, a wicked ruler was sinful; a murmur raised against him was in effect raised against God;[17] and the immense prestige of this saint made this view into a powerful prop of absolute and irresponsible monarchy throughout the Middle Ages. His contemporary, St Isidore of Seville, cited the prophet Hosea as authority for the doctrine that God gave a good ruler in mercy, a bad one in anger and as punishment for the

---

[16] *Ad Gebehardum* 47. Also ibid. 30, in which, reciting the deeds of an evil ruler who does the opposite of what he was chosen for, Manegold asks whether it is not clear that he should deservedly fall from the office entrusted to him, since he is seen to have been the first to violate the contract through which he was installed (*cum pactum, pro quo constitutus est, constet illum prius irrupisse*).

[17] *Expositio in librum Job* 22. 24.

people's sins; in either case the king was to be obeyed as God's appointed.[18] It can be seen, therefore, how revolutionary was the potential of Manegold's view of the ruler's continuing title depending on his keeping his side of a bargain with his people. It was to be in terms of their supposed violation of this original compact that the parliaments of seventeenth-century England stated their resistance to Stuart kings.

THE RULE OF LAW

It has been said that during the earlier Middle Ages, as the Germanic kingships absorbed the ideas of the late Roman world, the 'ascending' theory of government 'went underground'. Nevertheless one basic Germanic idea survived: namely, that the king reigns within the limits of his people's inherited laws and is bound by them. This principle (again, one which a thousand years later formed part of the English Commons' armament against Stuart pretensions) obviously assorted ill with the late Roman idea of the 'princeps legibus solutus', and there was never a neat theoretical reconciliation between them. Given however the Fathers' doctrine of non-resistance even to a wicked ruler—presumably, even therefore to one who exceeded the limits of the customary laws—it seems best to see the ancient German idea as surviving in the shape of a moral obligation on the king to respect the laws which he enforced on others; and this obligation is repeatedly stated in the Christian Early Middle Ages. St Ambrose (c.340–97), bishop of Milan, while holding that kings are immune from the operation of the penal law,[19] wrote also in two powerful rhetorical passages that the ruler ought to observe his own enactments: 'the emperor makes laws, and let him be foremost in respecting them.'[20] St Augustine wrote that while men might dispute about the shape of temporal laws in the process of enacting them, once they were in fact enacted and established, it was not permissible to sit in judgment on those laws, but only to judge according to them.[21] St Isidore of Seville admonished the ruler that he 'might hold his laws binding on all, as soon as he himself showed them respect'.[22] The Englishman Alcuin,

---

[18] *Sententiae* 3. 48.
[19] *Apol. prophet. Daniel* 16.
[20] *Epistulae* 21. 9.
[21] *De vera religione* 31.
[22] *Sententiae* 3. 51.

Charlemagne's tutor, admonished him on his coronation as emperor that he was bound by laws enacted by his late Roman predecessors, and thus, even in this strict sense, not *legibus solutus*. And a little later Sedulius the Irishman prescribed for the Christian ruler, in more general terms, that he who desired to command his subjects well and determined to correct the errors of others might not himself commit the evils which he strictly reproved in those others.

It is however futile to look in this period for more sophisticated expressions of the 'rule of law' idea, such as the notion that every exercise of power requires an unbroken chain of black-and-white legal authority, or that punishment can be inflicted only if the offence constituted a definite crime for which the law lays down a definite penalty. A wide, *ad hoc* discretion in the early medieval ruler was appropriate to what was regarded as his overriding commission from God to secure the spiritual salvation as well as the physical protection of his subjects. Thus, given the view that the justice of God created the law rather than was created by it, it was understandable that the maxim *nullum crimen sine lege* could find no place in Visigothic legal philosophy. To act in an unjust fashion was in itself an offence, even when no breach of the terms of an individual law was involved. It was this notion which made the provision of retrospective law a matter of ease.

LEGISLATION AND CUSTOM

It has been said that in the earlier Middle Ages the ancient German 'ascending' theory of the source of kingly power went underground, or was overlaid by the 'descending' late Roman theory, supplemented by the conception of God as the ultimate source of the king's authority; in other words, what has been called a 'theocratic' conception of kingship. Nevertheless in one respect at least the Germanic kings were not seen as free to depart from the primordial relation with their people which Tacitus had described. Unlike the late Roman emperor, described by Justinian as the sole *legis lator*,[23] the medieval Germanic king was never regarded as having an independent, arbitrary power to make new law. Indeed the notion

---

[23] C. 1. 14. 12.

of law itself was primarily visualized as the immemorial custom of the nation, which, so far from having been 'made' by any king, was the setting in which the king was placed, the landscape in which he moved. Obviously this or that occasion provided the need for change in, or addition to the existing body of law; but any such change appears in all the Germanic kingdoms to have been thought possible only with the agreement of others besides the king: as a rule, something like a council of the greatest men of the nation, whose approval was supposed to be reinforced by popular acceptance. An early example of legislation according to the German understanding are the laws of the Lombard King Rothari (636–52) which expressly declare that they were confirmed in the manner traditional among the Lombards, the beating of spears on shields, this warriors' applause signifying popular consent.[24] The theory of the necessity for this consent appears in the writings of the ninth-century Archbishop Hincmar of Reims, councillor of Emperor Charles the Bald, who speaks of laws promulgated by the emperor's predecessors 'with the general assent of their faithful subjects'.[25] Naturally this cannot mean that literally the entire nation was consulted; but certainly some substantial and influential section of it needed to be brought along in the process of enactment. Thus an account of *capitula* promulgated as additions to laws of Charlemagne of 803 shows them being read before all the *scabinei* (here this may be very roughly rendered as 'judges') at Paris, and, on their agreeing to obey these capitula, they signed them together with the bishops, abbots, and counts present.[26] Further instances from the ninth century are on record, before the *Edictum Pistense* of 864 summarizes the contemporary conception of lawmaking as a process involving both royal establishment and popular consent ('quoniam lex consensu populi et constitutione regis fit'),[27] a conception altogether at odds with the theory of absolutist late imperial Rome. It remains however the case that law as such presents itself to the earlier medieval mind as essentially something traditional and customary, rather than something constantly undergoing legislative innovation. The account of the laws drawn up for the brand-new kingdom which the Crusaders established in Jerusalem, captured in 1099, even if the account itself is not true, is

---

[24] Edict of Rothari, 386.   [25] *De ordine palatii* 8.
[26] *Monumenta Germaniae Historica (MGH) Leges* 2. 1. 39.
[27] Ibid. 2. 2. 273.

significant as reflecting contemporary standards: the Crusaders compiled their code from the customs of the various nations represented in their ranks, altering any of them only so far as necessary to bring it into harmony with the rest.[28] 'The whole story', wrote the Carlyles, 'illustrates very vividly the fact that the medieval conception of law was dominated by custom, for even when the jurists thought that the Crusaders had to legislate for a new political society, they conceive of them as doing this by . . . collecting existing customs.'[29]

NATURAL LAW IN THE EARLY MIDDLE AGES

The Graeco-Roman tradition, as has been seen, included the conception of a natural law accessible to man through his reason; the idea was given canonical expression by Cicero, in the language of the Stoic philosophy, in his *De republica*. After the Western Roman empire was overthrown by the German peoples, the intellectual world was dominated by the Christian Church, which had had to construct its own philosophical armoury on the basis of the teaching of Christ and his apostles. Christianity could feel an emotional affinity with many Stoic doctrines because of their high-minded moral content; and the Christian philosophy now built up represents in several ways a fusion between its own fundamental data and adapted teachings of the Stoics. Nowhere was the result more important for future civilization than in the area of natural law.

Here, however, there was a problem deriving from the very different forms in which the idea of God presented itself to the Judaeo-Christian and to the Graeco-Roman worlds. The God whom Cicero mentioned in his *De republica* is an entirely abstract force, separate from the numerous local and (if the word may be so used) sectoral deities whose worship waxed and waned in the ancient pagan world: an element, a cause, a source, about which no organized theology existed, but which made sense in contexts like Cicero's. The God of the Jews, on the other hand, who is continued in the Christian world in the dimensions which Christian theology

---

[28] Jean d'Ibelin, *Assizes of Jerusalem* 1.
[29] R. W. and A. J. Carlyle, *A History of Medieval Political Theory in the West,* 6 vols. (London and Edinburgh, 1903–36), iii. 44.

gave him, is a strongly personalized God, with a name, a history, a Son. Accordingly when Stoics talked of a higher law originating in God they had in mind something much less graphic and compelling than the Jews' and Christians' image of a God who dispenses fundamental law in the shape of commandments physically transmitted to the leader of his chosen people. This contrast had important results for natural-law theory, because it raised the question of primacy as between nature and a superior will. Had God so commanded Moses because the order of nature had, all along, already contained the precepts which the Decalogue expressed? If so, had the Decalogue been necessary? Conversely, if what was perceived as the law of nature was in fact itself only the outcome of God's will, it was open to God to change its rules: in which case nature could not be looked to as an infallible, invariable rule of conduct.

These problems were apparent to St Ambrose and St Augustine. But most of the early Fathers did not trouble to pursue theory to such a distance. For them, the identification of natural law, in its Stoic form, with the law of God was enough; and this identification was immensely facilitated for them by a crucial passage in St Paul's letter to the Romans in which, in a graphic phrase, he had written that the Gentiles, though without the law (of Moses), still displayed 'the effect of the law, written in their hearts'.[30] This image is not to be found in Stoic philosophy, but its (presumably unconscious) conceptual affinity with the Stoic doctrine of rationally perceptible natural law was so striking that it gave the latter an easy entrée into Christian teaching. Irenaeus (c.130–200) wrote that the source of the natural law was nature, God's creation, and that the Ten Commandments were, so to speak, only a summary and reminder of the natural precepts which had existed even before Moses received them.[31] Origen (c.185–c.254) also called the law of nature the law of God, written in men's hearts, where it showed as the force of reason.[32]

The most important aspect of natural law was, of course, its theoretical relation to positive human law; and Origen asserted that the state's laws, if contrary to natural law, were invalid.[33] Lactantius, about 300, cited with high praise the 'almost divine' words of Cicero in which the same implication was visible to the

[30] Rom. 2: 14–15.　　　[31] *Adversus omnes haereses* 4. 13–15.
[32] *Comm. in Epist. ad Romanos* 3. 6.　　　[33] Ibid.

Christian eye.[34] St Augustine (354–430)—although he later placed God's will in the central position—called the eternal law described by Cicero the establisher of natural law, the order with which human law must conform;[35] and St Isidore of Seville (*d.* 636) also taught that earthly law must be conformable to the law of God. Long before the systematization of natural law carried out by St Thomas Aquinas in the thirteenth century, there was therefore a firm tradition in Christian teaching of a standard higher than that of earthly law, against which the latter must be measured, and which might show it to be invalid. Naturally, in the actual practice of the Germanic kingdoms such points of view remained, as they had been in Cicero's Rome, mere theory without concrete impact. All the same, the early Christian Church was in fact the conduit through which the ancient idea of natural law travelled from classical Greece and Rome into the High Middle Ages, and from there ultimately into the secular modern environment of 'higher law' and 'fundamental rights', enforceable through processes of judicial review even against the positive enactments of a sovereign legislature.

THE THEORY OF HUMAN EQUALITY AND ITS CONSEQUENCES

It has been seen that, although the ancient pagan world recognized the theoretical equality of all men, it had difficulty in accommodating the universal institution of slavery in this recognition. Aristotle avoided the difficulty by saying that some men were slave-like by nature; the Roman lawyers by attributing slavery to the *ius gentium*, the general instinct of mankind, which was to regard the life of a conquered enemy as forfeit, and in consequence any terms on which he was permitted to live by his captor as licit. Under the earlier Roman empire, the law intervened more and more in the interest of humane treatment of slaves, and explicit statements as to the natural equality of humans appear in legal texts.[36] It may be that this liberal turn in doctrine was due to first Greek and then Roman experience in finding that peoples formerly thought simply barbarous were quite capable of assimilation to the civilized standards of Hellenistic kingdoms and of the Roman empire. At any rate, the

---

[34] *Divinae institutiones* 6. 8.   [35] *De libero arbitrio* 1. 3. 6.
[36] D. 1. 1. 4, 1. 5. 4. 1.

early Christian teaching on this subject, which was to the same effect, could not have seemed a foreign body in the Roman world, though the origins of the Christian doctrine were peculiar to Christianity itself.

The equality of men, in Christian eyes, arose not from rational consideration of the world but from the relationship of humanity to Christ, its Redeemer. St Paul once wrote to the Galatians, the Celts of Asia Minor, that all who are baptized, having put on the person of Christ, and being all one person in him, are 'no more Jew or Gentile, no more slave and freeman, no more male and female'.[37] The Fathers of the Church held fast to this principle, which was an important factor in the Church's early recruitment, as the humblest people, including slaves, were valued equally with their social superiors, whom perhaps for this reason they seem originally to have much outnumbered.[38] Language similar to St Paul's is found in St Gregory Nazianzen (*c.*329–90), and in his contemporary, St Gregory of Nyssa, who gave St Paul's thought sharper point by arguing that, as all men are made in God's image, all must be equal to one another: for 'who is so short of reason as not to see that things which are made like one thing, resemble also one another in everything?' This implied for him, too, the equality of man and woman. St Gregory the Great (*c.*540–604) also emphasized that by nature all men are equal, though by God's dispensation some are subordinate to others. Writers in the Frankish kingdom of Charlemagne are found in the same camp: Jonas of Orleans (who cites Gregory the Great), Agobard of Lyons (779–840), Hrabanus Maurus (776–856), Hincmar of Reims (*c.*806–82).[39] This universal theoretical commitment to human equality involved the Church, however, in the practical issues arising from the theory's corollaries.

SLAVERY

This was the most obvious point at which the world's practice diverged from Christian teaching, or so it seems to us. But the early Christians, although practising charity and mildness in a way which

---

[37] Gal. 3: 28.

[38] Robin Lane Fox, *Pagans and Christians in the Mediterranean World from the Second Century AD to the Conversion of Constantine* (Harmondsworth, 1986), 301.

[39] Carlyles, *Medieval Theory* (see n. 29), i. 199 ff., for references for these writers.

impressed the pagan world in spite of itself, did not practise or even advocate the wholesale manumission of slaves. Indeed St Paul, the same authority who had taught human equality, had also enjoined upon slaves obedience to their masters.[40] While the Church regarded the freeing of slaves as a virtuous act, and this was symbolized by the fact that Christian manumissions were commonly carried out in the assembly of the faithful (*in ecclesia*), no stigma can have attached to continuing ownership of slaves, as Christian bishops themselves might have servants of slave condition.[41] The Fathers in fact evolved a secondary theory, as a qualification to that of the natural equality of humankind, to explain and justify the institution of slavery. According to an unknown commentator on St Paul called only 'Ambrosiaster', slavery was the consequence of man's sinfulness;[42] and this theme is repeated with numerous shades of variation by many of the other Fathers, including St Augustine. There is no question of restoring the Aristotelian idea of some men being naturally inferior to others (though something like this does appear in Hrabanus Maurus in the early ninth century). The general view of the Fathers is that the essential equality of men is related to an ideal era before the corruption of human nature by sin, and it is the conditions of human society, as so corrupted, which have rendered the servitude of some men necessary.[43] This was not to be understood as imputing sinfulness to everyone of slave status; on the contrary, in the individual case the slave might be a better man than his master; but overall the institution of servitude was to be so understood, and its human effects mitigated by the clemency which the Church enjoined upon masters.[44] In another perspective, the Fathers emphasized that the real slavery under which a man might labour was not that of a human owner, but that of sin.[45]

One exceptional, if minor, figure stands out in the earlier Middle Ages as dissenting from the general willingness to accommodate slavery within the theory of general human equality. The ninth-

[40] Eph. 6: 5–9.

[41] See M. I. Finley, *The Ancient Economy* (London, 1979), 64 ff., 84 ff., in which the author emphasizes the relatively favoured condition of slaves in the ancient world by comparison with free labourers. Cf. Lane Fox, *Pagans* (see n. 38), 296.

[42] *Commentary on St Paul's Letter to the Colossians* 4. 1.

[43] Carlyles, *Medieval Theory* (see n. 29), i. 114, 116–18; Augustine, *De civitate Dei* 19. 15.

[44] Carlyles, *Medieval Theory*, 119; Isidore, *Sent.* 3. 4. 7.

[45] Ambrose, *De Joseph Patriarcha* 4.

century abbot Smaragdus from near Verdun (which was then the great European slave mart, through which numberless Slav captives were sold into Western Europe) urges the king to forbid the making of slaves in his realm, and admonishes Christians to set their slaves at liberty. He does not actually advocate the abolition of slavery as an institution, but represents it as so inconsistent with Christianity that he says the king would honour God by putting an end to enslavement.[46]

PROPERTY

The beginnings of Christianity are not associated with any special theory of property, nor was the connection between the equality proclaimed by St Paul and the unequal distribution of worldly wealth as obvious as the relevance of human equality to the institution of slavery. Christ's message showed indifference to property as an institution, though he constantly preached the virtue of charity and the foolishness of material acquisitiveness. The early Fathers also avoid any theory of property, but clearly regard the sharing of wealth as morally preferable to individual hoarding.[47] A similar note is struck in the common early Christian view that it is not wealth itself that matters, but the use one makes of it. The Fathers taught generosity and brotherly sharing with others, but certainly nothing like a dogmatic communism.

At the same time, it could not be said that the Christian teaching of the Early Middle Ages recognized individual private property as a natural right. The Church simply accepted the existence of private property as a contemporary condition of actual life, just like slavery, and concentrated its doctrine on its right use. So far as opinions were expressed on the origin and legitimacy of the institution, they were to the effect that in the primitive state of the world, everything in it was the common property of mankind, and that it was only by operation of human law—a human law which the Fathers do not condemn—that individuals acquired property rights in portions of the earth's goods. Private property, said St Ambrose, is not according to nature, for nature poured out its plenty to all men in common; but time and custom (*usurpatio*) created private

---

[46] *Via regia* 30.   [47] e.g. Cyprian, *De opere et eleemosynis* 25.

rights.[48] A similar point of view is found in St Gregory the Great.[49] The teaching of these early Fathers can by summarized as follows: private property is not an original, natural institution, for at the beginning all things belonged to men in common; but human law and practice allowed private property to emerge; it is not in itself wrong, but its legitimacy in an individual's case must depend on the use he makes of his goods.

To these propositions St Augustine added a very important corollary. If private property is the creation of human law, it can also be abolished by human law. 'By virtue of human law a man says, This is my villa, this is my house, this is my slave; by human law, that is, by the emperors' law . . . But take away the law of the emperors, and who will be able to say, That villa is mine, etc.?'[50] It is true that this passage comes from a controversial tract written to a special purpose; but it could not be more distant from an assertion of a natural right to private ownership. (The Donatists, against whom this tract was composed, appear to have come nearer a general theory of individual acquisition, by arguing that their labour in accumulating their property gave them a fundamental title to it: an anticipation, as the Carlyles pointed out, of the theory on which 1300 years later John Locke was to found the right of private property.)[51]

It may be here mentioned that although the Christian teaching of the Early Middle Ages was not communist, and did not exclude private property, the means commonly used to acquire property were often disparaged; at any rate, the means which could be broadly called commercial, as the Fathers tended to regard commerce as morally inferior to agriculture and artisanship. Their particular hostility was reserved for usury; the sinfulness of lending money at interest remained a prominent Christian theme into the Central Middle Ages and beyond. Other mercenary figures than the usurer also attracted their condemnation: the middleman, the speculator, and the monopolist. No doubt all this is best seen as particular examples of wrongful use of wealth (in which, in itself, there is no harm): wrongful because taking advantage of the difficulties or the relative economic weakness of others.

---

[48] *De officiis ministrorum* 1. 28.   [49] *Liber regulae pastoralis* 3. 21.
[50] *Tract. VI in Joannis Evang.* 25.
[51] Carlyles, *Medieval Theory* (see n. 29), i. 141.

POLITICAL SUBORDINATION

The inequality represented by political subordination and the compulsion to obey rulers was merely a dimension of the problem of the state. As has been seen, the early Fathers rationalised the state as being the consequence of sin, which rendered laws necessary so that the weak might be protected and the wicked punished. The later Fathers hold to the same theory. St Gregory the Great wrote that nature gave birth to all men as equals, but that on account of their differing merits, a 'hidden dispensation' placed some under the rule of others; to the extent that some men behave like animals, they must be subdued by the kind of fear that animals understand[52] (though he also thought that, even if the element of wickedness and sin were not in the picture, some form of hierarchy or subordination might properly exist, since even angels, though sinless, are divided into superior and inferior ranks).[53] St Isidore of Seville similarly made short work of the problem of human rule: 'kings and princes are chosen among the nations', he wrote, 'so that, by fear of them, they may restrain their people from evil, and constrain them by laws to a good life. If all men were free of fear, who would be able to keep anyone from wickedness?'[54]

EQUITY

There is very little in early medieval writing to correspond with, or continue the tradition of the Greek and Roman theories of equity as a standard capable of correcting the rigidity of the law. There is, however, a passage in the work of Hincmar of Reims which, certainly unconsciously, belongs in this tradition. This archbishop, adviser of Emperor Charles the Bald, had (as has been seen) strongly asserted the general subordination of the king to law. But in the later part of the same work Hincmar concedes to the king the power to transcend, or rather to 'squeeze' (*comprimere*) the positive law (*lex saeculi*) in order to effect the higher justice 'of God' by means of a judgment based on more general fairness or equity

---

[52] *Expositio in librum Job* 21. 15. [53] *Ep.* 5. 59.
[54] *Sent.* 3. 47. I have reversed the order of these two sentences.

(*iudicium aequitatis*).[55] This *iudicium aequitatis*, wrote Fassò, was 'the remedy which the legal conscience of that time applied to the eternal disharmony between strict law and substantial justice'.[56]

THEORY OF A LAW OF NATIONS

The Roman world recognized some rules, or had some understandings, which would today be classified within the category of international law: treaties with other peoples were concluded from the time of the early Roman republic, and were expected to be observed; and the inviolability of ambassadors was universally recognized. Nothing, however, like a theory of international law is to be found in Roman juristic or secular literature. But with the spread of the Christian Church the beginnings of such a theory are discernible in the writings of two of the foremost Fathers of the Church.

St Augustine saw the universal state which Rome had created— and which was crumbling around him under barbarian assault as he wrote—as dangerous. It was achieved only through bloody wars, and was constantly shaken by civil conflict. But 'if the condition of mankind were more fortunate, all Kingdoms would be small, enjoying a neighbourly harmony, and so there would be in the world a variety of dominions, just as in a city the citizens are distributed among a variety of homes'.[57] Although the thought does not become explicit, the parallel with families all of which live within the legal order of a single city (state) suggests the conception of a higher legal order encompassing a large variety of such states themselves. Within such an order the waging of war is justified (*bellum iustum*) only when the adversary had done wrong, and must be compelled to observe the law; the just war, therefore, is directed essentially to the establishment of peace.[58]

St Isidore of Seville does not repeat St Augustine's formula. But after giving examples of natural-law principles (as we have seen), such as human instinct everywhere suggests, he enumerates, as in a separate category, items of *ius gentium* in a way which completely diverges from the classical Roman usage of the phrase. By *ius*

---

[55] *De ordine palatii* 21: *MGH Leges* 2, capit. reg. franc. 2, 524–5.
[56] Guido Fassò, *Storia della filosofia del diritto*, 3 vols. (Bologna, 1966–70), i. 219.
[57] *De civitate Dei* 19. 5, 4. 15.   [58] Ibid. 19. 7, 11.

gentium the Romans meant the institutions of civil law which they supposed all peoples naturally respected (some of which figure in St Isidore's list of natural-law items, such as the restitution of things deposited or lent). St Isidore's *ius gentium*, on the other hand, consists of a series of matters which in fact are more or less the scattered timbers out of which the Renaissance world and ultimately Grotius constructed modern international law: the taking possession of land for settlement (*sedium occupatio*); the rights arising from constructing buildings and fortifications (*aedificatio, munitio*); wars, and rules about prisoners' captivity and their restitution to their former status after release (*bella, captivitates, servitutes, postliminia*); peace treaties and truces (*foedera pacis, indutiae*); the sacredness of ambassadors (*legatorum non violandorum religio*); and prohibitions of marriage with foreigners (*connubia inter alienigenas prohibita*).[59]

Soon after the age of St Isidore the political and economic conditions which would require an international law began slowly to appear. In the eighth century international trade, which had virtually ceased at the collapse of the Western empire, began to revive, and rudimentary codes of maritime law began to appear. And in the ninth, after the collapse of the empire of Charlemagne, the main nations of Western Europe began to draw apart, and to evolve into mutually independent states.

THEORY OF CRIMINAL LAW AND PUNISHMENT

The early medieval world affords no literature specifically devoted to the purpose, justification, or measure of criminal punishment; though, since human government is justified by the Fathers largely in terms of its necessity for the repression of evil-doers and the protection of their victims, the legitimacy of criminal sanctions in general is clearly taken for granted. St Augustine deplores the miseries and imperfections of the state, for example the cruelties and absurdities of the practice of torture (which nevertheless he does not condemn outright); and also the inherent weakness of any system in which one human being sits in judgment on another:

How deep and dark a question it is to adjust the amount of punishment so as to prevent the person who receives it not only from getting no good, but

[59] *Etym.* 5. 6.

also from suffering loss thereby! Besides, I know not whether a greater number have been improved or made worse when alarmed under threats of such punishment at the hands of men as is an object of fear. What, then, is the path of duty, seeing that it often happens that if you inflict punishment on one he goes to destruction, whereas, if you leave him unpunished, another is destroyed?[60]

His perplexity about the proportioning of punishment, his doubts about its effects, even his concern for the reclamation of the delinquent, are the sort of seeds from which theory on such matters would ultimately emerge, but scarcely amount to theory themselves. His clearest conviction remained that of the melancholy necessity, in so corrupt a world, for penal measures:

Surely, it is not without purpose that we have the institution of the power of kings, the death penalty of the judge, the barbed hooks of the executioner, the weapons of the soldier, the right of punishment of the ruler, even the severity of the good father . . . While these things are feared, the wicked are kept within bounds and the good live more peacefully among the wicked.[61]

In the earlier phases of the Roman empire (regardless of the philosophic penal theory expressed by Seneca and Aulus Gellius) actual criminal law had a simple retributive character, punishing the wrongdoer according to the quality of his act, and leaving to courts a certain discretion in the selection of the penalty. Occasionally, because of the exigencies of a particular time or place, a punishment might be specially intensified, or attended with unusual publicity, as an *exemplum*, a deterrence to others; but the fact that the jurists give the special justification for such cases shows that no general recognition of deterrence as the principal dimension of punishment had yet become established. But from about 300 onwards—i.e. from the time that the 'principate' changed into a more military and totalitarian 'dominate'—criminal law assumed an increasingly intimidatory character, reflecting the need to halt the growing lawlessness and disorder which accompanied the empire's decline. Under the pressure of this necessity, the sort of attitude reflected in St Augustine's words became general, and, understandably, the ideal of suiting the penalty to the subjective and objective conditions of the offender and his offence is not prominent.

[60] *Ep.* 95. 3; ed. Deane, p. 301.   [61] *Ep.* 153. 6. 16; ed. Deane, p. 139.

The Church, nevertheless, had some influence in mitigating the rigour of criminal law; in its eyes, the criminal was, firstly, guilty in a degree related to all the circumstances, including subjective ones— thus modifying the purely intimidatory aspect of the law—and, secondly, needed repentance and reclamation as a sinner, which tended to reduce the incidence of the death penalty after which reclamation was no longer possible. There thus lay in the early Church's attitude two crucial and civilizing influences, predisposing to the rationalist criminal theory of the distant future.

A roughly similar picture can be traced in the Germanic kingdoms. Among the Visigoths of Spain and southern France, the late Roman ferocity for purposes of deterrence survived; among the Franks and Anglo-Saxons the function of punishment as necessary to public order was uppermost, although among both peoples the delinquent was also required to satisfy the vindictive feelings of his victim or victim's family, and the feuds arising from this principle, themselves a source of further disorder and bloodshed, were only with difficulty repressed by government. Among the Lombards of Italy the subjective setting of the crime was irrelevant; material was only the objective harm, and the need to deter others from imitating its author. But among both Lombards and Anglo-Saxons the moderating influence of the Church, intent on repentance and reformation, pointed the way to an appreciation of all the circumstances of the injury, and to a less ferocious and final expiation of it.

4
The High Middle Ages
(1100–1350)

By 1100 the era of Germanic migration, understood in the widest sense to include the adventures of the Vikings and Normans which came long after the fall of the Western Roman empire, was more or less over. The waves had reached almost the last recesses of the shore. The first Crusade had ended in the foundation of a Frankish kingdom in Palestine (1099). A little earlier the Viking empire of Russia, centred on Kiev, had reached its greatest extent; the Normans had conquered England and, at the other end of Europe, southern Italy and Sicily; only their establishment in Ireland (1169), and the short-lived Frankish conquest of Constantinople and 'Romania' (1204),[1] were still to come. Something like a European stability, at any rate by comparison with the 'Dark Ages', was in sight. Challenges from non-European peoples had been contained and repulsed: the Arabs, who once had penetrated far into France, had first been confined south of the Pyrenees, and were now gradually receding towards southern Spain as the Christian princes of the north, successors of the Visigoths, commenced the *Reconquista* of the peninsula; the Magyars from central Asia, defeated in southern Germany by the German emperor Otto I in 955, had settled down on the territory which today is Hungary. To the east the Byzantine empire, confronting the Islamic Turks, still served as a bulwark against their expansion into Europe.

From the tenth century, also, and reflecting the somewhat more settled times, Europe's population and economy had begun to grow. The statistical basis for even a general statement like this is missing; the Domesday Book, for example, which was compiled soon after the Norman conquest of England and provides a survey

---

[1] Romania: the name applied not to the area of the modern Romania, but to what was left of the (eastern or Byzantine) Roman empire, i.e. mainly the area of the modern Greece.

of the value and ownership of the lands of the kingdom which does make possible some very approximate calculations, is unique: nothing else like it is to be found elsewhere at that date. But other kinds of evidence go some way to fill the gap: the continual pushing of German settlers further and further east of the Elbe, which formerly had been the frontier separating them from the Slavs; the widespread felling and clearing of forest and draining of marshland all over central Europe in order to reclaim land for cultivation; the improvement in agricultural methods, increasing the yield from the same area: all these reflect the need to feed more mouths and so point to rapid population growth. Surplus population also in the sense of more hands than those needed for the employment available can perhaps be read too into the disorderly exodus from Europe of multitudes of destitute people in the first phase of the first Crusade; and perhaps even in the numbers swelling the new monastic foundations which sprang up everywhere in the High Middle Ages—though among the monastic orders themselves the Cistercians (founded 1098) were the most progressive group in Europe in the reclamation of waste land and in the improvement of agriculture and its ancillary industries.

Trade, and with it communication between peoples of different cultures (though this was promoted also by the Crusades), grew in this era as strongly as did the population. Its spread is associated most strongly with the north Italian city-states; the maritime republics of Venice, Genoa, and Pisa, in particular, competed for control of the commerce of the East, establishing trading posts and colonies around the eastern Mediterranean and in the Black Sea. Of great importance too was the opening of new land routes from northern to southern Europe through the Alps; in the course of the thirteenth century many new roads through the passes in the central region from Switzerland and Bavaria to Lombardy had become established, sometimes under the incentive of avoiding the tolls imposed by local magnates on the better known roads. The same era contains the beginnings of the great German trading empire in the northern seas, formalised in the thirteenth century in the so-called Hanseatic League; and, in the late twelfth, the rapid growth of a money economy, evidenced for instance by an eight-fold growth in the number of mints at work in Germany.

The High Middle Ages had no more characteristic feature than the organization called the guild, formed by people pursuing the same craft or trade, partly for the advancement of common interests, partly for charitable purposes and common religious devotion, partly for purely social purposes. An expression of the tendency of medieval man to see himself within a corporate frame, it was also of historic significance for the evolution of European political thought, since these guilds were self-governing, the officers chosen by the members, and so were a living embodiment, at the ordinary man's level, of the 'ascending' theory of government. They were the familiar, working background against which new theories in the thirteenth and fourteenth centuries would recruit support.

The suggestion made above, that rapid population growth may have had something to do with the rise in the numbers of monasteries and monks, would not by itself explain this phenomenon, because it would take no account of the revival in religious sentiment, and reform in discipline, associated above all with the age of Pope Gregory VII (1073–85) and St Bernard of Clairvaux (1090–1153). It was Gregory who, in the so-called Investiture Conflict—about the claim of kings to designate bishops, and, conversely, the pope's claim to the right to depose kings—succeeded in freeing the Church from the temporal control under which it had lived since the late Roman empire; and in making stick the reforms in Church organization, resistance to which, mostly from Germany, had started the contest in the first place. St Bernard, abbot of the Cistercian abbey of Clairvaux, was the most powerful figure in Western monasticism and a tireless campaigner for Christian orthodoxy.[2] Their age was one of explosive intensity of faith and practice, symbolized by the idea of the Crusade and, in a form still visible, by the great Gothic[3] cathedrals of the twelfth and thirteenth centuries. The centrality of the Christian faith to all individual and corporate life, its universality throughout Latin Europe, the self-confidence with which occasional heresy was confronted and crushed, the fervour of worship, the large place in life occupied by auxiliaries to faith such as pilgrimages and relics, the splendour of the Church's rituals and monuments: all made up the intense

---

[2] He was a friend and supporter of St Malachi, archbishop of Armagh and reformer of the Irish Church, who died at Clairvaux in 1148.

[3] Originally so called by the Italian humanists of the 15th cent. in a disparaging sense, meaning 'barbaric' (by contrast with the style of classical antiquity) because deriving from the Germanic lands of northern France. Its principal architectural feature is the pointed arch, contrasting with the rounded and Roman and Romanesque arch.

atmosphere in which the high medieval intellect lived, and all contributed, too, to the reaction against it which was to bring the Middle Ages to a close, and announce the modern world.

Contemporaneously with, and causally related to the rapid growth in population and trade, a European urban civilization, of a strength not known since the fall of the Western empire, began to emerge. At about the date 1100 there were, indeed, two areas— Flanders and northern Italy—in which flourishing towns, large by the standards of the time, existed: in the case of Flanders, associated with the production of cloth (the wool mostly imported from eastern England, thus stimulating growth there too), and, in the case of Lombardy and Tuscany, with foreign trade. Italy was, however, a special case, because here the Roman urban tradition had never died out, being sustained into this period by the strong Lombard kingdom in the north, the papacy in Rome and central Italy, and the Greeks, the Muslims, and ultimately the Norman kingdoms in the south. 'During the gloomy and disastrous centuries which followed the downfall of the Roman Empire', wrote Macaulay with brilliant imagery,

Italy had preserved, in a far greater degree than any other part of Western Europe, the traces of ancient civilisation. The night which descended upon her was the night of an Arctic summer. The dawn began to reappear before the last reflection of the preceding sunset had faded from the horizon. It was in the time of the French Merovingians and of the Saxon Heptarchy that ignorance and ferocity seemed to have done their worst.[4] Yet even then the Neapolitan provinces, recognising the authority of the Eastern Empire, preserved something of Eastern knowledge and refinement. Rome, protected by the sacred character of her Pontiffs, enjoyed at least comparative security and repose. Even in those regions where the sanguinary Lombards had fixed their monarchy, there was incomparably more of wealth, of information, of physical comfort, and of social order, than could be found in Gaul, Britain, or Germany.[5]

In Italy, therefore, a high urban civilization—what had been the glory of the Graeco-Roman world—now began to revive. These cities were not only soon to become the setting for the resurgence of the European intellect which we call the 'renaissance'; they also

---

[4] Merovingians: the earliest of the Frankish kings, c.500–750. Heptarchy: the seven small kingdoms established by the Angles and Saxons in England at about the same era.

[5] *Critical and Historical Essays*, i. *Machiavelli* (London, 1843), 66–7.

gave Europe indispensable lessons in the conduct of business and hence in the fertilization of economies. Banking, bookkeeping, insurance, negotiable instruments, all kinds of commercial and financial methods, are traceable to north Italy in this period. They are also in part associated with the Jewish element in medieval populations; the Jews, generally prohibited from owning land and so from becoming assimilated in the basic economy, were driven towards commerce and finance (and then despised for it by the Christian neighbours whose bigotry had confined them to it), and here they fulfilled a vital role above all in the development of credit. This, because it involved the exaction of interest in some form, was forbidden anyway to Christians as usury, and only gradually, as its utility was recognized, did the Church relent and permit Christians too to engage in an operation crucial to economic growth.

Italy and Flanders, then, had the most urbanized societies at the start of the period; but they were quickly joined by other regions: southern Germany, eastern England, northern and parts of southern France, north-eastern Spain. Sometimes, as with southern Germany (where the trade-routes of the Rhine and Danube and the Alpine passes played a part), natural facts underlay the economic development on which cities began to rise; sometimes, indeed more often, there is a connection with a political phenomenon, namely the rise of what, by comparison with earlier times, were strong centralized monarchies. These certainly have something to do with the growth of London, Paris, and Palermo, already in the twelfth century much the biggest towns in their respective kingdoms (and probably also the three biggest in Europe). Leading the trend towards the nation-state, the earliest signs of which now appear, these monarchies began to settle in permanent 'capital' cities; they were no longer the fragile kingships of the Early Middle Ages, in which the king, often insecure on his throne and apprehensive of too-powerful local princes, had had to keep on a perpetual circuit of his territories if he was to maintain a minimum of order and obedience. Now, although even the stronger kings maintained administrations so tiny that they could scarcely staff a single section of a single modern department, the existence of a permanent court with its apparatus of justice, of military command, of exchequer, of ceremonial ritual, of patronage of arts and learning, of hospitality and diversion, and of religious observance, ensured a crowd of ancillary servants and dependants as well as providing work for various crafts and trades, in what today would be called a spin-off effect. Such conditions probably explain the great difference in size between the three capitals mentioned, and all other towns in those kingdoms.

A more subtle characteristic of these centuries, related partly to religious fervour and in particular to the cult of Our Lady, partly to more settled conditions, partly to codes of honour associated with the feudal relationship and with knighthood, is a general softening of manners, which even the horrors of war and persecutions of heretics and Jews could not conceal. The knightly ideal, expressions of the highest and most sacrificial forms of love, modes of music and poetry to celebrate refined and noble emotion all came into flower. The very word 'romance' belongs to this period, and took then the form of infusing episodes of the past—whether of the dimly recalled Graeco-Roman world, or of the Gothic and Frankish ages—with strong ethical and religious emotion. Its most famous epic, the *Chanson de Roland*, which was put together in the twelfth century, recounted with romantic emphasis a military tragedy of the eighth, from the still barbaric age of Charlemagne.

Finally, the better organized, stronger governments of the twelfth century, and a Church more disciplined and self-confident, had a close relationship with the birth of the European university. Civil and ecclesiastical administration more ambitious and efficient than the Dark Ages had known called for personnel capable of keeping accurate records, drafting charters and commissions and grants, supplying and servicing a judicature, conducting correspondence, in general able to organize and present material in lucid and forceful Latin.[6] This ability depended not just on bare literacy, but also on an understanding of grammar, logic, and rhetoric: studies which, weakly kept alive since the end of the Western Roman empire in the rudimentary schools attached to bishops' sees and monasteries, now formed the basis for the larger intellectual aspirations, as well as the governmental needs, of the twelfth century, and for a revival of legal studies. The polemics of the Investiture Conflict came through in a barrage of pamphleteering from the pope's and the emperor's camps; both needed people able to present and refute argument by

[6] Latin as the ordinary spoken tongue of the people had long since broken down into the dialects which were now evolving towards French, Spanish, etc. but something aspiring to be like classical Latin continued to be the official language of Church and state (and thus to serve as a medium of international communication between educated people) right through the Middle Ages and up to the 17th cent.

logic and authority, whether biblical or to be found in the writings of the Church Fathers. At the same moment philosophy received a new impetus from the rediscovery in Western Europe—via the Islamic and Jewish civilizations of Sicily and Spain—of the works of Aristotle, who now acquired a prestige so great that he came to be called (for example by Thomas Aquinas) simply 'the Philosopher', as though none other existed. Because of the need to defend Christian orthodoxy if possible with the aid of philosophy, theologians quickly appropriated it; and from the alliance of those disciplines the study of man's relation to God, his place in creation, and the purpose and end of both, emerged in the form of the so-called 'scholastic' philosophy which had its classical period in the thirteenth and fourteenth centuries and its classical exponent in St Thomas Aquinas (1226–74). From this complex of needs (governmental, political, religious) the higher schools of Europe emerged: at first, in the twelfth century, spontaneously and informally, as at Bologna, Paris, and Oxford, then as the result of deliberate foundation by princes, whose creations now came in quick succession all over Europe from Padua (1222) and Naples (1224) to Cracow (1364), and from Salamanca (1230) to Prague (1348) and Heidelberg (1386).

THE NEW LEGAL SCIENCE

The most important school of theology and philosophy was at Paris—its most famous early figure the tragic Peter Abelard—but the school most significant in the history of law is probably the most ancient of them all, that of Bologna in the papal territory of north central Italy.[7] This may have developed out of a grammar school attached to the bishop's seat, and may also have had some connection with a similar school in nearby Ravenna; all we know with certainty is that in Bologna, about 1100, a teacher called Irnerius (thought to be a Latinized form of the German name Werner) makes his appearance, and the subject which he expounds is not grammar or logic, but law. There had indeed been shadowy law-schools in northern Italy even earlier, in which the rules of Lombardic (i.e. the local Germanic) laws were taught, perhaps with

Except perhaps for schools of Lombardic, i.e. Germanic law.

some admixture of scraps of Roman law surviving in rudimentary (the so-called 'vulgar')[8] form. But what Irnerius pioneered was quite different: it was the study of Justinian's *Digest*, which, although it had been promulgated in Italy during the brief Byzantine reconquest of the sixth century, had then disappeared from view so completely that it is impossible to prove any knowledge of it in Italy from the seventh century until Irnerius' time. Very possibly there was not, in 1100, so much as a single manuscript copy of it in the whole of Italy; and it has been surmised that its reappearance at Bologna was connected with the westward migration of Byzantine scholars taking refuge from the empire of Constantinople, now under severe pressure from the Turks, and bringing books with them. At any rate, a huge demand for this infinitely richer legal material now developed; there was a ready market among princes and prelates for the knowledge which training in this inexhaustible mine of law conferred; a law, moreover, with all the authority and aura of the Roman empire, which the medieval world saw as somehow living on, both in an imperial German and in a papal embodiment. This *Digest*, together with Justinian's *Institutes* (a short student's textbook), *Codex*, and *Novellae* (collections of late imperial statute law) made up what the Middle Ages now came to call the *Corpus Iuris Civilis*; of its enormous influence Walter Ullmann wrote that 'its general principles relating to justice, to the concept of law, the division of law, its enforcement, and so on, became central to the medieval concept of law; whilst the *Code* (and the *Novellae*) set forth an unadulterated monarchic form of government in the guise of the law'.[9] From the point of view of the political usefulness of the *Corpus Iuris Civilis*, the Bologna law school was born at a particularly propitious moment; it was the height of the conflict between pope and emperor, and the contemporary needs of papal polemics may have done as much to stimulate the growth of legal proficiency as the more permanent needs of administrative and judicial civil government.[10]

---

[8] 'Vulgar law', a term coined by Ernst Levy (*Weströmisches Vulgarrecht: Das Obligationenrecht* (Weimar, 1956)) means the simplified law used in the 5th and 6th cents., with classical distinctions and classifications effaced and overlaid.

[9] *Medieval Political Thought* (see Ch. 3 n. 12), 47.

[10] For all this see Wieacker, *Privatrechtsgeschichte der Neuzeit* (Gottingen, 1952), 45 ff.; O. Robinson, T. Fergus and W. Gordon, *Introduction to European Legal History* (Abingdon, 1985), 71 ff.

The era of the studies inaugurated at Bologna—but of which Bologna did not long retain a monopoly, as other law-schools centred on the study of the *Digest* soon sprang up—is conventionally regarded as falling into two phases: the first, from about 1100 to about 1250, called that of the 'Glossators'; the second, from about 1250 until about 1400, that of the 'Commentators' (or, sometimes, 'post-Glossators'). These names express the different methods associated with the two phases. That used by the earlier teachers consisted in attaching simple explanatory side-notes, or 'glosses', to successive passages of the classical text; that of the later school ran to coherent commentries on whole subjects treated by the Roman jurists. The accumulated mass of various glossatores' work was edited and consolidated into a single collection about 1250 by Accursius, whose work became canonical under the name *Glossa Ordinaria*; the maxim 'Quod non adgnovit glossa, non adgnoscit curia' ('a rule unknown to the *Glossa [Ordinaria]* is not recognized by the court either') illustrates its authority. The most famous of the Commentators were Bartolus de Saxoferrato (1314–57) and his pupil Baldus de Ubaldis (1327–1400); the prestige achieved in particular by the former is seen in the (typically medieval) jingle 'Nemo romanista nisi bartolista' ('If you're not a follower of Bartolus, you're not a scholar of Roman law').

These pioneers established Roman law as the supreme expression of legal and political reason, and set it on a course which would lead to its reception into, and fusion with, the relatively less sophisticated native systems of the medieval states and statelets. Their influence caused the Roman law in its Justinianic dress to have the same sort of authority in civil affairs as the Bible had in spiritual. But both Glossators and Commentators were interested primarily in the practical application of law, and scarcely at all in legal theory, any more than their classical Roman predecessors had been. As with those, such theory as they held has to be glimpsed (as it will be here and there in this chapter) more or less between their lines.

Most legal theory in these years comes, as it had in the earlier medieval period, from churchmen rather than from lawyers: churchmen, as often as not, out to build a polemical argument, though sometimes too (especially with the scholastic philosophers) enunciating views of law as part of the greater picture of the relation of men to God and, in consequence of his creation, to one another. Important also in this connection is the maturing of canon law, a system which in that age had an impact on ordinary people's lives much greater than today, because the jurisdiction of the Church extended to several matters (mostly in the area of marriage, the family, and succession) which today belong to the civil jurisdiction. This maturing, another achievement of the twelfth and thirteenth centuries, was also associated with the school of Bologna and the revived interest in the *Digest*. It was here, around 1140, that a monk called Gratian collected, edited, and reconciled a mass of rulings of ecclesiastical authority (*canones*, from the Greek word *kanōn*, a rule) in a work formally entitled *Concordantia discordantium canonum*, but commonly known ever since as the *Decretum* of Gratian; this, as will be seen, is an important source of high medieval legal theory, and contains in particular, in its doctrine on natural law, a crucial milestone.

THE STATE IN THE THEORY OF THE HIGH MIDDLE AGES

About the year 1100 the concept of the state, of a permanent and independent frame for temporal government, scarcely existed, at any rate not with the sharply defined frontiers familiar today. Christian society was still seen essentially as a unity, of which the temporal government (*regnum*) and the spiritual direction (*sacerdotium*) were simply two aspects which in practice overlapped one another to a substantial extent; for example, kingship was regarded as an office with a priestly dimension. But 1100 was a year which fell in the midst of a revolution. Previously the Church had tended to be under the control of local kings and princes, and even the papacy under that of the German emperor, who in the eleventh century had actually deposed three popes. But the reform movement associated with the reinvigorated papacy had shaken off temporal control, and gone onto the counter-attack with the deposition by Gregory VII of Emperor Henry IV. The Church thus frustrated the vision of a universal state which the emperors' deliberate evocation of the ancient Rome was meant to inspire, and placed all rulers on the defensive; national monarchies were emerging in this era more clearly and strongly than before, but were confronted, throughout the twelfth and thirteenth centuries, by even stronger claims to papal dominance over them. These claims were symbolized, for example, by St Bernard's theory that the two swords mentioned in St Luke's Gospel (22: 38) represented allegorically Christ's identi- fication of the two domains of Church and state; that both swords were given by him to the Church; and that one of them, the 'temporal sword', was merely delegated by the pope (who reserved the wielding of the other, 'spiritual', sword to himself) to be employed at his direction by the kings who were his subjects. Papal assertiveness (and its frequent acceptance by temporal rulers) can be seen, again, in the grant of a crown to Roger, the Norman ruler of Sicily, in 1130, which was regarded as turning him into a king, with the special sacred aura which the title carried; in the grant by Pope Adrian IV in 1155 of Ireland to the English king Henry II, ostensibly for the reclamation of the Irish Church; and in the excommunication by Innocent III, in a quarrel over an episcopal election, of the English king John (the pope laid his kingdom under an interdict, reducing him in 1213 to surrender, whereupon he did feudal homage to the pope and became his vassal). The high point of papal encroachment was the issue of the decree *Unam sanctam* by Boniface VIII in 1302, which declared the universal lordship of Christ, and, on earth, of his vicar the pope; for salvation it was now necessary for every human creature to hold himself subject to the Roman pontiff.

The consequence of this phase of Church resurgence and papal pretension was, however, that the spheres of Church and state now began to pull apart, according as the partisans of monarchs replied to papal claims with equally vigorous assertions of the state's independence. There was a final abandonment of the early medieval view that the state had something unholy—man's sin—at its root, and was at best a necessary evil for the repression of wickedness and the punishment of wrongdoers; and it was now generally agreed to be (as indeed St Paul had considered it) an institution divinely ordained. The decisive step towards providing a philosophical basis for this view was taken by St Thomas, called Aquinas from his birthplace Aquinum near Naples (1226–74), who joined the newly founded Dominican Order, studied under Albertus Magnus at Cologne, and afterwards taught at Paris, Rome, and Naples. In the vast *Summa Theologica* which crowned his life's work he raised the question whether, had there never been a Fall and had mankind remained in its primal state of innocence, there would still have been subordination of some men to others. He mentioned, but did not rely on, the old argument that a hierarchy exists even among the angels; instead, he put forward, in a Christian format, Aristotle's assertion that man's nature inclines him to civic existence, so that some form of political organization would have been natural to him even without supposing the corruption of his nature by the Fall of his first parents:

Dominion is exercised over a free man by another when that other is directing him to his own [the free man's] proper good, or to the common good. And such dominion of man over man would have existed in the state of innocence, for two reasons. First, because man is naturally a social being (*animal sociale*), and so men in the state of innocence would have lived in social groups. But a social existence of many people would not be possible unless someone were in charge, to attend to the common good; for many people, of themselves, will have many different objectives, but a single person will have only one. And therefore the Philosopher [i.e. Aristotle] says that when many are directed towards one thing, you will always find one of them to be principal or director.

Secondly, because if one man greatly surpassed another in knowledge and justice, it would be wrong if he did not perform this function [of principal or director] for the benefit of the others; as it says in 1 Peter [4: 10], 'Everyone putting the grace he has received at the disposal of each other'. So Augustine too says that 'the just do not rule out of a lust to dominate, but out of the duty to look after affairs; this is what the order of nature prescribes, this is how God constructed man'.[11]

In another work, *De regimine principum* ('On Princely Government'), a tract addressed to King Hugh of Cyprus and of uncertain date, St Thomas advances the material self-insufficiency of the individual human being; unlike animals, which need no clothing or other goods, and can look out for their own food and shelter and safety, man needs the variety of others' production, and the protection of others' solidarity with him; hence he is a 'social and political being' (*animal sociale et politicum*), and from this the necessity of civic order—in a word, the state—results:

One man alone could not provide himself with all his needs; one man, of himself, could not live an adequate life. It is therefore natural to man, that he should live in the society of many ... And if it is natural to man to live in the society of many, it necessarily follows that there must be some arrangement whereby those many may be governed.[12]

[11] *Summa Theologica* 1a 2ae 96. 4.   [12] *De regimine principum* 1. 1.

The fusion which St Thomas thus achieves between Aristotle's doctrine about man's civic nature, and the Christian doctrine which imputes the creation of that nature to God, automatically legitimizes the state itself as a part of God's design. While the earlier medieval mind had seen in the kingdom only one facet of a unitary Christian society (and one which papal pretension threatened to make appear secondary) St Thomas, although no opponent of the papacy, now provided the state with an abstract and universal justification quite independent of the Christian fellowship on which the Church was based and which it expressed. And so St Thomas, as Walter Ullmann wrote, 'by absorbing Aristotle's ideas, effected in the public sphere not so much a metamorphosis of the subject as the re-birth of the citizen who since classical times had been hibernating'.[13] The citizen and the state, which was the frame of his existence, could now stand on their own feet; far from being a necessary evil, the consequence of man's Fall, the state, being the product of nature itself, carried *ab initio* the endorsement of God as nature's author.

It is worth noting that St Thomas effortlessly transposes the proposition of Aristotle, whose *politikon zōon* was conceived in the setting of the Greek *polis*, or city-state of modest dimensions, to the far larger frame of the medieval state which, if one excepts the city-republics of northern Italy, were as a rule kingdoms of substantial extent. St Thomas's construction, in turn, was made to do duty for a still more grandiose conception a generation later by Italy's national poet and the father of her literary language, Dante Alighieri (1265– 1321). Dante had taken part in the politics of his native city, Florence, but had to go into exile under sentence of death in 1302; and his bitter disillusionment with public life as it was in contemporary city-republics torn by the factions of Guelf (supporters of the pope) and Ghibelline (supporters of the German emperor) led him to see the best hope for Christendom in a universal empire, by which he meant the universal dominance of the revived Roman empire under its German leadership. The inspiration for this emotional commitment to a new Roman world order came from the Roman poet Virgil, contemporary and admirer of Augustus, who in his fourth Eclogue had celebrated the unique destiny of Rome which he saw unfolding under the new dispensation of his imperial patron. The tract in which Dante now revived this vision, the *De*

---

[13] *Medieval Political Thought* (see Ch. 3 n. 12), 176.

monarchia of about 1310, sees human society as destined by God and nature for an 'activity which individual men, or families, or neighbourhoods, or cities, or kingdoms by themselves would be incapable of carrying out', namely the pursuit of peace and justice; only the reign of a universal monarchy could assure these essentials to humankind.[14]

To the names of St Thomas and Dante may be added that of John of Paris, a Dominican who, in a work of about 1302 called *De potestate regia et papali*, also related the secular state to man's associative nature which was a sufficient justification for it. But the most radical assertion of the state's nature-based autonomy came from yet another Italian, Marsilius (Marsiglio) of Padua (*c.*1270–*c.*1342), at one time rector of the university of Paris. His famous book *Defensor pacis* ('Defender of the Peace'), published about 1324, led to his enforced flight from Paris, and was condemned by Popes John XXII and Clement VI as heretical. Its offence lay in its assertion, not just of the nature-based autonomy of the state, but also of the totally different spheres of temporal government and spiritual authority. Indeed Marsilius, who blamed the ambitions of the papacy for all the disasters of war and faction that had fallen upon his country, advocated the subordination of the Church to the state where temporal matters were concerned: the cleric, whatever his standing in spiritual affairs, was no less a citizen, with all the implications of obedience that that contained, than the layman. Marsilius's work had no lasting impact in his own era; but it lay like an unexploded mine among Europe's intellectual furniture, to be detonated two centuries later in the age of Reformation.

Thus the concept of the autonomous secular state, not beholden to religious authority, began to emerge through the medieval mist. A further dimension was given it—and by the pope himself— before the period closed, namely that of external sovereignty: the king is now seen as not merely sovereign *vis-à-vis* the other potentates within his kingdom, but sovereign also in the sense of being immune from the jurisdiction of all other kings, even that of the Holy Roman Emperor of Germany in whose office the vision of universal dominion more or less inarticulately survived (to be passionately advocated, as has just been seen, by Dante). The doctrine of the mutual sovereignty of kings can be traced back as far

[14] *De monarchia* I. 3; A. P. D'Entrèves, *Dante as a Political Thinker* (Oxford, 1952).

as the early twelfth century, and had established itself in the universities of Italy and France; but in the early fourteenth, in the context of a quarrel between the emperor and the king of Sicily, it was finally confirmed by Clement V. The papal decree *Pastoralis cura* (1313) is the first expression in legal terms of the concept of territorial sovereignty; as Ullmann wrote, 'it undercut the medieval idea of universality and set in its place the individual sovereign kings as lords who . . . could do within their kingdoms as it pleased them . . . It [thus] marked the beginning of the concept of state sovereignty'.[15] This concept was undoubtedly reinforced also by the emerging character of states as subjects of a slowly evolving international legal order (a matter to be dealt with in a later section).

THE BASIS OF POLITICAL AND LEGISLATIVE AUTHORITY

Justinian's *Digest*, together with the rest of the *Corpus Iuris Civilis*, provided ammunition for debate—now to be conducted by the newly arisen race of civilians and not merely by ecclesiastics—about the basis for temporal rule. There were now texts, chief among them Ulpian's account of the *lex regia* in the *Digest*, which offered an alternative to the purely theocratic and 'descending' theory which had dominated, albeit with qualifications, the earlier Middle Ages. All the civilians agreed in deriving the right to exercise rule from the people; the question of how its supposed original residence with, and then its delegation by, the Roman people could be imputed to the peoples of the Germanic kingdoms as well did not seem a problem. But this initial unanimity did not foreclose debate on the main difficulty in the Roman doctrine, namely: had the (actual Roman or putative Germanic) people made a permanent and irrevocable transfer of their right to government? Or had they delegated this to the monarch, broadly speaking, only on condition of his good behaviour, while retaining a residual right to resume their powers and to depose the monarch if he misbehaved?

Some of the Glossators took the former view, notably Irnerius, the founder of the new jurisprudence, and Placentinus (active about 1160); others, such as Azo and Hugolinus (active about 1200), held

[15] Ullmann, *Medieval Political Thought* (see Ch. 3 n. 12), 198–9.

that the people had never finally abdicated their authority, and that their enduring lawmaking capacity was to be seen in the legal force attaching to custom, which indeed (according to Hugolinus and others whom he cited) if universal, could even supersede positive law. So far as monarchs themselves and their advisers were concerned, assertions of absolutism were remarkably rare; although one reading of Ulpian's *lex regia* text, together with one or two other passages from the Roman corpus, would have made them colourable. Emperor Frederick I (Barbarossa) did say baldly in 1155 that 'it is for the prince to prescribe laws for the people, not the people for the prince';[16] and in thirteenth-century England absolutist ideas, or at any rate suspicions of them, seem to have been in the air.[17] But these instances are isolated. In practice, the old Germanic habit of expecting kings both to respect the ancestral laws, and to consult to the point of consensus before making new ones, operated to inhibit absolute rule, probably with more practical effect than any democratically oriented reading of Ulpian could supply. Bracton, emphasizing the law-based position of the king, wrote that this principle was not undermined by the saying *Quod principi placet*, etc., since this was referred in its turn to the enactment of a law by the people; in the terms of Bracton's time, this meant the product of debate and deliberation with the great men of the kingdom.[18]

The clerical philosophers of this age were also virtually unanimous against temporal absolutism. During the Investiture Conflict the ruler's position had been related by Manegold of Lautenbach to a contract with his people. In the thirteenth century St Thomas, while perceiving the state as the natural product of man's instinct for civic society, still used language which both suggested that royal power originated with the people, and construed it as resulting from an agreement with them. He justified resistance to a tyrant as follows:

If it is a people's right to provide itself with a king, and if that king tyrannically abuses the royal power, there is no injustice if the community deposes or checks him whom they have raised to the kingship, nor can it be charged with a breach of faith for abandoning a tyrant, even if the people had previously bound themselves to him in perpetuity; because, by not

[16] Otto of Freising, *Gesta Friderici imperatoris* 138 (*MGH SRG*, 1912).
[17] See Susan Reynolds, *Kingdoms and Communities in Western Europe, 900–1300* (Oxford, 1984), 46, 48 ff.
[18] *De legibus et consuetudinibus Angliae* 3. 9. 3.

faithfully conducting himself in government as the royal office demands, he has brought it on himself if his subjects renounce their bargain with him (*quod ei pactum a subditis non reservetur*).[19]

The notion of government founded on contract shows through clearly here. The same is found a little later in Engelbert of Volkersdorf; writing early in the fourteenth century he sees states as arising from men's rational perception of their own condition, which led them to choose one of their number to be ruler, and to bind themselves to him in a bargain and bond of subjection ('sub pacto et vinculo subiectionis');[20] and while his contemporary John of Paris does not use the image of contract, he equally relates the emergence of the state to reason, persuasion, and men's consent.[21] God as the author of creation had of course in this age not dropped out of the picture; but God and the human nature he had created—a nature political and social—were seen as the remote or ultimate factors, which worked through the mechanism of men's consent, sometimes expressed as their bargain or contract with the ruler they had accepted.[22]

The democratic implications of all this, and its incompatibility with the old 'descending' view of government, are clear. The writer in this period who drew the most radical conclusions in this direction, and whose work is a milestone in the history of constitutional freedom, is Marsilius of Padua, already mentioned. It has been seen that in his *Defensor pacis* he insisted on the separate spheres of Church and state, and even proposed the subordination of the former to the latter. But his republicanism went further. For him the sovereign in the state was the people, who set up a ruler not irrevocably, but to carry out such functions as the community, in the nature of things, was unable to discharge. This ruler can be checked or deposed by the people, of whom he himself remains only the 'secondary, instrumental or executive part'. Marsilius seems to have recognized the practical necessity of the majority principle; laws, he wrote, should be made by the citizen body 'or its preponderant part' ('aut eius valentior pars').[23] Just as with his

---

[19] *De regimine principum* 1. 6.

[20] *De ortu et fine Romani imperii*, ch. 2.

[21] *Tractatus de potestate regia et papali*, ch. 1. For this and the foregoing reference, see Gough, *Social Contract* (see Ch. 2 n. 48), 39.

[22] See O. von Gierke, *Political Theories of the Middle Age*, tr. F. Maitland (Cambridge, 1900), 89, 187.

[23] *Defensor pacis* 1. 12. 3, 5.

doctrine of the separate spheres of Church and state, this democratic teaching was to have a greater impact in later generations than it had in his own.

It is likely that the appearance of republican elements in real life in this era has a connection with the democratic element in its constitutional theory. The rules of the new religious orders such as the Franciscans (founded 1209) and the Dominicans (1216) were strongly democratic.[24] The so-called 'conciliar' movement in the central government of the Church tended in the same direction; it asserted the right of general councils, not the papacy, to decide important issues. Moves towards regularizing the role of the body of cardinals in electing (and deposing) popes belong to the same period. Similarly in lay life the High Middle Ages exhibit all sorts of collective activity in which self-government rather than submission to monarchic direction was the rule: in the new universities, in the guilds and fraternities which flourished in the towns, in the government of the towns themselves.[25]

THE RULE OF LAW

Alongside the democratic strain in constitutional theory, something like the modern theory of the *Rechtsstaat*, or the 'rule of law', now emerges in much clearer form than before. There are the same ethical propositions about how rulers should respect the laws they themselves enforce on others; but now there are also lawyers asserting the positive legal subordination of the ruler to the law of the land.

The contrary opinion—that the king is above the law, the *princeps legibus solutus* of Ulpian—did not simply lie down and die. The English bishop Richard fitz Nigel wrote in 1177–9 a guide to the operations of the royal exchequer (of which he was treasurer) called *Dialogue of the Exchequer* in which, addressing King Henry II, he declares that the actions of sovereigns 'ought not to be discussed or condemned by their subjects. For they whose hearts and the motions thereof are in the hand of God, and to whom the

---

[24] Mundy, *Europe in the High Middle Ages, 1150–1309* (London, 1973), 356–8.
[25] Reynolds, *Kingdoms* (see n. 17), *passim*.

sole care of their subjects has been by God himself committed, stand or fall by God's judgment and not by a human one.'[26]

The immense authority of St Thomas Aquinas in the following century was to the same effect. In the context of his division of the characteristics of law into directive and compulsive powers he declares the ruler immune from application of the latter:

A ruler is said to be above the law (*princeps dicitur esse solutus a lege*) with respect to its constraining force: for nobody can be constrained by himself; and the law derives its power of constraint only from the power of the ruler. So it is said that the prince is above the law, because if he should act against the law nobody can bring a condemnatory judgment against him. So, commenting on the text of Psalm 50 'To thee only have I sinned' etc., the [Accursian] Gloss explains that 'there is no man who can judge the actions of a king'.[27]

All the same, St Thomas immediately goes on to recommend, in the familiar way, that the ruler should as a matter of moral duty respect the law. He sees him therefore as subject to it in its directive even if not in its compulsive aspect:

But with respect to the directive power of law, a ruler is voluntarily subject to it, in conformity with what is laid down:[28] 'Whoever enacts a law for another should apply the same law to himself.[29] And we have it on the authority of the wise man that you should subject yourself to the same law which you promulgate'. And in the *Codex* of Justinian the emperors Theodosius and Valentinian write to the prefect Volusianus: 'It is a saying worthy of the majesty of a ruler, if the prince professes himself bound by the laws: for even our authority depends upon that of the law. And, in fact, the most important thing in government is that power should be subject to laws' . . . [And] in the judgment of God, a ruler is not free from the directive power of the law; but should voluntarily and without constraint fulfil it.[30]

St Thomas does, however, accord to the ruler the right to dispense from the application of laws in special cases in order to achieve justice. And in the fourteenth century, if Jason de Mayno (a civilian

---

[26] *Dialogue of the Exchequer*, preface, in *English Historical Documents 1042–1189*, ed. D. Douglas, (London, 1968), ii. 491.

[27] *S.Th.* 1a 2ae 96. 5. St Thomas also in a disconnected sentence at the end of qu. 96. 5 declares that 'the ruler is above the law also in the sense that he may, if it be expedient, change the law, or dispense from it according to time and place'.

[28] In the *Decretals* 1. 2. 6 (these were papal ordinances and decisions).

[29] Note the use of the Roman praetorian formula: D. 2. 2.

[30] *S.Th.* 1a 2ae 96. 5.

of the late fifteenth) is correct in his citations, the two most celebrated of the Commentators, Bartolus of Saxoferrato and Baldus de Ubaldis, seem also to have considered that the ruler was not himself subject to the law. Bartolus, according to Jason wrote that whenever the prince does something based on certain knowledge ('ex certa scientia'), this removes all obstacles of law ('tollit omne obstaculum juris'), which must mean in plain language that the prince is entitled to know better than the law and to act accordingly.[31] Baldus is cited as attributing to the prince

a fullness of power (*plenitudo potestatis*), and whenever he wills something on the basis of certain knowledge, no one may say to him, Why do you do these things? . . . In another place Baldus says that both Pope and prince may, out of certain knowledge, do all things above the law, or contrary to law or outside the law (*super jus et contra jus et extra jus*).[32]

But an opposite opinion was growing. In the thirteenth century, above all in England, there was strong resistance to the idea that the king might be above the law; and the contrary proposition passed definitively from the realm of admonition and moral precept into that of a supposed positive constitutional rule. A famous milestone (even if one which requires interpretation in the light of its own special historical setting) is Magna Carta, the 'Great Charter' conceded by the English King John in 1215, chapter 39, of which provides that 'no free man shall be taken or imprisoned, or disseised or outlawed or exiled or in any way ruined, nor will we go or send against him, except by the lawful judgment of his peers or by the law of the land (*per legem terrae*)'. 'The king', wrote J. A. P. Jones—though in relation to chapter 61 which provided for a process against the king if he misbehaved in regard to the terms which he had promised in the Great Charter—'the king was now under the law in the constitutional sense.'[33] This now became a commonplace. In 1258 Henry III's barons, as Susan Reynolds puts it, 'accused his half-brothers of whispering to him damnably that a prince was not subject to laws',[34] a detail which shows well enough how the opposite doctrine was digging itself in. At about the same time the churchman Henry of Bracton was writing his treatise *De*

[31] Com. on C. 1. 19. 1. [32] Comm. on D. 1. 4. 1.

[33] *King John and Magna Carta* (London, 1971), 105.

[34] *Kingdoms* (see n. 17), 49. Ullmann, *Medieval Political Thought* (see Ch. 3 n. 12), 150, points out that ch. 39 of Magna Carta owes something to an edict of the emperor Conrad (1036).

legibus et consuetudinibus Angliae ('On the Laws and Customs of England') in which he not only rehearsed the familiar arguments about how seemly it is for kings to obey the law which they enforce,[35] but also gave classical expression to an imperative version of this slogan:

The king should not himself be subject to man, but should be subject to God and the law (*rex non debet esse sub homine, sed sub Deo et sub lege*), seeing that it is the law that makes the king ... Let the king accord to the law what the law accords to him, namely sovereign power; for where will and not law is sovereign, there no king can be said to be.[36]

Opinion in the French world was similar, even if less trenchantly expressed. When laws were being fixed for the new crusaders' kingdom of Jerusalem in 1100 (by the process of selection from the various customs of the nations represented there) Godfrey of Bouillon, the new ruler, with the consent of his barons, established and accepted them as customs by which 'he and his people' were to be governed.[37] In the following century Bracton's French contemporary, Philippe de Beaumanoir, wrote that the nobles were bound to observe the customary laws and to see that their subjects did so too; and that if the nobles infringed the laws or allowed their infringement, the king must not tolerate this, 'for he is bound to keep, and to see kept, the customary laws of his kingdom'.[38]

THE NATURE AND PURPOSE OF LAW

Just as in the earlier Middle Ages, writers of the twelfth and thirteenth centuries and later continue to stress the connection between law and the common good, or between law and justice, values which are the object of human government. We find also, however, in the *Summa Theologica* of St Thomas Aquinas, the first systematic exposition of human law, which is defined and crucially related (as will be seen later) to the higher law of nature and of God.

St Thomas, like other writers before and after him, defines and describes law in imperative terms, or at least in terms which do not

---

[35] Bracton, ed. and trans. S. Thorne, 4 vols. (Cambridge, Mass., 1968), 3. 9. 3.
[36] Ibid. 1. 8. 5.
[37] Jean d'Ibelin, *Assizes of Jerusalem*, 1; Carlyles, *Medieval Theory* (see Ch. 3 n. 29), iii. 43.
[38] Beaumanoir, *Coutumes du Beauvaisis*, ed. Salmon (1899–1900), 24. 682.

reflect consciousness of the 'secondary' rules, in recent times classified by H. L. A. Hart, as characteristic parts of the legal system. Law, he says, is 'a rule or measure of action in virtue of which one is led to perform certain actions and restrained from the performance of others'.[39] Again, whereas a private person 'has no authority to compel right living, . . . law, to be effective in promoting right living, must have such compelling force . . . The power of compulsion belongs either to the community as a whole, or to its official representative whose duty it is to inflict penalties . . . He alone, therefore, has the right to make laws.'[40] From these and other premises we may, he says, 'gather the correct definition of law. It is nothing else than a rational ordering of things which concern the common good, promulgated by whoever is charged with the care of the community'.[41]

The relation of law to the common good is uniformly insisted on, sometimes with specific mention of law, sometimes with the idea of law merely implicit in the wider idea of rule and government; and often in emphatic repudiation of the abuse of law and government for a ruler's personal advantage. John of Salisbury, who died in 1180 and whose book *Policraticus* was 'an encyclopaedia of the institutional and intellectual imperatives of the time',[42] wrote that

the prince is said to be free from the bonds of law not in the sense that it would be licit for him to do wrong, but in the sense that—for love of what is right, not from fear of punishment—it is for him to practise justice, to attend to the best interests of the state, and in everything to put the benefit of others before his own private desires. Who will speak, in connection with public affairs, of 'the will of the prince', since in such affairs he is not allowed to have any will of his own, save what law and justice point out to him, and the common interest requires? . . . The prince is in fact the servant of the public good, and the slave of justice, and he represents the public in that, with justice and impartiality, he punishes the wrongs and injuries of all men, and puts down all crimes.[43]

Bracton, in the next century, wrote forcefully to similar effect;[44] as did Beaumanoir, with specific reference to royal legislation, which—among other conditions to be mentioned shortly—must be for the

---

[39] *S.Th.* 1a 2ae 90. 1.   [40] *S.Th.* 1a 2ae 90. 3.
[41] *S.Th.* 1a 2ae 90. 4.   [42] Mundy, *Europe* (see n. 24), 18.
[43] *Policraticus* 4. 2.
[44] Bracton, *On the Laws and Customs of England*, ed. Thorne, 3. 9. 2–3.

public benefit ('pour le commun pourfit').[45] St Thomas, also abstracting law from the ruler and legislator, wrote that

since every part bears the same relation to its whole as the imperfect to the perfect, and since one man is a part of that perfect whole which is the community, it follows that the law must have as its proper object the well-being of the whole community . . . Law, strictly understood, has as its first and principal object the ordering of the common good.[46]

Law for St Thomas had, however, a moral dimension which precludes the common good being understood in purely material terms, since 'the true object of law is to induce those subject to it to seek their own virtue. And since virtue is that which makes its possessor good, it follows that the proper effect of law is the welfare of those for whom it is promulgated: either absolutely or in some certain respect.'[47] For Marsilius of Padua, on the other hand, law 'had in itself no moral overtones and offered no short-cut to the achievement of salvation',[48] but its end was equally, even if purely in human terms, the welfare of the citizens from whom its authority was derived.

St Thomas also insisted on the connection of law with reason, the channel through which the law of nature could be apprehended by human intelligence: 'Human law has the quality of law only in so far as it proceeds according to right reason; and in this respect it is clear that it derives from the eternal law. In so far as it deviates from reason it is called an unjust law, and has the quality not of law but of violence.'[49] The justice of laws is appraised by reference to three tests by which they stand or fall:

Now laws can be considered just, either with respect to their object, that is when they are directed to the common welfare, or with respect to their author, that is when the law which is enacted does not exceed the powers of him who enacts it; or again with reference to their form, when the burdens they impose upon the citizens are distributed in such proportion as to promote the common welfare . . . Contrariwise, laws may be unjust for two reasons. Firstly, when they are detrimental to human welfare, being contrary to the norms we have just established. Either with respect to their object, as when a ruler enacts laws which are burdensome to his subjects

[45] *Coutumes* (see n. 38), 34. 1043; 49. 6, 1512; 48. 1499; Carlyles, *Medieval Theory* (see Ch. 3 n. 29), 3. 49–51.
[46] *S.Th.* 1a 2ae 90. 2.   [47] *S.Th.* 1a 2ae 92. 1.
[48] Ullmann, *Medieval Political Thought* (see Ch. 3 n. 12), 208.
[49] *S.Th.* 1a 2ae 93. 3.

and which do not make for common prosperity, but are designed better to serve his own cupidity and vainglory. Or with respect to their author; if a legislator should enact laws which exceed the powers vested in him. Or, finally, with respect to their form; if the burdens, even though they are concerned with the common welfare, are distributed in an inequitable manner throughout the community. Laws of this sort have more in common with violence than with legality . . . Secondly, laws may be unjust through being contrary to divine goodness: such as tyrannical laws enforcing idolatry . . .[50]

In addition, therefore, to the central value of the common good, St Thomas could be said in modern terms to point to the conceptions both of *vires* and of equality before the law as a requirement of legislative equity and non-discrimination.

CUSTOM AND LEGISLATION

In the passages cited in the foregoing section St Thomas might seem to speak as though he had only statute law, the conscious enactment of a ruler, in mind. But when he comes to speak about the conditions which justify a change in the law it is evident that he regarded law as the product of custom as much as of legislation. At the beginning of this chapter's period, indeed, Gratian's *Decretum* had spoken of custom as the only form in which human law existed, and, citing Isidore of Seville to this effect, Gratian wrote that what is right according to human law may be understood to result from 'customs lawfully recorded and handed down' ('mores jure conscripti et traditi').[51] St Thomas accorded a higher status to law when customary than when statutory, inasmuch as statute implies change, and with it the disturbance of customary observance:

As has been said, change in human law is justified only to the extent that it benefits the general welfare. Now the very fact of change in the law is, in a certain sense, detrimental to the public welfare. This is because, in the observance of law, custom is of great importance; so much so, that any action which is opposed to general custom, even if itself of little importance, always seems more serious. So when law is changed its coercive power is diminished, to the extent that custom is set aside. Thus human law should never be changed unless the benefits which result to the public

[50] *S.Th.* 1a 2ae 96. 4.
[51] *Decretum*, D. 1; Carlyles, *Medieval Theory* (see Ch. 3 n. 29), ii. 99.

interest are such as to compensate for the harm done. This may be the case if the new statutes contain great and manifest advantages; or if there is urgent necessity due to the fact that the old law contains evident injustice, or its observance is excessively harmful.[52]

But both customary observance and deliberate enactment are valid modes of lawmaking. Human reason and will lie behind both; in the latter case expressed by words, in the former by actions:

In the same way law can be changed and explained by means of actions, many times repeated, such as result in custom; and it can thus happen that new customs arise, which have the validity of law; in the sense that the multiplication of such exterior actions clearly manifests the interior movement of the will and the concept of reason. For whatever is done frequently would seem to result from a deliberate judgment of reason. In this sense custom has the power of law, it may annul law and it may act as the interpreter of law.[53]

Even a community which is not authorized to make laws for itself can, he held, develop a custom which may attain the status of law if it is tolerated by the legislative power; this toleration being taken to signify approval.[54]

The students of the newly arisen Roman legal science were not all of one mind with St Thomas about this. For them the question of the validity of custom was essentially related to the history of the *lex regia* attributed to Ulpian. If the people, in delegating their power to make laws to the *princeps*, had made an irrevocable surrender of it, then they could no longer make law by custom or otherwise. If on the other hand they retained a residual legislative power, then the *lex regia* could not prevent them from developing binding custom. The Glossators Azo, Hugolinus, Bulgarus, and John Bassianus held that the people had not, in fact, finally abdicated their power; and the last two even held that a universal custom abrogates statute, and does so even if it is only a local custom, provided that it has been adopted knowingly and deliberately.[55] On the other side of the question, Irnerius, the founder of the new jurisprudence, and Placentinus had denied the validity of custom as law,[56] at least its power to abrogate statute.

---

[52] *S.Th.* 1a 2ae 97. 2.   [53] *S.Th.* 1a 2ae 97. 3.
[54] Ibid.
[55] Passages cited in Carlyles, *Medieval Theory* (see Ch. 3 n. 29), ii. 63 ff.
[56] Ibid. ii. 60 f.

There was a certain unreality in these debates of the twelfth- and early thirteenth-century civilians, though one natural to students of a Roman law transmitted to the Middle Ages in the form which it had acquired in ages of absolutism when imperial legislation overshadowed all other sources of law. For in fact, as was seen in the previous chapter, the basic stock of law in medieval Western Europe was customary. The conception of law as primarily that which is made by a lawgiver was, as the Carlyles wrote, 'wholly foreign to the middle ages. To them the law was not primarily something made or created at all, but something which existed as a part of the national or local life. The law was primarily custom, legislative acts were not expressions of will, but records or promulgations of that which was recognised as already binding upon men.'[57] A good illustration of this, from the turn of the periods covered by this chapter and the last, is provided by the 'Assizes of Jerusalem'; in essence a statute formally promulgated, but put together from customary-law materials.

By the time St Thomas was writing, in the last third of the thirteenth century, the picture had begun to change; although he accords high rank to custom, his clear references to statute law, and to the essentially statute-related idea of conscious alteration of the law, may reflect the emergence of legislation as a factor in legal systems of greater significance than before. It was still possible at about the same time for Bracton to depict England as governed only by unwritten and customary law,[58] and for Beaumanoir to assume that in France all pleas were determined according to custom.[59] The great monument of medieval German law (and also the first prose work in the German language), the *Sachsenspiegel* ('Mirror of the Saxons') composed between 1215 and 1235 by Eike von Repgow, was simply a compilation of the customary law of the land, including feudal law; it served as a model for other similar works elsewhere in Germany.[60] But new influences were at work.

There was, first of all, the new acquaintance with the legislation-oriented legal world of Rome, which must have had its effect irrespective of disagreements about the role of custom. Secondly, and in practice probably of greater importance, there was the new kind of European kingdom, stronger and more self-confident than

[57] Ibid. iii. 40.
[58] Bracton (ed. Thorne), F1.
[59] *Coutumes* (see n. 38), 24. 727, 61. 1780.
[60] Heinrich Mitteis, *Deutsche Rechtsgeschichte* (Munich, 16th edn., 1981), 130.

in the earlier Middle Ages, and hence taking more on itself. 'Not only did kings often need to override custom in order to raise taxes and armies', wrote Susan Reynolds, 'but, as population grew, so government had to become more complex, and more laws and more enforcement were required. Legislation therefore became more frequent and more recognisable as such.'[61] Even early in the reign of the German emperor Frederick Barbarossa (1152–90) his chancery had declared that 'there are two things by which our empire is ruled: the divine laws of the emperors (*leges sanctae imperatorum*) and the good customs of our predecessors and ancestors (*usus bonus predecessorum et patrum nostrorum*)'.[62]

But the legislation which now begins to play a greater part in legal life was not regarded as the product of the king's sole will. Just as in the earlier age, in conformity with Germanic tradition, novelties in government were thought to require the assent of the people or of some body that could be taken to speak for them, so now too, in every state of which a record survives, consultation and even something like consensus were expected in the process of making new law or changing old. To this extent, as has been seen, the idea that the prince's will makes law was not accepted and was rarely even entertained. Already in 1187 or thereabouts the English law-book called 'Glanvill' had stated that laws, even if unwritten, are regarded as promulgated if they amount to the regulation of doubtful matters and carry the authority of the prince after he has taken counsel with the chief men (*proceres*).[63] The mid-thirteenth-century *Summa de legibus*, composed in Normandy, distinguished custom from enactments; the latter are not merely approved by the prince but are *conservate* ('taken up by', 'received'?) by the people.[64] Bracton wrote that there was no absurdity in calling the unwritten laws of England *leges*, since this rank belongs to 'whatever shall have been fixed and approved with the prior authority of king or prince, on the advice and consent of the great men and the general backing of the community (*reipublicae communi sponsione*)'.[65] In France Beaumanoir, after reconstructing the origin of government from a supposed state of general strife

---

[61] Reynolds, *Kingdoms* (see n. 17), 46.
[62] Fuhrmann, *Germany in the High Middle Ages*, tr. T. Reuter (Cambridge, 1986), 153.
[63] Prologue, ed. G. D. G. Hall, 2.
[64] *Summa de legibus* 10. 1.   [65] Bracton, 1. 1. 2.

ending in the creation of a king, attributed to this king the right to make laws for his subjects (*commandemens et establissemens*); these laws, however, must not only be made, as has been seen, for the common benefit—and for reasonable cause—but also *par grant conseil*, i.e. after consulting with a council of the kingdom's great men.[66] In Spain King Alfonso X of Castile (1252–84) promulgated a law-book called the *Siete Partidas* which formally prohibited a prince from making new laws without the consent of the people; what this may have meant is suggested by the king's confession to the Cortes of Barcelona in 1283 that 'if we or our successors should wish to make any general constitution or statute in Catalonia, we will do this with the approbation and consent of the prelates, barons, knights, and citizens of Catalonia or of the larger or saner of those summoned [to the Cortes]'.[67] In Germany, an imperial assembly at Worms in 1231–2 was asked

if any of the princes of the land can make constitutions or new laws without the consent of the better or more important people of the land? With the consent of the princes, it was so defined concerning this question: that neither princes nor anyone else can make constitutions or new laws unless the better and more important people of the land have first agreed.[68]

The Carlyles wrote of evidence like this that it was

characteristic of the whole medieval tradition. It is for the prince or king to issue or promulgate laws, and without his authority this cannot be done; but to make his action legitimate he must consult the great and wise men of the nation; and the people or whole community has its place, for they have to receive or observe the law.[69]

These conceptions are the roots of the European parliamentary tradition.

Natural Law

The doctrine that human law and actions should conform with an eternal, higher law, having survived from classical antiquity into the early medieval and Christian world, and having been there reinforced by a separate stream of specifically Christian teaching

---

[66] *Coutumes* (see n. 38), 45. 1453. [67] Mundy, *Europe* (see n. 24), 407.
[68] Ibid. 407–8. [69] *Medieval Theory* (see Ch. 3 n. 29), iii. 47.

centred on the Ten Commandments and the Gospels, underwent in the twelfth and thirteenth centuries a notable development, associated particularly with St Thomas Aquinas.

The *Decretum* of Gratian published not long after 1139, a collection and reconciliation of the canon laws in force and ultimately the basis of the *Codex Iuris Canonici*, distinguished divine or natural law from human law, but, like the writings of the earliest Church Fathers, related this natural law to the Decalogue and to Christ's commandment of love of one's neighbour: 'The law of nature is that which is contained in the Law and the Gospel, by which everyone is commanded to do unto others as he would wish to be done unto him, and is prohibited from doing unto others that which he would be unwilling to be done unto himself.'[70] This natural law

is antecedent both in point of time and in point of rank to all things. For whatever has been adopted as custom, or prescribed in writing, if contrary to natural law, is to be held null and void ... Thus both ecclesiastical and secular statutes, if they are shown to be contrary to natural law, are to be altogether rejected (*penitus sunt excludendae*).[71]

In the following century, under the influence of Aristotle whose writings were just becoming known in the West, this revelation-centred conception of natural law began to give way to a conception related to man's reason and what was discoverable by it. Thus William of Auxerre (d. *c.*1231), asserting the human capacity to recognize good and evil and God's will, made reason the criterion of natural law: this was that which natural reason, without much or even any need for reflection, tells us what we must do ('id quod naturalis ratio sine omni deliberatione aut sine magna dictat esse faciendum').[72] Similarly Alexander of Hales (d. 1245) saw human reason as the basis of the recognition of natural law, while he accepted that some of its parts might be adapted to meet actual conditions;[73] and St Bonaventure (d. 1274), reproducing a Stoic theme, wrote that what natural reason commands is called the natural law.[74] Natural law therefore in the thirteenth century is now seen as the law of right reason, which coincides with the biblical law

---

[70] *Decretum*, D. 1. This 'golden rule' as it was afterwards called, alludes to Matt. 7. 12.

[71] *Decretum*, D. 8. 2, 9 *ad fin.*   [72] *Aurea Doctons* fo. 169.

[73] See Felix Flückiger, *Geschichte des Naturrechtes* (Zurich, 1954), i. 426–8.

[74] Ibid.

but is not derived from it; and 'the germ of nature-based ethics, evolving from ancient philosophy, begins to part company with Christian morality and to form an autonomous department of its own'.[75]

The achievement of creating a total and organized synthesis of the natural law which is the product of reason, on the one hand, and Christian doctrine, on the other, belongs to St Thomas Aquinas. His contribution to legal theory, already mentioned in other connections, is most original in the area of natural law; it rests on both classical and Christian foundations, and some account of it must now be given.

First, St Thomas derived from Aristotle and ancient philosophy the notion of God as the highest good and the cause of all things which exist. These have an ideal potential; and 'partake' of good to the extent to which this potential is realized. The order of nature is the result; but, as order is the product of reason, a transcendent reason behind creation must be assumed. There exists also in creation, as a dimension of the principle of order, the principle of subordination, as e.g. the subordination of the individual to the collectivity, or of partial to principal objectives. The whole of creation—including the hierarchy descending from God through angels and then through men to beasts—acts according to the principle of subordination.[76]

The Stoic idea of an eternal universal law St Thomas presents as the external aspect of God's perfect wisdom, that is, his wisdom in its application to creation. It is essentially the law which flows from God's reason, from the ideal forms in the divine intellect, and is the first active principle of creation. This eternal law is received so to speak, is 'picked up'—in the world through two different media: partly through supernatural revelation (the *lex divina*)—here the specifically Christian doctrine is grafted to the ancient classical stock—which, when formulated by the Church, becomes positive law; and partly through natural law (*lex naturalis*), which is recognized as such by rational human nature and becomes the general norm of behaviour:

And so [rational creatures] have a certain share in the divine reason itself, deriving therefrom a natural inclination to such actions and ends as are fitting. [The Psalmist says] 'The light of Thy countenance, O Lord, is signed

[75] Ibid. i. 435.   [76] *S.Th.* 1a 1ae 96.

upon us': as though the light of natural reason, by which we discern good from evil, and which is the natural law, were nothing else than the impression of the divine light in us. So it is clear that the natural law is nothing else than the participation of the eternal law in rational creatures.[77]

The human reason

has to proceed from the precepts of the natural law . . . to other more particular dispositions. And such particular dispositions, arrived at by an effort of reason, are called human laws: provided that the other conditions necessary to all law, are observed[78] . . . Human law has the quality of law only so far as it proceeds according to right reason: and in this respect it is clear that it derives from the eternal law. In so far as it deviates from reason it is called an unjust law, and has the quality not of law but of violence.[79]

The precepts of the natural law are related to natural human inclinations, which for St Thomas include a natural inclination to good. From this starting-point, rational bases for human laws can be elaborated, such as the values of self-preservation, the propagation and upbringing of children, the desire for religious truth, the inclination to associate in organized society with others. Rules derived from the primary precepts of natural law (of which only one, namely: do good and avoid evil, is of the very highest rank) St Thomas called secondary natural law; these include what the Romans called *ius gentium*, and as an example St Thomas gives 'the norms governing buying and selling and other similar activities which are necessary to social intercourse: these derive from natural law because man is naturally a social animal'.[80] According as the natural law is applied in more and more particularized conditions—with what Kelsen might have called its progressive concretization—it becomes variable, and receptive of exceptions; local conditions, or changed conditions, may justify additions to or subtractions from it.[81] Impossible though it may be to codify its precepts in detail, however, the principle remains that a human law which conflicts with it is no law, but a corruption of law ('iam non erit lex, sed legis corruptio').[82]

Throughout the Middle Ages the concept of natural law was used as a sort of arsenal on neutral ground from which both sides to any controversy—such as those between pope and emperor, or later

[77] *S.Th.* 1a 2ae 91. 2.   [78] *S.Th.* 1a 2ae 91. 3.
[79] *S.Th.* 1a 2ae 93. 3.   [80] *S.Th.* 1a 2ae 95. 4.
[81] *S.Th.* 1a 2ae 94. 5.   [82] *S.Th.* 1a 2ae 95. 2.

between papacy and reformers—could draw weapons. But in the generation after St Thomas a quite different doctrine as to the source of human obligation arose, associated particularly with two Franciscans, the Scot John Duns Scotus (1265–1308) and the Englishman William of Occam, or Ockham (1290–1349). This doctrine centred on God's will, the expression of his infinite goodness, which was binding on human beings not for any supposed congruence with nature, or for any other particular objective reason, but simply because it *was* his will. But this had further implications certainly not intended by a devout Franciscan. For Ockham wrote H. Rommen,

an action is not good because of its correspondence with the essential nature of man, in which God's conception of Man in his essence and potential is reflected, *but because God wills it so*. God's will might equally have willed and prescribed that action's opposite . . . Thus Law is Will, pure Will, with no foundation in the nature of things.[83]

'Natural law', added A. P. D'Entrèves, '[thus] ceases to be the bridge between God and man; it affords no indication of the existence of an eternal and immutable order.'[84] But by floating off the idea of law from moral imperatives lying in nature, and attaching it to the idea of a superior will which cannot be questioned (albeit in this instance the will of an infinitely good God), an intellectual path seemed to have been smoothed out for the advance of will, generally and not with special reference to that of God, as a sufficient basis for legal obligation. This has been pointed to by modern writers as one of the intellectual roots of secular positivism, and of the notion—in its modern manifestations so destructive— that the state's will makes law.

A further, and very different, product of Ockham's thought is, according to Michel Villey, an emerging concept of the individual's natural *rights*. This arose in connection with a dispute about Franciscan poverty and how it was to be reconciled with the large possessions which the order in fact enjoyed. The pope conceded to the order the capacity to own property, a position which Ockham opposed, construing the Franciscans' situation in regard to property as one of use only. When the pope rejoined that this use was in fact a right (*ius*), Ockham undertook to distinguish *ius* from *usus*, and in

---

[83] *Die ewige Wiederkehr des Naturrechts* (Munich, 1947), 60.
[84] *Natural Law* (London, 1970), 69.

terms which gave the idea of a 'right' a more subjective colouration than had attached to the somewhat depersonalized Roman notion expressed by *ius*. This was the beginning of a trend which, as Villey put it, 'the individual . . . becomes the centre of interest for legal science, which henceforth strives to describe his legal attributes, the extent of his faculties, and of his individual rights'.[85]

EQUALITY

The theory that in principle all human beings are equal—as God's children—is held as universally among the writers of the High Middle Ages as it is among their predecessors. Ivo of Chartres (d. 1116) uses it to support the rule that if a free woman knowingly takes a slave in marriage, the marriage is to be regarded as valid, for 'we all have one Father in heaven'.[86] The *Decretum* of Gratian contains a canon which adds to this: 'and all men, rich and poor, free and slave, will have to render equally an account of themselves and of their souls.'[87] In the same era the Glossators expressed the same principle, if from the standpoint of the newly revived classical Roman law rather than from that of Christian doctrine. Bulgarus spoke of the 'law of nature by which all men are equal',[88] and Placentinus said that 'observation of nature' showed the equality of all.[89] The thirteenth-century compilations of German customary law, the *Sachsenspiegel* and the *Schwabenspiegel*, also acknowledge the original equality of men; as do Bracton and Beaumanoir in England and France.[90] But all those authorities address this topic in the first place only in order to concede, or explain, the contradiction of the principle of human equality visible all around them in the institution of slavery or in political subordination. The relevance of private property, and its uneven distribution, to the theory of human equality was still evident in this period, though the High Middle Ages had come to terms with private property as the early Church Fathers never did. Similarly there are references to what might today be called legislative equity, in the precept of St Thomas

---

[85] *Le Formation de la pensée juridique moderne: Le Franciscanisme et le droit* (Paris, 1963), 210.

[86] *Decretum*, D. 8. 52, 156.   [87] C. 29, qu. 2, c. 1.

[88] Comm. on D. 17. 22.   [89] *Summa Inst.* 1. 3.

[90] Beaumanoir, 45. 1453; Bracton, 1. 8. 1.

regarding a fair distribution of burdens in the state; and in that of Beaumanoir regarding the imposition of taxation in proportion to the means of those liable to it.

Equal treatment in the special context of criminal law is, however, not a value in this period with the same shape as it has today. St Thomas shows consciousness, and acceptance, of the relevance of rank to the criminal law in his reference to blows struck by or against a ruler. But he does not countenance differing treatment of persons, both delinquents in the same degree, by reference to their respective stations in life; though the appearance of widely separated classes in his time led in practice to discrimination of this kind. 'The problem of the jurist', wrote J. H. Mundy, 'was no longer so much to make the punishment fit the crime as to make it fit the status and means of the criminal. He therefore turned to his books to disinter the Roman distinction between the *honestiores* and the humbler folk.'[91] The magistrate Albert of Gandino thought the difference should turn on whether the penalty of the law was pecuniary or corporal: 'In the first case the rich ought to be punished more severely [whereas for the poor] the penalty should be restrained and diminished . . . In the second case, the poor should be more severely punished.'[92]

A more notorious differentiation was that which accorded to the (very numerous) persons entitled to rank as clergy an immunity— whose frontiers were sometimes angrily disputed[93]—from trial by secular tribunals, and the right to be dealt with by the ecclesiastical authority only, which as a rule imposed far milder penalties. Indeed it was partly out of repugnance for the barbaric penalties imposed by secular courts—which the Church writers constantly criticized—that the Church defended its privilege in this area so strongly.[94]

The period also contains, on the other hand, improvements in the administration of criminal justice which slowly tended to make it more rational and more equal for all. Resistance developed to old processes such as trial by battle and by ordeal. 'The attack on the old modes of proof and the lively prosecution of justice were favoured by those institutions and communities that had a strong

---

[91] Mundy, *Europe* (see n. 24), 250, 455.

[92] *Tractatus de maleficiis* 39. 22. 8; H. Kantorowicz, *Albrecht von Gandinus und das Strafrecht der Scholastik*, 2 vols. (Berlin, 1907, 1926).

[93] It was over this matter that the quarrel arose between Henry II of England and Thomas à Becket, archbishop of Canterbury, which ended in the latter's murder.

[94] Mundy, *Europe* (see n. 24), 337–9.

sense of the individual's responsibility and his citizenship or membership', wrote J. H. Mundy. 'Such entities were not only opposed to the protection of putative wrongdoers by family and local interests, but were also convinced of the advantage to be gained by making all members or citizens equal in rights or obligations, save for differences allowed to individuals in return for special functions or services.'[95]

Three particular institutions, slavery, political subordination, and private property, presented especial problems in relation to the doctrine of human equality, and require separate treatment.

SLAVERY

Throughout this period slavery was still part of ordinary life. It had, indeed, died out in northern Europe (except in England) by the twelfth century, merging in the status of villein, one tied to the land he worked largely for his lord's benefit, but at least free from being bought and sold; but in southern Europe it remained common, slaves being imported to Italy and Spain and Portugal from northern Africa and the Levant. The legal theory of the period could not overlook so flagrant a conflict with the doctrine of human equality. Both canon lawyers and civilians agreed that it was no part of the law of nature, but had grown up as part of the laws of mankind (*ius gentium*). The canonists said that sin, not nature, was at its root; 'the origin of slavery [was] to be found not in some inherent and natural distinction in human nature, but in the fact that sin, as it [had] depraved men's nature, so it [had] also disordered all the natural relations of human society';[96] and the Church, though its influence did much to mitigate the lot of slaves and contributed ultimately to slavery's disappearance, was itself at this period very frequently an owner of slaves.[97] Secular sources are more down-to-earth in explaining the phenomenon: Beaumanoir points to the capture of prisoners of war, to self-sale into servitude in order to relieve poverty, and to men's inability to resist the powerful men

[95] Mundy, *Europe* (see n. 24), 557.
[96] Carlyles, *Medieval Theory* (see Ch. 3 n. 29), ii. 119.
[97] Ibid. ii. 120 ff.

who reduced them to slavery;[98] and the *Sachsenspiegel* also attributed it to unjust violence.[99]

A very different note is struck, however, by St Thomas Aquinas, who, in the operation of importing Aristotle's teaching into the Christian theology and ethics, adopted also Aristotle's smooth explanation of slavery as a deviation from the natural order in terms of some men being born with a slave disposition anyway. This suggests two levels of 'naturalness': on the primary level, slavery is certainly not natural, but in its consequences in particular cases, it may be said to be so:

[What is naturally right or naturally just may emerge from looking at the relation of two things] not absolutely or in the abstract, but as involving a consequence . . . From the bare nature of the case there is no reason for this man rather than that man being a slave. It is only when it is looked at pragmatically in its results that, as is said in [Aristotle's] *Politics*, it is beneficial for one man that he should be ruled by another who is wiser; and beneficial for the latter that he should have the services of the former.[100]

St Thomas's followers, Ptolemy of Lucca and Egidius Colonna (also called Giles of Rome), took up and passed on Aristotle's doctrine quite openly. The former wrote that among men, as in other things there will be a stronger and a weaker variety, and so 'it is accepted that some will by nature be complete slaves. Then it happens that some are naturally deficient in reason, and these it is right to put to some sort of servile work, since they cannot use reason; and this must be called just and natural.'[101] The latter describes a natural slave as one who is physically powerful but weak in understanding; he will naturally live under another's rule (and may not even realize he is being ruled).[102]

POLITICAL SUBORDINATION

In regard to political subordination, on the other hand, there is a curious reversal of perspectives; here it is the secular lawyer who

---

[98] Beaumanoir, 45. 1453.
[99] Carlyles, *Medieval Theory* (see Ch. 3 n. 29), iii. 42.
[100] *S.Th.* 2a 2ae 57. 3.
[101] *De regimine principum* (attributed to St Thomas, but this part actually by Ptolemy), 2. 10.
[102] Ibid., preface and 1. 2. 7.

strikes the idealizing note, and the theologian who is more realistic. Beaumanoir, writing in the 1280s, thought that in the original state of nature all men were free and of the same degree of freedom ('franc et d'une meisme franchise'); but as it became obvious, what with every man thinking himself as great a lord as every other, that there was no hope of living in peace, they elected a king as their common lord.[103] St Thomas, writing a little earlier, did not share the idea of an original political equality (as distinct from an original natural freedom). Subordination (*dominium*), he wrote, came in two forms; that of personal slavery was incompatible with man's primal state of innocence, and arose only in consequence of his sin; but the same was not necessarily true of civil government and hence of political subordination:

Subjection [*dominium*] can be understood in two ways. In one sense it is understood as corresponding to slavery, and thus one to whom another is subjected as a slave is called *dominus*. *Dominium* is understood in a different sense when applied to those subordinate in any way, so that one who exercises civil government, and who controls free men, maybe called *dominus*. *Dominium* in the former sense, whereby one man is subjected to another, could not have existed in man's state of innocence; but in the latter sense it could. The reason is, that the slave differs from the free man in that the free man has his own sphere and purpose of existence, whereas the slave lives at another's pleasure [*ordinatur ad alium*] . . . and for his convenience.[104]

The reasons why the purely civil subordination might have existed in the state of innocence, and so be compatible with man's nature as a being tended towards civic existence, are entirely practical ones, already cited;[105] and such reasons also save political subordination from conflict with the natural law of equality.

PROPERTY

The *Decretum* of Gratian (*c*.1140) restates the early Christian opinion that the wealth of the earth was by nature the common property of all mankind, and that private property is one of the consequences of the Fall into sin; the communism idealized by Plato is praised, and the rise of the concepts of 'mine' and 'yours',

---

103 Beaumanoir 45. 1453.   104 *S.Th.* 1a 2ae 96. 4.
105 Above, in the section on 'Natural Law'.

now embodied in custom and ordinance, is ascribed to man's iniquity ('per iniquitatem alius hoc dixit esse suum, et alius istud').[106] But the philosophy of the age quickly came to better terms with private ownership, or, as Felix Flückiger said, to 'take the harm out of it'.[107] An early commentator on Gratian, Rufinus bishop of Assisi, wrote (c.1157) that natural law contains not only commands and prohibitions, but also what he called *demonstrationes*, indications of moral preference which stopped short of being obligatory, and gave as an example the ideal of community of property; long usage and statute had however sanctioned individual ownership, which must not be regarded as based in wickedness, but rather as blameless (*irreprehensibile*).[108] Thirteenth-century writers follow the same line. William of Auxerre (d. c.1231) and Alexander of Hales (d. 1245) both thought private property could be justified under natural law, the former pointing out that the institution of private property is presupposed by the commandment 'Thou shalt not steal'. This argument is also found in Azo (d. before 1235) and Accursius, the compiler of the *Glossa ordinaria* (d. c.1263), though the civil lawyers of the age are not unanimous about the status of private property in its relation to *ius naturale*.[109]

It is with St Thomas Aquinas that we encounter the first elaborate justification of private property, not indeed its ascription to natural law (he continues in the tradition of associating this rather with communal ownership), but its legitimate creation by positive human law as an addition to the law of nature.[110] In one passage he says that the naturally right or naturally just may be appraised both absolutely (as with reproductive biology) and having regard to consequences. He takes ownership of property as an example: 'considered in itself there is no reason why this field should belong to this man rather than to that man; but when you take into account its being put under cultivation and peacefully used, then, as the Philosopher [Aristotle] demonstrates, it is fitting that it should be owned by this and not that person.'[111] Later on he expands this in terms again recalling Aristotle.[112]

---

[106] D. 8. 1; C. 12, qu. 1 c. 2.
[107] 'Verharmlosung': *Geschichte* (see n. 73), i. 1407–8.
[108] *Summa Decret.* D. 1 Dict. Grat. ad c. 1; D. 8, Diff. quoque.
[109] Carlyles, *Medieval Theory* (see Ch. 3 n. 29), ii. 41 ff.
[110] *S.Th.* 2a 2ae 66. 2.   [111] *S.Th.* 2a 2ae 57. 2.
[112] Above, Ch. 1, 'Theory of Property'.

With respect to material things there are two points which man must consider. First, concerning the power of acquisition and disposal: and in this respect private possession is permissible. It is also necessary to human life for three reasons. First, because everyone is more concerned with the obtaining of what concerns himself alone than with the common affairs of all or of many others: for each one, avoiding extra labour, leaves the common task to the next man; as we see when there are too many officials. Secondly, because human affairs are dealt with in a more orderly manner when each has his own business to go about: there would be complete confusion if everyone tried to do everything. Thirdly, because this leads to a more peaceful condition of man; provided each is content with his own. So we see that it is among those who possess something, jointly and in common that disputes most frequently arise.[113]

He adds, however, the moral injunction that men should not hold material things as their own but to the common benefit, each readily sharing them with others in their necessity; and that urgent necessity may justify what otherwise would be theft.[114]

The special relation of labour to wealth, and the effort of production as justifying ownership, is occasionally noticed in this period. St Thomas appears to advert to it in the reference to cultivation of farmland cited above. So too does John of Paris, writing in the first years of the fourteenth century; in rejecting papal claims to an overriding dominion such as would justify the imposition of taxation, he held that the possessions of laymen were acquired by their own labour and diligence, by which they obtained true dominion over goods.[115]

It is in contexts like this that opinion hardened in favour of the legitimacy of property; and, consequentially, against arbitrary expropriation. The prince, wrote the civilian Odofridus in the late thirteenth century, is lord of what his realm contains not in the sense of ownership, only in the sense of being its protector ('non quoad proprietatem sed quoad protectionem').[116] William of Ockham similarly records the opinion that

the emperor is not lord of all temporal things . . . in such a way that it is licit or possible for him to dispose of all such things according to his will; however, he is in a certain manner the master of all things to the extent that,

---

[113] *S.Th.* 2a 2ae 57. 2.   [114] *S.Th.* 2a 2ae 66. 7.
[115] *Tractatus de potestate regia et papali* 7.
[116] Comm. on Digest, fo. 2. 5; 'Prima Constitutio', 2. 5; Carlyles, *Medieval Theory* (see Ch. 3 n. 29), v. 102.

in the teeth of any objection, he can use and apply them for the common benefit, whenever he judges that this is to be preferred to the interest of individuals . . . [He may not do this arbitrarily, but only] on account of the owners' guilt, or for good reason, i.e. for the public benefit.[117]

The civil lawyers generally emphasized that, even where public necessity justifies an expropriation, compensation must be paid; though some thought that, where the expropriating measure weighed equally on all, compensation was not called for, only when its burden fell on a single individual.[118] The utility of doctrine limiting expropriation in conflicts about taxation is evident.

EQUITY

A work which probably belongs to the very early twelfth century and so to the first generation of scholars of the rediscovered Roman law is the so-called *Petri exceptiones legum Romanorum*. In his prologue the author undertakes to 'trample underfoot' anything in the laws which offends equity (*aequitati contrarium*); and later on he says the law's precept should be observed, 'unless some reason shall appear, which may suggest the necessity of mixing some modification into what it says'; such a reason, justifying a judge in adapting the strict law, must lie in the highest of public or private interests.[119] Very similar expressions recur throughout the age of the Glossators; but it is not clear that the equity they have in mind is something suggesting itself to the judge in the circumstances of a particular case, or is rather something already well established in traditional authority as a modifying factor, i.e. itself now part of the law. Thus Bulgarus, in the middle of the twelfth century, wrote that the judge should give precedence to equity over strict law, but gave as an instance the rule that, 'in strict law, bargains are to be upheld. Yet equity differentiates cases: some bargains are not to be enforced, such as those induced by fraud, or duress, or violence, or those made with persons under disability.'[120] Here Bulgarus is

---

[117] *Dialogus*, pars 3, *Tractatus Secundus* 2. 23; Carlyles, *Medieval Theory* (see Ch. 3 n. 29), vi. 47.
[118] Gierke, *Political Theories* (see n. 22), 81, 179 ff.
[119] *Petri exceptiones*, prologue; 4. 3.
[120] Bulgarus, Comm. on D. 17. 90; Carlyles, *Medieval Theory* (see Ch. 3 n. 29), ii. 14.

parading modifying elements already entrenched in Roman law by the praetor, not giving his own suggestions for the operation of a free-floating judicial equity.[121]

It is with St Thomas Aquinas that we find a purer theory. Adopting Aristotle's doctrine about equity as a modification of strict law in order to do justice where the law unmodified would be unjust, St Thomas says we should not always judge according to written laws, for

judgment should be formed on the individual happening. But no written law can cover each and every such case, as Aristotle makes clear . . . Law is written down in order to manifest the lawgiver's meaning and intention. Yet sometimes it happens that, were he present, he would judge differently . . . Laws that are rightly enacted prove deficient where to observe them would be to offend against natural right. In such cases judgment should be delivered, not according to the letter of the law, but by recourse to equity, this being what the lawgiver aimed at . . . [If the legislator had foreseen such cases] he might have provided for them by law.[122]

In another passage St Thomas makes essentially the same point, though related rather to the needs of the public interest than to justice for an individual. Where some public emergency is such that the strict observance of a particular law would be ruinous, there ought to be dispensation from it; although, he says, the individual is not to be the judge of this for himself (so as to feel entitled to disregard the law) unless there is no time to refer the matter to 'princes, who on account of such cases have authority to dispense from statutes'.[123]

CRIMINAL LAW AND PUNISHMENT

In this connection, too, it is St Thomas who proposes a reasonably complete theoretical scheme, indicating the proper scope of criminal law, the legitimacy of punishment and its purpose, and the role to be assigned to the culprit's intent or lack of it. The scope of criminal law is to be determined bearing in mind 'the condition of the men who will be subject to it', that condition varying very greatly:

[121] Above, Ch. 2, 'Greek Philosophy and Roman Equity'.
[122] *S.Th.* 2a 2ae 60. 5. In this passage St Thomas cites also a Roman text, D. 1. 3. 25 (Modestinus).
[123] *S.Th.* 1a 2ae 96. 6.

Now human law is enacted on behalf of the mass of men, the majority of whom are far from perfect in virtue. For this reason human law does not prohibit every vice from which virtuous men abstain; but only the graver vices from which the majority can abstain; and particularly those vices which are damaging to others and which, if they were not prohibited, would make it impossible for human society to endure: as murder, theft, and suchlike, which are prohibited by human law.[124]

This emphasis on the element of 'harm to others' appears in another passage in a briefer form, where St Thomas derives the law against murder from the natural-law precept, 'Do harm to no man'.[125] It will be noticed that this theoretical basis for punishment, though St Thomas did not expressly declare it the only legitimate one, will not stretch far enough to cover the punishment of acts of moral turpitude not impinging on others—a curious premonition of the views of J. S. Mill in the nineteenth century.

Within the area where the criminal law legitimately functioned, its operation was for St Thomas mainly repressive and deterrent. There is also something of the reformative effect of criminal punishment, or the threat of it, on the actual or potential malefactor. In all these ways the innocent are made more secure.[126] There are, he says, some young men who, being virtuous, need only paternal guidance; but

there are others, of evil disposition and prone to vice, who are not easily moved by words. These it is necessary to restrain from wrongdoing by force and fear (*per vim et metum*) so that, they ceasing to do evil, a quiet life is assured to the rest of the community; and they are themselves drawn eventually, by force of habit, to do voluntarily what once they did only out of fear, and so to practise virtue. Such discipline which compels under fear of penalty is the discipline of law.[127]

The measure of punishment is to be proportioned to the wrong, though this may not imply an exact equivalence, since for a subject to strike his ruler is more serious than the reverse, and is not therefore adequately requited by the mere giving of a blow in return.[128]

A criminal penalty is unacceptable unless it is related to a moral fault; otherwise it is unjust; and the culprit's mental state is material

---

[124] *S.Th.* 1a 2ae 96. 2. Punishment 'a part of judging': 2a 2ae 60. 6.
[125] *S.Th.* 1a 2ae 95. 2.   [126] *S.Th.* 1a 2ae 95. 1.
[127] Ibid.   [128] *S.Th.* 2a 2ae 61. 4.

to the measure of his punishment. The chief reason against any mechanical equivalence of requital related to the nature of the injury, St Thomas says, 'seems to lie with the difference between involuntary and voluntary action; he who does an action involuntarily suffers the lighter penalty . . . The injury is augmented when the injurious action is voluntary, and is treated accordingly as a more important thing. Hence it calls for greater punishment in recompense.'[129] In a different context he says that 'whatever a man does in ignorance he does accidentally, and in consequence both human and divine law must consider the question of ignorance, in judging whether certain matters are punishable or pardonable'.[130]

THE INTERNATIONAL LEGAL ORDER

Nothing like a doctrine of a law of nations existed in the High Middle Ages. Nevertheless the period contains practical developments which, by disposing the European mind to the idea of a legal order transcending individual states, contributed to its emergence in a later age. For example, the revival of international trade which had begun in the earlier Middle Ages continued strongly in the era of the Crusades, and underlay the growth of rules of maritime law which were occasionally gathered into collections. The Rolls of Oléron, decisions given in the twelfth century by the maritime court at Oléron on the Atlantic coast of France, were widely recognized on the coasts of Western Europe and the Baltic, and were incorporated in the English 'Black Book of the Admiralty', parts of which go back to the twelfth and thirteenth centuries. Similarly the *Consolato del Mare*, a collection made at Barcelona in the fourteenth century, became canonical in the Mediterranean (and remained so right up to the nineteenth century).[131] Other examples are the occasional appearance of the pope or a king as arbitrator in disputes between princes not subject to a common jurisdiction;[132] the conclusion of

---

[129] *S.Th.* 2a 2ae 61. 4.   [130] *S.Th.* 1a 2ae 100. 9.

[131] A. Nussbaum, *A Concise History of the Law of Nations* (New York, 1962), 318 f.; A. Wegner, *Geschichte des Völkerrechts* (Stuttgart, 1936), 128 f.

[132] Nussbaum, *Law of Nations* 313; Wegner, *Geschichte* 121 ff.; W. Grewe, *Epochen der völkerrechtsgeschichte* (Baden-Baden, 1984), 119–30. Questions about the occupation, definition, and ownership of territory frequently arose. A symptom of what is perhaps a contemporary search for objective criteria rather than a genuine record of antiquity might be present in Giraldus Cambrensis's *Expugnatio Hiberniae*

treaties, most usually of a commercial character, between kings or between cities; and the growing custom, associated mainly with the Italian city-states, of placing standing consular representatives in other jurisdictions.[133]

On the plane of theory, both the civilians and the theologians contributed to the emergence of an international legal system. The most famous of the Commentators, Bartolus of Saxoferrato, yielded something from the Roman supposition of only one empire; the medieval emperor might be in title the 'dominus totius mundi' and 'rex universalis', but he acknowledged that, *de facto*, the world contained a number of independent kingdoms and principalities which 'recognized no superior', thus laying the ground for a system based on a plurality of mutually independent territorial sovereignties. His pupil and follower Baldus de Ubaldis consolidated this transition of thought by declaring that each king 'is an emperor in his own territory' ('rex in regno suo imperator regni sui'), thus making possible the application to the rulers of nations doctrines which Roman jurists had originally formed for the benefit of the emperor alone.[134]

Their younger contemporary, the Franciscan William of Ockham, also contributed to familiarizing in theory what had long been visible in practice, namely the coexistence and the equal status of a plurality of political bodies. In dealing, from the perspective of an opponent of papal pretension, with the passage of the imperial title from the Romans to the Greeks, and from them to the Franks and ultimately the Germans, he wrote that that title could be transferred by the body of humankind (the 'universitas mortalium') and that the Romans had, as such, no special privilege above 'all other nations' ('plus quam caeterae nationes'). The pope had no more God-given sovereignty over the emperor and his empire than over 'other kings and their kingdoms'. The imperial title, not being God-given, could be waived by the consent of the people in which it was vested; but it could also, in case of that people's fault and for

('Topography of Ireland')—written in the years shortly before and after 1200 and an immensely popular book in the High Middle Ages—in which, along with a lot of fabulous (and to the Irish disobliging) material, he describes how the ownership of the Isle of Man was once disputed between Ireland and Britain; the fact that poisonous reptiles lived on the island was thought decisive in Britain's favour (as none existed in Ireland). Part 2, ch. 48.

[133] Nussbaum, *Law of Nations*, 38–40.
[134] Grewe, *Epochen* (see n. 132), 19–30 and 148–56.

reasonable cause ('pro culpa Romanorum et ex causa rationabili') be withdrawn from them by the rest of humankind.[135]

Worth mentioning, finally, in this connection is the concept of the 'just war', which belongs especially to this period. The myriad doctrines on this have no place here; but a constant theme among writers on the subject is that, for a war to be just, it must (apart from other conditions) be waged by an authority with no superior, i.e. a sovereign state in the sense of modern usage.[136] The motive for this requirement was, in the twelfth and thirteenth centuries, the restriction of private warfare and brigandage between local war-lords. It must have contributed both to the notion of a plurality of sovereign states—since it takes two to have a fight—and, since 'just war' doctrines contain many other elements, to the idea of a transcendent order binding on them all.

---

[135] *Dialogus* 3. 2. 1. 29.
[136] F. H. Russell, *The Just War in the Middle Ages* (Cambridge, 1975), *passim*.

5
Renaissance and Reformation
(1350–1600)

Neither the opening nor the closing date of this chapter's period is a turning-point. But these later Middle Ages—if the expression may be allowed to cover a further century beyond the fifteenth[1]— enclose the two events which decisively condition intellectual life thereafter, namely, the revival of the Graeco-Roman tradition in art and literature, and the fracturing of the old Catholic unity of Western Europe with the Protestant Reformation. Both events eliminated factors which had been present in some form since the fall of the Western Roman empire and its replacement by the barbarian Christian kingdoms; and they brought into life the factors from which, in turn, the modern world was born: the secularization of public life and the emancipation of the lay individual from spiritual authority. Those features of the new age naturally found expression in its legal theory as elsewhere.

The external history of the period is most conspicuously marked by a rapid advance towards the nation-state, ruled by national kings of hitherto unknown strength, and tending to efface, in a larger territorial sovereignty, the independence of cities and other smaller units.[2] Germany and Italy were important exceptions: in the former the imperial position declined to one of mere prestige, its practical power reflecting merely that of the house of Habsburg, which monopolized the imperial title from 1438 on, but never set up as a purely German power or promoted a German nation-state; in Italy (though here too the larger powers such as Tuscany and Venice

---

[1] The Protestant Reformation, which is in a way the last act of the Middle Ages, ought as a 'period' to comprise also the Catholic reaction or 'Counter-Reformation': both were played out in the 16th cent., and indeed the curtain of settlement had not fallen on the scene even by 1600. The last volume of the Carlyles' *History of Medieval Political Thought in the West* is expressed in its title-page to cover the years 1300–1600.

[2] Fernand Braudel, *The Mediterranean and the Mediterranean World in the Age of Philip II*, pb. edn. (London, 1985), 338 ff.

were submerging the independence of the cities) the emergence of a national state was prevented by the division of the country between regional powers, the papal territory, and the southern kingdoms of Naples and Sicily, along with the continual conflicts of foreign powers on Italian soil.[3] But to the west, in England, France, and Spain, a new kind of kingdom was arising. The demands made in England and France by the Hundred Years War (1337–1453) between them[4] evoked in both a patriotic response to royal leadership in attack and in resistance, and left both by the mid-fifteenth century with national[5] kingships far stronger than before. These were also authoritarian in a high degree, their most celebrated representatives in this respect being the English monarchs Henry VIII (1509–47) and Elizabeth I (1558–1603)[6] and the French kings Louis XI (1461–83) and Francis I (1515–47); the latter is commonly regarded as the founder of the absolutist French monarchy. In Spain the marriage between Ferdinand of Aragon and Isabella of Castile in 1469 created the effective union from which a powerful Spanish state and empire arose, its most striking figure the austere Philip II (1556–98), front-line champion of the Counter-Reformation, master of the ill-fated Armada (1588), and oppressor of the Protestant Netherlands.[7] The Netherlands as a whole (corresponding to the area of the

[3] Between 1494 and 1559, in particular, Italy was the battleground of Spain and France. In 1559, with the treaty of Cateau-Cambresis, Naples and Sicily fell under the rule of the Spanish Habsburgs. In 1569 the Medici ruler of Florence, Cosimo, proclaimed himself Grand Duke of Tuscany, over which his family had now established total dominion, with Siena, Pisa, and many other ancient cities subject to their rule. In the previous century the republic of Venice had spread its power over its hinterland, the so-called *terra ferma* of northern Italy, subjecting cities such as Verona, Vicenza, Padua, Brescia, and Bergamo.

[4] This war, originating in the English king's claim to the French crown, ended in French victory and the expulsion of the English from the continent.

[5] Pride of nation can be seen emerging in this war in its heroes. The French national heroine is Jeanne d'Arc, the 'Maid of Orléans', who forced the English to abandon the siege of the town in 1429; the English king Henry V, victor of Agincourt in 1415, is celebrated as his nation's hero in Shakespeare's play.

[6] The conquest of Ireland was completed at the end of Elizabeth's reign, with the overthrow of the old Gaelic order at Kinsale in 1601.

[7] Parallel with the emergence of these strong national kingdoms, and a symbol of their centralization, was the tendency, within each linguistic area, for one particular dialect to become the standard national form of speech. English and French built their standard forms upon the dialects in use in the vicinity of the capital cities of each kingdom; Castilian became the standard form of Spanish. In Italy, despite the absence of a nation-state, the vernacular speech of Tuscany (because of the wealth and cultural predominance of Florence, and of her most famous poet Dante) became the standard educated speech of the whole peninsula.

modern Netherlands plus Belgium) had descended through accidents of marriage and inheritance from their former ancient sovereign the Duke of Burgundy to the Habsburg emperor Charles V (Philip's father); Philip, unwilling to tolerate the spread of the reformed religion there, provoked the seven northern and predominantly Protestant provinces into a long revolt, starting in 1566 and lasting throughout the rest of the century; from those seven provinces and their ultimately successful defiance of Spain there emerged not a kingdom[8] but nevertheless a very important new nation-state in the form of the Dutch republic, a great world force in the following era, no less in the sphere of the intellect than in that of material power.

While in Western Europe the ghost of the Roman empire still in titular being on German soil was overshadowed by this pattern of strong new nation-states, in the east its more authentic counterpart, the empire of the Byzantine rulers, came to an end in 1453 when its capital, Constantinople, was finally captured by the Turks. This people, whose remote origins were in central Asia, had long beleaguered the Eastern empire, and had thrust their way into the Balkans; by 1550 they were in control of what is now the modern Greece, Bulgaria, Romania, and southern Yugoslavia, not to speak of the eastern Mediterranean sea, over which Turkish ships ranged from end to end. Their siege of Malta (1566) failed, and they were defeated at the great sea battle of Lepanto in 1571 by the combined fleets of Spain, Venice, and the pope; but they remained an important factor in European politics for a further century.

The economic and social features of the closing Middle Ages left traces in the contemporary mind no less significant than did the purely political ones. In the late fourteenth century the expansion noted in the twelfth and thirteenth was, for a time, halted, and Western Europe experienced a recession. This was in part due to the ravages of bubonic plague. The 'Black Death' was carried by rats on board ships reaching southern Europe from the eastern Mediterranean; the first outbreaks were in Sicily and Genoa in 1348, but it travelled quickly north (reaching Ireland by 1349), and is estimated to have killed a third of Europe's population, emptying whole districts and towns of their people, extinguishing industry, and causing much farmland to lapse back into wilderness. But warfare, particularly the Hundred Years War which devastated France

---

[8] The house of Orange, which led the struggle, did not pretend to royal status, which it eventually attained only in 1815, at the conclusion of the Napoleonic wars.

intermittently and involved at times Flanders and Spain as well, had a lot to do with economic decline; as had the endemic banditry, often carried on by disemployed mercenary soldiers, which terrorized areas of Germany, Italy, and France. This economic recession, in its agricultural aspect, is thought to have caused the emergence of the system of succession based on primogeniture (which had never been part of either the ancient Roman or the ancient Germanic law); the continual subdivision of land between several sons being a less effective basis for production, intolerably so in depressed economic conditions, the principle of passing it to the eldest son undivided established itself in some regions. The landless younger sons often turned to mercenary soldiering for a living.[9]

In the fifteenth century economic activity picked up again; areas which had become derelict were reclaimed for agriculture; population, towns, trade, and industry began again to grow. But the bad times—particularly hard on the poorer people—led to a series of largely peasant revolts, notably the 'jacquerie' in France in 1358, and the risings led in England by Wat Tyler in 1381 and Jack Cade[10] in 1450. These were provoked by taxation and noble oppression, and (in England) by the system, deeply resented, whereby the peasant was compelled to perform labour services for his lord; they were marked, too, by an ominously egalitarian note.[11] It is to this age that the popular ballads about heroic outlaws, of which Robin Hood is the type, belong, with their unifying thread of complaint about social injustice, and approval of 'robbing the rich to feed the poor'.[12] A growing anti-clericalism (present in the Robin Hood world of fat abbots), centred on opposition to tithes and to low standards among the clergy, also played a certain part in the proto-revolutionary uprisings of this age, which were ruthlessly put down.[13] There were further violent social disorders elsewhere in Europe in the early sixteenth century, notably the Peasants' War in

---

[9] On the connection of primogeniture with the recession, see Mundy, *Europe* (see Ch. 4 n. 24), 274.

[10] Cade was an Irishman: *Dictionary of National Biography*, s.v.

[11] The rebel priest John Ball addressed the insurgent peasants at Blackheath in 1381 with the verse: 'When Adam delved and Eve span, Who then was the gentleman?'

[12] Maurice Keen, *The Outlaws of Medieval Legend* (London, 1961), *passim*.

[13] See Denys Hay, *Europe in the Fourteenth and Fifteenth Centuries* (London, 1989), 35–8.

Germany in 1525, and the rising of the communistic Anabaptists in the Netherlands ten years later. Both were suppressed with frightful brutality; of the former, V. H. H. Green wrote that 'peace and order had been restored at the cost of a continuance of social and economic injustice'.[14]

The earlier Middle Ages had seen very little technological change. To take the sphere of warfare (where necessity so often accelerates invention), an army of the late Roman empire might have confronted an equivalent force of thirteenth-century crusaders on terms not far from an equal footing. But in the closing Middle Ages technical innovation of immense importance now appeared. Advances in the art of navigation, partly stimulated by the desire to circumvent the Venetian monopoly of the overland routes to the East and its valuable spices by finding sea-routes there, opened up the world to Europe in the late fifteenth century, thus giving an enormous impetus to Europe's economy. The Portuguese rounded the Cape of Good Hope in 1488, and reached India in 1498 by that route. In 1492 also the Genoese Christopher Columbus, in the service of Isabella of Castile, crossed the Atlantic and discovered, in what he thought was an approach to the Indies from the other direction, the New World of America. In 1520 Magellan circumnavigated the globe. These achievements made possible the vast empires which the two Iberian kingdoms now built up, the Portuguese in the far East and in Brazil, the Spaniards in the rest of South and Central America and in the southern parts of North America; the wealth which these vast territories now poured back across the seas had powerful effects in European affairs.

The fourteenth century had seen the first common use of gunpowder in cannon (by both sides in the Hundred Years War). The mid-fifteenth produced an invention which was to be even more powerful in human affairs, that of printing with movable type. This wonderful technique, ascribed to Johann Gutenberg of Mainz, was crucial to the diffusion of literature and science, and thus of ideas, in a form which ordinary people could afford; it was, in particular, significant in the history of the Protestant Reformation, since it made possible the possession of a family Bible by most literate people, and thus gave access to the word of God (a cardinal point of the Protestant message) without the need to rely on a priest

[14] *Renaissance and Reformation* (London, 1964), 138.

to interpret it in its rare and expensive manuscript form. In the sixteenth century an important start was made in the scientific revolution (which was to unfold fully only in the seventeenth) when, from about 1540, ancient ideas about the universe were rejected by a new breed of astronomer, notably the Pole Copernicus, followed by the Dane Tycho Brahe and the German Johannes Kepler, who relied on observation not venerable authority, and set their science on the course of discovery which still continues.

These intellectual pioneers, trusting to telescopes and mathematics rather than the Book of Genesis and Aristotle, encountered the hostility of the Church,[15] which at the end of the Middle Ages was to pass through the greatest crisis since its foundation; indeed it is this crisis which draws the Middle Ages to a close. The rejection of traditional authority by the astronomers was not the cause of the crisis, though the spirit of intellectual self-reliance was an important aspect and symptom of it. The Church had been in trouble since the early fourteenth century, when the papacy, at that time under the thumb of the French kings, had moved from Rome to Avignon in France, where it remained for about seventy years. Gregory XI returned to Rome in 1377 and died in the following year; the question of his successor caused such bitter feelings between the pro- and anti-French parties that a chaotic scene developed, from which two, and later three, simultaneous and rival popes emerged. This so-called Great Schism lasted for half a century, to the great scandal of Christendom; the dimensions of worldliness and unscrupulousness which the papal institution now displayed, together with the general offence caused by clerical abuses, account for the appearance of rebel figures like John Wycliffe (c. 1330–84) in England and Jan Hus (c. 1372–1415) in Bohemia; these precursors of the Reformation not only questioned some areas of religious orthodoxy, but denounced the pope as Antichrist. Both were accused of heresy at the general council of the Church which met at Constance in 1414; Wycliffe was posthumously condemned; Hus— in breach of the safe-conduct under which he had travelled to the council—was burnt at the stake. This council had been summoned by the emperor to heal the Great Schism, and actually succeeded in doing so; but the so-called 'conciliar movement', which wished to establish for such councils an authority superior to that of the pope

[15] And of Protestant churches as well, which could not accept a version of the universe differing from the Bible's.

(and thus contained a democratic element), despite the councils held at Constance and, in 1431, at Basle, failed to achieve the reforms in Church government and religious practice—and above all in the standards of the papacy—which it was left for Martin Luther a century later to demand with revolutionary effect.

The consolidation of national kingdoms, the discovery of new worlds and new techniques, the stirrings of revolt within the Church against the medieval papacy and its pretensions to command men's minds: these are hugely important features in the historical tapestry of the fourteenth and fifteenth centuries. But of perhaps greater importance still—and intricately woven into the background of the others was the awakening of a new kind of lay intellect and of a new interest in the civilization of classical, Graeco-Roman antiquity. This awakening, or 're-birth' if we construe literally the word 'renaissance' which came to be applied to this epoch from the 1830s onward,[16] cannot be neatly dated or explained. It was perhaps in some degree endogenous, spontaneously showing in a few extraordinary spirits of the Italian fourteenth century such as the poets Dante and Petrarch and the painter Giotto; there had, after all, been intellectual leaps forward (though on a much humbler level) earlier in the Middle Ages, in the Carolingian ninth century, and again in the twelfth with the rediscovery of Aristotle and of the *Digest*. But the intellectual and artistic renewal which begins in the early fourteenth century, and is in full swing in the mid-fifteenth, is strongly related to a much larger, and more widely diffused, reacquaintance with classical and particularly with Greek culture. This was, at least, significantly helped on by the westward migration of scholars from the beleaguered empire of Byzantium, where Greek was still the ordinary language, and ancient Greek literature still read. The first fruits of this cultural fertilization were seen in the cities of northern and central Italy, where increasing prosperity created the basis for the emergence of a leisured class with the intelligence to value, and the means to pursue, its interest in learning and antique civilization; but the passion for reacquiring classical standards in art and literature quickly spread across the Alps, to France, Germany, and the Netherlands. The classical world had been a pagan world; its

---

[16] Previously it used to be called the 'revival of letters', or by some such phrase. The word Renaissance in its full modern meaning dates from the Swiss historian Jakob Burckhardt, who made it familiar in a work of 1860.

measure was man and his reason; its philosophy that which bade him live in accordance with the nature which his reason enabled him to interpret, rather than a personalized God and his revelation. Accordingly, the classical spirit which now begins to infiltrate the Catholic world—and which found patrons of rank, including several popes, in the Church itself—was a 'humanist' one; and the word humanist is used to describe the mind, and the man, cultivated in and devoted to the heritage of classical antiquity, which was now thrown ever wider open to his view as ancient manuscripts and works of art began to fill the libraries and great houses of Western Europe. Central, of course, to the humanist mind, indeed the unconscious deposit of its pursuits, was the spirit of calm, critical, independent judgment, of intellectual freedom and self-reliance, which was the very opposite of the old medieval mentality, accustomed to accept the Church's authority on everything. Thus the spread of humanism powerfully influenced the rise of the Protestant Reformation and, in particular, predisposed many cultivated rulers to accept it.

The crisis which now could be seen approaching can be graphically illuminated from both angles by reference to the career of one famous man, Erasmus of Rotterdam (*c.*1469–1536). A refugee from the religious life, he threw himself into the pursuit of classical learning. He corresponded and became friends with other cultivated men of the time, wrote spirited satire on ecclesiastical abuses such as fake relics and miracles and absurd superstitious practices, and became famous throughout Europe as the chief representative of the new spirit. His friends and correspondents included on the one hand Thomas More,[17] the English chancellor martyred for his Catholic faith by Henry VIII; but, on the other, Martin Luther, whose passionate rebellion against the scandals of the contemporary church and ultimate departure from the Roman fold he could not approve or accompany. By his Catholic allegiance, which he never finally abandoned, he remained bound to the Catholic Middle Ages; but by his humanist bent he looked to a future Europe, emancipated from spiritual and ultimately from all intellectual authority.

[17] Erasmus's influential attack on clerical abuses, *In Praise of Folly*, contained in its title an affectionate punning reference to More, through the Greek word for folly (*mōria*).

This emancipation had different roots, and took different forms, in different countries. An important factor in the revolt against Rome which broke out all across northern Europe[18] was the strength of the new national kingdoms, impatient of interference by the papacy and of papal financial demands, and favouring the establishment of national churches; this was decisive above all in the case of England and the Scandinavian kingdoms; but the principalities of Germany, too, had rulers whose desire to eliminate outside interference predisposed them to limit the role of Rome. It was, in fact, in Germany that the greatest figure of the Reformation, indeed its father, preached: Martin Luther (1483–1546), an Augustinian friar of Erfurt, whose fierce campaign for church reform focused first on the scandal of indulgences.[19] But other important and famous figures arose at about the same time, notably the Frenchman John Calvin (1509–64), whose rigorous, gloomy, and intolerant kind of church spread its ideas from Geneva in Switzerland, where he lived and ruled for the second half of his life, to his own homeland, to the Netherlands, to Scotland,[20] and to North America.[21] Protestantism, as the different kinds of theology and church organization which arose in and after the early sixteenth century are collectively called, displayed very large internal variety and a mutual intolerance almost as rigid as that of the medieval Catholic Church, and sometimes equally so. It did however have a certain common thread not only in the rejection of papal authority, but also an emphasis on the complete dependence of the individual on God, and his helpless exposure to the eternal destiny which God had ordained for him, which no priestly or saintly intercessions could modify. It is worth also noting in passing—because of its

[18] Except in Ireland, where Elizabeth's government, culturally and linguistically adrift from the people, relied not on preaching but on persecution of the Catholic clergy. The historian Macaulay (a Protestant but neither bigoted nor unsympathetic to Ireland) wrote: 'Alone among the northern nations the Irish adhered to the ancient faith: and the cause of this seems to have been that the national feeling which, in happier countries, was directed against Rome, was in Ireland directed against England': essay on von Ranke's *History of the Popes.*

[19] This was the practice of raising money, in this instance (1515–17) ostensibly to pay for the building of the new St Peter's in Rome, by selling, or purporting to offer for money, remissions of purgatory.

[20] In Scotland the Calvinist theology had its foremost exponent in John Knox. It was brought from Scotland to northern Ireland by the Presbyterian settlers of the 17th cent.

[21] Its spirit in early North America is portrayed in Arthur Miller's play *The Crucible.*

relevance to some departments of later legal theory—that the general psychological and social connection between the ethos of Protestantism, with its emphasis on the individual's direct relationship and answerability to God, and the rise of modern capitalist enterprise, is thought to be well established;[22] the link, roughly speaking, is supposed to lie in the idea that God's favour, the outward mark of his 'election' of an individual for salvation, will be visible in material prosperity here on earth; this transmutes subtly into the idea that God's favour attaches to whatever efforts the individual will make to bring that prosperity about: God helps those who help themselves.

The old Catholic Europe did not submit quietly to the fracture of its ancient unity, nor the papal dignity to defiance. Already in the lifetime of Luther and Calvin a vigorous response had been organized: this 'Counter-Reformation' (spearheaded by the Jesuits founded in 1540) checked the spread of Protestantism and reclaimed for the Catholic Church large areas which had been lost to it, notably Poland; and the Council of Trent (1545–63) established reforms in church discipline and practice of a kind thought likely to bring rebels back to the fold. This long convulsion in the life of Europe was in many places extremely violent: it provoked civil war in France, a long and terrible revolt in the Netherlands, persecution (by both sides) in England, rebellion in Ireland and Bohemia. Not until the Peace of Westphalia, which terminated in 1648 the war which had devastated Germany and the rest of central Europe for thirty years, was the new religious complexion of the continent tacitly accepted as being permanent.

THE STATE IN THE THEORY OF THE CLOSING MIDDLE AGES

In this era, even before the Reformation completed the adolescence of the independent nation-state and shattered the early medieval notion of the unitary Christian society for ever, the conflict about the status of individual kingdoms *vis-à-vis* papal authority was over. Reflection on the nature of the state and government is not

[22] The classic studies are those of Max Weber, *The Protestant Ethic and the Spirit of Capitalism*, tr. T. Parsons (London, 1976), and R. H. Tawney, *Religion and the Rise of Capitalism* (London, 1926).

concerned, in the way that Marsilius of Padua still was in the early fourteenth century, with simply defending its legitimacy. It goes deeper than this, and takes up again the theme first made explicit at the end of the eleventh century by Manegold of Lautenbach, namely, the foundation of temporal government in some sort of agreement. In the late fourteenth century John Wycliffe ascribed the introduction of civil government (*civile dominium*) to what he called the *ritus gentium* (which seems to mean the usage of all nations), and its coercive power to custom and agreement backed by the rational approval of the people: an uncertain enough message, it is true, barely to be read out of his notoriously rough Latin.[23] In the earlier fifteenth the German cardinal Nicholas of Cusa is more specific. Writing around the time of the Council of Basle (1431), when he was a supporter of the conciliar movement, he attributes the institution of government ultimately indeed to God, but brought proximately into operation by an 'elective accord of spontaneous submission'; all authority arises only from the agreement and common consent of the subject: 'For since by nature men are equal in liberty and in power, a true and regular common power in the hands of a single man, who by nature is simply an equal, cannot be established except by the choice and agreement of all the others.'[24]

A few decades later, about 1477, the Dutch cleric Wessel of Groningen writes that the subject's duty of obedience to the ruler is not absolute, but more in the nature of a contractual obligation towards him ('magis est pacti cum prelato'); and if the ruler scorns his part of the contract, the subject is no longer bound by it either.[25] At around the same date the English lawyer Sir John Fortescue in his *Governance of England* imagined an originally wild condition of mankind; from which however, when manners softened and virtue increased, 'great communities' arose, 'willing to be united and made a body politic called a Kingdom and having a head to govern it'; they chose a king, in a process he called an 'incorporation and institution of uniting of themselves into a kingdom'.[26] In the early sixteenth century the Italian Marius Salamonius visualized the state (*civitas*) as a kind of civil partnership, 'civilis quaedam societas' (the

[23] *De civili dominio* 1. 11; *De officio regis* 11.
[24] *De concordantia catholica* 3. 4, 2. 14.
[25] *De dignitate et potestate ecclesiastica* 18.
[26] *Governance of England* 2.

word *societas* being the technical Roman expression for the consensually formed business partnership) which comes into being through mutual agreements (*-pactiones*).[27]

In Spain the sixteenth century saw a late flowering of scholastic thought in the work of several jurist-clerics, of considerable importance (as will be seen) in the history of international law and of natural rights. These, too, present the state as the product of a mutual agreement to confer power on a ruler. Francisco de Vitoria (c.1485–1546), the earliest of them, is close to Aristotle and St Thomas in presenting the state not as the consequence of a human act of will, but as a natural organic growth founded on man's instinct to associate, and offering him obvious material advantages such as solidarity in defence against his enemies and the possibility of a great diversity of trades within a society.[28] Luis de Molina (1535–1600), on the other hand, while acknowledging the divine origin of the state's power, wrote that men came together of their own free will to form the state; and although they did not create its power themselves, this voluntary union was a necessary condition without which it could not materialize.[29] Francisco de Suárez (1548–1617) also saw the act of association as conscious rather than merely instinctual: men by common consent, he wrote, came together into a body politic for mutual aid towards a single political end, and with a common governance.[30] But with Suárez a definitely bilateral sort of obligation is visible (as it had been with Manegold), binding the ruler as well as the ruled: there is a pact between king and people, according to which, for as long as the king performs his duty, they may not renounce their allegiance to him; but if he turns into a tyrant, he is in breach of the condition on which he was accepted as ruler, and may be deposed (or, in extreme cases, even killed).[31] A similar justification of tyrannicide was offered in 1599 by the Jesuit Juan de Mariana (1536–1624), who also presented the state's order as having replaced man's original solitary savagery, once men had bound themselves in mutual partnership and agreed to obey one man of outstanding virtue.[32]

[27] *De principatu* 12–19.
[28] *Relectiones* 3. 1–8.
[29] *De iustitia et iure* 2. 22. 8.
[30] *De legibus ac Deo legislatore* 3. 2. 4.
[31] Ibid. 3. 4. 6: a 'just war may be waged against him'.
[32] *De rege et regis institutione* 1. 1–2.

In England, in 1594, the Anglican Richard Hooker published his *Laws of Ecclesiastical Polity*, 'the vehicle by which much continental political theory reached England',[33] in which, again, a contractarian rather than natural-instinct basis is ascribed to the state. 'To take away all such mutual grievances, injuries and wrongs' as afflicted men in their primordial condition, he wrote,

there was no way but only by growing unto composition and agreement among themselves, by ordaining some kind of government public, and by yielding themselves subject thereunto; that, unto whom they granted authority to govern, by them the peace, tranquillity, and happy estate of the rest might be procured. Without which consent there were no reason that one man should take upon him to be lord or judge over another; because, although there be, according to the opinion of some very great and judicious men, a kind of natural right in the noble, wise, and virtuous, to govern those which are of servile disposition; nevertheless, for manifestation of this, their right, and men's more peaceable contentment on both sides, the assent of those who are governed seemeth necessary.[34]

In the literature of the fourteenth and fifteenth centuries, wrote J. W. Gough (and he might have added the sixteenth, as the examples above show),[35]

it is clear that in spite of the mixture of Aristotelianism [i.e. the idea of the state resulting from man's natural associative instinct] the medieval, contractarian tradition was too strong to be overcome by it. That man is naturally political was a commonly repeated dogma, but it tended to be thrust into the background, while emphasis was laid on the voluntary origin of the state in a definite [contractual] act of subjection.[36]

This contractarian tradition survived vigorously into the seventeenth century, when it was to find its most famous representatives, despite the logical difficulties inherent in it, notably the problem of how an original contract of government could be taken to bind generations unborn at the time when it was made.

Although the closing Middle Ages added little or nothing to the theory of the state's basis, the state nevertheless emerges from the period with a sharper profile and heightened stature. This is partly because of Marsilius's assertion of its separate sphere, independent

[33] Gough, *Social Contract* (see Ch. 2 n. 48), 72.
[34] *Laws of Ecclesiastical Polity* 1. 10. 4.
[35] Further evidence from France, Scotland, the Netherlands, and elsewhere in Gough, *Social Contract* (see Ch. 2 n. 48), 51 ff.
[36] Ibid. 40.

of the Church; but also because of the doctrines of Noccolò Machiavelli (1469–1527). This characteristic Renaissance figure was a Florentine republican, who had to go into exile when the dictatorship of the Medici was restored in 1512; he was also an Italian patriot, who later urged the same Medici to lead a national effort to drive all foreign powers off Italian soil. These political interests were related for him to the public virtues of the best epochs of pagan classical antiquity, virtues which he thought were not the same as, or even compatible with, the virtues which inspired Christian society; and it was because of his preference for the morals of ancient Athens and Rome, his frank avowal of the classical republic rather than the Christian commonwealth as his model for the ideal state, that he became a byword for unscrupulous statecraft through the advice offered to rulers in his famous book *The Prince* (1513). His recommended methods were not of unheard-of wickedness, indeed they were familiar from contemporary Italian life, but later ages were scandalized by the cool, morally neutral way in which he expounded them. The importance of this work for the history of legal theory—as likewise of his *Discourses* on political questions suggested by the narrative of the Roman historian Livy—lies in this open elevation of the state and its interests and effective governance to a plane where they are the only values in sight. There is no pretence that the legitimacy of government's operations depends on their conformity with God's law, natural law, or any such transcendent standard; and even though, as will be seen, Machiavelli preferred a form of government in which the rulers are subject to the laws, this is not for him an overriding requirement—the state's interest may legitimately require their violation—and he does not state it with the pious emphasis which, say, Bracton had given it. Machiavelli is thus a significant figure (though no doubt without realizing it, any more than did his successors) in the intellectual march that was to lead through Hobbes and Rousseau towards the totalitarian state of the twentieth century.[37]

---

[37] Isaiah Berlin, 'The Originality of Machiavelli', in *Against the Current: Essays in the History of Ideas* (Oxford, 1989), 25–79.

THE SOURCE OF VALIDITY OF LAW

It has been seen that in the High Middle Ages the ancient Germanic idea of limited monarchy survived strongly: new law requires the consent of the ruled, expressed in one mode or another, and cannot spring from the will of the king alone. The elements of something like parliamentary representation of the people's wishes, operating side by side with the royal office, became visible in England, in Spain, in France, in parts of Germany; and the democratic principle found expression also in the rules of the new religious orders. Marsilius of Padua had wished to subordinate the authority of the pope to that of general councils in the main government of the Church; and in the early fifteenth century this desire was expressed in the so-called conciliar movement which had some success in its healing of the Church schism. Yet from the later fourteenth century the General European trend towards institutionalized sharing of government between king and assemblies weakened, evidently because the violent upheavals and the warfare which marked the age called for control by autocratic hands.[38] Therefore, it is probably not an accident that, on the plane of theory, the closing Middle Ages saw a shift in the trend of doctrine. Along with the traditional assertions of the non-absolute character of kingship, and of the monarch's duty to seek in some form the consent of the governed before promulgating new law, voices are heard which either express this idea in diluted and modified form, or which declare absolutely the absolute right of the king to legislate, to the same effect as Ulpian had declared it on behalf of the Roman emperor.

The older view is still stated by Nicolas of Cusa (1401–64). This German theologian in his *De concordantia catholica* recites the maxim 'quod omnes tangit, ab omnibus approbari debet' (that which affects everybody should be approved by everybody); the making of law ('legis latio') should be done by all those whom the law is to bind, or by the greater part of them.[39] In France the same idea appears in different form in a treatise of Jean Gerson (1363–1429): a

---

[38] Mundy, *Europe* (see Ch. 4 n. 24), 410–12.

[39] *De concordantia catholica* 3, proemium. This maxim comes originally from a Roman text (*Codex Justinianus* 5. 59. 5. 2) in which it referred to the quite special context of joint tutors; but it was taken from this context and generalized by the Glossators (see Robinson, Fergus, and Gordon, *Introduction* (see Ch. 4 n. 10), 79) and became a sort of democratic slogan.

law is without force unless approved by the usage of those who are to live by it ('moribus utentium').[40] In England Sir John Fortescue, describing the mixed form of the English constitution, declares that English kings cannot make laws without the assent of the three estates of their kingdom.[41] In Spain the Cortes of Castile and Leon repeatedly assert the principle that law was not simply the product of the king's will, but required also the authority of magnates and cities.[42] At the end of the sixteenth century the same was being written by the Spanish Jesuit jurist-theologians Molina and Suárez,[43] and it appears also in the anonymous but influential Huguenot tract of 1579 called *Vindiciae contra tyrannos*.[44]

But other tones, too, were being heard in those same centuries, and ones which signalled the shape of government in early modern Europe. Some of these, admittedly, do not address directly the question of legislation, but still they state the ruler's position in terms more absolute than anyone had stated them since the time of Pope Gregory the Great (except for some of the early civilians) and, therefore, at odds with the general Germanic outlook of medieval Europe which imputed a vital role to the consent of the people. In the late fourteenth century John Wycliffe taught the non-answerability of the earthly ruler to his subjects, who were bound to obey him, as being God's appointees, even when he was tyrannical.[45] Aeneas Silvius Piccolomini (1405–64), a humanist and writer who was pope (Pius II) from 1458, wrote a tract on the rise and authority of the Roman imperial office (1446) in which he presents the emperor as having power both to make and to abrogate law, without mentioning any necessity to secure anyone else's consent;[46] and in his bull *Execrabilis* of 1460 he condemned as heretical any appeal made from the pope's authority to a general church council. Martin Luther, at any rate in his earlier years and during the Peasants' War in which he called for the most ruthless suppression of these oppressed and desperate wretches, held that earthly authority was of divine origin, that earthly rulers had a divine title to unquestioning obedience, and that resistance to them was unconditionally wicked, however ill those rulers might themselves behave.[47]

---

[40] *Regulae morales* (*Opera* 1. 2. 10); *Liber de vita spirituali animae* (*Opera* 2. 2. 209).
[41] *De natura legis naturae* 1. 16.
[42] Carlyles, *Medieval Theory* (see Ch. 3 n. 29), vi. 133–6, 143.
[43] Ibid. 341 ff.   [44] Ibid. 338–41.   [45] Ibid. 52 ff.
[46] Ibid. 188 ff.   [47] Ibid. 272 ff.

The most important and finally influential statement of the right of kings was that of the French lawyer Jean Bodin (1530–96), the evangelist of the absolutism which the French kingship was now to display in its most strident form. In his famous work *De la république* (1576) he presents the idea that a state must contain a sovereign power, really sovereign in every department of positive law, and subject only to the laws of God, of nature, and of nations; the latter subjections being merely notional, Bodin's sovereign is in practice absolute, the source of law, and untrammelled by any necessity to secure the consent of others. He has reached this position by reason of the state's origin lying in force, in the violence which reduced men from their free state of nature to subjection; and indeed the very word citizen implies one who is subject to the sovereign rule of another. The view inherited from Aristotle, that citizenship implies a right to a share in public counsels and in the government of the state, is, thinks Bodin, a serious error. On the contrary, 'the first and most important feature of sovereignty (*maiestas*) is the capacity to give laws to the citizens, both singly and collectively; and moreover, this ought to be done without the need for consent of superiors, of equals, or of inferiors'.[48] In France, he found, matters were in fact managed like this; here

the prince's sovereignty shines forth, when the people and the estates with humble mien bring their petitions to him; they have no power to command or to forbid him anything, nor has their approval any significance; the prince ordains everything by his own will and judgment, and whatever he has decreed or commanded has the force of law. The opinion of those who consider him bound by the people's sovereignty—a view commonly found in books—must be put down; since it only gives ammunition to seditious men for their revolutionary projects, and brings turmoil into the life of the state.[49]

Other writers of the late sixteenth century, French, English, and Scottish, wrote to similar effect; among the Scots, notably their king, James VI, who became James I of England in 1603, and whose views on royalty's divine right had so fatal an influence on the Stuart dynasty which he inaugurated. A man of considerable intellectual cultivation, if few other qualities, he wrote in 1598 a treatise, *The True Law of Free Monarchies*, in which he attributed the royal sovereignty in Scotland to its original conquest,[50]

[48] *De republica* 1. 9.   [49] Ibid. 1. 8; see also 6. 4.
[50] 'By king Fergus, who came from Ireland': there was a legendary Irish king Fergus who invaded Scotland and is supposed to have died in about 330 BC, but

[whence] it follows, of necessity, that the kings were the Authors and Makers of the lawes, and not the lawes of the kings. . . . The lawes are but craved by his subjects and onely made by him at their rogation and with their advice. For albeit the king make daily statutes and ordinances, injoyning such paines thereto, as he thinks meet, without any advice of Parliament or Estates, yet it lyes in the power of no Parliament to make any kinde of lawes or statute, without his sceptre be put to it, for giving it the force of a Law.[51]

THE RULE OF LAW

Just as the fourteenth, fifteenth, and sixteenth centuries display the revival of doctrines, such as those mentioned above, departing from the older medieval idea that the assent of the governed, in some form, was necessary to the making of new law, and stating instead, in conscious or unconscious response to the disorders of social unrest and religious warfare, the claims of absolute monarchy, so too the same writers either dilute, or deny altogether, the doctrine that the prince is bound by the law of his country. There are, of course, familiar expressions about how right it is for a ruler to consider himself subject to the laws, by which the medieval world mainly meant the customary laws of the people; and about how the happiest state is that in which those conditions prevail. Jean Gerson pointed out that the king could slay no man except by due process of law (*iuris ordine*), i.e. no one who had not been charged, summoned, and convicted;[52] that the king of France submitted to the jurisdiction of the *parlement*[53] that he had himself established;[54] and that both prince and prelate, even if said to be free of law's binding force ('solutus legibus'), should allow themselves to be ruled by the law which they had enacted, as an example to their subjects and out of reverence for God.[55] The English judge

James probably meant the historical Fergus mac Eirc, the first Dalriada king of Scotland (of the northern Uí Néill, and so of the same clan as Colmcille, founder of Iona), who died in AD 501.

[51] *True Law of Free Monarchies* C.
[52] *Summa contra Ioannem Parisiensem* (*Opera* 1. 1. 399).
[53] The French *parlements*, of which that of Paris was the most important, were in the nature of judicial assemblies rather than legislatures.
[54] *Sermo pro viagio regis Romanorum* (*Opera* 1. 1. 152).
[55] *Sermo in die circumcisionis Domini* (*Opera* 1. 1. 240, 241).

Fortescue emphasizes that the king cannot override the law inasmuch as the judges must decide according to law even if commanded by the king to do otherwise.[56] A few years before Fortescue was writing, the rebels led by Jack Cade had wanted to get rid of the king's evil counsellors who 'filled him with such ideas as that our Sovereign Lord [the King] is above his laws . . . and may make them and break them as he list'.[57] The German Nicholas of Cusa, who as has been seen derived (in the setting of the conciliar movement) all authority from the people, presented the image of Jesus as an exemplar for rulers in this respect, that 'Christ was subject to the Law; He did not come to abolish it, but to accomplish it'.[58] Even Machiavelli, in his *Discourses* on Livy, accounts for what he thought the happy state of France by the people's knowledge that their king will in no circumstances break the laws:

that kingdom, more than any other, lives under and in accord with law and order. And that law and order is upheld most of all by the *parlements*, especially that of Paris. This *parlement* renews the laws when necessary, and gives judgment even against the prince of the kingdom, and in such judgments will condemn the king himself.[59]

Machiavelli's contemporary Baldassare Castiglione, who wrote a famous book on how a courtier ought to conduct himself, also thought that a good prince should respect the law.[60] The sixteenth-century school of Spanish jurist-theologians ('late scholastics', as they are sometimes called, for their adherence to the methods of the High Middle Ages and St Thomas) supported the same opinion; Vitoria, already mentioned, was quite clear that the law bound the king: royal decrees, he wrote, had the same authority as if they had been enacted by the whole people, but, just as a popularly enacted law would bind the king (who was himself part of the people), so too he was bound even by his own ordinances.[61] Suárez similarly thought the king was bound to observe his own laws; although he appeared to admit that the king was immune from compulsion in this regard, it has been seen that he thought even the compulsion of force might be justified against him if he degenerated into a tyrant.[62] Of the French humanist lawyers (shortly to be formally introduced)

[56] *De natura legis naturae* 1. 16.   [57] Keen, *Outlaws* (see n. 12), 167.
[58] *De concordantia catholica* 3, proemium.   [59] *Discourses* 3. 1.
[60] *Book of the Courtier* (Penguin Classics edn., London, 1928), 308.
[61] *Relectiones de potestate civili* 21.
[62] *De legibus ac de legislatore* 3. 35. 4, 28.

several, notably Cujas and Donellus, rejected the suggestion that the maxim 'princeps legibus solutus' implied the ruler's right to act contrary to the laws; though the precise quality of his subordination to them, whether legal or merely moral, is variously stated.[63]

But, just as in the matter of the title to legislate, here too other voices are now being heard. Aeneas Silvius, already mentioned, thought that, although it was a 'fine saying' ('quamvis pulchrum est dicere') that the emperor was subject to the laws, it could not be maintained as a serious proposition ('non asserendum'), since in fact he is above the law ('cum sit solutus').[64] The late civilian Jason de Mayno (1435–1519) thought so too, and cited the great authority of Baldus de Ubaldis in support; the prince was quite entitled to issue orders contrary to the law, as long as he included the formal phrase *non obstante* ('notwithstanding [that the ordinary law prescribes otherwise]').[65] The German–Swiss humanist Ulrich Zasius (1461–1535) was quite clear that the Roman emperor's power, now imputed to the modern ruler, had been unlimited ('immensa'), and not bound by the laws.[66] The famous French humanist Guillaume Budé (1467–1540) in his commentary on Justinian's *Digest* explains elaborately—bringing in, among other things, the analogy of a father's absolute authority over his children—that the ruler is exempted from the bonds of the laws, even though he may waive his privilege, and, putting on the spirit of a citizen ('civili animo'), may acquiesce in the jurisdiction of the parlement being invoked against him.[67] Martin Luther in his work *On Earthly Authority* (1523) affirmed the absolute authority of the ruler, ordained by God to protect the good and punish the evil-doer; even the law, he wrote, is not above this temporal power, since the prince, like Solomon, can seek direct guidance from God: a position in which the psychological connection between Ockham's voluntarism, which Luther expressly accepted, and political absolutism begins to be evident.[68] Naturally Jean Bodin considered that it was of the essence of sovereignty that the sovereign should not be bound by the laws;[69] though it may be noted that even this foremost apostle of absolutism thought that a kingdom ought to be governed 'as far as this may be possible'

[63] See Carlyles, *Medieval Theory* (see Ch. 3 n. 29), vi. 293–318.
[64] *De ortu et auctoritate imperii romani* 20.
[65] Comm. on Code 1. 19. 7.   [66] Comm. on Digest 1. 2. 2.
[67] *Annotationes in Pandectas* 1. 9. 12.
[68] *Von weltlicher Obrigkeit* (*Werke*, xi. 272).   [69] *De republica* 1. 8.

('quantum fieri poterit') by laws rather than by the arbitrary will of the ruler.[70] Lastly, King James VI of the Scots, in a vein similar to Bodin's and perhaps with knowledge of what Bodin had written, was quite clear about both royalty's rights, and the seemly way to exercise them:

A just prince will not take the life of any one of his subjects without a cleare law: yet the same lawes, whereby he taketh this, are made by himself, or his predecessors. And so the power flowes alwayes from himselfe . . . The king is above law, as both the author and giver of strength thereto; yet a good king will not onely delight to rule his subjectes by the law, but will even conforme himself, in his own actions thereunto, always keeping that ground, that the health of the commonwealth be his chiefe law. [The king has a dispensing and suspending power;[71] but] a good king, although he be above the Law, will subject and frame his actions thereto, for example's sake to his subjectes [but he does this] of his own free will, but not as subject thereto.[72]

LEGAL DEVELOPMENTS OF THE LATE MIDDLE AGES

These were the centuries in which the character of Europe's later legal systems was determined, above all in which the great division of the civilized legal world into the two families of 'civil law' and 'common law' began to emerge. The essential basis of the division was the permeation of continental Europe's jurisdictions[73] by Roman law, the *ius civile* in the Romans' own language; and, by contrast, the failure of Roman law permanently to penetrate the English legal profession, which persisted in the native traditional rules; these, uniformly applied throughout the kingdom by a single body of judges, were for this reason collectively called the 'common law'.

It will seem confusing, given this English usage, that on the continent, too, a *ius commune*, or 'common law', evolved. But the

[70] Ibid. 4. 4.
[71] The exercise of these powers by the Stuarts was highly controversial, and in the case of James II was a factor directly contributing to his deposition.
[72] *True Law of Free Monarchies* D. 1–2.
[73] The Scandinavian countries, however, remained outside this process; the generalizing term 'continental' also excluded Russia and the Balkans; though in the former Byzantine possessions, after the fall of Constantinople to the Turks in 1453, Roman law in its Byzantine form continued to be applied.

continental *ius commune* is something quite different. It does not mean, as in England, a uniform and comprehensive system enforced by a uniform judiciary; but rather those parts of the revived Roman law which, in varying measure and forms, and at a varying pace, were built into local systems and applied by local courts alongside the corpus of older law of Germanic customary or early medieval legislative[74] origin. This revived, 'learned' Roman law—'learned', because cultivated by the new race of university-trained canon and civil lawyers—tended to play a greater part in the fields of obligations (roughly, what English lawyers call contract and tort), property, procedure, and general principles, than in those of family and succession law, in which the ancient rules tended to hold their own. This generalization is very rough, and does not convey the wide differences, from kingdom to kingdom and from region to region, of the degree and form of absorption of Roman material. It can however be said that the Roman element more or less everywhere from Brittany to Poland and from Hamburg to Palermo was part of the local system's alloy, and provided a sort of conceptual lingua franca for lawyers of different nations, enabling them to understand one another's formulations.[75] This development, not having taken place in England, meant that English lawyers were excluded from this lingua franca; and the basis for the mutual sense of strangeness, as between the world of the English common law and that of what might be called the Romanesque civil law was laid.

Germany's development in these centuries needs special mention. Here, as has been seen, the High Middle Ages had produced written codes of native law, notably the *Sachsenspiegel*; and attachment to native tradition was so strong that it amounted to a cultural barrier less easily transcended by the new Roman law learning than anything encountered in Italy, France, or Spain. Indeed it could be said that the continental *ius commune*, in the sense given above, was formed at first without German participation. But suddenly, at the end of the fifteenth century, Germany 'received' Roman law. Certainly the spirit of the Renaissance with its enthusiasm for all things Roman, by now well rooted in Germany, played some part

---

[74] e.g. the codes of rudimentary Roman law promulgated, after the fall of the western empire, by the Visigothic and Burgundian kings for their Roman subjects.

[75] On all this see, in a convenient form, Robinson, Fergus, and Gordon, *Introduction* (see Ch. 4 n. 10), ch. 7, 'The *Ius Commune*'.

in this. But the main reason for this sudden and massive reception[76] appears to lie in political conditions: in the absence (by contrast with France) of a strong central monarchy, and the fragmentation of the huge country into numerous principalities, free cities, etc., just at the time when German industrial and commercial enterprise, and the urban civilization which subtended them, were beginning to grow explosively. There was a painful contrast between the cumbersome German rules and procedures observed by the ancient local courts, not the same in any two places, and the clear, simple, and intelligible rules and procedures, of Roman origin, observed by the courts of canon law. In an attempt, if not to impose a uniform jurisdiction throughout Germany (which would have been impossible to an authority so weak), at least to offer a model of improved regularity, Emperor Maximilian I reconstructed in 1495 the old imperial court with a new title (*Reichskammergericht*, 'court of the imperial (council) chamber'), half of whose judges were to be university (i.e. Roman-law)-trained lawyers; this half soon expanded in practice to the total membership of the court. This tribunal, though its own effective powers were very limited, inspired the emergence of others, equally 'Roman' and thus more satisfactory to litigants. Moreover, German courts took to referring many of their cases to the nearest university law faculty for its opinion; the faculties, naturally composed of Romanists, infused the Roman way of seeing and doing things into German practice. Thus this reception of Roman law in Germany, if later, was far more thoroughgoing than it had been anywhere else; indeed the modern German civil code, promulgated 400 years later but the fruit of 400 years of the same tradition, is in some of its parts the most purely Roman codification of any in the world.

While this evolution was proceeding in Germany throughout the sixteenth century, something quite new was happening (largely) in France. Here, the Renaissance had first taken hold north of the Alps; and here, too, the cool, critical Renaissance spirit had spread among French scholars. Some of these, led by the example of famous Italian scholars like Lorenzo Valla or Politian, now began to apply the techniques of philological and historical critical scholarship to the texts of Roman law, most notably of course to the *Digest*. In other words, instead of simply regarding this ancient

---

[76] The word is the one the Germans use: *Rezeption*.

material as an inexhaustible quarry from which legal doctrines might be mined for every eventuality (as the early Italian civilians had done), they looked at it, firstly, as a collection of texts probably full of corruptions which had encrusted it during the long centuries of manuscript-copy transmission, quite apart from the deliberate and unsignalled changes made by Justinian's codifying commission. These corruptions needed to be uncovered with the tools of scientific study of language, and scientific history which Renaissance scholarship had fashioned, and the original form of the texts re-established. Secondly, they looked upon the Roman texts as so much organic matter, the deposit of the age and society in which they had been composed, and therefore as encasing priceless evidence about the ancient Roman world which fascinated them so deeply. The studies pursued by the apostles of this so-called 'humanist' jurisprudence were certainly far from being a historical jurisprudence in the sense of the nineteenth century, emotionally charged with feelings for nature and nationhood. They represented an approach to antique civilization at a level similar in spirit, if different from it in mode, to the archaeological passion which seized so many humanists who excavated ancient remains, deciphered ancient inscriptions, and collected ancient coins and statuary;[77] but their contribution to legal science was enormous all the same. For the first time, law was studied as a phenomenon, rather than learnt in the way of one's calling, whether to administer a kingdom, persuade a court, or confute a political adversary. The earliest of these pioneers was the Milanese Andrea Alciato or Alciatus (1492–1550), who was professor of civil law at Avignon. Ulrich Zasius, already mentioned, who was professor at Freiburg and was a member of the circle of Erasmus at Basle, shared Alciatus's urge to recover the original classical texts from under later accretions. Most of the rest were French (most of them, too, were Huguenots, in other words French followers of Calvin's Reformation, and were obliged to leave their country and teach abroad): the most prominent names are those of Guillaume Budé, who was interested in the extent of Greek influence on Roman law and in the factors which produce legal change; Jacques Cujas (1522–90), who specialized in spotting corruptions in classical texts; and Hugues Doneau or Donellus (1527–91), who showed more interest than the

---

[77] See R. Weiss, *The Renaissance Discovery of Classical Antiquity* (Oxford, 1969).

others in the orderly arrangement of the Roman texts, and in their possible use as a basis for a modern working system.[78]

THE NATURE AND PURPOSE OF LAW

It has been seen that in every earlier era, with scarcely an exception, any writer offering a definition of law presents it in an essentially imperative formula—the point is worth drawing attention to because of the modern perception that such a presentation inadequately describes the phenomenon. The closing Middle Ages are in this respect no different from the preceding centuries. In England Sir John Fortescue (1394–1476), following the Accursian gloss mentioned in the last chapter, again calls law a 'sacred sanction' commanding those things that are right, and forbidding their opposite ('iubens honesta et prohibens contraria').[79] The Spanish jurist-theologian Domenico de Soto (1494–1560) spoke of law's 'coercive' force (*vis coerciva*);[80] his compatriot the Jesuit Juan Mariana (1536–1624) built a formula in essence the same as Fortescue's into a fuller definition: 'For law is reason, free from all passion (*omni perturbatione vacua*), deriving from the mind of God (*a mente divina hausta*), laying down those things that are upright and salutary, and forbidding their opposite (*honesta et salutaria prescribens, prohibensque contraria*).'[81] The English theologian Richard Hooker, writing his *Laws of Ecclesiastical Polity* at about the same time, equally concentrates on law's obligatory aspect. For fear of arbitrary government, he thought, men had been 'constrained to come unto laws, wherein all men might see their duties beforehand, and know the penalties of transgressing them . . . Laws do not only teach what is good, but they enjoin it, they have in them a certain constraining force'.[82] Thus both Catholic and Protestant Europe at the close of the sixteenth century saw law still in the manner of the High Middle Ages and before: essentially in the imperative terms of command and prohibition; no sign, as yet, of discomfort at the apparent difficulty of fitting 'rules of recognition'

[78] Robinson, Fergus, and Gordon, *Introduction* (see Ch. 4 n. 10), 284–300.
[79] *De laudibus legum Angliae* 3.
[80] *De iustitia et iure* 1. 1. 3.
[81] *De rege et regis institutione* 1. 2; also 1. 9: legislative power is 'auctoritas jubendi vetandique'.
[82] *Laws of Ecclesiastical Polity* 1. 10.

or 'power-conferring rules' into such a frame, though such rules of course existed.

The late Middle Ages imposed further, and again traditional, requirements for a valid law. Generally, it must conform with the law of God and nature (as will be seen later). It must be just; and the English lawyer Christopher St German (c.1460–1540) states the criteria for legislative justice in terms which come straight from St Thomas:

A human law is called just, by the standard of its end, its author, and its form (*ex fine, ex authore et ex forma*). Its end: when it is designed for the common good. Its author: when it does not exceed the powers of him who enacts it. Its form: when its burdens are laid upon the subjects in a due proportion, with the common good in view. And if its burdens are laid upon the people in an unfair way, even if its purpose be the common good, it does not bind him in conscience.[83]

His contemporary the French humanist lawyer François Connon (d. 1551) thought an unjust law was no law at all;[84] and Donellus, in the following generation, also insisted on the relevance of the common good (*utilitas publica*): a law tending to prejudice it ought not to be enforced by the judges.[85] At the beginning of the seventeenth century the English attorney-general Sir Edward Coke attributed to the age leading up to his own the practice whereby the courts would treat as null laws which were 'against common right or reason, or impossible to be performed'; although no one has found any clear case in which this was actually done, his statement attests the persistence of medieval doctrine on moral criteria for the validity of laws.[86]

CUSTOM AND LEGISLATION

Yet another criterion for law's validity appears in some late medieval writers—as it had among their predecessors—in the context of the relation of law and custom. The earlier Middle Ages, as has been seen, held fast to the ancient Germanic idea that law essentially *was* custom, the people's traditional observances, ante-cedent to the king, who lived within its meshes just as the rest of the

---

[83] *Doctor and Student* 4. 12.   [84] *Libri commentariorum iuris civilis* 1. 1. 8.
[85] *Commentarius de iure civili* 1. 9. 12.
[86] *Bonham's Case* (1610), 8 Co. CP 114a.

people did. Only from the thirteenth century does statute law, the enacting of new positive rules, begin to play a significant part, in response to new needs of the state; and even then the more democratically inclined interpreters of Ulpian and the *lex regia*, still saw the people—the authors of custom—as having a residual and final authority superior to the king's. In the late Middle Ages the spectrum of opinion widens: at one extreme there are assertions that even positive statutory enactments, to be valid, require the endorsement of customary acceptance; at the other, custom is demoted more or less to the marginal position which it occupies today.

In one system, certainly, custom in the ancient sense enjoyed a special institutionalized position. This was, of course, the system of England, where St German spoke of the various customs observed throughout England as one of the foundations of English law; 'these are the customs which are properly called the common law . . . and from those general customs, and other principles and maxims, the greatest part of the law of England arises'.[87] At the end of the sixteenth century Hooker records the general opinion that—even at that date—statute-law was supposed often only to declare and make concrete what was always common law anyway.[88]

In France the humanists for the most part accorded a high status to custom. Connon attributed an equal authority to law and custom, subject to the principle that a rule of later origin will prevail over an earlier;[89] Donellus stated a similar doctrine.[90] But two others place the claims of custom much higher. François Duaren, a contemporary of Connon, clearly held that custom could abrogate statute-law, in the sense that if the law were not enforced, and a contrary practice became customary, the law was in effect repealed; he cited St Augustine's dictum that statutes are confirmed (only) by the observance of those living by them.[91] Jacques Cujas, considered to be the greatest of the French humanists, writing in the next generation, stated the same position:

A custom based on a better reason, together with the common interest, and the passage of a long time in silent and unwritten agreement among the

---

[87] *Doctor and Student* 7: Carlyles, *Medieval Theory* (see Ch. 3 n. 29), 234.
[88] *Laws of Ecclesiastical Polity* 1. 10.
[89] Ibid.: Carlyles, *Medieval Theory* (see Ch. 3 n. 29), 303.
[90] *Opera omnia* 1. 10. 6: Carlyles, *Medieval Theory*, 309.
[91] Comm. on Digest 1. 3. 3: Carlyles, *Medieval Theory*, 304.

community, together with the authority of judicial decisions, has the effect of abrogating a statute the reason of which has disappeared, or is less substantial, or is of less benefit to the state . . . The disuse of the statute leaves the custom alone in force, and it acquires thus the same force as a statute . . . And no statute binds us, unless it has received the acceptance of custom.[92]

Cujas's contemporary Bodin, the apostle of absolutism, took a radically different view of custom's relation to legislation (which for him was of course the enactment of an absolute lawgiver). The force of statute, he wrote, was much greater than that of custom;

for customs are abrogated by statutes, but not statutes by custom; although it is within the power of the ruler to revive statutes into use which have fallen out of use. Custom can establish neither punishments nor rewards; this is the function of statute . . . Then, custom has a precarious validity, as seeming to owe its continued existence to the ruler's willingness [to tolerate it]; if he gives it his express sanction, he makes it in effect a statute.[93]

NATURAL LAW

The concept of a transcendent natural law enters the closing middle ages not merely in the vesture which St Thomas had given it; it wears also, for some philosophers, the colour which it had received from the voluntarism of William of Ockham, that is, the view that the root of human obligation is not what human reason perceives as right, but simply what God commands. The interplay between Thomist and Occamist thinkers, the formulas thrown up by writers on both sides, were to have important effects on later political and legal (and even scientific) theory.

Of the names which may be mentioned here the earliest is that of a General of the Augustinian Order, Gregory of Rimini, who died in 1358; a follower of Ockham, who still attempted an accommodation between God's will and reason in proposing a foundation for human obligation and a measure of human wrongdoing. Sin, he thought, is offence against the eternal law (this was St Augustine's definition); but the eternal law has two aspects, one indicative, the other imperative. The *lex indicativa* aspect simply points out to man

---

[92] *Paratitla* C. 8. 52: Carlyles, *Medieval Theory*, 314.
[93] *De republica* 1. 9: Carlyles, *Medieval Theory*, 423.

what is right and what wrong; the *lex imperativa* aspect commands man to perform the one and to abstain from the other. But sin, in its sense as an offence against the eternal law, is such only because of its offence against the 'indicative' aspect; offence against this aspect would be sinful even if God had issued no command corresponding with it. The eternal law, certainly, is divine reason and right reason; but offence against it is sinful because it is right, not because it is divine; if there were no such thing as divine reason, or if ('an impossible hypothesis') God did not exist, still an offence against whatever reason was available to man would remain sinful.[94] As will be seen, this turn of expression, 'if God did not exist', was to have a remarkable career in legal theory. Within the period of this chapter, it was cited by the German theologian Gabriel Biel (d. 1495)—who however followed Ockham in holding that God does not will something because it is right and just, but it is right and just because God wills it.[95]

Among the Spanish 'late scholastic' philosophers the lawyer Fernando de Vázquez (d. 1568) proposed a view which, though it takes its starting-point from Ockham, is in effect easily fitted into the Thomistic scheme. Natural law, he wrote, is right because God has commanded it. But the route by which humans can perceive this law is the faculty of reason which God has caused to be innate in them. Thus, whatever may be the truth about some existence of which we can have no idea, so far as we are concerned (and this must be enough for us) natural law as we perceive it through our God-given reason is simply the shape in which good and evil (as determined by God) present themselves to us.[96]

This, so to speak, rehabilitation of reason even within a voluntarist frame is taken further by Fernando's namesake (but no relation) the theologian Gabriel Vázquez (d. 1604). Neither God's will, nor God's reason, he wrote, is the prime standard for good and evil, but simply the nature of things, including rational human nature.[97] With this formula God becomes no more than a guide to what is right, not the creator of the standard; and natural law 'is freed from its God-appointed origin to the point that nothing

---

[94] *Expositio in secundo sententiarum*, dist. 34, art. 2; H. Welzel, *Naturrecht und materiale Gerechtigkeit* (Göttingen, 1951), 94.
[95] *Collectorium sententiarum* 1. 17. 1; Welzel, *Naturrecht* (see n. 94), 92.
[96] *Controversiae illustres* 1. 27. 11; Welzel, *Naturrecht* (see n. 94), 93.
[97] *Commentary on Summa Theologica* 2. 1, disp. 150. 3. 22–3, 26.

further would have been required for its complete secularisation',[98] such as was to come in the seventeenth century.

The role of natural law in the practical legal system, if it is not contradictory so to express it, was in the closing Middle Ages in theory the same as before: the orthodox view, that human law repugnant to the law of nature was void, was uniformly stated everywhere. In England Sir John Fortescue, who expressly cites St Thomas, wrote that the law of the realm derived from the law of nature as well as from custom and statute,[99] that the law of nature, along with the law of God, has supreme authority;[100] and that the law of nature takes precedence over both custom and statute, which, if they should conflict with it, deserved to be called not laws, but corruptions of laws.[101] Sir Frederick Pollock noted that, with the Reformation in England, the old scholastic philosophy and its language fell somewhat under a cloud because of its association with the Catholic Middle Ages;[102] but in the epoch of the Reformation Christopher St German, born a Catholic and holding office under Henry VIII, was still writing in traditional terms about the natural law's being 'written in the heart of every man'; against this law, neither prescription, statute, nor custom could prevail; such laws, if repugnant to it, were 'things void and against justice'.[103]

At about this time, however, the tone did change, perhaps because the evolution of thought noted in Spain also took place among English lawyers, or perhaps because, in Sir Frederick Pollock's phrase, 'talking of the Law of Nature' (because of its association with canon law) 'was not a good way to most English ears'.[104] 'It is not used', wrote St German,

among them that be learned in the law of England to reason what thing is commanded or prohibited by the law of nature, and what not; [instead,] when anything is grounded upon the law of nature, they say that reason will that such a thing be done; and, if it be prohibited by the law of nature, they say it is against reason, or that reason will not suffer it to be done.[105]

At the end of the sixteenth century natural law appears, not only in the simple dress of reason, but without any specific attribute of

[98] Welzel, *Naturrecht* (see n. 94), 97.   [99] *De laudibus legum Angliae* 8.
[100] Ibid. 16.   [101] *De natura legis naturae* 1. 5, 43.
[102] 'The History of the Law of Nature', in *Jurisprudence and Legal Essays* (London, 1961), 142, 144 ff.
[103] *Doctor and Student* 7. 21.   [104] *Jurisprudence* (see n. 102), 139.
[105] *Doctor and Student* 8.

primacy over human law; Hooker's *Laws of Ecclesiastical Polity* (1594) speaks of 'the Law rational, which men commonly use to call the Law of Nature, meaning thereby the Law which human nature knoweth itself in reason universally bound to, which also for that cause may be termed most fitly the Law of Reason'; its principles are 'investigable by Reason, without the help of Revelation supernatural and divine'.[106]

Natural rights, the aspect of natural law which today bulks largest, are not clearly developed. Yet the seeds of the idea are present among the Spanish jurist-theologians, who were horrified by their own countrymen's disregard for the human dignity of the American natives, and their cruel exploitation of them. Vitoria, the first of this school, asserted the natural right of even heathen peoples not to be enslaved or plundered, or attacked because of their unwillingness to accept Christianity; their entitlement to princes and political societies of their own was the same as that of Christian peoples.[107] Similar views were expressed by Molina and de Soto.[108]

EQUITY

As has been seen, in the High Middle Ages the Italian civilians had kept alive the ancient question as between strict application of the law, or its equitable adjustment to special circumstances; and the case for equity was much strengthened by the influence of the ecclesiastical courts, applying canon law but in this way also introducing the values of moral theology, in particular the duties of conscience and obedience to the moral instinct, as well as the principle of looking to the intent rather than to the word. These forces were still at work in the closing Middle Ages, up to and through the Reformation and beyond. The claims of equity and of conscience were commonplaces everywhere; in England, a special case, they gave birth to a separate jurisdiction within the same legal system, or perhaps it would be better to say, a second legal system within the same kingdom.

The French humanists of the sixteenth century were, moreover, aware of the ancient roots of the debate. Guillaume Budé—putting

---

[106] *Laws of Ecclesiastical Polity* 1. 8.   [107] *Relectio de Indis*, ii.
[108] See also the section on 'International Law' later in this chapter.

right a misunderstanding in the Accursian gloss which had arisen from inadequate knowledge of classical Latin—gave an exposition of the passages in Aristotle, including the image of the leaden rule of the masons of Lesbos, which explain the principle of *epieikeia*, that modification of strict legality which is made necessary by the inability of any general rule to meet the justice of every case. He reported also the somewhat corrupted form of the Greek word, and of a medieval Latin verb derived from that corrupt form (*epicaizare*), which was in current use, thus proving the vitality and familiarity of the idea. His English contemporary, the lawyer Christopher St German, although not a humanist in Budé's manner, also shows familiarity with the Graeco-Roman conception of equity in the discourse which he puts in his Doctor's mouth. 'I counsel thee', says the Doctor to his Student,

also that in every general rule of the law thou do observe and keep equity—all of which is in the law of reason; and if thou do thus I trust the light of thy lantern (that is thy conscience) shall never be extinguished . . .

Equity is a justice that considereth all the particular circumstances of the deed, which is also tempered with the sweetness of mercy. And such an equity must always be observed in every law of man . . . And the wise man saith: Be not overmuch legal, for extreme legality does extreme wrong (*summa iustitia summa iniustitia fit*),[109] as who saith, if thou take all that the words of the law giveth thee, thou shalt sometimes do against the law. Since the deeds and acts of men, for which laws are ordained, happen in divers manners infinitely, it is not possible to make any general rule of the law but that it shall fail in some case. And therefore makers of laws take heed to such things as generally happen, and not to every particular case, for they could not even if they wished to. Wherefore in some cases it is good and even necessary to leave the words of the law, and to follow what reason and justice require, and to that intent equity is ordained, that is to say, to temper and mitigate the rigour of the law. And it is called also by some men *epicaia* . . . And so it appeareth that equity rather follows the intent of the law than the words of the law.[110]

Thus the ideas of Aristotle and of the Roman orators ('summum ius summa iniuria'), kept alive both by the civilians and humanists and by the canonists and St Thomas, become one of the foundations of doctrine for English equity.

---

[109] A survival of the ancient Roman *summum ius summa iniuria:* Cicero, *De officiis* 1. 33.
[110] *Doctor and Student*, ch. 14.

The question of who is entitled to bypass the formal rules, as it were suspending the law *ad hoc*, naturally arose in the context of the rule of law, and was answered by the Spanish Jesuit Mariana (1536–1623) in the course of the traditional injunction to rulers to keep within the law. They may not turn the laws upside down for their own purposes; but 'it may still be permitted to kings, when the occasion requires it, to seek changes in the law, to apply old laws in a new way[111] and to soften their application (*emollire*), and to fill gaps (*supplere*) if some actual happening is not covered by the law as it stands'.[112]

EQUALITY

In the earlier epochs of the Middle Ages the ancient Christian teaching of the equality of humankind had had to be somehow reconciled with the visible inequalities of life in practice; and in the last period of that age we can still see the European mind working out formulas to give a logical and moral basis for its three principal aspects.

Political subordination presented the fewest problems. Firstly, the institution of government had been expressly countenanced by Christ himself, followed by St Paul (although St Paul was the originator of the Christian doctrine of equality). Moreover, common sense recommended it; Wycliffe thought that 'reason dictates that each people should set up one head for themselves . . . as we English have one blessed king'.[113] Vitoria cited St Thomas in allowing that 'dominion and pre-eminence were introduced by human law; they were therefore not by natural law'.[114] But they were a general feature of the world. Human nature demands society, he wrote in traditional vein, society in turn requires authority, for without authority there would be only confusion. The Protestant Hooker thought so too; 'to bring things into the first course they were in [i.e. in mankind's primitive condition] and utterly to take away all kind of public government in the world, were apparently to overturn the whole world'.[115] Indeed Hooker

---

[111] If 'interpretari veteres' may be so understood.
[112] *De rege et regis institutione* 1. 9.   [113] *De officio regis* 249.
[114] *Relectiones* 2. 1.   [115] *Laws of Ecclesiastical Polity* 1. 10.

attributed to government a natural-law origin as Vitoria had not done: 'the case of man's nature standing as it doth, some kind of regiment[116] the law of Nature doth require', even though it did not prescribe any particular form of government, but left the choice of this 'as a thing arbitrary'.[117] On the other hand, the Spanish theologians and jurists of this age, writing in disapproval of their countrymen's excesses in the New World, insisted that the institution of government must be freely accepted by those who are to be subject to it. No man, wrote Vitoria, has the right to force laws on others, since man is free by nature.[118] Fernando Vázquez, citing de Soto to the same effect, and in a context as relevant to political subordination as to slavery, held that by the law of nature 'all men are equal . . . No man whatsoever is or ever will be lawfully subject to the control (*iurisdictio*) of another without his own voluntary act: he can, of course, become subject to a ruler (*princeps*) by a voluntary act of submission to somebody'; and this is the only legitimate source for any man's subjection to another's will.[119] Naturally this doctrine is as applicable to the subjects of European monarchs as to the Indians whom the Spanish writers mostly had in mind; but here of course the theory of the social contract, or something like it even if not expressly identical (e.g. Vitoria's formula),[120] supplied the element of supposed consent of the governed, whatever the difficulty of imputing to later generations a consent thought to have been given in fact by their remote ancestors.

Writers of the voluntarist tradition, for whom God's will was the sole and sufficient justification for whatever they believed he had authorized, did not need to ground earthly government on anything so rational as an implied contract. Thus Luther in his earlier work wrote that coercive political authority was the expression of God's will working on earth; it was highly sinful to resist rulers, no matter how oppressive they were or what promises they might have broken; this was because many men are not good Christians and so require the restraint of government; were it otherwise, and all were

---

[116] Meaning 'institution of government', 'regime'.
[117] *Laws of Ecclesiastical Polity* 1. 10.
[118] *Relectio de Indis* 1.
[119] *Controversiae illustres* 1. 20. 24.
[120] Above, at the end of the section on 'Natural Law'.

good Christians, there would be no need of prince, sword, or law itself.[121]

Accordingly either their own implicit consent, or God's command, sufficiently explained the political subordination which modified men's natural equality. At the end of the age, Hooker in some measure combined both approaches: 'the lawful power of making laws to command whole politic societies of men', he wrote, is given either by God or by the subjects.[122]

SLAVERY

The period of this chapter was that in which slavery as a living institution—and as a living offence against the principle of men's natural equality—died out in Western Europe. There were still many slaves in fifteenth-century households, generally of Moorish or Balkan origin, and these were mostly to be found in the southern countries of Italy, southern France, Spain, and Portugal. In northern Europe, and then throughout the Western continent, the man of unfree status, who could be bought and sold, disappeared between about 1400 and 1500 or so; partly because an allowance of some measure of freedom and independence was seen to result in more efficient production by agricultural and other workers who could see some benefit for themselves arising from their labour; partly no doubt because of the humanitarian influence of the Church which, though it never condemned slavery outright and was often itself the owner of slaves, still preached the virtue of setting free the bondsman on the basis of the human equality which the very earliest Christians had proclaimed. Yet just as slavery was disappearing in the old world, it began a fresh and terrible life in the new, with the start of the slave trade to provide labour for the mines and afterwards for the plantations of America. The cruel human exploitation which accompanied Spain's colonizing across the Atlantic was the immediate stimulus for protests against the venerable legal theory on which slavery was justified notwithstanding its repugnance to the natural equality of all men.

---

[121] *Von weltlicher Obrigkeit* 247. For the later modification of his view on resistance, see Carlyles, *Medieval Theory* (Ch. 3 n. 29), vi. 280 ff.

[122] *Laws of Ecclesiastical Polity* 1. 10. 7.

Long before that episode, which belongs essentially to the late sixteenth century, Wycliffe in England had seemed to doubt the possibility of reconciling slavery with Christian teaching. Although I did say above, he wrote, that servants ought to obey their masters, 'it is a question whether masters can conform to Christ's precept in exacting this kind of servitude . . . Every man naturally desires freedom, which would not be the case unless freedom were part of the law of nature, that is, of God's law too.' He recites the 'golden rule' of St Matthew's Gospel, that one should do unto others as one would wish others to do to oneself, and continues: 'Every man is by nature unwilling to be reduced into human bondage, and therefore he ought not to reduce any of his brothers [*nullum confratrem suum*] into servitude either . . . No one should hold his neighbour in bondage by coercion.' The force of these expressions is not diminished by the arguments in the opposite sense which he then recites, which do not go to the root, namely the essential discordance between slavery and nature, any more than Aristotle's excuse (which Wycliffe also mentions) related to the supposed natural servility of some men.[123]

The latter easy palliation of slavery's offensiveness was probably a commonplace in the Italian Renaissance; it appears, for example, in Baldassare Castiglione's *Book of the Courtier*, where he says that men apt only for physical toil 'differ from men versed in the things of the mind as much as the soul from the body . . . These are essentially slaves, and it is better for them to obey than to command'. Even Francisco de Vitoria, the founder of the Spanish 'late scholastic' school, accepted Aristotle's formula (though he denied that the Indians of the New World could be classified as slaves for its purposes).[124] But with his disciple Domenico de Soto, and with the lay jurist Fernando Vázquez at the end of the sixteenth century, rebellion against 'the Philosopher's' doctrine is evident.

De Soto's approach was to modify the meaning of the words *dominus, dominium*, which in the Roman law and tradition had signified ownership of the sort exercised over a slave, so as to admit a master-and-servant relationship, but not servitude in the ancient sense. No law, he wrote, can repeal natural law; and by natural law all men are born free. Consequently, no law permits the human race to admit such a thing as slavery. On the other hand, both natural

---

[123] *De civili dominio* 1. 32.   [124] *Relectiones* 1. 24.

law and human law permit one man to be the *dominus* of another. But if so, this has to be understood in a manner not conflicting with the basic principle of natural freedom; and he sets out the conditions on which, within those limits, *dominium* can be admitted:

A man who is by nature a lord and master may not make use of those who are by nature servants, as though they were mere possessions, purely for his own enjoyment; on the contrary he must train them to virtue[125] like men free and *sui iuris*. Similarly his servants are not bound to serve him as though they were mere objects of property (*mancipia*),[126] but rather to give him fair and honest service—unless of course they have been hired out to him for money.[127]

With Fernando Vázquez we find Aristotle tackled head-on. Lamenting the open defiance offered to natural law by some of the actual practice of his time, he says in the preface to his book:

Who could endure the impudence—not to say the unforgivable offensive-ness—of Aristotle, when he says in the first book of his *Politics* that men of slow intellect should be considered to have been born slaves by nature, or for the service of people of greater wisdom? . . . What crime have we dullards committed? God made us, not those great brains . . . Quite a few of our nation follow that impious doctrine of Aristotle's. And surely a much truer and more worthy view is that of those upright and weighty jurists, who have written that slaves have been made so only by the legal systems of men (*iure gentium*), while by the law of nature they have continued to be free.[128]

Another passage from the same work, relating to human equality and subordination generally, has already been cited.[129]

---

[125] *in rem ac bonum instituendo*: the translation here offered of this odd phrase is a guess at Soto's meaning.

[126] *mancipia*: a Roman word meaning, in the plural, slaves; but as Roman slaves were items of property which could be bought and sold, the contrast seems to come through better with the translation here offered.

[127] *De iustitia et iure* 4. 2. 2. The reference to hiring presumably means that servants who are the subject of a temporary contract do not place their temporary master under the same moral obligation to them.

[128] *Controversiae illustres*, praefatio 9. The weighty jurists he mentions are of course the civilians repeating the Roman doctrine on this point.

[129] Above, the section on 'Equality'.

PROPERTY

The institution of private property had found theoretical justifications already in the days of the early Church Fathers; but it is interesting to note for how long its status in a Christian society seemed equivocal (its total adoption by the Catholic Church as part of natural law giving men the natural right to private ownership of 'external goods' was not to come until the late nineteenth century),[130] and how persistent is the idea that an innocent communism was the condition of the original race of man, and even now an optimum state for man to aspire to. The social unrest of the later fourteenth and the fifteenth centuries was largely provoked by the oppression of the poor by the rich, and so the abuse of property was a natural target for an early reformer like Wycliffe, who taught in his Oxford lectures in 1376 that private property was the consequence of sin: as Christ and the apostles had had no property, neither should the clergy, whose acquisitiveness provoked his particular anger; only righteous behaviour could justify property (or for that matter government). Two hundred years later Fernando Vázquez cited the Roman poet Macrobius' depiction of the primordial golden age, when it was unlawful to mark out ground as one's own, or to divide it with fences; Vázquez, too, thought that once all peoples had lived with neither kings nor laws, and had held the world's goods in common, with neither ownership or possession by individuals, nor any contracts nor any commerce (for which there was no need in the time of innocence).[131] This is still, in a way, the ideal of Thomas More (1478–1535), martyred under Henry VIII for his Catholic allegiance; his traveller Ralph Hythloday, giving an account of the dream-world of Utopia, shows a state in which 'all things being there common, every man hath abundance of every thing . . . [unlike countries] where every man calleth that he hath gotten his own proper and private goods'. This private greed is the cause of poverty; and, he is convinced, 'no equal and just distribution of things can be made, nor perfect wealth ever be among men, unless this propriety [i.e. this sort of private

---

[130] See section on 'Property' in Ch. 8 below.
[131] *Controversiae illustres* 1. 4. 3.

ownership] be exiled and banished'.[132] But More, who cast himself (under the simple name of 'the lawyer') as Hythloday's interlocutor, is enough of a practical man to see the problem here, as indeed Aristotle and St Thomas had seen it: when all things are held in common, he replies, there never can be wealth, 'for how can there be abundance of goods, or of any thing, where every man withdraweth his hand from labour? whom the regard of his own gains driveth not to work, but the hope that he hath in other men's travails makes him slothful'[133]—another way of saying everyone's business is no one's business. So human nature, whose altruism and civic sense cannot be depended upon as a rule for every day, enforces residence in a different world, however regretfully one may glance back at Utopia.

More's Spanish contemporary Domenico de Soto, far from thinking natural law required common ownership, thought more or less the opposite, though his reason was eccentric; liberality, the sharing of one's wealth with the more needy, depended on the existence of private property; it was not the meanest of human virtues, and if nothing belonged individually to anyone but everything was owned in common, there would no longer be any room for its exercise. Accordingly, he wrote, 'the assertion of the rightness of private property is so justified that its denial would be heretical'.[134] The last of the great generation of Spanish theologian-jurists, Suárez, stands more in the realist tradition. Natural law, he held, contained no particular command in favour either of common or of private ownership; 'the advantages which show that a division of property is better adapted to man's nature and the fallen state are proof, not that this division of ownership is a matter prescribed by natural law, but merely that it is adapted to the existing state and condition of mankind'.[135] From this position it is still a long way to the Catholic Church's enthronement of private property as an item of natural law.

---

[132] *Utopia*, Introduction. The name of this famous book, published in 1518, is composed from the Greek *topos*, 'place', plus either *eu-* 'good, well') or the negative particle *ou* (which would make Utopia mean 'nowhere', a 'non-place').

[133] Ibid.   [134] Soto, *De legibus* 3. 3. 1.

[135] *De legibus ac Deo legislatore* (1612), 2. 14.

CRIMINAL LAW AND PUNISHMENT

This age exhibits no advance on preceding ages so far as concerns a scientific interest in the theory of crime or the values to be pursued in its repression. De Soto and Molina, at least, put some theoretical shape on criminal law by relating it to the law of nature, and the necessity of supplementing it by positive human law. One of the basic functions of the body politic was for de Soto the 'checking of the boldness of evildoers';[136] the natural law, however, of which he appears to consider this function of society to be a corollary, 'cannot compel by punishment', and of course 'such penalties are necessary for man in the state of fallen nature, so that the work of the prince is to use penal laws'.[137] Molina attributed to the natural law the principle that malefactors should be punished by the public authority, so that peace, justice, and the common good of the community may be preserved;[138] presumably, either by removing the malefactors themselves from the scene, or by deterring them and others from repetition or imitation. On the other hand he held that it was not part of the natural law that thieves should be hanged or whipped, because the natural law is sufficiently preserved if they are punished by other penalties.

There are in this age some views worth mentioning on the proper approach of the criminal law, though a very far cry from the sort of debates which the nineteenth and twentieth centuries were to hear. Vitoria and de Soto both counselled against setting too high a standard (i.e. by proposing to punish all lapses from virtue) for frail humanity; anti-social vices—as well of course as offences against God—are the most important to prohibit. 'If all offences against virtue were punished', wrote Molina, 'the human race would be too much oppressed, and the courts and prisons unable to punish or contain all the crimes.'[139] A humane proportion of punishment to offence is recommended by Thomas More; at least he puts it in the mouth of Hythloday, the traveller to Utopia, and leaves it uncontradicted:

I think it not right nor justice, that the loss of money should cause the loss of man's life . . . Why may not this extreme and rigorous justice well be

---

[136] *De legibus* 4. 4. 1.
[138] *De iustitia et iure* 6. 5. 68. 1.

[137] *De iustitia* 1. 5. 1.
[139] Ibid. 6. 5. 72.

called plain injury? For so cruel governance, so strait rules, and unmerciful laws be not allowable, that if a small offence be committed, by and by the sword should be drawn: nor so stoical ordinances are to be borne withal, as to count all offences of such equality, that the killing of man, or the taking of his money from him, were both one matter, and the one no more heinous offence than the other: between the which two, if we have any respect to equity, no similitude or equality consisteth.[140]

The question of the mental element in wrongdoing, and its relevance to punishment or its quantum, is briefly treated by Hooker in his *Laws of Ecclesiastical Polity*. There may, he says, be a less than complete will to do wrong—as where the agent is the victim of duress or of madness, or is an infant—and 'in this consideration one evil deed is made more pardonable than another', in a degree related to the 'exigence', i.e. the compulsion affecting the will, or the difficulty of avoiding committing the injury. There is, however, an important qualification here; the offence, he thought, is not venial if 'this necessity or difficulty have originally arisen from ourselves', and in this connection he recalls the law attributed to Pittacus which doubled the penalty for an offence committed in drunkenness; this would not be reasonable if measured only by the gravity of the offence, but could be defended as being for the public good. In general, however, the relation of intent to guilt is plain: 'for who knoweth not, that harm advisedly done is naturally less pardonable, and therefore worthy of sharper punishment?'[141]

INTERNATIONAL LAW

It is to the end of this chapter's period, in other words to the sixteenth century, especially the later part of the century, that the emergence of a fairly clear concept of a legal system governing the relations of states with one another can be attributed. It has been seen that a few much earlier figures, like St Augustine and St Isidore of Seville, hinted at something like an international legal order; and some areas of practice, notably those of maritime and mercantile custom, and usage concerning heralds and ambassadors, predisposed to more comprehensive schemes; but it is not until the sixteenth century—and again, with the Spanish 'late scholastics' of

---

[140] *Utopia*, Introduction.   [141] *Laws of Ecclesiastical Polity*, 1. 9–10.

their country's 'golden age'—that something like a doctrine on the
subject appears, which shortly afterwards, in the early seventeenth
century, would be built by Grotius into a system.

This sixteenth-century date is not an accident. In the first place,
Spain's encounter with the strange peoples of the New World
presented problems to the reflecting Christian mind which forced
into existence some sort of reasoning about the rights of peoples.
Secondly, this was the first century in which Europe displayed a
fully developed pattern of clearly defined and powerful sovereign
states. The potential of the nations of Europe to evolve in this
direction had been obscured in the earlier Middle Ages by the idea
of Christian unity under pope and emperor; even in most of the
fifteenth century, as one authority puts it, European states were not
mature enough internally to have a clear external impact.[142] At the
end of that century, there was a change. Many writers actually
assign a date to it: 1494, the year of the French invasion of Italy and
the beginning of the long struggle with Spain for dominance there.
From that moment, 'the nations stand forth as full-grown personal-
ities' (particularly Spain, France, and England in the time of
Ferdinand, Louis XI, and Henry VII respectively) and a true
international system is born; a system, in the sense of habitual
intensive contacts between countries needing to have regard to one
another at all times.[143] The most characteristic feature of this new
Europe was the rapid spread of the practice (originated by the
Italian city-states) of maintaining standing embassies at foreign
courts, instead of merely dispatching them on some great occasion.
Thus new conditions both near at hand and across the Atlantic were
the ground on which a new Law of Nations was to be erected.

This expression, 'law of nations', is of course a rendering of the
Roman *ius gentium*; but *ius gentium* did not mean, either to the
Romans or the medieval civilians, international law in our sense.
This pressing of an old phrase into a new service is a sign of how
gradually, and at first only half-consciously, the concept of
international law in our sense emerged. When Vitoria wrote of the
right (here the right of the Spaniards) to travel, to trade peacefully,
to settle, as part of the *ius gentium*, he evidently meant that these
basic activities were lawful in the eyes of all mankind. When he

---

[142] Grewe, *Epochen* (see Ch. 4 n. 132), 34, citing W. Windelband, *Die Auswärtige
Politik der Grossmächte in der Newzeit* (Essen, 1936), 25.
[143] Grewe, *Epochen*, 33.

wrote that the Indians of the New World had true ownership of their land, that it was not at the disposal of either emperor or pope, and that they could not be despoiled of it, not even for their unbelief or refusal to hear the Christian message,[144] that they had legitimate princes just as Christians had,[145] that they could not be punished for their supposed sins against nature,[146] and that to wage war against them was permissible only with just cause,[147] he was evidently stating the rights of *nations* which other nations must respect. Here, to the extent that he imputed such conclusions to the *ius gentium*, he was pushing out the frontiers of the expression far beyond its classical limits. He also, in his lectures of 1532, used the new expression *ius inter gentes*; and, while this does not necessarily mean 'the law between, i.e. governing the relations of nations inter se' (more likely it conveys no more than 'the law among all peoples'), his exploration of rather new conceptual territory has caused him to rank as a founding father of international law, at any rate the leading pioneer before Grotius.

Alberico Gentili (1552–1608), who was that rare bird an Italian Protestant (he took refuge in England, where he was regius professor of civil law at Oxford), is also one of the pioneers. He was the first to write a treatise on the special subject of embassies, *De legationibus* (1585), and published a book on the law of war, *De iure belli* (1598), on the basis of lectures given originally in the year of the Armada (1588). This contained an important treatment of peace treaties, stating for example the principle that these are binding even when imposed under duress, and the notion of the so-called 'rebus sic stantibus' clause. The very title of the work implies a normative order transcending both belligerent powers; but it is only at the very end of the century, and shortly afterwards, that the idea of a legal order of which states are the subjects is put into words. Richard Hooker in the first book of his *Laws of Ecclesiastical Polity* (1594) envisaged a 'third kind of law which toucheth all such several bodies politic, so far forth as one of them hath public commerce with another'; this contains 'primary' rules relating to such things as laws of embassy, foreigners' rights, and 'commodius traffic', but also

---

[144] *Relectio de Indis* 2. 10, 11, 15.   [145] Ibid. 1. 4, 24; 2. 7.

[146] Ibid. 2. 16. The Norman Giraldus Cambrensis (see Ch. 4 n. 132) repeatedly charged the native Irish with crimes against nature (to wit, bestiality), just as the Spaniards accused the Indians of sodomy: were these routine medieval calumnies to justify conquerors?

[147] *Relectio de iure belli* 10, 13.

'secondary' rules, which apply when ordinary relations have broken down, in other words the laws of war. Those laws, he wrote, are based on nature and reason, and on the fact that 'we covet (if it might be) to have a kind of society and fellowship even with all mankind'.[148] But the clearest doctrinal foundation was provided by the Jesuit Suárez. In a phrase which cannot be misunderstood (as perhaps Vitoria's 'ius inter gentes' was) he spoke of the 'ius quod omnes populi et gentes variae inter se servare debent', 'the law which all peoples and diverse nations ought to observe among themselves'.[149] It was not part of the natural, but of human law; it was established by usage and custom; it was unwritten. Its basis he explained as follows:

No matter how many diverse peoples and kingdoms the human race may be divided into, it always has a certain unity, not merely as a species but even a sort of political and moral unity, which is indicated by the natural precept of mutual love and mercy which extends to foreigners, even to foreigners of any nation. No matter how a sovereign state, commonwealth or kingdom may be in itself a perfect society with its own members, *each one is also*, in a sense, as seen from the point of view of the human race, *a member of the universal community*; for states standing alone are not so self-sufficient that they never require some mutual help, association and intercourse . . . They therefore need some law to direct and order rightly this type of intercourse and association . . . and so certain specific laws could be introduced through the usage of the nations.[150]

The work containing these words was published in 1611. Both it and the other works of the Spanish school were known to Grotius, who a few years later was to clothe with system the ideas which his forerunners had brought into the world in the naked form of theory.

[148] *Laws of Ecclesiastical Polity* 1. 10.
[149] *De legibus ac Deo legislatore* 2. 19. 8.
[150] Ibid. 2. 19. 9.

6
The Seventeenth Century

The eighteenth century, being nearer us in time, and far more clearly visible for us in its architecture amid which we still live, evokes more numerous and more colourful images than does the seventeenth. Prominent among those images are the revolutions of America and particularly of France. The world was never the same again after the events of 1789; and this is why the half-century which starts at the fall of the Bastille is, for instance by the historian E. J. Hobsbawm in the title of a book, called the age of revolution. But these revolutions were not cooked up overnight. The peculiar political conjunctures which brought the powder to the flash on both sides of the Atlantic in 1776 and 1789 might have been avoided; those dates might not have become famous; but the events with which, as things happened, they are associated had an intellectual as well as a political history, and the direction in which Western thought had long been heading would sooner or later have produced a radical change in the state of the ancient monarchies and systems of government. It is in the seventeenth century, more than in any other that preceded it, that things were said and done which, to the eye of hindsight, make the events of the eighteenth inevitable; if not necessarily in quite the form they took, at least in substance; if not necessarily in just those years, at any rate in an age which would not be long delayed.

The century opened on a Europe not yet over the shock and rupture of Reformation. In England the fear of Catholic subversion of the Protestant establishment runs right through the century: the external threat from Counter-Reformation Spain ended at Kinsale in 1601 (the end also of the ancient Gaelic order in Ireland); but the sense of danger from within remained, not without reason. The Gunpowder Plot of 'Guy Fawkes' in 1605 was real, even if the 'Popish Plot' of 1679 was not, and the fear that the Catholic King James II would re-establish his religion as that of England led to his deposition and to the legal entrenchment of the Protestant succession in 1700. In Ireland the fall-out from national hatred was the more terrible for the added hatreds of religion; the rebellion of 1641, in which thousands of Protestant settlers were massacred, led to the awful vengeance of Cromwell at the decade's end, but remains to this day the leading item in the Ulster Protestant's chamber of Roman horrors; Irish Catholic support for James II led, after the Boyne (1690) and Aughrim (1691), to the departure of many Irish officers to service with the Catholic powers of Europe, and inaugurated at home the era of the Penal Laws. In France the religious wars of the sixteenth century had closed with the Edict of Nantes (1598), guaranteeing toleration for the Huguenots, the work of Henry IV (1589–1610), who having been himself a Protestant converted to Catholicism in order to win acceptance of his succession; but Louis XIV (1643–1715), both the archetypal absolute monarch and militantly Catholic, revoked the Edict of Nantes in 1685, provoking the emigration of Huguenots to every neighbouring country that would have them (to the great benefit of their new home countries and the impoverishment of France). In Germany the century was one of calamity originating in religious conflict; the attempt by the Protestant nobles of Bohemia to place a Protestant on the throne of that country—a coup which, had it come off, would have meant a Protestant majority in the college of seven imperial electors and the likely passage of the imperial crown of Germany into Protestant hands—detonated the terrible Thirty Years War (1618–48), still alive in the folk-memory of central Europe, which laid Germany in ruins, and involved at some stage virtually every power in Europe. The Peace of Westphalia which ended the conflict marked the end of all significance for the imperial title, henceforth only an ornamental trapping of the house of Habsburg, and the final settling-down of the old and the reformed religions in their respective zones of predominance; it marked, too, the final recognition by the Spanish crown of the secession of the northern Netherlands; as the United Provinces, these Protestant Netherlands experienced in the seventeenth century an age of military and commercial (and artistic) glory. To the north the Scandinavian kingdoms, to the south the powers of the Iberian and Italian peninsulas adhered with little disturbance to the new and to the old religions respectively. The fires of religious fanaticism burnt lower throughout Europe; and, though at the century's end Europe was very far from the easy pluralist tolerance which marks the continent today, the approaching age of reason and enlightenment would extinguish them, more or less completely, more or less everywhere.

On the purely political level, the seventeenth century saw the decline of Spain, none of whose subsequent kings after Philip II had his energy or capacity. Her absorption of Portugal (from 1580 to 1640) had added the huge Portuguese empire to her domains; but her fatal assault on the Dutch provoked this people into world-wide counter-attack. In the early part of the century they seized the rich Portuguese possessions in the East Indies, which they were to retain until the Japanese conquest of 1942 in the Second World War; they preyed on Spanish shipping coming from the new world; they were, for a time, the foremost maritime power in Europe. The Spanish state, handicapped by antique structures of government and by an aristocracy ridiculously inflated in numbers but too proud to do a useful day's work, sank under the pressures of the new age, yielding to France the position of incomparably the most powerful state in Europe. With the quelling of the wars of the Fronde—essentially, attempts to assert regional power and regional interests against the central authority of the crown and Paris—the French kingship advanced, under the early guidance of ministers such as Cardinals Richelieu and Mazarin, and above all in the long reign of Louis XIV, to the status of a byword for autocratic splendour. Louis XIV, however, in his insatiable appetite for military glory and expansion, involved his country in a long and exhausting series of wars which absorbed most of the fruits of his numerous[1] subjects' talent and industry; the patterns of taxation needed to sustain his gradiose career which then were solidified contributed decisively, along with patterns of intolerable privilege, to produce the explosion of the Revolution seventy years after his death. He interfered relentlessly in his neighbours' affairs, supporting James II of England in his contest with his Protestant subjects, and providing military help, above all an experienced officer corps from Europe's most redoubtable army, during James's Irish campaign; when James fled from Ireland it was with Louis that he sought refuge; and he lived in an exile court provided for him by Louis at Germain-en-Laye near Paris until his death in 1701. At the same time the age of Louis XIV

---

[1] France owed much of her power in this and the next century to her huge population, relative to that of other states. About the end of the reign of Louis XIV it was about 17 million, compared to Spain's 7 million. By 1789 it was 26 million.

was notable not only for military and diplomatic adventure, but also for achievements in science and the arts which won for France, her language, and manners, a prestige throughout the world not eclipsed until the twentieth century.

As for Germany and Italy, these two great cultural areas remained in the seventeenth century mere geographic expressions. In Germany the Thirty Years War ended in 1648 in universal desolation; in the remainder of the century its multiple statelets recovered only slowly from this convulsion, as trade and industry little by little revived, and the universities whose activity the war had mostly interrupted once again began to open their doors. Italy, where Protestant reformers had made virtually no inroads on the homogeneous Catholic culture, and where no religious wars had taken place, was divided into fewer mutually independent political units than Germany (virtually half the peninsula, the southern kingdom of Naples and Sicily, was under the rule of the Spanish Habsburgs throughout the century); but the rise of a sense of Italian nationhood and the emergence of a unified Italian state lay still far in the future.

In England the seventeenth century was the epoch of a revolution of the most cardinal importance in the history of political and legal theory. The very beginnings of the Stuart dynasty—the reign of James I who succeeded to the English throne on Elizabeth's death in 1603—were marked by conflict between crown and subjects on the questions of the origin and nature of royal authority, and the crown's power to dispense from application of the law or to act independently of it; in the reign of his son Charles I (1625–49) mutually irreconcilable doctrines on the source and limit of kingly powers and on the rule of law were the setting of the contest between king and parliament which ended in the king's execution; and the successive periods of Cromwell's republican commonwealth (1649–60) and of the restored monarchy, Charles II (1660–85) and James II (1685–8), did not see the harmonious resolution of these differences. James's obstinacy and insensitivity in dealing with his Protestant subjects, in particular his filling of offices with Catholics, provoked his deposition and (according to the previously understood rules of succession, illegal) replacement by the Protestant William of Orange and his wife Mary, James's Protestant daughter, as joint sovereigns. This 'Glorious Revolution' of 1688, no less than the convulsion of the Civil War in the 1640s, unfolded in a setting of conflicting legal and political theory. What emerged victorious from the Revolution was a body of principles about the supremacy of law, the fundamental rights of man, and the essentially democratic basis of political authority. These doctrines were at once transplanted to America, where they were to provide the intellectual armoury of the rebel colonials a century later; and to France, where they also furnished stimuli to progressive and ultimately to revolutionary thought. The Irish experience of the world which followed the Williamite wars and the Treaty of Limerick was a dark one; but the essential heritage of religious and political liberty, though at first withheld from the Irish people, was ultimately given reality among them in a more enlightened age, and, sometimes in American or in French dress, sometimes in that of the common law, passed in the twentieth century into the institutions of an independent Irish state.

Political revolution in the seventeenth century was confined to England (and, as an accompaniment of national liberation, Holland); but it was an age of scientific revolution everywhere. A start had been made in the previous century in the field of astronomy; there now followed a more general transformation of scientific thought, inarticulately inspired by the idea, strange to medieval man, that limitless discoveries might be made in every branch of knowledge, and limitless improvements in the condition of human life. This did not harmonize well with the universal and final certainties which the medieval Church had claimed to offer; and the rejection of papal authority, common to all forms of the reformed religion, was an important condition for the unfolding of the beginnings of modern science. But free enquiry implied the repudiation not just of ecclesiastical but of all authority, even that of Aristotle, the most venerable of the ancient pagan philosophers. In place of authority, the evidence of exploration and experiment was set, above all by the English lawyer[2] and philosopher Francis Bacon (1561–1626), whose book *Novum organum scientiarum* (1620) was of decisive influence, due mainly to its analysis of, and emphasis upon, the inductive method of reasoning whereby the observation of a number of individual instances is used in order to discover a general principle (rather than the method of deduction, by which a general proposition is used for a guide to particular instances). The century witnessed revolutions in astronomy (Galileo), physiology (Harvey,

[2] And corrupt judge: in 1621 he was convicted of taking bribes and removed from his office of lord chancellor, fined, and imprisoned.

discoverer of the circulation of the blood), physics (Newton), and mathematics (Newton and Leibniz both invented the differential and integral calculus at about the same time in the 1670s in ignorance of one another's work). The excitement caused by advances like these led to the creation in several countries of learned societies independent of the universities; the constant correspondence between their members contributed to still further discoveries and inventions. The conditions of ordinary life improved; better medical knowledge put an end to the plagues which had periodically decimated the European population (that of 1665–6 was the last to be seen in England); better agricultural methods contributed to a rise in population and the rapid growth of big towns. Ancient problems, wrote the philosopher R. G. Collingwood of the scientific revolution of the seventeenth century, suddenly could be

restated in a shape in which, with the double weapon of experiment and mathematics, one could now solve them. What was called Nature . . . had henceforth no secrets from man; only riddles which he had learnt the trick of answering. Or, more accurately, Nature was no longer a Sphinx asking man riddles; it was man that did the asking, and Nature, now, that he put to the torture until she gave him the answer to his questions.[3]

The Basis of the State and of Government

It has been seen that in the sixteenth century it was a commonplace to impute the origin of ordered society to an agreement of some kind between its members, or, to use the short expression which afterwards became usual, to a 'social contract'. It was, however, in the seventeenth century more than any other, and particularly in England, that social-contract theory played a central part in constitutional conflict; and it was that century also which produced its two most famous exponents in Thomas Hobbes and John Locke. It appears in varying formulations: sometimes it proposes no more than an account of how individuals previously unconnected by any civic tie came together to found some kind of society, what later German theorists called a 'contract of union'; sometimes a further element is added, and a further party, as where those individuals

---

[3] *An Autobiography* (Pelican edn.), 55.

agree not only to found a commonwealth, but also to constitute a ruler or ruling body, with whom further promises are exchanged: the ruler promises justice and protection to the new subjects, who in turn promise obedience in return and on condition that they actually receive those central values of good government; the same theorists called this a 'contract of subjection'. In either form of the social contract, a democratic or people-centred principle is apparent, its roots perhaps most obviously in ancient Germanic traditions, although (as was seen) the Graeco-Roman world too shows some inklings of it.

In either form, moreover, though more particularly in the form of the 'contract of subjection', social-contract theory did not accord with other ancient perceptions. It could, indeed, be got into harmony with Aristotle's (and Aquinas's) human being tending by his nature to civic existence by saying that, while man's instinct was political, it found realization by the mechanism of contract. But it was quite at odds with a theocratic view of government, one which saw kings as divinely appointed, and their subjects as divinely commanded to obey them, in other words with that which held government to be of God rather than of human contrivance. James I, king of England (1603–25), in his *True Law of Free Monarchies* written a few years earlier (when he was king of Scotland alone), mentioned the contract of subjection theory in the form which took each particular king to enter a bargain with his coronation oath, and, although admitting that a king ought to behave honourably, denied the conclusion that his ill-behaviour released his subjects from obedience:

For, say they, there is a mutuall paction, and contract bound up, and sworne betwixt the king and the people, whereupon it followeth, that if the one part of the Contract or the Indent bee broken upon the king's side, the people are no longer bound to keep their part of it, but are thereby freed of their oath. For (say they) a contract betwixt two parties of all lawe frees the one partie if the other breake unto him. As to this contract alledged, made at the coronation of a King, although I deny any such contract to be made then, especially containing such a clause irritant, as they alledge, yet I confesse that a King at his coronation, or at the entry to his kingdome, willingly promiseth to his people, to discharge honourably and truly the office given him by God over them. But presuming that thereafter he breake his promise unto them, never so inexcusable, the question is, who should be judge of this breake . . .

for everyone with the smallest knowledge of law knew that no one can release himself from a contract merely because he thinks the other party has broken it; there must first be an impartial trial, otherwise the self-releasing party is making himself a judge in his own cause. There is certainly no right 'in the headlesse multitude, when they please to weary of subjection, to cast off the yoke of government that God hath laid on them, and to judge and punish him by whom they should be judged and punished'.[4]

James's point about making oneself a judge in one's own cause (as the Commons were to do in 1649 when they put his son Charles I on trial) was well taken, even if it does not go to the root of the idea of a contract of subjection. But probably even for authorities with a less direct interest in the divine right of kings, all contract theory, if stated as an all-sufficient root of title for human governance, struck an unacceptably rationalist, even impious, note. The Canons of the Church of England, drafted in 1606, expressly denied that the state's legitimacy depended upon the people's acceptance of a ruler:

If any man shall affirm that men at the first, without all good education and civility, ran up and down in woods and fields, as wild creatures, resting themselves in caves and dens, and acknowledging no superiority one over another, until they were taught by experience the necessity of government; and that thereupon they chose some among themselves to order and rule the rest, giving them power and authority so to do; and that consequently all civil power, jurisdiction and authority was first derived from the people, and disordered multitude; or either is originally still in them, or else is deduced by their consents naturally from them, and is not God's ordinance originally descending from Him and depending upon Him; he doth greatly err.[5]

Yet even among the most pious people the contractual model was found appealing. It was put into service by the Pilgrim Fathers who sailed to North America in the *Mayflower* in 1620 in order to establish there a new commonwealth free of the disabilities which the rule of the Anglican Church placed on their worship in England:

In the name of God, Amen [*the Mayflower Compact ran*]. We whose names are underwritten, the loyall subjects of our dread soveraigne lord, King James, . . . doe by these presents solemnly and mutualy in the presence of

---

[4] See Carlyles, *Medieval Theory* (see Ch. 3 n. 29), vi. 437–40.
[5] See J. P. Kenyon, *The Stuart Constitution* (London, 1966), 11.

God, and one of another, covenant and combine oursselves togeather into a civill body politick, for our better ordering and preservation . . . and by vertue hearof to enacte, constitute and frame such just and equall lawes, ordinances, acts, constitutions, and offices, from time to time, as shall be thought most meete and convenient for the general good of the Colonie, unto which we promise all due submission and obedience.[6]

At the other extremity of the religious spectrum of Europe after the Reformation, in Catholic Spain, and in the same period, we find the contractual theory stated more or less exactly in the form in which King James had denied it, namely as a constitutional bargain between king and subjects. The oath taken to the crown by the members of the Cortes (parliament) of Aragon recited that 'we, who are as good as you are, take an oath to you who are no better than we, as prince and heir of our kingdom, on condition that you preserve our traditional constitutional rights (*fueros*) and liberties, and, if you do not, we do not'.[7]

The first great legal theorists of the century, the Spanish Jesuit Francisco Suárez and the Dutch Protestant scholar and diplomat Hugo Grotius, echo, with variations of their own, the contractrian formulations common in their age. Suárez in his *De legibus ac Deo legislatore* (1612) clearly attributes human rule to the consent and agreement of the people; the people come together into a political body by their deliberate will and common consent; they may then transfer their powers to a single person, or even to another state; if they adopt an original king, then that king will transmit his powers to his successors under the same conditions on which he himself received them from the people. It is not true that God is the immediate appointer of kings; He may indeed exceptionally have so acted, in setting up Saul and David, but not as a rule; though when, as is normally the case, the people constitute a governing authority for themselves, one can say that God has willed and allowed that it should be so.[8]

they who first entered into [political] society did (as may be presumed) contract a firm and immortal league among themselves, for the defence of their individual members . . . Such a society is constituted by mutual

[6] Cited by Edward S. Corwin, *The 'Higher Law' Background of American Constitutional Law* (Ithaca, NY, 1955), 65.

[7] E. N. Williams, *The Ancien Régime in Europe* (London, 1970), 87.

[8] *De legibus ac Deo legislatore* 3. 4. 2; cited by Carlyles, *Medieval Theory* (see Ch. 3 n. 29), vi. 345.

consent and agreement: and therefore its power over its parts depends wholly upon the will and intention of them who first instituted that society.[9]

But Grotius went, one might say, half-way to meet the King James position, because, once the people have chosen their form of government or ruler, they are not free to change their minds; he uses the analogy of marriage which, though freely entered into by a contract, then becomes indissoluble.

It was Grotius's slightly younger and much longer-lived contemporary, the Englishman Thomas Hobbes (1588–1679), who first offered a completely worked out construction of the supposed contractual basis of the state and the supposed motives which led to it. According to Hobbes (writing in the era of the English Civil War) the first precept of the law of nature, in the sense of the most urgent imperative instinct implanted in man by nature) is self-preservation. The primeval condition of man was one in which the individual, alone and unsupported by any association, was the potential prey of all others, which meant that the self-preservation instinct was felt in the form of constant apprehension and the life of this primeval man was, in Hobbes's most famous phrase, 'solitary, poor, nasty, brutish, and short'.[10] Always at war with his neighbours, man could enjoy neither security nor even the elementary amenities of life, and was deprived of all the advantages of an ordered and peaceful economy. From this intolerable state men ultimately devised a means of escape—as the Canon of 1606 had put it, they were 'taught by experience the necessity of government'—namely, the common surrender of their savage and perilous independence in favour of the rule of one of their number, who was now to guarantee the security of all. Hobbes's form of social contract is thus one of subjection, and the subjection was to a sovereign, whose name (and the name of Hobbes's book) has become proverbial for the ruler of an absolutist state: *Leviathan*.[11] The book appeared in 1651, during Cromwell's Commonwealth (and was suspected by some as intended to flatter Cromwell's military dictatorship). 'The only way', he wrote of his hypothetical primordial men,

to erect such a Common Power, as may be able to defend them from the invasion of Forraigners, and the injuries of one another, and thereby to

---

[9] *De iure belli et pacis* 2. 6. 4.   [10] *Leviathan* 1. 13.
[11] This name is taken from a Hebrew word in Job 12, where it signifies a monster.

secure them in such sort, as that by their owne industrie, and by the fruites of the Earth, they may nourish themselves and live contentedly; is, to conferre all their power and strength upon one Man, or upon one Assembly of men, that may reduce all their Wills, by plurality of voices, unto one Will: which is as much as to say, to appoint one man, or Assembly of men, to beare their Person; and every one to owne, and acknowledge himselfe to be Author of whatsoever he that so beareth their Person, shall Act, or cause to be Acted, in those things which concerne the Common Peace and Safetie; and therein to submit their Wills, every one to his Will, and their Judgments, to his Judgment. This is more than Consent, or Concord; it is a reall Unitie of them all, in one and the same Person, made by Covenant of every man with every man, in such manner, as if every man should say to every man, 'I Authorise and give up my Right of Governing my selfe, to this Man, or to this Assembly of men, on this condition, that thou give up thy Right to him, and Authorise all his Actions in like manner'. This done, the Multitude so united in one Person, is called a COMMON-WEALTH, in latine CIVITAS. This is the Generation of that great LEVIATHAN, or rather (to speak more reverently) of that *Mortall God*, to which wee owe under the *Immortal God*, our peace and defence. For by this Authoritie, given him by every particular man in the Common-Wealth, he hath the use of so much Power and Strength conferred on him, that by terror thereof, he is inabled to forme the wills of them all, to Peace at home, and mutuall ayd against their enemies abroad. And in him consisteth the Essence of the Common-Wealth; which (to define it), is *One Person, of whose Acts a great Multitude, by mutuall Covenants one with another, have made themselves every one the Author, to the end he may use the strength and means of them all, as he shall think expedient, for their Peace and Common Defence.*

And he that carryeth this Person, is called SOVERAIGNE, and said to have *Soveraigne Power*; and every one besides, his SUBJECT.[12]

Hobbes makes a perfunctory reference to God as the superior of the mortal ruler, but essentially his state is the utilitarian invention of man consciously devising for himself a structure which will afford him protection. 'From his political and legal theory', wrote Friedmann, 'emerges modern man, self-centred, individualistic, materialistic, irreligious, in pursuit of organised power'.[13] Hobbes's contract of subjection is an anomalous one, because the chosen ruler is not himself party to it, and so his subjects have no rights to enforce against him arising out of their contract with one another; even though it might be said that he lay under a sort of free-floating duty to provide the protection which was the object for which he

[12] *Leviathan* 2. 17.
[13] W. Friedmann, *Legal Theory* (London, 5th edn., 1967), 122.

was constituted; and even though, also, it was not illogical to insist that the ruler ought to act within and according to law, a standard recommended in the Middle Ages, as has been seen, even on the 'descending' theory of government. In general, Hobbes's Leviathan came to afford a plausible model of absolute government, a type of which later ages, into our own time, were able to show all too many examples: dictatorships for which, at any rate according to modern Western notions about the minimum civil rights of the individual, nothing could be said except that they provided a sort of peace, a sort of security, even if an arbitrary police power and the prison camp were its modes.

Hobbes's picture of the state as based essentially on a human nature dominated by fear found supporters on the continent, notably in the German universities reviving after the Thirty Years War. A very similar system was propounded by the Jewish–Dutch philosopher of an originally Iberian family, Baruch Spinoza (1632–77), who equally saw the state's legitimacy as founded on naked power, conferred on the ruler by agreement of the subjects, and for the same reasons as Hobbes had posited; though he held also that the state's power should be exercised reasonably, i.e. in conformity with man's nature, not as a moral but as a prudential principle.

Hobbes's system also met opposition; indeed, as J. W. Gough wrote, the main effect of his teaching and Spinoza's on their contemporaries was to antagonize them,[14] as it made no allowance for the moral side of man and society, which had been central to all accounts of the state and of law throughout the Middle Ages. His compatriot the earl of Shaftesbury pointed out in 1698 that Hobbes's picture of man's ruling instincts 'forgot to mention Kindness, Friendship, Sociableness, Love of Company and Converse, Natural affection, or anything of this kind'.[15] Much more influential was Samuel Pufendorf (1632–94), professor of law at Heidelberg and afterwards at Lund in Sweden, the most highly regarded German jurist of his time. Rejecting the idea that man's original disposition is savage, and his condition one of war with all his neighbours, Pufendorf visualized humans, in the moment before the formation of a political society, as having (much as Aristotle had said) a natural tendency to associate, and as understanding that the

[14] *Social Contract* (see Ch. 2 n. 48), 118.
[15] Introduction to Whichcote's *Select Sermons*; cited by Basil Willey, *The Eighteenth Century Background* (London, 1986), 59.

law of nature forbade them to injure one another. This alone did not explain the emergence of the state, as distinct from smaller (such as tribal) groups without the range of functions which must be attributed to even the simplest form of state; but a perception of the utility of such an organization as the state impelled men to its establishment, if only—and this is the sole point at which Pufendorf's views come within some short distance of Hobbes's— to restrain such men as would not obey the natural law of not injuring others. The mode of this establishment included submission to a ruler; but, unlike Hobbes's model, this contractual creation of the state required not only the people to promise submission, but also the ruler to promise protection. It is therefore a contract of subjection in the proper sense.[16]

By far the most influential exponent of social-contract theory thrown up in the seventeenth century, and the most significant for the history of the eighteenth, was another Englishman, John Locke (1632–1704), whose perspective and conclusions differed even more sharply from Hobbes's than did those of Pufendorf, and play an enormously important part in the development of Western ideas about human rights and the state's duty to respect them. Locke's main concern was the construction of a legal philosophy to underpin the English Revolution of 1688 which put an end to the Stuart dynasty with its pretensions to divine right in kingship and its denial of a popular base for government, and brought about a new settlement of the crown's descent, in violation of the established law of royal succession. This settlement was preceded by a resolution of the House of Commons (28 January 1689) which was couched in pure contractarian terms: King James, it alleged,

having endeavoured to subvert the constitution of the kingdom, by breaking the original contract between king and people; and by the advice of Jesuits and other wicked persons having violated the fundamental laws; and having withdrawn himself out of this kingdom; has abdicated the government; and . . . the throne is thereby vacant.

There was nothing original about this kind of language, except for its context; in spite of the scepticism of the Tories, who, believing in the immemorial transmission of the crown by divine right, rejected the artificial notion of a contract, the concept of an initial bargain between ruler and ruled had now achieved a quasi-constitutional

---

[16] See Gough, *Social Contract* (Ch. 2 n. 48), 122, 124.

status. The type of such a Tory was Sir Robert Filmer, a royalist who in the time of Charles I had written a tract, *Patriarcha*, in which the title of the king to absolute rule was derived ultimately from the paternal government of the family, which he took to be of divine institution. This work, published first in 1679 many years after Filmer's death, served as a soft target for Locke, who sarcastically demolished it in the first of his *Two Treatises of Government* (1690) by way of an introduction to the second. This offered an account of the state and government which modified the idea of contract by grafting on to it the element of a trust for the benefit of the governed, and established Locke as the authentic intellectual voice of the revolution.

Locke's original man, in the state of nature, resembled Pufendorf's rather than that of Hobbes. Living subject to the law of nature, which was accessible to him through his reason, he was bound not to injure the life, liberty, or property of others, and conversely might, in pre-civil society, avenge for himself any encroachments on his own rights in those areas;

But because no political society can be, nor subsist, without having in itself the power to preserve the property, and in order thereunto punish the offences of all those of that society, there, and there only, is political society where every one of the members hath quitted this natural power, resigned it up into the hands of the community in all cases that exclude him not from appealing for protection to the law established by it . . . Those who are united into one body, and have a common established law and judicature to appeal to, with authority to decide controversies between them, and punish offenders, are in civil society one with another.[17]

The members of this civil society must now choose a government for themselves, a ruler or rulers. In doing this, as in every other action, the community acts according to the will of the majority, who have a right to 'conclude the rest', i.e. the minority;

For, when any number of men have, by the consent of every individual, made a community, they have thereby made that community one body, with a power to act as one body, which is only by the will and determination of the majority. For that which acts any community . . . must move one way, it is necessary the body should move that way whither the greater force carries it, which is the consent of the majority . . .[18]

---

[17] *Two Treatises of Government* 2. 7.   [18] Ibid. 2. 8.

The community's government, once constituted, has only one function; and that is the protection of the members' property.[19] In this context Locke does not use the word 'property' in the narrow sense of external possessions; as he several times explains, he means it to comprehend the subject's entire legitimate interest; 'by property', he says, 'It must be understood here, as in other places, to mean that property which men have in their persons as well as goods',[20] or, as he calls it elsewhere, 'their lives, liberties and estates'.[21] This sole governmental function of protecting the subjects' property in this sense is conferred on the ruler or rulers— and here is the vital part of Locke's doctrine—not absolutely and irrevocably, but by way of a trust for the public good. Of the many references in the second *Treatise* to the fiduciary character of government, it will be enough to cite one:

Political power is that power which every man having in the state of Nature has given up into the hands of the society, and therein to the governors whom the society hath set over itself, with this express or tacit trust, that it shall be employed for their good and the preservation of their property.[22]

From this central perception of government as a trust several corollaries arise. Firstly, there is no question of admitting an arbitrary power in the government:

Though the legislative, whether placed in one or more, whether it be always in being or only by intervals, though it be the supreme power in every commonwealth, yet, first, it is not, nor can possibly be, absolutely arbitrary over the lives and fortunes of the people. For it being but the joint power of every member of the society given up to that person or assembly which is legislator, it can be no more than those persons had in a state of Nature before they entered into society, and gave it up to the community. For nobody can transfer to another more power than he has in himself, and nobody has an absolute arbitrary power over himself, or over any other, to destroy his own life, or take away the life or property of another. A man . . . having, in the state of Nature, . . . only so much [power] as the law of Nature gave him for the preservation of himself and the rest of mankind, this is all he doth, or can give up to the commonwealth, and by it to the legislative power, so that the legislative can have no more than this. Their power in the utmost bounds of it is limited to the public good of the society.[23]

[19] Ibid. 2. 7, 2. 9.   [20] Ibid. 2. 15.   [21] Ibid. 2. 9, 2. 11, 2. 19.
[22] Ibid. 2. 15.   [23] Ibid. 2. 11.

Thus the principle of 'nemo dat quod non habet' is deployed to limit the power of all government, which 'hath no other end but preservation, and therefore can never have a right to destroy, enslave, or designedly to impoverish the subjects'.[24]

Secondly, if a government does in fact exceed the legitimate limits of its power, it can be dismissed for this breach of its trust, and replaced with another, by the people who originally constituted it:

The legislative being only a fiduciary power to act for certain ends, there remains still in the people a supreme power to remove or alter the legislative, when they find the legislative act contrary to the trust reposed in them. For all power given with trust for the attaining an end being limited by that end, whenever that end is manifestly neglected or opposed, the trust must necessarily be forfeited, and the power devolve into the hands of those that gave it, who may place it anew where they shall think best for their safety and security.[25]

Further corollaries—relating to the rule of law and to taxation as a diminution of property—will be mentioned below.

All social-contract theory presents problems, for example as to the difficulty of fixing the contracting parties' successors with duties which *they* had never consented to assume, or the lack of historical evidence about any original contract; these cannot be solved without resort to a further range of artificial constructions. But they do not take from social-contract theory, at any rate in the form given it by Locke, a strongly illuminative power, that of presenting, even if only as a sort of allegory, something corresponding with instinct about the basis of ordered society: the element of mutual forbearance, or shared acquiescence, of the need to respect the solidarity of which all get the benefit. Moreover Locke's construction, though no less artificial than the others, offered in a politically useful form the ideal of government for the common good of the governed; this ideal, as has been seen, was known ever since the Early Middle Ages, but once combined, as Locke combined it, with the doctrine of government as a trust, breach of which will forfeit

---

[24] *Two Treatises of Government* 2. 13.

[25] He was 'sure 'tis not possible to shew a more fair original compact between a King and a people, than this between Henry the Second and the people of Ireland, that they should enjoy the like liberties and immunities, and be governed by the same mild laws, both civil and ecclesiastical, as the people of England': edn. by O'Hanlon (1892), 33.

the right to govern further, it cleared the ground for future democratic advance.

Locke's *Two Treatises* were published at first anonymously. They attracted enormous interest, and were mentioned by the Irish Protestant writer William Molyneux in his *Case of Ireland's being bound by acts of parliament in England stated* (1698); he was a friend and admirer of Locke's, and indiscreetly named him in this tract as the author of the *Treatises*. Molyneux's allusions to the social contract are not related to Locke's construction, but he strongly urged the principle of government by consent of the governed and for their benefit: 'On [men's natural equality] is founded that right which all men claim, of being free from all subjection to positive laws, 'till by their own consent they give up their freedom, by entering into civil societies for the common benefit of all the members thereof'; and cited Locke in support.[26] Molyneux was neither a revolutionary nor a separatist, but his very moderate plea for Irish legislative autonomy gave great offence;[27] the explosive potential of the doctrines it represented was clear. Already in the American colonies in the early part of the next century Locke was, 'after the Bible, the principal authority relied on by the preachers to bolster up their political teachings';[28] and his influence in France in the decades leading to the Revolution was to be no less.

BASIS OF THE VALIDITY OF LAW

The concluding passage of Molyneux's tract just mentioned contains an interesting comparative perspective of the constitutional complexion of Europe at the climax of the era of Louis XIV. So far from there being any justice in depriving the kingdom of Ireland of the right to legislate for itself,

the rights of parliament should be preserved sacred and inviolable wherever they are found. This kind of government, once so universal all over Europe, is now almost vanished from amongst the nations thereof. Our king's

[26] *Case of Ireland's being bound by acts of parliament in England stated* (1698), 100.
[27] 'Although in *The Case* . . . the Catholic people of Ireland are utterly ignored by the writer, who only pleads for the Protestant subject there it gave great offence': O'Hanlon, preface to 1892 edn., p. xxxvii.
[28] Corwin, *'Higher Law' Background* (see n. 6), 74.

dominions are the only supporters of this noble Gothick constitution, save only what little remains may be found thereof in Poland.[29]

The 'Gothick constitution' is of course the 'ascending', Germanic system so often adverted to in foregoing sections, supposed to have been brought on to the territories of the old Roman empire by the conquering barbarians of the Early Middle Ages, identified as the germ of European parliamentary institutions and of the idea that all law requires the consent of those who are to be subject to it. Molyneux's statement that this world of 'Gothick' freedom is in eclipse virtually everywhere in Europe except in English-ruled lands reflects the most important truth about the century at whose end he was writing: absolutism, with a doctrinal pedigree stretching from Jean Bodin back to Ulpian, was the rule; England, her early and modest revolution already behind her and her Gothick inheritance cast into a very acceptable theoretical form by Locke, was the exception. In France the ancient medieval parliament, the Estates General, met in 1614 under Louis XIII; they did not meet again until 1789, and then only to usher in the Revolution. In England, on the contrary, one of the main strands of the history of the seventeenth century was the assertion of parliamentary rights against royal prerogative, and the principal monuments of the theory relating valid law to popular consent are English.

From the ample polemical literature on this subject in the epoch of the Civil War the position of the Levellers, the extreme democratic wing of the Puritans, stands out: the so-called Agreement of the People (October 1647) proposed by them as a scheme of England's future government stipulated: 'That the power of [the elected] representatives of this nation is inferior only to theirs who choose them, and doth extend, without the consent or concurrence of any other person or persons, to the enacting, altering and repealing of laws . . .'.[30] In the debates at this time among the parliamentary army the Levellers' aim of a universal franchise was opposed by Henry Ireton (Cromwell's son-in-law) on the ground that it should be confined to men with a property stake in the country; but on the general principle of popular rather than despotic lawmaking Ireton was perfectly clear:

---

[29] *Case of Ireland* (see n. 26), 115.
[30] Kenyon, *Stuart Constitution* (see n. 5), 309.

I [will] tell you what the soldier of the kingdom hath fought for. First, the danger that we stood in was that one man's will must be a law. The people of this kingdom must have this right at least, that they should not be concluded [i.e. bound] but by the representative[s] of those that had the interest of the kingdom. Some men fought in this [war] because they were immediately concerned and engaged in it. Other men, who had no interest in the kingdom but this, that they should have the benefit of those laws made by the representative [i.e. passed by the House of Commons], yet fought [in order] that they should have [that] benefit.[31]

And the House of Commons, in the month of the king's trial and execution, declared

that the people are, under God, the original of all just power:
. . . that the Commons of England, in Parliament assembled, being chosen by, and representing the people, have the supreme power in this nation;
. . . and that whatever is enacted, or declared for law, by the Commons, in Parliament assembled, hath the force of law; and all the people of this nation are concluded [i.e. bound] thereby, although the consent and concurrence of King, or House of Peers, be not had thereunto.[32]

The constitutional ground of the crown and House of Lords thus encroached on was clawed back with the Restoration in 1660; but there was no royal recovery of the territory on which the ancient principle of popular consent, expressed through a representative body, to law was now entrenched. Even the use of what was thought to be the lawful prerogative of dispensing from a law's application by the Catholic king James II played a part in bringing about his deposition in 1688.

Two years after this event Locke's *Two Treatises of Government* appeared; and in the second treatise Locke stated, along with other principles of a kind which the revolution was supposed to vindicate, that of popular consent as a condition for the validity of a law. The legislature (or 'legislative', as he called it) cannot be absolute or arbitrary, as will be seen; but within its proper sphere it is the 'supreme power of the commonwealth, and unalterable in the hands where the community have once placed it'.

Nor can any edict of anybody else, in what form soever conceived, or by what power soever backed, have the force and obligation of a law which has not its sanction from that legislative which the public has chosen and appointed; for without this the law could not have that which is absolutely

---

[31] Ibid. 317.   [32] Ibid. 324.

necessary to its being a law, the consent of the society, over whom nobody can have a power to make laws but by their own consent and by authority received from them.[33]

Nothing else in Europe at this period can be compared with this English evolution of deed and doctrine. Yet here and there the embers of the ancient 'Gothick constitution' still smouldered; for example in Spain, where even Philip II had been obliged to respect traditional rights and privileges.[34] E. N. Williams cites a pamphleteer of 1622 who wrote that

in Catalonia the supreme power and jurisdiction over the province belongs not to His Majesty alone, but to His Majesty and the three estates of the province, which together possess supreme and absolute power to make and unmake laws, and to alter the machinery and government of the province . . . These laws we have in Catalonia are laws compacted between the king and the land, and the prince can no more exempt himself from them than he can exempt himself from a contract.[35]

NATURAL LAW

Alongside the question of the source of a law's validity, the more fundamental problem of law's relation to a higher or transcendent standard, that of 'natural' law, continued in this era to engage the interest of legal and political theorists. Already in the previous century, as has been seen, under the influence of the Protestant Reformation, 'natural law' discourse had begun to untie itself from that label and its associations with scholastic theology, and to use instead the language of 'reason'; and in this century a sort of secularized natural law was the base from which legal theory made notable advances. Locke offered, as a paraphrase of the law of nature, 'reason, which is that law';[36] he did not impute invalidity to a human law in conflict with it. But early in the century, in the reign of James I, Chief Justice Coke had gone to that length, when in *Bonham's Case* (1610)[37] he asserted that the English courts had an

---

[33] *Two Treatises* 2. 11. He here cited in support the passage from Hooker, *Laws*, quoted in Ch. 5.
[34] See Braudel, *Mediterranean World* (Ch. 5 n. 2), 957 ff.
[35] Cited in *Ancien Régime* (see n. 7), 87.
[36] *Two Treatises* 2. 6.   [37] 8 Co. Rep. 107a.

ancient jurisdiction to treat as void even Acts of Parliament which should be against natural justice:

> And it appears in our books, that in many cases the Common Law will control Acts of Parliament and sometimes adjudge them to be utterly void: for when an Act of Parliament is against common right and reason, or repugnant, or impossible to be performed, the Common Law will control it and adjudge such Act to be void.

This dictum (which fell on fertile soil in the young American colonies, where it bore fruit two centuries later) was cited in Coke's own time by Chief Justice Hobart in *Day* v. *Savadge*;[38] and although it is now agreed that the authorities referred to by Coke do not support his proposition, it does appear that both he and Hobart admitted in theory that a statute repugnant to natural justice could be disregarded.[39] At the end of the century, Molyneux in Ireland was pointing to Hobart as authority for saying that an Act against natural equity and reason was void,[40] and in 1701 Chief Justice Holt said it was 'a very reasonable and true saying' that no statute could make a man judge in his own cause[41]—the context in which Hobart had spoken.

The seventeenth century, however, also produced the first virtual denials of the existence of a higher order of natural law. As an advocate, Francis Bacon had invoked the law of nature; but generally he rejected medieval notions, intertwined with theology, which had tended to pre-empt empirical scientific exploration and experiment, and, in an uncompleted work, *Nova Atlantis*, he presented law as the product of simple considerations of human utility, not the reflection of, or something which should ideally conform with, some higher order. 'There thus emerges legal positivism', wrote Verdross, 'which regards law as a mere technique for the realisation of whatever objects men may wish, in other words as a means of organising political power.'[42]

Hobbes's system, too, was free of any trace of higher law; the 'natural law' which features in his *Leviathan* is not a transcendent ethical standard; on the contrary, it is simply the body of prudential

[38] (1615) Hob. 85.
[39] See C. K. Allen, *Law in the Making* (Oxford, 7th edn., 1964), 448, 623.
[40] *Case of Ireland* (see n. 26), 103.
[41] *City of London* v. *Wood* (1701), 12 Mod. 669, 687; but see Allen, *Law* (see n. 39), 449 n. 1.
[42] A. Verdross, *Abendländische Rechtsphilosophie* (Vienna, 1958), 98.

maxims suggested by the observation of, and the desire to improve, the bestial condition of man in the original state of nature which Hobbes supposed for him:

And consequently it is a precept, or generall rule of Reason, That every man ought to endeavour Peace, as farre as he has hope of obtaining it; and when he cannot obtain it, that he may seek, and use, all helps, and advantages of Warre. The first branch of which Rule, containeth the first, and Fundamentall Law of Nature; which is, to seek Peace, and follow it. The Second, the summe of the Right of Nature; which is, By all means we can, to defend our selves.

From this Fundamentall Law of Nature, by which men are commanded to endeavour Peace, is derived this second Law; That a man be willing, when others are so too, as farre forth, as for Peace, and defence of himselfe he shall think it necessary, to lay down [his supposed primitive right, in the wild state of nature,] to all things; and be contented with so much liberty against other men, as he would allow other men against himselfe . . .[43]

Spinoza's denial of natural law in the ancient sense was even more radical; he considered that

every natural thing has only as much right from nature, as it has the capacity to exist and to function . . . By the law of nature I understand the laws or rules of nature according to which all things come about, that is, what is naturally possible . . . Nothing is by the law of nature absolute prohibited, unless it is physically impossible.[44]

'In [thus] denying the reality of natural law, and recognising no obligation but that imposed by power', wrote J. W. Gough, '[Hobbes and Spinoza] had made a clean break with medieval and post-Renaissance beliefs'.[45]

There was, however, a middle way between the Thomistic conception of a divinely implanted natural law, still alive (if in disguise) even in Protestant England, and the merely prudential systems of Bacon or Hobbes. This middle way had, as has been seen, been prefigured by several catholic writers of the later Middle Ages, but was first thoroughly elaborated into a system by the Dutch Protestant Hugo de Groot, or Grotius (1583–1645), regarded as the founder of modern international law.

Grotius had been a youthful prodigy at the Dutch national university at Leiden (founded in 1575, during the rebellion against

[43] *Leviathan* 1. 14.   [44] *Tract. Pol.* 2. 3–5, 18.
[45] *Social Contract* (see Ch. 2 n. 48), 118.

Spain, to provide a humanist élite for the united provinces). An involvement in politics on the losing side of a dangerous conflict forced him to spend much of his life in exile; his famous work *De iure belli et pacis* ('On the Law of War and Peace'), published in 1625, he wrote while living at Paris in the diplomatic service of the king of Sweden. This work was partly inspired by an urge to find rules which might lessen the horrors of war, far worse (he noted) in the contemporary Thirty Years War in Germany than even in the Dutch revolt; though his system aimed at a system of law for peacetime as well. Many earlier writers, notably the Spanish jurists mentioned in the last section, had conceived a law binding nations in a common legal order; Grotius's work was the first to put the subject on a thoroughly organized and scientific basis.

The specifically international dimension of his work will be outlined below. In the present context it is enough to notice that the work's centre and foundation was his doctrine, in itself not original, of a natural law which would have had validity even if God had not existed, or had not interested himself in human affairs. Grotius, although a Protestant, was no fanatic, and wished for the healing of the wounds that had divided Christendom. At the same time, this characteristic turn, hypothetically divorcing natural law from a divine being (though he himself disclaimed belief in any such separation, and actually ascribed natural law to God as its author) was bound to recommend his construction to a Protestant world suspicious of all doctrine carrying a whiff of the medieval Catholic world of St Thomas.

Grotius's starting-point, in elaborating this natural law into a set of usable principles for the mutual relations of states (and, so far as applicable, individuals), was the perception—later adopted by Pufendorf, as has been seen—that man is by nature sociable:

Among the traits characteristic of man is an impelling desire for society, that is, for the social life—not of any and every sort, but peaceful, and organised according to the measure of his intelligence, and with those of his own kind . . . Stated as a universal truth, therefore, the assertion that every animal is impelled by nature to seek only its own good cannot be conceded . . .[46]

The maintenance of the social order . . . which is consonant with human understanding, is the source of law properly so called. To this sphere of law belongs the abstaining from that which is another's, the restoration to

[46] *De iure belli et pacis, prolegomena,* 6.

another of anything of his which we may have, together with any gain which we may have received from it; the obligation to fulfil promises, the reparation of a loss incurred through our fault, and the infliction of penalties on men according to their deserts.[47]

Even though this law issues forth from man's inmost being—and so ought to receive obedience whatever one may wish to believe about how it got there—it is still (he says, asserting his own personal faith) deservedly attributed to God, whose will it was that such principles should exist within us.[48] And so, summarizing his position, though again without prejudice to the hypothesis that God might not exist, he writes that

the natural law is the command of right reason, which points out, in respect of a particular act, depending on whether or not it conforms with that rational nature, either its moral turpitude, or its moral necessity; and consequently shows that such an act is either prohibited or commanded by God, the author of that nature.[49]

Despite this repeated statement of his own Christian belief, his hypothesis, however qualified, was to be decisive in unhooking the doctrine of natural law—in the ethical sense, not as a prudential derivative of desire to cure a savage state of nature—from theology. Grotius's famous formula *etsi daremus* ('even if we were to concede' the non-existence of God) served to make harmless later essays in his own century towards elaborating what he has been credited with inaugurating, namely, an entirely secular natural law.

Of these later seventeenth-century writers, Pufendorf may serve as a typical example. For him, natural law was free of any connection with divine revelation, and was purely the product of reason. The moral precepts derivable from the use of reason had an inner binding quality of their own. A central such principle, not unlike that which Immanuel Kant was later to propound, was: 'Let no one act towards another in such a way that the latter can justly complain that his equality of right has been violated.'[50] More precise rules derived from reason and hence nature were: not to harm others, and, where harm is inflicted, to make reparation; to treat others as having naturally equal rights by reason of the dignity of all

---

[47] *De iure belli et pacis, prolegomena*, 8.
[48] Ibid., *prolegomena*, 11–12.   [49] Ibid. 1. 1. 10. 1–2.
[50] Pufendorf, *Elementa jurisprudentiae* 2. 4. 4.

men; to help others as far as one is able to do so; and to discharge the obligations one has assumed.[51]

NATURAL RIGHTS

The most significant seventeenth-century contribution to jurisprudence, alongside the placing of the law of nations on a scientific footing, and the definitive expression of the social contract as one binding the ruler as well as the ruled in a conditional structure of trust, was the concept—to some extent correlative to the doctrine of limited government—of individuals' natural rights. Whereas the medieval Catholic world knew a theory of natural law in which the main emphasis was on man's duties to his sovereign or to his fellows (and even the secular natural law of Pufendorf, as has just been seen, still comes through in terms of social duty) the individualist atmosphere of Europe after the Protestant Reformation, an atmosphere which had been gathering since Ockham, gave a new turn to natural-law doctrine by extending it to comprehend also man's rights against his sovereign and everyone else. R. H. Tawney in his celebrated *Religion and the Rise of Capitalism* pointed to the 'rejection by social theory of the whole conception of an objective standard of economic equity' in favour of the assertion of subjective rights, especially in the area of property. 'The law of nature had been invoked by medieval writers', he wrote, 'as a moral restraint upon economic self-interest. But [by the seventeenth century] . . . "nature" had come to connote, not divine ordinance, but human appetites, and natural rights were invoked by the individualism of the age as a reason why self-interest should be given free play.'[52] It is true that already in the sixteenth century the jurists of Catholic Spain had asserted the natural right of even heathen peoples not to be maltreated and plundered, but that was rather different: a protest against cruel exploitation, and thus in the medieval tradition (to use Tawney's words) of invoking the law of nature as a moral restraint. The newer trend was one by which the combined influence of nominalism and the Reformation, which both stressed the unique importance of the individual, led to a change of emphasis from natural law to natural rights.

---

[51] Pufendorf, *De officio hominis et civis* 1. 3. 9. 6–9.
[52] *Rise of Capitalism* (see Ch. 5 n. 22), 183.

The first step in this direction had indeed been taken even before the Reformation, by one of its precursors, William of Ockham (if Villey is correct in attributing to him the earliest use of the word *ius*, 'right', in a subjective sense; Richard Tuck believes this new usage goes even further back, as has been seen, to the papal bull *Quia vir improbus* of 1329). But the real inaugurator of natural-rights thinking was Grotius. In his work on the law of his own country, written in its own language—*Inleidinghe tot de Hollandsche Rechts-gheleerdtheydt* (1619–20)—he offered, in Tuck's words, 'the first reconstruction of an actual legal system in terms of rights rather than laws'; consequently, it was 'the true ancestor of all the modern codes which have rights of various kinds at their centre'.[53] From this position Grotius could move, in his great work *De iure belli et pacis* (1625), to view the law of nature as essentially the injunction to preserve peace by way of showing respect for the rights of others; and so 'rights [had] come to usurp the whole of natural law theory'.[54]

Grotius attributes to nature the right of self-defence.[55] A natural right to punish a wrongdoer must also be assumed, otherwise it could not be enjoyed by the state by cession from individuals.[56] Private ownership of goods Grotius accounted for in a special way (as will be seen later), but in his early work *De iure praedae* he imputed this, too, to the law of nature.[57] Acts which human life requires, such as the seeking of a marriage partner, or the purchase of necessaries of life at a fair price, are the subjects of natural rights.[58] So too are the rights of parents in regard to their children,[59] and the right of the majority in any association to have its will prevail over that of the minority.[60] The law of nature is also the source of the validity of various modes of acquisition,[61] and underlies rights arising through promises and contracts.[62] The right of sepulchre, i.e. of burying one's dead, also exists by nature.[63]

Locke, although the prophet of natural rights in England, does not draw up a formal catalogue in the manner of Grotius. But his language necessarily implied the elaboration of values to countervail the royal prerogative; the rights of Englishmen show through in his

---

[53] R. Tuck, *Natural Rights Theories* (Cambridge, 1979), 66.
[54] Ibid. 67.   [55] *De iure belli et pacis* 2. 1. 3.   [56] Ibid. 2. 20. 1–2.
[57] *De iure praedae* 214; Tuck, *Theories* (see n. 53), 61–2.
[58] *De iure belli et pacis* 2. 2. 21, 2. 2. 19.   [59] Ibid. 2. 5. 1.
[60] Ibid. 2. 5. 17.   [61] Ibid. 2. 3. 4 ff.   [62] Ibid. 2. 11. 4.
[63] Ibid. 2. 19. 1.

developing fluid (so to speak) as shaded fields enclosing and delimiting the rights of the crown. Locke, as will now be seen, concentrated chiefly on the right of property; but the route to other rights, today more easily classified as personal or political, lay through his extended employment of the word 'property' to include men's 'lives, liberties, and estates'.

THE THEORY OF PROPERTY

The seventeenth century saw, perhaps in response to Reformation theology, a strong interest in property rights both in theory and practical contexts. In 1604 a committee of the House of Commons declared, at a time when crown-granted monopolies were a widely felt grievance, that

all free subjects are born inheritable [capable of inheriting]; as to their land, so also to the free exercise of their industry, in those trades whereto they apply themselves and whereby they are to live. Merchandise being the chief and richest of all other, and of greater extent and importance than all the rest, it is against the natural right and liberty of the subjects of England to restrain it into the hands of some few.[64]

In 1609 Grotius, writing about the right of booty (in the context of Dutch seizure of a Portuguese ship in the East Indies), dealt with the principle of acquisition by occupation as of a right whose exercise 'imitated nature'; all that was necessary to make oneself owner of something now without an owner was to do some overt act of appropriation, such as seizing it or making something else out of it or putting a fence around it;[65] though later, in *De iure belli et pacis*, he altered his position somewhat; he now thought that although unilateral appropriation was the exercise of a right, some kind of further agreement between men was needed to ratify this instinct:

[After the Deluge] all things . . . formed a common stock for all mankind, as the inheritors of one general patrimony. From hence it happened, that every man seized to his own use or consumption whatever he met with; a general exercise of a right, which supplied the place of private property. So that to deprive anyone of what he had thus seized, became an act of

---

[64] Cited by Tawney, *Rise of Capitalism* (see Ch. 5 n. 22), 183.
[65] *De iure praedae* 216; Tuck, *Theories* (see n. 53), 61.

injustice . . . It must have been generally agreed that whatever anyone had occupied should be accounted his own.[66]

Either with or without the contractual element, Grotius's account ultimately derives from the Roman doctrine of *occupatio*, a mode of acquisition which Gaius classifies[67] as being by natural law (*naturali ratione*). Grotius, it should be noted, thought in connection with the supposed agreement that in a situation of emergency or urgent necessity, any such agreement was tacitly rescinded, and a state of nature revived, so as to allow people to use (or perhaps to destroy) the property of others.[68]

In mid-century, during the parliamentary army's 'Putney Debates' of 1647, the natural right to contract and inherit, indeed the centrality of natural property rights generally, was repeatedly stressed by Ireton; he opposed the Levellers' demand for a universal suffrage unrelated to property qualification, 'because I would have an eye to property . . . Let every man consider with himself that he do not go that way to take away all property. For here is the case of the most fundamental part of the constitution of the kingdom, which if you take away, you take away all by that.'[69] He spoke of the origin of property as Grotius had done (perhaps he had read him):

If you will resort only to the law of nature, you have no more right to this land, or anything else, than I have. I have as much right to take hold of anything that is for my sustenance . . . as you. But [the foundation of all right between men is that] we are under a contract, we are under an agreement, and that agreement is, what a man has for matter of land that he hath received by a traduction from his ancestors, which according to the law doth fall upon him . . . he shall have the property of, the use of, the disposing of . . .[70]

Grotius had required an overt act of appropriation. But Locke moved a step further. Contract is not the basis of acquisition, but the axiom that one's labour is indisputably one's own; what one has 'mixed one's labour with', by capturing it or picking it up, is one's rightful property. Indeed, it was in order to make such original property rights secure that civil society was instituted:

---

[66] *De iure belli et pacis* 2. 2. 2. 1, 5. [67] *Inst.* 2. 66 ff.
[68] *De iure belli et pacis* 2. 2. 6 ff.
[69] Kenyon, *Stuart Constitution* (see n. 5), 314. [70] Ibid. 312.

Though the earth and all inferior creatures be common to all men, yet every man has a property in his own person. This nobody has any right to but himself. The labour of his body, and the work of his hands, we may say, are properly his. Whatsoever then he removes out of the state that nature hath provided, and left it in, he hath mixed his labour with it, and joined to it something that is his own, and thereby makes it his property. It being by him removed from the common state nature placed it in, it hath by this labour something annexed to it, that excludes the common right of other men. For this labour being the unquestionable property of the labourer, no man but he can have a right to what that is once joined to, at least where there is enough, and as good left in common for others.[71]

This labour-based theory of property has been called Locke's most influential contribution to jurisprudence.[72] Certainly to the widening class of merchants and industrialists in the years after 1700 it was a highly acceptable proposition of natural right; while among the pioneer American colonists, mixing their labour with the newly broken earth of a new continent, it came into its own. This was especially true of an important corollary of the theory, namely, that as one has an absolute right to the fruits of one's labour, so no one is entitled to diminish one's possessions by taxing them, unless one has consented to this being done:

The supreme power cannot take from any man any part of his property without his own consent. For the preservation of property being the end of government, and that for which men enter into society . . . [and] men, therefore, in society having property, they have such a right to the goods, which by the law of the community are theirs, that nobody hath a right to take them, or any part of them, from them without their own consent; without this they have no property at all . . .

It is true governments cannot be supported without great charge, and it is fit every one who enjoys his share of the protection should pay out of his estate his proportion for the maintenance of it. But still it must be with his own consent—i.e. the consent of the majority, giving it either by themselves or their representatives chosen by them; for if anyone shall claim a power to lay and levy taxes on the people by his own authority, and without such consent of the people, he thereby invades the fundamental law of property, and subverts the end of government.[73]

On this text the colonies could later take their stand in their struggle with the government of George III.

[71] *Two Treatises* 2. 5.
[72] D. Lloyd, *Introduction to Jurisprudence* (London, 5th edn., 1985), 120.
[73] *Two Treatises* 2. 11.

This celebration of property—in these passages obviously to be understood in the narrow rather than the broad sense—does not however amount to a theoretical charter for unlimited acquisition. A more traditional, medieval conception is present in Locke's restriction of legitimate acquisition to what one can reasonably use; the claim of others, already glimpsed in the second last passage cited, comes through more clearly in the following one:

It will, perhaps, be objected to [the labour-based theory], that if gathering the acorns or other fruits of the earth, etc. makes a right to them, then any one may engross as much as he will. To which I answer, Not so. The same law of Nature that does by this means give us property, does also bound that property too ... As much as any one can make use of to any advantage of life before it spoils, so much he may by his labour fix a property in. Whatever is beyond this is more than his share, and belongs to others. Nothing was made by God for man to spoil or destroy.[74]

THE RULE OF LAW

In the constitutional conflict and debate which ran right through the seventeenth century in England the ideal of government according to the known law was quite as central as the rights of the subject discussed in the last section. Arbitrary government, exercised outside the law by pretended virtue of the royal prerogative, was the core of the case against the Stuarts: the reason why Charles I perished and part at least of the reason why James II was deposed.

James I, the first of the Stuart kings of England, acknowledged in the manner of the Middle Ages that the king ought to govern according to the law, but expressed this merely as an ideal to which his subjects had no right to constrain him. In addressing Parliament in 1610 he declared it was

sedition in subjects to dispute what a king may do in the height of his power, but just kings will ever be willing to declare what they will do, if they will not incur the curse of God. I will not be content that my power be disputed upon, but I shall ever be willing to make the reason appear of all my doings, and rule my actions according to my laws.[75]

[74] *Two Treatises* 2. 5. 31.
[75] Kenyon, *Stuart Constitution* (see n. 5), 14.

In 1612 the principle of the rule of law—to give the concept its modern name—was asserted to his face by Chief Justice Coke in a celebrated confrontation. The occasion was a conference of the king with a number of judges on the subject of the scope of competing ecclesiastical jurisdictions. James asserted that, since he was supreme judge under God, he could arbitrate between them. He was contradicted by Coke, who said that such questions were and, by the immemorial law of the kingdom, always had been the province of the courts:

Then the King said, that he thought the law was founded upon reason, and that he and others had reason, as well as the judges: to which it was answered by me, that true it was, that God had endowed his Majesty with excellent science, and great endowments of nature; but his Majesty was not learned in the laws of his realm of England, and causes which concern the life, or inheritance, or goods, or fortunes of his subjects, are not to be decided by natural reason but by the artificial reason and judgment of law, which law is an art which requires long study and experience, before that a man can attain to the cognisance of it: and that the law was the golden met-wand and measure to try the causes of the subjects; and which protected his Majesty in safety and peace: with which the King was greatly offended, and said, that then he should be under the law, which was treason to affirm, as he said; to which I said, that Bracton saith, *quod Rex non debet esse sub homine, sed sub Deo et lege.*[76]

James swallowed this rebuke (though a few years later he removed Coke from office for his persistent obstruction of his wishes).

In 1641 an act to abolish the court of Star Chamber recited as that court's principal offence that it did not operate according to the ordinary law; its judges, it was said, had 'not kept themselves to the points limited by [the act of 1488 which constituted the court for certain purposes], but have undertaken to punish where no law doth warrant, and to make decrees for things, having no such authority, and to inflict heavier punishments than by any law is warranted'; the court's operations had been found to be 'the means to introduce an arbitrary power and government', and it had 'adventured to determine of the estates and liberties of the subject, contrary to the law of the land'.[77] In 1649 the indictment of Charles I by the Commons charged that he, 'being admitted King of England, and therein trusted with a limited power to govern by and according to

[76] *Prohibitions del Roy* (1607), 12 Co. Rep. 63.
[77] Kenyon, *Stuart Constitution* (see n. 5), 223.

the laws of the land, and not otherwise', had nevertheless made war on his people 'out of a wicked design to erect and uphold in himself an unlimited and tyrannical power to rule according to his will. Forty years later, after the last of the century's convulsions had replaced his son James II on the throne with William of Orange, the Bill of Rights of 1688, which made appropriate declarations against such abuses, recited the practices of King James in terms of their illegality. He was said to have 'endeavoured to subvert . . . the laws and liberties of this Kingdom' by dispensing with and suspending laws (i.e. purporting to take certain persons out of the application of laws without the consent of Parliament); and similarly without the consent of Parliament levying money and keeping a standing army in peacetime; also by violating the freedom of elections, by causing prosecutions in the courts for matters cognizable only by Parliament, and by countenancing excessive bail and excessive fines, 'all which are utterly and directly contrary to the known laws and statutes and freedom of this realm'.[78]

These documents are no more than samples, though very important ones, of common English theory on the rule of law; many more evidences could be adduced.[79] It will be enough to conclude on this subject with Locke, of whose picture of government the rule of law was an important part. 'Whoever has the legislative or supreme power of any commonwealth', he wrote, 'is bound to govern by established standing laws, promulgated and known to the people, and not by extemporary decrees, by indifferent and upright judges, who are to decide controversies by those laws; and to employ the force of the community at home only in the execution of such laws . . .'.[80] This principle, twice repeated in summary or in paraphrase,[81] is supplemented by his views against the exercise of a pretended power to dispense anyone from the law's application. He is, somewhat surprisingly, hesitant about declaring the ruler's own acts to be bounded by law ('I will not dispute now whether princes are exempt from the laws of their country'),[82] since certainly their persons are sacred and not available for the punishment which the law threatens against other wrongdoers; no very great harm may come through an occasional princely crime

[78] See E. Wade and G. Phillips, *Constitutional Law* (London, 6th edn., 1960), 6–7.
[79] See J. Gough, *Fundamental Law in English Constitutional History* (Oxford, 1961).
[80] *Two Treatises* 2. 9. 131.
[81] Ibid. 2. 11. 136–7; also 2. 9. 124.   [82] Ibid. 2. 16. 195.

going unpunished;[83] but he is quite clear that no pretended dispensing power can have the effect of authorizing a subordinate to do something illegal with impunity. Whatever personal privilege of immunity a prince may enjoy

hinders not but they may be questioned, opposed, and resisted who use unjust force, though they pretend a commission from him which the law authorises not; as is plain in the case of him that has the king's writ [if the mode of its execution exceeds] the limitations of the law, which, if any one transgress, the king's commission excuses him not. For the king's authority being given him only by the law, he cannot empower any one to act against the law, or justify him by his commission in so doing.[84]

The kernel of the rule of law appears in the next sentence:

The commission or command of any magistrate where he has no [lawful] authority, being as void and insignificant as that of any private man, the difference between the one and the other being that the magistrate has some authority so far and to such ends, and the private man has none at all; for it is not the commission but the authority that gives the right of acting, and against the laws there can be no authority.[85]

But Locke does not deny the ruler a certain prerogative discretion, outside the four corners of the law, if exercised for the public good; and he justifies this in the same way as systems of equity (equally outside the ordinary law) had been conventionally justified, namely the impossibility of making full legal provision for all possible future contingencies:

For the legislators not being able to foresee and provide by laws for all that may be useful to the community, the executor of the laws, having the power in his hands, has by the common law of Nature a right to make use of it for the good of the society, in many cases where the municipal law has given no direction . . . nay, it is fit that the laws themselves should in some cases give way to the executive power, or rather to this fundamental law of Nature and government, viz. that as much as may be all the members of the society are to be preserved;

thus the ruler can justify pulling down a house to stop a fire from spreading,[86] or prevent the punishment of someone whose action, though technically unlawful, in fact deserves commendation, or pardon an offender.[87] Locke's rule of law, therefore, is a theory

---

[83] Ibid. 2. 18. 205.   [84] Ibid. 2. 18. 206.   [85] Ibid.
[86] Ibid. 2. 14. 159.   [87] Ibid.

whose central values are clear, but whose application at the margins is elastic, though governed by the idea that 'prerogative is nothing but the power of doing public good without a rule'.[88]

EQUALITY BEFORE THE LAW

This, again, is a value which, in a Europe full of privilege, found a full expression only in the voice of the English revolution. The republican programme, the 'first Agreement of the People', presented by the Levellers in 1647, contained the principle that 'as the laws ought to be equal, so they must be good'; what they meant by equality came through in the proposition 'that in laws made or to be made every person may be bound alike, and that no tenure, estate, charter, degree, birth or place do confer any exemption from the ordinary course of legal proceedings whereunto others are subjected'.[89] Locke combined this conception with his rule of law in stating the first of the 'bounds which the trust that is put in them . . . have set to the legislative power of every commonwealth' as follows: 'They are to govern by promulgated established laws, not to be varied in particular cases, but to have one rule for rich and poor, for the favourite at Court, and the countryman at plough.'[90]

THE CHARACTER OF LAW

As in preceding centuries—it would not be worth insisting on the point, except to show an unbroken habit of mind long before Bentham and Austin gave formal shape to an imperative theory of law—all references to law's character were built around the idea of command. Grotius explains at the outset of *De iure belli et pacis* that *ius* can mean what is just, or it can mean a subjective right, or it can mean the same as *lex* (a law in the sense of a statute). In this third sense it means 'a rule of moral actions constraining the subject to what is right (*obligans ad id quod rectum est*)'. It is true that this expression seems vague; but equally it is clear that *obligans* contains the element of imperativeness, because Grotius distinguishes this

[88] *Two Treatises* 2. 14. 166.
[89] Kenyon, *Stuart Constitution* (see n. 5), 310.
[90] *Two Treatises* 2. 11. 142.

sort of rule from counsels or precepts which stop short of being obligatory. In England Coke in his *Institutes* was content to cite the medieval and ancient definition of law, again an imperative one, as a rule commanding what is right and forbidding what is not.[91]

Hobbes's conception of law, as one would expect in a scheme dominated by Leviathan, is similarly an imperative one. In his tract *On the Citizen (De cive)*, first published in 1641, he explains the difference between a mere counsel, on the one hand, and a law, on the other, as the difference between a counsel and a command, the latter being 'a precept, in which the cause of my obedience depends on the will of him who commands . . . The law is not a counsel, but a command, and is defined thus: law is the command of that person, whether man or court, whose precept contains in it the reason of obedience'.[92] In the *Leviathan*, more briefly, he calls law 'the word of him, that by right hath command over others'; in the parallel passage from the *Philosophical Rudiments Concerning Government* this is stated more fully: 'A law, to speak properly and accurately, is the speech of him who by right commands somewhat to others to be done or omitted.'[93] The figure of the sovereign, and his will, stand forth in Hobbes in a way in which they do not in Coke or Grotius or their predecessors. So too does the idea of punishment in the case of disobedience: 'every civil law', wrote Hobbes in the *De cive*, 'hath a penalty annexed to it, either explicitly or implicitly'; the implicit penalty is the one not specified, but left to the arbitrary will of the legislator as 'supreme commander'.[94] Moreover it is law, so understood, which determines what is justice, not the other way round; 'they that have sovereign power', we read, 'may commit iniquity, but not injustice, or injury in the proper signification'.[95] A notion like iniquity thus belongs to a plane of moral order which law, as such, does not inhabit.

Seventeenth-century discourse on the character of law was still devoid of the scientific dimension which the following century was to add. Yet brief mention may be made of the first stirrings of the relativist interest which later would see law as the conditioned product of its time and place and social setting: the French free-thinking Huguenot exile Pierre Bayle (1647–1706), by his rationalist and comparatist critique of established religion, laid an important

[91] 2 *Inst.* 588.
[92] *De cive* 14. 1.
[93] *Philosophical Rudiments* 3. 33.
[94] *De cive* 14. 8.
[95] *Leviathan* 2. 18.

part of the foundations on which the French and European Enlightenment would arise, and, more specifically, made familiar the kind of enquiry which Vico and Montesquieu shaped into the beginnings of anthropological jurisprudence.

CRIMINAL LAW AND PUNISHMENT

What might be called the first extensive self-contained treatise on criminal punishment is embedded in Grotius's *De iure belli et pacis*; and in this long chapter[96] he has been seen as propounding the first modern theory of criminal jurisprudence.

First, Grotius defines, by way of exclusions, the proper sphere of the criminal law. There is no right to punish internal acts, i.e. thoughts (though they may be taken into account in weighing the external acts which they have influenced).[97] Acts which 'neither directly nor indirectly affect human society, or another human being', are not to be punished, but left to God (unless the chastisement is meant for the improvement of the offender).[98] Moreover there can be no general principle of punishing sin, acts which human frailty cannot avoid; men are imperfect, and the less serious consequences of their imperfection ought not to be treated as crimes[99]—a view which, though Grotius does not mention him in this connection, St Thomas had also held. Secondly, although he identifies vengeance as the root of criminal punishment, he disapproves of its infliction with a merely vindictive motive, and adopts Seneca's threefold account of its purposes: reformation of the delinquent, deterrence and instruction of others, and serving the public safety by putting the culprit out of the way.[100] Punishment ought not to be inflicted by the victim of crime by way of personal requital.[101] A proportion in punishments, related to the gravity of the offence, he takes for granted;[102] but holds also that, even within the confines of this principle, penalties should be related to their likely effects on those punished, since 'the fine that will burden a poor man will not burden one who is rich; and to a man of no repute ignominy will be a trifling harm, while for a man of

---

[96] *De iure belli et pacis* 2. 20; also 2. 21; applied by Grotius also to the waging of war by way of punishment.
[97] Ibid. 2. 20. 18.   [98] Ibid. 2. 20. 20.   [99] Ibid. 2. 20. 19.
[100] Ibid. 2. 20. 5–7, 9.   [101] Ibid. 2. 20. 8.   [102] Ibid. 2. 20. 28.

consequence it will be serious'.[103] The right to inflict punishment on another human being in the first place Grotius thought was a right by natural law; it was the primordial possession of this right by individuals which was the origin of the state's right, obtained by cession from those individuals;[104] this cession was not however irreversible, as the individual's right to punish revives in a legal or political vacuum, as where men find themselves in a desert place.[105]

Hobbes, too, devoted a part of his great work to crimes and punishments. In this latter point he differed from Grotius; the state's right to punish did not, he thought, arise from general cession of individual rights, since no individual could be taken to have given 'any right to another to lay violent hands upon his person'; it was not the cession to the sovereign of the original right of the individual to avenge wrongs committed on him, but rather their total abandonment of this right, thus 'strengthening the Soveraign to use his own', that grounded the sovereign's claim to punish.[106] *Leviathan* shows less philosophy than Grotius, in excepting from the legitimate reach of the punishing power only inward thoughts; there is no exclusion in principle of the lesser and common moral failings inseparable from man's nature; though by implication he recognizes their exclusion in practice, when he ranks as sins by the law of nature 'Violation of Covenants, Ingratitude, Arrogance, and all Facts contrary to Morall vertue'.[107] A crime is defined only by reference to the positive law as 'a sinne, consisting in the Committing (by Deed, or Word) of that which the Law forbiddeth, or the Omission of what it hath commanded'.[108] As for the punishment of crime, this is 'an Evill inflicted by publique Authority, on him that hath done, or omitted that which is Judged by the same Authority to be a Transgression of the Law; to the end that the will of men may thereby the better be disposed to obedience'.[109] As for the precise purposes of punishment, there is in Hobbes no careful analysis of these; though he does say that 'the end of punishing is not revenge, and discharge of choler; but correction, either of the offender, or of others by his example'.[110] Punishments are to be graded in severity by reference to the degrees of danger to the public that crimes represent;[111] but, looked at from the point of view of the offender, there are several factors

[103] Ibid. 2. 20. 33.
[104] Ibid. 2. 20. 7.
[105] Ibid. 2. 20. 8.
[106] *Leviathan* 2. 28.
[107] Ibid. 2. 27.
[108] Ibid.
[109] Ibid. 2. 28.
[110] Ibid. 2. 30.
[111] Ibid.

which will excuse or at any rate extenuate the offence,[112] factors, too, which will aggravate it, such as premeditation,[113] or being in a position to know better; so that 'in a Professor of the Law, to maintain any point, or do any act, that tendeth to the weakning of the Soveraign Power, is a greater Crime, than in another man'.[114]

This latter factor is stressed also by a very different writer, Locke, when he denounces the exceeding of their lawful authority by those in offices of government. 'The being rightfully possessed of great power and riches', he wrote, 'is so far from being an excuse [for unlawful oppression], that it is a great aggravation of it'; exceeding the bounds of authority, in a great man, '[is] so much the worse in him as that he has more trust put in him, is supposed, from the advantage of education and counsellors, to have better knowledge and less reason to do it, having already a greater share than the rest of his brethren'.[115] This of course applied in Locke's sense to misgovernment rather than to crime generally, though the analogy is close. In general, Locke's very brief references to criminal behaviour are related to his restrictive, even minimalist picture of government's purpose, namely the preservation of the subjects' property (in the sense including their lives and liberties as well as estates) his legislature has only

a power to make laws, and annex such penalties to them as may tend to the preservation of the whole [society], by cutting off those parts, and those only, which are so corrupt that they threaten the sound and healthy, without which no severity is lawful. And this power has its original only from compact and agreement and the mutual consent of those who make up the community.[116]

The conservation of society is seen by Pufendorf also as the legitimate end of punishment, rather than retribution; security is achieved by incapacitating the criminal from causing further harm, and deterring others from imitating him.[117]

Other principles of punishment, ancillary but still important, find expression in this age. Hobbes wrote that, though a law which did not specify the punishment for a crime must be taken to have left this to the ruler's discretion, still 'Harme inflicted for a Fact done before there was a Law that forbad it, is not Punishment, but an act

---

[112] *Leviathan* 2. 27.   [113] Ibid.
[114] Ibid.   [115] *Two Treatises* 2. 202.   [116] Ibid. 2. 171.
[117] Pufendorf, *De iure naturae et gentium* 8. 3. 12.

of Hostility', in other words, a retroactive penalization is simply an act of aggression outside the law;[118] the same was true of an infliction more severe than one specifically provided by the law.[119] In their programme for the government of England, the Levellers' 'Humble Petition' of 1648 contained the demand that all men should be 'freed from being questioned or punished for doing of that against which no law hath been provided'.[120] Very much the same sector of the principles of legality in punishment was in the minds of the House of Lords in 1642, when, on the impeachment of the 'Five Members' of the Commons whose arrest by the king had been frustrated and against whom general charges of treason were now laid, the Lords resolved to take into consideration 'whether any person ought to be committed to custody upon a general accusation from the King or the House of Commons, before it be reduced into particulars'.[121] The necessity, also, for punishment to follow upon a regular adjudication of guilt was stated by Hobbes: 'the evill inflicted by publique Authority, without precedent publique condemnation, is not to be stiled by the name of Punishment; but of an hostile act; because the fact for which a man is Punished, ought first to be Judged by publique Authority, to be a transgression of the Law'.[122]

THE LAW OF NATIONS

We have seen that the idea of a community of nations bound by law is ancient. Articulated in a shadowy way by St Augustine, latent in medieval mercantile and later diplomatic practice, it began to form the subject of separate works in the sixteenth century, after the emergence of the European system of large sovereign states conventionally dated to the beginning of that century, or the end of the preceding one. In the early seventeenth century it was at last placed on a full and systematic foundation by Grotius.

Grotius's famous work *De iure belli et pacis* (1625) was conceived and written at a time when the Thirty Years War in Germany, which had broken out in 1618, was displaying horrors of a kind

---

[118] *Leviathan* 2. 28.   [119] Ibid.
[120] Kenyon, *Stuart Constitution* (see n. 5), 322.
[121] Ibid. 241.   [122] *Leviathan* 2. 28.

even worse than those of the Dutch revolt against Spain. 'Throughout the Christian world', he wrote in his introduction,

> I observed a lack of restraint in relation to war, such as even barbarous races should be ashamed of; I observed that men rush to arms for slight causes, or no cause at all, and that when arms have once been taken up there is no longer any respect for law, divine or human; it is as if, in accordance with a general decree, frenzy had openly been let loose for the committing of all crimes.[123]

His dismay was the emotional inspiration to undertake the work which, as he says at the outset of his book, no one had yet treated in a comprehensive and systematic way; though he does acknowledge the work of Gentili in the previous century, and his own indebtedness to it.[124]

The foundation of all order is man's sociable nature, which Grotius attributes to God; but, even if one were to suppose that God did not exist, there still would be rules and standards, flowing from that human nature, which require obedience. The maintenance of the social order is the source of all law; and law, properly so called, consists in the discharge of one's duty to others in this social context. But, he says,

> just as the laws of each state have in view the advantage of that state, so by mutual consent it has become possible that certain laws should originate as between all states, or a great many states; and it is apparent that the laws thus originating had in view the advantage, not of particular states, but of the great society of states. And this is what is called the law of nations, whenever we distinguish that term from the law of nature.[125]

This law of nations, which he relates to the basic precepts of natural law (keeping promises, restoring unjust gains, making reparation for injury), is in force among states by their mutual consent. There is an advantage for states in observing this law

> just as the national, who violates the law of his country in order to obtain an immediate advantage, breaks down that by which the advantages of himself and his posterity are for all future time assured, so the state which transgresses the laws of nature and of nations cuts away also the bulwarks which safeguard its own future peace. Even apart from this, it would be a mark of wisdom, not of folly, to allow ourselves to be drawn towards that to which we feel that our nature leads.[126]

[123] *Prolegomena* 28.   [124] Ibid. 1, 38.   [125] Ibid. 17.
[126] Ibid. 18, 30.

The fact that the law of nations carries no sanction to enforce it does not mean it has no effect (and, as has been seen, he had defined law as *obligans* without any reference to its issuing from the command of a superior, which Hobbes was to make central), obedience to it has the rewards of a good conscience, the approval of other nations, and the protection of God.[127] War, he recognized, sometimes had to be waged; but the just war must be waged with the same scrupulousness, as to the occasion for it and the methods by which it was conducted, as if one were administering the judicial justice which, as it is unhappily not available, one has been forced to replace with belligerence.[128]

This, in outline, is the theory on which he erected a mass of detailed precepts, some bearing on war; some, as they are not parts of international but of municipal law, are incorporated so as to suggest their application by analogy in the relations between states.

Grotius's work inaugurated a new science, and in the century or so which followed many notable jurists wrote on the law of nations and occupied chairs which now began to be created in this new subject. Of those who came after him within the seventeenth century, Pufendorf's is the most important name (he occupied at Heidelberg the first university chair ever created in the 'law of nature and of nations'). Unlike Grotius, who accorded to treaties and to common practice the status of sources of the law of nations, Pufendorf denied binding authority to these, and derived the law of nations from natural law alone.[129]

---

[127] Ibid. 19–23.   [128] Ibid. 25.
[129] *De iure naturae et gentium* 8. 9.

7

The Eighteenth Century

GENERAL HISTORICAL INTRODUCTION

The eighteenth century is near enough to our own time to allow us to use its name as a phrase to conveniently evoke familiar impressions of its arts and life-styles. It is not, any more than any other century, a self-contained 'period' in political and intellectual history. But it is the one in which the ancient European structures of authority and legitimacy were irreparably fractured by the French and American Revolutions. The century also contained the high point of the intellectual epoch which prepared the ground for revolution, the so-called 'Enlightenment', whose central feature was a rejection of all spiritual and intellectual authority and of the position of the Christian faith and obedience in the civilization it had done so much to mould.

Looked at on the purely political and constitutional level, the British Isles were exceptional among the states of Europe in having accomplished, at the close of the seventeenth century, a revolution which the eighteenth would spend in stabilizing and digesting. By the 1701 Act of Settlement the British crown passed on Queen Anne's death in 1714 to the elector of Hanover, a German great-grandson of James I—a person further down the order of legitimate succession (according to the older law) than the son left by James II, but artificially promoted by that Act, which excluded from the crown in perpetuity all persons of Roman Catholic allegiance. The elector, assuming the British crown as George I, was succeeded in 1727 by his son, George II, who was succeeded in 1760 by his young grandson, George III, and the sons of the latter, George IV (1820–30) and William IV (1830–7). By the time these 'Hanoverian' sovereigns were succeeded in 1837 by the young Victoria, the dynasty had long been accepted by all but cranks as legitimate. But the reigns of the first two Georges whose hearts lay in Germany, were troubled by flickers of Jacobite loyalty to the ousted Stuarts, which went in 1715 and 1745 to the length of rebellion. During the first half of the century, too, the frontier between royal and parliamentary rights was uneasy, and did not settle down in a stable relationship until the time of the third George. It was in this unsettled period that party politics, in the modern sense, first began to emerge; the 'Whigs' representing broadly those who stood for the revolution of 1688 and the liberal and parliamentary rights and traditions supposed to be associated with it, the 'Tories' those who still felt loyal to the older doctrines which accorded a wider scope to royal prerogatives, or were still attached to the banished Stuarts.[1] For some time after the Hanoverian settlement the aura of disloyalty, of only grudging acceptance of the new order, hung around the Tories, who were out of office for most of the century; but ultimately their equal attachment to the monarchy, even as reconstituted, was accepted, and political conflict, while often bitter, remained bloodless (except in the case of actual rebellion, as in the Jacobite risings, or the Irish rebellion of 1798). Peaceful political opposition to the crown and its ministers became safe and normal. The phrase 'His Majesty's Opposition', which would have seemed a grotesque and subversive one in the seventeenth century, had to wait until the early nineteenth to be invented,[2] but the reality which it expresses, the possibility of political hostility to the crown's ministers (the government of the day) coexisting with perfect loyalty to the crown itself and the state's institutions, was the product of the Hanoverian eighteenth century in England.

Britain succeeded in the course of this century in hugely extending her overseas possessions, driving the French out of India and North America (though losing her own colonies in the latter, after their rebellion in 1776 against the home government's taxation policies and their independent confederation as the United States). The later eighteenth century was also the age of the British industrial revolution, most phases of which were ahead of the corresponding phases in the foreign economies competing with hers. Founded upon several factors, such as the scientific revolution (though most of the decisive technical advances were the innovations

[1] 'Tory': from the Irish *tóiridhe*, a robber or highwayman, i.e. one of the dispossessed native Irish who preyed on English settlers; applied abusively to the followers (because so many of them were Irish) of James II. The etymology of 'Whig' is more obscure.

[2] Apparently by the Whig Lord Broughton, in the 1820s: see *The Concise Oxford Dictionary of Quotations*, 105. 11.

of practical craftsmen, not scientists), great stores of formerly underemployed capital, plenty of cheap (and often cruelly exploited) labour, as people were driven off the land by the private enclosure of commonage and the destruction of cottage industry by new techniques of concentrated mass production, the natural resources of coal and iron, and the Protestant ethic, this industrial revolution was to promote Britain to the economic leadership of the world.

Ireland, abandoned after the Williamite wars by a great part of her ancient nobility, oppressed by the disabilities of the penal laws against Catholics, so miserably ill-governed that even her Protestant people developed a sense of Irish patriotism in indignation at the destruction of Irish industry to suit that of England, most of her people sunk in the abject poverty that kindled the memorable compassion and rage of Jonathan Swift, shared nothing of her conquerors' glory. At the century's end she was absorbed by Britain in a Union, a measure largely prompted by the alarm which the independent spirit of Grattan's Parliament, and then the rebellion of 1798, had caused to a British government locked in combat with revolutionary France.

This revolutionary France had experienced a very different century. It had begun as the reign of Louis XIV, the very image of untrammelled power and pride of royalty, was drawing to a close amid a series of military reverses. At his death in 1715 he left a state exhausted by the unproductive wars which his grandiose ambitions had wished upon his people. The almost equally long reign of his great-grandson and successor Louis XV (1715–74) was marked by a further train of defeats, particularly overseas. Internally the royal absolutism of Louis XIV was perpetuated; the medieval French parliament, the Estates General, which had last met in 1614 under Louis XIII, was not convoked again until Louis XVI did so in 1789, when it turned itself into the Constituent Assembly from whose work the Revolution and the destruction of the monarchy would follow. This absolute kingship was surrounded by a very numerous nobility, descendants of the powerful local lords whose turbulence had long delayed the rise of a strong French monarchy, together with many more recently ennobled families promoted by their wealth, military prowess, or legal and administrative abilities. These aristocrats, often absent from their estates in order to attend Louis XIV's splendid court at Versailles (where the immense palace had been built in part to facilitate their concentration there and to keep them from mischief-making far away), traditionally enjoyed and jealously preserved the most odious and abusive privileges, notably freedom from taxation; this, together with the Church's similar freedom in respect of its own vast wealth, meant in modern language an impossibly narrow tax base from which the royal government was left to squeeze the revenue to support world-wide wars. This chronic financial asthma, made worse by the weak condition of French trade and industry relative to that of Britain, was an important factor in bringing on revolution; together with the sense of national humiliation arising from repeated military failures, it conditioned the climate in which the ambitions and resentments of an underprivileged middle class could finally explode. Paradoxically, the last straw was supplied by the one episode in which French military involvement was material in causing a British defeat, namely, the revolt of the American colonies; this was so powerfully and effectively supported by the French that the royal government's finances were fatally overstretched, and it was to deal with the ensuing crisis that Louis XVI convoked the Estates General in the summer of 1789, thus erecting the stage on which the revolution would unfold around a demand, not for mere fiscal reforms, but for change in the whole structure of government and society.

Across the Pyrenees the once mighty Spanish kingdom continued throughout the eighteenth century in the decline which the seventeenth had inaugurated. Louis XIV had engineered the passing of the Spanish crown in 1700 to his grandson, Philip of Anjou, who reigned as Philip V until 1746; but the settlement at Utrecht in 1713, which ended the European war fought over this succession, cost Spain her European possessions; the southern Netherlands (modern Belgium) together with the Italian territories of Naples and Milan and the island of Sardinia passed to Austria, and Sicily went to Piedmont-Savoy. The American empire remained; but its produce and trade did not compensate Spain for the chronic weaknesses of her own economy: the largely barren soil, poor internal communications, and a huge class of gentry which (in total contrast to the hard-headed English upper class) regarded all gainful occupation as beneath its dignity. This Spanish aristocracy, like the French, enjoyed considerable privilege (which did not prevent many of its members from being impoverished); the Spanish king was nearly as absolute as the French. The main organ of government was the Council of Castile, which discharged simultaneously legislative, administrative, and judicial functions. The Church retained enormous power which, together with Spanish geographical isolation, pride, and distrust of foreign influences, made in this century for an intellectual stagnation unique in Western Europe.

Germany in the eighteenth century remained a patchwork of many states and statelets. The largest political complex and, at the beginning of the century, the most significant was the Habsburg-ruled Holy Roman Empire. This stretched far beyond German-speaking lands, and had many Magyar, Slav, Italian, Romanian, and Belgian subjects; but its core was the ancient Habsburg territory of Austria, and its capital Vienna. By mid-century a new German power had arisen, destined ultimately to unite all German lands west and north of Austria into a mighty, world-class state: Prussia, a lean, efficiently governed, militaristic kingdom built around the flat, sandy country of Brandenburg with its capital Berlin, but including also territories on the Rhine far to the west. Under its famous King Frederick II ('the Great') Prussia advanced to the front rank of European powers, capable of confronting and defeating the Habsburg empire, the Russians, and the French. There were important differences in the levels of prosperity in the German regions; recovery from the devastation of the Thirty Years War was slow and uneven. Culturally, eighteenth-century Germans, despite their numerous universities and an acknowledged pre-eminence in music, felt themselves upstaged by the brilliance of France: this irksome sense of inferiority was to play some part in the unfolding of German intellectual and political history, with very mixed results for themselves and for others.

Italy remained throughout the century politically fragmented and to a substantial extent under foreign control. The papal states of central Italy, the republics of Genoa and Venice in the north, and a few other principalities, were under rulers of their own; but the kingdom of Naples—in other words, all the south of Italy—together with Sicily were, after 1713, first under Austrian, then Spanish control, and Austria acquired also the important territories of Parma and Milan. In 1737, too, the once proud Grand Duchy of Tuscany, built on the dynasty of the Medici of Florence, passed into Austrian Habsburg hands. On the other hand, though Italy was no longer pre-eminent in the arts and sciences, she was to a far greater extent than Spain in touch with the larger European civilization. Naples, in particular, was an active intellectual centre; the presence of Rome and the papacy meant a continued centrality of Italy for the culture of Catholic Christendom; the presence and the tradition of the classical world in its ruins, and of the Renaissance in its most splendid monuments of art and architecture, assured the love and passionate attention of educated people in every part of Europe, and a continuous and intimate contact with them.

Across the Atlantic, the British colonial settlers who had, as a matter of course, supported the mother country in her struggles with the French for the mastery of North America, were progressively alienated from her by resentment of her policy of taxation. The emergence of a competent local leadership, among whom lawyers were prominent, assured the degree of organization that made possible the colonies' joint Declaration of Independence of 1776 followed by the successful armed revolt, the War of Independence, in which the American rebels were given decisive assistance by the France of Louis XVI, as well as by Spain and the Netherlands. The impression made in Europe by this American Revolution, with its apparatus of ideology in which old European ideas of the social contract and of the rights of man converged, was profound; and while the French crisis of 1789 was largely provoked by the financial strains of intervention in America, the recent American example of successful revolt, and the ideas which had fuelled it, also made a contribution to the spirit of immediate revolution.

THE EIGHTEENTH-CENTURY 'ENLIGHTENMENT'

Looked at in a longer perspective, perhaps more significant in human history even than the French Revolution was the intellectual movement which conditioned and equipped many of those who led or inspired it: the so-called 'Enlightenment', expression of the 'Age of Reason' with which on the level of the intellect the eighteenth century is more or less coextensive, which had representatives all over Europe, but whose principal home was unquestionably France. Even to call the Enlightenment a 'movement' may be misleading; it was more a shared mood or temper, or attitude to the world, in which the dominant note was one of profound scepticism towards traditional systems of authority or orthodoxy (especially those of religion), and a strong faith in the power of the human reason and intelligence to make unlimited advances in the sciences and techniques conducive to human welfare. The decisive immediate impulse to the rise of this mood is often attributed to the French Calvinist writer Pierre Bayle (1647–1706), whose deeply sceptical *Dictionnaire Historique et critique* (1695–7), rejecting orthodoxies of all kinds and insisting on empirical proof for every proposition, became a sort of secular, free-thinkers' Bible for the French Enlightenment. But the ultimate ancestry of the Enlightenment must be traced from much further back: the Renaissance, the Reformation, the scientific revolution in the era of Bacon, Galileo, and Newton, the empirical philosophy of Locke and Descartes, all were steps on the way to it. Its most significant and typical monument in France was the *Encyclopaedia*, planned and supervised by Diderot; this immense work, to which all the principal representatives of what counted as progressive thought contributed, was intended not only as a huge repository of technical information (presented, naturally, free from the views and interpretations of church authority) but also as 'an anthology of "enlightened" opinions on politics, philosophy and religion . . . The sheer number of the contributors ensured that it would not express any narrowly sectarian viewpoint, but there was sufficient agreement on a rationalist and empirical approach to ensure a certain convergence of aim'.[3] These 'enlightened' opinions were what conservative, church-guided people in France, Britain, and elsewhere called 'infidel' views. But those who held them had a very important effect on the climate of political as well as of religious feeling. The French writer and politician Alexis de Tocqueville (1805–59) in his work *The Ancien Régime* described the political attitude of the eighteenth-century Enlightenment thus:

[French men of letters] took no part in public business, as English authors did; on the contrary, they had never lived so much out of the world. They held no public office, and, though society teemed with functionaries, they had no public functions to discharge.

But they were not strangers to politics, or wholly absorbed in abstract philosophy and belles-lettres, as most of the German literary men were. They paid sedulous, and, indeed, special attention to the subject of government. They were to be heard day after day discoursing of the origin and primitive form of society, of the primordial rights of the governed and governing power, of the natural and artificial relations of men one to the other, of the soundness or the errors of the prevailing customs, of the

[3] Norman Hampson, *The Enlightenment* (Pelican edn., Harmondsworth, 1968), 86.

principles of the laws. They made thorough inquiries into the Constitution, and criticised its structure and general plan. They did not invariably devote particular or profound studies to these great problems. Many merely glanced at them in passing, often playfully, but none omitted them altogether . . .

The political systems of these writers were so varied, that it would be wholly impossible to reconcile them together, and mould them all into a theory of government.

Still, setting details aside, and looking only to main principles it is readily discerned that all these authors concurred in one central point, from whence their particular notions diverged. They all started with the principle that it was necessary to substitute simple and elementary rules, based on reason and natural law, for the complicated and traditional customs which regulated society in their time . . . The whole of the political philosophy of the eighteenth century is really comprised in that single notion.[4]

These writers, as Tocqueville goes on to explain, saw all round them innumerable ancient anomalies, privileges, and injustices, under which, at some point or other, every section of French society suffered. Having no experience of practical affairs, and in the absence of any representative institutions which might have been capable of carrying out reforms, the politically interested writers of the French Enlightenment thought only in terms of making a clean sweep of the ancient structures (though certainly not by means of a violent revolution such as actually took place) and starting again from scratch, building this time on purely rational principles. This was the cast of mind, willing to sacrifice traditions with a history of a thousand years to the mere theories of the day, that Burke was to attack so fiercely when the fruits of this philosophy became visible after 1789.

Some aspects of the Enlightenment mind are of especial interest for the history of legal theory. The very idea that political or legal institutions might be critically appraised, and their suitability questioned, resided in Montesquieu's perception that laws are contingent, likely to reflect the conditions of life of the peoples who live by them rather than to conform to a single universal standard; both Vico a little earlier, and Voltaire a little later displayed a similarly relativist attitude towards human rules, in Voltaire's case sharpened by burning hatred of their frequent absurdity and cruelty. The standard by which they were to be replaced by ideal

---

[4] *The Ancien Régime* 2. 13 (Everyman Classics edn., London, 1988, p. 110).

structures was that of reason and 'natural law' in its eighteenth century form, as Tocqueville wrote in the passage just cited. The conviction of the age in this regard finds expression in the utilitarian ideas of Bentham (though Bentham despised the notion of natural law), the humanitarian critique of criminal law pioneered by Beccaria and foreshadowed by Voltaire, and the codifying enthusiasm of the Prussian king Frederick the Great and the Austrian emperor Joseph II.

The references in the foregoing paragraph hint at the strongly international character of the Enlightenment, far transcending the France where its spirit first became established. In the Iberian peninsula, insulated against it by the forces of a powerful Catholic tradition, it made small impact. But everywhere else in Europe, and in America where Benjamin Franklin can be reckoned its prime representative, its influence was profound. From the Anglo-Ireland of Grattan to the Russia of Catherine the Great the doctrines and attitudes of the Encyclopaedists were in varying degrees the fashion, and were familiar even to those who did not adopt them. There arose a kind of European freemasonry of the intellect of a sort until then unparalleled on the secular plane, symbolized most memorably in the friendship of Frederick the Great and Voltaire. The earlier works of Bentham were first published by an admirer in France; a visit to Voltaire, forced into exile, was a sort of pilgrimage undertaken by advanced thinkers of all nationalities; Gibbon, the infidel historian of the Roman empire's long decay and thus of the whole Middle Ages, was a European celebrity at his home in the Swiss town of Lausanne. Indeed, even on the purely political level the sense that events were moving, under the impulse of reason affronted by ancient injustice and absurdity, towards some irreversible revolution was felt in some sense everywhere. Burke's famous polemic, *Reflections on the Revolution in France*, and his use of the word 'in', suggests a consciousness that everywhere a great wheel of history was turning, of which only the French phase need at present attract his interest and indignation.

The same century which we think of as the Age of Reason, however, saw also the rise of a very different and dissenting spirit, that of the 'romantic' mood in art and letters, though one which also left its mark on legal theory. Its dominance belongs rather to the nineteenth than to the eighteenth century; but its principal founder was a younger contemporary of Voltaire. This was the Swiss Jean-

Jacques Rousseau (1712–78), native of Geneva but for most of his life resident in France. Like all cases where an individual is singled out as a founder, it is possible to point to premonitions of his outlook, as here perhaps in the rise of the popular novel in the early part of the century in England. It was, however, indisputably Rousseau who established, particularly with his very influential book *La Nouvelle Héloïse* (1761), the claims of human sentiment as against mere reason. He was the first important rebel against the formalized, classicizing, and (as it was easy to represent it) somewhat dehumanized conventions of manners, of art, and of literature which we associate with the pre-revolutionary eighteenth-century world: the periwig, the minuet, the alexandrine couplet, the endless recycling of themes from Greek and Roman antiquity. In enthroning in their place 'nature' and 'feeling'—by which he meant what was fresh, wild, primitive, spontaneous, not amenable to mere rational appraisal, in everything from manners to landscapes—he inaugurated a whole aesthetic movement, not even now extinct, which a later age called Romantic. He struck a chord on the frontiers of the emotions and the intellect: the preference, which he made fashionable, for what had grown free-range rather than under cultivation, for the spontaneous rather than the artificial, lent a sort of authority to whatever had the quality of the pristine and the unforced and original; but incidentally, too, tended to exempt what could be passionately felt, and passionately expressed, from the scrutiny of reason. The impact of all this on his theory of law and the state, which may have thought ultimately baneful, will be outlined below.

THE CONCEPTION OF THE STATE AND ITS BASIS

The eighteenth century had outgrown the need which the previous century had evidently still felt to justify the existence of the state and of government. Even now an occasional anarchic dream could be given utterance, particularly in non-conformist America; the Anglo-American radical Tom Paine wrote in 1776 that 'government, like dress, is the badge of lost innocence'.[5] But no Hobbes or Locke

---

[5] References in I. Krammick (ed.), *The Federalist Papers* (Penguin Classics edn., Harmondsworth, 1987), Introduction, 23.

now arose to attribute its institution to men's fear for their persons
or for the protection of their property.

On the other hand, the state now started to emerge as an entity in
its own right more clearly than before. It is true that we have been
watching this process gradually unfold since the High Middle Ages;
the Investiture Conflict might be seen as inaugurating the cleavage
of the spiritual from the temporal powers, the consolidation of a
stable system of national kingdoms around 1500 and the Reformation
shortly afterwards, in part a rejection of Rome's influence in the
affairs of kingdoms, as further steps on the road. But even in the
seventeenth century the abstract idea of the state had not at all
clearly emerged, and the very use of the word state, in this sense,
was no older than the sixteenth. Louis XIV is supposed as a young
man to have uttered before the Parlement of Paris the famous phrase
'L'État, c'est moi': this however was not intended as a supreme
expression of personal absolutism but simply as a statement of the
simple medieval view which sought no abstraction more profound
than the crown, and saw the powers of government concentrated in
its incumbent. In the mid-eighteenth century a change seems to take
place towards the notion of an impersonal, corporate entity,
abstracted from the organs and centre of government; a significant
moment in this development is thought by some writers to be the
so-called 'Diplomatic Revolution' of 1748, in which, for reasons
related purely to perceptions of the interests of the kingdoms
concerned rather than to the traditions of their dynasties, France
and Austria found themselves for the first time in alliance without
regard to the hereditary rivalry of Bourbon and Habsburg.

The social-contract model, in one or other form, continued to be
used by many writers as an explanation of the state's basis.
Montesquieu believed that, in man's original condition, although
'fear would induce men to shun one another, the marks of this fear,
being reciprocal, would soon engage them to associate': a conscious
collective act, therefore, towards which however he thought the
natural instinct for the society of other humans would have
contributed.[6] The civil state ('l'état civil': civic existence) was the
result of the 'conjunction of all the wills of individuals'; again, a
conscious collective act is visualized.[7] Frederick the Great, writing
in French on the political state of contemporary Europe, saw

---

[6] *De l'esprit des lois* 1. 2.   [7] Ibid. 1. 3.

government as resulting from a conscious choice by the people of someone to govern them 'as a father', and, near the end of his life, presented the 'social compact' as emerging from a primitive Hobbesian condition of general violence.[8] Similar expressions are found among jurists such as the German Christian Wolff[9] and the highly influential Swiss writer Emmerich de Vattel.[10] The Austrian professor Karl Anton von Martini, important in the history of the pioneering efforts of the empress Maria Theresia and her successor Joseph II towards achieving a codification of the empire's laws, wrote of the social contract very much in the spirit of Locke: by their contract of submission, he held, the people do not surrender their rights finally, nor does their appointment of their ruler entitle him to exercise any more power than is necessary for the social purpose he is charged with achieving.[11] Across the Atlantic, too, the language of the social compact is sometimes heard, though for example in the *Federalist Papers* it appears subordinate to the simpler principle that 'the fabric of American empire ought to rest on the solid basis of THE CONSENT OF THE PEOPLE';[12] the 'genius of republican liberty' demanded both that 'all power should be derived from the people', and that its exercise should be regarded as the discharge of a trust subject to a system of careful checks and controls.[13] Here too the echoes of Locke are too strong to miss.

The social contract thus continued in this century to be a handy model for exposition or polemics. But it was impossible that the age of reason and enlightenment could accept the notion of an original contract as the state's basis as a serious historical hypothesis. Even in the early seventeenth century, as has been seen, the Church of England had ridiculed the notion of a primitive state of nature when men had 'run up and down' as isolated savages. And in the eighteenth century the atmosphere of scepticism thickened around the concept of a supposed contract. The Scottish philosopher David Hume, in an essay published in the same year (1748) as Montesquieu's *Esprit des lois*, while supposing that men at first voluntarily abandoned their native liberty for the sake of peace and order, still thought the idea of a 'compact and agreement expressly formed for

---

[8] Cited by Gough, *Social Contract* (see Ch. 2 n. 48), 157–8.
[9] Ibid. 158–61.   [10] Ibid. 161.
[11] See Williams, *Ancien Régime* (Ch. 6 n. 7), 469.
[12] Krammick (ed.), *Federalist Papers* (see n. 5), 184: no. 22, Alexander Hamilton.
[13] Ibid. 243: no. 37, Alexander Hamilton.

general submission' was 'far beyond the comprehension of savages'; the real foundation of government was rather the general acquiescence in it, which in time led to habitual obedience'.[14] Something similar appears in the *Commentaries on the Laws of England* of William Blackstone (1765), who seems to present the social contract not as a strictly historical hypothesis, but as a sort of useful allegory illuminating the reasons why ordered society persists, constraining the individual passions of its members to its discipline:

The only true and natural foundations of society are the wants and the fears of individuals. Not that we can believe, with some theoretical writers, that there ever was a time when there was no such thing as society, either natural or civil; but that, from the impulse of reason, and through a sense of their wants and weaknesses, individuals met together in a large plain, entered into an original contract, and chose the tallest man present to be their governor. This notion, of an actually existing unconnected state of nature, is too wild to be seriously admitted . . .

Families and tribes coalesced by conquest or by accident, 'and sometimes, perhaps, by compact':

But though society had not its formal beginning from any convention of individuals, actuated by their wants and fears: yet it is the *sense* of their weakness and imperfection that *keeps* mankind together, that demonstrates the necessity of this union, and that, therefore, is the solid and natural foundation, as well as the cement, of civil society. And this is what we mean by the original contract of society; which, though perhaps in no instance it has ever been formally expressed at the first institution of a state, yet in nature and reason must always be understood and implied, in the very act of associating together, namely, that the whole should protect all its parts, and that every part should pay obedience to the will of the whole . . .[15]

At about the same period that Blackstone was writing, there appeared across the English Channel a famous work whose title suggests an affinity with the sort of social contract tradition with which Blackstone was coming to terms, but whose burden was something which would have been entirely strange to Locke, or Hobbes, or their predecessors back through the Middle Ages to antiquity. This was Rousseau's *Du contrat social* (1762). It is in many ways an obscure and contradictory book; but there emerges from it clearly the idea of the sovereignty of the people, an idea now

---

[14] Cited by Gough, *Social Contract* (Ch. 2 n. 48), 186–7.
[15] *Commentaries on the Laws of England* 1. 47; see Gough, *Social Contract*, 189–90.

naturally coloured by the bias against traditional authority characteristic of the age of reason (despite Rousseau's rejection of the cult of
reason) and by his awareness of the apparently incurable abuses of
the *ancien régime*. There is a significant difference between
Rousseau's form of social contract and that presented either by
Hobbes or Locke. Far from being a bargain to exchange simple
submission for simple protection, and still further from being the
creation of a limited and revocable trust, Rousseau's contract
envisaged

the total alienation of each associate, together with all his rights, to the
whole community; for, in the first place, as each gives himself absolutely,
the conditions are the same for all; and, this being so, no one has any
interest in making them burdensome to others. Moreover, the alienation
being without reserve, the union is as perfect as it can be, and no associate
has anything more to demand . . .

If then we discard from the social compact what is not of its essence, we
shall find that it reduces itself to the following terms: Each of us puts his
person and all his power in common under the supreme direction of the
general will, and, in our corporate capacity, we receive each member as an
indivisible part of the whole.

At once, in place of the individual personality of each contracting party,
this act of association creates a moral and collective body, composed of as
many members as the assembly contains voters, and receiving from this act
its unity, its common identity, its life, and its will.[16]

It will be seen that Rousseau's social contract is not just an
explanation of the state, but a justification, in a shape more
worrying than that advanced by Hobbes for his Leviathan, for a
particular kind of state. Rousseau's contract has a curious, quasi-
chemical effect. There emerges from it neither a personal sovereign
nor a determinate assembly governed on a principle of simple
majority; the entity to which the individual has made a total
surrender of his autonomy, and to whose compulsion he is now
subject, is a mysterious construct called 'the general will' (*la volonté
générale*). This is something which, as it is not equivalent simply to
the majority will—and even contains within itself somehow the real
wishes of an apparently dissenting minority—is evidently an
abstraction transcending both, and, ultimately, independent of
either. It is easy to see how such a theory earned Rousseau credit for

[16] *Du contrat social*, 1. 6, tr. G. D. H. Cole (London, 1973).

being a major intellectual influence on the Revolution which he did not live to see; and how such a conception, though requiring initially an act of faith, can readily be made to serve any sort of tyranny which prefers to dispense with the ballot-box. It was certainly not so intended by its author, but Rousseau's 'volonté générale' is one of the philosophical ancestors of the totalitarian regimes of the twentieth century.

Not so far distant from Rousseau's picture of the state's formation is that of the philosopher Immanuel Kant (1724–1804), who near the end of his life wrote formally on legal theory. In a work of 1797 he presented the act by which a people constituted itself into a state as an original contract; in virtue of this contract each individual surrendered his external freedom, so as then to resume it again as a member of the commonwealth, i.e. of the total community considered as a state. In this state the sovereign legislative power belongs to the 'united will of the people', and this power is an unlimited one, since (as the individual will is subsumed in the general will) no one can be thought to commit an injustice upon himself. The unease which such a construction might excite is heightened by the fact that Kant's state contained as active citizens only those persons of independent economic substance; minors, women, and mere wage-earners were not admitted to the franchise. On the other hand, as will be seen later, the picture is relieved by Kant's concern for individual freedom, and for the separation of powers in the state which he thought essential for the safeguarding of freedom.[17]

NATURAL LAW

Throughout the eighteenth century, writers on legal subjects tended to offer a routine salute to natural law in one form or another. It was seen in Chapter 6 that, beginning with Grotius, the idea of a transcendent system of values with which human law ought not to conflict was gradually dissociated from the medieval theology which had given it shape, and acquired a secular existence of its own, based simply on reason. Such a construction was peculiarly congenial to the eighteenth century, the very age of reason, and most of the century's legal writers acknowledge a law of nature in

---

[17] *Die Metaphysik der Sitten*, in *Werke*, ed. E. Cassirer, 11 vols. (Berlin, 1912–18), vii. 120–5.

terms, essentially, of reason; its occasional ascription to God or a divine being seem purely perfunctory. All the same, the ancient format died hard, even in a Protestant environment. In 1765 we find Sir William Blackstone (1723–80), at the outset of his *Commentaries on the Laws of England*, writing in terms which (as Friedmann says)[18] might have been used by St Thomas, and hark back beyond him to Cicero: the law of nature,

being coeval with mankind and dictated by God himself, is of course superior in obligation to any other. It is binding over all the globe in all countries, and at all times: no human laws are of any validity, if contrary to this; and such of them as are valid derive all their force, and all their authority, mediately or immediately, from this original.[19]

Unfortunately, as will be seen later, Blackstone did not mean this to be taken as having any practical effect.

More usually, reason is in the foreground, the Divinity or the Creator hardly more than a decorous adjunct to a presentation essentially rationalistic. Thus Montesquieu in the opening chapter of *L'Esprit des lois* (1748) argues the existence of eternal standards of some kind, antecedent to the positive laws of men, and recognizable to human intelligence:

Before laws were made, there were relations of possible justice . . . We must acknowledge relations of justice antecedent to the positive law which establishes them: as, for instance, that, assuming human societies, it would be right to conform to their laws; that, if there were intelligent beings who had received some benefit from another being, they ought to show gratitude; that, if one intelligent being had created another, the one so created ought to remain in his original state of dependence; that an intelligent being who had done harm to another, ought to suffer requital; and so on.

This intelligent being, indeed, 'incessantly transgresses the laws set by God'. Nevertheless (he goes on in the next chapter) 'the law which, impressing on our minds the idea of a Creator, inclines us towards Him, is the first in importance . . . of natural laws', though on a different plane from what might be called the practical natural laws, which he enumerates as four in number. All result from rational interpretation of the human condition in a state of nature. Man is individually weak and vulnerable, and so the first natural law

---

[18] *Legal Theory* (4th edn., 1960), 84.   [19] *Commentaries* 1. 41.

is the maintenance of peace. He has physical needs, so a second natural law will animate him to provide for himself. A third law results from his instincts of affection and sexual attraction towards other humans; and a fourth, supported also by man's capacity to acquire knowledge, directs him towards existence in society.[20] This brief and rather insipid scheme, however, as will be seen, is entirely subordinate and extraneous to the more original reflections on human laws which made Montesquieu's book famous.

But natural-law doctrine in the eighteenth century went far beyond the merely decorative or platitudinous. Particularly in Germany, natural law was taken—of course in the secular sense which Grotius had given it—to be a material from which whole systems of municipal law could be fashioned, just as Grotius had extracted from it a structure of international law. It also provided a standard by which existing rules might be corrected or supplemented (though this happened only to a very limited degree). The setting of the formidable labours which now unfolded was the German universities, in this century leading Europe: the first chair formally devoted to the law of nature had been Pufendorf's at Heidelberg in the previous century, but such professorships now proliferated, and in the eighteenth century were standard features of the German centres of learning.

The most famous representative of this fashion was Christian Wolff (1679–1754), professor at Marburg and at Halle. In the 1740s he produced an eight-volume work in which he offered an entire system of law based on human nature; this material, together with a system of international law, was reworked in the *Institutiones* of 1752, a treatise on 'the law of nature and of nations, in which all rights and all obligations are deduced, by an unbroken chain of connection, from man's own nature' (so read the long Latin title). That nature, he wrote—recycling the *entelecheia* concept of Aristotle and St Thomas—tended always to its own perfection, so the primary law to be derived from it was the precept of advancing human beings to their most perfect condition possible. Accordingly man's own primary obligation was to strive towards this condition for himself, and to avoid all acts prejudicial to this progression. He was obliged also to assist in the perfection of his neighbours, though, since his capacities were limited, this duty must take second

[20] *L'esprit de lois* 1. 2.

place to his duty of perfecting himself. On the other hand the obligation not to do anything prejudicial to his neighbour's similar progression was absolute; and even the originally imperfect, less than absolute duty to assist his neighbour could be hardened into something absolute by contract. These general propositions represented man's goals set by the law of nature; but as the achievement of a goal requires access to appropriate means, the law of nature also authorizes the provision of such means. Moreover, as men are all by nature equal, a range of human rights can be deduced from their equality: for example, liberty, security, the right of self-defence. Into this frame of theory Wolff was able to fit, under one head or another, the entire body of contemporary positive law; but this did not mean that his system was really a means of sanctifying with the aura of the law of nature what a human lawgiver had prescribed. On the contrary, the law of nature bound the ruler as much as the ruled, and the subject owed no obedience to the ruler who commanded what the law of nature forbade; a justified disobedience might even take the form of active resistance.[21]

Wolff had considerable influence on contemporaries, for example on Vattel in his work on international law, and on the German lawyers who were to take the first steps towards codification of the civil law in the later part of the century. But the most celebrated of all German thinkers of the eighteenth century, Kant, offered something altogether different: not a rationalist system worked out from a purely theoretical starting-point, but a simple, all-purpose moral precept, suggested by the moral sense innate in human nature. This is the 'categorical imperative', the operative aspect of the moral law which Kant could recognize in himself as partaking of an order quite as real as, though different from the order of the material universe: both the expression of God. The categorical imperative is stated by Kant thus: 'Act only on that maxim through which you can at the same time will that it should become a universal law'; and again, in slightly different words, 'Act as if the maxim of your action were to become through your will a universal law of nature'.[22] This certainly appears to have no content more specific than the old 'golden rule' of the Middle Ages—do unto others as you would wish them to do to you—but in another work Kant restates his imperative in a somewhat more concrete form:

---

[21] References in Verdross, *Abendländische Rechtsphilosophie* (see Ch. 6 n. 42), 132 ff.
[22] Ibid. 139–40.

'Act in such a way as to treat humanity, whether in your own person or in that of another, always as the end, never merely as the means.' As Verdross says, this raises respect for the human person to become the measure of an action's morality.[23]

THE FIRST EUROPEAN CODES

The rationalist spirit of the eighteenth century produced not only academic works on the law of nature, but also the first legislative attempts at codifying national legal systems on lines suggested by the natural-law ideal. The most famous and influential of these codifications is of course the French civil code, which came into force just after the turn of the nineteenth century (commonly called the 'Code Napoléon', at least by foreigners, though this was its official title only during a few years),[24] but this work had been anticipated by efforts elsewhere, notably in Prussia and in Austria, to reduce to order a heterogeneous civil law, inherited with a bewildering penumbra of local custom and Roman accretions from the Middle Ages.

The Prussian *Allgemeines Landrecht* ('General Law of the Land') of 1794 was the first national legal code actually to come into force. It was intended to give a measure of (though not total) uniformity to the legal systems of the Prussian king's territories, which lay scattered from the Rhineland in the west to Pomerania in the east, and has been regarded as a textbook product of the Enlightenment, or rather of the enlightened absolutism of Frederick the Great. Frederick, deeply influenced by the French writers Voltaire and Montesquieu—he had a short but famous friendship with the former, wrote an essay on the latter, and generally admired French intellectual achievements as heartily as he despised those of his own nation—issued in 1780 the edict ('Cabinetts-Ordre') which authorized the work of codification; according to this edict, natural law was to take precedence over the Roman law which had been adopted generally in Germany since the sixteenth century; only as much Roman law as was compatible with this natural law, and with the existing constitution, was to be included. In the text of the code,

---

[23] References in Verdross, *Abendländische Rechtsphilosophie* (see Ch. 6 n. 42), 139–40.

[24] In 1807–16 (under the first Napoleon) and 1852–70 (under Napoleon III).

compiled by a number of distinguished jurists led by Carl Gottlieb
Svarez,[25] the general rights of the individual were declared to rest
upon his 'natural freedom to pursue and promote his own welfare,
without injury to the rights of others';[26] and all activity was
declared permitted which was forbidden 'neither by natural nor by
positive laws'.[27] The part of the code dealing with criminal law was
evidently composed under the influence of Beccaria's principles of
humanity, moderation, and proportion.[28] Tocqueville wrote of the
code as a whole that no other of Frederick's works 'throws as much
light on the mind of the man or on the times in which he lived, or
shows as plainly the influence which they exercised one upon the
other'.[29] It was brought into force under his successor, Frederick
having died in 1786.

This code, although parts of it survived in force here and there
until well into the twentieth century, is generally reckoned not to
have been a success; its provisions were too voluminous and too
minute, reflecting in this very attribute the contemporary belief that
every conceivable conjuncture in human affairs was amenable to
rational regulation. It was, moreover, only a few years old when the
rise of the historical movement in Germany created doubts as to the
whole notion of purely reason-based codification, and a critical
atmosphere in which the shortcomings of the Prussian code
appeared to justify those doubts.

The efforts made towards codification in Austria, though they
began earlier than those in Prussia, did not result in a code with the
force of law until some years later (1811), when the *Allgemeines
bürgerliches Gesetzbuch* ('General Civil Code') was promulgated.
The movement was inaugurated under Empress Maria Theresia
(1740–80) and continued, with an indiscreet enthusiasm which left
everyone discontented, by her son Joseph II (1780–90), who, like
his brother and successor Francis (at this time Grand Duke of
Tuscany), was the very model of the modern enlightened and
reforming monarch. By 1766 a draft code had been prepared, the
Codex Theresianus, by a commission which had been at work since
1753. The *Principles of Compilation* which it had published when it

---

[25] Nothing to do with the Spanish name Suárez; the German Svarez is a form of
the name Schwartz.

[26] Introduction, § 83.   [27] Introduction, § 87.

[28] James Heath, *Eighteenth Century Penal Theory* (London, 1963), 135–6; Olwen
Hufton, *Europe: Privilege and Protest, 1730–89* (London,1980), 217.

[29] *Ancien Régime* (see n. 4), 183–4.

began work recited that it had been instructed to choose the 'most natural and equitable' of the existing laws in the very heterogeneous provinces of the Habsburg empire, and to supplement them 'according to the rules of reason and natural law'. While stopping well short of a wholesale replacement of existing rules by other, purely reason-based ones, this still shows an automatic veneration of, and belief in, the rationally discoverable natural law in the form enunciated by Christian Wolff and others.[30]

In France, home though it was of the eighteenth-century Enlightenment, the role played by natural law and pure reason in the construction of the Civil Code was extremely modest. This, when it finally emerged in 1804, turned out to consist largely of the old law—i.e. a combination of the ancient Germanic customs of northern France, of Roman law (some of it in the form it had received in the Visigothic codes), and of canon law, each predominant in its own sectors of the system. There was very little innovation; and, where there was, the code 'did not devise and sanction whole new theoretical systems; the break with pre-revolutionary rules and ideas was less clear than was supposed'.[31] The reason was that those who had drafted the code were mostly men in their sixties who had grown up and received their professional formation far back in the eighteenth century under the old regime; for them, 'written reason was the law they had always known'.[32] Nevertheless, while the practice of codification was conservative in this way, as it had been in Austria, the atmosphere in which it was carried out was still heavy with belief in reason-based natural-law doctrine. Repeated salutes to the law of nature and of reason came from speakers in the National Convention,[33] while the opening article of the draft civil code published in the Year VIII of the Revolution (1799) declared that 'there exists a universal and unchanging law, the source of all positive laws: none other than natural reason'. By that date, however, disillusionment and scepticism induced by the Revolution's course had already, even in France, begun to cool the ardour for reason which had fuelled the codifying movement.

---

[30] See Henry E. Strakosch, *State Absolutism and the Rule of Law* (Sydney, 1967), 65–6. According to Strakosch, however, the influence of natural law on the Theresian Code was a superficial one.

[31] R. David and H. de Vries, *The French Legal System* (New York, 1958), 13.

[32] Ibid.

[33] See J. van Kan, *Les Efforts de codification en France* (Paris, 1929), 366–7.

England remained untouched by all this. It is true that, in the general abhorrence of the French Revolution and all its terrible works, there would have been no market among the British establishment for anything bearing the label of reason. But even before 1789—and later, after the Napoleonic wars had ended—English interest in codifying the common-law was minimal. All the same, it was an idea which attracted, and was all his life passionately promoted by, one of the most remarkable English spirits of the age, Jeremy Bentham, a genuine 'child of the Enlightenment'.[34] His starting-point, though, was very different from that of the continental natural lawyers; the idea of natural law, indeed, meant nothing to him. But he was revolted by the muddle, the unreason, the absurdity, the frequent injustice of the laws and procedures which he saw in operation all round him, and which he had heard complacently extolled by Blackstone at Oxford. He saw codification (a word which incidentally he invented) as the only way to cure English law of its haphazard and uncertain character, profitable only to the lawyers; he wished to reconstruct it in codified form, purged of its unreason, and shaped on his guiding principle, namely the aim of the greatest happiness of the greatest number. His effort to promote codification (abroad as well as in Britain) came to nothing in his lifetime. But the nineteenth century would see the triumph of his fundamental message of reform.

THE LAW OF NATURE AT WORK

It is worth saying something about how, apart from the codification movement, natural-law theory impinged on the actual practice of the law. Its effect was not negligible, as can be seen from the examples of Germany and England.

In Germany, as a modern study has suggested,[35] contrasts between the existing, essentially Roman law and the reason-based constructions which added up to natural law in the contemporary German sense (*Naturrecht*) were generally resolved in favour of the law in force, which, because of its largely Roman origin, got the

---

[34] He is so described by H. L. A. Hart: *Essays on Bentham* (Oxford, 1982), 22.
[35] Klaus Luig, 'Der Einfluß des Naturrechts auf das positive Privatrecht im 18.Jahrhundert', *Zeitschrift der Savigny-Stiftung*, 96 (1979), 38. (Germ. Abt.).

benefit of the aura which had accompanied Roman law since the Middle Ages, i.e. that of being the very embodiment, in writing, of reason itself (*ratio scripta*). Thus, to take a striking example, German law contained the Roman rule that where landed property changes owners by sale, the new owner is free to eject tenants from the holdings let to them by the former owner, leaving the tenants with no more than a personal remedy against the latter. But *Naturrecht* suggested the argument that, once the former owner had promised the letting of a holding for a term to a tenant, he had disposed of that much of his rights of ownership, and was not free to promise the same thing—in other words, was not free to promise the totality of ownership rights implicitly including the aspects he had already bargained away—to a third party. Here the Romano-German rule prevailed. Again, writers on natural law from Grotius onward had been against the Roman idea (not part of classical law, but established in the *Corpus Iuris Civilis* by Justinian) that there was, in sale, a notional 'just price' and that where a sale had taken place for a price far below the object's real value, the vendor ought to have a chance to rescind or have the price topped up; their view, on the contrary, was that parties should be free to make their own bargains, the principle of freedom of contract being seen by them as one of natural law. Here, too, they failed to uproot the Justinianic concept; though the doctrine of freedom of contract seems to have had an influence in disposing courts to apply very strict tests to allegations of an unfairly low price, and, in practice, to reject most cases brought on grounds of supposed *laesio enormis* (as Justinian called this situation); and so here *Naturrecht* could claim a modest achievement. Much more substantial was the success of argument based on *Naturrecht* in establishing in German law the concept of contracts for the benefit of third parties and capable of being enforced by those third parties. This principle, based simply on the natural-law principle that promises should be kept, supplanted the Roman rule which resembled English doctrines on privity of contract.

In England the most conspicuous conquest of the law of nature was made in the admiralty jurisdiction, particularly as developed by Lord Stowell at the century's end, during the Napoleonic wars. The law administered by this famous admiralty judge was '*ius gentium* in the fullest sense, a body of rules not merely municipal, but cosmopolitan . . . a law founded on cosmopolitan principle of reason, a true living offshoot of the Law of Nature'.[36] But even within municipal areas of law there was a silent or disguised recourse to the same plane of values. The law merchant, founded on the general custom and usage of traders and approved by that usage as reasonable, 'was a branch of the Law of Nature, and was constantly described as such'.[37] The emergence in the eighteenth century of an enforceable obligation not based on contract but arising *quasi ex contractu* is part of the same history; Lord Mansfield, in *Moses* v. *Macferlan*,[38] had approved the count for money had and received to the plaintiff's use on the basis that 'the defendant, upon the circumstances of the case, is obliged by the ties of natural justice and equity to refund the money'; according to Blackstone, this obligation arose 'from natural reason and the just construction of the law'.[39] Thus, wrote Pollock, 'the whole modern doctrine of what we now call quasi-contract rests on a bold and timely application, quite conscious and avowed, of principles derived from the Law of Nature'.[40]

Pollock, following the passage from St German's *Doctor and Student* which was quoted in Chapter 5, also identified as a manifestation of the law of nature in English dress the whole conception of the 'reasonable' standard throughout the common law, particularly marked in sale and mercantile law (the reasonable price, a reasonable time, etc.) and in negligence (reasonable care, reasonable foreseeability, etc.): 'thus natural law may fairly claim, in principle though not by name, the reasonable man of English and American law and all his works, which are many'.[41] Moreover, the notion of natural justice in the procedural sphere, importing essentially the rules *audi alteram partem* (hear what the other side has to say) and *nemo iudex in causa sua* (no one to be a judge in his own cause), together with their obvious corollaries, is applied as of course in both judicial and quasi-judicial matters, and is the most explicit instance of the 'natural' standard in the common-law system. Both the concept of reasonableness and the concept of natural justice, in the sense just mentioned, were much solidified in the practice of the eighteenth-century English courts.

---

[36] Pollock, in *Jurisprudence* (see Ch. 5 n. 102), 147–8.
[37] Ibid. 140.   [38] (1760), 2 Burr. 1005.
[39] *Commentaries* 3. 161.
[40] *Jurisprudence* (see Ch. 5 n. 102), 149.   [41] Ibid.

NATURAL RIGHTS

The historically most significant area in which natural-law thought operated in the eighteenth century was that of natural rights. It has been seen that this idea played no part in the scheme of natural law worked out by St Thomas, that its origin can be traced (though with difficulty) only from William of Ockham, that its substance is latent in the protests uttered by the sixteenth-century Spanish jurist-theologians against the maltreatment of the peoples of the New World by their countrymen. But it was the dogmatic and definite shape given it by Locke, in his apologia for the English Revolution of the late seventeenth century, that chiefly influenced the practical statesmen and political writers of the eighteenth. Locke's teachings, particularly on the central role of rights of property, were, along with Coke's affirmations on natural justice and the rule of law, the main intellectual armament of the discontented American colonists. They were famous also in France, where they had been made so above all by Voltaire, who used to mention Locke in the same breath as Newton and other natural philosophers to whom he gave credit for the liberation of man from ancient, and wrong-headed, authority.

It would be wrong to imagine that natural rights talk in this century was a monopoly of sceptical or radical spirits. As has already been seen, Christian Wolff derived a range of rights from man's nature and natural equality: liberty, security, self-defence. Edmund Burke, emphatically no *philosophe*, had imbibed enough of Locke to write in the 1760s that 'a conservation and secure enjoyment of our natural rights is the great and ultimate purpose of civil society, and therefore all forms whatsoever of government are only good as they are subservient to that purpose to which they are entirely subordinate'.[42] In 1778 he presented the right to earn a livelihood— in this context, related to Ireland's right not to be denied the possibility of doing so by the restraints imposed by the British parliament on her trade—as something which 'the Author of our nature has written strongly in that nature', as well as promulgating it by revelation.[43] Two years earlier, a royal proclamation of Louis XVI, aimed against the restraints which the system of industrial corpora-

---

[42] *Tracts on the Popery Laws*; in *Irish Affairs* (Cresset Library, London, 1988), 39.
[43] *Letters to Gentlemen in Bristol*, in *Irish Affairs*, 111.

tions imposed on workmen, had declared that 'the right to labour is the most sacred of all properties' and that 'any law which infringes that right is essentially null and void, as being inconsistent with natural right'.[44]

But it was other voices, added to that of Locke, which mainly inspired the resounding declarations of man's natural rights with which the century ended. One of these was that of Rousseau, though his writings contain very little that could plausibly be called legal theory, and that little is not unambiguous. Still, his contribution to what might be called the emotional department of natural-law doctrine was considerable. His references to natural law as superior to and inviolable by positive law were mere commonplaces; but the source of his natural law was not. For Rousseau, natural law was not dictated to the individual by reason, but by his heart; it rested on principles anterior to reason, namely, love of oneself and love of others.[45] The individual has certain innate natural rights; but these he surrenders to the collectivity in the social contract, in order to receive them back from that collectivity in the form of positive law rights.[46] The key to all this is not reason, but sentiment, just as it is sentiment which gives its force to his most famous aphorism, 'Man is born free, yet everywhere he is in chains';[47] words like these gave what might be called the plain chant of natural rights, as Locke had intoned them, a polyphonic charm.

The revolutionary developments in America and France were closely related to one another, as has been said, and so too were the formal declarations of human rights which accompanied them. The model of the English Bill of Rights of 1689 was of course there, as was, much closer to the revolutionary epoch, the declaration of rights prefixed to the constitution adopted for the state of Virginia in 1776. But the states' joint Declaration of Independence of the same year is the main American document. In it Locke's concept of man's natural rights (together with his construction of the social contract) is distilled: men, it declared, are created equal, and are endowed by their Creator with certain inalienable rights, among which are life, liberty, and the pursuit of happiness; the purpose of the institution of government is to guarantee those rights; that institution rests on the consent of the governed; and if government becomes destructive of those rights, it can be abolished and replaced

---

[44] Tocqueville, *Ancien Régime* (see n. 4), 144.
[45] *Contrat social* 1. 2.   [46] Ibid. 1. 6.   [47] Ibid. 1. 1.

with a new form. The bill of rights, consisting of the first ten amendments annexed in 1791 to the United States Constitution of 1787, although using as its practical model the English Bill of Rights of 1689, clearly belongs in the doctrinal tradition shaped by Locke.

The French Declaration of the Rights of Man and of the Citizen, made by the National Convention in 1789, obviously stands in the same general tradition. It proclaimed men free and equal in their rights; identified as the object of all political association the conservation of 'the natural and imprescriptible rights of man: liberty, property, security, and resistance to oppression'; and defined liberty as the freedom to do whatever does not injure others, who also enjoy the same freedom. The principles of fair trial, or due process of law, were guaranteed; the making of retroactive penal sanctions forbidden; the presumption of an accused person's innocence established. Freedom of conscience as well as of expression and communication were proclaimed; property was enthroned as 'an inviolable and sacred right'.

At the same time, this famous Declaration was not a pure expression of natural rights ideology nor a mere imitation of admired English or American precedents. The rights which it asserted all recalled the abuses of the *ancien régime* and of an era of privilege, injustice, intolerance, and arbitrary government.

[The declaration of] liberty of the person was a reference to the Bastille and to *lettres de cachet* [i.e. arbitrary imprisonment without trial]; that of the freedom of expression and of the press recalled [Rousseau's book] *Émile*, burned by the hangman, and Rousseau himself exiled for having written one of the greatest books of the age; that of freedom of conscience recalled the Protestants who had been driven from the kingdom and deprived of their civil status. The affirmation of the natural right of property was the counterpart of the ancient feudal exactions to which it had been enslaved. Equality before the law was the opposite of the special jurisdictions [enjoyed by the old nobility]; equal access to public office, the opposite of the privileges of rank reserved for the nobles; the proportional incidence of taxation [on all ranks] recalled the *taille*, paid exclusively by the Third Estate [the commons].[48]

While the doctrines of Locke and Rousseau strongly influenced the American and French declarations, the format of the latter was only

---

[48] P. Janet, *Histoire de la science politique*, 3rd edn., 2 vols. (Paris, 1887), i, p. xlvi, cited by G. del Vecchio, *La Déclaration des droits du l'homme et du citoyen dans la Révolution Française* (Paris, 1968), 22.

a mould in which armour was cast to protect against patterns of government which even men who had never heard of the law or rights of nature might have recognized as abuses and rebelled against.

THE REACTION AGAINST NATURAL-LAW THEORY

At the middle of the eighteenth century there was already taking place in Europe a profound intellectual shift which, from various points of departure, represented the abandonment of the concept of natural law accessible through reason; an abandonment which was to become so complete that in the nineteenth century scarcely any idea was less fashionable. On the purely philosophical level its most effective critic was the Scottish writer David Hume (1711–76). His analysis of reason, in the sense of an unfailing route to the perception of natural law, suggested that experience did not accord to it the role that theory did. Human behaviour, according to experience, is not dictated by an unvarying antecedent standard of natural law, but is the product of human motives and inclinations; if, again according to experience, it is found to follow certain patterns, this is no more than a matter of habit or convention. This denial of universal, uniform reason as the basis of action naturally undermined belief in reason-based natural-law doctrine; his analysis, first published in 1740,[49] introduced a new era 'which is predominantly anti-metaphysical, scientifically minded and utilitarian'.[50]

The scientific mind, brought to bear on law, is visible in the repeated observation throughout the century that laws in fact differ from one country to the next, that there are objective and discoverable factors which cause this to be so, and that laws ought to be suited to the particular conditions of the people for whom they are intended. The finding of the relativity of law now served, not as with the ancient sophists to support a denial of universal moral values, but to draw attention to the elements in the life of particular peoples which were likely to have determined the shape of their institutions; in other words, to the raw materials of what would later become the independent sciences of comparative law, anthropology, and sociology.

[49] *Treatise of Human Nature.*
[50] Friedmann, *Legal Theory* (see Ch. 6 n. 13), 130.

The earliest writer to express such ideas was Giambattista Vico (1668–1744), who spent most of his life in his native Naples and was for long scarcely known outside Italy (which at this epoch was something of an intellectual backwater). In his *Scienza nuova*, first published in 1725, he advanced the perception that, far from there being a natural law setting the same standards for men at all times and places, each society grew organically in its own peculiar environment, and its institutions, including its laws, reflected its own peculiar history. 'The nature of institutions [he wrote] is nothing but their coming into being at certain times and with certain guises; whenever the time and guise are thus and so, such and not otherwise are the institutions that come into being.'[51] This perception was revolutionary in the intellectual conditions of his time; with it, wrote Isaiah Berlin, Vico 'denied the doctrine of a timeless natural law the truths of which could have been known in principle to any man, at any time, anywhere . . . He preached the notion of the uniqueness of cultures [and thereby] laid the foundations at once of comparative cultural anthropology and of comparative historical linguistics, aesthetics [and] jurisprudence';[52] although it is hard to prove that he had any influence on his contemporaries, and had to wait until the next century for wide recognition.

In a more general way other eighteenth-century writers drew attention to the diversity of laws and to the desirability of their suiting those to whom they applied. Voltaire, writing to the future Frederick the Great, touched on the variety of national laws; some items, he thought, were common to all peoples, e.g. abhorrence of murder and respect for promises, and that such instincts flowed from a divinely implanted sense of justice; beyond this, laws varied as widely as taste; and, while he did not advance a general theory about the influence of environment as Vico had done, he suggested, in order to explain why theft had been no crime in ancient Sparta, a feature of the Spartan social system.[53] In his *Dictionnaire philosophique* (1764) he returned, satirically, to the perverse mutual discordance of legal systems.[54] Meanwhile, however, the subject had provided the

---

[51] *Scienza nuova* (Bergin and Fisch edn.), 147–8.
[52] Berlin, in *Against the Current* (see Ch. 5 n. 37), 5.
[53] In *The Portable Voltaire*, ed. B. Redman (Harmondsworth, 1977), 452.
[54] See s.v. 'On laws'.

theme of one of the greatest books of the century, *De l'esprit des lois* by Charles de Secondat, baron Montesquieu.

Montesquieu (1689–1755) became a European celebrity after the publication of this work in 1748, though a hint of his interest in the critical appraisal of institutions by reference to those of other societies was already visible in his *Lettres persanes* published in 1721. His *De l'esprit des lois* reads today like a rather quaint and rambling collection of odds and ends of legal and institutional curiosities, but it performed the important function of drawing attention to the varying customs of different nations (while giving the usual perfunctory salute, noted above, to the supremacy of the law of nature) and suggesting that their variety was explained by the variety in their surrounding conditions. Indeed, the adapting of laws to suit the actual condition of the people concerned amounted to a principle:

[Laws] should be adapted in such a manner to the people for whom they are framed that it will be a mere accident if those of one nation should suit another. They should be in relation to the nature and principle of each system of government; whether they actually form it, as may be said of constitutional rules, or merely support it, as in the case of civil law. They should be related to the climate of each country, to the quality of its soil, to its situation and extent, to the principal occupation of the natives, whether husbandmen, huntsmen, or shepherds; they should be related to the degree of liberty which the constitution will bear; to the religion of the inhabitants, to their inclinations, riches, numbers, commerce, manners and customs. They ought also to be related to each other, as well as to their origin, the intent of the legislator, and the order of things on which they are established; in all of which different lights they ought to be considered . . . [All these relations] together constitute what I call the *Spirit of Laws*.[55]

This perspective quickly became a commonplace. When the government of Maria Theresia formed the idea of a unified code for the heterogeneous peoples of the Habsburg empire the learned commission in charge of the project observed, in their *Principles of Compilation* (1753), that the difference of laws in the various provinces of the empire was to be attributed to their different ways of life, and that if the divergences could be traced to their historical origin, a common principle might be uncovered.[56] A counter-petition, aimed at dissuading Maria Theresia's government from

[55] *De l'esprit des lois* 1. 3.
[56] Strakosch, *State Absolutism* (see n. 30), 66–7.

imposing any rigid legal uniformity, pointed out that 'the geographical situation of the provinces is not the same, nor is the air they breathe, the food they consume or the way they live; but all these things have a great influence on their constitution [i.e. legal systems]'.[57] Montesquieu's work, according to M. S. Anderson, 'seems to have appealed particularly to statesmen and diplomats, men with direct experience of government and its problems'.[58]

So far in this account of the movement away from the idea of law as something which can or ought to be ideally shaped by a purely rational perception of nature, we have seen the views of dispassionate observers or improvers, anxious to explain or to accommodate variety without finding the individual distinctiveness of a system, in itself, either good or bad. At the end of the century, however, there appeared from the pen of the Irishman Edmund Burke (1723–95), star of the British parliament and of society, a passionate claim for the superiority of organically grown systems over those constructed from purely rational, or supposed 'natural', materials. At first sympathetic to the reform of French institutions—as he had been to the cause of the American colonists, as well as to the grievances of his native country[59]—he was so appalled by the course taken by the Revolution (and this was while Louis XVI was still alive and still king, and long before the Terror) that he turned into a fierce opponent of movements to uproot long-established systems in the name of reason and put artificial, purely rational constructions in their place. His famous *Reflections on the Revolution in France* (1790) is a classic rhetorical statement of the conservative position; but in the course of this polemic he made points which go beyond the modest observations and prescriptions of his Italian, French, and Austrian forerunners, and give him some claim to rank— though he could not have foreseen that such a significance would be assigned to his insights—as the father of historical jurisprudence. This science was not pursued consciously until the early nineteenth century (unless one counts the humanist jurisprudence of Renaissance France); but it rested on perceptions which he was the first to state in terms of certain values.

[57] Strakosch, *State Absolutism* (see n. 30), 58.
[58] *Europe in the Eighteenth Century, 1713–1783* (3rd edn., London, 1987), 424.
[59] See the collection of tracts and letters published as *Irish Affairs* (Cresset Library, 1988).

The *Reflections*—formally constructed as a long open letter in reply to a French correspondent—are, curiously enough, although an assault on systems based on reading off what 'nature' is supposed by the rationalist mind to recommend, nevertheless a celebration of nature in another sense; of that in institutions which is rooted in history; of the slow, organic progression and development of a nation in response to its own environment and in the forms suggested by its own genius. Central to it is the contrast between the British constitution, unembarrassed by rationalistic constructions, and quietly, as it were at a human pace, adapting itself simply and slightly as it went along to changing surroundings, and that of France, where structures which had been a thousand years in building were rashly pulled down overnight to make way for something thought up by theorists, although ample and far less destructive reform would have been possible by simple grafts upon and excisions from the old body:

By a constitutional policy working after the pattern of nature, we receive, we hold, we transmit our government and our privileges, in the same manner in which we enjoy and transmit our property and our lives . . . By the disposition of a stupendous wisdom, moulding together the great mysterious incorporation of the human race, the whole [is] in a condition of unchangeable constancy, [and] moves on through the varied tenor of perpetual decay, fall, renovation and progression . . .

You [the French] might have repaired those walls . . . built on those old foundations . . . [but] you began ill, because you began by despising everything that belonged to you; [whereas by] respecting your forefathers, you would have been taught to respect yourselves . . . Is every landmark of the country to be done away in favour of a geometrical and arithmetical constitution?[60]

Basil Willey quotes from elsewhere in Burke's work: 'Politics', said Burke, 'ought to be adjusted, not to human reasonings, but to human nature; of which the reason is but a part, and by no means the greatest part'. 'This celebrated remark', says Willey, 'illustrates the manner in which Burke counters "Nature" the abstraction with "Nature" the actuality, the metaphysical with the historical . . . and it may stand as a symbol of the transition from the eighteenth century mental climate to that of the nineteenth.'[61]

---

[60] *Reflections on the Revolution in France* (Pelican edn., Harmondsworth, 1968), 120–2.
[61] *Eighteenth Century Background* (see Ch. 6 n. 15), 243.

The reaction against the law of nature also brought the doctrine of natural rights within the range of fire. 'We have not', wrote Burke in the course of his *Reflections,* 'been drawn and trussed, in order that we may be filled, like stuffed birds in a museum, with chaff and rags, and paltry blurred shreds of paper about the rights of man'—though a quarter of a century earlier he himself had seen the conservation of man's natural rights as the great end of civil society. Bentham wrote in 1791 an impassioned, even hysterical, attack upon the notion of natural rights, evidently by way of reply to Tom Paine's *Rights of Man,* in which the Anglo-American revolutionary had listed the 'natural and imprescriptible rights of man' as 'liberty, property, security, and resistance of oppression': such talk, said Bentham, was nonsense: ' "Natural rights" is simple nonsense; "natural and imprescriptible rights", rhetorical nonsense—nonsense upon stilts'.[62] In the following paragraph he called such talk 'terrorist language'. Bentham's objection to natural-rights theory was partly rational; he thought it made no sense to speak about a 'right' which could not be presented in terms of a duty (to respect such a 'right') imposed by the command of law upon others; and that in any case to speak about, say, a 'right of property' was contradictory, since any such 'right' of mine implies a corresponding ouster of the right of all others in the same object. But in addition he saw something far more sinister in the doctrine of natural rights, namely, a crude weapon of bullying demagogy:

When a man is bent upon having things his own way and can give no reason for it, he says: I have a right to have them so. When a man has a political caprice to gratify . . . when he finds it necessary to get the multitude to join with him . . . he sets up a cry of rights. I have a right to have it so; you have all a right to have it so: none but tyrants can refuse us. Give us then our rights. The dictates of reason and utility are the result of circumstances which require genius to discover, strength of mind to weigh, and patience to investigate; the language of natural rights requires nothing but a hard front, a hard heart and an unblushing countenance. It is from beginning to end so much flat assertion: it neither has any thing to do with reason nor will endure the mention of it.

The great end of government was to restrain selfish passions and induce sacrifices for the common benefit; but declaration of man's

[62] *Anarchical Fallacies,* in *Works,* ed. J. Bowring, 11 vols. (Edinburgh, 1838–43), ii. 501.

'natural rights' could only 'add as much force to those passions, but already too strong'.[63]

THE EMERGENCE OF NEW CONSTITUTIONAL THEMES

The eighteenth century saw the rise of several practices and doctrines of a constitutional kind which are today familiar but which before that age either were wholly unknown or were present, or were articulated, in only obscure or rudimentary form. These themes stand out, because of their novelty, from other themes, equally of constitutional rank, but which by the eighteenth century already had a very ancient history, such as the rule of law, or equality before the law; there has been something to say about both of those matters in every chapter of this book. Three or four new constitutional subjects require to be mentioned briefly here.

First, it is now that written constitutions make their appearance. It is of course true that English documents such as the Bill of Rights of 1689 correspond with important parts of modern written constitutions (and in Britain still do adequate duty for them). But a document which actually determines the functions and relations of the organs of the state, or which even purports to establish the state, is in a different category. Here the first example is provided by Sweden, whose King Gustavus III organized in 1772 a sort of *coup d'état* against the nobility, and forced the Riksdag to accept a constitution in the form of a single comprehensive document. This, because of the marginal position of all Scandinavia to the main European theatre, might have remained an isolated instance. But shortly afterwards the world witnessed the revolt of Britain's American colonies, their declaration of independence, and their creation of a union with the Constitution of 1787. The whole American development, as has been said, was followed with keen sympathy and urgent interest in France; and one of the first works of the French revolutionaries was the production of their own written Constitution of 1792. From that era onwards the movement towards political reform, or national independence, or both, was in every country (except Britain, the great mother of anomalies) bound up with the idea of anchoring the structures of liberty in a written charter with the force of law.

[63] Ibid.

Although the United States Constitution was virtually a world novelty, the fact that it took written form does not seem to reflect any particular theory, but arose from its history. There were in the contemporary world already two well-known federal polities, those of the Netherlands (or the United Provinces, as they were still called) and Switzerland; neither of them, as yet, had written constitutions, but then their systems were of ancient organic growth, and were as well understood and accepted by their peoples as the British system was by the people of Britain. In America, on the other hand, everything arose from a crisis. The colonies there, all of which had their own colonial legislatures, were driven into contriving a system of co-operation in resistance to Britain; this took the form of a Continental Congress, which, in order to get some basic structure of common government into place, drafted Articles of Confederation and submitted them to the individual colonial assemblies for approval. These Articles disclosed weaknesses in operation; and from a plan for their amendment the draft constitution of the United States ultimately emerged. All this happened in an atmosphere of strong disagreement between what were now to be the States of the Union, and the separate ratification by those States of this document was a slow process and one which seemed for a time by no means certain of success. The whole episode, from this point of view, was one of adjustment, compromise, persuasion, in order to get all the States tied down in agreement and it was this resemblance to the effort to negotiate a very complex partnership or treaty and the natural desirability in those conditions that it should be embodied in a written and permanent instrument, that account for a constitution-format which today seems so normal but was then a novelty. The French situation was different in so far as here there was no problem of federation; but the French were equally starting from constitutional scratch, building on a constitutional *tabula rasa*, and this alone, even if the American example were not to hand, could explain the project of casting the new state in a mould of permanent written rules.

Secondly, it was in this century that the doctrine of separation of powers established itself as a formula against tyranny. There was, as has been seen, an incomplete foretaste of this in Locke; but its classic statement is found in Montesquieu's *Esprit des lois*. He placed it in his chapter entitled 'The Constitution of England' (he had visited England in 1729–31 and had been much impressed by its institutions, though had in part misunderstood them) and began by explaining that 'in every state there are three kinds of power: the legislative power, the executive power in matters governed by the law of nations, and the executive power in matters governed by the law of the state'.[64] The next paragraph explains that the first of these is the power to make temporary or permanent, or repealing or amending laws; the second is the function of making war or concluding peace, sending or receiving envoys, assuring security, preventing invasions; the third is that of punishing crimes, or deciding disputes between individuals. Put in modern form, these correspond with, respectively, the legislative, the executive, and the judicial power, though a modern writer would define them somewhat differently. At all events, Montesquieu perceived that political liberty could not exist where any two of these three powers were in the hands of the same organ of the state, and considered that the liberty which he believed the English enjoyed (as they unquestionably did by comparison with his own or most other peoples of Europe) sprang from their having dispersed the exercise of the three governmental powers among different organs. His theory, carried by the vehicle of his famous book, found acceptance in both America and France, whence it afterwards became a constitutional commonplace elsewhere; though not, of course, in Britain itself, where any application of a meter based on Montesquieu's scheme would produce to this day a rather muddled reading.[65]

Thirdly, although the first concrete instance of the scrutiny by a court of a duly enacted statute for its possible infraction of a written constitution had to await the pioneer American case of *Marbury* v. *Madison*[66] in 1803, the theory of judicial review had already emerged in the eighteenth century. It first appears, not in America, but in France, in the 1760s, among a group of Enlightenment authors whose principal importance was their interest in economics (at this epoch only beginning to assume the lineaments of a science); they were known as 'Physiocrats'. Several Physiocrat writers contended that judges, before enforcing the laws, ought to satisfy themselves that the laws they were being called on to apply actually conformed with the dictates of the 'natural laws of the social

---

[64] *De l'esprit des lois* 2. 6.
[65] e.g. the lord chancellor is a member of all three arms of government.
[66] 1 Cr. 137.

order'[67] and of justice. One passage may be cited from probably the best known of the school:

> It is clear that any judge who took it upon himself to inflict penalties on his fellows by virtue of obviously unjust laws would be guilty of fault. Judges, therefore, should measure the ordinances of positive law against the laws of essential justice which govern the rights and duties of all men . . . before taking it upon themselves to give judgment according to those ordinances.[68]

Einaudi found no evidence that American ideas about judicial control owed anything to the Physiocrats, and noted that the Physiocratic position would seem to undermine the principle of separation of powers which the Americans had made central to their constitutional thinking (though this of course is breached in any case by the development after *Marbury* v. *Madison*). It seems hard to believe that in the very decade in which American resistance to British government was hardening, the literate American public was not reached by these ideas. But whatever their genesis or provenance, the theory of judicial review was alive in America even before the coming into force of the Constitution. In the 1780s, wrote Corwin, it was a 'rapidly spreading idea'.[69] A single passage from the celebrated *Federalist Papers* (a series of articles published during the time when the ratification of the Constitution by the States hung in the balance, and written by Alexander Hamilton, James Madison, and John Jay) states the theory in essentially the form which it still has

> Some perplexity respecting the rights of the courts to pronounce legislative acts void, because contrary to the Constitution, has arisen from an imagination that the doctrine would imply a superiority of the judiciary to the legislative power . . .
> There is no position which depends on clearer principles than that every act of a delegated authority, contrary to the tenor of the commission under which it is exercised, is void. No legislative act, therefore, contrary to the Constitution, can be valid . . . If it be said that the legislative body are themselves the constitutional judges of their own powers and that the construction they put upon them is conclusive upon the other departments it may be answered that this cannot be the natural presumption where it is

[67] Charles de Butré (1768), cited by Mario Einaudi, *The Physiocratic Doctrine of Judicial Control* (Cambridge, 1938), 37.

[68] Pierre Samuel Dupont de Nemours, *De l'origine et des progrès d'une science nouvelle* (1767), cited by Einaudi, *Physiocratic Doctrine*, 44–5.

[69] E. S. Corwin, *The Doctrine of Judicial Review* (Princeton, NJ, 1914), 49 n.

not to be collected from any particular provisions in the Constitution ... It is far more rational to suppose that the courts were designed to be an intermediate body between the people and the legislature in order, among other things, to keep the latter within the limits assigned to their authority. The interpretation of the laws is the proper and peculiar province of the courts. A constitution is, in fact, and must be regarded by the judges as, a fundamental law. It therefore belongs to them to ascertain its meaning as well as the meaning of any particular act proceeding from the legislative body. If there should happen to be an irreconcilable variance between the two, that which has the superior obligation and validity ought, of course, to be preferred; or, in other words, the Constitution ought to be preferred to the statute, the intention of the people to the intention of their agents.

Nor does this conclusion by any means suppose a superiority of the judicial to the legislative power. It only supposes that the power of the people is superior to both ...[70]

The United States Constitution did not, however, expressly provide for judicial review; the implicit residence of the principle in the Constitution was established by *Marbury* v. *Madison*. There is of course also the difference between the French and the American theory that the former proposes a free-floating judicial right to reject statutes felt to offend against the unwritten principles of justice, while the latter makes conformity with the written constitution the only criterion of the validity or invalidity of a law.

Lastly, the effect of a revolution on the legal order (a theme well worn in recent decades) while not the subject of any eighteenth-century theory, was evidently in practice confined within as narrow limits as possible. Questions of legitimacy of the operations of subordinate state organs after a radical shift in the constitution do not seem to have disturbed the age at all. Tocqueville, writing about the *ancien régime* in the early nineteenth century, pointed out that France had seen since 1789

several revolutions which have altered the whole edifice of government. Most of them have been very sudden, and have been achieved by violence, in open violation of existing laws. Yet none have given rise to long continued or general disorders: they have been scarcely felt, in some cases hardly noticed by the majority of the nation.

The reason is that, since 1789, the administrative system has always remained untouched in the midst of political convulsions. The person of the sovereign or the form of the central power has been altered, but the daily

[70] No. 78: Alexander Hamilton.

transaction of business has neither been disturbed nor interrupted. Each citizen has remained subject to the laws and usages which he understood, in the small matters which concerned him personally. He had to deal with secondary authorities, with which he had done business before, and which were rarely changed. For if each revolution struck off the head of the government, it left its body untouched and alive, so that the same functionaries continued to perform their functions, in the same spirit, and according to the same routine, under every different political system. They administered justice or managed public affairs in the name of the king, then in that of the republic, lastly in that of the emperor.[71]

THE RULE OF LAW

In the late seventeenth century, as has been seen, Locke's very influential voice had articulated the old idea that the state ought to be governed according to certain laws, not arbitrarily. In the eighteenth this was a commonplace; M. S. Anderson records as 'universal in the political thinking of the Enlightenment' the belief that 'the best form of government is one in which the individual is subject to known and clearly expressed laws'; this ideal 'ruled out the arbitrary and uncontrolled "oriental despotism" which every thinker of the age agreed in rejecting'.[72]

In England the great authority on this was Blackstone. Notwithstanding the prerogative immunity from suit that the crown enjoyed, he was clear that the crown and its ministers ought to respect the ordinary law and were in no way outside it. Exhibiting as evidence the coronation oath, he wrote that

the principal duty of the king is, to govern his people according to law. *Nec regibus infinita aut libera potestas*, was the constitution of our German ancestors on the continent. And this is not only consonant to the principles of nature, of liberty, of reason, and of society, but has always been esteemed an express part of the common law of England . . .[73]

At about the same time as Blackstone was writing, a notable assertion of the rule of law came also from the courts. It had been still thought possible for agents of the executive (in modern terms,

---

[71] *Ancien Régime* (see n. 4), 161–2.
[72] Anderson, *Europe in the Eighteenth Century*, 184.
[73] *Commentaries* 1. 6. The Latin sentence is from Tacitus' *Germania*: see Ch. 3 above.

the police), equipped with 'general warrants' (warrants not alleging a specific breach of the law by a specific person), to break into and search premises; this practice was resorted to against printers during the conflicts with government associated with John Wilkes, a political agitator and MP, but it was finally declared illegal in the classic case of *Entick* v. *Carrington.*[74]

In France, writing in the middle of the reign of Louis XV, Montesquieu noted that 'in a monarchy . . . he who commands the execution of the laws generally thinks himself above them':[75] no unjust reflection on the state of affairs in his own country, where some years earlier Voltaire had been set upon and beaten by agents of a nobleman against whom he had no effective redress. Tocqueville described the lax and unequal enforcement of law by the government of the *ancien régime*; the government 'rarely broke the law, but it daily bent it to either side, to suit particular cases or facilitate the transaction of business'.

Complaints are heard [he wrote] that Frenchmen show contempt for law. Alas! when could they have learned to respect it? It may be broadly said that, among the men of the old régime, the place in the mind which should have been occupied by the idea of law was vacant. Petitioners begged that established rules might be departed from in their case as seriously and as earnestly as if they had been insisting on the honest execution of the law . . .[76]

These were conditions to which clauses both of the Declaration of the Rights of Man and the Citizen of 1789, and the Constitution of 1792, were intended to put an end.

In Prussia, on the other hand, recognized by contemporaries as the best-governed state in Europe, it was possible to sue the ruler; this principle was given formal expression in the *Allgemeines Landrecht* prepared under Frederick the Great, which provided that such disputes were to be decided in accordance with the law, and by the ordinary courts.[77] In America James Madison emphasized that the House of Representatives could make 'no law which will not have its full operation on themselves and their friends, as well as on the great mass of the society'.[78]

[74] (1765) 19 State Trials 1030.
[76] *Ancien Régime* 2. 6.
[78] *Federalist Papers*, no. 57.

[75] *De l'esprit des lois* 3. 3.
[77] Introduction, § 80.

PRINCIPLES OF LEGISLATION

Throughout the eighteenth century there are frequent echoes of themes long familiar as to the principles which should govern the enactment of new law; there are also one or two statements of principle which are less familiar, and these are probably attributable, for example where they occur in the *Federalist Papers*, to the rising spirit of constitutionalism.

The ancient doctrine that the common good must be the object of all law and government is heard in this age over and over again. 'The public good, the real welfare of the great body of the people, is the supreme object to be pursued', wrote Madison; 'and no form of government whatever has any other value than as it may be fitted for the attainment of this object'.[79] The principle is stated with transcendent power by Burke in his tracts against the injustice of the penal laws against the Catholics of Ireland, which were designed to leave the majority of the Irish population without property, influence, education, or the social position accessible through the professions. All these tracts from the 1760s amount to an indictment of laws framed on principles of injustice, and the selection of one passage for quotation rather than another is not easy.

In reality there are two, and only two foundations of law, and they are both of them conditions without which nothing can give it any force—I mean equity and utility. With respect to the former, it grows out of the great rule of equality which is grounded upon our common nature, and which Philo,[80] with propriety and beauty, calls the mother of justice. All human laws are, properly speaking, only declaratory; they may alter the mode and application, but have no power over the substance of original justice. The other foundation of law, which is utility, must be understood not of partial or limited, but of general and public utility, connected in the same manner with, and derived directly from our rational nature. . . . If any proposition can be clear in itself, it is this, that a law which shuts out from all secure and valuable property the bulk of the people, cannot be made for the utility of the party so excluded . . . But if it were true (as it is not) that the real interest of any part of the community could be separated from the happiness of the rest, still it would afford no just foundation for a statute providing exclusively for that interest at the expense of the other; because it would be

[79] *Federalist Papers*, no. 45.
[80] Philo of Alexandria (13 BC–c.AD 45), Hellenistic Jewish philosopher.

repugnant to the essence of law, which requires that it be made as much as possible for the benefit of the whole. If this principle be denied or evaded, what ground have we left to reason on? We must at once make a total change in all our ideas, and look for a new definition of law.[81]

It by no means followed from this that a statutory scheme was to apply with an undifferentiating rigidity to all sections of the people. On the contrary, whereas the general principle of tailoring legislation to the people for whom it was intended was, as has been seen, something of a commonplace, Burke felt that laws needed also to have regard to the existence of different elements within the same population. Writing to his son about 1790 on the subject of the Anglican Protestant church which was by law the established Church of Ireland, he said:

Instead of prating about Protestant ascendancies, Protestant Parliaments ought, in my opinion, to think at last of becoming Patriot Parliaments. The Legislature of Ireland,[82] like all legislatures, ought to frame its laws to suit the people and the circumstances of the country, and not any longer to make it their whole business to force the nature, the temper, and the inveterate habits of a nation to a conformity to speculative systems concerning any kind of laws. Ireland has an established government, and a religion legally established, which are to be preserved. It has a people, who are to be preserved too, and to be led by reason, principle, sentiment and interest to acquiesce in that Government. Ireland is a country under peculiar circumstances. The people of Ireland are a very mixed people; and the quantities of the several ingredients in the mixture are very much disproportioned to each other. Are we to govern this mixed body as if it were composed of the most simple elements, comprehending the whole in one system of benevolent legislation? or are we not rather to provide for the several parts according to the various and diversified necessities of the heterogeneous nature of the mass?[83]

In 1764 Voltaire in his *Dictionnaire philosophique* reproduced several themes on legislation which hark back to the Early Middle Ages and beyond. These are all brief maxims, contained in an entry headed 'Civil and ecclesiastical laws', which he pretended to be 'notes found among the papers of a jurist', which 'perhaps deserve

---

[81] *Tracts on Popery* (see n. 42), 27–8.
[82] This was the old Irish Parliament, in which only Protestants sat. It was abolished in 1800 by the Act of Union.
[83] *A Letter to Richard Burke, Esq.*, in *Irish Affairs*, 360–1.

some attention'. Most of them are shots aimed at the Church; the more general, and familiar, ones are:

That the whole of the law should be clear, uniform and precise: to interpret it is nearly always to corrupt it.

That taxation should never be anything but proportional.

That law should never conflict with custom; for if the custom is good the law is superfluous.[84]

Many less concise expressions of the same values could be cited from the literature of the century.

The *Federalist Papers* contain three legislative principles worth citing. The first, not entirely original because it has an analogue in early Roman law and is occasionally mentioned later, is apparently now re-emerging in the common-law world after a long period of eclipse in practice. It is the rule against the enactment of bills of attainder (whereby an individual is convicted and condemned by parliament, without judicial trial) and *ex post facto* laws (i.e. with retroactive penal effect) contained in a clause of the draft United States Constitution restricting the powers of the States. Of this class of laws Madison wrote that they were 'contrary to the first principles of the social compact and to every principle of sound legislation . . . and prohibited by the spirit and scope of these fundamental charters [i.e. the several State constitutions]'.[85] The same judgment applied to laws impairing the obligations of contract, prohibited by the same clause, which he described as a 'constitutional bulwark in favour of personal security and private rights'.[86] Lastly, there is a rejection, this time from Hamilton, of the idea that a legislative reversal of a judicial decision is admissible:

The theory, neither of the British, nor the State constitutions, authorises the revisal of a judicial sentence by a legislative act. [It was true that the proposed Constitution did not explicitly prohibit it; but] the impropriety of the thing, on the general principles of law and reason, is the sole obstacle. A legislature, without exceeding its province, cannot reverse a determination once made in a particular case; though it may prescribe a new rule for future cases. This is the principle and it applies in all its consequences [both to the State and to the Union legislatures].[87]

---

[84] *Dictionnaire philosophique*, s.v. 'Of civil and ecclesiastical laws'.
[85] *Federalist Papers*, no. 44. See also, on retroactive penal laws no. 84 (Hamilton).
[86] Ibid.   [87] Ibid. no. 81.

Certainly the most famous eighteenth-century essay in the area of legislative principles was that of the Englishman Jeremy Bentham (1748–1832), a youthful prodigy who decided early in life that he had a 'genius for legislation'. His phenomenal influence on the world did not become fully visible until the nineteenth century, when his name, and the slogan of 'utilitarianism', were associated with all kinds of rational and beneficial law reforms. But his notion that law was an instrument capable of indefinite improvement, and of effecting indefinite improvement in the world, was already implicit in his early work, and the ultimate triumph of his ideas, due no doubt in part to his very long and active life, rested largely on the appealing simplicity of his startling insight. This was his identification, as the proper standard of government activity, of the 'principle of utility', which he paraphrased (in a formula which he did not invent but apparently derived, perhaps at one remove, from Beccaria), as 'the greatest happiness of the greatest number'. He also called this the 'felicific calculus'.

The occasion of Bentham's first statement of the principle of utility was the (originally anonymous) publication in 1776 of his *Fragment on Government*, a critique of, or rather an attack upon, Blackstone's recently published *Commentaries on the Laws of England*. The 28-year-old Bentham exhibited these, with what must have been a wounding severity, as founded on assumptions which were complacent, untrue, or even meaningless: in particular, he assailed the supposed contractual origin of society and the transcendent authority of the law of nature, both of them ideas which Bentham took to be finally exploded, and which Blackstone had certainly presented in a manner so confused that it was easy to make his work seem ridiculous. This was not Bentham's only concern; his point was rather that an exposition of a legal system which starts from such dubious references is unlikely to get a useful result in its assessment of the system's values and the reasons underlying the concrete rules, whatever success it may have in simply setting out the rules themselves.

Instead of using these antique theories as the base from which to applaud the British constitution and the existing laws, he urged the necessity of a censorial jurisprudence which would measure every rule against the standard of utility; and he developed this theme at great and even wearisome length in the book to which the *Fragment on Government* was really only an introduction, namely, his

Principles of Morals and Legislation, printed in 1780 but not published until 1789. Here he wrote:

Nature has placed mankind under the governance of two sovereign masters, *pain* and *pleasure.* It is for them alone to point out what we ought to do, as well as to determine what we shall do. On the one hand the standard of right and wrong, on the other the chain of causes and effects, are fastened to their throne. They govern us in all we do, in all we say, in all we think: every effort we can make to throw off our subjection, will serve but to demonstrate and confirm it. In words a man may pretend to abjure their empire; but in reality he will remain subject to it all the while. The *principle of utility* recognises this subjection, and assumes it for the foundation of that system, the object of which is to rear the fabric of felicity by the hands of reason and of law . . .

A measure of government (which is but a particular kind of action, performed by a particular person or persons) may be said to be comformable to or dictated by the principle of utility, when . . . the tendency which it has to augment the happiness of the community is greater than any which it has to diminish it.[88]

Bentham thought that that debate about the balance of utility of an actual or proposed law—naturally he did not suppose that the balance would seem to every eye, and without debate, to tilt in the same direction—could be based on concrete instances drawn from experience; and that this was a more fruitful way to thrash out disagreements about a law's virtues than to argue whether it was or was not in accordance with nature; a pernicious law could be simply described as such, without entering into argument as to whether, having regard to its possible repugnance to a supposed transcendent standard, it was a law at all. Why turn aside into a wilderness of sophistry, when the path of plain reason (i.e. discerning whether the law conduces to greater or to less felicity) is straight before us?

This perception, which needless to say does not require the idea of happiness to be understood in any base or unworthily material sense, may seem banal today, but in the eighteenth century the idea of appraising legislation, actual or potential, not by the porous standard of the common good (into which suspect values can easily percolate) but by that of the number of people it does or may make happier, was strikingly original. As, however, the era of Benthamism triumphant is essentially that of his later life, and of the ninteenth

---

[88] *Principles of Morals and Legislation* 1. 1.

century generally, further reference to Benthamite legislative principles will be left for the next chapter.

THE DEFINITION OF LAW

Bentham must, however, be mentioned once or twice again in other connections before we leave the eighteenth century behind. One of these is the definition of law. We have seen virtually throughout the history of Western legal thought that, when law is defined, it receives a definition in which the imperative element, in other words the element of command, is central. The eighteenth century both continues this tradition and, in Bentham, solidifies it in a theoretical form.

Blackstone, for example, defined law as a 'rule of civil conduct prescribed by the supreme power in a state, commanding what is right and prohibiting what is wrong', thus perpetuating a formula going back through scholastic theology to the Romans.[89] A command or prohibition could, in theory, be issued independent of a sanction;[90] but the element of a sanction is insisted on by Alexander Hamilton in the *Federalist Papers*:

Government implies the power of making laws. It is essential to the idea of a law that it be attended with a sanction; or, in other words, a penalty or punishment for disobedience. If there be no penalty annexed to disobedience, the resolutions or commands which pretend to be laws will, in fact, amount to nothing more than advice or recommendations.[91]

Possibly Bentham read and was struck by this remark. At any rate, his own view of the making of a true law is clearly cast in the mould of command in its strong, not merely admonitory, form.

The history of this view is curious. For a hundred years the systematizer of the idea of law as the command of a sovereign, equipped with the power to punish for disobedience, was thought to be not Bentham, but a disciple of his, John Austin (1790–1859). In 1945, however, a previously unpublished work of Bentham's, which had lain unremarked among his voluminous manuscripts at

---

[89] *Commentaries* 1. 30.
[90] For a modern example, see the Irish Documents and Pictures (Regulation of Export) Act, 1945.
[91] *Federalist Papers*, no. 15.

London University, was finally published; this was now seen to be the second part of his *Principles of Morals and Legislation*, and carries the title *Of Laws in General*.[92] In this work Bentham takes up the thought already visible in the *Fragment on Government* in which, in the context of combating the social contract theory, he had written:

When a number of persons (whom we may style *subjects*) are supposed to be in the *habit* of paying *obedience* to a person, or an assemblage of persons, of a known and certain description (whom we may call *governor* or *governors*) such persons altogether (*subjects* and *governors*) are said to be in a state of *political* SOCIETY.[93]

The conception here stated is echoed in chapter 4 of *Of Laws in General* when he describes a 'sovereign' as 'any person or assemblage of persons to whose will a whole political community are (no matter on what account) supposed to be in a disposition to pay obedience'; and this figure of the sovereign is central to his idea of law itself, because, rejecting any higher notion of law, he sees it wholly in the form of a command issued by the sovereign to his habitual subjects, and ultimately therefore in terms of the ruler's simple will. A law, he says, may be defined as

an assemblage of signs declarative of a volition conceived or adopted by the *sovereign* in the state, concerning the conduct to be observed in a certain *case* by a certain person or class of persons, who in the case in question are or are supposed to be subject to his power: such volition trusting for its accomplishment to the expectation of certain events which it is intended such declaration should upon occasion be a means of bringing to pass, and the prospect of which it is intended should act as a motive upon those whose conduct is in question.[94]

From this ponderous formula there results a theory of law as the command of a sovereign, likely to be obeyed because of the sanction (the 'expectation of certain events') with which it is equipped. This picture of law was however (because of the non-publication of Bentham's work) first propagated by Austin in the 1830s, and its further discussion will therefore be taken up in the next chapter.

---

[92] Edn. by H. L. A. Hart (1970).

[93] *Fragment*, § 10. The format of the proposition obviously owes something to Hobbes.

[94] Ibid. ch. 3.

EQUALITY BEFORE THE LAW

The natural equality of all men is a theoretical commonplace of the Enlightenment, which involves, again in theory, the proposition of their equality before the law. Examples might be found in Vico, who wrote of 'the desire of the mass of men to be ruled with a justice corresponding with the equality of human nature';[95] and about 'human governments, in which, by reason of the equality of their intelligent nature, which is man's own nature, all men are treated as equal by the laws'.[96] Christian Wolff also declared the natural equality of all men, with the same innate rights and duties. Voltaire's maxims of 'civil and ecclesiastical laws' in his *Dictionnaire philosophique* include the precepts 'that the magistrates, labourers and priests should equally pay the expenses of the state, because all equally belong to the state', and 'that there should be only one weight, one measure, one law'.[97] This commonplace theoretical ideal of equality passed into statutory and constitutional formats. Thus the Introduction to the Prussian *Allgemeines Landrecht* of 1794 stated the principle that 'the state's laws bind all its subjects, without regard to status, rank, or family'.[98] The most celebrated statement in this area is Article 3 of the French Constitution of 24 June 1793: 'All men are equal by nature and before the law', but the Constitution of 3 September 1791 which preceded it (and which still envisaged a king as part of the constitution) had also declared that 'men are born and remain free and equal in rights; social distinctions may be founded only in what is useful to the community' (Article 1). The United States Constitution contained by contrast no such article, nor did equality as a value receive explicit mention in it until the enactment of the Fourteenth Amendment after the Civil War; perhaps this silence reflects acceptance of the realities which might seem to mock the theory of equality.

---

[95] *Scienza nuova* 1. 2. 37 (1725 edn.).
[96] *Scienza nuova* 2 (3rd impression of 1744 edn.).
[97] *Dictionnaire*, s.v. 'Of civil and ecclesiastical laws'.
[98] Introduction, § 22.

PROPERTY

The most conspicuous of those realities was the institution of private property, unaccompanied by any system for preventing its very uneven distribution. The philosophy of Locke on the origin and duties of property seemed perfectly satisfactory to the eighteenth century, and the century contains vigorous defences of private ownership, and of the attribution of extra political weight to the possession of wealth. There were, however, some dissenting voices; the most famous was that of Rousseau, who saw the individual appropriation of the world's resources as the origin both of civil society and of vice. The opening passage of Part 2 of his *Discourse on the Origins of Inequality among Men* (1754) contains the following celebrated sentences:

The first person who, having fenced off a plot of ground, took it into his head to say: 'This is mine', and found people simple enough to believe him, was the true founder of civil society. What crimes, wars, murders, what miseries and horrors would the human race have been spared by someone who, uprooting the stakes or filling in the ditch, had shouted to his fellow men: 'Beware of listening to the impostor; you are lost if you forget that the fruits belong to all and the earth to none!'

All vice, he thought, derived ultimately from the unnatural inequality arising from the engrossment of property by individuals. The institution of laws, in turn, and therewith the emergence of civil society, were simply means towards perpetuating and protecting the situation of the possessors. In 1767 S. N. H. Linguet published his *Théorie des lois civiles*, which attacked Locke's idea that the admixture of the individual's labour with the resources of the earth could create a right of private property; on the contrary, he believed that property rested on superior force, and that civil institutions which protected property rights were simply a conspiracy against the majority of the human race.[99] Both Rousseau and Linguet influenced Marx in the following century.

As against this interpretation of property, the institution was presented by Kant in 1797 as something necessitated by practical reason. This forbade the conception that objects external to us could not be owned, for there could be neither 'mine' nor 'yours', since

[99] Anderson, *Europe in the Eighteenth Century*, 416.

this would involve the idea of something inherently capable of use for human benefit yet excluded from such use. The acquisition of individual ownership derives, he held, originally from the claim of the first taker, and the agreed admission of his claim by others; including the recognition that he may now exclude all others from what he has pre-empted.[100] Inequalities of possessions are explained and justified by inequalities in the distribution of human talents, for which possessions are the reward.

The principle of private property found strong defenders not merely among the philosophers but among the political writers of the later part of the century. William Paley, in a book published in 1785, founded the right to property in prescription, i.e. in the status conferred by long undisturbed possession.[101] So too did Burke, who thought property, together with inequality in its distribution, was both inherent in and a condition of civilization; the confiscation of property was something totally unjustifiable, even under the pretext of the common good.[102] The same opinion was a staple across the Atlantic, where in 1787 Madison was writing about safeguards against 'a rage for paper money, for an abolition of debts, for an equal division of property, or for any other improper or wicked project'.[103]

As for the political role of property, it was defended by all who feared an excessive admission of the democratic principle—and these were by no means all conservatives. On the one hand Burke is found in 1792 writing that 'it is one excellence of our constitution, that all our rights of provincial election regard rather property than person . . . By admitting settled, permanent substance [in the case of extending the franchise to Irish Catholics] you would avoid the great danger of our time—that of setting up number against property'.[104] That was Burke, the philosopher of conservatism. But even the revolutionary French constitution of the same year did not propose a universal suffrage; the right to vote was limited to the owners or tenants of property of a minimum value expressed in terms of the value of numbers of days' labour.[105]

---

[100] *Metaphysik der Sitten: Rechtslehre*, §§ 11 ff.
[101] *The Principles of Moral and Political Philosophy* (1838 edn.), iii. 224–31.
[102] *Reflections* 35, 102, 240 f.; speech on the reform of representation (1782).
[103] *Federalist Papers*, no. 10.
[104] *Letter to Sir Hercules Langrishe*, in *Irish Affairs*, 273–4.
[105] Art. 35.

CRIMINAL LAW AND PUNISHMENT

It is in the eighteenth century, and as one of the fruits of the Enlightenment, that theory as to the basis, objects, and measures of criminal law and punishment first assumes the aspect of an independent science. Several factors conduced to its emergence. First, the rise of scepticism about ancient authority and tradition undermined the acceptance of immemorial practice, and of un-examined values, as a sufficient warrant for the infliction of punishment. Secondly, the retreat of religious extremism, and of belief in occult forces, destroyed the confidence which once had sustained the prosecution of witches and sorcerers. Thirdly, while there was a steep rise in crime, particularly property-related crime, throughout the century, resulting in the application of ferocious penal repression, there was also, partly in reaction to this, a general advance in humane feeling (visible also in the movement against the slave trade), and this raised up powerful critics of European systems of criminal justice. In the ages of Bach and of Mozart these were still presenting Europe with frequent scenes of appalling public cruelty.

Thus a question mark now began to form over the extent of the state's right to punish, in particular whether it was entitled to punish acts which had no injurious effects on others or on society, or which could be looked at more as sins or moral failings than as offences. Both Voltaire and the great Italian pioneer of penal reform, Cesare Beccaria (1738–94), thought that only offences against man, and not those against God, should attract human punishment; Voltaire protested notably in 1766 against the putting to death of a wild young man whose offence was a blasphemy which caused no material harm to anyone.[106] In the same decade Edmund Burke had proposed, as part of his argument against the oppressive laws under which Irish Catholics lived, a view of the criminal law in which what he presents as the actual state of English law seems to be the ideal:

[The criminal law] considers as crimes (that is, the object of punishment) trespasses against those rules for which society was instituted. The law punishes delinquents, not because they are not good men, but because they

---

[106] Voltaire, 'Relation de la mort du Chevalier de la Barre', in *Œuvres complètes*, ed. L. Moland (Paris, 1877–85), xxv. 504.

are intolerably wicked. It does bear, and must, with the vices and the follies of men until they actually strike at the root of order.[107]

The French Constitution Assembly's Law of 8–9 October 1789 declared similarly that the law has the right to prohibit only actions harmful to society. The idea of the law should not try to enforce perfection on an imperfect human race was not new; but the idea that only that is punishable which injures others would become a controversial theme in the following two centuries.

As to whether the state was in any case justified in punishing individuals, the social-contract-based theories of Grotius and Hobbes were still heard. The idea that the sovereign was endowed with the sum of individual rights of reprisal, ceded to him as a corollary of the original contract, was repeated, more or less, by the Italian jurist Gaetano Filangieri (1752–88), and by Blackstone, at least as far as *mala in se* (things wicked in themselves) are concerned; in a state of nature, he wrote, the right of punishing such wrongs is vested in every individual, but in a state of society it is transferred to the sovereign power.[108] The right to punish mere *mala prohibita*, things originally indifferent but forbidden by the lawgiver, he also derived from a supposed contractual source.[109] The same conception is found in Beccaria's famous work, *Dei delitti e delle pene* ('On Crimes and Punishments'), published in 1764, in terms of the pooling by all the subjects of a certain amount of their individual liberty: 'Every individual would choose to put into the public stock the smallest possible portion of his own liberty; as much only as was sufficient to engage others to defend it. The aggregate of these, the smallest portions possible, forms the right of punishment; all that extends beyond this is abuse, not justice.'[110] But this very formulation suggested to him also the illegitimacy of capital punishment, of which, horrified by the cruelty of its frequent infliction, he was a passionate opponent: as no one had a natural freedom to yield up his own life, so no one could hand over to a sovereign the right to take it away.[111]

It is in this century that the range of purposes attributed to criminal punishment begins finally to depart from the earlier almost universal concentration on deterrence and retribution. It is true that, even at the end of the century, the high-minded philosopher

---

[107] *Tracts on Popery*, in *Irish Affairs*, 46.   [108] *Commentaries* 4. 1.
[109] Ibid.   [110] *Opere*, i. 49.   [111] Ibid. 80.

Immanuel Kant thought the state had not only the right but the duty to inflict retaliation for its own sake.[112] But now the reform of the criminal—his reclamation, as a moral value in its own right—begins to establish itself as a standard element in penal theory. So, too, does the perception that, as society itself must carry some of the blame for the delinquent's emergence, neither the retributive nor the deterrent motive of punishment is morally adequate. The great English philanthropist John Howard (c.1726–90) wrote that 'we have too much adopted the gothic mode of correction, viz. by rigorous severity, which often hardens the heart; while many foreigners pursue the more rational plan of softening the mind in order to its amendment'.[113] His first-hand studies of foreign penal systems (which drew Burke for their originality and humanity) led him to call attention particularly to the relatively humane criminal regime of the (Dutch) United Provinces, under which criminals while in prison were given 'religious instruction and enforced work in a puritanical combination'.[114] The English lawyer Samuel Romilly (1757–1818) saw society as often itself responsible for leaving people in such hopeless deprivation that delinquency was the natural consequence; instead of handing out brutal repression, it would be better to supply the poor with employment, and thus relieve them of the motive for crime.[115] The philosopher William Godwin, writing in 1793, condemned the whole theory of criminal punishment, whether based on retribution, reform, or deterrence, and rounded on society more passionately than Romilly had done: 'What can be more shameless than for society to make an example of those whom she has goaded to the breach of order, instead of amending her own institutions which, by straining order into tyranny, produced the mischief?'[116] Indeed he went further and advocated the abolition of law and its replacement by reasoning addressed to the facts of the individual case.[117]

Jeremy Bentham, finally, subsumed the whole problem into the general system of his 'felicific calculus'. His *Introduction to the Principles of Morals and Legislation* (1789) recognized that punishment is itself an evil which can be admitted only in order to avert a greater evil; it should be based on reformation as well as on its

---

[112] *Account of the Principal Lazarettos in Europe.*
[113] *Speech at the Guildhall in Bristol*, in *Irish Affairs*, 140.   [114] Ibid.
[115] *Observations* (1786) (on Madau's pamphlet *Thoughts on Executive Justice*).
[116] *An Inquiry concerning Political Justice* (1793), 713.   [117] Ibid. ch. 8.

disabling and deterrent elements; retribution was an illicit motive, since (weighed in the utilitarian balance) the pleasure it gave those whose vindictive instincts were satisfied did not equal the pain which its infliction caused.[118] Even Blackstone, complacent rather than indignant with the system under which he lived, had in his *Commentaries on the Laws of England* excluded retribution from the list of legitimate penal purposes, and had tentatively included what he appears to mean as reformation of the offender himself rather than his deterrence:

[Punishment] is not by way of atonement or expiation for the crime committed; for that must be left to the just determination of the Supreme Being; but as a precaution against future offences of the same kind. This is effected three ways: either by amendment of the offender himself . . . or by deterring others by the dread of his example from offending in the like way . . . or, lastly, by depriving the party injuring of the power to do future mischief.[119]

Three other matters deserve brief mention. The relevance of the delinquent's state of mind to his guilt, or the degree of his punishment, is now universally admitted (though, surprisingly, in one passage Beccaria seems to have thought the seriousness of an offence ought to be assessed not by reference to the offender's state of mind but to the degree of public injury he had caused).[120] In general, however, Blackstone was representative of his age in approving the English view, that factors operating on the delinquent's mind, such as violence of passion, or temptation, or extreme need, ought to extenuate his crime.[121]

Secondly, there was virtual unanimity on the need for punishment to be proportionate to the offence. One or two English writers urged a scarcely discriminating severity, and this in fact was a scandalous feature of the English system which, at the century's end, prescribed the death penalty for over a hundred different offences; but most of the minds of the age advocated moderation in both senses of the word. Montesquieu as early as 1721 had asserted in his *Lettres persanes* the importance of a reasonable proportion between crime and penalty, and he stated the same proposition more formally in 1748 in his *Esprit des lois*.[122] The following year

[118] *Principles of Morals and Legislation* 13. 1.
[120] *Opere*, i. 96 ff.
[122] *Lettres persanes* 102; *De l'esprit des lois* 6. 16.
[119] *Commentaries* 4. 1.
[121] *Commentaries* 4. 1.

Frederick the Great made the same point in his *Dissertation sur les raisons d'établir ou d'abroger les lois*. In 1764 Beccaria repeated it, basing it however on the unwisdom of undermining the moral sense of difference between the gravity of different crimes, and removing any incentive to refrain from a greater rather than a lesser crime.[123] In 1765 Blackstone recommended a due proportionality, also on a utilitarian ground, namely that undue severity is likely to lead to non-execution of the law because of the humane instincts of the public (and so of juries).[124] Disproportion was condemned also in 1771 by the penal reformer William Eden,[125] and in 1785—with special reference to the English penal system—by Benjamin Franklin.[126]

Finally, it was generally held that criminal statutes should be clear, leaving no room for ignorance on the part of the public or arbitrary interpretation on that of the judge. Montesquieu wrote that

the nearer a government approaches towards a republic, the more the manner of judging becomes settled and fixed . . . The very nature of the constitution [of republics] requires the judges to follow the letter of the law; otherwise the law might be interpreted to the prejudice of every citizen, in cases where their honour, property, or life is concerned.[127]

Voltaire similarly stressed the need for clarity in criminal laws.[128] Beccaria took up in particular the same theme as that stated by Montesquieu in connection with criminal laws in monarchies, that, where these are not explicit, the judge 'endeavours to investigate their spirit'. There is nothing, said Beccaria,

more dangerous than the common axiom that 'the spirit of the law should be considered'. To adopt this is to give way to the torrent of opinions . . . An explicit code [on the other hand] which must be observed to the letter leaves to the judge only the function of examining the actions of citizens, and deciding whether they conform to, or infringe, the law as written.[129]

---

[123] *Opere*, i. 96 ff.   [124] *Commentaries* 4. 1.
[125] *Principles of Penal Law* 49–51.
[126] Letter of 14 Mar. 1785 to Benjamin Vaughan.
[127] *De l'esprit des lois* 6. 3.   [128] *Œuvres*, xix. 626.
[129] *Dei delitti e delle pene*, ch. 4.

INTERNATIONAL LAW

The eighteenth century and its cult of reason found the idea of wars, and the unregulated relations between states which gave rise to wars, repugnant. To the systematized doctrine of international law created by Grotius it added proposals for ensuring peace and stability. Writers on the subject, in the words of M. S. Anderson, 'started from the assumption that the governments of Europe were still in a "state of nature" and that some means must be found of restraining their innate propensity to attack and injure one another'; for this purpose a pragmatically maintained 'balance of power' was simply inadequate.[130] The best known of these publicists was the abbé de St Pierre, who in 1713, at the end of the war-ridden reign of Louis XIV, produced his 'Project for Making Peace Perpetual in Europe'; this urged that all European states should form a federation, with a senate to adjudicate their disputes, and with a system of enforcement by arms against any state infringing the rights of another.[131]

The theoretical aspect of this scheme was contractual, though the contract was something ideally to be concluded, not taken as already existing. For Christian Wolff something like a social contract had already arisen between nations; they were members of what he called a *civitas maxima*, a 'superstate', and this rested on a 'pact or quasi-pact'[132] which could be read out of the body of rules which in fact were observed by nations in their mutual relations. The end of the individual human, namely his or her perfection, Wolff applied to states as well; they were to strive for their own perfection, and for the perfection of their fellows, whom they must love as themselves, freely transferring their superfluity of resources to the needier members of the *civitas*. Just like human individuals, states were all equal by nature; and, again like human beings in the state of nature, each had the right to defend itself and to punish an offender, presumably, until such time as the *civitas* evolved a common mechanism of defence and repression.[133] Much of Wolff's scheme was adopted by the Swiss writer Emmerich de Vattel (1714–67), whose compendium of the international law of his day developed

---

[130] *Europe in the Eighteenth Century*, 250 f.   [131] Ibid.
[132] *Jus gentium methodo scientifica pertractatum* (1764), §§ 10–20.
[133] Ibid., §§ 31 ff.

enormous authority in the later eighteenth and nineteenth centuries, for some reason particularly in Britain and in the United States.[134]

Among all his other interests, Jeremy Bentham wrote on the law of nations, and indeed has the credit of inventing the word 'international' in this context.[135] His theory here is simply the application of his general principle of utility to the conduct of nations: this should be regulated towards the end of achieving the greatest possible welfare of all nations on earth. Putting himself in the position of a hypothetical lawgiver to the nations, he reduced this generality to five subordinate propositions, which can be summarized thus: each nation must seek the general good by committing no injury upon, and conferring as much benefit as possible on, other states, consistent with its own welfare; by accepting no injury from, and deriving as much benefit as possible from, other states, consistent with regard for *their* welfare; and, in a state of war, to do as little harm as is consistent with achieving its objective.

Finally, the views of Kant on international law must be noted. In his *Metaphysics of Morals* (1796) he observed that practical reason suggested the principle that there should be no such thing as war. Even if this ideal is unrealizable, the conduct of states should be directed nevertheless towards its achievement. This would require the foundation of a federation of states, 'according to the notion of an original contract', and a union of peoples, committed to not interfering in one another's affairs, and to protection against external enemies. Such a congress of states would make reality of the idea of a public law between nations, which would decide disputes in a civilized manner, and not by the barbarous recourse to war.[136]

---

[134] *Le Droit des gens ou principes de la loi naturelle* (1758).
[135] *Principles* 17. 25.   [136] *Metaphysik der Sitten.*

8
The Nineteenth Century

The nineteenth century opens in Europe on a scene of war. The French Revolution had terrified the rest of the old Europe into attempts to quench or at least to contain it, but these efforts led only to the embattled republic giving the world its first sight of a 'people in arms': the revolutionary armies which at first defeated the attacks launched from foreign thrones, and then, under the generalship and later the imperial rule of Napoleon Bonaparte, carried the French flag to every corner of the continent, where it at first seemed the banner of liberation for subject peoples. The final defeat of Napoleon in 1815 by the combined power of Britain, Prussia, Russia, and Austria was succeeded by a general settlement worked out at the Congress of Vienna; this established a balance in European affairs which lasted more or less until the outbreak of the First World War a century later. There were several localized and generally short conflicts, such as the Crimean war (1853–6) and that between France and Prussia (1870–1), but no widespread and protracted convulsion such as the Napoleonic wars had been, and such as the twentieth century was again to produce. It was thus, compared with what had gone before and what was to come later, a relatively tranquil century.

Its most significant political developments took place in Germany and Italy. In Germany there emerged, under the hand of Bismarck working on the romantic nationalism of the age, a united German empire led by the militarist and expansionist Prussian kingdom. In Italy the revolutionary soldier Garibaldi, the agitator Mazzini, and the liberal politician Cavour managed to put together a national unitary kingdom under the House of Savoy, rulers of Piedmont and Sardinia; the process involved above all the expulsion (with French help) of the Austrian power from northern Italy and of the Bourbon dynasty from Naples and Sicily, together with the reduction of the papal dominions to a small fragment around Rome. Other changes were the creation of a Belgian state (1831) on the territory of the old Austrian (and formerly Spanish) southern and Catholic Netherlands; the emergence in the same year of the kingdom of the Netherlands from the old United Provinces of the Calvinist north; and, in Eastern Europe, the establishment of several independent kingdoms and principalities in former provinces of the crumbling Ottoman empire.

Although the 1815 settlement created relative stability in the mutual relations of the European powers, the century was still one of enormous political change. The defeat of Napoleon and the restoration of Louis XVIII on the throne of France, together with the peace which seemed to allow the old regimes of Europe to breathe easily once again, could not quench the popular thirst for reform, and, in some countries, for national independence; nor the romantic enthusiasm, expressed in the art and literature of the age, which converged with it everywhere from Dublin to Budapest. The internal stability of the old kingdoms was continually disturbed by tremors of revolt; in 1848, the 'year of revolutions', almost every European regime was unseated, though everywhere except in France the old order re-established itself quickly, and even in France the Second Republic soon gave way (1852) to a Second Empire under Napoleon III, great-nephew of the great emperor. Nevertheless, under the influence of the bourgeois liberalism which was the century's dominant force, political reforms made headway everywhere. Most European states acquired written constitutions; and, though some monarchies such as that of the Habsburg empire remained virtually absolute, most were 'constitutional', i.e. their powers were defined by a written charter, by the century's end. The parliamentary franchise tended to be continuously extended to greater circles of population, in other words towards universal adult suffrage at least for males; this point was established in Germany by the constitution of 1871, in France by that of 1875. In Britain, where the House of Commons counted for more than did continental assemblies, the right to vote at parliamentary elections remained tied to what may (roughly speaking) be called a property qualification; but the size of the electorate was progressively enlarged in 1832 (by the Great Reform Act), 1867, and 1884.[1] In Ireland the great reform of

---

[1] For a general picture of the democratization of European states, see E. J. Hobsbawm, *The Age of Empire* (London, 1989), ch. 4, esp. pp. 85–6.

the century on the political plane was the removal of Catholic disabilities in 1829, which meant that for the first time representatives of the Irish majority could sit in the House of Commons. But the century passed, despite the efforts of Mr Gladstone, with Irish home rule still unachieved, and other small nations also remained without their independence: Poland, the Baltic peoples, and those of the Austro-Hungarian empire.

Nineteenth-century economic and technological changes were vast. Capitalist enterprise appeared on a scale altogether dwarfing the business activity of earlier times. European populations, increasingly urbanized, grew rapidly, partly because of the relatively cheaper corn which spread of free trade guaranteed, partly because better public sanitation, medical knowledge, and personal hygiene reduced the diseases which previously (above all by way of a terrific infant mortality) had wiped out natural increases; only exceptionally, as in Ireland, was rapid population growth checked and reversed by local factors. In the cities, these populations, living mostly only just at the level of subsistence, provided cheap labour for the industrial revolution inaugurated in the preceding century; this now reached a paroxysm, particularly where (as in Britain above all, but also Belgium, Germany, northern France) there were resources of coal to run the steam engines and fuel the foundries and steel mills. To the ordinary man, the most revolutionary product of the century was the steam locomotive railway; in the space of a generation, say from 1830 to 1870, a European system of unimaginably rapid transport had grown from nothing, opening all kinds of possibilities in economic, political, and private life. Scarcely less important was the improvement in communications brought about by the electric telegraph, and, in the last quarter of the century, by the telephone.

International free trade was more or less the central article of faith in liberal *laissez-faire* ideology, and was much facilitated by these improvements in communications. It tended to force the division of labour, and the concentration of different forms of production in the areas which best suited them, and thus led to cheaper goods. European business now had access to cheap imports of basic foodstuffs and industrial raw materials, while the inventions and the aggression of the age had opened up vast markets for its products both near home and overseas. The prospects of new markets, together with national pride, changed the attitude of European powers towards overseas possessions; at the beginning of the century these had not played a vital role in the national policies of the home states, but towards its end these powers became locked in competition for colonies. The British converted the Indian possessions of what was once a purely commercial company into an empire (1877); and they reorganized constitutionally the sparsely settled Canada, Australia, and New Zealand, and, after a war (1899–1902) with the long-settled Boers (of mostly Dutch descent), combined the rich Transvaal with Natal, the Orange Free State, and the old Cape colony, into the Dominion of South Africa. Egypt, the Sudan, other parts of East and West Africa were also gradually coloured red on the map. What was left was divided between France (in North and West Africa: though France had also acquired an empire in south-east Asia) and Portugal, the pioneer of European settlement in Africa; together with the new imperial Germany, which insisted on being admitted to the colonial club, and even Belgium, whose immensely rich King Leopold II acquired the Congo territory as a sort of personal dependency in 1885. Europe—including Russia, which had built up a considerable industrial potential in the course of the century, mostly through foreign entrepreneurs, and had acquired an empire of its own in central Asia—thus possessed a vast economic stage on which the forces of its capitalism could play: accompanied (or even preceded) though these usually were by Christian missionaries, and by the conviction, entertained no doubt with varying degrees of sincerity, that European civilization could do nothing but good, moral and material, to those among whom it arrived.

THE CONCEPTION OF THE STATE

Presenting a picture of nineteenth-century theory about the state is a far more complex undertaking than its equivalent for any earlier century. In previous eras, as has been seen, the idea of a structure resting on something whose various forms could all be subsumed in the notion of 'social contract' constantly recurs, and, since the High Middle Ages, had been dominant. But those days were now gone. With the nineteenth century, the problem of the nature and the proper function of the state had to be rethought from scratch. The 'social contract' had been attacked by Bentham as not only a fiction but a falsehood; and as it was part of the vocabulary of the French

Revolution, it was discredited anyway, along with natural law and natural rights, as having given intellectual sustenance first to the Terror, then to the Napoleonic tyranny. The powerful conservative reaction which set in after 1815 had as its Bible the writings of Burke, and his picture of political institutions as organically rooted in and growing with a people's values and history, not as susceptible to planning on the basis of pure theory. Moreover, the nineteenth century could draw on the new sciences such as economics, opened up by British and French writers in the preceding age; sociology, a pursuit first defined by the Frenchman Auguste Comte (1798–1857); and the evolutionary biology of Charles Darwin (1809–82). All these sciences forbade the reduction of the state's nature to a simple formula, or the statement of its functions by a simple precept. We can therefore only look at some of the leading attitudes and theories towards and about the state; these naturally all entailed corollaries as to the nature and the role of law.

One might begin by trying to describe the kind of state aimed at by the dominant political theory of the earlier part of the century— economic liberalism—and to show how it evolved in the later part, under the pressure of newly enfranchised political forces but also in prudent response to the fears of revolution (from which the governing bourgeois classes were never free), towards increased regulation of economic processes for socially inspired purposes. One can then add the particular philosophies of the state which, originating in the nineteenth century, were to be of special significance in the twentieth, namely, those of Hegel and of Marx.

The economic liberalism of the earlier part of the century went back at least to Locke and his placing of the rights of property at the centre of the state's title to exist. Rights of property included naturally freedom of contract; and freedom of contract was at this time held in such reverence that it inhibited the erection of even very slight limitations on the operation of the market. Thus interventions and reforms which to a late twentieth-century eye seem to have been inadequate or scandalously delayed (if they were made at all), such as laws prescribing minimum conditions or maximum hours for workers in various industries, or reform of the landholding system which made the failure of a single crop (as in Ireland with the potato) the occasion of devastating famine, or even timely measures to rescue a starving and diseased population, were resisted not just by inhumanity and greed, but from the conviction that the state had no business to interfere in the relationships of master and workman or landlord and tenant, any more than in any other form of private contract. This position was reinforced by the economic theory of the time, going back to the Scottish pioneer economist Adam Smith and his *Wealth of Nations* (1776), which saw the unimpeded operation of free market forces, not only in international trade but in internal economic relations too, as likely in the long run to best promote economic growth and thus the happiest overall result, whatever the temporary hardship to this or that individual or group: a theory which moreover, so far as it implied a guide for legislators, passed the test which Bentham had enunciated for all state regulative activity.

But a reaction set in. In Britain, which had led the world in industrialization and which now astonished the world by its wealth, the traces can be seen in the earliest factory acts of the 1800s, and in the relaxation of the laws against combinations of workmen by the Combination Act, 1825. Critics of the 'freedom of contract' religion arose, who pointed out that there was no real freedom in a relationship where the starting positions of the two sides were grossly unequal. In particular the Oxford philosopher T. H. Green (1836–82), restated the liberal faith in a form which made it include respect for the dignity of the individual, recognition that he should have the chance of fully unfolding his capacities, and an acknowledgment that the state had a role, which might take the form of legislative interference and regulation, in affording him the basic conditions in which this ideal might be achieved. The force of this reconstructed liberalism was joined, in the 1880s, by beginnings of organized socialism, and both were sustained by the philanthropic and humanitarian movements, religious or secular, which in Britain were many and influential. The net result was the rise, over the whole course of the century but especially in its latter half, of 'social legislation' in all kinds of fields, and the rapid growth of subordinate mechanisms of government for its administration. Even as long ago as 1905 it was possible for A. V. Dicey, best known as a constitutional lawyer, to call this development the 'transition from individualism to collectivism' and to document the course which it had taken in England.[2] Other European countries displayed a

---

[2] In *Lectures on the Relation between Law and Public Opinion in England during the Nineteenth Century* (London, 1962).

similar progression; imperial Germany, indeed, was well ahead of England in such matters as the acceptance by the state of responsibility for elementary education, and the construction of a system of social insurance (the latter undertaken in Bismarck's time, as a measure for taking the wind out of the sails of the rising socialist movement). Accordingly, if one generalizes and if one ignores the degree to which some states were more or less authoritarian or democratic in the working of their systems, one might say the dominant theory of the nineteenth-century state supported its emergence from the minimal role which social-contract theory had suggested, and its acceptance of a large role of social interventionism and economic control both exceeding and conflicting with the protective function once seen as its sole reason to exist.

This shifting liberal theory of the state was focused on its function. Far deeper was the examination to which it was submitted by the German philosopher Georg Wilhelm Friedrich Hegel (1770–1831), successively professor at Jena, Heidelberg, and Berlin. Hegel's philosophy is of extreme difficulty; but one central feature of it is that he proposed the essential interdependence of everything, literally everything, in the universe, whether material or metaphysical. This interdependence of all things subsists in countless sequences of 'unfolding' from the 'Absolute Spirit', each of its individual parts or stages having been inevitably produced by one anterior to it, and itself being inevitably compelled to spawn a further part or stage. The dynamic in this process is what he called the 'dialectic', a word taken from the setting in which we first encountered it, namely the method used by Socrates, in the dialogues reported by Plato, to arrive at truth: one position or argument implied, or provoked, its opposite, and from the confrontation of this pair of opposites a third position emerged, which was seen to be the truth; this third position thereupon in its turn must encounter contradiction, and so would itself become a first position confronted by its opposite, from which conflict a new third position would emerge, and so on *ad infinitum*. In this process—in which Hegel believed he had uncovered the key to all development in physical nature and in history as well as in philosophy—the initial position is called the 'thesis', its opposite the 'antithesis', and the resolution of the conflict of both the 'synthesis' (which then becomes a 'thesis' in its own right, and so on). It is worth outlining this notion of infinite series of self-propagating triangles here, not because of its relevance to Hegel's idea of the state, but because of the epoch-making use to which Marx would afterwards put it.

The state, for Hegel, is not a simple, unitary concept, but one with three separately conceived characters, all interconnected because all subsisting amongst the same population on the same territory, but still all conceptually distinct. There is the state in the sense nearest to our own common usage, the 'political' state which can be described by pointing to its institutions of government and lawmaking. There is then the 'civil' state, consisting of the mass of arrangements (most of them would register with us, since they are protected by state institutions, as part of the legal order and hence of the political state as we would conceive it) which individuals make with one another rather than have imposed upon them, such as contracts, marriages, the establishment of corporations: things perhaps which might have been spontaneously evolved even if the political state did not exist. And then there is the state in a far wider and less concrete sense, the state as the sum of all the ethical values, all the shared experiences and responses, the consciousness of belonging together through history, reinforced by religious and cultural homogeneity: this 'ethical' state—though his usage is not precise and uniform—is the one to which Hegel accords supreme value and importance. It is in this alone that the individual achieves freedom and self-fulfilment through participation in its transcendent life. The expressions Hegel used to convey his ideas about the state, in this very special sense, are of an intoxicating vagueness:

The state in and by itself is the ethical whole, the actualisation of freedom; and it is an absolute end of reason that freedom should be actual. The state is Mind on earth and consciously realising itself there . . . The march of God in the world, that is what the state is. The basis of the state is the power of reason actualising itself as will. In considering the Idea of the state, we must not have our eyes on particular states or on particular institutions. Instead we must consider the Idea, this actual God, by itself . . .

What the state demands from us as a duty is, *eo ipso*, our right as individuals, since the state is nothing but the articulation of the concept of freedom. The determinations of the individual will are given an objective embodiment through the state and thereby they attain their truth and their actualisation for the first time. The state is the one and only prerequisite of the attainment of particular ends and welfare.[3]

---

[3] *Philosophy of Right*, tr. T. Knox (Oxford, 1967), 279–80.

In the same book, *The Philosophy of Right*, Hegel makes it clear that he genuinely believes in individual freedom also in our sense, and in the value of the individual, and deplores evil or oppressive states; the state, he says, is 'no ideal work of art; it stands on earth and so in the sphere of caprice, chance, and error, and bad behaviour may disfigure it in many respects', and he disapproves the state as Plato had ideally envisaged it, because, in it, 'subjective freedom does not count', and subjective freedom must be respected, as for example by letting people choose their own calling in life.[4] But it is easy to see how heady rhapsodies like those in the passage just quoted could lead, as they did, to the glorification, by later writers, of the state in crude and simple terms, without regard either to the fact that it is the ethical, not the political state on which Hegel lavished these expressions, or to his express declarations in favour of the liberty of the individual in the fullest of modern senses.

The connection between Hegel and one of the most revolutionary thinkers of all time, Karl Marx, lies not in their conceptions of the state, but in the dialectical method, which Marx used in order to construct a radically different theory of political institutions. Marx (1818–83) was born into a Rhineland family originally Jewish but converted to Protestantism. He began his career as a journalist; his subversive opinions caused his forced withdrawal to Paris, then his expulsion from France; ultimately, after the failure of the 1848 revolutions, he settled in London. At first attracted by proto-socialists like Saint-Simon, he came to despise 'Utopian' socialism, and evolved instead a creed which was both a philosophy of history, purporting to lay bare the ineluctable processes by which history had thus far moved, and by which it was destined to continue, as well as an action programme, whose participants were to discharge their own part in bringing about what was in any case inevitable. The historical process was one of conflict and evolution, and so conformed to the Hegelian dialectic; the forces in conflict, however, were not ideas or concepts or beliefs, but material interests, namely, the interests of *classes*, understood as groups defined in terms of their relation to the ownership and control of the society's material resources. When history was looked at in this way, the institutions of each society could be seen to correspond to the interest of whatever class was dominant from time to time; so that the state

----

[4] Ibid. 280.

(and, as will be seen, the legal system) was merely a structure arranged to suit the needs of those in control of the society's resources. 'I was led by many studies', wrote Marx,

> to the conclusion that legal relations as well as forms of state could neither be understood by themselves, nor explained by the so-called general progress of the human mind, but that they are rooted in the material conditions of life, which are summed up by Hegel after the fashion of the English and French writers of the eighteenth century under the name 'civil society', and that the anatomy of civil society is to be sought in political economy [i.e. in economic forces] . . . In the social production which men carry on they enter into definite relations that are indispensable and independent of their will; these relations of production correspond to a definite stage of development of their material powers of production. The totality of these relations of production constitutes the economic structure of society—the real foundation, on which legal and political superstructures arise, and to which definite forms of social consciousness correspond.[5]

Accordingly, the state of the feudal age reflected in its arrangements the concentration of its forces of economic production, which were mostly agricultural, in the hands of the nobility; when the feudal age was superseded, most markedly at the epoch of the French Revolution, the ruling class which succeeded the feudal nobility, namely the bourgeoisie, shaped the institutions to accommodate its control of the new forms of industrial production, so that the liberal bourgeois state of the mid-nineteenth century was what it had to be, given the shift in the nature of wealth; but this kind of state depended on the exploitation of the working class, the proletariat,[6] who were systematically robbed of the value of their labour over and above what was needed simply to keep them alive and working; and the conflict now opening between the bourgeois exploiter and the proletarian exploited would lead to a further, and final, revolution, in which the means of production, concentrated at last in the hands of the actual producers, would (since there was no further, inferior class left to exploit) draw this dialectical process to a close. The state corresponding to the victory of the working class in this last revolution would necessarily be a 'dictatorship of the

---

[5] *A Contribution to the Critique of Political Economy*, tr. N. I. Stone (Chicago, 1904), preface, p. 11.

[6] This word is a construct based on the Latin *proles*, 'offspring', and is supposed to convey the idea of a class with no function but the endless procreation of a labour force.

proletariat'; but once this period of pacification and transition had been completed, and the new order established beyond fear of counter-revolution, the state (as it was put by Marx's friend and younger contemporary, Friedrich Engels) would simply 'wither away'. As there would now be a classless society, there would be no further fuel for the engine of dialectical conflict. Government would disappear, there would remain at most an 'administration of things'. All this would necessarily happen, as anyone could see who had grasped the secret of the process; but naturally, as the event was in itself desirable, it called for activists to help the process on. G. H. Sabine pointed to the affinity between the Marxist valuation of wealth, and its control by a class, and the Calvinist valuation of the will of God, by which equally future events, such as the destiny of the individual soul, were predetermined: historical necessity meant 'not merely cause and effect, or desirability, or moral obligation, but all three at once'; but 'while Calvinists called this theology, Hegelians and Marxists call it science'.[7] At all events, in Marx's scheme it is clear that any idea of the state's neutrality as between competing economic interests, or of its leading an existence on a different plane from them, is an illusion or a fraud.

CODIFICATION AND THE CONCEPT OF LAW

It was seen in Chapter 7 that the movement towards the incorporation of law in planned and stable codes, originating in Austria and Prussia, was partly a response to the problems of states in which a variety of local legal systems coexisted, but partly also an expression of the contemporary belief in the organizing power of pure reason, the leading certainty of the age of Enlightenment. Its most famous achievement in this field was the French *Code civil*, planned since before the end of the eighteenth century and coming into force in 1804 (though in content, as has been seen, largely sticking to traditional French rules and by no means an exercise in wholesale rationalistic innovation). This code won world-wide admiration, and was an important influence in the drafting of the later codes of Belgium and Holland, Italy, Spain, and the states of the former Spanish colonial empire. Moreover, the spirit and the

[7] *A History of Political Theory* (London, 1973).

historical circumstances in which it had been conceived had important results in forming the dominant nineteenth-century conception of law itself, which was a 'positivist' one, seeing the essential and only authentic form of law in legislation (in 'law laid down', *ius positum*, whence 'positivism').

The leading idea of the French codifiers had been to exclude uncertainty and arbitrariness in the administration of law, and for that purpose they wished to reduce as far as possible the interpretative and creative function of judges, which they distrusted. The judge was to be no more than a machine intelligently applying a body of clear and stable rules; and these were therefore to be a complete, smooth, seamless network, the measurement of any problem against which would automatically indicate its solution. In the careful building of this network reason was, of course, to be the guide; and the finished construction was to be reason's supreme accomplishment. But the result of this process was curious. The Reason of the eighteenth century, though secular not to say godless, was rooted in a European tradition which before the seventeenth century had ascribed a divine pedigree to it, had not been willing to dissever it clearly from the law of nature, nor the latter from man's conscience, which may command him to regard a wicked law as a nullity. What was now, however, distilled from the long worm of that history, was a code which was to be the sole guide of the judge, whose mere enactment was the sufficient warrant of its validity, and to values beyond or outside which neither judge nor citizen had any business to look.

The result, even in the academic world, was the discouragement of theoretical reflection, or historical research, which might destabilize, and rob of its effects, this 'organic body of norms, planned and in their logical order'.[8] There emerged in France the so-called 'school of exegesis' (*école de l'exégèse*), a generation of law professors who saw themselves as having only one function, namely, the explanation of the code, article by article, following the order adopted by its drafters. The spirit of this 'school' was epitomized in a famous dictum of one of its representatives: 'I know nothing of the "civil law"; I teach the *Code Napoléon*.' It is easy to see the end effect of this paradoxical progression from nature to the written code: the lawgiver's will, as expressed in the code, came

---

[8] Fassò, *Storia* (see Ch. 3 n. 56), iii. 26.

first, higher values nowhere. What was originally projected as a stable statement of natural law ended in natural law's eclipse. 'As a matter of history', wrote Guido Fassò,

the initial assumption on which this process rested was that the legislator need only translate into the form of a statute the precepts of reason, and that this positive law would be no more than the public declaration, the ascertainment with obligatory force, of natural law. What actually happened was that the source of law was seen to be the legislator's will; and that natural law, after being for a short time hailed as the very essence of the code, was soon forgotten, then rejected and mocked. The ancient conflict between reason and will ended only in appearance with the acceptance of the claims of the former, but in reality with the complete victory of the latter.[9]

In England, despite the lifelong efforts of Jeremy Bentham, there was no codification or any other external development to which one could point as explaining the positivist spirit. But Bentham's own formulation of law as a sovereign's command (notwithstanding that it remained unpublished until 1945) was taken up, and built into a system, by his young disciple John Austin (1790–1859), first professor of jurisprudence in the newly founded University of London. Austin's lectures on this subject, published in 1832 as *The Province of Jurisprudence Determined*, are far from being a monument of literature, but they came to dominate the teaching of jurisprudence in England and the rest of the common-law world well into the twentieth century. 'The matter of jurisprudence', he wrote at the outset of his lectures,

is positive law: law, simply and strictly so called: or law set by political superiors to political inferiors . . . A law, in the most general and comprehensive acceptation in which the term, in its literal meaning, is employed, may be said to be a rule laid down for the guidance of an intelligent being by an intelligent being having power over him.[10]

Law so understood encompasses both laws set by God to man (which elsewhere Austin appears to regard as more or less the same as the principle of utility), and laws set by man to man; and such of those laws as are set by virtue of the lawgiver's status as a political superior compose 'the appropriate matter of jurisprudence'. To the

---

[9] Ibid. 25.
[10] *The Province of Jurisprudence Determined*, ed. H. L. A. Hart, pp. 9–10.

aggregate of such rules 'the term *law*, as used simply and strictly, is exclusively applied'.[11]

Every law, in this simple and strict sense, is a command; as it had been for Bentham, and for writers in every age since the beginning of the history of legal thought. But Austin now was more explicit than his predecessors, more explicit even than Bentham's convoluted description, in explaining a command: 'If you express or intimate a wish that I shall do or forbear from some act, and if you will visit me with an evil in case I comply not with your wish, the *expression* or *intimation* of your wish is a command.'[12] A law is, then, a command backed with a threatened sanction, issuing from a political superior. This political superior is a 'sovereign', not necessarily an individual but possibly a group or assembly of individuals; and the existence of such a 'sovereign' is a condition of the existence of a political society. Essential, moreover, to the status of the sovereign element is its not being in the habit of obedience to any other authority, while being in the habit of receiving it from its own subjects: 'If a determinate human superior, not in a habit of obedience to a like superior, receive habitual obedience from the bulk of a given society, that determinate superior is sovereign in that society, and the society (including the superior) is a society political and independent.'[13]

Such an understanding of law, the 'matter of jurisprudence', automatically excludes several items conventionally labelled 'law' but not fitting the above specifications. Not only are laws only metaphorically so called, such as the 'laws' of nature, obviously not in the picture—and one might be glad to see the end of a muddle going back to Aristotle—but the law of God, the law of nature, the law of morality, are also outside the range of Austin's jurisprudence, together with what are merely called 'laws' by way of an analogy, such as the laws of good society, or of chess. More troublesome still, bodies of rules which have a clear functional affinity with law strictly so called, rising far above the mere level of analogy or metaphor, and which are called 'law' by lawyers engaged in legal discourse without any sense of straining language, are seen, in Austin's scheme, to have their licence to avail of this name withdrawn because they have not been set by political superiors to their subjects: customary law, for instance (unless one admits that

[11] *The Province of Jurisprudence Determined*, ed. H. L. A. Hart, p. 11.
[12] Ibid. 13–14.   [13] Ibid. 194.

by tolerating it, the sovereign is to be taken implicitly to command obedience to it); or the law of primitive societies, ancient or modern, in which no sovereign is visible; or (above all) international law, which Austin was willing to regard as law only 'by analogy', and distinguished from positive law also by placing it in a category which he labelled 'positive morality'. Whatever criticisms of Austin's concept of law may suggest themselves (and in the present century his scheme, as will be seen, has received its most radical critique ever), it can still be said that he pioneered the analytical form of positivist jurisprudence, and was the first writer to suggest the presentation of a legal system as a structure of 'laws properly so called'[14] considered without regard to their goodness or badness.

THE INFLUENCE OF UTILITARIANISM: MILL'S REFINEMENT OF 'UTILITY'

While Jeremy Bentham had no success in his own country (or anywhere else) with his proposals for codification, his long advocacy of reforming the existing law in the spirit of utility, in other words on the criterion of the solution likely to maximize happiness and minimize its opposite, had revolutionary results even in his own lifetime, and continued to produce a rich harvest of law reforms long after his death. 'The age of law reform and the age of Jeremy Bentham are one and the same', wrote the Liberal politician and reforming lawyer Lord Brougham;

he is the father of the most important of all the branches of reform, the leading and ruling department of human improvement. No one before him had ever seriously thought of exposing the defects in our English system of jurisprudence. All former students had confined themselves to learn its principles—to make themselves masters of its eminently technical and artificial rules; and all former writers had but expounded the doctrines handed down from age to age . . . He it was who first made the mighty step of trying the whole provisions of our jurisprudence by the test of expediency, fearlessly examining how far each part was connected with the rest; and with a yet more undaunted courage, inquiring how far even its most consistent and symmetrical arrangements were framed according to the principle which should pervade a code of laws—their adaptation to the

[14] Ibid. 1.

circumstances of society, to the wants of men, and to the promotion of human happiness.

Not only was he thus eminently original among the lawyers and the legal philosophers of his own country; he might be said to be the first legal philosopher that had appeared in the world.[15]

The age of law reform thus identified with Bentham's influence unquestionably owed something also to other facts: religion (particularly of the evangelical variety which had achieved in the early nineteenth century a powerful hold on the more modest classes of the English population), humanitarianism, the fear of revolution and the anxiety to avert it by conceding reforms, all exerted great force: for example in extracting from a British parliament, theoretically committed to the doctrine of freedom of contract, the legislation which prescribed minimum conditions of humanity in the hours and conditions of industrial employment; and in forcing that parliament, too, despite its prejudices against Catholics in general and the Irish in particular, and in favour of the rights of property, to concede Catholic Emancipation and the measures of Irish land reform which, in the end, expropriated the Irish landlords and made their tenants the owners of the fields they lived on. But spanning all those forces, and contributing a momentum of its own independent of them, was the spirit of Bentham and his followers, always insisting that neither long-standing usage nor entrenched interest and privilege ought to stand in the way of reform based upon the principle of utility; and never basing their programme on theories which recent experience had made suspect to English ears. Benthamism, as Dicey wrote,

exactly answered to the immediate want of the day. In 1825 Englishmen had come to feel that the institutions of the country required thorough-going amendment; but Englishmen of all classes, Whigs and reformers, no less than Tories, distrusted the whole theory of natural rights, and shunned any adoption of Jacobinical principles . . . The teacher who could lead England in the path of reform must not talk of the social contract, of natural rights, of rights of man, or of liberty, fraternity, and equality. Bentham and his disciples precisely satisfied this requirement; they despised and derided vague generalities, sentiments, and rhetoric . . . The first of legal philosophers was no agitator, but a systematic thinker of extraordinary power, and a thinker who kept his eyes firmly fixed, not upon vague and

[15] Quoted by Dicey, *Law* (see n. 2), 126–7.

indefinite ideals, but upon definite plans for the practical amendment of the law of England.[16]

Inasmuch as a core belief of the Benthamites was the sacredness of individual freedom, including freedom to contract, on the grounds that the individual must know best for himself what was most conducive to his own welfare, some of the laws which can be ascribed to Benthamite influence would today seem intolerable, and have in fact long since been overlaid by new systems based rather on socially conscious, 'collectivist' values: such as the laws inhibiting trade union activity (as tending to overbear employers and distort the terms of the labour bargains they would make if left undisturbed) and those reforming the old Elizabethan method of poor relief (which was felt as leading to the industrious members of a parish being obliged at painful cost to maintain the idle) by erecting central workhouses. But in other areas the Benthamite revolution conferred permanent benefit. 'Utility, efficiency, economy and quantitative evaluation', wrote Oliver MacDonagh, 'were all challenging the prescriptive, reverential and hereditary views of law and its institutions':[17] this in connection with reforms in the administration of justice and poor relief in the 1830s and 1840s, but the principle applied in every field. It became the practice now to institute proper parliamentary or governmental commissions to enquire first into the facts of a situation in order that it might receive as rational a legislative regulation as possible. The structures of parliament and government were themselves reformed, with the Acts of 1832 and 1867 which both broadened the franchise and rationalized the distribution of seats, and that of 1836 which gave English towns a proper system of self-administration. Laws for reforming (and humanizing) criminal law, civil and criminal procedure, the courts system; for removing archaic restraints on trade and on the disposal of landed property; for creating a divorce jurisdiction; for punishing cruelty to animals: all can be ascribed to the influence of Bentham and his school.

That school contained no more famous and prominent disciple than John Stuart Mill (1806–73), who coined the word 'utilitarianism' to denote the position of those attached to the doctrine of utility as

---

[16] Ibid. 171–3.
[17] "'Pretransformations": Victorian Britain', in E. Kamenka (ed.), *Law and Social Control* (London, 1980), 118.

the measure of laws and institutions. But Mill added dimensions to the notion of utility which must be mentioned here. Firstly, he emphasized that commitment to the doctrine of utility does not mean imputing to the individual an interest in pursuing only his own pleasures and in averting pains threatening himself; this is far too base a reading of human nature. Altruism, concern for others, is no doubt less strongly and urgently developed in man than concern for himself; yet his natural social instinct tends to encourage this element in his nature, and to prevent a purely selfish approach to the world and thus a purely selfish understanding of utility. His own happiness is bound up with that of those among whom he lives and cannot be pursued in total independence from theirs. Again, common experience shows that humans—no doubt inconsequence of training, but then none the less naturally—desire virtue, a desire 'not as universal, but as authentic a fact, as the desire of happiness';[18] indeed, for some it is 'desired and cherished, not as a means to happiness, but as a part of their happiness'.[19] Utility, as the principle of subserving happiness, becomes thus a refined and elevated conception.

Secondly, Mill constructed an important relationship between utility and justice. He recognizes the elusive nature of the concept of justice—one only has to consider problems such as the justification for the infliction of punishment, or the proper measure of punishment, or the just measure of remunerating people for work of equal quantity but different market value, or the just principle for levying taxation, to see that minds equally honest can radically differ in their perceptions of it. Yet a shared fundamental idea of justice must subsist, as is evident in our readiness to agree that, speaking generally, to deprive another of his legal rights, or his moral rights, or of his deserts, or to break faith with him, or to behave with partiality when performing a judicial function, or to treat people unequally, are all actions which attract the name of injustice. Even now, we have still not isolated justice's essence. But Mill thinks he can put his finger on something just as good, which will inarticulately unite all such cases: namely, the *resentment* which injustice evokes, not merely for our own sakes—because an individual might well selfishly resent an injury even though it was not undeserved, in other words, even though it was justly

---

[18] *Utilitarianism*, ed. H. Acton (London, 1972), 33.   [19] Ibid. 34.

inflicted—but for the sake, or on the behalf, of others too. Here then there is a value, impossible to define, but instinctively recognized, which suggests that it can be presented also in the dress of moral right: my claim on just treatment is something I can raise against all the world, and all the world, because of its common instinct to resent injustice, must recognize, uphold, and defend my claim. In doing so, however (here Mill rejoins his utilitarian theme) the world is doing no more than recognizing its own interest; because security from injustice is vital for everyone, and the solidarity shown by others in defending me against it is essentially and ultimately directed to securing the utility and happiness of all. 'It has always been evident', he concludes, 'that all cases of justice are also cases of expediency . . . Justice remains the appropriate name for certain social utilities which are vastly more important, and therefore more absolute and imperative, than any others are as a class.'[20]

It may be briefly added that in the course of presenting this thesis of justice as an expression of the utility principle Mill lays particular stress on the value of *equality*, adopting, as something which 'might be written under the principle of utility as an explanatory commentary', Bentham's dictum: 'everybody to count for one, nobody for more than one'. The claim of everybody to happiness, he wrote, so far as it must be taken into the consideration of the moralist or the lawgiver,

involves an equal claim to all the means of happiness, except in so far as the inevitable conditions of human life, and the general interest, in which that of every individual is included, set limits to the maxim; and those limits ought to be strictly construed . . . All persons are deemed to have a *right* to equality of treatment, except when some recognised social expedience requires the reverse.[21]

From this generality Mill developed, in a few lines, an interpretation of past history, and a prophecy of future evolution of ideas, of great perceptiveness:

And hence all social inequalities which have ceased to be considered expedient, assume the character not of simple inexpediency, but of injustice, and appear so tyrannical, that people are apt to wonder how they ever could have been tolerated; forgetful that they themselves perhaps tolerate other inequalities under an equally mistaken notion of expediency,

[20] Ibid. 60.   [21] Ibid. 58–89.

the correction of which would make that which they approve seem quite as monstrous as what they have at last learnt to condemn. The entire history of social improvement has been a series of transitions, by which one custom or institution after another, from being a supposed primary necessity of social existence, has passed into the rank of a universally stigmatised injustice and tyranny. So it has been with the distinctions of slaves and freemen, nobles and serfs, patricians and plebeians; and so it will be, and in part already is, with the aristocracies of colour, race, and sex.[22]

The culmination of this passage reflects the championship of the cause of women's emancipation, of which Mill was a pioneer, particularly through the publication of his tract *The Subjection of Women* in 1869, an era when the notion of equality of the sexes was highly unfashionable.

THE RISE OF THE HISTORICAL SCHOOL

Contemporaneous with the rise of utilitarianism, and with the movement towards positivist conceptions of law, the nineteenth century saw also a powerful reaction, with its roots in those eighteenth-century intellects which had not been in sympathy with the rationalist enthusiasms of the Enlightenment. This reaction had found a famous voice, though not a programme, in Edmund Burke; and, at the end of the century, found a quite special embodiment in a generation of young German intellectuals. Here, inspired to some extent by the patriotic instinct to resist the French emperor who trampled back and forth across the prostrate and disunited German lands, a new mood developed among writers and poets, turning their interests inward upon their own nation, their people, their race (this latter still far from having any élitist or threatening sense). For them the people, the *Volk*, was endowed not merely with a history, which obviously every people possesses, but with a sort of mystical essence and value transcending both the merits of the nation's present members and the external facts of its past. To this depersonalized but emotionally powerful entity Rousseau's idea of the *volonté générale* as something different from the mere opinion of the majority, something which rather subsumed majority and minority in an irresistible higher element which defied numerical analysis, supplied a further dimension. But the mystical sense of the

[22] *Utilitarianism*, ed. H. Acton (London, 1972), 59.

nation was more than a fuel for later political struggles. Among scholars it awakened a genuine historical sense and a genuine passion to penetrate and understand the German past: and between scholarship and literature no hard frontier was drawn. A whole constellation of intellects inspired by national feeling now appeared, many of them associated in a sort of sentimental attachment with the picturesque streets and ruined castle of Heidelberg (whence their collective assignment, in German cultural history, to the 'Heidelberger Romantik'); leading names were those of Achim von Arnim and Clemens Brentano, who collected old German folk-song and poetry, and the brothers Jacob and Wilhelm Grimm, whose collection of German folk-tales became world famous. Jacob Grimm also became the founder of Germanic philology, the study of the history of the language. The cast of mind of such men was just as marked among lawyers in Germany as among secular writers and poets; and the consequence was the emergence of the 'historical' school of jurisprudence, by which expression is meant the tradition, now almost 200 years old, of studying not merely the law in force, but the special history, the folk-roots, the conditioning factors, the environment at different epochs, of a nation's legal institutions.

The immediate occasion for the visible emergence of this school, as distinct from its intellectual origins, was a difference between two German scholars. In 1814 Anton Thibaut (1772–1840), professor of law at Heidelberg, published an essay *On the Necessity for a General Civil Code for Germany*, in which, evidently inspired as much by the recent example of the *Code Napoléon* as by national ambition related to his own country and hopes for her unity, he urged the point expressed by this title. Germany was of course still divided into a large number of more or less mutually autonomous political entities, but, in the spirit of the Enlightenment, Thibaut argued that a law founded upon reason would be applicable successfully everywhere. He was at once contradicted by the Berlin professor Friedrich Carl von Savigny (1779–1861)[23] in a work entitled *On the Vocation of our Age for Legislation and Legal Science*. This work, which substantially announced the programme of what was to be the historical school, declared Thibaut's proposal premature. According to Savigny, one could not successfully codify

[23] Both Savigny and Thibaut belonged to families of French Huguenot origin.

what one had not yet properly understood; and there could be no complete understanding of the mass of law in force in the different parts of Germany until the history of each part of the mass had been fully penetrated and explored, a task which had not yet even begun, but which Savigny, fired with the romantic spirit in its nation-centred aspect of historical enchantment, was determined to take up. What Germany needed was not a rationalistic corpus of legal mechanisms, but a thorough insight into the history of her existing institutions. Only when this had been gained could a start be made on putting together the elements most suitable for reduction into a code.

The axiom from which Savigny proceeded was that each people had its own individual character, its own spirit—the *Volksgeist*, or national soul, as it was later compendiously called by one of his disciples in a phrase that stuck—and this spirit left its mark upon all the people's institutions, including their law. Implied here was the idea, attractive to the ear but exceedingly difficult to prove, that some institutions which were actually in force would turn out, on investigation, to be peculiarly 'natural' to that particular people, and to have grown out of their history; while others would turn out to be spurious, grafts from an alien stock, not 'natural' to the people and hence with no claim to perpetuation in the rigid form of a code. Savigny's own country was in fact unsuitable terrain from which to make such a point, because some areas of the law in all its regions, notably the law of contracts and other obligations, was notoriously not of native origin at all, but had been consciously 'received' into the practice of the German courts, or at any rate those of them in which enough of Renaissance learning was present, at about the end of the fifteenth and the beginning of the sixteenth century (as has been seen above): would Savigny propose to excise this vast mass of Roman material to which many generations of German lawyers had become accustomed? Savigny's answer was that the Roman institutions thus absorbed had had a sufficient affinity with the German national spirit to be, so to speak, implanted in German national life without rejection. This answer is not very satisfying, and seems to explode the very axiom which was his starting-point; this axiom is doubly hard to keep on its feet in the twentieth century, which has seen successful transplants of entire legal systems, or almost entire systems, into territories with far less affinity with the exporting culture than medieval Germany had with the late Roman empire: for example, the adoption by Turkey and Japan of large tracts taken straight from the civil codes of Switzerland and of Germany respectively. Nevertheless, Savigny's influence in halting, in the cause of historical understanding, the movement for codification was decisive; only in the latter years of the century, and after German political unification had been achieved, was a German civil code finally drafted; it came into force as the *Bürgerliches Gesetzbuch* on 1 January 1900.[24]

The historical school was thus originally focused on German law. But its basic postulate applied to all nations and their institutions, and it did in fact animate research into the legal history of many countries. It was especially important in inspiring the scientific historical study of the Roman law which formed a substantial element in the existing systems throughout most of Europe. This Roman law, however, was in essence the compilation of Justinian, encrusted of course with the work of the medieval commentators; a generation of so-called 'humanistic' jurists had, at the era of the Renaissance, recognized the difference between the text of the *Digest* and what the classical jurists there excerpted (who had mostly worked 350 or more years before Justinian's time) had probably originally written; but their work rested rather on philological than on institutional critiques, and its chief value for them was the light which the texts threw on the ancient world; they did not suspect any greater complexity in the historical layers of text than adaptations by the Justinianic commission might have given them. The new historical jurisprudence now explored these texts, particularly the *Digest*, with the tools of a much more subtle analysis, and began to construct a picture of Roman law as of course it was, namely, an intellectual monument with a thousand years of history behind it by the time Justinian's compilers sat down to their task. The progress of this scientific study (in which the Germans were during all the nineteenth century pre-eminent, though in the twentieth the Italians have rivalled them in volume of scholarly output, with significant contributions also from France, Spain, England, and the Low Countries) was marked by prodigies, not to say extremes, of ingenuity in the unpicking of texts and the exposure of non-original elements layered upon the classical jurists' original

[24] The date of coming into force was chosen by the Kaiser, Wilhelm II, who could not be persuaded that the first day of the 20th cent. (a day which seemed of psychological value) was not 1 Jan. 1900 but 1 Jan. 1901.

words (such elements were called indiscriminately, and with a sense wider than ordinary usage would support, 'interpolations'). But despite the excesses committed in the hunt for interpolations ('Interpolationenforschung'), which around the turn of the twentieth century occupied so many scholarly careers that it might almost be called an academic industry, the insight on which the whole school rested—that law should be seen as an organic and developing phenomenon in the history of a civilization, of which every stage demanded study— was a permanent and fruitful enrichment of legal science.

It was seen earlier that, by a paradoxical evolution, the legal culture of France, having initially proposed to express in the new *Code civil* the perfection of reason, the last word of the natural-law tradition, ended in an extreme positivism which looked on the words and will of the legislator as the sole basis for the law's validity. The nineteenth-century development of German legal culture offers, in a way, a parallel; because the historical movement quickly generated a school of jurists whose work also culminated in a form of positivism. The call to historical exploration of German law did lead to a specifically Germanic historical jurisprudence, but also, as explained above, to a new intensity of juristic archaeology in the Roman law which, in the form given it in the Middle Ages, was the dominant element in the contemporary German systems. Savigny himself in particular, but later many others, approached this Roman law in a classicizing spirit; nothing would do for them but the careful peeling away not just of the medieval but also of the Justinianic accretions, and the laying bare of the Roman rules of the classical period, in other words, of the first two centuries AD. From this approach there then sprang the conception of a *system*—the more appealing to these German lawyers concerned to assist in the unification, including the legal unification, of their politically fragmented country, since the law of the high Roman empire had also assumed the quality of a system observed throughout its many regions. Such a system, for these lawyers, would be a vast structure of mutually interconnected, harmoniously articulated *concepts*: principles, rules, doctrines, in the elaboration of which this classical Roman material was to serve as the quarry from which suitable blocks could be hewn. The activists of this school, since they concentrated their attention chiefly on the *Digest* (which also bore the equivalent Greek name of Pandects, *Pandectae*), were called in

German *Pandektisten*, their science *Pandektistik*. Their classicizing
approach conflicted with that of the modern practical lawyers who
worked with the 'impure' Roman law which had been knitted into
municipal German systems since the Middle Ages; not to speak of
their collision with the *Germanisten*, the fundamentalist scholars
who had taken Savigny with excessive literalness and were fighting
for a maximum of input, into the ultimate German code which
everyone knew must come in the end, from ancestral Germanic
sources. But it was the Pandectists who in the end were most
influential in the drafting of the *Bürgerliches Gesetzbuch*. Some
ground was gained and held by the Germanists in the parts of the
code governing the law of property, the family, and succession; but
the general shape and style of the code, together with the part on the
law of succession, and above all the first, 'general' part in which the
fundamental groundwork, the concepts basic to the whole code, are
laid down, was Roman in the sense which the Pandectists had
elaborated by their long decades of abstraction from the essentially
concrete, casuistic classical Roman material. How far all this was
from the first romantic conception of exploring, and identifying
with, the principles organically growing with the people and rooted
in their spirit, can easily be seen. So, too, can the positivist character
of the struggle—reminiscent of the work of Christian Wolff, at the
height of the Enlightenment, in creating an entire system on purely
rational postulates—to attribute the force of law, and of law
cemented into a standing code, to a network of norms built from the
abstractions distilled out of the classical Roman sources.

THE ANTHROPOLOGICAL APPROACH

A further offshoot of the historical school, and distinguished from it
by a strongly comparative approach as well as by the absence of
romantic belief in the *Volksgeist*, is the sometimes so-called
'anthropological' school. It is possible to point to forerunners of
this school in the previous century, such as Vico and Montesquieu.
But the first person to erect insights like theirs into something like a
science was the Englishman Henry Sumner Maine (1822–88). Maine
was an academic lawyer who also wrote very many essays on
contemporary political and economic issues, and served for some
years as legal member of the council of the viceroy of India. His first

and most famous book, *Ancient Law* (1861), was written in the era in which the principal intellectual excitement had been provided by the recently published masterpiece of the biologist Charles Darwin, *The Origin of Species* (1859), and thus it reflects to some extent the current interest in evolution; another, remoter influence has been identified in the Hegelian philosophy of history, mentioned earlier, which perhaps suggested to him the idea of uniform principles of development.[25] At any rate, in *Ancient Law* Maine proposed something like an evolutionary theory of law, complete with a pattern of growth to which all systems, though geographically or chronologically so distant from one another as to exclude the possibility of extraneous inspiration, could be shown to conform. Basing his theories on some knowledge of Roman, Greek, biblical, and other ancient law (including the laws of ancient Ireland),[26] as well as on native institutions of contemporary India, he presented the notion, firstly, that societies of all kinds tend to develop, so far as their legal life is concerned, by passing through certain stages which are the same everywhere. He thought that the earliest stage—that visible in the Homeric poems—was in one sense pre-legal: kings uttered judgments about actual disputes, and some element of divine inspiration, or of mediation through the kings of judgments of divine origin, hung about these isolated *themistes*, or 'dooms' (the Germanic equivalent). The next stage was the solidifying of these judgments, presumably when repetition and pattern made this possible, into custom, of which the oligarchies which had succeeded the era of kingship were custodians: this sequence of judgments preceding custom being the reverse of what the uninstructed layman might suppose a priori to have taken place. The third stage, associated with a more or less democratic movement to break the oligarchic monopoly of expounding the law, is that of codes (of which in fact Greece offers a number of examples, of roughly the same era as the Twelve Tables of Rome). At this point some societies cease to develop further; their legal institutions never evolve new dimensions beyond their petrified code: these societies

---

[25] Julius Stone, *Social Dimensions of Law and Justice* (London, 1966), 120.

[26] The great publication of ancient Irish law in an English translation by O'Curry and O'Donovan had not yet taken place when Maine wrote *Ancient Law*. His subsequent work *The Early History of Institutions* (1875) resulted from a visit to Ireland and study of the Brehon laws, which, he thought, reflected pan-Aryan institutions spread from Ireland to India, and further illustrated the historical patterns he had outlined in *Ancient Law*.

Maine called 'static'. Other societies, however, had the ability to adapt their laws to new circumstances; these, the 'dynamic' societies, tended, he found, to employ three mechanisms of change, namely, fictions, equity, and legislation. Unfortunately this orderly and appealing scheme was found by later scholars to rest on evidence too slender to support such giant generalizations; above all, other, newly available evidence from primitive societies still to be found in remote parts of the contemporary world would show a much greater variety in patterns of legal development than Maine had assumed.

Some of his particular insights have a strong illuminating force. The most celebrated of them is his view of the general direction which he thought the dynamic or progressive societies had been taking up to his time:

The movement of the progressive societies has been uniform in one respect. Through all its course it has been distinguished by the gradual dissolution of family dependency, and the growth of individual obligation in its place. The Individual is steadily substituted for the Family, as the unit of which civil laws take account . . . Nor is it difficult to see what is the tie between man and man which replaces by degrees those forms of reciprocity in rights and duties which have their origin in the Family. It is Contract . . . The word Status may be usefully employed to construct a formula expressing the law of progress thus indicated . . . All the forms of Status taken notice of in the Law of Persons were derived from, and to some extent are still coloured by, the powers and privileges anciently residing in the Family. If then we employ Status . . . to signify these personal conditions only, and avoid applying the term to such conditions as are the immediate or remote result of agreement, we may say that the movement of the progressive societies has hitherto been a movement *from Status to Contract.*[27]

In fact, even as Maine was writing this, the process which he discerned had already begun to go into reverse; the world had begun, under the impulsion of humanitarian and other considerations, to turn from belief in the individualist notion of the sacredness of

---

[27] *Ancient Law*, 173–4. R. C. J. Cocks, *Sir Henry Maine: A Study in Victorian Jurisprudence* (Cambridge, 1988), draws attention (p. 15) to the Irish scholar James Caulfield Heron's work, *Introduction to Jurisprudence* (1860), as anticipating in several ways the ideas Maine published in *Ancient Law* the following year. Heron is however forgotten; or remembered, if at all, only for obtaining a writ of mandamus against Trinity College, Dublin, which had refused him a scholarship, to which he was otherwise entitled, on the sole ground of his Roman Catholic faith.

contracts freely entered into. In Britain, for example,[28] Parliament had long ago interfered with the contractual freedom which resulted in inhuman conditions for ocean passengers (mainly emigrants) and had imposed minimum standards, in the interests of health and safety, on shipowners. The earliest Factory Acts were also long on the statute-book and were equally an infringement on the sacred freedom of wretched men, women, and children to agree to work under any conditions in order to stay alive. The first significant interference with the Irish landlord class had not yet taken place, but were shortly to come (and were strongly opposed, on the principle of contractual freedom, by Maine in his publicistic activity); so were laws favourable to the trade unions through which the individual worker could, by combination and collective bargaining, avoid isolated exposure to 'freedom of contract' with employers. This kind of process swelled, in the later decades of the nineteenth century, into a huge volume of social legislation tending to reduce more and more the 'freedom of contract' which, illusory wherever economically inferior groups were forced into contracting with economically dominant interests, now gave ground rapidly to the 'collectivism' which Dicey would document.

THE MARXIAN UNDERSTANDING OF LAW

An outline has been given above of the general Marxian view of the state as an expression, in structural form, of the interest of the class dominant in society from time to time. The place occupied by law in the Marxian scheme is chastening for the lawyer who thinks he deals in timeless, changeless, classless values, or transcendent, 'natural' rules; to Marx, law as it existed in the bourgeois societies around him in the middle of the nineteenth century was merely a mechanism whereby the dominant class perpetuated their grip on the means of production and sources of wealth, and which conferred an apparent legitimacy on their exploitation of the labouring masses, who, to the extent that they received for their labour only the minimum reward which the freely operating forces of the market obliged their employers (in competition with other employers) to pay, were robbed of the surplus value, over and

[28] This example is documented, with others, by O. MacDonagh, *A Pattern of Government Growth, 1800–60* (London, 1961), 122 ff.

above this wage, which their labour brought into being. Recalling an idea which we have already encountered in classical antiquity, Marx associated the emergence of laws with the emergence of private property, in other words, with the private appropriations which ended the golden age of humankind's common access to the world's resources:

Civil law develops concurrently with private property out of the disintegration of the natural community.[29]

If power is taken on the basis of right . . . then right, law, etc., are merely the symptoms of other relations upon which state power rests. The material life of individuals . . . their mode of production and form of interest which mutually determine each other . . . this is the real basis of the State . . . The individuals who rule in these conditions, besides having to constitute their power in the form of the State, have to give their will . . . a universal expression as the will of the State, as law.[30]

These brief quotations almost exhaust Marx's own direct references to law, whose place in Marxian theory is essentially implicit in the Marxian view of the state. However, Marx's view of the role of law comes through more forcefully in the famous Communist Manifesto (more properly, *Manifesto of the Communist Party*), which he wrote in collaboration with his friend Friedrich Engels (1820–95), and which was published in London in 1848, the 'year of revolutions'. To the proletarian, announced the Manifesto, 'law, morality, religion, are so many bourgeois prejudices, behind which lurk in ambush just as many bourgeois interests'.[31] Apostrophizing the bourgeoisie, it goes on:

Your very ideas are but the outgrowth of the conditions of your bourgeois production and bourgeois property, just as your jurisprudence is but the will of your class made into a law for all; a will, whose essential character and direction are determined by the economic conditions of existence of your class . . . The selfish misconception that induces you to transform into eternal laws of nature and of reason, the social forms springing from your present mode of production and form of property—this misconception you share with every ruling class that has preceded you.[32]

Engels, in his *Principles of Communism* (written, at about the same time, in a question-and-answer form, rather like a confessional catechism), presents the lofty legal values of liberal Europe—the

---

[29] *The German Ideology*: Marx and Engels, *Collected Works*, v. 90.
[30] Ibid. 329.   [31] Communist Manifesto, ch. 1.   [32] Ibid., ch. 2.

rule of law, equality before the law, and so on—as mere cosmetic and fraudulent masks for the harsh truth that law is just a means of entrenching the system which serves the dominant class. The immediate mode of entrenchment adopted by the bourgeois class had been the 'establishment of the representative system' (this was of course when the electoral franchise was still narrowly restricted everywhere on the basis of a property qualification); this in turn rested 'upon bourgeois equality before the law, and the legal recognition of free competition', fitted into a European format of constitutional monarchy.[33]

The liberal fetish of this 'free competition' and the freedom of contract which it presupposed, Engels (like T. H. Green, as has been seen) regarded as a fraud. Many years after his *Principles of Communism* he published, in 1884, a tract which incidentally denounced the cant of free contract in the context of labour:

The labour contract is to be freely entered into by both partners. But it is considered to have been freely entered into as soon as the law makes both parties equal *on paper*. The power conferred on the one party by the difference of class position, the pressure thereby brought to bear on the other party—the real economic position of both—that is not the law's business. Again, for the duration of the labour contract, both parties are to have equal rights in so far as one or the other does not expressly surrender them. That economic relations compel the worker to surrender even the last semblance of equal rights—here again, that is no concern of the law.[34]

It was, of course, one thing to present legal systems as formal entrenchments of dominant and selfish interests at a time when no revolution had yet taken place on communist principles, nor any state been called upon to apply them. What, on the morrow of the revolution when it eventually came, would be law's replacement? And in what ways would this replacement differ from what it had replaced? These were the questions with which Marxist jurisprudence would grapple in the following century, after the Russian Revolution of 1917.

[33] *Principles of Communism*: Marx and Engels, *Collected Works* (London, 1976), vi. 345–6.
[34] *The Origin of the Family, Private Property, and the State*, 2. 4.

SOCIOLOGICAL JURISPRUDENCE

The so-called 'sociological' branch of jurisprudence has only become conscious of itself in the twentieth century, but its origins can be traced in the nineteenth, among writers with very various kinds of interest.[35] Indeed, there is no very clear line around the concept of sociological jurisprudence which would force us to exclude figures like Savigny, Maine, or Marx from it; these have been mentioned in the contexts where they seem especially important as pioneers, but inasmuch as all three of them, in their varying ways, drew attention to the way in which law is rooted in, or conditioned by, the society which it regulates, no doubt they can be credited with 'sociological' forms of theory. There are, however, some other nineteenth-century figures who promoted the study of society, and law's relation to it, more centrally, and these may be briefly considered, loosely speaking, as founders of a new department of legal theory.

The earliest of them, the Frenchman Auguste Comte (1798–1857), was actually the inventor of the word 'sociology'. Comte was one of the many thinkers of his time who were impressed, firstly, by the huge strides which had been made by the physical sciences since the seventeenth century, and which led his age generally into a blind confidence in the capacity of science to effect limitless improvements in man's condition; and secondly, by the social transformation brought about by the industrial revolution, itself in some degree a product of the preceding scientific revolution. He, like Maine, was writing at a time when biological evolution was in the air, and, although he was dead before Darwin's greatest work was published, he proposed the view that society developed and changed in response to certain laws, analogous to the great biological principles governing the development of individual species. To the understanding of society's development no ideology, no transcendent 'law', could contribute anything, but only the observation of empirical facts.[36] A science of society, thus conducted—in his word,

---

[35] A sort of catalogue of the different senses in which legal theory is called 'sociological' is given by Lloyd, *Introduction* (see Ch. 6 n. 72), 548–9.

[36] This belief in the exclusive value of concrete facts Comte called 'positivism', and thus provided a further sense for a word already overladen. For a list of its different meanings (not exhaustive: it omits the Italian school of criminologists called

sociology—could, he thought, reach a point of perfection such that law itself would become redundant, or rather that the function it now discharged would be subsumed in a sort of scientific social management.

A somewhat similar approach was that of the English philosopher Herbert Spencer (1820–1903), who also proposed a variety of social Darwinism. He believed that man, by an inherited mechanism, succeeded to the sum of earlier generations' experience in the matter of adapting to the requirement of living in society, and so acquired from generation to generation a deepening sense of his social duty. There was, therefore, a hidden engine of continuous and irreversible improvement at work, to which legal and social development could simply be left, without state interference, to evolve by a sort of social natural selection. Pending the natural emergence of a perfect society, only one essential rule bound men, namely, that while each may do what he likes, he may not injure the equal freedom of others—a kind of restatement of Kant's formula. From this maxim, however, certain natural rights of individuals result as corollaries: property, free speech, religious worship, and so on. It was the state's business to protect those rights; but apart from this the state had no legitimate role in steering society along the path which the principle of social evolution destined it to follow in any case.

The relevance of Comte and Spencer to legal theory lies in their vision of law's ultimate supersession, not (as in Marxian theory) through the resolution of the class conflict in which law is just the armament of the bourgeoisie, but through the perfection of society achieved (according to their respective theories) by a science-based manipulation, or by a natural evolutionary process. With the German lawyer Rudolf von Jhering (1818–92)[37] a different focus of interest is apparent, though one equally related to society. In his earlier life Jhering had promoted an approach to law of the analytical positivist kind associated with Austin, centred on the reduction of a legal order to a system of concepts. Later, however, he came to feel the inadequacy of such an approach (and went so far as to ridicule it, in a satirical work of a kind rare for his age,

positivists) see Stig Strömholm, *Short History of Legal Thinking in the West* (Stockholm, 1985).

[37] This name, sometimes written Ihering, has two syllables, and is pronounced 'Yaring' (to rhyme with 'daring').

profession, and nation).[38] Central to his view of law was now the idea that legal science must address itself to social relations, and to the social purpose which underlay every rule. Ideally, this purpose should be the protection of 'interests', among which he distinguished the interests of the individual and of society; the task of both the legislator and the judge was to bring these into harmony—in the case of the judge, by looking less at the bare text of a law than at what he took to be the social purpose behind it. There was, however, no necessary opposition between the interests of the individual and society, for the individual has an interest of his own in society's welfare, and it is society's interest, in turn, to protect the individual's rights. Jhering did not provide any calculus of the relative weight of interests which would be any use to a judge or legislator in a concrete case (any more than did his twentieth-century successors); and the idea of the social role of law in a society of interdependent individuals may now seem banal. But he was the first to present law as society's mechanism for the harmonization of individual and group purposes, and the balancing of individual and group interests.

NATURAL LAW IN HIBERNATION

If we scan the nineteenth century for any trace of the natural-law belief which had survived from the ancient world until well after the Reformation, being eclipsed only by the rational and scientific spirit of the Enlightenment, we will find it difficult to locate anywhere outside the teaching of the institutional Catholic Church, which never abandoned the Aristotelian–Thomistic tradition. One figure, however, should be mentioned as having represented the natural-law tradition more fully than merely as an expression of the obedience in which, as a Catholic priest, he stood: Antonio Rosmini (1797–1855), who for his sympathy with the ideals of the *Risorgimento* was in occasional disfavour with the Church authorities. Rosmini asserted the presence in man of an insight of transcendental origin, informing his moral conscience; at the moment when the moral law, so perceived, 'recognises a person's right to an activity, it

---

[38] He envisaged a heaven composed of concepts ('Begriffshimmel') in *Scherz und Ernst in der Jurisprudenz* ('Joking and in Earnest about Legal Science') (1884).

prohibits others from interfering with it'.[39] This general duty of respect for the rights of others, anchored in the moral worth and dignity of the person, is the source of the law itself. This perspective reverses the approach of the eighteenth century, which, Rosmini said, 'derived duties from rights, not rights from duties', and was thus 'a most dismal doctrine of dehumanised egoism'.[40] There could not, however, be any right to do something morally impermissible; and, in saying this, Rosmini criticized the seventeenth- and eighteenth-century German natural lawyers who had separated law from morality. Favourable to the idea of a codified civil law common to all the different parts of the still disunited Italy, he wished this code to be prefaced by a declaration that the state was bound by the precept of justice, in the form in which this was proclaimed by reason illuminated by the Gospel;[41] in no sense would this code be simply an expression of the state's own will. The religious inspiration of Rosmini's writings, however, allowed him to identify this instinct for justice with the love of God, so giving them a flavour to which the spirit of the age was unsympathetic. It could not be said that he exercised any noticeable influence outside the Church or his own country.

PROPERTY

It has been seen that even the most radical revolution in world history to date, that of France, had not only been free of any element of communism or levelling in the field of property, but actually attributed a positive status to private ownership via a franchise based on property qualification. The turn of the eighteenth to the nineteenth century saw, in this respect, the spirit of Locke still dominant. Hegel, for example, despite the sacredness which he imputed to the (ethical) state, was 'before everything else a good bourgeois, with rather more than the usual bourgeois respect for stability and security'. Private property, for him, was 'not created by the state or even by society', but was 'an indispensable condition of human personality'.[42] He saw it, in his *Philosophy of Right*, as essentially the product of the individual will operating upon an object, the basic instance being the act of the first taker in

---

[39] *Filosofia del diritto*, 107.   [40] Ibid. 127.   [41] Ibid. 10.
[42] Sabine, *History* (see n. 7), 599.

appropriating something not previously owned, with corollaries in the right of alienation and the right to acquire by contract, which derives its force from the operation of two wills.[43] But the rise of capitalism and the quite new contrasts of social condition brought on by the industrial revolution caused new voices to be heard, which raised again, and in much more urgent form, the ancient question of man's right to appropriate as an individual large quantities of the earth's resources apparently left by nature to man as a race.

The earliest of these voices belonged to writers which the post-Marxian age labelled as 'utopian' socialists, that is, thinkers whose protests were linked to the desire that society might reform itself on a basis which excluded private property along with the exploitation associated with it, but did not rest upon any comprehensive theory which explained its abuse in terms of an inevitable process. Mention may be made, in this connection, of the figure regarded as the founder of the 'anarchist' tradition, Pierre-Joseph Proudhon (1809–65), famous for coining the phrase 'property is theft'. In his tract *What is Property?* (1840) he undertook to justify this proposition, which in the first instance he asserted was no more implausible than the statement that slavery is murder: inasmuch as the enslaver takes from the slave all that makes life valuable, the hyperbole is not extreme, and the analogy with his expression about private property sufficiently appealing. Instead, however, of sticking to mere rhetoric, Proudhon examined in turn the various justifications of private property which had been long familiar, and denounced them all as dishonest or inadequate. It stands in the catalogue of the natural and inalienable rights of man proclaimed in 1793 along with liberty, equality, and security; but how was it that no one had ever felt the need to justify the presence of the three other values in that list? Why was the natural-right status of property still problematical? Was it because the old explanations of it were not sincerely believed in? Cicero had likened private property to the occupancy, for the duration of the performance, of a seat at the theatre; but was it possible simultaneously for a single man to occupy three seats? And if this image corresponded with what could frequently be witnessed in the world, then Cicero's analogy could not be relied on to justify it. The fact that private property is universally recognized in actual

---

[43] *Philosophy of Right*, §§ 45–50, 63–71.

legal orders does not legitimate it either. The argument based on the 'mixing of one's labour' with the product of the earth is a visible hypocrisy; since what is owned privately is often not the product of one's own labour, but of that of others which one has appropriated.[44] Nevertheless Proudhon did not advocate communism; against this kind of system (of which the world at that time afforded only marginal or purely theoretical examples: he mentions Plato's ideal state, and the regime of the Jesuits in seventeenth-century Paraguay) he uses the strongest denunciation:

The disadvantages of communism are so obvious that its critics never have needed to employ much eloquence to thoroughly disgust men with it. The irreparability of the injustice which it causes, the violence which it does to attractions and repulsions, the yoke of iron which it fastens upon the will, the moral torture to which it subjects the conscience, the debilitating effect which it has upon society; and, to sum it all up, the pious and stupid uniformity which it enforces upon the free, active, reasoning, unsubmissive personality of man, have shocked common sense, and condemned communism by an irrevocable decree.[45]

Later he calls 'property the exploitation of the weak by the strong', but 'communism the exploitation of the strong by the weak'; communism, he says, is 'oppression and slavery'. The conclusion which he reaches is that individual possession, not individual ownership, is the condition of social life; the one must be maintained, the other suppressed. On such a state of society liberty will arise, a liberty which in fact, in asmuch as the institutions of conventional government will now have become redundant, will be identical with anarchy.[46] It is easy to see how visions of such a kind earned the epithet utopian.

Marx, on the other hand, saw the contemporary pattern of the distribution and concentration of wealth (as has been seen) in terms of its inevitable role in history whose stages unfolded in an ineluctable dialectical process. But the characterization of private property which he and Engels built into the Communist Manifesto a few years after Proudhon's tract recalls the latter's attack on the labour-based justification of it: 'the existence of property for the few is due solely to its non-existence in the hands of nine-tenths'.[47] Not sharing Proudhon's fears about the tyranny inseparable from

44 *What is Property?* ch. 3.   45 Ibid., ch. 5. 2.
46 Ibid., ch. 5. 2. 3.   47 Communist Manifesto, ch. 2.

communism, they stated its distinguishing feature as being 'not the abolition of property, but the abolition of bourgeois property', i.e. that property which is based on exploitation.[48]

Such opinions about private property naturally caused alarm in a Europe to which even the worst nightmare so far experienced, the French Revolution, had not proclaimed the illegitimacy of individual ownership but had rather endorsed it. Two examples of the reinforcement of intellectual barriers against penetration by such new ideas may be given, from the Catholic and the Protestant ends of later nineteenth-century Europe. The latter may be represented by a passage from Maine's *Village Communities in the East and West*, published first in 1871, in which he presents the institution of private property as lying at the core of civilization itself:

There are a few perhaps who may conceive a suspicion that, if property as we now understand it, that is, several property, be shown to be more modern, not only than the human race (which was long ago assumed), but than ownership in common (which is only beginning to be suspected), some advantage may be gained by those assailants of the institution itself whose doctrines from time to time cause a panic in modern Continental society. I do not myself think so. It is not the business of the scientific historical enquirer to assert good or evil of any particular institution. He deals with its existence and development, not with its expediency. But one conclusion he may properly draw from the facts bearing on the subject before us. Nobody is at liberty to attack several property and to say at the same time that he values civilisation. The history of the two cannot be disentangled. Civilisation is nothing more than a name for the old order of the Aryan world, dissolved but perpetually re-constituting itself under a vast variety of solvent influences, of which infinitely the most powerful have been those which have, slowly, and in some parts of the world much less perfectly than others, substituted several property for collective ownership.[49]

Maine was a Protestant who, as has been seen, was highly hostile both to indiscriminate democracy and to breaches in the Liberal doctrine which forbade state interference for social purposes. In 1891 the head of the Catholic world, Pope Leo XIII, issued his encyclical letter *Rerum novarum*, whose very title alluded to apprehensions of revolution,[50] and whose central message was one of social conciliation through a new consideration for the just claims

---

[48] Ibid.   [49] *Village Communities*, 229–30.
[50] The opening words are: 'The longing for revolution (*res novae*)'.

of the working class on a world dominated by the wealth which they sweated to produce but did not own. Such a social disposition implied of course restraint upon instincts of acquisitiveness and greed; and the idea that wealth should not be needlessly accumulated for its own sake, but should be used also with the benefit of others in mind, had always been present in Christian treatments of the theme of property. Now, however, Leo XIII prefaced his social message—perhaps in order to render it less suspect to the owning classes he was primarily addressing—with a statement of the right of private property far more downright than anything heard before from the supreme authority of the Church. In a section headed 'The settled ownership of property is from the natural law' he wrote:

It is right and proper for a man to have ownership, not only of the fruits of the earth, but also of the earth itself, because of his awareness that the earth is the source from which his future needs will be supplied. Because his needs are forever recurring . . . nature must have given to man access to a stable source of supply.

A rationale going no further than this would, of course, equally apply to communal forms of ownership. But he went on: 'An objection to private ownership cannot be based upon the fact that God has given the earth to the whole human race for them to use and enjoy.' Custom and law may, in different countries, determine the precise modes of distributing property, while the earth continues to feed everyone. Labour earns wages which are exchanged for the fruits of the earth, so the earth is the source of labour's livelihood too:

All this affords further proof that it is fully in accordance with nature to own property privately . . . When a man expends the activity of his mind and the strength of his body in procuring the goods of nature he makes his own that part of nature's resources which he brings to completion, leaving on it, as it were, in some form, the imprint of himself. This being so, it cannot but be right for him to possess that part as his very own, nor can it be lawful for anyone to violate that right in any way.

To this view of property's basis (surprisingly but obviously in the liberal and Lockeian tradition) the Pope added the evidence both of civil law's uniform recognition of private property, and, from the Church's point of view enough to carry the entire argument, the authority of God's own Tenth Commandment, forbidding men to covet the goods of another and thus implicitly recognizing the right of that other to their ownership.[51] From now on the right of private property, however tempered by the duty of social responsibility in the use of wealth, was part of the natural law in the Church's teaching.

CRIMINAL LAW AND PUNISHMENT

The eighteenth century had seen, with Beccaria, the first stirrings of the scientific conscience (as distinct from the simple promptings of humanity) in regard to the application of criminal law; and the nineteenth saw the opening of a debate, still in progress, as to whether that application had any natural or theoretical boundaries. The debate originated in the camp of the English utilitarians, and specifically with John Stuart Mill, generally regarded as having taken up the leadership of that intellectual and political movement after Bentham's death. Mill, an intellect force-grown by the insulated and intensive education imposed by his father, had already made a name in philosophy and economics when he published in 1859 his celebrated essay *On Liberty*, which caused a sensation in an England dominated by a very constrictive social morality whose harshness, despite a generation of humanitarian-inspired reform, was still reflected in its criminal law. This essay for the first time advanced the proposition that the criminal law had no right to punish acts merely because they were acts which society disapproved of and wished to repress; and that the frontier beyond which the force of the state had no title to advance was that which separated 'other-regarding' acts, i.e. those causing harm to others, which the law was indeed entitled to put down, from the 'self-regarding' acts, which, since they affected no one but the doer, were not the state's or society's business and hence represented territory on which the criminal law was a trespasser. The core of this theory has always been seen as summarized in this passage from the Introduction to the essay:

The object of this Essay is to assert one very simple principle, as entitled to govern absolutely the dealings of society with the individual in the way of compulsion and control, whether the means used be physical force in the form of legal penalties, or the moral coercion of public opinion. That

---

[51] *Rerum novarum* 1. 6–8.

principle is, that the sole end for which mankind are warranted, individually or collectively, in interfering with the liberty of action of any of their number, is self-protection. That the only purpose for which power can be rightfully exercised over any member of a civilised community, against his will, is to prevent harm to others. His own good, either physical or moral, is not a sufficient warrant. He cannot rightfully be compelled to do or forbear because it will be better for him to do so, because it will make him happier, because, in the opinions of others, to do so would be wise, or even right. These are good reasons for remonstrating with him, or reasoning with him, or persuading him, or entreating him, but not for compelling him, or visiting him with any evil in case he do otherwise. To justify that, the conduct from which it is desired to deter him must be calculated to produce evil to some one else. The only part of the conduct of any one, for which he is amenable to society, is that which concerns others. In the part which merely concerns himself, his independence is, of right, absolute. Over himself, over his own body and mind, the individual is sovereign.[52]

In the sections which follow the Introduction, Mill argues for toleration of dissenting opinions and for the encouragement of human individuality and diversity. It is the appreciation both of human dignity and of human limitations and fallibility, rather than any strict proof of his main proposition, which leads him back in the final section to assert once more, with concrete instances, the wrongfulness of imposing sanctions on anyone save for the purpose of preventing harm to others. His theory, however, proposes limits not merely for criminal law, but even for the operation of the moral force of social disapproval: a large extension of his front which naturally offered his critics an easy target. Moreover it is worth noticing that there appears to be no necessary connection between Mill's conception of liberty, as something which it is not permissible to interfere with except to preserve others from harm, and the general utilitarian test of law by the standard of its tendency to maximize pleasure and minimize pain;[53] inasmuch as the application of the 'liberty' standard in a particular case might fail to pass this test of 'utility'.

Mill's most forceful critic was in fact himself a utilitarian. The exceedingly austere lawyer (later judge of the English High Court) James Fitzjames Stephen (1829–94) published in 1873 a book whose title—*Liberty, Equality, Fraternity*—was a purely sarcastic allusion

[52] *On Liberty*, Introduction.
[53] J. W. Harris, *Legal Philosophies* (London, 1980), 117.

to the revolutionary motto, as the author's purpose was a radical questioning of what passed for those values. Taking to pieces Mill's arguments and pronouncing them inadequate, he put forward his own view on what justified punishment, over and above the protection of society: punishment, he wrote, also had the function of

gratifying the feeling of hatred—call it revenge, resentment, or what you will—which the contemplation of such conduct excites in healthily constituted minds . . . Criminal law is [thus] in the nature of a persecution of the grosser forms of vice, and an emphatic assertion of the principle that the feeling of hatred and the desire of vengeance above-mentioned are important elements of human nature which ought in such cases to be satisfied in a regular public and legal manner.[54]

Yet Stephen did not assert that in every case where society's hatred might be excited the criminal law should apply. The law was, of course, entitled to repress vice; but subject to important qualifications, one being 'that those who have due regard to the incurable weaknesses of human nature will be very careful how they inflict penalties upon mere vice, or even upon those who make a trade of promoting it, unless special circumstances call for their infliction'.[55] Generally, too, there were many reasons against extending the sphere of criminal law, but these were reasons altogether independent of general considerations about liberty.[56] He appeared in fact to accept that the balance of toleration and repression exhibited by contemporary English law was about right: 'Criminal law . . . has found its level in this country, and, though in many respects of great importance, can hardly be regarded as imposing any restraint on decent people which is ever felt as such.'[57]

He seemed even to accept 'the principle that criminal law ought to be employed only for the prevention of acts of force or fraud which injure others than the agent', but this was only a 'rough practical rule'; by no means would he accept it as an unvarying criterion arising from the idea of liberty. The considerations which might, then, limit the play of criminal law did not spring from any theory at all, but from the nature of the criminal law and process themselves, which must prevent their extension into anything like a system of moral police. For instance, some morally censurable

---

[54] *Liberty, Equality, Fraternity*, 149.
[55] Ibid. 152–3.　　　[56] Ibid. 136.　　　[57] Ibid.

behaviour (like ingratitude or perfidy) is too vague and unmeasurable
to be the subject of legal regulation; the law ought not to go in for
officious, petty meddling; problems of an entirely practical order in
the law of evidence must put some kinds of sin out of reach anyway;
criminal law should not express a standard of morality too far above
the current popular level; and the privacy of individuals is a value in
its own right, excessive disruption of which by too energetic a
criminal law ought to be avoided.[58] Mill died very soon after
Stephen's tract appeared, and never had an opportunity of replying
to it. In the retrospect of more than a century, however, it does
seem that Stephen, in spite of his expressions of Gothic rigour about
crime and criminals, was still dealing—once notions like 'meddling'
and 'privacy' emerge—with values near enough to liberty, in the
practical understanding of ordinary usage, while avoiding any
theoretical analysis of it. In the present century, as will be seen, the
issue thus debated by Mill and Stephen has again been an academic
battle-ground.

So much for the role of criminal law, its right to exist. But another
theme, related and overlapping with that one, is the motive of
criminal punishment. We have just seen that Stephen wrote in this
connection of vengeance, the gratification of feelings of hatred for
the criminal. This would later become unfashionable, but it was a
sentiment not strange to nineteenth-century English ears; in the
earlier part of the century it was heard, for example, from the poet
Shelley and the essayist Hazlitt.[59] A much more rarified version of
retributivism appears in Hegel's *Philosophy of Right* (1821). In the
section of the book dealing with 'Wrong' Hegel advances, in
characteristically difficult language, a picture of a crime creating a
sort of disequilibrium which it is the job of punishment to put right;
the punishment 'annuls' the crime. Not only that, but it happens
with the implied consent of the criminal, to whom a sort of
participation in the whole plan of restoring the balance is
mysteriously imputed; indeed, the criminal has a 'right' to be
punished. Here are brief excerpts from the passages which appear to
mean all this: 'The sole positive existence which the injury possesses
is that it is the particular will of the criminal. Hence to "injure" [by
penalizing it] this particular will, as a will determinately existent, is

---

[58] *Liberty, Equality, Fraternity*, 147.
[59] References in Séamus Deane, *The French Revolution and Enlightenment in England* (Cambridge, Mass., 1988), 115, 155, 173–4.

to annul the crime, which otherwise would have been held valid, and to restore the Right.' Merely to treat punishment as a sort of necessary evil, to be justified in terms of deterrence, prevention, reformation, and so on, is inadequate. While these elements may be legitimately borne in mind, especially in connection with determining modes of punishment, essentially 'the only important things are, first, that crime is to be annulled, not because it is the producing of an evil but because it is the infringement of a right as right; and secondly, the question of what that positive existence is which crime possesses and which must be annulled'.[60] Criminal punishment is to be thought of not simply as just, because, 'as just, it is *eo ipso* [the criminal's] implicit will, an embodiment of his freedom, his right'. Beccaria's argument against the death penalty based on social contract (the idea that no one can be assumed to have entered a contract making possible his own execution) is to be rejected, as the state is not based on contract in the first place. On the contrary, 'punishment is regarded as containing the criminal's right, and hence by being punished he is honoured as a rational being. He does not receive this due of honour unless the concept and measure of his punishment are derived from his own act'.[61]

A more characteristic—and incomparably more influential—figure in nineteenth-century criminal-law theory is Bentham, one of whose lifelong preoccupations was the rational reform of that law and of its enforcement.[62] It has been seen that the utility test, applied to criminal punishment, tended to weigh anyway in favour of a humanitarian bias: the pain endured by the criminal far exceeded the gratification produced in those beholding or conscious of his punishment. The same test showed the proper principal end of punishment to be deterrence, not retribution: deterrence both of the criminal, and of others tempted to imitate him:

General prevention ought to be the chief end of punishment as it is its real justification. If we could consider an offence which has been committed as an isolated fact, the like of which would never recur, punishment would be useless. It would be only adding one evil to another. But when we consider that an unpunished crime leaves the path of crime open, not only to the same delinquent but also to all those who may have the same motives and

---

[60] *Philosophy of Right*, §§ 99.   [61] Ibid., § 100.

[62] This interest extended even to prison design. He conceived a prison building which he called the Panopticon ('see-all'), a set of radiating passages which could be easily surveyed by a single watching eye at the centre.

opportunities for entering upon it, we perceive that punishment inflicted on the individual becomes a source of security to all. That punishment which considered in itself appeared base and repugnant to all generous sentiments is elevated to the first rank of benefits when it is regarded not as an act of wrath or vengeance against a guilty or unfortunate individual who has given way to mischievous inclinations, but as an indispensable sacrifice to the common safety.[63]

Reform of the English criminal law, at the beginning of the century the most ferocious in Western Europe, proceeded throughout the latter three-quarters of the century very much in Bentham's spirit and under his influence; Maine wrote in 1875 that 'he did not know a single law reform effected since Bentham's day which cannot be traced to his influence'.[64] In particular, Peel's 'Five Acts' of 1825, simplifying criminal law and much reducing the number of capital offences, are attributed to Bentham's influence; so too are later laws penalizing (for the first time) cruelty to animals, and abolishing archaic sanctions such as forfeiture for treason and 'corruption of blood'.[65]

The nineteenth century has a further claim on our interest in the context of criminal theory inasmuch as it was now that the foundations of the science of criminology were laid. The father of that science is generally considered to be Cesare Lombroso (1836–1909), a doctor and anthropologist who became professor of forensic medicine at Turin. He is best known for his theory that crime is the necessary product of an individual's unlucky physiological and psychological constitution, and that certain physical characteristics, capable of measurement, can indicate a criminal 'type'. This general theory, presented in a famous book *L'uomo delinquente* ('Criminal Man', 1876), was later entirely demolished; but, like all pioneers whose particular views have been afterwards refuted, he deserves the credit of initiating a science. His ideas, since they tended to nullify the concept of moral guilt, thus depriving the criminal law of its moral title to punish, encountered instinctive suspicion. But they were a stimulus to the wide range of sociologists, anthropologists, psychologists, and pathologists, whose research on the associations of criminality with predisposing genetic or environ-

---

[63] *Principles of Penal Law*, in *Works*, ed. Bowring, p. 383.
[64] *Early History of Institutions* (1875), 397.
[65] See Margery Fry, 'Bentham and English Penal Reform', in G. Keeton and G. Schwarzenberger (eds.), *Jeremy Bentham and the Law* (London, 1948).

mental causes, and generally on the roots of crime, are a characteristic adventure of the twentieth-century intellect.

INTERNATIONAL LAW

On the plane of practice international law expanded enormously in the nineteenth century, with the law of war tending to be now much overshadowed by developments belonging rather to the law of peace. There was, especially from about the 1860s, a huge growth in the number and range of international treaties, which now tended to be more businesslike and technical, free too of the ceremonial flourishes and precedencies with which in earlier ages diplomatic usage had encumbered them. These treaties—another modern development—were now frequently 'open', in other words, available for accession by states other than the originally concluding powers. Large areas of economic life were brought in this way under international regulation: copyright, patents, maritime law, and so on; the best and standard example is the world-wide convention on the international carriage and delivery of mails, originating in 1874 and given a form which has lasted ever since as the Universal Postal Union in 1878. Humanitarian movements also frequently sought for their objectives the stability of an international agreement; the best-known example here is the Red Cross organization, inspired by the Swiss Henri Dunant after he had witnessed the horrors of Italian battlefields in the 1850s; the first Geneva convention on the mitigation of warfare was concluded in 1864. There was also in this century a huge growth in the settlement of disputes (such as over a contested frontier or territory) by international arbitration.[66]

On the theoretical side, however, the status of international law was equivocal. In 1821 Hegel could not admit that it was a 'law' in any sense which implied subjection to it of individual states: 'The nation-state is mind in its substantive rationality and immediate actuality and is therefore the absolute power on earth. It follows that every state is sovereign and autonomous against its neighbours.'[67] The principle of 'pacta sunt servanda' (agreements must be observed) was said to be fundamental to the law of nations, but as in fact all states are sovereign, i.e. not answerable to any external

[66] Nussbaum, *Law of Nations* (see Ch. 4 n. 131), 192 ff.
[67] *Philosophy of Right*, § 331.

authority, this rule is only an 'ought-to-be'. The 'League of Nations' suggested by Kant, if it were to be a reality, would need what, given the nature of states, it cannot have, namely a supreme sovereign will.[68]

The role assigned to international law a few years later (1832) by John Austin is in substance no different, though founded not on a doctrine of the state so much as on an exclusively imperative definition of law. Since law 'strictly so called' is for Austin the command of a political superior, backed up by a threatened sanction in the event of disobedience, international law, as it evidently does not conform to this definition, must fail to qualify as law strictly so called; Austin relegates it to a category labelled 'positive morality', where its companions are other systems called law more or less by courtesy, such as the laws of honour or of fashion. It is no more than the 'opinions and sentiments current among nations generally'; though of course in England, since English courts considered the established rules of international law to be part of the law of the land, these rules could certainly be called 'law' in this municipal context.[69] This position, based purely on definition, naturally deprived international law of the psychological impact normally delivered by the word 'law', and was correspondingly resented.

Worth mentioning is the so-called 'nationality' theory of the Italian nationalist lawyer Pasquale Stanislao Mancini (1817–89). Working in the era before Italian unity and independence had been won, he delivered a lecture in 1850 in which he advanced the idea that nations, not states, are the real subjects of international law. Nations, that is, communities united by natural and historical factors such as territory, race, and language, as well as by consciousness of shared nationality, are entitled (he held) under international law to organize into states and to live independent of, and equal to, other nations. As the idea of substituting nations for states as the subjects of international law was impractical in actual conditions, not to speak of the problem of defining nations (more complex than he imagined), Mancini's theory had no large-scale success: except within the more modest area of private international law, or conflict of laws—a discipline which in this era was beginning to hive away from what now would be called, for purposes of distinctness, 'public' international law. Here the notion

---

[68] *Philosophy of Right*, § 333.
[69] *The Province of Jurisprudence Determined* (1832), 12.

of nationality was adopted in the general practice of states in areas like divorce and marriage, inheritance, and contracts; only in the twentieth century was the practice reversed in favour of the now generally accepted criterion of domicile.[70]

[70] Fassò, *Storia* (see Ch. 3 n. 56), iii. 141–3; Nussbaum, *Law of Nations* (see Ch. 4 n. 131), 225–7.

9
The Earlier Twentieth Century

The world order established in 1815 at the Congress of Vienna, and the political and social structures which the nineteenth century had made seem permanent, did not finally crumble until the First World War (1914–18). The origins of the Great War are controversial, but some factors cannot be left out of any account of it: the basic instability of the multinational Habsburg empire of Austria-Hungary, constantly shaken with the ambitions and rivalries of its peoples, and thinking a war the shortest way to re-assert itself; the position of Russia as the patron of the smaller Slav nations, and her probable involvement once Serbia was attacked; the emergence of bloc alliances, the balance between which was upset when Britain, despite having no traditional hostility towards Germany, joined the alliance of France with Russia; French antipathy to her eastern neighbour, fuelled with eagerness to avenge the disasters of the war of 1870; the militarism of imperial Germany, lately united under Prussian leadership, and locked in alliance with Austria; British jealousy of the growing German sea-power, of German industry and economic influence, of her own security which she saw threatened by the rise of this mighty state just across the North Sea. There seems also to have been a fatalistic mood in the European air, a resignation to good times ending, to the long summer breaking in a storm; this mood had even an element of impatience, impatience to bring on the thunder and lightning, get it over with, clear the air; though very few of the soldiers and statesmen who allowed the war to grow out of an episode in itself so relatively petty imagined that it would last so long or cause such horrific suffering.

When the war ended, it resulted not merely (like previous wars) in changes in the political map as the victors helped themselves to the territory of the beaten; though several new states—Hungary, Yugoslavia, Czechoslovakia, and the rump republic of German Austria—arose on, or with components taken from the former Habsburg territory. More significant was the transformation of

Europe's political texture. The imperial regimes of Germany and Russia had disappeared as well as that of Austria; and had in Russia been replaced, in the October Revolution of 1917, by a Marxist dictatorship under Lenin.

The peace settlement reached in 1919 with the Treaty of Versailles was dominated by the influence of the United States, which had entered the war against Germany in 1917, and by the principle, which the Americans in particular promoted, of national self-determination. It was, however, fatally harsh on the defeated Germany, made to bear the entire burden of war-guilt which the German people by no means felt. Germany was made to surrender her entire colonial empire and to pay such colossal reparations to the probably equally guilty victors that the German economy and people suffered most severely. A frightful inflation in 1923 destroyed the savings of the middle class; this, when it was followed by the world economic depression which set in in 1929, created an acute sense of national grievance and resentment which the extreme Left and Right of German politics were able to exploit. Adolf Hitler's National Socialist Party was better at street violence than its Communist rivals; and gained support at first especially among the smaller bourgeoisie, whose impoverishment made them susceptible to expert propaganda against the victor nations and their supposedly Jewish-dominated capitalism. Hitler also made allies among the German industrialists, who saw opportunities for themselves in his programme of massive state-led expansion. He came to power first by electoral means, in 1933; and by 1935 had completely undermined the democratic institutions of the so-called 'Weimar' Republic which had succeeded the German monarchy in 1919. His aggressive foreign policy, conducted in the name of asserting the rights of the German people, degenerated into war with his invasion of Poland in 1939; Britain and France thereupon declared war upon Germany. The Second World War which now developed (1939–45) caused far more civilian (although fewer military) casualties than the first, ended in Germany's defeat and the pulverization of most of her cities, and brought Russian influence, for the first time since 1815, into the heart of central and almost into Western Europe.

The National Socialist tyranny in Germany was only one of the many European dictatorships which arose after 1918 from the discontents which liberal parliamentary democracy proved unable to cure. It was Mussolini's Fascist Party, which took power in Italy in 1921, that provided an inspiration and model for Hitler in Germany; support from both these countries facilitated the victory of General Franco in the Spanish Civil War (1937) and the emergence of a similar regime there. Other countries, under the mere pretence of democracy, were in fact also dictatorships. From this pattern only Britain, France, Switzerland, the Low Countries, Scandinavia, and Czechoslovakia remained exempt; as well as the Irish Free State, the product of the Treaty of 1921 which terminated the struggle of Sinn Fein with the British which had started with the Easter Rising of 1916. The new, independent Irish state got off to a rocky start, its constitution coming into force (6 December 1922) in the middle of a civil war; but it managed to preserve free institutions through a period of controversial constitutional change, and ultimately to assert its autonomy in the most signal manner of all, by remaining neutral (alone among the nations of the Commonwealth, to which it still nominally belonged) in the Second World War.

Economically, the twentieth century brought an enhancement of trends inaugurated in the eighteenth century and continuing in the nineteenth: a continued shift of population away from the countryside and into the towns in which continuously expanding industrial activity offered employment; the diffusion of greater and greater varieties of relatively cheaper and cheaper consumer goods, the production of which was facilitated by the rapid advances in science and technology which the two World Wars had occasioned as a by-product of competition in slaughtering efficiency; further huge improvements in transport and communications (flying as well as wireless telegraphy were inventions of the first decade of the century). As a function of the expanding role of the state in the typical Western society, the proportions of populations employed neither in industry nor in agriculture nor the traditional private services, but in some department of the state or its dependent organizations also greatly increased (though some nineteenth-century states, notably Austria-Hungary, had already maintained huge bureaucracies).

Between 1900 and (about) 1950 there emerged, finally, a quite new global arrangement of forces. Behind the Soviet armies advancing in 1945 into the heart of Germany there arose, all over central and Eastern Europe, regimes dominated by communist parties, in other words by totalitarian dictatorship. In the polemics soon heard in the West when disillusionment with the Soviet ally set in (which was almost immediately) these states were called Soviet 'satellites' and the line which divided them from the West was called the 'Iron Curtain'. Beyond the Soviet Union's Far Eastern frontier a long Chinese civil war ended in 1948 with the victory of the Communists; the Chinese regime some years later distanced itself from Soviet Russian patronage (as, in Europe, Yugoslavia's communist regime had already done), but nevertheless the world now contained a bloc of Marxist states stretching from the Elbe to the Pacific; and that bloc was soon to be enlarged by extensions in the Caribbean and south-east Asia. Scarcely had the world begun to recover from the Second World War, therefore, when it was divided into two mutually hostile, ideologically irreconcilable camps. Moreover, a new element appeared as soon as the Western powers began to disengage from their colonies, led by Britain which relinquished its huge Indian empire in 1947. This disengagement was not substantially complete until the 1970s; but already by 1950 the emergence of an ex-colonial, non-white 'Third World' could be foreseen, economically and politically backward, and resentful of the Western colonial exploitation to which its handicaps, with some justice, could be attributed; a world in theory 'non-aligned', but psychologically more accessible, for obvious reasons, to the influence of the non-capitalist, Marxist powers than to that of their rivals.

THE WESTERN STATE OF THE EARLIER TWENTIETH CENTURY

The bourgeois liberal states of the West evolved in the first half of this century in ways which, though not revolutionary in method, were just as striking in effect as anything produced by a dictatorship. This evolution was in some ways a forced growth brought on by the two World Wars. Huge numbers of people—far more than those involved in many earlier wars put together—suffered so much, and for so long, that they were able, in an age of easy communications, to make effective their common unwillingness to return to systems of excessive privilege on the one hand, and of economic insecurity and neglect on the other; though it is true that already by 1900, as has been seen, the basic directions in which the liberal Western state was moving were clear.

The general notion of human equality, the presumption against privilege, of course had very ancient roots, but had been stated most stridently at, and since, the French Revolution. The wars of 1914–18 and 1939–45 were decisive in the final overthrow of whatever remained of medieval regality. In 1900 every European state, East and West, with the exceptions of France and Switzerland, had a crowned head, but by 1950 they had all gone except for the north-western sector (Britain, the Low Countries, and Scandinavia) and Greece (where, however, the monarchy disappeared in 1967). Whereas at the earlier date women were excluded from the parliamentary franchise almost everywhere, and in some of them men had votes only if they reached a certain property qualification, by the later date universal adult suffrage was the almost invariable rule. The franchise extension, which as has been seen was already in progress in the previous century, owed something to the spread and improvement of popular education, as the strongest arguments of the opponents of democracy had been based on the fear of entrusting political power to people who were illiterate and ignorant. This improvement in public education, in its turn, was based partly on Benthamite and philanthropic opinions, but partly also on the correct perception that the health of a national economy increasingly industrial in character depends on the availability of an educated labour force.

The extension of the state's functions which had taken place by 1900, though dramatic when measured against the *laissez-faire* orthodoxy of 1800, was still fairly modest. Some areas of economic activity had already seen state monopolies, e.g. railway transport (though in Ireland and Britain the railways had all been built by private enterprise and were still privately owned); and a certain spread of state intervention had taken place in response to political perceptions of social need, usually however not going much further than the assuring of minimum standards. But over the following half-century, under the pressures generated by two wars and the concomitant rise of the parliamentary left (which the extension of the franchise in any case guaranteed, allowing for example in Britain the Labour Party to replace the Liberals as one of the two great political forces), official intervention and state paternalism had spread into nearly every area of life. As early as 1938 an Irish judge had declared that 'the days of laissez-faire are at an end';[1] a very

---

[1] J. Hanna in *Pigs Marketing Board* v. *Donnelly*, 1939 IR 413.

large range of economic activity was commonly either state-owned or state-monopolized. In 1900 the average European structures of social responsibility in the form of support in unemployment, disability, or old age, or the provision of housing and health services at public expense, were very modest; by 1950 the reality expressed by the new phrase 'welfare state' was general (though in some countries at a much humbler level than in others).

These transformations in the Western liberal state were accompanied also, after the Second World War, by a generalization of constitutionalism, parliamentary democracy (except in the Iberian peninsula), and the rule of law. The outrages committed in the 1930s and 1940s in the name of the state against elementary human rights reached such a paroxysm that, as soon as the war was over, significant movements took place towards strengthening the institutional safeguards against abuse of authority. The idea of objective individual rights and an objective principle such as the rule of law remained incompatible with the theory and practice (as will be seen) of Marxist-ruled states, but in the democratic West these values now received both doctrinal acceptance and practical application in an unprecedented degree. The new constitutions which formed the basis of the Italian Republic (1946) and German Federal Republic (1949), and were intended to give these countries a fresh start, rejecting the spirit and the deeds of the earlier dictatorships, each provided for judicial review of laws on constitutional criteria (and are today, along with the 1937 Constitution of Ireland, the only constitutions within the European Communities to do so). The European Convention on Human Rights and Fundamental Freedoms (1950), created in the framework of the Council of Europe which had the specific ideal of reconciling former enemies in a new European community of feeling, was the first instrument to establish a supra-national jurisdiction for the enforcement of human rights in the member states. Even in the one European state without a written constitution, and recognizing no authority in any court to invalidate laws for supposed conflict with the unwritten constitution—Great Britain—the courts have shown, since the war, a tendency to keep the organs of executive government in their place, and to interpret restrictively even acts of parliament in which they detect encroachments on understood standards of fairness and freedom.

THE STATE IN THE THEORY OF THE EARLIER
TWENTIETH CENTURY

All early twentieth-century theory on the state is the offspring of nineteenth- or eighteenth-century thought. Sometimes the parentage is to be located in the romantic and historical movements, sometimes in the sociology of Comte and Durkheim, sometimes in the scepticism of Hume; also, of course, in the doctrines of Marx and Engels and the ineluctable force of dialectic materialism.

The major representative of the first of these categories is Otto von Gierke (1841–1921). Gierke belonged to the historical school inaugurated in Germany by Savigny; but whereas Savigny himself, having at first proclaimed the organic growth of law as an expression of the nation, dedicated himself to the study and defence of the Roman element in the legal orders of his native country, Gierke was a passionate adherent of the Germanistic branch of the movement, which struggled in the years in which the German Civil Code was being incubated, to rescue for the future German legal order as much as possible of the indigenous German legal past. In this connection Gierke—professor of German law at Berlin in these years—stressed particularly the contrast between what he saw as the central element of Roman law, namely the individual and hence an 'atomistic' conception of society, and that of German law, in which community and 'fellowship' were far more prominent values. The native German idea of the 'group' he interpreted in essentially biological terms. So far from the state, or any other group, being the product of a supposed social contract, it was a real, quasi-palpable person, generated by the common act of its members. At the same time it is not just 'a psychological tissue, connecting the threads of individual minds', but 'a sort of higher reality, of a transcendental order, which stands out as something distinct from, and something superior to, the separate reality of the individual'.[2] In Gierke's own words, 'human group-life is a life of a higher order, in which the individual life is incorporated'; and this Whole has a higher value than the individuals which subtend it.[3]

---

[2] Ernest Barker, Introduction to his translation of Gierke, *Natural Law and the Theory of Society* (Cambridge, 1950), p. xxxi.

[3] Gierke, *Das Wesen der menschlichen Verbände* (Berlin, 1902), 10; cited by Barker (see n. 2).

This interpretation of the group, based on ancient German concepts of fellowship, applied to all groups, not just the state; and even the subordinate groups, voluntary associations of all kinds, which subsisted within the state's jurisdiction, did not owe their juridical existence to the state, merely the recognition of that existence, into which not the state but the collective act of their members had breathed a life quite as real as their own individual existences. Moreover the state itself, no less than the groups which it did not create but could only supervise, was bound by the object of its creation; and thus Gierke subscribed to something like the state keeping itself within the limits of those values which had inspired its birth: the *Rechtsstaat*, or 'rule of law'. Nevertheless it was evidently only a short step from this almost mystical conception of the state to its glorification; Gierke himself did not take this step, nor perhaps foresee that others might do so; but in the decades after his death, his doctrine of the state as the supreme group, with a real and transcendent existence, was put to sinister use: 'strengthened', as Friedmann wrote, 'in the eyes of German nationalists by its deduction from Germanistic origins, [it] formed an important stepping-stone towards that merger of the individual in the collective, which is an essential and vital aspect of modern totalitarian government'.[4]

A somewhat similar fate befell the teaching of his younger contemporary, the Frenchman Léon Duguit (1859–1928). Duguit stood in the relatively modern tradition of the sociology of Comte and Durkheim, and became well known above all for his doctrine of 'social solidarity'. What he meant by this was not merely a statement of the value of what we in the later century might recommend under such a phrase used as a slogan (though he meant this too). At a more fundamental level, Duguit was asserting that the interdependence of individuals and groups (including vocational groups, economic sectors, and classes) was a primary, unarguable datum of society, and that this fact was so to speak antecedent to the concept of a state. Indeed this very concept was suspect. The state was neither sovereign nor a person. The only reality, he thought, which existed within the word 'state' was the will of those who ran it; and this will, so far from being 'sovereign' or unbounded, should be directed strictly and solely to the maintenance and improvement

---

[4] *Legal Theory* (see Ch. 6 n. 13), 238.

(especially by way of division of labour) of the relations between society's various interdependent groups and interests.[5] This approach naturally led him to insist on the necessity for strict control of state authorities so as to guard against any abuse of their powers. But this did not prevent his doctrine from being taken up by the Italian Fascists in the construction of their 'corporative' state—so called because a central feature was a pattern of corporations representing both capital and labour in the same economic sector, and also of trans-sectoral corporations of capital and of labour. In the result (again in the words of Friedmann) 'Fascism and National Socialism radically altered the basis of Duguit's system, by subordinating syndicalism to a state even more powerful, godlike and arbitrary than any that Duguit had in mind, and abhorred'.[6]

The earlier twentieth century produced also, in the work of the Austrian Hans Kelsen, a notable depiction of a legal system in terms evidently in the long run inspired by Hume. Hume, it will be recalled, had drawn attention to the illegitimacy of deriving an 'ought'-proposition from an 'is'-statement, in other words, of purporting to deduce ethical or similar norms from mere observed facts; this had formed part of his demolition, at the time considered decisive, of the general natural-law position. Kelsen proposed the analysis of a legal system *simply* as a structure of norms, in other words of 'ought'-propositions, which could be, within its own terms, valid and illuminating, regardless of the moral quality of those norms, and indeed independent of all extraneous ethical, social, economic, or political values. The pattern in which, and the principle according to which, he disposed his norms will be outlined later in this chapter; here it is enough to say that Kelsen's scheme had the result of effacing the distinction between public and private law (and for that matter between any other pair of categories of law denominated by their functional areas) and between law itself and the state. For what is the state itself but a complex of norms? Each one of the norms that, collectively, amount to everything we mean by 'the state', is no more and no less an 'ought'-proposition than any rule located in any other part of the legal system; stripped down to this minimum quality, all are of the same character.[7]

---

[5] A. W. Spencer (ed.), *Modern French Legal Philosophy* (New York, 1968), 254.

[6] Friedmann, *Legal Theory* (see Ch. 6 n. 13), 231.

[7] On Kelsen generally see the section on 'Analytical Positivisms', later in this chapter.

The theory of the state associated with Marx and Engels—that at any particular time it reflects, through its laws, merely the interest of the dominant class, that the contemporary Western state reflected bourgeois dominance, and that once real socialism had emerged, after a period of dictatorship of the proletariat, the state and law would wither away—was official doctrine in the Soviet Union after its emergence in 1917. It received a certain qualification in the admission of Lenin that, even after the final triumphant emergence of socialism, something resembling the structures of the bourgeois state would need to be kept in place for a certain transitional period, until, so to speak, socialism had become second nature to everyone, its values completely understood and accepted, its goals spontaneously pursued. The best known of the pre-war Soviet jurists, Yevgenyi Pashukanis (1891–1937),[8] stated the classic doctrine, and that of the transition (emphasizing that during the transitional employment of the bourgeois structures no one should be in any doubt as to their true basis) as follows:

The constitutional state (*Rechtsstaat*) is a mirage, but one which suits the bourgeoisie very well, for it replaces withered religious ideology and conceals the fact of the bourgeoisie's hegemony from the eyes of the masses . . . The free and equal owners of commodities who meet in the market are free and equal only in the abstract relation of appropriation and alienation. In real life, they are bound by various ties of mutual dependence. Examples of this are the retailer and the wholesaler, the peasant and the landowner, the ruined debtor and his creditor, the proletarian and the capitalist. All these innumerable relationships of actual dependence form the real basis of state structure, whereas for the juridical [i.e. the conventional *Rechtsstaat*-related] theory of the state it is as if they did not exist . . . One must, therefore, bear in mind that morality, law, and the state are forms of bourgeois society. The proletariat may well have to utilise these forms, but that in no way implies that they could be developed further or be permeated by a socialist content. These forms are incapable of absorbing this content and must wither away in an inverse ratio with the extent to which this content becomes reality. Nevertheless, in the present transition period the proletariat will of necessity exploit this form inherited from bourgeois society in its own interest. To do this, however, the proletariat must above all have an absolutely clear idea—freed of all ideological haziness—of the historical origin of these forms. The proletariat must take a soberly critical attitude, not only towards the bourgeois state and bourgeois morality, but

---

[8] The date 1937 is not certain, but likely; in the Stalinist purges of that year Pashukanis simply disappeared.

also towards their own state and their own morality. Phrased differently, they must be aware that both the existence and the disappearance of these forms are historically necessary.[9]

FORMS OF TWENTIETH-CENTURY LEGAL THEORY

There is a huge contrast between even the first half of the twentieth century (not to mention the second) and, say, the eighteenth, so far as concerns the profusion of new legal theory, all of it generating in turn a vast critical literature of assent, dissent, qualification, and refinement. It may be suspected that this has a good deal to do with the explosion in higher education: the foundation of new universities, the growth of new law schools, the establishment of new law journals, the association of academic promotion with volume of publication—and, though this is far more marked in the later part of the century, the large increase in law-school staff numbers, and the fact that political involvement or identification seems, at any rate, to be commoner among academic lawyers than it was in earlier times. In other words, far more people now have the time, the means, the professional incentive as well as duty, and sometimes also the political motive to speculate on the nature and the roots of law, apart from merely teaching students the cases, statutes, and constitutions which formally compose it. But even if this factor had not been present, other factors would have led to the same result (though it might not have been documented in such stupefying bulk). These were the accelerated industrial and social change of the twentieth century, accompanied by the convulsions of two World Wars; the reaction against the purely formal, section-and-paragraph-based apprehension of law associated with the *école de l'exégèse* in France and the German Civil code based on the conceptual structures put together by the Pandectists; a new appreciation, produced in the peculiar conditions of the United States, of the relevance of the life of the courts to an understanding of the law they were supposed to be administering; together with advances in the relatively new sciences of psychology, sociology, and anthropology. The theories of law born in the early century, to the extent that they (for the most part) looked behind the black-

[9] *Law and Marxism* (London, 1978), 143–60; cited in Lloyd, *Introduction* (see Ch. 6 n. 72), 1079–81.

and-white letter of the law, could collectively be called, in the phrase used by Guido Fassò, 'anti-formalistic'. But formalistic presentations of law also appeared, most notably that of Kelsen already mentioned; the Marxist vision of law, if indeed it is possible to speak of this as something different from the Marxist vision of the state, was (as has just been seen) still in the field; and the ancient doctrine of natural law, driven back in the early twentieth century to small pockets of essentially Catholic resistance, underwent a powerful renewal among the ruins to which Europe was reduced by the Second World War.

THE 'FREE LAW MOVEMENT' AND SOCIOLOGICAL JURISPRUDENCE

An important influence in the first third of the century was the *Freirechtsbewegung* ('free law movement') in Germany, whose roots are to be found in a lecture given in 1903 by Eugen Ehrlich (1862–1922) and in an essay published in 1906 by Hermann Kantorowicz (1877–1940), entitled 'The Fight for Legal Science'. The movement (also called the 'free law school') was in essence a reaction against the excessively literal, and therefore often absurd and unjust adherence to the letter of the codified law, of which the son of one of the school's principal figures, Ernst Fuchs, recorded some examples from the period before 1914. One turned on a section of the Code of Civil Procedure, which exempted from distraint on a debtor's goods any things (*Sachen*) which belonged to him and were used by him as the tools of his trade; the German Supreme Court refused the benefit of the section to a fisherman too poor to own a boat of his own, but who had a half-share in a boat along with another fisherman, on the ground that the half-share, being incorporeal, was not a thing or a *Sache*. Another case resulted in a will being invalidated because of non-conformity with a section of the Civil Code; this required a signature by the testator (*Unterschrift*, literally, a 'signing-below' or 'subscription'), but here the testator had written his name level with the date, hence not 'below' the entire document. Hence it did not qualify as an *Unterschrift* or signature.[10] Such grotesque absurdities, the new school thought, were the natural result of the *Begriffsjurisprudenz*,

[10] Albert S. Foulkes, 'On the German Free Law School (Freirechtsschule)', *Archiv für Rechts- und Sozialphilosophie*, 55 (1969), 367.

the 'jurisprudence of concepts', which imagined it had constructed a seamless network of rules which answered all problems scientifically, and excluded all extraneous values. Kantorowicz intended the expression 'free law' as a sort of analogy to (religious) 'free thinking', in other words non-dogmatic, and by no means believed that judges should simply ignore or disobey a statutory rule; but he and the others did believe that no statutory system, however elaborate, could possibly meet all cases which could arise—incidentally the perception on which ever since antiquity the case for equity had been based—and recommended that where such an unusual case arose a judge ought to be free to apply the solution which seemed right, having regard to the nature of the area of law within which the problem fell and which the law was an attempt to regulate. Indeed there were areas in which the German Civil Code itself had specifically provided for the application of wide equitable standards; for example, by § 42 contracts were to be construed in the light of good faith ('Treu und Glauben'). But to the free law movement this was not enough; where the inevitable lacunae appeared in practice, a judge should have the same freedom as that given to him by § 1 of the Swiss Civil Code (which came into force in 1912), according to which, while the law was to be applied 'in all cases which come within the letter or the spirit of any of its provisions', still 'where no provision applies, the judge shall decide according to the existing customary law, and, failing which, according to the rules which he would lay down if he had himself to act as legislator'. In a larger perspective, the movement aimed at the modernization of law, 'especially by advocating the mutual permeation of law and sociology'.[11]

Unfortunately, under the National Socialist regime the idea of departing from the strict language of statute and looking instead at values (which were likely to be subjectively and unpredictably appraised) like the 'spirit' of the law—long ago condemned as dangerous by Beccaria—was taken to sinister extremes. In one famous instance it invaded German criminal law. An amendment of the German Criminal Code on 28 June 1935 imported a new § 2 which read as follows:

Punishment is to be inflicted on any person who commits an act declared by the law to be punishable, or which, *in the light of the basic purpose of*

[11] Albert S. Foulkes, 'On the German Free Law School (Freirechtsschule)', *Archiv für Rechts- und Sozialphilosophie*, 55 (1969), 367.

criminal law, and according to healthy popular feeling [gesundes Volksemp-finden], *deserves to be punished.* If no specific criminal law applies directly to such an act, it is to be punished according to whatever law, in its basic purpose, best applies to it.

The commentary of Schäfer and von Dohnanyi on the new German criminal legislation of the years 1931–5, published in 1936, spoke with apparent enthusiasm about the principle underlying this new article. The old rule—'nullum crimen sine lege'—was, they said, a mere relic of the Enlightenment, which had seen in it a safeguard against judicial arbitrariness; and it had become 'a sort of Magna Carta for the criminal'. But now,

in line with the transformation which has taken place in our attitude to the relationship between the national community and the individual, the legislator has given the protection and security needs of the national community priority over the interests of the individual, and given the idea of material justice precedence over that of formal justice. The legislator moreover declares himself unreservedly in favour of the principle of 'analogy', as we call it, in the broad sense, that he has placed by the side of the written statute a second source of law—or rather a source of recognition of law—of equal rank and value.

This change they summed up in the chilling formula that '*nullum crimen sine lege* has given way to *nullum crimen sine poena*'.[12] No wonder, in this kind of atmosphere, that Gustav Radbruch, who had been at first a supporter of the free law movement, and was after 1945 a vehement opponent of positivism,[13] wrote in 1939 that positivism appeared to be again the ideal of which Germans stood in bitter need; inflexible words at least gave certainty, and a protection against arbitrary oppression. After the Second World War the movement—which had received approval also in the Soviet Union—had disappeared in the West.

The doctrine of the original apostles of free law hardly amounted, in reality, to more than a plea for an equitable creativity in the courts, related to the facts of life. Ernst Fuchs tried to christen this approach 'sociological jurisprudence' (*soziologische Rechtswissenschaft*). This phrase is however effectively identical with one used by the Austrian jurist Eugen Ehrlich (1862–1922) in the title of his *Fundamental Principles of the Sociology of Law* (1913), in which

---

[12] *Die Strafgesetze der Jahr 1931 bis 1935* (1936), 184–5.
[13] R. Dreier and W. Sellert, *Recht und Justiz im Dritten Reich* (1989), 344 ff.

something much more radical was proposed. His central position was that law in the ordinary sense, 'lawyers' law', exists side by side with other factors in society which may heavily influence or even in practice override it; such factors, inasmuch as they are recognized and influence behaviour, are equally law and should be studied by lawyers; examples might be the practical role of poverty in making it not worth while to sue certain kinds of defendant, or of the presence of an insurance company standing behind other classes of defendant in inflating both the frequency of claims and the size of awards against them; or the social composition of juries; or the disuse or disregard of this or that code of statutory regulations under the influence of this or that social prejudice or economic impracticability. 'Lawyers' law', moreover, is only one of a series of normative orders which society itself has evolved, and which are historically prior to it; institutions such as marriage, succession, business relationships preceded all state regulation of them, and can only be understood in the setting, and with the forms, which society gives them. 'The centre of gravity of legal development', he wrote, 'is at all times to be found, not in legislation nor in legal science or in the decisions of the courts, but in society itself';[14] the organization of society, its values, its structures, its instincts, and habits— including its disobedience to what seems to be law—are the basic components of the legal order, rather than its set of ostensible rules.

In France, François Gény (1861–1938) demonstrated before the turn of the century that, in the application of the Code Civil by the courts, so far from its text being able to provide an automatic answer to every problem, it had been necessary for judges to draw also on their understanding of social factors, and other values, in order to make the legal order work satisfactorily. From this perception he proceeded, in his *Science et technique en droit privé positif* (1914–24), to distinguish the 'technique', the mere knowledge of the machinery of legal rules, from the 'science' which is the understanding of the non-legal, but highly relevant, values in the law's environment, in other words the sociological material which must accompany the strictly legal material in the solution of legal problems. This sociological material consists of data, what he calls *donnés* ('given facts'); while the legal rules which operate in their midst are merely a 'construct' (*construit*). These given facts can be

[14] Foreword to *Fundamental Principles of the Sociology of Law* (Cambridge, Mass., 1936).

divided into those of concrete physical reality (*le donné réel*), of history (*le donné historique*), of reason (*le donné rationnel*), and of society's aspirations (*le donné idéal*). Both the making and the judicial application of law require a role for these *donnés*, which are to be balanced in the correct relation. No formula or rule is offered for guidance in this operation, over which honest opinions may differ (though we might feel the average parliamentary debate on a new bill, together with the departmental studies and advices, and the politically coloured discussions within government which precede it, would approximate fairly well to the process of balancing Gény's *donnés*). Their analysis and elaboration are, no less than the work of the 'free law' movement and the early sociological school of Ehrlich, a testimony to the legal formalism against which they were a protest. This particular branch of legal theory, incidentally, scored a notable triumph in the world of practice: Gény's teaching, in an earlier phase, influenced the inclusion of the 'legislator-judge' concept in § 1 of the Swiss Civil Code, to which attention was drawn above.

The best known of the 'sociological' jurists in the common-law world is the American Roscoe Pound (1870–1964). Pound was impressed by the degree to which legal concepts formed in a simpler era, and aiming essentially at individuals and the adjustment of their relationships, were still in service in the early twentieth century, despite the huge transformations of society and the economy which had taken place, and the rise of all kinds of new and competing claims and interests. In an essay published in 1921 he wrote, in response to this perception, that it was now important to 'construct a theory of social interests which courts may use, just as in the past they have used the schemes of individual interests which we call theories of natural rights'. The central idea of the theory of social interests which he now advanced was that lawmaking, legislative or (within obvious limits) judicial, should be seen as a kind of 'social engineering'—a famous phrase, and, it may be said, a characteristic American piece of imagery, its deliberately unpretentious evocation of blue overalls and functional workshop contrasting with the elaborate abstractions of European jurists: 'For jurisprudence, for the science that has to do with the machinery of social control or social engineering through the force of politically organised society, it is no less true that individual interests are capable of statement in terms of social interests and get their significance for the science from this fact.' The engineering metaphor is explained in terms of getting those interests into well-oiled synchronism, with wear and waste minimized:

Looked at.functionally, the law is an attempt to reconcile, to harmonise, to compromise these overlapping or conflicting interests, either through securing them directly and immediately, or through securing certain individual interests . . . so as to give effect to the greatest number of interests, or to the interests that weigh most in our civilisation, with the least sacrifice of other interests . . . I venture to think of problems of eliminating friction and precluding waste in human enjoyment of the goods of existence, and of the legal order as a system of social engineering whereby these ends are achieved.[15]

In another work, Pound allowed that other agencies, such as one's household, church, school, voluntary organizations, professional associations, social fraternities, and so on, also performed a certain role in the social engineering process; but 'the brunt of the task falls on the legal order', with its political apparatus of regulation and compulsion.[16] As for what he had in mind as the kinds of social interest fit for the legislator's recognition, he listed, in his 1921 essay, six general heads. There is first the social interest in general security, i.e. the law-and-order area. Secondly, there is the social interest in the security of social institutions, such as the complex of domestic relations including marriage and the family; thirdly, a social interest in general morals; and fourthly, the social interest in the conservation of society's resources (not just material ones: he included here the interest in educating the rising generation). There is then, fifthly, the social interest in general progress, in which he included the spread of aesthetic fulfilment as a component value. Sixthly, there is the social interest in individual life: the freedom, dignity, fulfilment of the individual. Unfortunately this scheme does not, and cannot, offer a calculus enabling us to read off the respective weights to be attached to this or that interest in this or that setting. It cannot for example settle the perennial problem of the proper limits to the criminal law's rights in the enforcement of morality, nor tell us how far civil rights may be overridden in the interest of state security. It is essentially an exercise in analysing the

---

[15] 'A Theory of Social Interests', *Proceedings of the American Sociological Society*, 15 (May 1921), 16; cited in J. Hall, *Readings in Jurisprudence* (Indianapolis, 1938), 243, 245–6.
[16] *Contemporary Juristic Theory* (Claremont, NH, 1940), 8C.

task of the modern legislator once social and economic change had pushed him into activity in fields which earlier ages had not considered to be any business of the state's. It was also anything but revolutionary; it took as a starting-point the values of liberal Western society ('our civilisation') and its institutions, and took for granted the importance of their defence. The social engineer was evidently to be himself a solid family man, and one with a stake in the country.

LAW AND THE COURTS

Even more 'anti-formalistic' than the exponents of sociological jurisprudence were the founders of the school of American 'realism' which flourished particularly in the first half of this century. For them, as for the sociological jurists, the letter of the law had diminished significance. But the special feature of the 'realists', and the reason for their being so called, was that they pointed to the realities of the judicial process through which all law, in a case of dispute, must be applied. Disputes, litigation whether civil or criminal, was thus the terrain over which realist theory ranged; 'disputes', as one of the school's major figures, Karl Llewellyn, wrote, 'are the eternal heart and core of law; they do not mark its circumference, but they will always mark its centre'.[17] This concentration on what actually happens in courts, and why, as distinct from what a statute by itself might lead us to expect to find happening, is sometimes called 'scepticism', in the sense that it places a question mark over the dependability of the naked norm; or 'relativism', a less helpful expression, also intended to suggest the uncertainty of the black-and-white rule, the application of which, in any given case, will depend on a number of factors, not all of them legal or even predictable.

This court-focused approach was given its first and classic expression in 1897 by Oliver Wendell Holmes (1841–1935), who a few years later was to become (and remain for thirty years) a justice of the United States Supreme Court. In a paper entitled 'The Path of the Law' he suggested that, in order to see what the law is *in reality*,

---

[17] *Legal Tradition and Social Science Method* (1931); cited in Hall, *Readings* (see n. 15), 790.

one might adopt the standpoint of a hypothetical 'bad man' facing trial:

Take the fundamental question, What constitutes the law? You will find some text writers telling you that it is something different from what is decided by the courts of Massachusetts or England, that it is a system of reason, that it is a deduction from principles of ethics or admitted axioms or what not, which may or may not coincide with the decisions. But if we take the view of our friend the bad man we shall find that he does not care two straws for the axioms or deductions, but that he does want to know what the Massachusetts or English courts are likely to do in fact. I am much of his mind. The prophecies of what the courts will do in fact, and nothing more pretentious, are what I mean by the law.[18]

The object of legal study was simply 'the prediction of the incidence of public force through the instrumentality of the courts'.[19] The perception of law's uncertainty, of the potential influence, on its application in a particular case, of undeclared factors, has been thought characteristically American for the reason that there were factors at work in the United States which were unknown in England (from which the Americans had taken over the common law) or the European continent. First, the country was divided into a large number of independent jurisdictions, all administering common law, but all free to shape it judicially in their own way; secondly, the subordination of both state and federal legislatures to the Constitution as interpreted by the Supreme Court, which could easily—and not infrequently did—declare acts of those legislatures to be invalid, acts in reliance on which all kinds of expectations and commitments might have arisen; thirdly, the unprofessional judicial note supposed to be imported into the standards of the lower courts by the fact that the judges of those courts were popularly elected. At any rate, there was obviously more likelihood in the United States of circumstances arising where it would be absurd to talk of there being any pre-existing law at all. Jerome Frank (1889–1957)[20] saw this insight as being as revolutionary in jurisprudence as some epoch-making demonstration might be in the natural sciences:

---

[18] *Harvard Law Review*, 10 (1897), 457; cited in Lloyd, *Introduction* (see Ch. 6 n. 72), 717.
[19] Ibid.
[20] 'Mr Justice Holmes and Non-Euclidean Legal Thinking', *Cornell Law Quarterly*, 17 (1932), 568; cited in Hall, *Readings* (see n. 15), 368.

As Copernicus caused men to drop a geocentric notion of the universe and to take up a heliocentric notion, so Holmes's bad man will, sooner or later, compel all intelligent persons to acknowledge that the centre of the legal world is not in the rules but in specific court decisions (i.e. judgments, orders, and decrees) in specific lawsuits.[21]

Indeed the very idea that law needs to be 'certain' in the sense of perfectly predictable was ridiculed by Frank as a survival into adulthood of the child's craving for certainty and reassurance which he seeks in his father's strength and wisdom.[22]

Frank himself distinguished the realists into two groups which he called respectively 'rule-sceptics' and 'fact-sceptics' (it was among the latter that he himself belonged). The rule-sceptics are those whose disbelief in the certainty and predictability of law goes no further than holding that behind the 'paper' rule other, unseen and undisclosed, values are at work which will be likely to determine the outcome of a particular case; these values operate in the minds of judges, and the judges on whom the rule-sceptics concentrate are those of appellate courts. The more radical fact-sceptics accept, of course, the rule-sceptics' doubts about the reliability of the paper rule, but go further; the establishment of the bare facts of a case—which must take place before anyone purports to apply a rule to it—is itself a highly erratic process; all kinds of elements, many of them quite unconscious, may determine what a judge (for this branch of the realists, typically the trial judge) or jury will accept as the 'facts'. Not just inaccurate or forgetful or untruthful witnesses, but all kinds of prejudices operating for or against this or that witness or party, or even momentary personal dispositions of the judge or juror, may be decisive. Frank advocated much greater attention for the workings of the lower, first-instance courts and study of the fact-finding process; though, as has often been said, particularly by English critics, neither he nor any of the other realists can be credited with insights which are not already second nature to any practising lawyer, who does not need to be told how important such elusive personal factors are in the administration of human justice.

The work of Karl Llewellyn (1893–1962) may also be mentioned. His position (presented in rebarbative English) is that the law is no more than the pattern of behaviour of a range of official persons,

[21] *Cornell Law Quarterly*, 17 (1932), 578.
[22] *Law and the Modern Mind* (1930).

'official' being understood in a very wide sense: 'This doing of something about disputes, this doing of it reasonably, is the business of law. And the people who have the doing in charge, whether they be judges or sheriffs or clerks or jailers or lawyers, are officials of the law. What these officials do about disputes is, to my mind, the law itself.'[23] Llewellyn's special addition to realist thought lies in his picture of what he calls the 'law-job'. Every group, but of course the state in particular, needs a mechanism to ensure its stability; 'to *stay* a group, you must manage to deal with centrifugal tendencies, when they break out, and you must manage, preventively, to keep them from breaking out. [Thus] you must *effect* organisation, and . . . you must *keep* it effective.' This task is the overall Law-Job. But it can be broken down into separate law-jobs, which he lists as:

I The disposition of trouble-cases.
II The preventive channelling and the re-orientation of conduct and expectations so as to avoid trouble.
III The allocation of authority and the arrangement of procedures which legitimatise action as being authoritative [this includes the apparatus of judicial decision].
IV The net organisation of the group or society *as a whole* so as to provide direction and incentive.[24]

The manner in which these law-jobs are performed by those involved in them at different levels, and not a mass of mere rules, amount to the law itself; though it may be added that in later years Llewellyn came round to the view that there was, in fact, a fair element of predictability in the work of appellate courts at least, and that the presence of a number of 'steadying factors' made their decisions reasonably 'reckonable'.[25] In the result, then, American realism in its earlier phase seems to have stabilized around a sort of compromise perception: certainty in law, in the sense of predictability, is unattainable; nevertheless, a good measure of security is offered by higher courts genuinely attempting to apply objective norms, in an atmosphere governed by precedent; while the study of life's

[23] *The Bramble Bush* (1930; Dobbs Feny, NY, 1969), 12.
[24] 'The Normative, the Legal and the Law-Jobs: The Problem of Juristic Method', *Yale Law Journal*, 49 (1940), 1355; cited in Lloyd, *Introduction* (see Ch. 6 n. 72), 758.
[25] *The Common Law Tradition* (Boston, Mass., 1960); cited in Lloyd, *Introduction*, 747 ff.

realities and the way they can impinge on the administration of justice is encouraged.

SCANDINAVIAN REALISM

More or less contemporary with the years of greatest activity in American realism there emerged in Scandinavia a quite different school of 'realists'. To a certain extent the Scandinavians drew the judicial process into their accounts of law, but courts were not central to their position, nor were the economic and social factors which might condition courts' workings. They earned the name 'realists', like the Americans, because they proposed to explain what the law 'really' is; but they explained it essentially in psychological terms, in terms, that is, of a set of mental responses to words like 'right' and 'duty' which training and habit had developed among the subjects of a legal system and those who administer it.

The inspirer of this school was the Swedish philosopher Axel Hägerström (1868–1939), and the point of departure of its doctrine was his work on the Roman concept of an obligation.[26] Hägerström belonged to the empirical philosophical tradition which declined to admit the reality of propositions which could not be verified by the experience of the senses. Accordingly, talk of duties, rights, the binding force of law, and so forth, was empty, since such concepts depend on propositions which are really only assertions of one's own individual or group habit or preference. Of course it is true that these words and phrases evoke special responses among those who use or hear them. But then all one can do is to describe law as the totality of the collective psychological response of individuals— here is to be found the only verifiable fact, i.e. that if I am persuaded I have a duty, or believe I have a right, and so on, a certain mental state will arise in me, with probable external consequences. The emergence of such a mental state is probably the result of the conditioning and training I have received, but by now I cannot shake this conditioning off, and so a 'right' or 'duty' appears to me to mean something objectively valid. This conviction on my part is what is 'real' in law. The connection with Hägerström's studies in Roman law lies in his belief—very much in tune with the intellectual world

[26] *Der römische Obligationsbegriff* (Uppsala and Leipzig, 1927 and 1941).

of the early twentieth century, the era of J. G. Frazer's *Golden Bough* and a rapidly growing interest in anthropology—that for early peoples, including the ancient Romans, the use of what we would call legal forms was in reality the activation of magic, and the relationship between parties to a conveyance or a contract was in reality one in which one party believed he was exerting a magical or supernatural leverage or hold on the other. By the time belief in such supernatural forces had faded, people's mental responses to words like 'right', 'duty', and so on, had become ingrained, and the mass psychological reality which law represents today is simply what has been deposited by millennia of conditioning, first by magic, then by habituation.

Other significant figures in this school were two further Swedes, Vilhelm Lundstedt (1882–1955) and Karl Olivecrona (1897–1980), along with a Dane, Alf Ross (1899–1979). Olivecrona built on Hägerström's work by offering a view of legislation, of lawmaking, adapted to the notion of law as a communal set of psychological responses. Legislation, he wrote, may be presented as a process of 'commanding', but only in a very special sense; in the modern state there is no individual, or manageable group of individuals, who can be reasonably exhibited as uttering commands coextensive with the entire body of law. The law is certainly *felt* by its subjects to be non-optional, and it may be convenient to speak about it using the metaphor of 'command', but if so, the law's commands are depersonalized, free-floating, 'independent' imperatives; he compares them with the Ten Commandments handed out by Moses, regarded as 'binding' even though there is in reality no commanding will behind them (God's authorship of them he of course dismisses as a superstition). Accordingly, the force of the law is to be found in the *effect* on the subjects' minds, conditioned as they are by words of primordial magical import, and the legislature, in making new laws is simply mobilizing a set of such psychological effects: and the legislature, or rather the constitution on which it stands, is able to appeal to the deposit of primordial responses to concepts like kingship:

The effect of the attitude towards the constitution is first, that the constitutional law-givers gain access to a psychological mechanism through which they can influence the life of the country; secondly, that only they gain access to this mechanism and that everybody else is debarred from using it or building up another of the same kind . . . The effect of legislation is conditioned by the psychological attitude which we ourselves and the millions of other people maintain [viz. *certain feelings evoked by the deployment of words like 'offence', 'unlawful', and so on*]. Because of this attitude the law-givers can play on our minds as on a musical instrument.[27]

Lundstedt is regarded as the most extreme of the Scandinavian realists. For him, expressions like 'right' or 'duty' conveyed nothing which could be verified by experience. They merely served as labels, perhaps convenient ones, indicating the courses of action which would be taken, above all by judges, in different sets of circumstances; rights, accordingly, are simply positions of advantage which are such because they are generally protected by the state through its judicial machinery. The presence of the courts in Lundstedt's picture does offer a point of affinity with American realism, but in his rejection of legal concepts as illusory he was infinitely more radical. The latest of the school, Ross,[28] placed judges also in a prominent position, inasmuch as he thought, for example, that a law student learning about a norm in the legal system was really merely being trained to expect that the citation of such a norm to a judge would generate in the judge's mind a reaction which would induce him to make a particular kind of decision; but Ross, like the other Scandinavians, also refused to admit an independent reality in a legal rule. Needless to say, the Scandinavian realists rejected not only all absolute ideas of justice, but *a fortiori* the entire natural-law position; the absence of natural-law thought in Scandinavia is attributed by Friedmann to the non-existence of a Catholic element there.[29]

MARXIST JURISPRUDENCE

The classic Marxist view of the legal order of any state, as has been seen, is that it expresses, and subserves, the interest of the dominant class; apparently impartial values like the rule of law, or equality before the law, are mere cosmetic pretences disguising this reality;

---

[27] *Law as Fact* (1st edn., Copenhagen, 1939), 42–3, 54–6; cited in Lloyd, *Introduction* (Ch. 6 n. 72), 833–4.

[28] Many of Ross's contributions in fact date from the later 20th cent. In later years the Scandinavian realist movement, apart from the work of Ross, has attracted little attention. Strömholm refers to its 'short and now fading glories' in the preface to *Short History* (see Ch. 8 n. 36).

[29] *Legal Theory* (see Ch. 6 n. 13), 305.

but when classes finally disappear altogether, as they are supposed to do on the realization of perfect communism, then law and the state will be redundant and will wither away. In the years immediately after the Russian revolution of 1917, however, it was quickly understood that something like a legal order would have to be maintained, particularly when, in 1921, the 'New Economic Policy' was introduced in order to meet the production crisis which had resulted from radical nationalizations in the first era of revolution. This policy (usually called NEP) was a compromise between communism and private enterprise, which was permitted to survive in certain areas. Traditional patterns of relations, of the kind expressed through law, could not be dispensed with overnight. The official theory used for explaining this perpetuation of bourgeois forms was that the new legal order was indeed the expression of the interest of the dominant class; but this, of course, was now the proletariat. And this legal order would be operated in the light of that class's overriding objectives and destiny. This general position was stated as early as 1921 by the People's Commissar for Justice in the first revolutionary government, the lawyer Pyotr Stuchka (1865–1932); he summarized it in 1928 in a formula stating that Soviet law was bourgeois law minus the bourgeoisie, maintained by the state during the period of transition.[30]

The NEP was abandoned at the end of the 1920s and what had remained of private enterprise was eliminated. But meanwhile it had become clear to the ruling sections in the Soviet Union that even an undiluted communist regime would need some regular 'administration of things', even if it bore disquieting superficial resemblances to bourgeois structures; nor could the state be allowed to fall into disrepair as long as the Soviet Union was encircled by states based on a hostile ideology. It was in this atmosphere that, unfortunately for himself, Yevgenyi Pashukanis, already mentioned, continued in his writings to expect the ultimate disappearance of state and law, thus exposing himself to lethal disfavour. He was, however, the only significant Soviet lawyer to offer what could be called a theory of law which was to the effect that law's core consisted in the exchange of commodities:

---

[30] *Kurs sovjetskovo grazhdanskovo prava* (1928), 1. 69; cited by Fassò, *Storia* (see Ch. 3 n. 56), iii. 368.

The legal subject is an abstract owner of commodities raised to the heavens. His will, in the legal sense, has its real basis in the desire to alienate through a purchase transaction and to profit through alienation. For this desire to be fulfilled, it is essential that the wishes of commodity owners meet each other halfway. This relationship is expressed in legal terms as a contract or an agreement concluded between autonomous wills. Hence the contract is a concept central to law . . . The act of exchange concentrates, as in a focal point, the elements most crucial both to political economy and to law . . . If development began from appropriation, as the organic, 'natural', relationship between people and things, this relation was transformed into a legal one as a result of needs created by the circulation of goods, primarily, that is, by buying and selling.[31]

Outside the Soviet Union the most significant Marx-oriented jurist in the earlier twentieth century is the Austrian Karl Renner (1870–1950), who had the distinction of presiding, as Chancellor, over the provisional government which succeeded the abdication of the last Habsburg emperor in 1918, and also over that formed after the collapse of the Third Reich in 1945. Renner, in politics a moderate socialist, contributed to jurisprudence a study of the institution of property in capitalist society.[32] In this he pointed to the supposed process by which capitalists first developed from individuals who, having amassed a surplus from the sale of their own personal production, were able to hire others to expand that production, the fruits of which however were now to belong not to the physical authors of the extra production but to those who had hired them. Moreover, the original surplus was used in more subtle ways—contractual bargains, shares in enterprises, mortgages, etc.—to hollow out the apparent property of X and transfer control of it, effectively, to Y. By this process relatively small numbers of persons were able to engross large areas of economic activity. This very phenomenon, however, necessarily has a public dimension, and so calls for the transfer of such areas to public legal control; ultimately, for the domination by public interests of all the means of production, leaving to the private sphere only items for personal consumption. Thus Renner's Marxist appreciation of the process whereby the fruits of one man's labour are appropriated by another, and legal institutions used for the purpose of expropriation under other names, brings him to an unorthodox position (in Marxist

---

[31] *Law and Marxism*, 120–2; cited in Lloyd, *Introduction* (Ch. 6 n. 72), 1076–7.
[32] *The Institutions of Private Law and their Social Functions* (London, 1949).

terms), namely, the conception of property being split into two modes, radically differentiated on the basis of their respective economic functions. Renner's ideal programme accordingly envisages the preservation of law, albeit adapted to this kind of split, rather than its disappearance. Indeed he acknowledged—pointing to the manifold interventions already made by the state, since the end of the *laissez-faire* era, for social purposes, and tending to limit the ancient freedoms of capitalist power—that the process had in a way already been inaugurated.

NATURAL LAW

In the nineteenth century natural-law theory had disappeared from every school of thought not directly influenced by the Catholic Church (which in 1879 had declared the teaching of St Thomas Aquinas to be its own official doctrine). In the twentieth it continued to flourish in Catholic environments; but also experienced, particularly in the period immediately after the Second World War, a powerful revival not confined to the specifically Catholic World.

In the newly independent Irish state, unique in this respect among Western countries, natural law actually attained a certain status in the secular legal system; this was undoubtedly due to the overwhelmingly Catholic environment, the effortless influence of the Catholic Church, and the Catholic upbringing and convictions of most of the legislature and judiciary. A remarkable declaration for natural law in the full Thomistic sense was made in 1934 by the chief justice, Hugh Kennedy,[33] in his dissenting judgment in *The State (Ryan)* v. *Lennon*.[34] This case concerned the validity of the amending act which had interpolated a new article into the Constitution of the Irish Free State; although ostensibly a constitutional article, it was in substance an elaborate and drastic public safety act, which not only provided for a special court of army officers to try persons charged with a range of (essentially subversive) offences, but so constructed their jurisdiction as to permit them to inflict any sentence, even one greater than that

[33] Formerly the legal adviser of the provisional government (1921–2) and a member of the committee which drafted the Constitution, then the state's first attorney general.
[34] 1935 IR 170.

provided by law, up to and including the death sentence, where they thought this 'expedient'; and brought within that jurisdiction any offence whatever, even one committed before the amending act was passed, in respect of which a Minister certified that he believed it had been committed with the object of 'impairing or impeding the machinery of government or the administration of justice'.[35] The chief justice held the amending act to be invalid on the following ground:

The Constituent Assembly[36] [conferred] on the Oireachtas [an amending] power . . . but that power is limited and circumscribed . . . In the first place, what I may describe as an overall limitation arises in this way. The Constituent Assembly declared in the forefront of the Constitution Act . . . that all lawful authority comes from God to the people . . . It follows that every act, whether legislative, executive or judicial, in order to be lawful under the Constitution, must be capable of being justified under the authority thereby declared to be derived from God. From this it seems clear that, if any legislation of the Oireachtas . . . were to offend against that acknowledged ultimate Source from which the legislative authority has come through the people to the Oireachtas, as, for example, if it were repugnant to the Natural Law, such legislation would be necessarily unconstitutional and invalid, and it would be, therefore, absolutely null and void and inoperative.

On this criterion he found repugnant the aspects of the new law mentioned above. The English constitutional lawyer, O. Hood Phillips, in a contemporary comment called this 'eloquent judgment' a 'tribute to the continued vitality of natural law theories'.[37] As a judicial declaration of faith it remained isolated (until the 1960s, as will be seen in Chapter 10). Nevertheless, the year of the chief justice's utterance was that in which work started on the drafting of a new and more elaborate constitution, which was enacted by plebiscite in 1937; this not only recognized God as the source of all lawful authority, but stated several fundamental personal rights in terms which clearly acknowledged their source in the law of nature. Article 41 declares the Family to be the 'natural primary and fundamental unit group of Society, and a moral institution possessing inalienable and imprescriptible rights, antecedent and

---

[35] This military tribunal however did not make use of its most extreme powers.

[36] i.e. the Dáil, which had no legal standing in the eye of the regular law, but which nevertheless was accepted as having enacted the Constitution.

[37] *Law Quarterly Review*, 52 (1935), 214.

superior to all positive law'; Article 42 calls the Family the 'primary and natural educator of the child' and guarantees to respect the 'inalienable right and duty of parents' in this connection; and Article 43 acknowledges that 'man, in virtue of his rational being, has the natural right, antecedent to positive law, to the private ownership of external goods'.

Academic natural-law theory in the Catholic world in this era is best represented by Jacques Maritain (1882–1972), who was one of a circle including several celebrated musicians, artists, and writers (e.g. Stravinsky, Rouault, Cocteau), and who after his conversion to the Church devoted himself, in his professorship at the Catholic university of Paris, to the revival of the doctrines of St Thomas Aquinas and their application to the modern world. Since man, he wrote, is

endowed with intelligence and determines his own ends, it is for him to attune himself to the ends that are necessarily demanded by his nature. This means that there is, by force and virtue of human nature itself, an order or disposition which human reason can discover and according to which the human will must act in order to attune itself to the essential and necessary ends of the human being. The unwritten law, or natural law, is nothing more than that.[38]

The maxim that one must do good and avoid evil is not the natural law itself so much as its 'preamble and principle'. Its concrete application may and must vary, but even then retains its character as natural law as 'a right or a duty existing for certain men by reason of the human and contingent regulations proper to the social group of which they are a part'. As an example of this natural law with variable content he takes the institution of property:

The right to the private ownership of material goods pertains to natural law, in so far as mankind is naturally entitled to possess for its own common use the material goods of nature; it pertains to the law of nations, or *ius gentium*, in so far as reason necessarily concludes in the light of the conditions naturally required for their management and for human work that for the sake of the common good those material goods must be privately owned. And the particular modalities of the right to private ownership, which vary according to the form of a society and the state of the development of its economy, are determined by positive law.[39]

[38] *Man and the State* (London, 1954), 78.   [39] Ibid. 91.

Outside the Catholic world the usual attitude to the idea of a transcendent natural law was dismissive. The pre-Revolution Russian jurist N. M. Korkunov attributed belief in natural law to the ancient philosophical error of supposing that to everything conceived in the mind, some reality must correspond: 'The notion of natural law springs from the simple antithesis to variable law which we recognise in our experience, and from the tendency of the mind to attribute external reality to all our notions.'[40] The Italian Vilfredo Pareto thought, in the manner of Bentham, that natural law was 'simply that law of which the person using the phrase approves'.[41] Justice Oliver Wendell Holmes saw the persistence of natural-law ideas as due to the fact that 'there is in all men a demand for the superlative . . . It seems to me that this demand is at the bottom of the philosophers' effort to prove that truth is absolute, and of the jurist's search for criteria of universal validity which he collects under the head of natural law'.[42]

Yet in the early years of the century, even in quarters not under Catholic influence, there was already a certain stirring, a certain reaction against positivism, a certain search for the criteria which Holmes had described. Even Holmes himself, in the paper which has just been quoted, accepted that, at any rate on the assumption that Western man and society were to survive in the form they appeared to value, certain kinds of legal rule would necessarily, and to that extent 'naturally', be entailed and would be accepted as indispensable:

No doubt it is true that, so far as we can see ahead, some arrangements and the rudiments of familiar institutions seem to be necessary elements in any society that may spring from our own, and that would seem to us to be civilised [*he gave as instances the regulation of the relations between the sexes, individual property, security of contract, protection of the person*] . . . As an arbitrary fact people wish to live, and we say with various degrees of certainty that they can do so only on certain conditions. To do it they must eat and drink. That necessity is absolute. It is a necessity of less degree, but practically general, that they should live in society. If they live in society, so far as we can see, there are further conditions. [*Rules of some kind must result, even if based merely on the individual's fear that his neighbours will 'put the screws' on him if he disturbs the common safety.*] I not only accept

---

[40] *General Theory of Law* (Boston, Mass., 1909); Hall, *Readings* (see n. 15), 262–3.
[41] *The Mind and Society*, 4 vols., tr. A. Bongiorno and A. Livingston (London, 1935); Hall, *Readings*, 265.
[42] 'Natural Law', *Harvard Law Review*, 32 (1918), 40; Hall, *Readings*, 259.

the rules, but come in time to accept them with sympathy and emotional affirmation, and begin to talk about duties and rights.[43]

This is hardly natural-law theory, or at any rate it is too pedestrian and demystified to belong in its main stream. None the less, it bears a very strong resemblance to what H. L. A. Hart forty years later would present as a natural law of 'minimum content'. So too does the proposal of François Gény, advanced at about the same time as Holmes was writing, to identify a sort of natural law in 'the nature of things'; this 'irreducible natural law', equivalent to respect for the 'given facts' or *donnés* mentioned earlier, is 'the sum of the rules of law drawn by reason from the nature of things' and 'the precepts of human external conduct which arise from the ideas of moral perfection, utility, and suitability' in the light of those 'given facts'.[44] Reaction against code-centred positivism emerged also in Germany and Italy, where Rudolf Stammler (1856–1938) and Giorgio Del Vecchio (1878–1970) respectively proposed theories, if not of natural law, at least of legal idealism. Stammler's highly abstract theory centred on justice, which he called 'right law' (*richtiges Recht*); this 'right law' in turn amounted to 'natural law with variable content'; in other words, a purely formal conception, suggesting no particular rules, even the most general.[45] Del Vecchio, on the other hand, came very close to traditional natural-law notions in placing the autonomy of the individual in the centre of his theory of justice; the maximizing of the human being's capacity for free development, and the protection of the rights which naturally belonged to him because entailed by this end, was the main business of the state; the state, indeed, had no title to any activity incompatible with this purpose, which was its only justification for existence; and he described a state which acted contrary to justice in this sense as a 'delinquent state'.[46] Even in England, this revival of legal idealism found an echo; C. K. Allen thought that 'the New Natural Law' did not really say anything very new, but it had been valuable in 'counteract[ing] the tendency to exaggerate the purely historical and fortuitous circumstances of legal growth, at the expense of the moral principles from which law

---

[43] Ibid.
[44] *Science et technique en droit privé postif*, 4 vols. (Paris, 1914–24), ii, §§ 176–7.
[45] See Friedmann, *Legal Theory* (Ch. 6 n. 13), 179 ff.
[46] For Del Vecchio's later Fascist affiliations see ibid. 189.

may sometimes be judicially separated, but can never be divorced *a vinculo matrimonii*.[47]

In the period immediately following the Second World War, with the recent horrors fresh in the world's mind, the revival of natural-law thought moved into a higher gear. A significant figure at this juncture was the highly respected German jurist Gustav Radbruch (1878–1949), who had been briefly Minister for Justice under the Weimar Republic, and was at the end of his life involved in the drafting of the Constitution, or 'Basic Law', for the new German Federal Republic. Deeply religious (though not committed to any particular Christian denomination), a humanist by training, tolerant by temperament, in politics a lifelong social democrat, he was appalled by what had happened in Germany since 1933. Although he had earlier approved the 'free law' movement, he wrote in a lecture course published in 1947 that the Nazi regime had 'done a very complete job in taking over for its own ends' the ideas of that movement, not just in supplying the law's commissions, but in overriding law altogether. As for positivism, the doctrine that law was whatever a statute said had rendered German justice helpless when confronted with cruelty and injustice once these wore statutory vesture. What now was to be said of crimes committed during the Nazi period under cover of such laws? The objection to punishing the criminals (based on the impermissibility of retroactive penal justice) could be overcome only if one simply said that the post-war decrees invalidating Nazi laws did not qualify as retroactive penal sanctions because 'even though [those decrees] themselves were not in force, their *content* was already binding before those deeds were committed; and in their content such rules correspond to a law which is above statute, however one may like to describe it: the law of God, the law of nature, the law of reason'. In his own reaction and in that of others, Radbruch saw a revival of belief in a transcendent law by which evil positive laws may be condemned as 'legal injustice'. He ended this final lecture by reminding his students that, once upon a time, the title of this course in the syllabus had been 'The Law of Nature'.[48] Such sentiments, no longer associated necessarily with any denominational religious belief, underlay both the judicial review features of the new German

[47] *Law in the Making* (see Ch. 6 n. 39), 27.
[48] *Vorschule der Rechtsphilosophie* (Willsbach, 1947), § 36: this section is entitled 'Supra-statutory Law' (*Übergesetzliches Recht*).

and Italian Constitutions and the 1950 European Convention on Human Rights and Fundamental Freedoms.

LAW AND THE PHILOSOPHY OF HISTORY

The idea that history can be interpreted as unfolding according to a pattern, or in response to 'laws', is found in various forms since classical antiquity; studies in this area have been called 'philosophy of history' since the eighteenth century (Voltaire originated the phrase). The philosophies of both Hegel and Marx represent contributions to this category of thought. In the earlier twentieth century, especially in the period immediately after the First World War, there was strong public interest in the genre, of which the most elaborate example was Arnold Toynbee's twelve-volume *Study of History* (1934–61). In Germany there appeared between 1918 and 1922 a work entitled *Der Untergang des Abendlandes* ('The Decline of the West') which enjoyed a peculiar vogue during the following couple of decades; its author, Oswald Spengler (1880–1936), offered a pattern explaining the rise and fall of societies, a scheme not confined to the youth and maturity of a culture, but providing a pathology of decay as well. The contemporary condition of Western civilization he classified as moribund, which found some echo in the mood of the time. His scheme included an account of the role of law, which passes in any particular culture through similar phases of youth, maturity, and senile decay. His panorama of Western legal history—from which he regarded English law as an exceptional and fortunate deviation—is idiosyncratic as well as eccentrically expressed. It contains three phases, the last of them not yet complete. The first phase is essentially Roman; and Roman law grew out of the life, practice, and experience of the Roman people. Its vigorous period was that in which it remained connected with this real life. With the later Roman empire, however, the second phase began, highlighted by the shift of the empire's centre of gravity eastward; many of the leading late classical jurists were natives of the Levant, so he called this phase 'Aramaean' or 'Arabian'. This period of 'orientalization' is characterized by a petrification of the Roman law into formulas whose effect was felt as magical rather than rational or suggested by day-to-day practical necessity; the whole law is a sort of oracle which may not be arbitrarily changed; hence the unacknowledged interpolations of Justinian's compilers (those exponents of 'Arabian jurisprudence') are 'secret modifications which outwardly kept up the fiction of unalterability' of the canonical texts. The third phase arrives with the Germanization of the West and the 'unfortunate accident' by which Justinian's law was rediscovered there; the West, instead of permitting its own native systems of Germanic law to evolve in response to its own practical needs, took over this petrified code (quite unsuitable as it was, having evolved in totally different social and economic conditions) and applied it by main force to its own subjects. This amounted to 'the highly civilised law of an aged culture being forced upon the springtime of a young one'. The more natural course, and one which Spengler now advocated, would have been 'to build up *our* law out of *our* experiences'; what he meant by this was the shaping of institutions to fit not the 'static', person-centred conditions of antiquity, but the 'dynamic' real forces important in the modern world: the potentialities of creativity, inventiveness, organization, and enterprise.[49] It may be added that Spengler, though no Marxist, saw the shape of law as dictated by the dominant sector of any society:

Law always contains in abstract form the world-picture of its author, and every historical world-picture includes a social and economic *tendency* dependent, not upon what this man or that thinks, but upon the practical intention of the class which in fact commands power and, with it, the making of laws. Every law is established by a class in the name of the generality . . . Law is the property of the powerful. Their law is the law of all.[50]

LEGAL ANTHROPOLOGY

In Chapter 8 it was seen that nineteenth-century enthusiasm for anthropological inquiry and evolution theory had the effect of producing a new branch of legal study in which the work of Sir Henry Maine was the most prominent. This new legal science made headway in the twentieth century with the spread of field-work among contemporary primitive societies. Although Maine's ideas were largely discredited, a strong emphasis was still placed on the

[49] *The Decline of the West* (Knopf edn.), ii. 60–83.
[50] Ibid. 64, 345.

enterprise of identifying patterns in legal evolution. Thus the Russian[51] legal historian Paul Vinogradoff (1854–1925) thought work in this direction up to the time of his writing (1920) suggested chronological strata in the evolution of law, beginning with 'totemistic' society (in which human associations are built on supposed shared magical affinity with some animal or other natural object), evolving then through tribal law, civic law (i.e. the law of a city-state), 'medieval law in its combination as canon and feudal law', 'individualistic', and then finally 'socialistic' jurisprudence;[52] a scheme which, as Friedmann observed, combined elements of both Maine and Dicey.

It was about this time that there was a great increase in the volume and sophistication of field-work among the primitive peoples still to be found in the world; the results of this work could now be added to what was yielded to modern scholarship by the discovery and decipherment of law-codes far more ancient than anything so far known (in 1902 the laws of the Babylonian ruler Hammurabi (*c.*2000 BC) were unearthed and published; in the late 1940s the evidence of even older laws, those of Eshnuna (*c.*2250 BC) were added from the same region). The Polish ethnographer Bronislaw Malinowski (1884–1942) laid particular emphasis on the importance of the new field-work, pointing out that the findings of the modern specialist were simply not available at the time when Maine or the early German students of primitive law were writing.[53] The English lawyer A. S. Diamond summarized the dual task of legal anthropology in his criticism of Maine: 'such a title as Ancient Law [*he wrote*] fails to indicate the important truth that the study of the origins of law must look for its evidence to the beginnings of law both as we know of them in the past and as we see them in the present'.[54]

In 1915 the ethnographers Hobhouse, Wheeler, and Ginsberg had published an influential book in which they had proposed a way of classifying early or primitive societies according to their method of obtaining food; thus they identified, on the basis that such groups relied wholly or mainly on the capture of wild animals

---

[51] After holding a professorship at Moscow he moved to England and a chair at Oxford (1902–23). He was knighted in 1917 and took British nationality in 1918.

[52] *Outlines of Historical Jurisprudence*, 2 vols. (London, 1920, 1922), i. 157–8.

[53] *Crime and Custom in Savage Society* (London, 1926), 2–3.

[54] *Primitive Law* (1st edn., London, 1935), 1.

or the gathering of wild fruits, a First and a Second Hunters' Grade; there followed, according as these groups learnt to cultivate the earth with increasing sophistication, First, Second, and Third Agricultural Grades; with a parallel development, in response to different environmental conditions, of a First and Second Pastoral Grade, which entered this collateral path at a point higher than the First Hunters. The significance of this pattern here is that those authors believed that to each level of development certain kinds of institution, including law or pre-law, were likely to be attached.[55] This scheme was taken up by the legal anthropologists. Diamond thought it revealed a kind of evolutionary pattern or process, played out by every society at different times and places. There was obviously no such thing as a chronologically simultaneous development among all peoples, but there was an 'order of important stages of progress': 'Some parts of the story are being enacted today in West Africa just as they were enacted 2,300 years ago in Rome and some 5,000 years ago in parts of Mesopotamia. The whole history has perhaps never been enacted in one place, for progress achieved in one country is transmitted to the inhabitants of another.'[56] But the character of the evidence now emerging was 'universal', and showed a 'uniform progress' everywhere and always, by which 'law advances with material culture'. As for the point at which we can recognize something that we would call law, most of our evidence came, he thought, from the Third Agricultural Grade—in other words the stage at which techniques such as ploughing and irrigation become known—and it is this Grade which tends to be found with its law cast into the shape of a code.[57]

As for the detailed conclusions arrived at by this generation of writers, they all tended to reject Maine's generalizations as being based on inadequate or misunderstood evidence. Diamond recited the salient Maine doctrines—the early identity of legal, moral, and religious rules; the developmental sequence of themistes, custom, oligarchic interpretative monopoly, codes; the subsequent progress through the modes of fiction, equity, and legislation; the early peoples' attachment to technicality and rigid formalism; the secretion of substantive law in the interstices of procedure—and denounced them all as being without substance and capable of being

[55] *The Material Culture and Social Institutions of the Simpler Peoples.*
[56] *Primitive Law* (see n. 54), 175 ff.   [57] Ibid.

disproved by evidence. The most misleading of Maine's conclusions he considered to be the idea that law had evolved from religion.[58]

Malinowski's most influential work, *Crime and Custom in Savage Society* (1926), was based on his living among and studying the inhabitants of the Trobriand islands near New Guinea. He found that the islanders' social arrangements were a lot more subtle than anything which we would call law, nor were they (as other ethnographers had thought) a kind of criminal law to which obedience was secured by magic, taboo, or punishment. The binding forces behind their conformity to certain patterns of life were, he thought, 'concatenations of obligations', 'chains of mutual services'. There were also 'self-interest, ambition, and vanity, set into play by a special social mechanism into which the obligatory actions are framed'. He predicted that, elsewhere too, 'reciprocity, systematic incidence, publicity, and ambition will be found to be the main factors in the binding machinery of primitive law'.[59] Another anthropologist working on Pacific islanders, H. I. Hogbin, came to similar conclusions in his *Law and Order in Polynesia* (1934). More recent research, however, differs in its findings both from these early twentieth-century writers and from Maine.

ANALYTICAL POSITIVISM

Austin's picture of law as a system of commands issuing from a sovereign and backed by a sanction encountered dissent commonly on the ground that it did not account adequately for several areas generally labelled 'law', or that his sovereign was an unsatisfactory construct. Nevertheless, the analytical approach to what we call law, that is, the effort to apprehend it independent of the historical, social, economic, or ethical dimensions which are central to the interest of other schools, maintained its position as, at the least, a healthy exercise; in the common-law world, indeed, the study of jurisprudence in the universities regularly began with the study of Austin. In this century the analytical-positivist approach has had a very notable exponent in the Austrian Hans Kelsen (1881–1973), born in Prague, professor at Vienna in the period of the First World War, in later life resident in the United States.

---

[58] *Ancient Law*, 4 ff.   [59] *Crime and Custom* (see n. 53), 63–4.

Kelsen's years in Vienna coincided with the extraordinary flowering of science, art, and philosophy which attended the last phase of the Habsburg empire and were concentrated in its capital. More directly connected with the direction of his thought was probably the situation which developed from the empire's disintegration in 1918: revolution, the rise of new states on the old imperial territories, the creation of new constitutions, generally therefore the problem of legitimate authority and its exercise. The 'pure theory' of law, which Kelsen had actually begun to expound from his chair as early as 1911 and for which he is most famous, he brought to maturity in this post-war period—when, incidentally, he had the major role in drafting the constitution for the new Austrian Republic—and ultimately published, in a book bearing that title (*Die reine Rechtslehre*) in 1934.

The foundation upon which Kelsen's 'pure theory of law' stands is the distinction, going back to Kant and beyond him to Hume, between 'is' and 'ought to be' (*sein* and *sollen*): to the former category the natural sciences belong, the 'normative' sciences (prescribing behaviour rather than describing it) to the latter. But whereas in another normative science, say ethics or even grammar, it is possible to state a norm or rule so as to convey what people 'should' do or how they 'should' speak, the legal 'should', or 'ought', despite its looking rather like one of the others, is not charged with any element of morality or propriety. It disclaims, so to speak, the carrying of any message other than its own bare words. And those bare words are reducible to the proposition, which can have any material content, that if fact A comes about, then the consequence is to be B. The entire legal system of any country is thus a mass of linked ought-propositions or norms and nothing else; such a depiction of law can be called a 'pure' theory of law because of its abstraction from everything except the naked norm; because it is a theory of law as it is, not as it 'should' be (on some standard perhaps of morals, or economic or social utility, matters whose value Kelsen does not deny, but which are extraneous to the law itself and to legal science properly so-called). The service performed for legal science is the provision of an illuminating and clarifying mode of analysis which strips down a legal system to its bare norms, examines their mutual relation, and shows the artificial and adventitious character of some traditional divisions of the law.

The mutual relation of norms is one of dependence. Every norm in the system depends for its authority on a superior norm. Thus the humblest application of law—say the infliction of a fine for prohibited parking—depends, looked at in its substantive dimension, on breach of a police regulation or local authority by-law; the power to make such a regulation or by-law depends on a parliamentary statute which confers it on some subordinate authority; the power of the parliament to enact such a statute depends on the functions assigned to it by the state's constitution. When this point is reached, and it is asked: on what, in its turn, does the authority of the constitution depend, the answer which must be given is one which crosses the frontier, out of the strictly legal sphere, and enters the sphere, perhaps, of group psychology or sheer political force (or inertia), namely, some proposition such as 'One should obey the constitution'. This ultimate proposition, laying thus somewhat outside the legal order, Kelsen called the 'basic norm' (*Grundnorm*). A similar chain of norms, on the procedural side, will lead back from the parking fine to the *Grundnorm* by way of the statutory sections providing for the formalities of prosecution and conferring an appropriate jurisdiction on a particular court, then the constitution authorizing such enactments. If, on the other hand, one traces this chain not from the bottom up, but from the *Grundnorm* down, passing through the same stages in the reverse order, the process by which more general norms are followed by more specific ones, focusing, as the chain develops, on a narrower and narrower area, can be looked at as one of gradual 'concretization of law'; its ultimate, most individuated concretization, in the instance suggested, being the infliction of a parking fine on an individual for a specific offence. The image which results from this account of a legal system—which will accommodate every last department of it—is one of a series of steps which can be ascended or descended; this image was expressed by one of Kelsen's followers in the phrase 'Stufenbau des Rechtes' ('the step-structure of the law'). This step-structure, it may be noted, is not confined to statute-law (although of course Kelsen like all continental jurists was oriented primarily to a code-based system); assuming the penultimate authority of the national constitution—even an unwritten one—it is possible to reduce to Kelsen's model bodies of law consisting of rules of common law, rules emerging from a series of judicial decisions, or a single such decision, or the rules which tell us when such decisions are to be regarded as binding.

It will be seen therefore that Kelsen's legal 'ought', his norm, and the legal system into which the mass of norms cumulate, are of a purely formal character, admitting no appraisal deriving from sciences or value-systems outside the law itself (as so understood). This reduction of law is so extreme and so drastic, its purging of everything except form is so complete, that it is hard to come to terms with it at first acquaintance. Kelsen himself gave the best possible example of its non-contamination by values when he showed how, on the 'pure' theory, the traditional frontier between 'public' and 'private' law dissolves: seen in this light, 'private' law is revealed as just as much part of the seamless total system as 'public' law, and as equally an expression of the society's political premises:

That which we call 'private law', when looked at from the point of view of the function performed by this part of the legal system in the setting of the legal whole, is no more than the special legal shape given to economic production and the distribution of the product by capitalism; a function, therefore, eminently political and in fact a function of power. In a socialist economic order a different form of law would be required, not based on autonomy and democracy, such as the private law of today represents, but, presumably, one based on autocratic dictation, a form of law which would be rather nearer that of our present administrative law. Whether this would be a more satisfactory or more just kind of regulation must remain here an open question; it is something which the pure theory of law cannot decide, nor does it aim to do so.[60]

For the ruthlessly limited purposes of the pure theory, one kind of law is just as good as another; both are simply multiple staircases of norms. In another passage he emphasizes again the difference between moral and legal norms: the former are a matter for humans in their ethical or political dimensions to respect or to mobilize as seems best to them, but the latter exist on an entirely separate plane, on which 'any material content whatever can be law; there is no such thing as a human activity which, because of its content, is disqualified from being built into a legal rule'.[61]

In the passage cited above it was seen that law's skeleton, when revealed by the Kelsen X-ray in clear dissociation from all

---

[60] *Die reine Rechtslehre* (1934), § 45.   [61] Ibid., § 28.

surrounding ethical or other tissue, exhibits no essential difference between public and private law. But other conventional dualisms also disappear from his eerie screen. No difference can any longer be seen between subjective and objective 'right', for instance; what we call an individual's 'right' to something is only 'a special formulation, a personalised representation of the objective law' which is simply, in any such context, the norm or cluster of norms obliging others to abstain from interfering with this individual in this or that way.[62] The distinction of natural from juristic persons, indeed the idea that a natural person as such is a fundamental element in the legal system, are equally dissolved: the notion of 'person' is merely an 'auxiliary device created under the influence of anthropomorphic ideas', and is no more than a personification of the complex of legal norms affecting X or Y; and the legal quality of artificial or juristic persons (corporations and so on) can be resolved into the legal qualities of the individuals subtending them.[63] Even the doctrine of separation of powers scarcely shows on the plate; both judicial decisions and administrative orders represent the realization of public policy, and both are engaged in the process of 'concretizing' prior norms.[64] Finally, the distinction between 'the state' and 'law' also vanishes, because the state can be described only in terms of—and has no meaning apart from—the norms which set out its structure and mechanisms, and these, *qua* norms, do not differ in kind from the other norms in the total legal system.[65]

It has often been remarked that, despite this stripping-down of a legal order to its minimum formal essence as a complex of chains of successively dependent norms, Kelsen's model is forced, at the point of its initial hypothesis, into the sphere of those very elements—psychology, ethics, social behaviour, and so on—which lower down the hierarchy of norms are so rigorously excluded. His original suggestion as to the nature of the *Grundnorm*, far from clear anyway, does not dispose of this problem (if indeed it is a problem, as his scheme is coherent and illuminating in spite of it). The same difficulty (again, if it really is one) surrounds his condition for the existence of a legal order and so of a *Grundnorm*, very necessary to get straight in order to make sense, in his terms, of a revolution: namely, that it should be generally effective in that human behaviour conforms by and large to the legal order in

---

[62] *Die reine Rechtslehre* (1934), § 26.
[63] Ibid., § 25.   [64] Ibid., § 31.   [65] Ibid., § 41.

question.[66] This is an appeal to the standards of public international law, by which revolutionary regimes are recognized on that criterion, but, apart from introducing the problem of where international law is to be accommodated in his total scheme it again cannot avoid recourse to extra-legal factors in order to measure the effectiveness required for a legal order to exist and so for a *Grundnorm* to be presupposed.

CRIMINAL LAW AND PUNISHMENT

The penal theory of the earlier twentieth century could not feel entitled to the ancient certainties about human wickedness; the difficulties surrounding the subject, wrote the leading English author on criminal law, C. S. Kenny, had grown greater since the time even of the reformer Sir Samuel Romilly, not less. The development of the science of criminology had 'disclosed to us the unexpected complexity of the problems of crime'; the jurists of the eighteenth and nineteenth centuries had 'earned a just fame through their successful efforts to purge medieval criminal law of its aimless severities', but experience had shown that

they exaggerated the simplicity of the problem they were dealing with. They treated the human race as if all its members were possessed of equal moral responsibility, except a few abnormal individuals, all of whom were equal in their abnormality. And they supposed that, if punishment were but aptly selected, the threat of it would effectually restrain all human beings from crime.[67]

The new science of criminology now became a recognized neighbour of other sciences—medicine, sociology, above all psychology, which Sigmund Freud's work had endowed with special significance in this context because it revealed the role of the unconscious, the 'uncomprehended conflicts within the personality', which could inflict damage on the mental constitution and might issue in anti-social behaviour of a kind to attract criminal punishment on traditional standards.[68] Genetic biology, too, was now recognized as relevant to the study of criminal behaviour. The

---

[66] *General Theory of Law and the State*, 119.
[67] *Outlines of Criminal Law* (12th edn., Cambridge, 1926), 516–17.
[68] Margery Fry, *Arms of the Law* (London, 1951), 64–5.

pioneer in this area, Cesare Lombroso, fell out of fashion; his theories as to the association between physical characteristics and criminal tendencies were refuted by an English prison doctor, Charles Goring, in 1913; his studies of several thousand convicts enabled him to disprove them. But other kinds of research took their place; for example, the study of identical twins, conducted in several countries, which showed a far higher concordance in delinquency than non-identical twins displayed (the point here being that *all* twins were likely to experience the same familial and environmental conditions at the same point in upbringing, thus making it possible to eliminate environment as a factor possibly accounting for behaviour, and suggesting that the identical genetic structure of identical twins extended to those elements determining their behavioural patterns).[69] All such studies were naturally mobilized in argument by criminal-law reformers, as all of them tended to diminish the moral imputability of offences to their authors, and hence to place a question mark over society's title to inflict suffering on a delinquent and to call the process justice.

The most conspicuous revolutionaries in this area were the 'positive school' in Italy, inspired originally by Lombroso. Central to its position was a refusal to treat all offenders as responsible, and a tendency instead to regard them as victims of their genetic inheritance, upbringing or environment. It was, as Kenny wrote, 'obvious that [in such theories] criminal law, properly so-called, disappeared from view', to be 'replaced by civil law in some cases, and by the art of medicine in others'. There were too many rational objections to so radical an approach. On the other hand, the era was no more successful than any other in formulating a firm theory on which to ground the infliction of punishment; according to Kenny, neither the contemporary (1926) English modes of punishment, 'nor the abstract doctrines which have given rise to them can be regarded as having attained a final—or even a temporarily stable—form.[70] And he cited Sir Henry Maine from the previous century, and a High Court judge and a former Prime Minister from his own, in similar confessions.

All the same, shaky and discordant though individual justifications of punishment might be, and all of them looking morally problematical in the light of the associations which criminology had

---

[69] Nigel Walker, *Crime and Punishment in Britain* (2nd edn., Edinburgh, 1969).
[70] *Outlines* (see n. 67), 521, 523.

established between delinquency and non-imputable background factors, some theory there had to be if courts were to have any guide. Accordingly we find Sir John Salmond listing four ends of criminal justice to which four aspects of criminal punishment corresponded: (1) deterrence of others, 'the chief end of the law of crime is to make the evil-doer an example and a warning to all that are like-minded with him'; (2) prevention, by disabling the delinquent temporarily or permanently from repeating his crime; (3) reformation, and here Salmond thought this feature would develop increasing prominence because of the tendency of the new science of criminology towards identifying crime with disease, thus 'delivering many classes of criminal out of the hands of the men of law into those of the men of medicine'; and finally (4) retribution, which 'serves for the satisfaction of that emotion of retributive indignation which in all healthy communities is stirred up by injustice [and] gratifies the instinct of revenge or retaliation, which exists not merely in the individual wronged, but also by way of sympathetic extension in the society at large'.[71] How the latter dimension of punishment is to be reconciled with the insights of criminology (which at the very least must counsel humility and caution to those making or administering criminal law) Salmond did not explain. Neither did Kenny: arranging his subject differently, he pointed foremost to prevention and deterrence (of the delinquent himself and others), but added to this two further purposes, namely, retribution, and also public edification, or 'the effects of Punishment in elevating the moral feelings of the community at large'. On retribution, he quoted James Fitzjames Stephen as saying that 'criminal procedure may justly be regarded as being to Resentment what marriage is to Affection—the legal provision for an inevitable impulse of human nature . . . The modern community, like those ancient ones which Maine depicts, measures here its own public vengeance by the resentment which the victim of the crime entertains.' But this vindictive aspect of punishment, he granted, was 'distasteful to the great majority of modern writers'.[72]

[71] *Salmond on Jurisprudence* (7th edn., 1924), § 33.
[72] *Outlines* (see n. 67), 32.

The Later Twentieth Century

Until a very few years ago it would have been possible to sketch the decades since the end of the Second World War as a continuation of the conditions which 1945 produced. They were marked by the confrontation of two power-blocs, and the allegiance of two competing ideologies: the Western democracies, whose systems are all variants of liberalism, though a liberalism which had come to accept a large degree of redistributive social support, as well as the state's involvement in areas of economic activity once considered outside its legitimate scope; and the professedly Marxist, authoritarian, one-party regimes which spanned the northern hemisphere from central Europe to the Pacific, with late outcrops in Africa and Latin America. Outside those blocs a heterogeneous array of states contained right-wing dictatorships, as until lately in Spain, Portugal, and parts of Latin America; authoritarian regimes, not classifiable in ideological terms, where the coup was the only known mode of change, as in many of the ex-colonial territories of Africa; and a small number of genuine multi-party democracies standing clear of alignment with either major bloc, of which India is the most important instance. The poorer, less developed areas of the world—the 'Third World'—usually with regimes of an authoritarian kind, tended to look rather to the Marxist bloc, less identified with past colonialism, for moral support than to the West from which most material assistance reached them.

This setting produced a certain world stability, in spite of wars such as those in Korea and Vietnam and the continual conflict in the Middle East. When elements of change began to show themselves, they did not (as a Marxist determinist might have predicted) occur in the West but in the Marxists' own camp. Dissent began to appear where before there had been only uniformity: a dissent now grudgingly tolerated or at least not repressed by liquidation or the concentration camp, and one which found an audience among populations whose economy, state-owned and centrally controlled, was falling further and further behind that of the West, with harsh consequences for standards of living. Countries formerly reckoned as Soviet satellites found a voice of their own, most notably Poland, where in the late 1970s successful trade union revolt, together with the election of a Polish pope, powerfully contributed to a resurgence of self-confidence. The Marxist states of Eastern Europe subscribed the Helsinki accords on human rights (1976), and while their performance in this area long fell short of what Western citizens took for granted, still there was a great improvement in personal freedom in most of them.

Since the middle of the 1980s this process has accelerated with dizzying, even unsettling speed, led by the Soviet Union itself, in which, under the slogans of 'openness' and 'reconstruction', something like a system of free electoral democracy as well as of free economic enterprise seems in process of establishment. At the same time the Soviet Union, by disengaging itself from the control or support of its former satellites, has hastened the demolition of Marxist autocracy in those countries, leading to a reunification of Germany and even to the prospect of including some of those states in the European Communities. But the whole evolution, which of course has had world-wide political and military repercussions, seems in many ways out of control and therefore unstable in itself and potentially destabilizing for the entire globe. Its general direction, inasmuch as evidently corresponding with the wishes of the peoples concerned, is benign; but its ultimate outcome is impossible to predict, as is, too, the interpretation which it will ultimately receive in this or that philosophy of history.

There is no question but that a crucial role has been played in these developments by the late twentieth-century revolution in communications. Cheaper and faster travel, but even more the pervasiveness of the electronic media, made it impossible to insulate people from new facts and opinions; and this has had political consequences in the West also. Here a whole new trend of dissent has been seen, in a form not known in the 1950s, much facilitated by the media which reflected and amplified it. Incapable of being labelled as communist fellow-travelling—at least without great injustice to most of its representatives—this dissent embraces a wide spectrum of interests without perhaps much in common except a rejection of Western axioms, and of the military and industrial strategies which Western societies have thought necessary for their defence and material prosperity. Probably the earliest movement to be prominent in this loose 'front' was the campaign against nuclear armaments; this has evolved in more recent times into hostility to nuclear technology in any form, overlapping with groups concerned about the cumulatively very negative effects of modern industry on the environment and the 'ecology' of nature; this strand of feeling takes an organized form in movements like the various national Committees for Nuclear Disarmament and the 'Green' parties. Intellectually interlocking with this trend there has arisen a very powerful movement against discrimination, whether racial—here of course connected with rejection of the tradition of Western colonialism—or sex-related, the latter branch of the movement issuing often in a strident feminism; real changes have taken place under its impact, reflected in law, in culture, even in language. At a deeper, less specific level there has been a mood of protest, among certain sectors of Western populations, against Western political habits and structures of authority; this was perhaps at its height in the late 1960s and early 1970s, with the not too clearly focused wave of student unrest in Europe and the United States, and protest against the Vietnam war. Recording, amplifying, perhaps further inflaming the temper animating all those movements were the media, now immeasurably more immediate and influential because of cheap and universal television reporting, with instant comment and debate: media personnel naturally regarding it as their business to report dramatic events, and often enough, too, presenting the phenomena of dissent with that slight leftward sympathy which seems to be, perhaps rightly, their professional psychological bias.

That part of late twentieth-century Western existence which the foregoing is an attempt to convey had and has such varied facets that it cannot be comprehended by a simple definition, and so Western verbal shorthand has had recourse, for easy reference, to a range of caricatures which point at essentially quite secondary, but regular external concomitants, such as newspaper allegiance, habits of dress, tastes in food or music, addiction to neologisms from psychology and sociology, 'non-judgmental' attitudes towards activity formerly or still forbidden by criminal law or social convention. These details merely add touches to an impressionistic picture of the late twentieth-century Left in Western society, an important contributor to the Western intellectual climate, and one to which some parts of contemporary Western legal theory appear related.

THE BASIS AND CHARACTER OF THE STATE

The general Western conception of the state has not for a long time taken the form of a simple picture like social-contract theory or a theory as to whether the state's authority is to be located above or below the ruler (though elements from those earlier kinds of thinking are part of the cement of Western constitutionalism). What can certainly be said about the modern Western state is that—in reaction against the totalitarianisms of the 1930s and 1940s—it has become less authoritarian, more 'user-friendly', no doubt therefore also weaker. Here, too, the media have certainly played an important part in bridging the gap between government and people and in enforcing a visible answerability on the former. It is possible to point, as well, to certain values, formerly less well articulated, which the Western state has come to accept without question, and has helped to entrench in institutional structures.

A much stronger recognition now exists that the rights of a majority, while they must include the determination of the state's general policy, cannot extend to invading a range of irreducible individual and hence also minority rights. This is reflected in the European Convention on Human Rights and Fundamental Freedoms mentioned in the last chapter; the jurisdiction of the Commission and Court established under it has now been accepted by nearly all the signatory states, and these organs have built up an impressive volume of decisions unfavourable to signatory states but accepted by them. These states, allowing themselves to be sued before an international tribunal not only by their own nationals but by foreigners too, have thus accepted practical limitations to their own sovereignty of a kind that the pre-Second World War states of Europe would have considered unthinkable.

Far more substantial encroachments on national sovereignty are entailed by membership of the European Communities (originally the European Economic Community set up by the Treaty of Rome in 1957). These Communities from the beginning aspired to goals transcending mere economic integration, including the harmonization of laws and the stability of general European standards of human rights; for example, consideration of admitting Spain, Portugal, and Greece was regarded as impossible for so long as those countries contained authoritarian regimes), and the Court of Justice of the Communities has begun to apply such standards in its decisions which are binding on all the member states.[1] There is now general agreement on achieving a full European union, though the timetable of such a development, and the practical dimensions which it would probably display, are not yet settled; the consequence for the sovereignty of member states is clear in principle if not in detail. Britain alone stands on older conceptions of statehood and appears to be against further radical integration, but her dissent is not enough to mask the widespread abandonment of pride of state.

Within individual European states there has been an equally strong move away from 'internal' sovereignty, by way of entrenching constitutional values against legislative or governmental attack, and opening up the processes of government to popular control and independent inspection. The constitutions of the new Italian and German Federal republics contain provisions for special courts to adjudicate on laws and to declare them invalid if found unconstitutional; a similar mechanism was grafted on to the Austrian Constitution of 1919. In Britain, although majority legal and political opinion and the strength of ancient tradition are against a written constitution or judicial control, a respectable body of feeling now exists in favour of something like the latter to enforce, even as against acts of parliament, a bill of rights. In France, where judicial control of legislation in the strict sense would be repugnant to the doctrine of separation of powers, a special Constitutional Council has nevertheless been created, which reviews, on constitutional criteria, laws while still in draft and there is a somewhat similar mechanism in the Netherlands. The originally Swedish institution of the 'Ombudsman'—an independent officer empowered to investigate alleged abuses of executive authority—has been imitated since the late 1960s in several other European states. In the United States there have been no comparable innovations, but the 1960s and 1970s saw notable initiatives by the Supreme Court

---

[1] The landmark case is *Firma Nold* v. *Commission of the European Communities*, 1974 CMLR 338, in which the Court of Justice of the Communities held that fundamental rights, as generally understood in the jurisprudence of the member states, formed part of the general principles of law which it would enforce.

towards ending discrimination, particularly that based on colour, and dismantling legal structures which the Court saw as intrusions on personal rights in the service of a religious ideology which it was not the Constitution's business to countenance.

There has also been, by comparison with pre-war Europe, far more use of direct consultation of the people by plebiscite or referendum. This mechanism was before the war virtually confined—a rare exception was the Irish plebiscite of 1937 which enacted the Constitution—to settling the future of border areas, such as Silesia (1921) and the Saarland (1935). But since the war, not counting referenda required by constitutions for their own amendment, the use of the referendum to decide some major issue of national policy has emerged in several countries. Even in Britain, the bastion of parliamentary supremacy, an *ad hoc* consultation of the people (which could have been of no legally binding effect) was carried out in 1975 in connection with European Community membership; equally ineffectual legally, though politically significant referenda were held in Wales and Scotland in 1978–9 in order to determine the people's wishes in regard to regional parliaments; and in Northern Ireland in 1973 on the issue of continued integration in the United Kingdom. In 1987 Italian voters decided on a single day six separate issues submitted to referendum.

Apart from these evidences of the late twentieth-century Western state's submission to formal controls, a sort of consensus has arisen that some things, even if not the subject of specific guarantees, have come to be characteristic of Western democracy, and indeed required by it. This can be seen in the Irish constitutional jurisprudence built up since the mid-1960s on the idea that there exist latent, unenumerated personal rights, which Article 40.3 of the Constitution protects in merely general terms,[2] but which may be specifically identified and enforced by the courts as occasion arises; these rights, according to the judgment which initiated the trend,[3] are such as are implied by 'the Christian and democratic nature of the State'. That a state of this sort will respect, for instance, the right to quit its territory at will was assumed by the President of the Irish

---

[2] '(1) The State guarantees by its laws to respect and, as far as practicable, by its laws to defend and vindicate the personal rights of the citizen. (2) The State shall, in particular, protect as best it may from unjust attack and, in a case of injustice done, vindicate the life, person, good name and property rights of every citizen.'

[3] *Ryan* v. *Attorney General*, 1965 IR 294.

High Court in *The State (M.)* v. *Minister for Foreign Affairs*[4] when he said:

> One of the hallmarks which is commonly accepted as dividing states which are categorised as authoritarian from those which are categorised as free and democratic is the inability of the citizens of, or residents in, the former to travel outside their country except at what is usually considered to be the whim of the executive power.

The general principle of freedom to leave was described by the German constitutional lawyer Reinhold Zippelius as 'rooted, in terms of political philosophy, in the conception that although a citizen may find occasional laws unacceptable while being ready to accept the system as a whole, once he finds himself fundamentally at odds with that system he should be free to withdraw himself from it'.[5]

Another proposition latent in general Western conceptions of the democratic state (anything else would have been inconsistent with the general honour paid to those who resisted tyranny in Germany in the years 1933–45) is the legitimacy of resistance to a system which violates justice and human rights; this is formally recognized in the German Constitution of 1949, of which Article 20, after reciting the principle of constitutional order and the rule of law, proclaims that 'all Germans have the right to resist whoever attempts to destroy that order, if no other recourse is open'. The practical value of this licence, should the occasion of invoking it arise, may be slight; but from the point of view of legal theory it is a strong restatement in modern terms of the medieval arguments for tyrannicide or at any rate deposition of the oppressive ruler.

Along with readjusting the relations of state and people in the ways just described, the general Western theory of government now attributes a strong social role to the state. It is seen as having the function of reconciling the needs and interests of classes and sectors, of abolishing structures of privilege or unreasonable restraint left over from the past, of promoting solidarity and mutual support among its people. The Constitution of Italy speaks in Article 2 of 'inalienable duties of political, economic and social solidarity' and in Article 3 of the 'equal social dignity' of all the citizens; the same Article requires the state to 'overcome the obstacles of economic

---

[4] 1979 IR 79, 81.   [5] *Allgemeine Staatslehr* (7th edn.), 381.

and social character which, limiting in effect the citizens' freedom and equality, impede the full development of the human person and the participation of all workers in the country's political, economic and social organisation'. The leading German writer of the theory of the state sees the contemporary problems of the state's purpose to be those of 'promoting the development of the human personality, social justice, economic prosperity and stability, assuring law and order and external security; [to be achieved by placing these objects] in a properly balanced relationship to one another, and establishing between them a correct scale of precedences and the best possible compromise'.[6] These contemporary conceptions of what the state is all about recall the pre-war teaching of Roscoe Pound on the status of law as a mechanism of 'social engineering' aiming to minimize 'friction and waste'. But in their emphasis on the importance of the human individual and the unfolding of his or her personality they seem also to echo the specific Catholic teaching, going back in the first instance to Leo XIII's encyclical *Immortale Dei* (1885) and beyond that to St Thomas, whereby the state has the function of providing the setting for this human development.

Catholic teaching derives from this doctrine an important political principle, that of 'subsidiarity'. What is meant by this is that, since the development of the human personality is to be promoted, the autonomy of the human individual and the area of his autonomy are to be maximized. Every function implied by society's existence is to be exercised by the smallest group capable of its exercise; the state, so far from assuming responsibility for every function, must devolve functions as far as possible downwards, the notionally optimal goal being the exercise by the individual of as many as possible of such functions at the highest practicable level of initiative and responsibility. As will be seen later, in the context of justice, this conception of 'subsidiarity' is an aspiration reached, by a different route, by the American philosopher Robert Nozick, who struck a very unusual note in this age by presenting in 1974 an elaborate argument for a 'minimal state' which would have retreated to the very modest area of competence which states still had in the mid-nineteenth century.[7]

---

[6] Ibid. 385.
[7] In his *Anarchy, State and Utopia* (Oxford, 1974), 26–7; Lloyd, *Introduction* (see Ch. 6 n. 72), 538 ff.

Western in its origins, but fundamentally at odds with the values nowadays commonly so called, is the Marxist philosophy of the state which, until very recent times, was still being vigorously professed by many writers in Europe and America. As has been seen, practical experience in the Soviet Union in the early decades after the Revolution had enforced the acceptance of a far longer time-scale for the withering-away of law and the state. In the earlier years after the Second World War not only did Soviet law assume aspects of extreme severity—as for instance in the infliction of the death penalty for 'economic crime', such as corruption or embezzlement in state enterprises—but the scope of law was extended so as to achieve what might be called a moral effect. Formerly the idea of morality had been thought (like law) to be a fetish, the mere expression of contemporary material forces; but now there arose the ideal of 'socialist morality', the morality which is obedience to the inner voice of social obligation; this morality, said the Programme of the 22nd Party Congress in 1961, would under communism remain permanent even when the state had eventually withered away. Meanwhile the law was mobilized to repress conduct denoted by a morally pejorative term: 'parasitism', an idle, socially useless way of life.[8]

Marxist theory had to digest also the apparent failure of its predictions as to the inevitable collapse of capitalism. Capitalism did not collapse, but, on the contrary, delivered models for the reconstruction of the broken-down economies of the socialist world. Long before the events of 1989, the more advanced of these states were admitting increasing elements of private ownership and enterprise as, apparently, the only remedy for the rigidity and inefficiency which seemed inseparable from a centrally planned socialized economy. In capitalist countries, on the other hand, the class cleavage which was supposed to be the root of inevitable revolution has been narrowed in many ways: by the social mobility which free or at any rate cheap education tends to promote; by generous structures of social support; by redistributive taxation; by large measures of control which put limits on capitalist acquisitiveness; in some countries, by a level of material prosperity among wage-earners which gives them access to virtually the same, or at any rate a comparable, range of goods and services as their employers enjoy.

[8] See *Natural Law Forum*, 8 (1963), 1.

Herbert Marcuse, who was a cult figure for a time in the 1960s, saw the last-mentioned feature in terms of technological advance enabling the ruling class to buy off the workers with 'consumerism';[9] other Marxists see social legislation similarly, as a system of calculated bribery, cynically intended to stifle what would otherwise be the irresistible demand for fundamental change. During most of the past forty years, however, the basic Marxist predictions have continued to be heard. In 1963 the Soviet writers Ioffe and Shargorodsky wrote that 'communism is a society that will have neither state nor law'; there would have to be, it was true, some 'normative regulation' even so, but this 'will not rest upon state compulsion but solely upon public opinion, the strength of the group, social influence'.[10] The American Marxist Richard Quinney was a little less positive in 1974: 'with the achievement of a socialist society . . . the state may no longer be necessary. And following this, there may be no state law.'[11] But as late as 1977 he had no doubts as to the fate of the capitalist world: 'We are reaching the end of an age. An advanced capitalist society with its dehumanising conditions of existence and its highly secular and utilitarian sensibility is coming to an end. The contradictions of the existing social and moral order and the personal and collective struggle are bringing about a new human history.'[12] Yet there has appeared a thesis by Christine Sypnowich, written in 1987, arguing to the contrary that 'law is not merely congenial to socialism. It is an essential precondition of its attainment. Whether or not a socialist society is stable and effective will depend on the stability and effectiveness of its legal institutions.'[13]

But since the events of 1989 there has been a retreat from Marxian ideology on law at the highest practical level. An essay by the Chairman of the Supreme Court of the USSR, Yevgenyi Smolentsev, contains in its 2,000 words no reference whatever to Marxism, and only one (heavily qualified) to socialism; if any ideology at all is visible in this article, so critical of Soviet lawmaking and law enforcement, it is well within the main European tradition, right

---

[9] *One-Dimensional Man* (London, 1964).

[10] 'The Significance of General Definitions in the Study of Problems of Law and Socialist Legality'; quoted by Lloyd, *Introduction* (see Ch. 6 n. 72), 1082–5.

[11] *Critique of Legal Order: Crime Control in Capitalist Society* (Boston, 1974); Lloyd, *Introduction*, 1090–5.

[12] *Class, State and Crime* (New York, 1977), p. vii.

[13] *The Concept of Socialist Law* (Oxford, 1990), 155.

down to the rule of law and the separation of powers, once rejected by Marxist theory as a sham and a superstition:

Democratic and humane socialism is only possible in a state ruled by the law which is based on two fundamental principles—the supremacy of the law and the division of power into legislative, executive and judiciary. Unfortunately, there was no due respect for the law in this country for a long time. It is clear to everyone that the attitude to law should be radically changed if we want to preclude new acts of arbitrariness and abuse of power and create guarantees against encroachments on human rights. The nihilistic attitude to law negatively affects the legal conscience of not only officials but also ordinary citizens. Instead of trust in the law, its strength, justice, and supremacy, people were taught for decades to trust in their superiors on whose will and team their work and life depended. Law could be of no importance at all . . .

The decision of the court can only be fair if the law is fair. If a law has grown outdated and does not take into account the changes which have occurred in society and its new requirements, a court decision based on this law cannot be trustworthy . . .

The court system also needs radical improvements. Under the undivided domination of the bureaucratic system of administrative management, the division of power into legislative, executive, and judiciary was simply impossible. Power was indivisible. It was determined and exercised by the very same bodies and officials who held its levers in their hands . . .

The loss of independence by judges was manifested in the almost complete disappearance of acquittal from court practice: when undecided, courts, instead of acquitting the innocent, preferred to return cases for further investigation to procurators' offices where they were just dropped as a rule . . . [But] the independence of the judges is being restored and the quality of the personnel has started to improve, although this process is rather slow . . . Our court reform . . . is aimed at guaranteeing the independence of the judiciary authority, and . . . strengthening the foundation of a law-based state.

THE CONCEPT OF LAW

Since the time when Austin, following Bentham, had defined law as the command of a sovereign, addressed to those habitually obedient to him, and backed by the threat of a sanction in the case of disobedience, this had tended to be the starting-point for the study of jurisprudence in the common-law world until after the Second

World War. In the Britain of the early 1950s, wrote Neil MacCormick, 'jurisprudence as the general study of law and legal ideas was in the doldrums'. What transformed this scene, awakening much interest also outside the common-law world, was the infusion into jurisprudence of the new philosophy of linguistic analysis which had arisen from the work both of Ludwig Wittgenstein, an Austrian who worked for some years at Cambridge, and of a group of Oxford philosophers, notably J. L. Austin and Gilbert Ryle. This came about through the appointment to the Oxford professorship of jurisprudence of H. L. A. Hart, a lawyer with a strong interest in philosophy, who in his inaugural lecture, 'Definition and Theory in Jurisprudence', more or less announced his programme: whereas earlier legal science had struggled to penetrate concepts by first establishing a definition, erecting a theory 'on the back' of the definition, and then beating off challenges, Hart proposed—following the language-centred approach of the new philosophy—to study instead the usage and setting of the *words* used in legal discourse, hoping to arrive, via an understanding of what people actually meant when they used a term and the role assumed by their usage in social existence, at a more useful picture of the legal reality they had in mind. The definitive statement of this jurisprudence appeared in 1961, when Hart published *The Concept of Law*, which at once established a central position in Anglo-American legal theory, and has retained it for the past thirty years. Neither very long nor very elaborate, it provoked an immense literature and must be reckoned, whatever faults may be found with it, one of the seminal works of twentieth-century jurisprudence; in the case of this book alone, the authors of *Lloyd's Introduction to Jurisprudence* offer no extracts, on the ground that the book in its entirety should be read by every student of the subject.[14]

Hart's starting-point is a radical critique of the Austin model of law as command backed by sanction. Some of the inadequacies of this 'imperative' conception of law had long been notices; for instance, it could not account—except by including them in the sub-legal grade of 'positive morality'—for international law, or for early (or contemporary primitive) legal systems; and the identification of the sovereign, who was central to the theory, was not a simple

---

[14] *The Concept of Law* (Oxford, 1986), 79.

matter. But Hart concentrated on the theory's failure to cover many parts even of a municipal system of what we call law. It may fit well enough a simple criminal law, which defines an offence by statute and attaches a penalty to it. But there is much else in a legal system, as that phrase is commonly understood, which cannot be reduced to the Austin formula. There are, for example, 'rules of change', rules which enable either private individuals to alter their legal position, e.g. by assuming obligations which they did not previously have, or the legislature to alter the law generally. A simple instance of such a 'power-conferring' rule in the private sphere is the rule allowing people to make binding contracts with one another; another is the law which prescribes the formalities necessary for making a valid will. The bundles of rules on wills and contracts cannot be called the 'commands' of anyone, still less can they be said to be backed by sanctions, without distortion of language and obscuring of the place which such rules actually occupy in social existence (the objection to any theory which misrepresents real life recurs over and over again with Hart). The 'command' model cannot be rescued in the case of wills, for example, by saying that failure to comply with the statutory requirements for testation (e.g. in regard to witnesses), since it will mean the instrument is invalid, carries the sanction of nullity, because the nullity is simply the inseparable logical concomitant of, and not a logically independent and separately prescribed penalty for failing properly to activate the facility, offered by the legal system, of determining the posthumous disposition of one's estate. In the public sphere, the constitutional, statutory, and procedural rules by which a legislature works in changing the law (by addition, subtraction, or modification) are for similar reasons not reducible to commands.

The imperative model is also no good for explaining the 'rule of recognition' which every legal system has, and which is a short way of denoting the complex of constitutional rules, statutory provisions, and judicial precedents which tell us what is to count as law. A document may purport to be the 'Finance Act, 1990', but criteria are needed in order to distinguish it, as being *law*, from something which, say, a hoaxer has dreamt up and printed himself. These criteria result from the constitutional rules about the composition, range of authority, and mode of functioning of the legislature, together with whatever subordinate rules on these subjects have been made by the legislature itself; and the interpretation of the Act will proceed by canons, mostly of judicial origin, assigning legal force to a section (but denying it to the section's side-note) and defining its true reach. That such a rule of recognition is indispensable is evident from considering even the simplest case of a law which can be admitted, for the purpose of argument, to conform to the Austin model, a penal statute. Such a law, in a state like ours, applies to everyone, including the individual members of the parliament who made it. The resulting apparent absurdity of a sovereign (supposedly not in the habit of obedience to anyone else) commanding himself, under threat of punishing himself, is avoided if we distinguish the capacities of a member of parliament in his role as such, and as a private citizen. But such a distinction is possible only by resort to a prior rule of recognition, which is not amenable to formulation as a command. It is something capable only of being generally accepted by the people who work the system.

This system also needs rules of adjudication, in other words an apparatus for deciding, in cases of conflict, how the law is to be applied; rules of adjudication also cannot be reduced to the model of orders backed by threats. Hart associates the rules of adjudication, along with those of change and recognition, in a category which he calls 'secondary rules' and which in any legal system must accompany the 'primary', obligation-imposing rules. The idea of a rule—which Hart freely admits to have psychological ('internal') and social dimensions (the latter that of 'acceptance'), thus locating it on a quite different plane from Kelsen's 'pure', formalistic theory of a hierarchy of norms—is central to his system: his concept of law is a 'union' of these primary and secondary rules, and in this union he thinks 'there lies what Austin wrongly claimed to have found in the notion of coercive orders, namely "the key to the science of jurisprudence"'. It is true that the removal of the idea of command-plus-sanction from the scene would, by itself still leave the problem of how to distinguish legal from merely moral rules but Hart does not make heavy weather of it. It is all a question of the status of this rule or that in the acceptance and usage of the society, and the degree of pressure it exerts to get conformity:

Rules are conceived and spoken of as imposing obligations when the general demand for conformity is insistent and the social pressure brought to bear upon those who deviate or threaten to deviate is great. Such rules may be wholly customary in origin; there may be no centrally organised system of punishments for breach of the rules; the social pressure may take only the form of a general diffused hostile or critical reaction which may stop short of physical sanctions. It may be limited to verbal manifestations of disapproval or of appeals to the individuals' respect for the rule violated; it may depend heavily on the operation of feelings of shame, remorse, and guilt. When the pressure is of this last-mentioned kind we may be inclined to classify the rules as part of the morality of the social group and the obligation under the rules as moral obligation. Conversely, when physical sanctions are prominent or usual among the forms of pressure, even though these are neither closely defined nor administered by officials but are left to the community at large, we shall be inclined to classify the rules as a primitive or rudimentary form of law.[15]

In a fully developed society, of course, with sophisticated rules of recognition to mark off what is strict law from what are only moral precepts, it will not be necessary to inspect social usage; but even here, the rules of recognition themselves depend on the support of acceptance.

Hart devotes special attention to the sovereign presupposed by the Austin model. Briefly, his attack on this conception is marshalled from two directions: the problems of the supposed 'habitual obedience' accorded to the sovereign; and of finding any person, or any body of persons, in any state, whose area of power is truly legally unlimited. The 'habitual obedience' difficulty arises in several ways. If we can imagine a sort of Hobbesian Leviathan receiving, long enough for it to become habitual and automatic, the obedience of subjects, does this not involve an anarchic interregnum after Leviathan's death until such time as another person succeeds in building up for himself a similar habit of obedience in others? This can be avoided only by positing a rule of recognition, accepted before Leviathan's demise, which regulates the succession to him; and this rule cannot be an Austinian command because, *ex hypothesi*, Leviathan is no longer there to enforce it. Moreover, the old model cannot, without another rule of recognition providing for the continuance of law, explain how statutes made under one sovereign or parliament continue in force indefinitely under their successors. As for identifying a 'sovereign' with unlimited power, one need only look at the written constitutions common in the Western world which impose limitations on the legislature by commanding it to observe certain standards or by forbidding it to make laws of a certain kind; even if one goes a step further back and

[15] *The Concept of Law* (Oxford, 1986), 84.

identifies the sovereign in the people, or the electorate, they too are circumscribed, at the very least, procedurally, since an array of laws regulate the modes by which they make their will known and translate it into effect; in addition to enabling us to distinguish (as we had to do in the case of the parliament) the citizen wearing the citizen's hat from the citizen as an effective agent in lawmaking (in which role, of course, he is giving orders to the former, albeit at one or two removes, and perhaps threatening to punish him if he disobeys).

This must suffice as a summary of Hart's opening position (though *The Concept of Law* will reappear later in this chapter in the contexts, which he worked into his total picture, of legality and the rule of law, of legislative justice, of natural law, of natural rights, and of realism). Of the many reactions, that which has been most influential is that of his own successor in the Oxford chair of jurisprudence, the American Ronald Dworkin. Dworkin's central point of criticism presented in a volume of essays called *Taking Rights Seriously*, was that legal systems are not capable of exhaustive reduction into patterns of rules alone. Along with rules, and often operating so as to modify them or even nullify their effect in particular cases, there are also general *principles*, to which courts will have recourse in order to decide 'hard cases', i.e. cases to which the unmodified application of a 'rule' would not be possible without injustice. In fact attention had been drawn to this feature of legal systems much earlier, not only before Dworkin but several years before Hart's *Concept of Law*, by the German professor Josef Esser, whose book *Grundsatz und Norm* ('Principle and Rule') appeared first in 1956. Esser's concern was to study the interaction between statute-law—in continental tradition, a term virtually coextensive with law itself—and its interpretation. In the course of his work, which was based on a large comparative foundation, he was able to show that the supposed difference between the civil-law judge, bound to the text of his code, and the common-law judge, free to construct new solutions for new cases, was largely imaginary. The civil-law judge also in fact created and shaped law under cover of merely applying the book; and he did this by giving expression to extra-statutory principles in selecting and deploying paragraphs of his codes. Not that this meant that transcendent natural law got into his court by the back door. But what were seen as 'general principles of law' kept being used in judicial decisions, where the words of statute seemed inadequate to cover the case, or as a starting-point for giving a quite new evaluation of it.[16] What may have begun as a moral precept can become a sort of maxim, and rise from there to become a principle of law as well: he instanced the maxims of English equity, and gave expressly (in English) the principles that 'No man should profit by his own iniquity or take advantage of his own wrong'—an example relied on afterwards by Dworkin—and 'He whose interests are advanced by the act should bear the cost of doing it'.[17]

Dworkin identified another kind of standard, which in some contexts needs to be kept distinct from the notion of principles, namely, 'policies', general goals which courts attribute to society and the recognition of which may play some part in shaping their decisions in difficult cases. Briefly, his challenge to Hart's position was built on consideration of such 'hard cases', in which lawyers in fact

make use of standards that do not function as rules, but operate differently as principles, policies, and other sorts of standards. Positivism, I shall argue, is a model of and for a system of rules and its central notion of a single fundamental test for law forces us to miss the important roles of these standards that are not rules . . . I call a 'policy' that kind of standard that sets out a goal to be reached, generally an improvement in some economic, political, or social feature of the community (though some goals are negative, in that they stipulate that some present feature is to be protected from adverse change). I call a 'principle' a standard that is to be observed, not because it will advance or secure an economic, political, or social situation deemed desirable, but because it is a requirement of justice or fairness or some other dimension of morality.[18]

Principles and policies are fundamentally different from rules, Dworkin thinks, because whereas a rule falls automatically to be applied once the paradigm conditions of the rule are met, these other standards are merely values or considerations to be put in the balance; sometimes they will be decisive, sometimes they will be ousted or outweighed by other, countervailing values. Such elements are therefore—as Esser had shown twenty years before— outside a structure built of rules, but are complementary to them in the legal system. Accordingly, any satisfactory statement of a concept of law must accommodate them. In particular, they are

[16] *Grundsatz und Norm* (Tübingen, 1956; 3rd edn., 1974), 8.
[17] Ibid. 99.   [18] *Taking Rights Seriously* (London, 1978), 22.

indispensable if we are to explain judicial innovation, judicial 'lawmaking' of the kind that can be seen in a landmark case like *Donoghue* v. *Stevenson*,[19] in which what had become a regular fact of life—the sale by retailers of products received from manufacturers in a sealed, uninspectable condition—was treated as generating a duty of care owed by the manufacturer to the ultimate consumer, on a 'neighbour' principle, breach of which now became actionable despite there being no privity of contract between them; in other words, this principle, in those special conditions, ousted what formerly would have been the decisive privity rule.

Of course it could be said that the notion of a rule can be given a wide meaning so as to embrace the principle-based qualifications to which it may, in a particular case, turn out to be subject, and that Dworkin's distinction is more verbal than substantial. On the other hand, there *is* a real difference—akin to that between a legal and a moral precept—between a rule in the narrow sense and a principle (or a policy): rules are felt to be amenable to deliberate change or repeal, say, by legislation, whereas what is meant by a principle is something we do not think of as susceptible to deliberate alteration. Its relative weight in society may change over time, in the way for example that the principle that people should be free to make what bargains they choose has been eroded in the light of new social perceptions, and this change will be reflected in judicial as well as in legislative responses. But at any particular time a body of principles will be thought of as underlying, or transcending, a body of rules, and inherently possessing a stability which rules do not enjoy.[20]

THE RULE OF LAW: REVOLUTIONS AND LEGALITY

Just as the experiences of the era which, in Western Europe, closed in 1945 led to a firmer entrenchment of constitutionalism and of human rights, as well as to a revival of interest in natural law, so the idea of legality (the rule of law, the *Rechtsstaat*) increased in value and acceptance. This in turn sharpened the problem of how to evaluate or justify the exercise of power in a revolutionary regime— not necessarily merely one emerging from violence, but any system

---

[19] [1932] AC 562.
[20] See Harris, *Legal Philosophies* (see Ch. 8 n. 53), 172–7; Neil MacCormick, *Legal Reasoning and Legal Theory* (Oxford, 1978), 244.

of which it could be said that the *Grundnorm* in Kelsen's sense (or the ultimate rule of recognition, in Hart's) and hence the root of validity of all other norms had changed. This problem might have presented itself to legal theory even before the war (it was for example latent in several aspects of the Irish constitutional transitions of 1922 and 1937) but only since then, and probably due to the greater sensitivity to the value of legality, has it become a familiar theme: most notably in the 1960s, when events in the British Commonwealth made it topical (especially in Rhodesia in the conditions following the 'unilateral declaration of independence' by the dominant white minority in 1965).

There are two ways of looking at this matter. When the successful revolutionary regime is in the saddle, and there has been a shift in the ultimate rule of recognition, this new rule can be accounted for in Hart's terms by saying it 'rests simply on the fact that it is accepted and used as such a rule in the judicial and other official operations of [the country's] system whose rules are generally obeyed'; by this rule, the fact of enactment by the revolutionary legislative authority may be an ultimate criterion of validity.[21] The new rule of recognition might also include the practice of holding valid whatever dispositions of the old regime the new regime had chosen not to alter. This may be an adequate account of the new regime's legal system. On the other hand, the revolution may have taken the form (as in Rhodesia) of breaking loose from a prior, but continuing, legal system (in Rhodesia's case, that of the United Kingdom, whose parliament had in English law the power to legislate for the territory and whose ultimate rule of recognition could not, of course, be affected by what the local usurpers did). It is not necessary to treat this as a dilemma, because, as Hart says

as a matter of fact there [are now] two legal systems, [even though] English law will insist that there is only one. But, just because one assertion is a statement of fact and the other a proposition of (English) law, the two do not necessarily conflict. To make the position clear we can, if we like, say that the statement of fact is true and the proposition of English law is 'correct in English law'.[22]

But does this mean that there is no route of legal reconciliation between the two systems, and that an English court is compelled (until parliament lays down some legislative accommodation) to

[21] Hart, *Concept* (see n. 14), 117.   [22] Ibid. 118.

treat all the works of the new regime as null and void? In *Madzimbamuto* v. *Lardner-Burke*[23] the problem reached the Judicial Committee of the Privy Council in London, when it had to consider the validity of a constitution promulgated by the political leadership of the Rhodesian white minority, and of acts done under regulations purportedly authorized by it. The majority of the Committee took the view that the only lawful constitution of the territory was that represented by a British statutory instrument of 1961 made under a British act of 1948; and that the purported laws being operated by the breakaway regime—though they were being administered in fact, and without effective resistance—were void. The case was one in which, even under the old regime, the plaintiff had been lawfully detained, and might even still have been detained; but his detention under regulations made by the new regime was held invalid. However, the dissenting judge, Lord Pearce, enunciated a principle which he called that of 'necessity or implied mandate' from the lawful sovereign (i.e. the queen in Parliament) in cases of this kind, which meant that even formally invalid acts done by those in actual control may be recognized by the English courts as valid if they are intended for the orderly running of the country, do not impair ordinary rights under the lawful constitution, and do not, in themselves, further the usurpation. Were it otherwise, he thought, and if the local Rhodesian judges (appointed under the old but still, in the British eye, legitimate regime) were to declare such acts invalid merely because of their formal lack of legal title, the result would be chaos.

This dissent was followed by academic treatment of the theme to much the same effect. A. M. Honoré suggested several routes by which judges might be justified in making orders which, in effect, went to uphold the violation of the constitution under which they themselves had been appointed; the most attractive of these was an expansion of the notion of implied mandate from the sovereign, and was expressed as resulting from a tacit constitutional term. This can be envisaged—for example in the case of a constitution originally resting on its adoption by a popular vote—as the people's assumed assent to an unspoken understanding that, where brute facts render the constitution partly or even largely inoperative, those still actually discharging the duties of pre-existing offices are to do the

[23] (1969) 1 AC 645.

best they can to preserve, in the interest of public security and stability, as many portions and fragments of the old order as possible.[24] J. M. Eekelaar related the problem of revolutions to the models of legal systems presented by Kelsen and Hart, and argued (as Dworkin had done in another context) that, as those models did not encompass characteristic features of legal systems such as general values and principles (of varying weight relative to one another, depending on circumstances such as only the judge could appraise in a particular case) the dissolution of an 'old' *Grundnorm*, or the abandonment of an 'old' rule of recognition, could not touch elements which did not depend on them, and which accordingly remained valid and capable of deployment, as might be appropriate, in support of the acts of a revolutionary regime.[25] J. M. Finnis reached a similar practical conclusion by another route: legal systems, he wrote, are not in fact systems of rules, but sequences, or successive sets of rules, changing every minute, and cohering in what society accepts is a continuous system not by virtue of any perennial rule of recognition, but as a function of the existence of society itself, which is an organic structure responding to laws of growth, change, and decay analogous to those governing the individual organism. Consequently, a revolution is 'neither a necessary nor a sufficient condition for anything that should be described as a change in the identity of the state or the legal system'. Accordingly, both of the latter can be presented as surviving a revolution, and not implying the invalidity of all the revolution's dispositions in areas conventionally regulated by law:

Hence it is usually reasonable to accept the new rules of competence and of succession of rules [i.e. *rules about the exercise of official acts and about how old laws are to be changed*] proposed by the revolutionaries [and there is similarly reason to accept] the validity of the remaining bulk of the legal system, unaffected by the revolution.

But justice, he concedes, has other demands, so that 'sometimes the character of a revolution is such that allegiance to the revolutionary order of society is unreasonable'; the reasonableness which he thus makes the basis of his society-oriented, non-formalistic approach is 'the reasonableness of justice and *philia politikē* [i.e. *the solidarity*,

---

[24] See A. M. Honoré, 'Reflections on Revolutions', *Irish Jurist* (1967), 268 ff.
[25] 'Principles of Revolutionary Legality', *Oxford Essays in Jurisprudence*, 2nd ser. (Oxford, 1973), 22 ff.

or mutual affection, of those sharing the same state] which demands legal coherence and continuity and respect for acquired rights'.[26]

Mention may be made, lastly, of Karl Olivecrona, whose reading of revolutions is equally non-formalistic, and, in the tradition of Scandinavian realism, presented largely in terms of psychology:

New leaders step in and proclaim that they have 'assumed power'. They begin to issue laws and administrative decrees. To succeed they need, of course, organisation and a special political and psychological situation in the country . . . In actual fact, the revolutionaries make use of the foundations of the old order. Most of the law is left as it is; only the constitution is put aside . . . [But] the respect for the previous constitution may easily be transferred to the new one . . . A new constitution, enacted without reference to an old constitution, therefore, needs no other justification than its being willed by the people.[27]

LEGISLATIVE JUSTICE[28]

One of Hart's central concerns, in constructing his *Concept of Law*, was to contradict the ancient proposition of natural law in its strongest form, that a measure conflicting with that transcendent standard of rightness, implanted in human nature by God, and accessible to man through his reason, ought to be denied the title of law. Such a theory, he thought, led only to muddle. On the other hand, there was nothing to prevent us from *both* recognizing such a measure to be indeed law—on the criteria offered by our local rule of recognition—*and* at the same time condemning it as evil, seeking its repeal, refusing it obedience, resisting those who had enacted it. Nothing was gained by allowing our moral repugnance to subvert our analytic perception; each could play its part in its own sphere. At the same time, he acknowledged the universal instinct which insisted on a necessary connection between morality and law; and, more specifically, between law and that dimension of morality (as the terms are not coextensive) called justice. Now justice, since

[26] 'Revolutions and Continuity of Law', *Oxford Essays in Jurisprudence*, 2nd ser., 44 ff.

[27] *Law as Fact* (2nd edn., London, 1971), 104.

[28] This was the expression proposed by Éamon de Valera, during the Dáil debate on the draft Constitution of 1937, to distinguish one facet of 'equality before the law' from mere procedural or judicial impartiality: J. M. Kelly, *The Irish Constitution* (2nd edn., Dublin, 1984).

Aristotle, has been divided into 'distributive' and 'corrective' or 'commutative', more or less corresponding with it as a value, respectively, in legislation and in judicial processes; and Hart follows Aristotle in seeing the connecting link between the two in the idea of equality,[29] of treating alike things that are like, and treating differently things that are different. But where 'distributive', or legislative, justice is concerned, this maxim does not take us far:

Any set of human beings will resemble each other in some respects and differ from each other in others and, until it is established what resemblance and differences are relevant, 'Treat like cases alike' must remain an empty form. To fill it we must know when, for the purposes in hand, cases are to be regarded as alike and what differences are relevant. Without this further supplement we cannot proceed to criticise laws or other social arrangements as unjust.

In a society such as that in which he was writing it would be possible to identify many differences (such as those of colour or religion) as enjoying a public consensus that they ought to be irrelevant, in other words that a law which effected a discrimination on such a basis would be unjust. But this might not be so in another kind of society. It was therefore 'clear that the criteria of relevant resemblances and differences may often vary with the fundamental moral outlook of a given person or society'. On the other hand, and at a more modest level, if one at least knew the general purpose for which legislation was contemplated, the injunction to treat like cases alike could be given some content:

If a law provides for the relief of poverty[30] then the requirement of the principle that 'Like cases be treated alike' would surely involve attention to the *need* of different claimants for relief. A similar criterion of need is implicitly recognised when the burden of taxation is adjusted by a graded income tax to the wealth of the individuals taxed.

A further aspect of distributive justice, again a very general one, he identified as essential to any legislation which purports to be for the common good: it is that the claims of all the different competing interests likely to be affected by it should be 'impartially considered': 'For here what is justly "distributed" is not some specific benefit

---

[29] *Concept* (see n. 14), 155.
[30] It would have been better for the purpose of his argument to say, 'if a law is contemplated for the relief of poverty'.

among a class of claimants to it, but impartial attention to and consideration of competing claims to different benefits.'[31]

The American professor Lon Fuller (1902–78) contributed something to the idea of legislative justice in his book *The Morality of Law* (1969). He constructed an elaborate parable about a king (called Rex, namesake of the king whom Hart depicted as building up a habit of obedience to himself); Fuller's king unhappily embarks on a 'bungling career as legislator and judge', and he shows that there are eight different ways in which his government miscarries. Only one of these is evidently a failure in the judicial sphere (the 'failure of congruence between the rules as announced and their actual administration'). From the remaining seven failures it is possible to distil seven criteria for laws if they are to be just in even the most elementary way. First, they must *exist*; the most obvious failure is to leave every issue to *ad hoc* settlement. But in addition, they must be promulgated, i.e. made known to those who are to be bound by them; they may not be retroactive so as injuriously to affect persons who innocently relied on the earlier state of the law; they must be intelligible; they must be internally consistent; they must not 'require conduct beyond the power of the affected party'; and they must not be so frequently changed 'that the subject cannot orient his action by them'.[32] This list (curiously reminiscent of the criteria of a just law propounded in the seventh century by St Isidore of Seville) states only the criteria for what Fuller calls the 'internal morality of law'; all the items on it might be respected in the course of producing a code whose material content was oppressive. All the same, it looks like a catalogue of what could be called legislative natural justice, although Fuller did not subscribe to any traditional natural-law theory.

A far more radical adventure in stating a basis for the whole plan and construction of the state and law was undertaken by the American philosopher John Rawls, whose book *A Theory of Justice* (1972) made a sensation. This theory uses as a starting-point something like the ancient social-contract hypothesis, except that it is one not limited to explaining the origin of ordered society or its subordination to a sovereign. Indeed these matters are not central to Rawls' interest at all. Under his kind of social contract, we are asked to imagine people in an 'initial situation' considering with one

[31] Ibid. 153 ff.
[32] *The Morality of Law* (New Haven, Conn., 1969), 39.

another what sort of society they would accept as just, assuming (as we must do) that justice, meaning 'fairness', would seem to them a central, unarguable value. The assumption that they would, so to speak, all vote for justice first is made easy in the Rawls scheme, because, while an ordinary person who knows himself to be better endowed, in one way or another, than most of his fellows might not vote for justice unless he knew it meant something that would leave him no worse off, in the Rawls initial hypothesis the contracting parties are not ordinary people, but people operating behind a 'veil of ignorance' which conceals from them all knowledge of their own actual situation in even its most rudimentary dimensions: no one knows anything about his/her own sex, age, nationality, level of intelligence, physical characteristics, material possessions, or anything else which might distort his/her pure concentration on finding principles, which all could agree to be just, as a basis for the political society which they propose to create.[33] The rules at which Rawls arrives by this route—via, to take a striking landmark of the road, the proposition that the total of individuals' talents of intelligence and other personal advantages should be looked at as a common resource just like the total of the territory's natural material resources—are, that while

each person is to have an equal right to the most extensive total system of equal basic liberties compatible with a similar system of liberty for all, [yet] all social primary goods—liberty and opportunity, income and wealth, and the bases of self-respect—are to be distributed equally unless an unequal distribution of any or all of these goods is to the advantage of the least favoured.[34]

The most radical critique of Rawls's utopian egalitarianism came from another American, Robert Nozick, located at the opposite end of the political spectrum. In his book *Anarchy, State, and Utopia* (1974) he rejected in particular Rawls's idea that differences in natural talents (and in the character it takes to exploit them) should be neutralized on the ground that, being the product of genetic

---

[33] There is said to have been an instance of an attempt to reproduce, for a limited purpose, Rawls's 'veil of ignorance' on the premise of universal acceptance of fairness, for the purpose of securing a just distribution. When an estate was to be divided among a number of brothers, the youngest was given the task of dividing it into the appropriate number of shares but all the others then chose their own shares, leaving the last to him.

[34] *A Theory of Justice* (Oxford, 1972), 302–3; Lloyd, *Introduction*, 526 ff., 537–8.

inheritance and environment and upbringing, they are undeserved. On the contrary: according to Nozick, not only does something like simple envy lie at the root of this desire to eliminate the advantages of natural talent and character, but if these dimensions of human beings are subtracted, even for the sake of argument, no coherent conception of a 'person' remains. Nozick's own claim is that the principle of acquisition enunciated by Locke is still valid and should be respected by the state; this, although not free of problems, essentially proclaims that when a man has 'mixed his labour' with the earth's resources, the resulting thing is his, provided that there is 'enough and as good left in common for others'. Accordingly there is no room for any system of justice which starts by attempting a radical redistribution. Central to Nozick's theory is the notion of 'entitlement' in the sense implied by the Locke formula; and, 'if the world were wholly just', one might summarize justice in the area of property ('holdings') as follows:

1. A person who acquired a holding in accordance with the principle of justice in acquisition is entitled to that holding;
2. A person who acquires a holding in accordance with the principle of justice in transfer, from someone else entitled to the holding, is entitled to the holding;
3. No one is entitled to a holding except by (repeated) applications of the foregoing two rules.

From proposition 3 it follows also that the rectification of its breach will be a further ground of entitlement. As for what will accord with 'the principle of justice in transfer', Nozick presents a formula impossible to summarize neatly, but evidently pretty well equivalent to the free operation of the market (plus of course what may be transferred gratuitously out of love or charity). As a political background for these arrangements he proposes a 'minimal state', to which the average state of today could present no greater contrast; it will retreat to its primitive role of simply keeping order, and will be justified in imposing taxation or other coercive mechanisms only so far as is necessary to enable it to discharge this minimal role. Anything like taxation for the purpose of redistributing wealth is impermissible, as it boils down, in effect, to making me work for the support of others; as much of my earnings as is appropriated by the state for such a purpose represents in effect an exaction of 'forced labour' from me.[35]

We may mention also Dworkin's treatment of the Rawls thesis. He regards the initial position of a hypothetical contract, concluded behind a veil of ignorance, as inadequate to ground compellingly a structure of equality of Rawls's kind: it is a bad argument to say that 'because a man would have consented to certain principles if asked in advance, it is fair to apply those principles to him later, under different circumstances [i.e. after the veil of ignorance has been lifted] when he does not consent [because he now knows of his circumstances of advantage, and is unwilling to sacrifice them]'. He detects, however, a fundamental feature underlying (and not resulting from) the theory: it is 'rights-based' (as distinct from political theories which are 'goal-based' or 'duty-based'), and the right which he sees concealed in its foundations is the 'natural right to equality of concern and respect'. Inasmuch as this must involve him in supporting a 'liberal constitution' and 'an idealised form of present [U.S.] economic and social structures', the practical implications of his theory must seem less radical than his starting-point would lead his readers to apprehend.[36]

NATURAL LAW

As was seen in the last chapter, the idea of a transcendent law of nature, having fallen completely out of vogue—except in spheres of institutional Catholic influence—in the nineteenth and early twentieth centuries, underwent a revival which began immediately after the Second World War; though—again, except in the Catholic world—in a form independent of denominational doctrine. The new natural law, of which the first apostle was perhaps Gustav Radbruch, found expression in the fourth edition of his *Rechtsphilosophie*, which appeared in 1950 shortly after his death; an appendix contains an essay entitled 'Legal Injustice and Supra-statutory Law', a phrase which, he wrote, expressed the guiding maxim of those who were 'everywhere taking up the struggle against positivism'. The Nazi laws which had ignored the central legal value

[35] *Anarchy* (see n. 7), 157–60.
[36] *Taking Rights Seriously* (see n. 18), ch. 6 ('Justice and Rights').

of treating like cases alike, while differentiating cases which were not alike, did not, he said 'partake of the character of law at all; they were not just wrong law, but were not law of any kind'; examples were measures authorizing the treatment of some human beings as sub-human, and the undifferentiated infliction of a single punishment (death) for a wide range of offences from motives of pure deterrence. In another essay in the same appendix he again asserted that when laws deliberately defy the instinct for justice, then they are void; 'the people owe them no obedience, and lawyers, too, must find the courage to deny them the character of law'. Another German jurist, Helmut Coing (born 1912), dealt in recent times (1985) more systematically with the question of resistance: 'Deliberate violations [of natural law] must be met with passive resistance. Active resistance, extending to the use of force, is not *required* by morality. But in the face of a criminal government, deliberately acting in a manner forbidden by the natural law, resistance is by natural law both permissible and legitimate.'

The principal French representative of the revived natural law is Michel Villey, who is in much the same Thomist tradition as his compatriot Maritain in the previous generation. Villey, in an essay praising Gény's work at the beginning of the century, still faulted his attempt to build (from his scheme of *donnés*) a body of rules to be independent of jurists' lawmaking and law-interpreting efforts; something more subtle was needed, in which there was room both for recognizing natural imperatives, and for choosing among a wide range of possible concrete ways of regulating life:

[Classical natural law] was not a totalitarian doctrine; it sought rather to allot their proper roles to positive law and to other sources; and in the idea of law, to distinguish between that which is set, positive law, and that which is not. In a word: if the highest source of law lies in the observation of the order which is thought to lurk in nature, it is easier to understand the role played by legal opinion, judicial precedent, creative development of law; and, on the other hand, if political authority is a natural feature of existence, one can better appreciate, and appraise the extent of, the function which normally devolves upon this authority of giving expression to the natural law and to supplement it by giving it the necessary precise concretisations. You will find in the authentic natural law very pertinent guide-lines for helping us to decide in which kinds of conditions the law of the state is to be strictly followed, and in which conditions, on the contrary, the interpretation of law is to give precedence to the quest for the naturally just solution.

Far more radical essays in natural law came from Anglo-American jurisprudence. Chronologically first is H. L. A. Hart's construction, presented as part of his *Concept of Law* (1961); this, in one sense, is not part of the natural-law tradition at all, inasmuch as the phrase, in his usage, does not prescribe a standard, but only explains why, as a matter of fact, we can expect to find certain types of rule in every human society. There is a certain small number of unalterable factors in the human condition; and if humans desire to go on living (which we must assume), it is 'natural' to have rules which are a response to those factors, reconciling them with the goal of survival. (Perhaps therefore his approach should be catalogued as a sort of speculative anthropology rather than under natural law.) Anyway, Hart's central features of human existence are, first, that men are vulnerable; secondly, that they are approximately equal in physical strength; thirdly, that they have only limited altruism; fourthly, that they have at their disposal only limited material resources; and fifthly, that they have only limited understanding and strength of will. If things had evolved differently, for example if men were not vulnerable to their own species, or if the earth yielded an unlimited abundance of everything they needed, and without toil, then their survival might be assured with an even more rudimentary legal apparatus. As things are, their actual condition will require, if they are to survive, *some* kind of rules aimed at protecting persons from one another, and from the consequences of their own weaknesses of body or mind; as well as *some* kind of regime (not necessarily one of private property) for the management and conservation of the earth's resources, and the safeguarding and distribution of what it yields. This proposition Hart calls a 'minimum content' natural law, and his 'simple truisms' about human existence disclose the 'core of good sense' in natural-law doctrine.[37] But it might be said that his truism-based theory might have been more interesting and fruitful if—as would have been easily possible—a number of further truisms had been added, for example, that human young remain for a very long time physically and educationally dependent, or that humans' mental processes are inscrutable to their fellows, or that human beings are infinitely various in a huge number of respects. In other words, Hart's survival kit would do just as well for animals, but does not seem to be sufficiently focused on the *human* person

[37] *Concept* (see n. 14), 188–95.

and personality in dimensions which seem just as inherent as physical vulnerability. It is, after all, survival of human persons in all their essential aspects which concerns us, and if these had been further explored, Hart's minimum-content list might have grown considerably, as well as perhaps looked like converging with more traditional natural-law perspectives.

It was seen earlier in this chapter that the American Lon Fuller put forward, in his book *The Morality of Law* (1969), a catalogue of criteria on which the justice of a law might be appraised. It is worth noting here that these, for him, added up to a kind of natural law, though one equally divorced from the tradition established by St Thomas. 'Do these principles', he asked,

represent some variety of natural law? The answer is an emphatic though qualified, yes. What I have tried to do is to discern and articulate the natural laws of a particular kind of human undertaking, which I have described as 'the enterprise of subjecting human conduct to the governance of rules'. These natural laws have nothing to do with any 'brooding omnipresence in the skies'. Nor have they the slightest affinity with any such proposition as that the practice of contraception is a violation of God's law.[38] They remain entirely terrestrial in origin and application . . . They are like the natural laws of carpentry, or at least those laws respected by a carpenter who wants the house he builds to remain standing and serve the purpose of those who live in it . . . As a convenient (though not wholly satisfactory) way of describing the distinction being taken we may speak of a procedural, as distinguished from a substantive natural law. What I have called the internal morality of law [i.e. *his justice criteria*] is in this sense a procedural version of natural law.[39]

As for the search for a substantive natural law, Fuller dismissed Hart's initial hypothesis, the centrality of the aim of survival, with small ceremony: 'As Thomas Aquinas remarked long ago, if the highest aim of a captain were to preserve his ship, he would keep it in port forever.' He believed, instead, in something more eccentric but also more moving: that

if we were forced to select the principle that supports and infuses all human aspiration we would find it in the objective of maintaining communication with our fellows . . . Communication is something more than a means of staying alive. It is a way of being alive. It is through communication that we inherit the achievements of past human effort. The possibility of communi-

---

[38] The phrases quoted are allusions, respectively, to words used by O. W. Holmes (cited in Ch. 9) and to the papal encyclical *Humanae vitae* (Paul VI) issued in 1969.
[39] *Morality of Law* (see n. 32), 96; Lloyd, *Introduction*, 190–1.

cation can reconcile us to the thought of death by assuring us that what we achieve will enrich the lives of those to come . . . If I were asked, then, to discern one central indisputable principle of what may be called substantive natural law—Natural Law with capital letters—I would find it in the injunction: Open up, maintain, and preserve the integrity of the channels of communication by which men convey to one another what they perceive, feel, and desire.[40]

To these two modern, earth-bound versions of natural-law theory must be added a far more elaborate and densely constructed system, that of the British (originally Australian) lawyer and philosopher John Finnis. Finnis, though himself a declared and convinced Catholic, does not build on his own belief or on the authority of the Church, but, like Grotius, on reason; the chain of natural law which he presents has God not as its first link, but as its last. The first link is the identification, which for Finnis results not from empirical observation but from introspection or 'reflection' (though it is not easy to see how an adult's reflection can proceed uninfluenced by his general experience), of certain basic values of existence; these are 'indemonstrable but self-evident principles shaping our practical reasoning' accessible to 'reflection on one's own character'. The first of these (and the only one enjoying a logical impregnability) is the value or good of *knowledge*; we cannot deny this, because to do so—thus evincing a concern in whether the proposition is true or false—automatically undermines our dissent. But apart from truth or knowledge, there are other things which, in one form or another, all societies seem to value *and* which we ourselves find intuitively obvious: the 'universality of a few basic values in a vast diversity of realisations'. These are: life, play ('each of us can see the point of engaging in performances which have no point beyond the performance itself, enjoyed for its own sake'), aesthetic experience, friendship and sociability, practical reasonableness, and religion (which is the importance of reflecting on, and if possible achieving the harmonization of, the orders of existence in oneself and the cosmic order and its origin). All the other values of existence, which are innumerable, Finnis believes can be reduced into departments or corollaries of one or other of these central seven values.[41]

---

[40] *Morality of Law* (see n. 32), 96; Lloyd, *Introduction*, 199.
[41] *Natural Law and Natural Rights* (Oxford, 1980), chs. 3, 4.

This list, while no one would call it arbitrary, is perhaps arguable (Hart, for example, would not accept it),[42] as is the method of arriving at it. A more interesting aspect of the book which carries Finnis's theory, *Natural Law and Natural Rights* (1980), is his elaboration of the value he calls 'practical reasonableness'; this is 'the basic good of being able to bring one's own intelligence to bear effectively (in practical reasoning that issues in action) on the problems of choosing one's actions and life-style and shaping one's own character'.[43] This practical reasonableness, for someone whose problem is to choose a course of action in lawmaking, shows in following requirements which are 'fundamental, underived, irreducible'; the ' "natural law method" of working out the (moral) "natural law" from the first (pre-moral) "principles of natural law" '. These requirements are, first, acceptance that life should have a 'rational plan' (something that Rawls had also said). Then, there should be no 'arbitrary discounting or exaggeration of any of the basic values' (but on this basis, Rawls's four primary goods add up to a programme which is 'too thin'). There should be no arbitrary preference as between persons. A balance should be preserved between commitment and detachment; both fanaticism and indifference (what perhaps might be called 'cop-out') are to be avoided. The means chosen should be efficient to achieve a reasonable purpose (here Finnis turns aside to blast the facile utilitarian formula of 'the greatest good of the greatest number', neglecting perhaps to notice its importance in its day as a standard of revolt against ancient unfairness and unreason). The legislator (or judge) should do nothing 'which of itself does nothing but damage'; all his acts should show respect for every basic value, and he may never choose directly against one of them. He must respect the requirements of the common good. And he must not violate his own conscience by doing something which he feels 'all in all, should not be done'.[44]

In this list, the most intractable element is the 'common good'; Finnis says this is the maximization of the subjects' participation in the basic goods of life already described. Participation, in his philosophy, is active; one is not there just to experience, but to do and to achieve. Accordingly, a law which deprives the subjects of chances of participation in this sense, for example by centralizing

---

[42] *Essays in Jurisprudence and Philosophy* (New York, 1983), Introduction.
[43] *Natural Law* (see n. 41), 88. [44] Ibid. 125.

functions which they, or small numbers of them, can perform for themselves (the Catholic principle of subsidiarity) is a failure in the justice which requires the lawgiver to afford the people this basic good. Similar reasoning must maximize personal autonomy; and, together with common experience, will suggest the superior virtue of a regime of private ownership of goods (which are thus more likely to be well and efficiently used). But similar reasoning will also condemn the pure acquisitiveness which leads men to amass wealth without making it available for use; this, moreover, violates the first principle of 'distributive' justice, which is equality. The same goes for the waste of resources. On the other hand, an inequality in distribution may be justified on the basis that the party who gains is distinguished by his function, or his capacity, or his deserts, or even by his acceptance of risk, so as to make his greater share fair. The common good, in addition, will require the existence, in society, of some *authority* (as being the only alternative, in regulating human affairs, to unanimity); but Finnis does not elevate to the plane of natural law any particular configuration of authority, i.e. it is not necessarily parliamentary democracy. As for laws which offend against Finnis's canons, unjust laws, it is, he says, a distortion of natural-law thought to summarize it in the maxim that such laws are not laws at all. There are several different levels on which they may be appraised, and he fully accepts the distinction between laws as they are and laws as they ought to be. The question, a practical and often dangerous one, of whether one ought to disobey an unjust law cannot be answered in absolute terms, because it is 'highly contingent upon social, political, and cultural variables',[45] but one must weigh up, for example, whether one ought not to obey a law which is itself unjust but is part of a system which, on the whole, is just; or whether one's disobedience—by influencing others and bringing the whole system into disrepute—may be doing more harm than good.[46] Such a summary is all that can be attempted here, and it no doubt does poor justice to so formidable and closely argued an enterprise as Finnis's, the only weakness of which is, perhaps, that its insights have the look of being conditioned by his personal conditioning.

The only place in the Western world where natural law in the Thomistic sense still survives outside (though certainly due originally

---

[45] *Natural Law* (see n. 41), 362.   [46] Ibid. 361.

to the influence of) the Catholic church is Ireland and the jurisprudence of the Irish courts. Many years passed, after the spectacular assertion of natural-law values by Kennedy CJ in *The State (Ryan)* v. *Lennon*,[47] before such a note was again heard from the bench. But a new generation of judges arrived in the 1960s, not overawed as their predecessors had been, by the positivist tradition of (at any rate) the post-Reformation common law. The first sign of what was to come was seen in an article contributed to a legal periodical by a barrister who, in the interval between its writing and its publication, was appointed to the High Court (and later to the Supreme Court); in this, it was flatly asserted that 'if a judicial decision rejects the divine law or has not as its object the common good, it has not the character of law'.[48] This frame of mind became commonplace in the courts from the 1960s onward. In both *Murphy* v. *P. M. P. A. Insurance Co.*[49] and *The State (Healy)* v. *Donoghue*[50] judges of the High Court asserted the existence of 'natural rights' (in the context, respectively, of a person's natural right to confidentiality, and an accused person's right to be treated fairly). In *G.* v. *An Bord Uchtála*[51] another High Court judge said 'the emotional bonds between [mother and child] give to her rights which spring from the law of nature'. And in *Northants County Council* v. *ABF*[52] the President of the High Court said (again in the context of parental rights) that 'the natural law is of universal application and applies to all human persons, be they citizens of the State or not'.

RIGHTS

Allied to and from one point of view a part of natural-law theory is the question of natural or fundamental rights, which has a large place in the jurisprudence of the late twentieth century. Its profile, especially in North America, is conditioned by the fact that several issues of political debate in the 1960s and later were rights-centred:

---

[47] 1935 IR 490.
[48] 35 MLR (1962), 544, 557 (Séamus Henchy). He added: 'This idea is no strange addition to the common law. It is as old as Coke.'
[49] Unreported; High Court (Doyle J.), 21 Feb. 1978.   [50] 1976 IR 325.
[51] 1980 IR 32. (An Bord Uchtála: 'the Adoption Board').
[52] 1982 ILRM 164.

civil rights for people disadvantaged by their colour, equal rights for women, the rights in play (on both sides) in the era of protest against United States involvement in the Vietnam war, against nuclear armament, against conscription, against environmental degradation, and so on. Here the leading name has been that of the American Ronald Dworkin, and the leading text his collection of essays entitled *Taking Rights Seriously* (1978). Taking up the line of argument of John Rawls already mentioned, he construes it as, and assents to, the proposition that 'justice as fairness rests on the assumption of a natural right of all men and women to equality of concern and respect, a right they possess not by virtue of birth or characteristic or merit or excellence but simply as human beings with the capacity to make plans and give justice'. The sphere within which this right to equal concern and respect operates is that of the 'design of political institutions'.[53] But from this generality Dworkin (writing in an age of civil disobedience, which he was inclined to place in a defensible light) elaborates a range of rights which are not necessarily capable of abridgement merely because this would be in the general interest. On the contrary, they resemble what he calls 'trumps', which will 'beat', or prevail over, official acts done in pursuance of some policy judged to conduce to some desirable public goal. This, to take what may seem a provocatively chosen example, 'if someone has a right to publish pornography, this means that it is for some reason wrong for officials to act in violation of that right, even if they (correctly) believe that the community as a whole would be better off if they did'. Rights, he says, are not a gift of God, but are entailed by the primordial right to equality. It is up to the state to establish their integrity, and this will necessarily be 'a complex and troublesome practice that makes the government's job of securing the general benefit more difficult and more expensive'.[54] In other words, as becomes clear in different parts of his output, rights once identified cannot be abated (unless there are 'special grounds', not however specified); and the state must simply take the consequences in good part. This approach, very much in tune with the liberal end of American thinking in the 1960s, necessarily involves the state and community in accepting, where individuals' consciences dictate such behaviour, the burden of civil disobedience as legitimate.

[53] *Taking Rights Seriously* (see n. 18), 182.   [54] Ibid. 198.

For John Finnis, rights fit neatly into the overall scheme already described. Although he thinks that, in explaining the requirements of justice, the notion of duty has a 'more strategic explanatory role' than that of a right (and he draws attention too to the relative late-comer, i.e. post-medieval, status of the idea of someone *having* a right), still modern 'rights-talk' is convenient. But when we see manifestos of human rights, such as the Universal Declaration or the European Convention, we are really only seeing a sort of analytical X-ray of the common good (which, as was seen, is a principal pillar of his natural-law structure). On the one hand, 'we should not say that human rights, or their exercise, are subject to the common good; for the maintenance of human rights *is* a fundamental component of the common good'. But on the other hand, of course, 'we can appropriately say that most human rights are subject to or limited by each other and by other *aspects* of the common good, aspects which could probably be subsumed under a very broad conception of human rights but which are fittingly indicated . . . by expressions such as "public morality", "public health", "public order" '. As for the question whether there are any *absolute* human rights, whose abridgement nothing can justify, an answer lies in one of his precepts of practical legislative reasonableness, namely, that which forbids the doing of anything directly contrary to one of the basic values of existence: this entails an absolute human right (as against the persons lying under this prohibition) 'not to have one's life taken directly as a means to any further end'; but also

the right not to be positively lied to in any situation in which factual communication . . . is reasonably expected; and the related right not to be condemned on knowingly false charges; and the right not to be deprived . . . of one's procreative capacity; and the right to be taken into respectful consideration in any assessment of what the common good requires.[55]

This is a fairly modest list of unconditional rights, but realistic, because Finnis accepts, in a way that Dworkin does not, that the public good etc. inevitably limits the exercise of most of the conventional personal and political rights, and is expressly recognized, by most if not all human rights manifestos, whether in national constitutions or international instruments, as doing so. He calls attention also to the practical limitations imposed, for example, on freedom of speech from considerations much more pedestrian, less

[55] *Natural Law* (see n. 41), 225.

politically sensitive (and hence mostly forgotten), than upholding public decency and the state's authority, such as 'the law about patents, copyright, contracts in restraint of trade and protection of trade secrets and intellectual property; misleading or dangerous advertisements, and consumer protection generally; libel, slander; . . . conspiracy to commit any and every crime, incitement to commit any and every serious crime; official secrets, etc.'[56] The point, presumably, is that those who think laws against pornography or political subversion are unjust inroads on free speech would find this formidable list a good deal more difficult to argue away. Nevertheless we may note that Finnis shares at any rate this much common ground with Dworkin, that he sees rights as rooted essentially in human equality: 'The modern usage of rights-talk rightly emphasises equality, the truth that every human being is a locus of human flourishing which is to be considered with favour in him as much as in anybody else. In other words, rights-talk keeps justice in the foreground of our considerations.'[57]

A word may be said, just as in the more general field of natural law, about the modern jurisprudence of the Irish courts, influenced certainly here by the US Supreme Court, in the area of rights. In both Ireland and the United States there has taken root a judicial theory to the effect that the rights which the courts may uphold are not confined to those expressly enumerated in the state's written constitution, but include also a 'penumbra' of unspecified personal rights which it is the courts' function to identify and vindicate as fundamental according as the occasion may arise. In the American case this doctrine has at least the support of the Ninth Amendment of the US Constitution, which expressly says: 'the enumeration in the Constitution of certain rights shall not be construed to deny or disparage others retained by the people.' In Ireland the Constitution contains no such saver; but it does have the feature—overlooked during the Dáil debate on the draft, and probably not intended by anyone to have the effect later attributed to it[58]—that, apart from the specified fundamental rights individually enumerated in Articles 40–4, Article 40.3 speaks of the 'personal rights' of the citizen in general terms (without identifying them with the former), and commits the state to 'respect' and 'vindicate' them. The evolution of the 'penumbra of rights' doctrine has some more remote origins,

---

[56] Ibid. 229.   [57] Ibid. 221.
[58] See Kelly, *Irish Constitution* (see n. 28), 473 ff.

but its modern shape in the United States can be ascribed, first, to the dissenting judgment of Douglas J. in *Poe* v. *Ullman*[59] in 1961, then to the judgment of the Supreme Court in *Griswold* v. *Connecticut*[60] in 1965. In the *Griswold* case Goldberg J. addressed the problem of whence the courts' justification of establishing a right as fundamental was to come, and cited words of Douglas J. in the earlier case, while also relying on the Ninth Amendment:

[This amendment] shows a belief of the Constitution's authors that fundamental rights exist that are not expressly enumerated in the first eight amendments, and an intent that the list of rights included there not be deemed exhaustive . . . In determining which rights are fundamental, judges are not left at large to decide cases in light of their personal and private notions. Rather, they must look to the 'traditions and [collective] conscience of our people' to determine whether a principle is 'so rooted [there as] to be ranked as fundamental' . . . ['Liberty'] also 'gains content from the emanations [of] specific [constitutional] guarantees' and 'from experience with the requirements of a free society'.

It can be seen that the American doctrine keeps away from natural-rights theory, and allows effectiveness to the Ninth Amendment through what could be called judicial introspection on the *Volksgeist*. In Ireland, on the other hand, the tradition of allegiance to Thomistic natural law has spilled into the 'penumbra of rights' area. In the very first Irish case in this development, *Educational Co.* v. *Fitzpatrick (No. 2)*,[61] Kingsmill More J. (himself a Protestant) said: 'The right to dispose of one's labour and to withdraw it seems to me a fundamental personal right which, though not specifically mentioned in the Constitution as being guaranteed, is a right of nature which I cannot conceive to have been adversely affected by anything within the intendment of the Constitution.' This was a case between an employer and a trade union attempting to enforce a closed shop; the state was not directly involved. But a couple of years later a citizen who considered that the addition of fluorine to the public water supply (which had just been authorized by statute) was a threat to her health and her family's, sued the state for a declaration that the authorizing Act was unconstitutional for violating her 'right of bodily integrity', a right not specified in the Constitution but which, she said, was latent in the general reference to the citizen's 'personal rights'.

---

[59] 367 US 497, 516–22.   [60] 381 US 479.   [61] 1961 IR 345.

She failed to discredit the Act; but the High Court and Supreme Court successively agreed with her that such things as unenumerated rights lurked in the Constitution and, at a deeper level, in nature, and that the courts could identify and enforce them as occasion arose. As a guide to finding them, Kenny J. in the High Court proposed the 'Christian and democratic nature of the State', and cited a recent encyclical letter of Pope John XXIII, *Pacem in terris*, which had emphasized the natural rights of man, in particular that part which had given the plaintiff inspiration: 'Beginning our discussion of the rights of man, we see that every man has the right to life, to bodily integrity, and to the means which are necessary and suitable for the proper development of life.' Since the time of that case, *Ryan* v. *Attorney General*,[62] the Irish courts have identified several further unenumerated rights, in some cases letting the traditional commitment to the law of nature show through. In *The State (Nicolaou)* v. *An Bord Uchtála*[63] the Supreme Court said it was 'abundantly clear that the rights referred to in Article 40.3 are those which may be called the natural personal rights'.

In *G.* v. *An Bord Uchtála*[64] O'Higgins CJ said that the right of the unmarried mother to her child was 'clearly based on the natural relationship which exists between mother and child'. In *Attorney General* v. *Paperlink*[65] Costello J. said that 'as the act of communication is the exercise of such a basic human faculty . . . a right to communicate must inhere in the citizen by virtue of his human personality and must be guaranteed by the Constitution'. And in *Norris* v. *Attorney General*,[66] in which the plaintiff failed by a 3–2 margin to persuade the Supreme Court that laws penalizing homosexual acts were an invasion of his unenumerated right to privacy, one of the dissenting judges, Henchy J, said that 'a right of privacy inheres in each citizen by virtue of his human personality' and so he thought, would attract the protection of Article 40.3.

REALISM AND THE JUDICIAL FUNCTION

Among the many facets of Hart's *Concept of Law* is a confrontation with American realism, at any rate in the form called 'rule-scepticism'. To the mere fact (recognized in every age, as we have

---

[62] 1965 IR 294.   [63] 1966 IR 567.   [64] 1980 IR 32.
[65] 1984 IRLM 373.   [66] 1984 IR 36.

documented in the sections of earlier chapters devoted to equity) that no law can make specific provision for every possible case, with the consequence that judges must retain an area of discretion, a freedom to select one of several possible applications, and the room that this leaves for the assertion that equates law with prediction of which way a court will jump, Hart attaches no significance: 'In all fields of experience, not only that of rules, there is a limit, inherent in the nature of language, to the guidance which general language can provide . . . Uncertainty at the borderline is the price to be paid for the use of general classifying terms.'[67] This uncertainty involves us in recognizing that all rules have an 'open texture' (though the degree of openness will vary from rule to rule; for example, peculiarly important social ends like protecting life may mean laws against killing which have very little area of open texture). Nevertheless, judges start out from rules, and take themselves to be administering rules, which they internally accept. To pretend that there is no limit to the area of open texture, i.e. to judges' freedom to wander at large, is to ignore the way rules work in ordinary real life. Hart draws a telling analogy, as often elsewhere, from the world of sport: in a game which involves scoring the referee cannot be challenged, but the players can keep the score even without him (though they may sometimes disagree with his ruling) by reference to rules which both he and they are supposed to recognize; and the players' running calculation of the score means something more than a mere prediction of what the referee will announce. It is, of course, possible that a judge or referee will ignore a rule, but this is not a reason for denying the rule's validity, and a judge who does this will be thought to misbehave through his failure to apply it.[68]

It is true, Hart concedes, that even the ultimate rule of recognition (i.e. the complex rule which tells us what is, and what is not, true law) may itself contain uncertainties, have an area of open texture; for instance, there is no clear consensus as to whether the British parliament may or may not 'redefine' itself for future purposes, by changing some requirement of form in certain cases, as, say, by requiring a two-thirds majority vote in the House of Commons for the enactment of laws bearing on a certain subject-matter. If such a thing were done, the question of its force might fall to be decided by a court, which, in the absence of a clear pre-

[67] *Concept*, 123, 125.   [68] Ibid. 138 ff.

existing rule, might have to do something never done before, and for which its own authority was not visible. Here, Hart thinks, the court's authority to decide as it has may be allowed only after the decision has been 'swallowed'; and here, too,

at the fringe of these very fundamental things, we should welcome the rule-sceptic, as long as he does not forget that it is at the fringe that he is welcome; and does not blind us to the fact that what makes possible [such] striking development by the courts of the most fundamental rules is, in great measure, the prestige gathered by courts from their unquestionably rule-governed operations over the vast, central areas of the law.[69]

CRITICAL LEGAL STUDIES

The most radical representatives of American realism in modern times are to be found in what is called the 'critical legal studies' movement, whose cradle in the 1970s and 1980s was the Harvard law faculty. The essence of critical legal studies theory is that it denies to law and judicial decisions any special character separating them from politics and political decisions. It does not adopt the Marxian position that law in a capitalist society is no more than a mechanism for sustaining the structures which suit the ruling classes; but it holds nevertheless that law is politics under another guise, and its pretensions to objectivity, transcending political commitments, are a sham. But so far from merely advocating a fresh start by way of devising a genuinely objective legal system, the critical legal studies school aim to merge law and politics institutionally, and to involve them in a process of conscious, perpetual, transformation. As things stand, both public and private law are designed to insulate both the current modes of democracy and the current practice of the market from the 'conflict' which is generally inherent in life; these insulated structures represent 'hierarchies', or 'hegemonies', which it is the movement's business to liquidate. Marxist-oriented societies of course also possess such 'hierarchies' and 'hegemonies', and so critical legal studies theory is equally directed against them; nevertheless, the movement is clearly of the left. Marxist insights as well as those of the older American realists

[69] *Concept*, 150.

are both among the parental influences of this highly controversial school.[70]

The standard exposition of what this movement is all about is taken to be that provided by Roberto Unger (himself one of its originators after he joined the Harvard faculty) in a very long article, not easy to read—indeed in parts nearly impenetrable—because of his use of many abstract words, and phrases, in unfamiliar ways, evidently suggested by the school's contacts with other disciplines such as modern sociology and literary analysis. One of his concerns is what appears to him to be the injurious alternation of political power in a democracy between, broadly speaking, conservative and property-regarding forces on the one hand, and socialist-redistributivist forces on the other. Each side, because of the need to conciliate a large middle ground of the electorate, is obliged to sell its soul by adopting some of the positions of the other; and this weary see-saw, sustained at the expense of the citizen who is unable to break out towards anything better, is made inevitable by fireproofed constitutional structures, the 'entrenched institutional order'. Unger wants to move instead towards something more fluid,

an institutional structure, itself self-revision, that would provide constant occasions to disrupt any fixed structure of power and coordination in social life. Any such emergent structure would be broken up before having a chance to shield itself from the risks of ordinary conflict . . . [It would be] a polity . . . open to self-revision and more capable of dismantling any established or emergent structure of social division and hierarchy.[71]

Not only, then, would Unger's new kind of state be in a condition of provisional stability so far as its institutions were concerned; it would impart (by its compulsory intervention) the same instability to every structure in the non-state areas of society. It would do this because, in the new dispensation, people would have four orders of rights, of which one order would be what he calls 'destabilisation rights, to prevent petrification of any new structure out of reach of competitors':

The central idea of the system of destabilisation rights is to provide a claim upon governmental power obliging government to disrupt those forms of

---

[70] For an interesting account of the impact of the critical legal studies movement on a traditional law school, see an article entitled 'Harvard Law' in the *New Yorker*, 26 Mar. 1984.

[71] 'Critical Legal Studies', *Harvard Law Review* (1983), 561, 592, 607.

division and hierarchy that, contrary to the spirit of the [new-modelled] constitution, manage to achieve stability only by distancing themselves from the transformative conflicts that might disturb them. Such a doctrine would do the work undertaken by [current US 'equal protection' court interventions, but would do it more rationally].[72]

A central value for the critical legal studies school is that of 'community', by which Unger means the social or altruistic element in the world (and also in the law). He presents, merely in order to illustrate his position, an area of constitutional and an area of private law, and tries to show that in both of these the 'community' element, quite wrongly and arbitrarily—or rather, not so much arbitrarily, as to suit the perpetuation of the structures represented by democratic government on the one hand and by the market principle on the other—appears as subordinate to, no more than a modification of, what are supposed to be the primary principles inherent in the law of each; whereas, if we could look at the whole scene with a fresh eye (and with the ability to 'disrupt' and 'correct' it from the ground up), in fact the 'community' element could easily and more satisfactorily be made the central one, with the supposedly primary rules being placed in a far more modest perspective. Thus, in constitutional law, while the state's measures must be general in application (the primary principle), certain groups will appear so typically disadvantaged as to require special treatment via the 'equal protection' jurisprudence developed by the Supreme Court, these groups (blacks, women) are arbitrarily selected (so as to keep the idea of 'equal protection' intervention in the role of a merely secondary modification of the primary principle). His point is that there are many other disadvantaged groups, e.g. those generally with low bargaining or lobbying or decision-making power. Why not then start with the notion of relieving all disadvantage, of fairness for everyone and not just blacks and women, as the central source of government and law, whatever the consequences for the value of generality? In other words, why not invert the present respective roles of the (present) primary and secondary principles? Though the secondary ones, or 'counterprinciples', 'may be seen as mere restraint upon the principles, they may also serve as points of departure for a different organising conception of this whole area of law'.[73] The same operation is carried out in the central legal idea on

---

[72] 'Critical Legal Studies', *Harvard Law Review* (1983), 612.
[73] Ibid. 618.

which the market depends, namely that of contract. Here, says Unger, the primary principle is freedom of contract. But there is a counterprinciple, which (he says) is secondary: namely, that that freedom 'will not be allowed to work in ways that subvert the communal aspects of social life'. The counterprinciple comes through in various modifications of freedom of contract, all connected by being rooted in the idea of fairness. But why relegate this 'community' value of fairness to a secondary role? Why not, here too, make a fresh start and construct this area of law from scratch on fairness, which now will extend into contexts where at present freedom of contract reigns unchecked? Why not, here too, invert the roles of principle and counterprinciple, letting the supposed value of freedom of contract fend for itself in the reconstructed contractual world? Thus in both public and private law, Unger's counterprinciples 'may even serve as the points of departure for a system of law and doctrine that reverses the traditional relationship and reduces the principles to a specialised role'.[74]

The implication of all this (even if it rested on an accurate analysis of the existing system) is of course revolutionary, and perhaps will also seem likely to end in anarchy, a plausible comment on a scheme informed by the urge for endless disruption and remodelling. Even Unger's choice of language suggests a spirit emotionally attuned to destruction, as when he chooses the phrase 'negative capability' to describe the desirable condition of society:

Negative capability is the practical and spiritual, individual and collective empowerment made possible by the disentrenchment of formative structures. Disentrenchment means not permanent instability, but the making of structures that turn the occasion for their reproduction into opportunities for their correction. Disentrenchment therefore promises to liberate societies from their blind lurching between protracted stagnation and rare and risky revolution. A thesis of this article is that the formative contexts of the present day [i.e. Western democracy, the market economy, with the legal apparatuses through which they work] impose unnecessary and unjustifiable constraints upon the growth of negative capability.[75]

Objections to Unger's thesis lie however also in his depiction of the existing system. John Finnis, concentrating on his analysis of Anglo-American contract, rejects the idea that fairness in some way

---

[74] 'Critical Legal Studies', *Harvard Law Review* (1983), 633.   [75] Ibid. 650.

is only grudgingly admitted into a world where over most of the area self-interest, 'pitiless business deals', are by and large upheld; on the contrary, even business deals are an aspect of the civil affection, the *philia politikē*, which we saw Finnis expounding in his *Natural Law and Natural Rights*; and in fact 'existing contract law and doctrine is rich in concern for moral principles of fairness, and can expand or contract its specification of those principles without engaging in any struggle between conceptual frameworks'. Unger he charges with 'not understanding the moral underpinnings of existing pre-critical contract law and theory . . . The [critical legal studies] movement's criticism of substantive and procedural social institutions fails to subvert those institutions because it fails to understand their relationship to principles of practical reasoning which not only justify them but could justify their reform.[76] A more general attack on the critical legal studies movement, relating it to the spirit of the age in which it grew up, is that of Owen M. Fiss; it will be briefly cited at the end of the next section, on the 'law and economics' school, against which it is also directed. It remains a major movement in the United States, and has been joined by European disciples as well. Despite the triviality which its opponents see in it, the editors of *Lloyd's Introduction to Jurisprudence* think it is most unlikely to have simply fizzled out by the time of their next edition.[77]

LAW AND ECONOMICS

The 'law and economics' movement, shorthand for those whose interest is the 'economic analysis of law', can be regarded, in crude terms, as the right wing of modern American Jurisprudence, critical legal studies being its left. Its remote ancestry is the utilitarianism of Bentham and Mill, more proximately it descends from the realism of the earlier twentieth century and from Pound's 'social engineering'. The link with classical utilitarianism lies in the attempt to find a formula for lawmaking more scientific and precise than the elusive 'greatest happiness of the greatest number'; the latter is really no more than an emotive demand for rational, general-interest-

---

[76] J. Finnis, 'The Critical Studies Movement', in *Oxford Essays in Jurisprudence*, 3rd ser. (Oxford, 1987), 157, 159, 165.
[77] Lloyd, *Introduction*, 716.

oriented legislation, and incapable of yielding a concrete guide to the right solution in any particular instance. The link with realism lies in the movement's study of what judges actually do; and the link with 'social engineering' (the satisfaction of wants with the least waste or friction) in its identification of the 'maximization of wealth' as the best key to successful lawmaking. Into the notion of 'maximization of wealth' the school has fed criteria invented by economists, notably the formulas proposed by the Italian pioneer Vilfredo Pareto (1848–1923); and underlying it is the assumption that all people (except those under some disability) are rational maximizers of their own satisfactions. The notion of wealth, or of satisfaction, is understood in a sense wider than the purely monetary; and 'rational' does not necessarily mean something consciously calculated.

The claims of the law and economics school—extreme at first sight, more plausible on reflection—are twofold, 'positive' and 'normative'. The 'positive' doctrine originated in the early 1960s. It was perhaps at first suggested by contemporary study of anti-trust legislation to see whether or not it tended to be 'efficient' in the economist's sense, i.e. tending to increase rather than to reduce social wealth. Next, a study of the almost entirely judge-made law of nuisance claimed to show that the rules which had been judicially worked out, when analysed on economic criteria, in fact turned out to meet the same standard.[78] And then, in the 1970s, this insight was generalized over the entire span of the common law, not excluding criminal law; in particular, by the school's foremost representative, Richard A. Posner, lecturer in the University of Chicago law school as well as a federal judge. This school now claims to show that, when we carefully examine what the common-law judges have been doing in shaping the doctrines which have been perfected over the last hundred or so years, we will find that they have—albeit unconsciously, in response to an instinct as beneficent as that which leads a fish to cover its spawn with gravel against predators—been working out the rules which best tend to maximize wealth. In the leading law and economics text, *Economic Analysis of Law*, Posner wrote that 'many of the doctrines and institutions of the legal system are best understood and explained as efforts to promote the efficient allocation of resources . . . It would not be surprising to

[78] Richard A. Posner, *Economic Analysis of Law* (Boston, Mass.: 1st edn. 1972; 3rd edn. 1986), 20–1.

find that legal doctrines rest on inarticulate gropings towards efficiency.'[79] In his more recent work, *The Problems of Jurisprudence* (1990), he says of judge-made law that it

exhibits, according to the economic theory I am expounding, a remarkable . . . substantive consistency. It is as if the judges *wanted* to adopt the rules, procedures, and case outcomes that would maximise society's.wealth . . . No doubt most judges (and lawyers) think that the guiding light for common law decision making should be either an intuitive sense of justice or reasonableness, or a casual utilitarianism. But these may all be the same thing, and if pressed such a judge would probably have to admit that what he called utilitarianism was what I am calling wealth maximization.[80]

In fact one American judge, Justice Learned Hand, had as long ago as 1947 virtually recognized this in terms foreshadowing Posner's doctrine when he defined negligence as 'the failure to take cost-justified precautions',[81] an instance which Posner uses to illustrate his point. If the possibility of an accident, which if it occurs will occasion a cost or loss of $100, can be assessed as one chance in a hundred, while the cost (to a potential defendant) of taking the precautions needed to avoid it will be $3, the court will tend to recognize the diseconomy of taking those precautions by way of holding that they would go beyond what would be required on the standard of reasonable care. In other words, in such apparently non-material, morality-oriented standards as reasonable care, in fact an instinctual economic appraisal lies buried. If the figures in this hypothetical example were reversed, i.e. if the chances of the accident were three in a hundred, and the avoidance cost only $1, the liability would be reversed; what the court would actually say, however, would be merely that the standard of reasonable care, if it had been met in the present circumstances, would have meant taking these relatively cheap precautions; by making the defendant liable in such conditions, as Posner puts it, 'the law would be overcoming transaction-cost obstacles to wealth-maximising transactions—a frequent office of liability rules'.[82] He sees all this in a historical frame: 'It probably is no accident . . . that many common-law doctrines assumed their modern form in the nineteenth century, when laissez-faire ideology, which resembles wealth maximisation, had a strong hold on the Anglo-American judicial imagination.'[83]

[79] Ibid.
[80] *The Problems of Jurisprudence* (London, 1990), 356, 390–1.
[81] Ibid. 358.   [82] Ibid.   [83] Ibid. 359.

All kinds of objections to this will occur; but Posner allows for exceptions, indeed draws attention to them, and does not claim perfection for his theory. There is no denying that some human behaviour is not rational; or that incommensurable elements such as unwillingness to take risks play a part in it—for example to take up again the accident example, many people would not be willing, in exchange for $3, to assume even a 1 per cent chance of a $100 accident-loss. Moreover, he points out that several actual rules in the law would not be there if pure maximization of wealth were pursued throughout: for example, some aspects of fault-liability are less 'efficient' economically than strict liability would be; and probably the law excluding forced confessions from criminal evidence is not 'efficient' either. Generally, too, as he puts it, 'freedom appears to be valued for reasons that escape the economic calculus'.[84] Nevertheless economic analysis of law has a value: 'There may well be definite although wide boundaries on both the explanative and reformative power of economic analysis of law. Always, however, economics can provide value clarification by showing the society what it must give up to achieve a non-economic ideal of justice. The demand for justice is not independent of its price.'[85]

The 'normative' dimension of law and economics amounts essentially to the proposal that legislation should be guided by regard for the maximization of wealth, in other words, the doctrine moves from the claimed observation of how judges in fact have worked, to the ought-proposition that this is how legislators too should work. Here of course the school is obliged to recognize that, as it does not purport to offer a theory of initial distribution of goods (in the way, say, that Rawls does), neither has it anything to say about principles of redistribution. Nevertheless it is interesting to see how Posner regards legislation, or much legislation, as having been undertaken with the express purpose of blocking or circum-venting the market which, if left alone, will tend to be wealth-maximizing; this is because legislators do 'deals' with (i.e. enact statutes to suit) lobbies which are powerful enough electorally to induce this intervention on their behalf—intervention which can often be expressed in terms of transferring wealth to them out of the hands of others. Accordingly,

[84] Ibid. 379.   [85] *Economic Analysis of Law*, 26.

the economic analysis of law implies that fields of law left to the judges to elaborate, such as the common law fields, must be the ones in which interest-group pressures are too weak to deflect the legislature from pursuing goals that are in the general interest. [But where the legislature does take it into its head to make law] the analyst will urge—on any legislator sufficiently free of interest-group pressures to be able to legislate in the public interest—a program of enacting only legislation that conforms to the dictates of wealth maximisation.[86]

Posner's lucidly written work, moderate in its assertions and evincing full acceptance that there is more to both life and law than wealth maximization, has still come under attack, with that of the other law and economics writers, for its supposed crude materialism, as offensive as the supposed anarchism of the critical legal studies movement. In 1986 both were bitterly assailed, as misbegotten products of their unhappy period, by Owen M. Fiss. The 1970s, in which both movements flowered, he called a time

of difference and disagreement, in which the emphasis was not on what we shared, our public values and ideals, but on how we differed and what divided us. Although in the 1960s we undertook the Second Reconstruction and tried to build the Great Society, and we were drawn to law as public ideal, in the next decade we took refuge in the politics of selfishness. The prospect of understanding and nourishing a common morality seemed hopeless . . . We will never be able to respond fully to the negativism of critical legal studies or the crude instrumentalism of law and economics until a regenerative process takes hold, until the broad social processes that fed and nourished those movements are reversed.[87]

In regard to Posner's idea that a court, faced with a choice of solutions, ought to choose the one which market considerations would recommend—ought, as he put it, to replicate or 'mimic' the market—Fiss stiffly commented that 'the duty of the judge is not to serve the market, but to determine whether it should prevail'. Alluding to the things other than wealth maximization that humans think important, he says 'Values are values'. But Posner's school, as has been seen, does not deny this. Admitting that any absolutely consistent application of the 'wealth maximization' principle would (as the movement's critics had said) tend to treat human individuals as if they were merely cells of an organism, he frankly writes that the implications of such a construction would be 'contrary to the

[86] *Problems of Jurisprudence*, 359.
[87] 'The Death of the Law', *Cornell Law Review*, 72 (1986), 14.

unshakeable moral intuitions of Americans, and . . . conformity to intuition is the ultimate test of a moral (indeed of any) theory'.[88]

NEW STUDIES: LAW, STRUCTURALISM, SEMIOTICS

In very recent years theories originally proposed by anthropologists and linguistic scientists have been tentatively tried out by some scholars on law. This field of study has not yet 'settled down', but one or two of its centres of interest may be very briefly signalled here.

First, the doctrine of 'structuralism'—its most celebrated pioneer the anthropologist Claude Lévi-Strauss—appears to have potential for explaining, among other things, the forms typically assumed by legal regulation. 'At its most general', wrote Bernard Jackson, 'structuralism asserts the existence within the human mind of a "rational subconscious", which shapes but does not determine human culture. This rational subconscious has a genetic or physical base, and operates as an innate structuring mechanism, guiding the "surface" manifestations (i.e. human culture) towards expression in certain forms.'[89] According to Lévi-Strauss, one dimension of this ingrained human structuring mechanism is the instinct for 'binary opposition', that is, the built-in tendency to perceive the realities of the outside world in terms of pairs of opposites or correlatives (examples are the contrasts between form and content, implicit and explicit, abstract and concrete, constant and variable, stable and changeable, nature and environment) instead of as continual shading into one another. 'It is of the essence of structuralism', again in the words of Bernard Jackson, 'that it strives to explain culture in terms of the structures of the mind', and so, if the instinct for binary opposition really is one such structure, we evidently possess a hint as to one powerful formative element in the construction of our typical patterns of law, in which pairs of mutually exclusive classes or concepts are exceedingly common. There may be others; Jackson, at any rate, thinks

the whole direction of structuralist thought concerning the range of the subconscious and the levels of mind and meaning would appear to lead to

---

[88] *Problems of Jurisprudence*, 376–7.
[89] *Structuralism and Legal Theory* (Liverpool, 1979), 2.

the conclusion that the search *must* be mounted for the mental structures that guide the production of law, whether or not they are likely to follow the pattern discerned for systems of communication.[90]

Semiotics (from the Greek *sēma*, a sign) is a similarly modern, and related, field devoted to the study of modes of communicating meaning. Such study shows that a mass of words or sentences, such as is represented by a legal text like a statute or judgment, may transmit to those to whom it is addressed a total 'message' over and above the sum of meanings of its parts; in the way that, say, a novel imparts to a reader habituated to literature an impression which transcends that available to someone merely capable of understanding one sentence or paragraph at a time as he goes along. This in a structuralist view, suggests that the human mind, or at least the human mind in a given culture, is equipped or conditioned with deep-level locks to which particular forms and arrangements of language offer the keys. In its application to law, semiotics thus suggests that a statute or judgment may in fact be saying something rather different from, or something additional to, what the text says on its surface, its deep-level meaning being of course accessible to those who inhabit the same cultural, and semiotic, group.[91]

FUNCTIONAL ANALYSIS OF LAW

Modern continental jurisprudence exhibits an interest in the study of law in relation to the functions assigned to it by society. In Italy the most important writer in this area has been Norberto Bobbio (born 1909), who drew attention to the changed role of law—and in particular to the fading of the frontier between law and politics—resulting from the growth of the social and welfare state. In Germany Niklas Luhmann (born 1927) published in his *Rechtssoziologie* (1972) a highly abstract functional analysis of law centred on 'expectations' and the evolution by which they are generalized. Our expectations (in Luhmann's presentation) are of two kinds, cognitive and normative; the former relate to the supposed qualities of the real world, the latter to the behaviour of people. Both kinds are liable to 'disappointment'. But whereas if a cognitive expectation is

---

[90] *Structuralism and Legal Theory* (Liverpool, 1979), 26.
[91] Bernard Jackson, *Semiotics and Legal Theory* (London, 1985), ch. 1.

disappointed, e.g. if it turns out that the earth is after all not flat as we had thought, we handle this 'disappointment' by changing our expectation, in other words by learning better. But the disappointment of a normative expectation does not lead us to abandon it. We must, indeed, come to terms with it (*verarbeiten*; 'process', 'digest' it); and social systems have the function, *inter alia*, of facilitating the handling of such disappointments. Here the major role is played by the 'generalization' of expectations of behaviour. Generalizations have several different dimensions; in their social dimension, they are represented by institutionalization. Once an expectation is institutionalized (i.e. given the vesture of law) it no longer depends on individual or even active group assent, which explains why an institutionalized expectation, or law, may sometimes survive long after the disappearance of the consensus which originally supported it. This whole process, Luhmann wrote, can be seen in the context of an evolution concerned with managing a world growing ever more complex and developing constantly fresh sets of 'expectations'. The decisive moment historically in this evolution he placed in the era of 'positivization', of the rapid growth of the bourgeois state with its accompaniment of huge productions of new statute-law. The element of *complexity* in the evolution rules out as impractical the old appeal to natural law and instincts of justice.

THE CRIMINAL LAW AND MORALITY

The question debated in the nineteenth century between schools of which John Stuart Mill and James Fitzjames Stephen were respectively the leading representatives, namely, the title of the law to repress immoral behaviour even when it caused no harm to others, attracted little notice in the earlier twentieth century, but revived in the late 1950s in England. The occasion was an entirely practical one. The existing law on two quite separate areas of sexual practice—homosexuality and prostitution—was felt to be unsatisfactory, but before legislating for change the British government established a committee (usually called the Wolfenden Committee after its chairman) to consider these matters. The committee recommended liberalizing the law in the former area, tightening it up in the latter; but as well as giving its practical reasons it declared a philosophical position:

[The function of the criminal law in these areas] is to preserve public order and decency, to protect the citizen from what is offensive or injurious, and to provide sufficient safeguards against exploitation and corruption of others, particularly those who are specially vulnerable because they are young, weak in body or mind, inexperienced, or in a state of special physical, official or economic dependence.

It is not, in our view, the function of the law to intervene in the private lives of citizens, or to seek to enforce any particular pattern of behaviour, further than is necessary to carry out the purposes we have outlined ... [We think to be decisive] the importance which society and the law ought to give to individual freedom of choice and action in matters of private morality. Unless a deliberate attempt is to be made by society, acting through the agency of the law, to equate the sphere of crime with that of sin, there must remain a realm of private morality and immorality which is, in brief and crude terms, not the law's business.[92]

These passages were picked up by the English judge Sir Patrick Devlin in a lecture delivered in 1959. Devlin rejected the simplicity of what was, in essence, a modern and almost official restatement of the Mill position. He observed, first, that the existing criminal law did, in fact, in various ways display a moral concern independent of the question of harm to a victim. For example, it did not admit consent as a defence to a charge of murder or assault; and it treated euthanasia, suicide pacts, sibling incest, abortion, and so on as criminal, despite the absence of harm to other persons. The system in fact was seamed through with moral ideas which collectively reflected a shared public morality; and this was as necessary to the continuance of a civilized society as was a stable government. This morality was admittedly Christian in character, and so left room for the argument that, since orthodox Christian belief now existed only among a minority in Britain, it ought not to determine the shape of a criminal law applying to a non-believing majority. But such an argument overlooked the fact that Christian morality had long since been inseparably mortared into the masonry of British society. English marriage law one could recognize as originally built on the Christian doctrines of marriage; but this was an unalterable historical fact. It did not have its modern shape *because* it was Christian; 'it has *got* there because it is Christian, but it remains there because it is built into the house in which we live and could not be removed without bringing it down'. Accordingly, no

---

[92] *Report of the Committee on Homosexual Offences and Prostitution*, § 13.

formula such as the Wolfenden Committee had suggested was admissible:

The suppression of vice [wrote Devlin] is as much the law's business as the suppression of subversive activities; it is no more possible to define a sphere of private morality than it is to define one of private subversive activity. There are no theoretical limits to the power of the State to legislate against treason and sedition, and likewise I think there can be no theoretical limits to legislation against immorality.[93]

In this passage it is the word 'theoretical' which requires emphasis; because it was only the impossibility of assigning *theoretical* limits that Devlin was asserting. He did, in fact, go on to admit a series of *practical* limits (much as Stephen had also done) in the shape of some 'elastic principles' whose application might, in fact, produce a criminal code in effect quite as liberal as anything in the Wolfenden Committee's concrete proposals. These principles, briefly, were 'toleration of the maximum individual freedom that is consistent with the integrity of society'; a recognition that 'the limits of tolerance shift'; a respect, as far as possible, for the privacy of individuals; and an acceptance that 'the law is concerned with the minimum and not with the maximum'—as he put it, 'there is much in the Sermon on the Mount that would be out of place in the Ten Commandments'.[94]

In spite of these practical 'elastic principles' Devlin's general position was very much out of tune with the mood of the 1960s. The foremost of the critics who now rose up was H. L. A. Hart, who embodied his contrary view in three lectures published as *Law, Liberty, and Morality*. These were a reply to Devlin, but also, belatedly, to Stephen. With regard to Devlin's instances of how the criminal law did in fact express moral values, Hart denied that this construction could be put on his points about consent no defence, euthanasia, and so on; each of these parts of the law 'may perfectly well be explained as a piece of paternalism, designed to protect individuals against themselves . . . a perfectly coherent policy . . . and instances of paternalism now abound in our law, criminal and civil [he mentioned as an example the laws on drug abuse]'.[95] He then turned back to an argument which Stephen had used, namely

---

[93] 'The Enforcement of Morals', repr. as ch. 1 ('Morals of the Criminal Law') in a collection of papers entitled *The Enforcement of Morals* (London, 1965), 9, 13–14.
[94] Ibid. 19.   [95] *Law, Liberty, and Morality* (London, 1968), 31–2.

that a court would have regard, in measuring the punishment awarded to two defendants convicted of the same crime, to their differing degrees of moral guilt so far as this could be assessed: even if this were so, thought Hart, it did not show that the enforcement of moral standards was central to the constitution of a crime. As for the instance of bigamy—adduced by Dean Rostow in an essay in support of Devlin[96]—this, he thought, was criminal not because it was immoral but because the confusion of status records was a public nuisance.[97] He laid, more generally, special emphasis on the human misery attributable to criminal punishment as a reason for restricting its infliction to the cases which Mill had admitted, i.e. those where harm is caused to others. But his main criticism was aimed at Devlin's picture of society and the state as vitally dependent on the maintenance of a given moral code (and thus entitled to enforce it through law). Devlin, he wrote,

appears to move from the acceptable proposition that *some* shared morality is essential to the existence of any society to the unacceptable proposition that a society is identical with its morality as that is at any given moment of its history, so that a change in its morality is tantamount to the destruction of a society . . . No doubt it is true that if deviations from conventional sexual morality are tolerated by the law and come to be known, the conventional morality might change in a permissive direction . . . But even if the conventional morality did so change, the society in question would not have been destroyed or 'subverted'. We should compare such a development not to the violent overthrow of government but to a peaceful constitutional change in its form, consistent not only with the preservation of a society but with its advance.[98]

Devlin in his rejoinder[99] took up Hart's handling of Stephen's point on gradation of sentences: it would contravene a central principle of law if a power given for one purpose (on Hart's hypothesis, the mere repression of crime harmful to others) were to be used for another (viz., on the same hypothesis, in the context of sentencing, for the vindication of moral standards); on the contrary, the whole criminal process must be seen as informed by those standards throughout. Hart's dismissal of various crimes as mere exercises in paternalism, Devlin said, 'tears the heart out of his doctrine'; it was

---

[96] 'The Enforcement of Morals', *Cambridge Law Journal*, 74 (1960), 190.
[97] Hart, *Law, Liberty, and Morality*, 41.   [98] Ibid. 51–2.
[99] The last chapter ('Morals and Contemporary Social Reality') in *Enforcement of Morals* (see n. 93).

impossible to disentangle meaningfully the notion of paternalism from the upholding of morality, as in every paternalistic act there must reside a moral conviction—as Neil MacCormick an admirer of Hart's wrote, 'in deciding what is "harmful" to a person, we necessarily make an evaluation, and the evaluation belongs to morality'.[100] A law directed at drug abuse obviously rests on the conviction that wanton inducement of narcosis is morally wrong.

Hart's more general criticism of Devlin, that a change in moral convictions does not amount to a subversion of society, was hardly necessary to answer, since Devlin in his initial statement had acknowledged that 'the limits of tolerance shift', not quite the same thing as admitting that moral convictions wax and wane, but near enough, as a practical 'elastic principle', to inhibit officious moral policing or the enforcement of laws after the moral consensus which once supported them has dissolved. The debate (which was joined by many others)[101] dragged on for a while; but as Devlin's initial assertions had been modest, so they seemed at the end to have stood up well. A parting shot was particularly telling:

> Mill's doctrine has existed for over a century and no one has ever attempted to put it into practice . . . [John Morley, Mill's disciple] had opportunities rarely obtained by a rationalist philosopher of putting his theories into practice. He was a Member of Parliament for a great many years and one of the four men who formed the dominant group in Mr Gladstone's last Cabinet. But he does not appear to have made any use of them.[102]

CRIMINAL LAW AND PUNISHMENT

We have seen that throughout Western history the purpose predominantly attributed to punishment has been deterrence; retribution, or reformation of the offender, are much less regularly mentioned. In the 1950s, with the insights which modern criminology was gaining, the whole idea of inflicting punishment under whatever ostensible justification was being challenged by those who were impressed by the degree to which delinquent behaviour

---

[100] *H. L. A. Hart*, 153.
[101] Bibliography in R. W. M. Dias, *Bibliography of Jurisprudence* (3rd edn., London, 1979), 70–6; K. Greenwalt, *Conflicts of Law and Morality* (Oxford, 1987).
[102] *Enforcement of Morals* (see n. 93), 125, 127.

seemed preconditioned by factors not imputable in justice to an offender, such as genetic inheritance, environment, and early upbringing. This suggested to Barbara Wootton, for example, a British penal reformer who had herself been for many years a magistrate, the futility of continuing to ground criminal justice in the supposed fault of delinquents; she argued instead for a system of strict liability which would bring within the law's reach anyone who was the physical author of prohibited acts, irrespective of fault. Such a person would be referred to a board for assessment and for further referral for appropriate treatment, perhaps medical, perhaps rehabilitative, perhaps ending in dismissal without treatment at all, as the case might suggest.[103] In her idea that the notion of criminal responsibility might thus be allowed to wither away there is an evident affinity with the Italian 'positivist' school of criminal theory of the earlier part of the century.

But since about 1970 a quite unfamiliar, and in the preceding era unfashionable, tone began to be heard: retributivism as a legitimate element in criminal punishment was taken up by writer after writer. Possibly this fits into the larger picture which shows a resurgence in the 1970s of right-wing economic and political thinking. There had always, of course, been voices which scorned to rest punishment on some utilitarian calculation of deterrent value: a well-known such voice in Britain was that of Lord Denning, who in his evidence to the Royal Commission on Capital Punishment, whose report was published in 1953, had said:

The punishment for grave crimes should adequately reflect the revulsion felt by the majority of citizens for them. It is a mistake to consider the object of punishment as being deterrent or reformative or preventive and nothing else. The ultimate justification of any punishment is not that it is a deterrent but that it is the emphatic denunciation by the community of a crime.[104]

This 'denunciation' theory of punishment was itself denounced by Hart in *Law, Liberty, and Morality*.[105] But the new wave of retributivist theory which set in a few years later had more formidable philosophical foundations. From Kant it took the principle that it is never permissible to treat a human being as a means rather than as an end; applied to this context, it cut the

---

[103] *Crime and the Criminal Law* (London, 1963), 41 ff.
[104] Report, § 53.   [105] See above, n. 95: pp. 60–9.

ground from under deterrence as a respectable pretext for punishment. 'If we take seriously', wrote Jeffrie G. Murphy,

the Kantian demand that persons (including persons convicted of a crime) are owed basic respect, then surely we owe it to them that our harsh treatment of them can be justified by reasons that they (in so far as they are rational beings) can understand and accept. Here is where the utilitarian theory seems to be in trouble, for it must say to the criminal: 'We are punishing you in order to use you as an example to others and thereby deter crime'. But surely the criminal can at this point well ask the question: 'What gives you the right to use me in this way? . . . Are you not simply proposing to use me as a means only, as an instrument toward the social good; and do I not have, as a rational being, a right not to be so used?'[106]

The Kantian principle of retribution simply as something required by justice—memorably stated as demanding the execution of all remaining condemned prisoners before a state could be dissolved— now also reappeared. 'Some of our conclusions may seem old-fashioned', said the (American) Report of the Committee for the Study of Incarceration, '[but] we take seriously Kant's view that a person should be punished because he deserves it.'[107] The same practical conclusion was reached, from a very different starting-point, by Finnis. In his *Natural Law and Natural Rights* he presents crime rather as a form of unjustified enrichment, a disequilibrium produced by the criminal's disregard of others' rights, which must be rectified by punishing him (and thus curing the diminution of his own personality which he has brought on himself): the whole process sounding like some corrective mechanism in hydraulics:

Sanctions are punishment because they are required in reason to avoid injustice, to maintain a rational order of proportionate equality, or fairness, as between all members of the society. For when someone, who really could have chosen otherwise, manifests in action a preference . . . for his own interests, his own freedom of choice and action, as against the common interests and the legally defined common way-of-action, then in and by that very action he gains a certain sort of advantage over those who have restrained themselves, restricted their pursuit of their own interests, in order to abide by the law . . . If the free-willing criminal were to retain this advantage, the situation would be as unequal and unfair as it would be for him to retain the tangible profits of his crime . . . Punishment, then, characteristically seeks to restore the distributively just balance of

---

[106] *Philosophy of Law* with Jules L. Coleman (Totowa, NJ, 1990), 121.
[107] *Doing Justice: The Choice of Punishments* (1976), 6.

advantages between the criminal and the law-abiding . . . What is done cannot be undone. But punishment rectifies the disturbed pattern of distribution of advantages and disadvantages throughout a community by depriving the convicted criminal of his freedom of choice, proportionately to the degree to which he had exercised his freedom, his personality, in the unlawful act.[108]

A very similar view comes through in Wojciech Sadurski, who sees the law as imposing the burden of self-restraint on each citizen so that every other citizen can have the benefit of his rights within his own protected sphere. A wrongdoer 'arrogates to himself part of his victim's benefits and renounces some of his own burdens [of self-restraint]', and so earns punishment; the object of punishment is neither deterrent nor reformative but 'to restore the equilibrium of benefits and burdens' by increasing the burdens which the wrongdoer must bear.[109] Whether there is any commensurable relation between a prison sentence (not to speak of a death sentence) and the offence of, say, rape or causing an explosion, or, in general, whether this whole subject-matter can realistically be presented in terms of disequilibria, is another question.

CRIME AND CRIMINOLOGY

Criminology is a science in which field-work, as well as the insights of other sciences, yields theories as to the roots of the social disorder we call crime: 'constitutional' theories, which focus on the evidence for genetic predisposition to delinquency; theories which seek pathological explanations in terms of mental weakness and illness; theories which see delinquency rooted in the maladjustment which faulty upbringing can saddle on a child; environmental theories which attribute importance to social and economic conditions such as overcrowding, ghetto subculture, and so on.[110] It is not itself the material on which theory operates, unless it be any form of scepticism as to all men being equally responsible, and to the same extent, for their actions, which no one believes. The only

---

[108] Natural Law (see n. 41), 262–3.
[109] 'Distributive Justice and the Theory of Punishment', Oxford Journal of Legal Studies, 5 (1985), 47, 53.
[110] The typology of theories listed here is based on Walker, Crime and Punishment (see Ch. 9 n. 69).

qualification which need be made here is based on the general Marxian interpretation of the state and law; this necessarily entails a view of crime, and of criminology as pursued in the West, which deviates from the general Western perception in a predictable way. The American Marxist writer Richard Quinney restated in 1977 the traditional Marxian position that 'crime is essentially a product of the material and spiritual contradictions of capitalism'; while crime control was essentially a form of capitalist domination.[111] This in turn entailed a disobliging estimation of Western criminology and those who pursue it:

> Criminology has been, and continues in large measure to be, a body of thought and practice that seeks to control anything that threatens the capitalist system of production and its social relations . . . The objective task of the criminologist [in capitalist society] is to transmit bourgeois ideology to the working class as a whole, to ensure harmonious relations between the working class and the capitalist class according to the interests of the latter . . . Only in a working-class consciousness, coming from an affiliation with the working class, can a socialist-Marxist criminology be pursued.[112]

How doctrine of this kind will survive the events of 1989–90 in the states of Eastern Europe—or how it will explain the lately soaring criminality in the Soviet Union—remains to be seen.

INTERNATIONAL LAW

This chapter will conclude with a brief account of Hart's application of his *Concept of Law* to the law of nations. In the closing section of his book he deals with two obstacles which the Austin conception of law, as the orders of a sovereign backed by threats, had been traditionally seen as blocking the title of 'international law' to be called law at all: namely, the obvious difference, in regular enforceability, between its rules and the primary rules of a municipal legal system (a difference which had led to its being classified, on the Austin principle, as no more than 'positive morality'); and, secondly, the apparent impossibility in the proposition that a *sovereign* state might be capable of being the *subject* of a superior system under which it could be said to carry obligations.

---

[111] *Class, State and Crime* (see n. 12), 176. [112] Ibid. 177, 180.

The first of these obstacles Hart surmounts by pointing simply to his disposal of the Austin position, in particular his seeing in legal obligation not simply a prediction of sanction in case of disobedience but an internal normative statement as well: 'Once we free ourselves from the predictive analysis and its parent conception of law as essentially an order backed by threats, there seems no good reason for limiting the normative idea of obligation to rules supported by organised sanctions.'[113] It might make perfectly good sense, therefore, to impute an obligation to a state even though no one had commanded its performance, or was in a position to enforce it. As for the problem with 'sovereign' states, it all arises from an unwarranted preconception that such entities are the basic building-blocks of the international order. In fact what are loosely called 'states' display a wide variety of degrees of independence. And instead of letting this preconception dictate our estimate of international law, it would be more rational to start from the other end.

For if in fact we find that there exists among states a given form of international authority, the sovereignty of states is to that extent limited, and it has just that extent which the rules allow. An uncritical use of the idea of sovereignty has spread similar confusion in the theory of both municipal and international law, and demands in both a similar corrective . . . In both cases, belief in the necessary existence of the legally unlimited sovereign prejudges a question which we can only answer when we examine the actual rules.[114]

As for the relegation of international law to the status of mere 'positive morality'—required by the Austin formula—this also arises from inadequate attention to what is implied, in ordinary usage, in the notion of morality. Claims based on international law, or on others' supposed violation of it, are not couched in terms of (though they may be accompanied by rhetorical invocations of) morality. The content of most rules of international law is morally indifferent (say the extent of territorial waters) until fixed by convention or practice; and similarly (as was seen earlier) while rules of morality are not thought or spoken of as susceptible to deliberate overnight repeal or amendment, rules of international law do not exist on this plane of transcendence but rather resemble

[113] *Concept* (see n. 14), 213.   [114] Ibid. 218.

conventional rules of municipal law, like the rule of the road, which we might legislatively alter at will.[115]

Hart's main concern, however, is to disengage international law from debates whose form is preconditioned by any theory which originally arose in a municipal-law setting (and culminated in an understanding, or definition, of law into which international law will not fit). For him, there is as little reason to despair because it sits equivocally in Kelsen's scheme as there is because it does the same in Austin's. There is, certainly, no visible *Grundnorm* in international law; even the suggested 'States should behave as they have customarily behaved says nothing more than that those who accept certain rules must also observe a rule that the rules ought to be observed. This is a mere useless reduplication of the fact that a set of rules are accepted by states as binding rules.'[116] What is to stop us—once we throw away the fetish that all rules must fit somewhere into a chain leading back to a basic norm which gives the rest their validity—from seeing international law as simply a 'set' of rules, all binding (and thought and spoken of as such, reflecting their internal aspect), but lacking, as yet, a basic norm or rule of recognition, which can be looked on as 'not a necessity, but a luxury, found in advanced social systems' which the international order does not yet fully match?

It is not the case that there is some mystery as to why the rules in such a simple social structure are binding, which a basic rule, if only we could find it, would resolve. The rules of the simple structure are, like the basic rule of the more advanced systems, binding if they are accepted and function as such. These simple truths about different forms of social structure can, however, easily be obscured by the obstinate search for unity and system where these desirable elements are not in fact to be found.[117]

The point about international law for Hart, and the one which his search for a *concept* rather than a definition of law—in other words a frame of linguistic usage with a core of typical meanings, shading all round the edges into a penumbra of others less typical in a wide variety of ways—makes accessible to him, is its very strong *analogy* in function to the rules of a domestic legal system:

Bentham, the inventor of the expression 'international law', defended it simply by saying that it was 'sufficiently analogous' to municipal law. To

---

[115] Ibid. 223–4.   [116] Ibid. 230.   [117] Ibid.

this, two comments are perhaps worth adding. First that the analogy is one of content not of form; secondly that, in this analogy of content, no other social rules are so close to municipal law as those of international law.[118]

[118] *Concept* (see n. 14), 230.

Index